The Iliad: a commentary

Volume I: books 1-4

THE ILIAD:
A COMMENTARY

GENERAL EDITOR G. S. KIRK

Volume 1 : books 1–4

G. S. KIRK

REGIUS PROFESSOR EMERITUS OF GREEK
IN THE UNIVERSITY OF CAMBRIDGE

CAMBRIDGE
UNIVERSITY PRESS

PUBLISHED BY THE PRESS SYNDICATE OF THE UNIVERSITY OF CAMBRIDGE
The Pitt Building, Trumpington Street, Cambridge, United Kingdom

CAMBRIDGE UNIVERSITY PRESS
The Edinburgh Building, Cambridge CB2 2RU, UK
40 West 20th Street, New York, NY 10011–4211, USA
10 Stamford Road, Oakleigh, VIC 3166, Australia
Ruiz de Alarcón 13, 28014 Madrid, Spain
Dock House, The Waterfront, Cape Town 8001, South Africa

http://www.cambridge.org

First published 1985
Reprinted 1987, 1990, 1993, 1995, 2000, 2001

Library of Congress catalogue card number: 84-11330

British Library Cataloguing in Publication Data
Kirk, G. S.
The Iliad: a commentary
Vol. I, Books 1–4
I. Homer, Iliad
I. Title
883'.01   PA4037

ISBN 0 521 23709 2 hard covers
ISBN 0 521 28171 7 paperback

Transferred to digital printing 2004

For Kirsten
and to the memory of Adam Parry

CONTENTS

MAPS

PREFACE

This is the first instalment of a six-volume Commentary on the *Iliad*, of which I hope to undertake the second volume also, the rest being committed to four other authors – J. B. Hainsworth, R. Janko, M. W. Edwards and N. J. Richardson – with myself as general editor. Subsequent volumes should appear at close intervals in some four years' time.

The Commentary has always been envisaged as one that develops as it goes along, rather than one in which everything has been decided once and for all. The latter may be simpler for the user, but the present kind has compensating advantages. Different emphases will emerge, in a more or less logical order, through the six volumes, as poem and Commentary unfold. That is why there is a strong emphasis in this opening volume on poetics, especially at the level of rhythm and diction. Another important aspect of composition, at least of the oral kind, is the varied use of standard themes and 'typical scenes' – the equivalent, on a larger scale, of the standard phrases we call 'formulas'. These are less obtrusive in the epic's opening Books than later, and will accordingly be more fully treated from the second volume on. Again, the overall structure and dominant emotional impulse of this enormous poem – its metaphysical aspect, almost – only emerge as the epic approaches its conclusion, and consequently are left undefined, or open, in the present volume. Homer's methods and aims are in any case unusually complex, and I am not sure that single-minded interpretations in terms of tragic essence or human predicament (for instance) are either justified or particularly helpful – although such dimensions undeniably exist. These matters will begin to require special consideration in connexion with the Embassy in book 9, if not before, but will be most fully analysed and discussed in the closing volume.

One of the commentator's overriding duties is to examine the Greek text in detail and make it as clear as he can. The relation of any part of it, however small, to the *Iliad* as a whole and its literary and imaginative background is always relevant; that goes without saying, but it is a basic emphasis of the present Commentary, and not least of its opening volume, that the better understanding of Homeric poetry in its stylistic and expressive aspects, from phrase to phrase, verse to verse and sentence to sentence, is a fundamental need – the precondition of all other and more abstract modes of appreciation.

Substantial although not massive in scale, the Commentary is directed primarily to those with a reasonable reading knowledge of Homeric Greek. Further discussion of the kinds of help intended is remitted to the editorial introduction which follows; but it may be noted here, too, that in this opening volume there is relatively slight reference to modern secondary literature on the *Iliad*, outside a repertoire of important and standard works; and that heavy bibliographical coverage will not be sought in the Commentary as a whole. From the commentator's viewpoint that is mainly because such references, difficult in any event to render comprehensive or well-balanced for Homer in particular, can so easily distract one from squarely facing the problem under discussion. I have always tried to do that, often with the *Iliad* and *Odyssey* themselves as main guide; naturally many problems remain where the available evidence is incomplete. Sometimes a wider use of other critics' work will turn out to have been desirable; some such omissions, at least, especially over formulas, can be corrected in later volumes.

The spelling of Greek names presents the usual problems. Here, *direct transliteration* has been widely adopted, but with the following exceptions: all ancient authors (and their birth-place), regional names like Boeotia or Locris, names of people like Achaeans, Phrygians (although e.g. Lukie and Boiotoi may occur when there is direct reference to the text). Priam, Helen, Apollo and Odysseus, as well as Troy, Athens and Rhodes, are retained (since 'Helene' etc. would be rather affected); but old friends like Achilles, Hector and Ajax are replaced by Akhilleus, Hektor and Aias. Some may find this initially distressing, but I can assure them they will become used to direct transliteration once they have read a few pages. Latinization throughout, as it seemed to me, would have led to almost as many exceptions, producing curious results with many Homeric names of unfamiliar places and characters. More positively, there is no room in a work that aims at keeping close to the Greek text for such wholly un-Greek forms as Ajax and Teucer; and there is little purpose in pretending, by altering his interesting and ancient termination, that Akhilleus has a different kind of name from that of Tudeus or Peleus.

It remains to thank two enlightened institutions and several individuals for their help and support. The British Academy through its Small Grants Fund provided welcome initial aid with equipment and other facilities. The Leverhulme Trust, by electing me to a Leverhulme Emeritus Fellowship for two years, has generously enabled me to meet other expenses of research and, in particular, to have a part-time research assistant. Dr Janet Fairweather has provided invaluable assistance in this role, and I owe many excellent suggestions to her, not least over geographical questions, especially in Strabo, and the whole field of rhetoric in which she is an expert. Professor A. M. Snodgrass provided encouragement and authoritative advice over part of the commentary on the Achaean catalogue, and David Ricks improved the 'methods and aims' introduction. My future collaborators kindly read the first proofs, and Dr Neil Hopkinson generously volunteered to read the second. Between them they have removed a heap of errors; those that remain will mostly be of a more insidious kind, and are the author's unaided achievement. The staff of the Cambridge University Press have been as helpful and efficient as ever. Finally I record my affectionate thanks to Trinity College and the Cambridge Faculty of Classics.

G. S. K.

ABBREVIATIONS

Books

Allen, *Catalogue*   T. W. Allen, *The Homeric Catalogue of Ships* (Oxford 1921)

ANET   J. B. Pritchard, ed., *Ancient Near Eastern Texts relating to the Old Testament* (3rd edn, Princeton 1969)

Arch. Hom.   *Archaeologia Homerica: die Denkmäler und die frühgriechische Epos*, edd. F. Matz and H. G. Buchholz (Göttingen 1967–)

Bolling, *External Evidence*   G. M. Bolling, *The External Evidence for Interpolation in Homer* (Oxford 1925)

Burkert, *Griechische Religion*   W. Burkert, *Griechische Religion der archaischen und klassischen Epoche* (Stuttgart 1977)

Chantraine, *Dict.*   P. Chantraine, *Dictionnaire étymologique de la langue grecque* (Paris 1968)

Chantraine, *GH*   P. Chantraine, *Grammaire homérique* I–II (Paris 1958–63)

Cook, *Troad*   J. M. Cook, *The Troad: an Archaeological and Topographical Study* (Oxford 1973)

Denniston, *Particles*   J. D. Denniston, *The Greek Particles* (2nd edn, Oxford 1951)

Desborough, *Last Mycenaeans*   V. R. d'A. Desborough, *The Last Mycenaeans and their Successors* (Oxford 1964)

Erbse   H. Erbse, *Scholia Graeca in Homeri Iliadem* I–V (+index vols.) (Berlin 1969–)

Fenik, *Typical Battle Scenes*   B. C. Fenik, *Typical Battle Scenes in the Iliad* (*Hermes* Einzelschriften 21, Wiesbaden 1968)

Frisk   H. Frisk, *Griechisches Etymologisches Wörterbuch* (Heidelberg 1954–73)

Giovannini, *Étude*   A. Giovannini, *Étude historique sur les origines des catalogues des vaisseaux* (Berne 1969)

Griffin, *HLD*   J. Griffin, *Homer on Life and Death* (Oxford 1980)

Hainsworth, *Flexibility*   J. B. Hainsworth, *The Flexibility of the Homeric Formula* (Oxford 1968)

Hesiod, *Erga*   = Hesiod, *Works and Days*

Hoekstra, *Modifications*   A. Hoekstra, *Homeric Modifications of Formulaic Prototypes* (Amsterdam 1965)

Hooker, *Iliad III*   J. T. Hooker, *Homer Iliad III* (Bristol 1979)

Hope Simpson, *Mycenaean Greece*   R. Hope Simpson, *Mycenaean Greece* (Park Ridge 1981)

HSL   R. Hope Simpson and J. F. Lazenby, *The Catalogue of Ships in Homer's Iliad* (Oxford 1970)

HyDem, HyAp, HyHerm, HyAphr   *Homeric Hymns* to Demeter, Apollo, Hermes, Aphrodite

Janko, *HHH*   Richard Janko, *Homer, Hesiod and the Hymns* (Cambridge 1982)

Kirk, *Songs*   G. S. Kirk, *The Songs of Homer* (Cambridge 1962)

Leaf   W. Leaf, *The Iliad* I–II (2nd edn, London 1900–2)

Leumann, *HW*   M. Leumann, *Homerische Wörter* (Basel 1950)

LfgrE   *Lexicon des frühgriechischen Epos*, edd. B. Snell and H. Erbse (Göttingen 1955–)

Lorimer, *HM*   H. L. Lorimer, *Homer and the Monuments* (London 1950)

L–P   E. Lobel and D. L. Page, *Poetarum Lesbiorum Fragmenta* (Oxford 1955)

LSJ   H. Liddell, R. Scott and H. S. Jones, *A Greek–English Lexicon* (9th edn, Oxford 1940)

Macleod, *Iliad XXIV*   C. W. Macleod, *Homer, Iliad Book XXIV* (Cambridge 1982)

Meister, *Kunstsprache*   K. Meister, *Die homerische Kunstsprache* (Leipzig 1921)

Moulton, *Similes*   Carroll Moulton, *Similes in the Homeric Poems* (Hypomnemata 49, Göttingen 1977)

M–W   R. Merkelbach and M. L. West, edd., *Fragmenta Hesiodea* (Oxford 1967)

Nilsson, *GgrR*   M. P. Nilsson, *Geschichte der griechischen Religion* I (3rd edn, München 1967)

OCT   *Oxford Classical Texts: Homeri Opera I–V*: I–II (*Iliad*) edd. D. B. Monro and T. W. Allen (3rd edn, Oxford 1920); III–IV (*Odyssey*) ed. T. W. Allen (2nd edn, Oxford 1917–19); V (*Hymns*, etc.) ed. T. W. Allen (Oxford 1912)

Odissea   Omero, *Odissea* (general editor, A. Heubeck; Fondazione Lorenzo Valla, 1981–): I (libri I–IV) ed. Stephanie West (1981); II (libri V–VIII) ed. J. B. Hainsworth (1982)

Page, *HHI*   D. L. Page, *History and the Homeric Iliad* (Berkeley and Los Angeles 1959)

Parker, *Miasma*   Robert Parker, *Miasma*: Pollution and Purification in Early Greek Religion (Oxford 1983)

Parry, *MHV*   A. Parry, ed., *The Making of Homeric Verse*. The Collected Papers of Milman Parry (Oxford 1971)

Shipp, *Studies*   G. P. Shipp, *Studies in the Language of Homer* (2nd edn, Cambridge 1972)

van der Valk, *Researches*   M. H. A. L. H. van der Valk, *Researches on the Text and Scholia of the Iliad* I–II (Leiden 1963–4)

Vernant, *Problèmes de la guerre*   J.-P. Vernant, ed., *Problèmes de la guerre en Grèce ancienne* (Paris, Mouton, 1968)

Ventris and Chadwick, *Documents*   M. Ventris and J. Chadwick, *Documents in Mycenaean Greek* (2nd edn, Cambridge 1973)

von Kamptz, *Personennamen*   Hans von Kamptz, *Homerische Personennamen* (Göttingen 1982)

Wace and Stubbings, *Companion*   A. J. B. Wace and F. H. Stubbings, *A Companion to Homer* (London 1962)

West, *Theogony*   M. L. West, *Hesiod, Theogony* (Oxford 1966)

West, *Works and Days*   M. L. West, *Hesiod, Works and Days* (Oxford 1978)

Willcock   M. M. Willcock, *The Iliad of Homer, Books I–XII* (London 1978)

Journals

AJP	*American Journal of Philology*
BCH	*Bulletin de correspondance hellénique*
BSA	*Annual of the British School of Archaeology at Athens*
CQ	*Classical Quarterly*
GGN	*Nachrichten von der Gesellschaft zu Göttingen* (phil.-hist. Klasse)
JHS	*Journal of Hellenic Studies*
TAPA	*Transactions and Proceedings of the American Philological Association*
YCS	*Yale Classical Studies*

NOTE

The numbers of occurrences of words and formulas (in the form e.g. '10x *Il.*, 6x *Od.*') are provided for ostensive purposes only, see p. xxiii. The abbreviation '(etc.)' after a Greek word in such a reference indicates that the total given is of all relevant terminations; '(*sic*)' in such circumstances means 'in that position in the verse'. '2/11x', for example, means 'twice out of a total of eleven occurrences in all'.

| is used to mark the beginning, or the end, of a verse; occasionally, too, the central caesura.

On 'Arn/bT' (etc.) references see pp. 41f.

EDITORIAL INTRODUCTION:
THE METHODS AND AIMS
OF THE COMMENTARY

Over eighty years have passed since Walter Leaf's two-volume commentary on the *Iliad* appeared, and a replacement has long been needed. The present volume initiates a series of six which may or may not succeed in filling that need. Naturally one hopes that it will; but at the same time it is fair to emphasize that it is not, in any case, envisaged as 'definitive', any more than Leaf's great individual effort was. For how *could* there be a definitive commentary on a poem of such length, brilliance and complexity, one that is always open to being experienced in fresh ways? That idea of the definitive has occasionally damaged classical scholarship, and it is as well to concede without delay that many of the judgements to be made in these pages will inevitably be personal, inadequate and idiosyncratic. The intention, of course, is to make a commentary which provides most of what is needed by serious readers of this remarkable poem; but it is in the nature of the *Iliad* itself, and of the present still defective state of Homeric studies in general, that much will eventually require to be amended.

Homer, in any case, presents special problems. The critical literature is enormous, and has passed through historical phases some of which are best forgotten. The idea that the *Iliad* and *Odyssey* are in an important sense oral poetry, and that the formular systems revealed most fully by Milman Parry from 1928 onward result from that, has brought a degree of welcome relief, not only by demonstrating important new dimensions in criticism but also by rendering obsolete its polarization into 'analytical' and 'unitarian'. Most scholars now accept that the Homeric epics are the result of a developing oral epic tradition on the one hand, the unifying and creative work of an exceptional monumental composer on the other. There is still room for disagreement about the way these two forces interact, and much of the commentator's task must be to show in detail, from passage to passage and episode to episode, what is traditional and what invented, altered or adapted by the main composer for his large-scale plan.

Anyone who works on the early Greek epic must be prepared to enter into detailed and difficult questions concerning the history of the late Bronze and early Iron Ages, including social and political developments; into the political geography of the eastern Mediterranean world during those periods; into heroic morality and religion, including the ritual background of life and death and developing beliefs about the gods; into the niceties of armour and warfare in general, as well as the technicalities of seafaring – at least as they were understood by poets; into the aims and limitations of oral singers, and the probable effects of new writing-systems; into many other technical matters, but above all into the language, metre and style of the poems, on which so much of the rest, as well as the essence of the epic as literature, depends. Ideally, a new and thorough commentary on even a part of the *Iliad* should be written by a team of scholars, including at least a philologist, an archaeologist-historian, and a specialist on the oral epic; and preferably a historian of religion, a specialist in myths and folklore and a metrician as well. But the difficulties are great, and one can easily imagine the colourless and miscellaneous comments that might emerge from such a collaboration – not to speak of the organizational problems of getting it started. Computers are already altering the ways in which such problems might be tackled, but in any event some kind of single personal plan and overview is essential.

The reader will quickly observe that the present volume of commentary is not overloaded with references to modern secondary literature or elaborate comparisons with later developments in Greek. This is partly due to the conviction that the practical limits of a commentary published in English in 1985 preclude a massive scale; and that, given the need for a medium scale, it was better to use most of the available space for the author's own interpretations, based primarily on the Homeric text, rather than for references to the remoter kinds of modern or not-so-modern speculation.

The disadvantages of an overloaded commentary are well known; which is not to say that full commentaries, especially on short works (or on single Books, for example, of a long one), cannot be of great scholarly value. But the serious reader of Homer needs to be provided, above all, with the materials for making up his own mind about problems, and for reaching a more satisfying understanding of the text. He does not require to be bombarded with lists of articles and parallel passages, with strings of references which he may never look up – or rather, when a reference *is* given it should be one he will know to be profitable if he does decide to track it down. Recent commentaries have made good progress in this respect, but some of them still refer to other works without even outlining the kind of help they offer; this is sometimes used as a means of avoiding the type of explanation that should be summarized, at least, in the commentary itself. Another common fault of the overloaded commentary arises out of the laudable desire to provide a complete classical education *en passant* by recording every possible influence either on the work in question or by that work on later literature. This would be commendable were it possible to achieve it, but only too often the result is a commentary which loses sight of the real problems requiring illumination. The Homeric epics are in any event a special case, since they stand at the beginning of known Greek literature and the influences on them are hard, if not impossible, to gauge; while literature and culture after them were so manifestly affected by the epic background that tracing detailed influence at every point becomes self-defeating.

In the end, any commentary is a personal selection of what should be discussed and what should not; and yet another argument against the idea of the definitive is precisely that it stifles this personal approach, which has its positive side. For there is no complete and objective code to the *Iliad* waiting to be cracked. There are concrete problems, especially at the linguistic level, which can be more or less definitely solved, but otherwise the text presents a mass of ideas which elicit responses from the reader, and about which he needs to compare his own reactions with those of the commentator. Perhaps he will sometimes adjust his feelings as a result – that would be a reasonable consequence, since, after all, the commentator is setting himself up as a professional, and at the very least has had time to study the poem in depth, in most of its ramifications, in a way that even dedicated students cannot easily match. The present writer is conscious that his own views have often been elicited by quite untheoretical difficulties, and that his awareness of the range of possible reactions to Homeric poetry has sometimes prevented him from proposing a single and definite literary interpretation. The reader will often have strong feelings about the poetry and its effect, and the author does not see it as his function to be always trying to shape those feelings, beyond the range of language and hard fact, by urging a single line of interpretation or a particular aesthetic theory.

Moreover the study of Homer presents special problems which make a-historical criticism, of whatever sort, hard to apply. For oral poems are in important respects different from literate ones, or from those invented by a single poet with a self-conscious creative intent. The complicated mode of creation of a passage of the *Iliad* – dependent as it is likely to be both on the traditional development of oral heroic poems through several generations, and on the particular needs and feelings of the monumental composer with the plot of a large-scale, composite *Iliad* in mind – needs to be worked out, so far as that may be possible, in order to assess the text, to 'read' it even, in a manner analogous to that which would apply to a literate poem. To take a very simple instance, the frequent repetitions which are an essential element of oral poetry need 'explaining' in that sense; if they are simply viewed as part of a text without a history (and almost inevitably by unconscious comparison with other but literate texts the reader has experienced), they will appear either as meaningless, or as eccentricities of style which, if they have a meaning, are almost certain to be wrongly interpreted – that is, in some other way than as necessary devices of oral composition and 'hearing' (for the very concept of 'reading' is obviously misleading, and in a more than pedantic way, for oral poetry).

Another obvious instance of the effects of ignoring the oral background and special mode of composition of the *Iliad* arises out of the interpretation both of character and of customs and practices. Agamemnon emerges from the text as complex and at times highly erratic; but the chances are that some, at least, of the erratic quality stems from the imperfect conjunction of originally distinct elements of the oral tradition. Some kind of critical discussion about whether the testing of the troops' morale in book 2 (on which see pp. 124ff. of the Commentary) arose in this way or for some other reason *is* valid and necessary, in order to attain a response to the text that is not too dogmatic or seriously distorted; and this is to be achieved not so much through the re-creation of the author's intention (although that is not unimportant) as by the identification of possible accidents of transmission which may leave the implications of 'the text' quite different from those obtained, or intended, by Homer. For it is more than likely that the character of Agamemnon in the *Iliad* is an amalgam of attitudes (towards rulers, for instance) and actual descriptions (whether of him or of other great leaders) that existed in earlier poems and were part of the oral singer's storehouse of themes, phrases, verses and passages. Such elements can become imperfectly sorted and assembled in a process of monumental composition, and it is reasonable, indeed necessary, to ask whether something like that is likely to have happened in this particular instance. The incomprehensible reactions to the testing-motif by various of the parties involved in the action of the poem may suggest a positive answer, and that is likely to alter in some degree the quality of one's response to the vulgate text and indeed to the king's character itself.

For similar reasons many matters of concrete detail in the *Iliad* require a kind of examination and explanation which is usually unnecessary in the case of the nineteenth-century novel, for example. The notes provided by English literature scholars to such a work often seem quite simple; that is because we already know so much of the work's background. With an epic poem composed in a wholly unfamiliar manner and in a foreign, indeed a 'dead', language, and concerning a mode and view of life distinct from our own – an artificial one, moreover, in that it is partly compounded of elements, attitudes and motifs derived from different generations of men over a period of some three hundred years if not more – the matter is bound to be very different. In this case there are all sorts of problems concerning the text to which a whole battery of philological, historical, archaeological, theological, mythological and sociological knowledge has to be brought to bear. It may sound excessive; but, unless he can do this, the commentator will leave many of his readers open to all the confusions and misunderstandings that a simple confrontation with this very complicated and often arcane text inevitably produces.

In the interest of economy, apart from anything else, it has been decided not to print the Greek text of the *Iliad*, thus allowing more space for the Commentary. Most readers will in any case already have their own texts – the 1920 Oxford Classical Text of D. B. Monro and T. W. Allen, for example, is readily available – and it is far more convenient to have the text in front of one in a separate volume, next to the volume of commentary.

Such a decision has important advantages for the commentator himself, chief among them being that it allows him to concentrate on his primary task. The *Iliad* and *Odyssey* are special cases, since their text, unlike that of many surviving works in Greek, is in generally excellent condition; this is because of the special status of Homer in antiquity and the operations on the stabilization of the text carried out in the sixth and fifth centuries B.C. and especially in connexion with the Panathenaia, and in the third and second centuries B.C. in the libraries of Alexandria and, to a minor extent, Pergamon (see Chapter 3). The *Iliad* is particularly fortunate since a full range of scholia is preserved in some of the great medieval manuscripts, expecially in A (Venetus Graecus 822, written in the tenth century A.D. and now in the library of St Mark's at Venice). That MS alone would offer the reader a usable text of the *Iliad*; it has of course been improved by modern scholarship, and the OCT of Monro and Allen, based on a consideration of the whole range of MSS and on the then known papyri, as well as on fundamental work on the scholia by Lehrs and Ludwich in the nineteenth century, has come to be accepted more or less as the modern vulgate. That does not mean that it is perfect; Allen's system of classification of the MSS by 'families' is agreed to be sometimes misleading, many Homeric papyri have become known in the last fifty years, and H. Erbse's edition of the scholia vetera has resolved some outstanding problems. The *apparatus criticus* could be substantially improved and a new editor would wish to alter a number of readings and spellings in the text itself, and probably to remit a dozen or so whole verses from the text to the *apparatus*: nothing very much in the way of *actual* change in a work of nearly 16,000 verses. Most of the alterations would be relatively minor in their effect, and the more substantial ones, especially those of the status of whole verses, will be fully discussed as they occur throughout the present Commentary – based as they are likely to be not on crucial changes in the manuscript evidence (whatever the improvements that could be made in analysing the relations of MSS), or even on new papyri (which only rarely affect actual readings), but rather on a reassessment of the internal evidence of the poems themselves and, to a lesser extent, of the attitudes of the ancient critics as recorded in the scholia.

The production of a new edition of the text of the *Iliad* may be desirable by the highest scholarly standards; it would, of course, be an enormous task. It is not one which the present author could conceivably undertake, even if he were qualified in codicological matters (especially) to do so; the writing of a commentary is enough by itself. The only possible alternative to producing a complete new text would be to reproduce the Monro and Allen text with a few verses omitted, with references to the very small number of subsequently-published papyri which make any difference, with fuller reports of the views of the ancient critics, especially Aristarchus and Zenodotus, but with no radical review of the medieval manuscript evidence. That is what P. Von der Mühll has done with the *Odyssey*, and Dr Stephanie West and Dr J. B. Hainsworth have proceeded along similar lines, although more concisely, in their texts of books 1–4 and 5–8 respectively in the admirable new Italian edition of the *Odyssey* (*Omero, Odissea*, I and II). All these are impressive in their different ways, but the resulting *apparatus criticus* is in no case really satisfactory, leaving even more than usual to the subjective judgement of the editor and being at many points somewhat mystifying to the reader. It is the present writer's firm opinion that all important matters pertaining to the Greek text can be adequately discussed in the Commentary, and indeed are better presented there than through a necessarily incomplete and highly selective *apparatus*.

To turn now to the Commentary itself: having established that it is not intended as definitive, that it does not offer complete bibliographical coverage, that it rejects the idea of 'the text' as autonomous, and that it requires the reader to have the OCT Greek text, *vel sim.*, at hand, its author may reasonably be asked *what sort* of commentary it is intended to be. The answer, obvious as it may seem, is that it aims at helping serious readers of the poem by attempting to identify and deal with most of the difficulties, short of those assumed to be met by a general reading knowledge of Homeric Greek, which might stand in the way of a sensitive and informed personal response to the *Iliad*. It is also hoped that the present volume may help other scholars toward a better understanding of the epic style, its formular and rhythmical elements in particular, as well as of many well-known thematic problems on a larger scale; needless to say the two aspects are connected and cannot reasonably be treated in isolation. The catalogues in book 2 obviously present a special challenge to the commentator, and again it is hoped that the relatively full treatment accorded them will clarify certain issues in a confused area of research. Overall, however, succinctness must be the goal (even at the cost of elegance) because of the ultimate restriction on space, itself the result of what publisher, author and readers can from their different viewpoints accept.

Editorial introduction: the methods and aims of the Commentary

Ultimately it is hoped that the whole *Iliad* will be covered in a further five volumes each dealing with four Homeric Books. Each volume is envisaged as being of not much more than 300 printed pages – the present volume has exceeded that, partly because of the need to comment on many common words and phrases occurring for the first time in the poem, partly because of the special demands of the two catalogues. Subsequent volumes will be prepared simultaneously by separate authors, with the present writer taking responsibility for vol. II and for the general shape and consistency of the whole. With four Books and some 40–50 pages of introductory essays to each volume, that will amount to little more than 60 pages of commentary on an Iliadic Book of average length. That is not very much; not so much as might be found on a Greek play or indeed in a special commentary on a single Homeric Book, like C. W. Macleod's welcome *Iliad Book XXIV* (Cambridge 1982). Succinctness is therefore especially important, together with careful selection; many words, phrases and verses on which something useful could be written, given more space, must be passed over in silence. All commentaries must do that to a greater or lesser degree; the trouble is that their authors are liable to pass over genuine difficulties, too, at least on their first occurrence. It is an advantage of the present arrangement that there will sometimes be a chance of repairing the omission in a subsequent volume; and the same is so, to an extent at least, with important items of secondary literature which may have been overlooked.

The author has relied heavily on certain standard works and makes frequent reference to them; for example, on language, to P. Chantraine's brilliant *Grammaire Homérique* and *Dictionnaire étymologique de la langue grecque* (with less frequent citation of Frisk, Leumann, Shipp, the *Lexicon des frühgriechischen Epos* and H. von Kamptz, *Homerische Personennamen*); on archaeological matters, as a last resort, to *Archaeologia Homerica*; on topography (particularly in book 2) to R. Hope Simpson and J. F. Lazenby, *The Catalogue of Ships in Homer's Iliad* (Oxford 1970), a particularly clear presentation of the evidence to that date (and also to D. L. Page, *History and the Homeric Iliad* (Berkeley and Los Angeles 1959) and J. M. Cook, *The Troad* (Oxford 1973)); and on battle-poetry to B. Fenik, *Typical Battle Scenes in the Iliad* (Wiesbaden 1968). Of earlier commentaries, Walter Leaf's outstanding *The Iliad* (2nd edn, 2 vols., London 1900–2), although obsolete in important respects and extremely 'analytical', contains many observations that are still valuable, and some of these are cited with due acknowledgement in the present Commentary. Short commentaries like M. M. Willcock's on *Iliad* books 1–12 can also contain, as his certainly does, useful insights. The multi-author Italian *Odissea* contains valuable material on various matters common to both epics; for topics common to Homer and Hesiod M. L. West's commentaries on the latter are an essential source.

The list could be continued: for example Milman Parry's collected works in A. Parry, ed., *The Making of Homeric Verse* (Oxford 1971), is bound to be among the commentator's 'bibles' on formular matters, as are the concordances of Prendergast–Marzullo and Dunbar–Marzullo. The point is that the Commentary is supported by reference to a limited number of key works to which readers will have relatively easy access. On linguistic matters something further needs to be said; compared with e.g. Leaf's commentary there are far fewer notes on debatable constructions and forms of words, and that is deliberate. One of the key discoveries about Homeric language is embodied in K. Meister's *Die homerische Kunstsprache* (Leipzig 1921), a work whose main conclusion, that the language of the *Iliad* and *Odyssey* is indeed an artificial affair, combining elements from different dialects and periods and using great freedom over metrical adjustment and the use or neglect of contraction and digamma, has seldom been disputed. It is completely confirmed in Chantraine's *Grammaire*, for example; as L. R. Palmer put it (in *The Greek Language* (London and Boston 1980), 83), '...the Epic language betrays not only its artificial and conventional character but also that it is the product of a long and complex history'. The artificiality is further confirmed by study of the formular systems and their adaptations, from Milman Parry on (for example by J. B. Hainsworth, *The Flexibility of the Homeric Formula* (Oxford 1968)). The epic singer evidently had great freedom in adapting older forms, combining different dialect elements, and so on. The result is that it is usually impossible to assign an individual and unusual construction or form to a particular stage of syntactical or morphological development. The introduction of new forms seems to have increased somewhat in the later stages of the oral epic tradition – especially around the lifetime of Homer – but, even so, certainty is impossible precisely because the normal logic of linguistic development does not necessarily apply. It is for that reason that the long notes on such apparent abnormalities which were a feature of Homeric commentaries down to the 1930s, at least, now seem unnecessary and often misleading. Arguments about such matters can occasionally reach a conclusion in the pages of, say, *Philologus*, but usually even there they tend to be both over-complicated and uncertain in results. The user of an ordinary commentary is scarcely helped by that kind of speculation, whatever its possible value in the long term; and the same is so of some of the more hypothetical discussions of Mycenaean words and forms as revealed in the Linear B tablets.

There is a very distinct emphasis in the present volume on the detailed workings of metre and of style at the level of diction, especially in relation to the 'cumulative' or adding technique of oral heroic singers; to the sound and rhythm of the verse as indicated by its pattern of word-breaks and rhythmical cola; to the varying degrees of enjambment and ways of creating longer sentences; to the effects of whole-sentence verses, and flowing ones against internally interrupted ones; and to syntactical (or subordinated) and paratactical (or co-ordinate) modes of expression. The emphasis on such points is partly because of their neglect by commentators in general, but more importantly because they reveal how Homeric verse was constructed and how the formular and conventional language of the tradition was deployed by the main composer to form the rich texture of his *Iliad*. Much of the enormous range and variety of this poetry is completely lost if one fails to notice such things, which pass beyond the 'mere' mechanics of versification – or rather move continuously from there into the depths of meaning and style in the broader sense. Sometimes, admittedly, the observation of 'rising threefolders' and the like (that is a term applied here to verses composed of three progressively-lengthening cola, through absence or weakness of a third-foot caesura and the presence of a strong fourth-foot one) might seem irrelevant or intrusive, but the reader is asked to read the verses in question out to himself, aloud as it were, before he dismisses the comment as excessive.

Care is also taken to present necessary information, not at every point but from time to time, about the formular status of phrases and verses – of single words, even, because they can sometimes have an inherited tendency, not solely dictated by their length and metrical value, to a particular position in the verse. The frequency of occurrence, usually in both epics, is suggested in crude numerical terms (as e.g. '10x *Il.*, 7x *Od.*'), where the numbers are merely the simplest way of briefly indicating the initial facts and providing some check on the commentator's use of the concept of formularity. The whole question of the formular, conventional or traditional component in the Homeric language is extremely important for the exact appreciation of any particular passage, and of course of the whole poem. Something of a reaction is detectable at present from the extreme claims and inconclusive statistics that proliferated after the Milman Parry revolution, but it remains true, nevertheless, that the deployment of a partly fixed phraseology is a fundamental aspect of Homer's style and technique – one that shaped his view of life, almost. One can as well ignore Homer's 'use of phrases' as an ordinary poet's 'use of words'.

Another aspect of many individual notes in the Commentary that will strike readers is the close attention paid to the Homeric scholia vetera – that is, to the ancient critical comments recorded in a few medieval manuscripts, most fully in A (p. 39); and particularly to those which, according to the authoritative work of H. Erbse, were derived from Aristonicus and Didymus (in particular) and so record, indirectly for the most part, the views of Aristarchus himself. Further discussion of these matters will be found in chapter 3; meanwhile some preliminary justification may be needed of what might appear as at times pedantic in a commentary that does not set out to be either definitive or heavily loaded with peripheral learning. There are three main reasons for it: first, the Homeric criticism of the Alexandrian era was in touch, at times, not so much through manuscript evidence as through looser scholarly and popular tradition, with views and problems concerning the epic from as early as the sixth century B.C.; at its best – rarely, it is true – it may reflect ideas that go back close to the time of Homer himself. Secondly, this school of criticism is part of the history of the poems in a way in which 'the higher criticism' of the nineteenth century, for instance, never could be; moreover it reflects much of the attitude not only of the Hellenistic but even of the classical period to these great national epics (as they had become), and therefore offers a taste of epic 'influence', in a particular form, which is worth noting even in a commentary primarily focused on the *Iliad* itself. Even the aberrations of this kind of scholarship have occasionally been noticed; there were plenty of those, and in general the standard of criticism, Aristarchus apart, was depressing; but even such obvious aberrations can be instructive or diverting, and remind us of how sceptical we should often be about the level of judgement in the rest. Thirdly, Aristarchus himself was a superb scholar whose operations on the text succeeded in establishing an ancient vulgate which is also substantially the modern one. His work on punctuation and prosody (preserved in many of the comments ascribable to Nicanor and Herodian) has been largely taken for granted here, but his views on the status of debatable verses and passages, as well as on specific Homeric expressions and episodes, are a necessary part of any survey of the evidence for such important matters.

Two final observations need to be made. The first is that the preliminary chapters in this first volume will be essays on various aspects of the *Iliad* and its composition; since it *is* the first volume, these will deal with essential preliminary topics like Homer's date and background, the problems of orality and literacy, and the rhythm, formulas and other more concrete aspects of his style; as well as adding something more on the scholia and on the first four Books in their general context. Each subsequent volume will contain other critical essays, and the intention is that they should eventually cover the various aspects of the *Iliad* and so provide a complete background to the Commentary. Inevitably some of these essays will have to be delayed beyond the first point at which they might become relevant; for example similes will be treated in a later volume, although it would have been useful to have a general discussion even in this one as background to the detailed comments on the developed similes that occur in books 1–4. Similarly the battle-poetry begins in book 4, but a general discussion of it will be delayed until (probably) volume III, when fighting becomes the predominant part of the action. The reader is asked to accept this inconvenience, which it is hoped is outweighed by positive advantages.

The second observation is that the author may be thought to be adopting in this volume a somewhat more 'unitarian' approach to the *Iliad* than he has in earlier writing. That reflects, perhaps, a small change in his own position, but primarily it is because, other things being equal and for one who is trying to produce helpful and objective comments, it is better to err on the side of conservatism, of treating the text as a reasonable reflection of Homer's own poem, except where there is a strong case to be made on the other side and for one or other of the various possible kinds of distortion. It remains true, as the author has stressed before, that in a monumental poem created substantially in an oral tradition, and then passed through at least a couple of generations of transmission by decadent and quasi-literate singers and rhapsodes, a degree of looseness, of departure from the *ipsissima verba* of Homer at any single performance, is almost inevitable in any surviving version whatever.

INTRODUCTION

1. The making of the *Iliad*: preliminary considerations

No commentary on the *Iliad* can avoid discussing, in a preliminary way at least, the poem's author and the manner of its creation. That is all the more necessary with what will turn out to be a substantially oral composition, the text of which cannot be treated with the disregard of circumstance which is sometimes applied nowadays, as a reaction against historicism and psychologism, to the assessment of fully literate works. The difficulties of the old 'Homeric Question' in its traditional form are all too familiar and will not be entered into here – the systematic study of the Greek text will, indeed, help to clarify many of the remaining problems more satisfactorily than any isolated general consideration could. On the other hand the objective evidence concerning composition and date deserves summarizing; for an account of the basic facts I have sometimes drawn on my earlier book *The Songs of Homer* (Cambridge 1962), especially chapter 13, 'The circumstances of Homeric composition', as well as on 'Objective dating criteria in Homer', *Museum Helveticum* 17 (1960) 189–205, to both of which the reader is referred for supporting references. These matters occupy sections (i) and (ii) below; (iii) sets out some fundamental considerations relating to Homer's possible use of writing, and the chapter closes with a suggestion in (iv) about Greece's unusual and perhaps unique status in respect of oral poetry.

(i) The external evidence for Homer's date and background

Antiquity knew nothing definite about the life and personality of Homer. Little about him that is at all plausible is found in the ancient traditions whose proliferation we can trace back to the sixth century B.C., except only that he was an Ionian particularly associated with Smurne and Khios. The *horror vacui* that was an endemic disease of ancient biographers caused a mass of spurious details to be invented, many of them palpably based on innocent passages in the poems themselves, others supplied by local interests or designed to reconcile divergent conjectures. The commonest version to be found in the various Lives of Homer, eccentrically created from the Hellenistic period onward but sometimes incorporating stories from the classical age, is that Homer was born in Smurne (an Aeolic foundation which became Ionic early in its history), lived in Khios and died in the insignificant Cycladic island of Ios; his name was originally Melesigenes, his father being the river Meles (!) and his mother the nymph Kretheis; he was also descended from Orpheus and contemporary with, or even a cousin of, Hésiod, with whom he had a poetical contest in Euboea. Much of this information is recognizably fantastic and nearly all of it is probably worthless; but the tale about Meles and Kretheis was already being discussed, according to Harpocration, as early as the genealogical historian Hellanicus in the fifth century B.C. Even in the relatively critical environment of classical Athens it was possible to say, or deny, almost anything about this almost wholly mysterious figure. Not even the association with Smurne and Khios, the latter backed by the existence there from at least the late sixth century B.C. of a rhapsodic guild called the Homeridai or 'descendants of Homer', can have been watertight – or there would not have been so many rival claimants, of which Kume, Ephesos and Kolophon were the chief but to which several others had been added by the Roman period.

The association of Homer with both Khios and Smurne is said (in the second pseudo-Plutarchan Life) to have been already made by Pindar, whose older contemporary Simonides of Keos (more probably than Semonides of Amorgos, somewhat earlier) ascribed a famous Iliadic verse, 6.146, to 'the man of Khios'. Similarly a 'blind man...from rugged Khios' was claimed (in verse 172) as author of the Delian part of the 'Homeric' *Hymn to Apollo* – that is likely to be a Homerid claim, and implies the connexion of Homer with Khios as early as this Hymn, which R. Janko in *HHH* places in the mid-seventh century B.C. but I hesitantly retain in the early sixth. Pindar also wrote of the Homeridai as 'singers of stitched tales', ῥαπτῶν ἐπέων...ἀοιδοί (*Nem.* 2.1f.); and the scholium on this passage states that they were at first members of Homer's family, but later were rhapsodes who claimed no blood descent; one of them was Kunaithos of Khios, who first recited the poems of Homer to the Syracusans in 504 B.C. The last part of this could be accurate; much of the rest may be speculative, but that there was some sort of guild-organization in Khios as early as the sixth century at least, claiming a special relationship with Homer and his works, need not be doubted. It survived there, apparently in a degenerate form, at least until Plato's time. Unfortunately we do not know the origins of these eponymous or guild organizations, or precisely how loose and fortuitous they may have been. Certainly the Homerid connexion need have been little closer than that which related doctors who called themselves Asklepiadai to the semi-divine Asklepios, or even the Homeric herald Talthubios to the Spartan clan of Talthubiadai. It can however be concluded that the associations of Homer with Khios were claimed at least as early as the earlier part of the sixth century B.C. and seemed to have some supporting evidence. On the other hand the lack of detailed biography concerning their founder and supposed ancestor suggests that there was no continuous Homerid tradition in Khios; otherwise it would surely have been disseminated at some stage, if only to bolster the group's own disputed claims. The Smurne connexion, by contrast, managed to maintain itself in the tradition even without such an assumed family connexion; perhaps that had something to do with the presence of Aeolic forms in the predominantly Ionic dialect-mixture of the epic.

The absence of serious discussions of Homer's life and person from the surviving literature of the classical era remains surprising. His name happens not to be directly cited before Simonides, Heraclitus and Pindar, but there was obviously much incidental speculation about his date and background. Thus the elegiac poet Callinus in the middle of the seventh century B.C. is said by Pausanias (9.9.5) to have ascribed a Theban epic to him; Theagenes of Rhegion at the end of the sixth wrote an allegorical treatise on his works; and his chronological relation to Hesiod was discussed by the poet Xenophanes at about the same time. This question of date was obviously of great interest, and a whole range of possibilities, from close to the Trojan War itself down to 500 years after it, was advanced at different times. Much the most important contribution to the debate was made by Herodotus, who at 2.53.2 expressed the firm opinion that 'Hesiod and Homer were 400 years older than me and not more'; it was they, he thought, who created a theogony for the Greeks and gave the gods their names and functions. Here he is thinking of the Homeric picture of the Olympian gods, and of the Hesiodic *Theogony* in particular; and since Hesiod deals with the earlier stages of divine development, that is perhaps why Herodotus names him first (and why in other lists of divine authorities from Orpheus downwards Hesiod often precedes Homer). Herodotus' opinion about Homeric religious innovations is pure speculation, but the date he offers so confidently, in its upper limit at least, seems to depend on harder information. It is an attractive modern conjecture (by H. T. Wade-Gery, *The Poet of the Iliad* (Cambridge 1952) 25–9) that the phrase 'and not more' in his '400 years...and not more' implies that he was basing this computation on a chronological factor which he himself regarded as probably excessive, and that concerning the length of a generation. For Herodotus the 40-year generation, which seems to have been quite commonly accepted, was unrealistic; at 2.142.2 he states his own feeling that 'three generations of men are a hundred years'. If so, then his maximum of 400 years (which is likely in any event to be based on some kind of genealogical count) may represent ten 'stretched' generations, and his own

3

lower estimate would make those same ten generations represent not 400 but about 330 years before his own time. Given that he was writing around 435 B.C., that would put Homer around 760 – not a bad shot! But we should remember that, even if Wade-Gery's idea is correct, the calculation would still depend on the unassessable assumption of a genealogy for Homer (perhaps a Homerid one?) reaching back precisely ten generations – a conveniently round number.

Homer, then, was as much a remote figure to the ancient world as he is to us. Of all the speculations about him of which evidence survives, only Herodotus' calculation of his date and the general agreement that he came from somewhere in Ionia are of much value; the former being supplemented by the date of around 700 B.C. given for the *floruit* of Arctinus of Miletus, composer of the *Aithiopis* which started where the *Iliad* left off, by the annalist Artemon of Clazomenae (Kirk, *Songs* 286). One also wonders whether the idea of him as blind, the τυφλὸς ἀνήρ of the Delian hymn (*HyAp* 172), had any special authority – but then blindness was often associated with singers (no doubt partly for real reasons), and Demodokos, one of the two singers in the *Odyssey* itself, was blind, which arouses some suspicion.

That the *Iliad* and *Odyssey* were widely known by the middle of the seventh century B.C., if not earlier, is supported by other considerations: mainly the quotations and echoes in surviving poetry of that time (in Archilochus, Alcman, Callinus and Tyrtaeus especially), but also a couplet referring to Nestor's cup of *Il.* 11.632ff. which was inscribed around 725 B.C. on a cup excavated in Ischia in 1954. This is confirmed by the appearance of heroic scenes as decoration on vases from around 735 B.C. onward. The earliest of these (Herakles and the Stymphalian birds on a late-Geometric jug in Copenhagen; a specific battle-scene, arguably the end of the duel in *Iliad* book 7, on another jug in the Louvre; Kirk, *Songs*, pl. 5, *a* and *b*) are either non-Homeric in subject or are not certainly identifiable in themselves; but by soon after 680 B.C. topics like the blinding of Poluphemos or Odysseus' subsequent escape from his cave tied underneath the ram are inescapably 'epic' in inspiration, and it takes a determined sceptic not to see them as inspired by the increasing popularity of the Homeric poems themselves. Artistic fashion, and an equal or greater interest in subjects described not in the *Iliad* and *Odyssey* but in poems of the epic Cycle, have to be taken into account; but overall, and in combination with the quotations and echoes in other poets, there can be no serious doubt that both *Iliad* and *Odyssey* were quite well known, not only in Ionia but also on the mainland, by 650 B.C. The increase from around 700 in cults of epic heroes and heroines, like those of Agamemnon at Mukenai and Menelaos and Helen at Sparta, points in the same direction.

4

(ii) **Internal evidence: language and content**

So far we have been dealing with various kinds of external criterion for dating and placing Homer and his poetry. Clearly the poems themselves reveal much about their own environment and mode of composition, if virtually nothing about their main author (or authors, this being a subject about which nothing further will be said here except that the intuition of pseudo-Longinus, that the *Odyssey* belongs to Homer's old age, cannot be disregarded). This internal evidence may be divided into two kinds: first that of the language of the poems, and second that of the theoretically datable or placeable objects, customs and beliefs to which they allude. Both kinds are susceptible to a caution that applies to all traditional literature: that the existence of an archaic feature does not necessarily mark its whole context, let alone the whole poem, as equally archaic, since such things can survive in traditional phrases or passages that were incorporated much later into their existing context. The formular nature of much Homeric poetry (on which see chapter 2 (ii)) increases the likelihood of such survivals, as does the artificial and composite nature of the epic language (on which see p. xxii). On the other hand relative modernisms, which once again only implicate their immediate setting, must be judged in relation to the length of the entire tradition, obviously including its final or monumental stage; and in the case of a work like the *Iliad*, which had to undergo a further period of fluid transmission before it was provisionally fixed in an accepted written text (this probably happened in the second part of the sixth century B.C. and as a result of rhapsodic competitions at the Panathenaia at Athens), there was the possibility of limited alteration and corruption after the lifetime of Homer himself. Finally, as with any ancient text, there were further changes in spelling and other minor matters which even the critical work of Aristarchus and his school could not entirely eradicate.

(a) *Language*

The language of the poems, as has been remarked, is an artificial amalgam of words, constructions and dialect-forms from different regions and different stages in the development of Greek from the late Bronze Age until around 700 B.C. Yet the predominance of Ionic forms is a strong argument in favour of locating this particular oral tradition in Ionia itself – that is, in the central part of the east Aegean seaboard including the large offshore islands of Khios and Samos; for the dialect spoken there developed in certain ways which were not paralleled in the Attic-Ionic of the mainland, and a mainland origin for the Homeric oral tradition is out of the question for this and other reasons. That the *Iliad* was composed primarily in the ambience of Ionia is confirmed not only by this consideration but also by the traditions about Homer's birthplace, confused as they are; and by an additional factor which needs handling with equal caution, namely the references in the *Iliad* itself to specifically east Aegean landscapes and seascapes. These are confined to the probable awareness that the peak of Samothrake was visible from the plain of Troy on a clear day, above Imbros (13.12ff.); to the observation of birds in the Asian meadow at the mouth of the Kaüstrios river (2.459ff.), of storms in the Icarian sea (2.144ff.) and of north-westerly gales from Thrace (9.5); and to isolated bits of knowledge about Asia Minor, not only in the Trojan catalogue in book 2 but also e.g. in the idea of Niobe petrified on Mt Sipulos (24.614ff.).

The Homeric language contains many elements which demonstrate the long period of its formation and also its artificial and literary quality (of which the metrical lengthening of vowels more or less on demand, as in εἰλήλουθα, Ἀπόλλωνα, πουλυβότειρα, ἠϋγένειος, ἀπονέεσθαι, is another aspect). Thus Arcado-Cypriot forms like αἶσα, φάσγανον, ἦμαρ, αὐτάρ, ἰδέ, ἠπύω, survived the collapse of the Mycenaean world only in isolated Arcadia and Cyprus and must have been absorbed into the poetical vocabulary either before or not too long after that collapse. These can be found in the *Iliad* beside mainland Aeolisms like infinitives in -μεν, and ποτί (for Ionic and Lesbian πρός), and more broadly diffused Aeolisms like πίσυρες, φῆρες, αὐερύω, ζάθεος, ἴα for μία, κεκλήγοντες etc. as perfect. There are even occasional Atticisms, most of them, like ἀγξηράνῃ or ἐνταῦθα (for Ionic ἀγξηρήνῃ and ἐνθαῦτα), mere spelling-variants introduced in an Athenian stage of the transmission of the text; of apparent Atticisms which cannot be changed without affecting the metre most are nowadays found questionable, like δενδρέῳ (on which see the comment on 3.152), although 23.226 ἑωσφόρος (Ionic ἠωσφόρος, Aeolic αὐωσφόρος) more persuasively demonstrates Attic remodelling at that point. Conspicuous above all are the many Ionic forms which give the dialect-mixture its predominantly Ionian character: forms like ξυνός, ἔσαν or ἀγκυλομήτεω; or τέσσαρες, ἡμεῖς and εἶναι existing side by side with Aeolic πίσυρες, ἄμμες and ἔμμεν or ἔμμεναι. Usually the Aeolism is retained only where it offers a useful metrical variant, and in purely literary inventions we can find an Aeolic ending, like dative plural -εσσι, tacked on to a genuine Ionic stem as in νέ-εσσι or an artificially distended one as in ἐπέ-εσσι.

Two important elements in the Homeric language reflect real changes in pronunciation and can be approximately dated by some complicated arguments that come under the general heading of dialect-geography. First, contraction (the amalgamation of adjacent vowel-sounds) is not only absent from the Mycenaean dialect of the Linear B tablets but is demonstrably later than the foundation of the Ionian settlements in Asia Minor from *c.* 1000 B.C.

onwards, since e.g. εο contracts to ου in Attic-Ionic but remains open, or becomes a sound later written as ευ, in Ionia. Moreover the Ionic change of α to η was still operating by the time the Μᾱδᾱ first impinged upon the Greeks, not before 1000 B.C., since the Ionians called them Μῆδοι, Medes; yet the Ionic contraction of αε was to α (as in Attic-Ionic νίκα) and not η; therefore the contraction itself was subsequent to *c.* 1000 B.C. The second argument concerns the gradual disappearance of the semi-vowel digamma, whose metrical effects were still felt, as often as not, in the language of Homer. This, like contraction, began to affect Ionic pronunciation only after the completion of the α → η change, since the classical Ionic (and Homeric) version of what was originally spelled and pronounced καλϝός was κᾱλός and not κηλός. In many cases the neglect of digamma can be seen to have preceded contraction; for example ἄκων is the contracted form of ἀέκων which was earlier ἀϝέκων.

That is important because it reveals that, notwithstanding the occasional Mycenaean word or even formula (φάσγανον ἀργυρόηλον or ξίφος ἀργυρόηλον being the strongest candidates to be the latter) which survived into the mixed language of the *Iliad* and *Odyssey*, certain all-pervading dialectal characteristics, which are often organic in the sense that they cannot be removed by simple spelling-changes, can only have accrued after the Ionian migrations (and in Ionia itself, in many cases). Further attempts to date specific passages, or complete Books or epics, more narrowly by comparing the occurrences of neglected or observed digamma, for instance, or of especially significant contractions like -ῶν for -άων or -ου for -οο or -οιο, are more dangerous, although when carefully handled (see now R. Janko, *Homer, Hesiod and the Hymns* (Cambridge 1982)) they can produce some interesting indications here and there. Yet the main conclusion from the Homeric language remains unshakeable: that it was developed for the most part during the early Iron Age, down to the time no doubt of Homer himself.

(b) Content

The material objects mentioned in the poems, and sometimes the description of customs and beliefs, offer a striking analogy to the mixed nature of the language. The cultural picture as a whole is an artificial one. Actual people never fought in quite the way the *Iliad* suggests, and their customs in relation to giving brides or disposing of the dead, although complicated and no doubt changing somewhat from region to region and epoch to epoch, are unlikely to have had exactly those inconsistencies which appear in the *Iliad* and *Odyssey*, most of which result from the conflation of different poetical accounts originating at different periods. For just as the language of the *Iliad* appears as the product of many generations of oral poetry, in which archaic features are preserved here and there, new developments are introduced from time to time from contemporary spoken dialects, and new kinds of artificial pronunciation are at first tolerated and then conventionalized in the interests of metrical flexibility, so the material and social background is gradually compounded into one belonging to an essentially fictitious 'heroic age'. We shall examine the cultural mixture with special attention to the detection of extreme archaisms on the one hand (since they raise the possibility of a stage of the oral tradition contemporary with the Trojan War itself) and of relatively late innovations on the other (since, if they are suspected of being later than about 700 B.C., they raise the possibility of post-Homeric additions).

The unambiguously Mycenaean objects mentioned in the epics are few: the tower-like body-shield chiefly associated with the greater Aias, of a kind made not later than *c.* 1200 B.C.; the 'silver-studded sword', which became increasingly rare toward the end of the Bronze Age and then fell out of use until the late eighth to early seventh century (its developed formular status, quite apart from its possibly Mycenaean wording, precludes the latter period); the boar's-tusk helmet described at *Il.* 10.261ff. – evidently an unusual object even there, but certainly Mycenaean and unparalleled in the Iron Age; Nestor's dove-cup at *Il.* 11.632ff., which has some resemblance to a famous silver cup from the fourth Shaft-grave at Mukenai and reproduces Bronze-Age design and workmanship (like the boar's-tusk helmet it may have been an heirloom); finally the technique of metal inlay, exemplified in the famous Shaft-grave daggers and described with some misunderstanding when Hephaistos makes Akhilleus' new shield in *Iliad* book 18. Other things are probably or possibly Mycenaean but could be later: the metallic corslet and metallic greaves, the work-basket on wheels of *Od.* 4.131f., the knowledge of the wealth of Egyptian Thebes revealed at *Il.* 9.381–4 and *Od.* 4.126f. Other more general conditions are Bronze-Age in origin but would have persisted here and there into the Dark Age: the undeniable element of late-Mycenaean political geography in the Achaean catalogue in *Iliad* book 2, and the use of bronze not only for defensive armour and spear-heads etc. (which continued virtually through antiquity) but also for swords and cutting-tools.

The immediately post-Mycenaean Dark Age, in broad terms from 1100 to 950 B.C., was probably of great importance for the development of the heroic oral tradition and also for the transmission of information and ideas from the preceding Mycenaean age; but it left no very specific trace in the material and cultural amalgam of the epics (even though it may have done so in one or two linguistic phenomena; see Kirk, *Songs*, ch. 7). Subjects which can be assigned to the early Iron Age down to the time of Homer – that is, to the Protogeometric and Geometric phases of Greek art and manufacture – and to no other period are again quite few. First, the *pair* of throwing-spears as martial equipment seems to have been adopted around 900 and to have gone out of fashion again within a further two hundred years, with the development of hoplite fighting and the reintroduction of the thrusting-spear (references to which in the confused Homeric picture could be of various dates). Secondly, the single Iliadic and five Odyssean mentions of Phoenician ships around the Aegean indicate a state of affairs unlikely to be earlier than *c.* 900 B.C., when the Phoenician trade-routes to Carthage via Cyprus, Crete, Kuthera and Sicily were established, or to have lasted longer than the early eighth century. Thirdly, cremation as the normal way of disposing of the dead at home and in peacetime begins in the early Iron Age and goes out of fashion again by the end of the eighth century; yet most Homeric mentions of cremation refer to war overseas and are not significant – only Antikleia's statement at *Od.* 11.218ff. that burning is the δίκη...βροτῶν is unambiguous. Fourthly, the absence of any reference to writing, with the exception of the mysterious 'baneful signs' of the Bellerophon-tale at *Il.* 6.168 (supplemented by the omission of scribes from the quite complicated household of Odysseus in the *Odyssey*), must reflect conditions in Greece after the obsolescence of Linear B and before the wide dispersion of alphabetic writing; it could, of course, be an intentional archaism by the monumental composer, in whose time the new script was establishing itself.

There are several other practices which probably belong to this period, but could theoretically be later in their introduction into the Homeric corpus. One of the most important is hoplite fighting, something resembling which is presupposed in three passages in the *Iliad*, at 12.105, 13.130ff. and 16.212ff. (with the possible addition of 4.448f. = 8.62f.). Arguments among historians about when massed hoplite tactics were 'introduced' still continue (see for example P. Cartledge and J. Salmon, separately, in *JHS* 97 (1977) 11ff. and 84ff.); generally speaking, about 675 seems to be the preferred date, but the fact is that a developed bronze cuirass and helmet of about 725 B.C. were found at Argos in 1953, and suggest that early experiments in the side-by-side deployment of fully armed warriors – although something short of the developed hoplite line depicted on Protocorinthian jugs around 650 – could have been under way at that time. Then four-horse chariots are implied a few times in Homer (at *Il.* 8.185, 11.699 and *Od.* 13.81); two-horse chariots are the norm, but four-horse ones are depicted in art after about 750. Horseback riding, fishing and the use of trumpets in warfare are supposedly 'late' practices, but they too are rare in the epic because they were unheroic rather than because they were unknown.

It is only, after all, the *certainly* datable items which have much value

9

as dating criteria; the supposedly post-Homeric ones are nearly all chimerical. Thus Odysseus' brooch as described at *Od.* 19.226ff. is not likely to be seventh-century Etruscan after all; the gorgon's-head decoration on Agamemnon's shield at *Il.* 11.36f. and in three other Homeric passages is not necessarily later than 700, since gorgon-masks were probably much older and several found at Tiruns were made very early in the seventh century; only one lamp is mentioned in Homer, at *Od.* 19.33f., and surprisingly few lamps have been found from *c.* 1100 to *c.* 700 B.C. – but lamps can never have gone out of use and could be mentioned in poetry, if necessary, at any time; finally the seated statue of Athene in her temple at Troy (*Il.* 6.297–304) has been curiously claimed as post-Geometric, but the cult-statue of Athene at Lindos was probably of a seated figure and seems to go back to the mid-eighth century B.C., and doubtless there were others; free-standing temples, of course, were relatively rare to begin with but are known from the late Minoan age onwards. One phenomenon and one only can be securely dated after 700, and that is Nestor's proposal at *Il.* 7.334f. (in an inorganic couplet athetized by Aristarchus) that the Achaean dead should be burned 'so that each man may bring home the bones for the children, whensoever we return to our native land' – a custom apparently initiated by the Athenians in 464 B.C.

The absolutely datable phenomena in the *Iliad* and *Odyssey* turn out to be surprisingly few, and suggest precisely what we should conclude from other kinds of evidence: that the subject-matter of the poems was gradually formulated over several centuries, beginning soon after the Trojan War itself and ending with the period some five hundred years later when Homer set about making a monumental *Iliad*, with a monumental *Odyssey* following within a generation or so. Post-Homeric details, later than around 700 B.C., whether of language or of content, are virtually absent. That does not absolutely prove, in a generally conservative tradition, that the composition of the poems could not be somewhat later, say around 650 B.C.; that it was, has been argued by M. L. West in support of the view (certainly false on linguistic grounds, cf. G. P. Edwards, *The Language of Hesiod in its Traditional Context* (Oxford 1971) 190ff.) that Hesiod was earlier than Homer; but few people have been won over so far.

(iii) The possible contribution of literacy to the monumental *Iliad*

If the artificial language of the *Iliad* was formed over a period lasting from the end of the Bronze Age, or shortly before, until Homer's own lifetime in the eighth century B.C., then it was formed for the most part in a non-literate environment and by *aoidoi*, ἀοιδοί, singers or bards, something like Phemios and Demodokos in the *Odyssey*. That is confirmed by the highly-developed formular system on which so much of Homer's language and style depend. And yet it is a curious fact that a new kind of writing, based on the development of the alphabet, started to take hold in Greece either shortly before or even during Homer's own lifetime. That naturally raises the question whether Homer himself used the new writing, indeed whether the whole creation of a monumental epic in some sense depended on it. This is an important question, as any must be which concerns the manner in which these great masterpieces were composed; yet, unlike the oral techniques implicit in the *Iliad*, it does not have a very direct bearing on the way we experience the poem itself. Nor, since Homer is in any case such a shadowy figure, and the cultural and social background of Ionia in the eighth century B.C. so largely unknown, does it greatly affect either the biographical issue or the assessment of historical elements in the epic. Our understanding of the early history of alphabetic writing would undoubtedly be greatly improved if the question could be settled one way or the other; so would the generalizations we tend to make about the effects of literacy on oral traditions. But the close study and literary experience of the text would remain largely unchanged, and that is what most directly affects a commentary.

I propose, therefore, to set out quite briefly some of the basic facts and considerations. My own opinion has always been that Homer made little use, if any, of writing, and some reflection of that is probable in this brief presentation of the issues; but that opinion could be proved wrong by new evidence at any time, and it would be imprudent as well as pointless to argue it at length all over again.

(1) Linear B writing, which seems to have been confined to bureaucratic uses in the Mycenaean palaces of the mainland and of Knossos, disappeared with the destruction of the palaces themselves and of the social and economic system they represented. That happened by about 1050 B.C.

(2) There is no sign of any replacement writing system in Greece until the introduction of the new alphabet, of which the first direct evidence is of around 750 B.C.

(3) The artificial language and dialect-mixture of the *Iliad* were under formation during much or all of this period – see the arguments from both language and datable content presented in section (ii) above.

(4) Therefore the oral poetical tradition concerning the Trojan War and its aftermath was continuously developing during this broad period. Whether it goes back to the Mycenaean age itself is disputable, but at least there must have been some tradition, not necessarily poetical, about life and warfare in that epoch.

(5) The 'Dark Age' of the eleventh and early tenth centuries was not

so totally disrupted as to prevent the continuity, in places at least, of such a tradition, and indeed it is likely that the poetical narrative tradition was itself under development by then.

(6) An oral poetical tradition is maintained by professional singers whose usual stock-in-trade is likely to have consisted of narrative songs lasting an hour or so – a short evening at the most. This conclusion is based partly on comparative evidence, most fully from the Serbo-Croatian singers studied by Parry and Lord in the 1930s, partly on the descriptions of Phemios and Demodokos in action in the *Odyssey*, and partly on common-sense considerations of a general sort. It is affected, admittedly, by the kinds of audience and occasion that are envisaged: aristocratic banquets are only one possibility, and heroic singers in modern times have had informal popular audiences, in coffee-houses, at weddings and so on. A singer can be described as a δημιοεργός, 'a worker for the community', at *Od.* 17.383–5.

(7) The monumental *Iliad* is of a totally different order of magnitude from those 'normal' songs, and must have been performed in a special way at which we can only guess. It was still designed for a listening audience, since the spread of literacy cannot possibly have been such, by say 700 B.C., as to allow for a proliferation of copies and readers.

(8) There is no special occasion which could of itself accommodate, let alone promote, such a mammoth enterprise. A religious festival like the Delia or the Panionia might seem like a possible environment. The Delian Hymn tells of Apollo's maidens singing of men and women of ancient times and somehow mimicking their accents (*HyAp* 156–64), and there was a tradition about Homer and Hesiod composing hymns to Apollo in Delos according to the scholium on Pindar, *Nem.* 2.1. Considerably later, in the sixth century B.C., competitions of rhapsodes were organized at the Panathenaia at Athens in which large sections, at least, of the Homeric poems were recited. Yet the Ionians who with their wives and children enjoyed themselves with 'boxing and dancing and singing' at the Delian festival, according to lines 147–50 of the Hymn, can hardly be imagined as sitting or standing through 16,000 verses of the *Iliad*, which would take at the very least 20 hours of continuous singing, and that without taking account of pauses for rest or musical decoration. Assuming three-hour sessions as the longest any audience would be likely to endure, at least six or seven such separate sessions would be required for the *Iliad*, and more probably nine or ten.

(9) Since no special occasion can be imagined which would easily accommodate the performance of the *Iliad*, it must be accepted either that the poem was never intended to be heard as a whole, which is unlikely; or that it was regarded as such a prodigious affair that people would accept discomfort, and a certain amount of interruption, in order to hear it over

a period of two or three or four days. Homer must have had an extraordinary reputation in order to be able to impose his epic on audiences despite its unnatural size; but then an extraordinary reputation for such a man of genius is only to be expected. Other oral traditions suggest that a brilliant singer can become very widely known, and is easily encouraged by an enthusiastic public to extend his scope beyond that of ordinary oral songs and performances.

(10) The problem of performance is only loosely connected with that of whether Homer used writing in some way to help him compose the monumental *Iliad*, unless of course the epic was not performed but read. But that is out of the question, since there can have been no general reading public at this stage of the development of literacy, and at least until the growth of a book-trade in Athens in the fifth century B.C.

(11) That Homer used writing to create, either in person or through a scribe to whom he dictated, the whole *Iliad*, for his own purposes and not for a reading public, seems unlikely for these reasons: (a) the newness of the alphabet; (b) the indications that in Homer's time it was used for simple practical purposes; (c) the evidence suggested by Hesiod, Archilochus and the Milesian Presocratics that its use for literary composition developed gradually; (d) the probably high cost and erratic availability of papyrus, the clumsiness of papyrus rolls (of which an enormous number would be needed to accommodate the whole *Iliad*, especially when written in a probably large majuscule script), and the implausibility of such a massive experiment in book-production in the earliest days of literacy.

(12) Those objections do not apply to the possibility that Homer used writing on a small scale for lists of themes and topics, or even the points to be made, for example, in a long and complicated speech.

(13) There is one single argument, but an important one, in favour of a much more substantial use of writing by the monumental composer, and that is precisely the length, complexity and subtlety of the *Iliad* as a whole, together with the feeling they produce of being beyond the scope of wholly oral techniques. Very long oral or primarily oral poems are known from other cultures (for example *The Wedding of Smailagić Meho* by the Yugoslav singer Avdo Međedović), but they are far simpler, more restricted in theme and vocabulary, more repetitive and generally vastly inferior to the *Iliad* and *Odyssey* – which by contrast may seem to develop their central plot and various sub-plots, as well as the complex interplay of characters, all kept in place by accurate foreshadowing and retrospect, in a way no singer however gifted could achieve.

(14) That kind of feeling, which some Homerists experience all the time and all must experience some of the time, is one belonging to habitual literates, which is a reason for regarding it with some suspicion.

(15) Moreover our knowledge of the possible range and powers of exceptionally gifted singers is less than adequate for any firm judgement to be made. Nothing remotely approaching the quality of Homeric poetry is known from any other oral tradition; but it is a reasonable conjecture that not only was the monumental composer himself wholly exceptional, but so also was the local tradition of heroic poetry on which he depended.

(16) The highly-developed formular structure of the *Iliad* is matched by an analogous theme-structure and system of thematic variations (for instance in the battle-poetry) which would make the handling of this material much easier for a skilled singer than would appear on first consideration. Moreover the general circumstances of oral poetry in Greece are fundamentally different in one respect, to be considered in section (iv) below, from those of any other developed oral tradition known.

(17) The evidence, to repeat, is insufficient for a firm conclusion at this stage. Relevant details will be considered from time to time in the Commentary, where, however, it is normally assumed that the *Iliad* was composed by predominantly oral means and not written out in full either by, or at the behest of, the main composer.

(iv) Greece's backwardness over writing: a factor in the development of the monumental *Iliad*

There is another side to the problem of the introduction of alphabetic writing which has been generally neglected by writers on Homeric topics, yet is highly relevant to the understanding of how the *Iliad* might have developed against its oral background. I have already stated the argument in my chapter on Homer in *The Cambridge History of Classical Literature*, vol. I, and have deliberately followed that statement very closely, although with certain modifications, in what follows here.

The truth is that ancient Greece acquired a fully practicable writing-system (which the Linear B syllabic script never was) unusually late in its general cultural development, in comparison with the transition from non-literacy to literacy in other observable societies. Both Mesopotamia and Egypt were already quite advanced technically when they developed the art of writing ages before, back in the third millennium B.C.; but some of the Achaean kingdoms, if they lagged behind them in many respects, had already in the second half of the second millennium reached a stage of sophistication in art and administration, at least, comparable with that of their Near Eastern neighbours. Yet they could do no better in the way of writing than imitate the most cumbersome features of the hieroglyphic and cuneiform systems in order to develop a syllabary which could never have coped with anything beyond basic documentary uses, even though the

Mesopotamian and Egyptian models had been applied to historical, religious and purely literary purposes long before.

In many respects this strange Greek backwardness over writing (presumably due in part to Minoan influence) and the insistence on clinging to the worst available system – and then dropping even that without immediate replacement – must have been disadvantageous. In respect of poetry, however, it had some paradoxical merits. For the oral tradition, which would have been killed off by any immediate and serious extension of literacy, continued and expanded in the Greek world of the late Bronze and early Iron Age far beyond the modest requirements of village or even baronial entertainment. The heroic tradition based primarily on the exploits at Thebes and at Troy, established in some form by the end of the Bronze Age itself, not only survived the disturbed period which followed but was evidently carried overseas in some form with the migrations to Aeolis and Ionia from shortly before 1000 B.C., to develop there in an era of social, political and economic consolidation and expansion. How far the range and techniques of oral poetry kept pace with cultural progress in other fields is a matter for speculation; but it seems probable that they did so to a worthwhile degree. The heroic poetry of the eleventh century B.C., probably already expressed in comparatively developed dactylic hexameters, may well have consisted, as in most other oral heroic poetry, of short and primarily whole-verse sentences; and similes and speeches are likely to have been similarly rudimentary. Two or three whole centuries of further development in a modestly expansionist environment, and before any intervention from literacy, may well have brought enormous advances in formular and thematic resources, so as to carry the standards of Homer's more immediate predecessors far beyond those of ordinary oral singers.

Even the creation of the monumental poem, more or less without warning, was now made possible. What had hitherto kept heroic poems short had presumably been not one but two main causes: not only functional limitations but also the conservative effect of tradition itself. The functional desirability of shorter poems still applied, but tradition had been already broken in many important sectors of the cultural environment. Oral poetry always originates, and is most conservatively maintained, in a traditional society; but Greek society in the ninth century probably, and the eighth century certainly, was no longer that. Economic change, foreign contacts, colonizing and exploration, the growth of the polis and the decline of kingship: these and other factors must have seriously disrupted a traditional way of life which had evidently persisted, even in the settlements overseas, for centuries – as is suggested by the preservation of religious institutions, decorative and architectural forms and the heroic tradition itself. Largely, then, through the failure to develop the technique of writing, traditional poetical methods survived into an age when traditional restraints on the scope and form of oral verse had virtually disappeared.

Thus the monumental epic was made feasible – functional considerations apart – by a prevailing spirit of experiment and expansion (exemplified also in art and architecture, not least in Ionia) that was still, in this particular field of culture, compelled to operate within the limits of orality. In an important sense, therefore, the alphabet and Homer are likely to have been not so much cause and effect as parallel products of the new expansionism. A generation or two later, the impulse had gone. Writing had spread too far by the early years of the seventh century B.C. for the creative oral genius to flourish much longer. One result was the derivative Cyclic poems and the Homeric Hymns, even the earliest and best of which show signs of self-conscious and laboured imitation of the oral style. In short, the eighth century B.C. was exactly the period in which conditions were at their best for the production of a monumental oral epic.

2. The structural elements of Homeric verse

That the *Iliad* is poetry may seem to need little further comment. The idea may arouse various kinds of excitement in the modern reader – but also, perhaps, a degree of dread, a mild distaste at the thought of special barriers to be overcome. This is, after all, a narrative poem, and it may be said of most narrative that it is better done in prose. Enthusiasm is more easily aroused by lyric poetry, rhythmically less severe and better adapted to the personal and emotional expressiveness for which poetry can claim to be a privileged medium. Against that, it can be said that the Homeric hexameter is a metre both lively and surprisingly flexible; that the *Iliad*'s brilliant combination of speech with objective narrative substantially removes the monotony of most such epics; and that the 'oral' characteristics which are such an important feature of Homeric style, far from making it merely naive, give it a liveliness and a sheer pleasurable quality that most desk-bound narrative poems tend to lack.

Far more can be gained from reading and listening to this Homeric poetry if certain technical aspects of versification, beyond what is revealed by that basic acquaintance with the dactylic hexameter which most users of a commentary such as this can be assumed to possess, are examined and described. It is an initial assumption of the present work that one of its most important functions is to help the reader understand and appreciate the Homeric style – those special ways of conveying facts, images and ideas that are unique to the *Iliad* and *Odyssey*. It is a style which has been often imitated but (mainly through the separate influences of rhetoric, literacy, politics and religion) never equalled, even if Milton and Vergil, in that order, may be felt to have occasionally come close to doing so. This, even more than in the adducing of archaeological, historical or strictly philological explanations, may be where a commentator can offer most to the reader whose Greek is more or less adequate and whose perceptions in general are, like those of all of us, theoretically beyond reproach.

This second introductory chapter, accordingly, deals in a preliminary way with four basic and interlocking aspects of Homeric verse and style: (i) word-groups and rhythmical cola; (ii) the formular style and its operation; (iii) the relation of verse to sentence; and (iv) what I have called the cumulative technique. These are not the only components, needless to say, of Homeric style, but they constitute the essential groundwork for other and less concrete exercises in the interplay between diction and meaning.

The initial section, on rhythmical cola, might seem a little pedantic to those unfamiliar with this kind of approach – to those content, perhaps, with the idea of an all-important central caesura. But, although the approach can be misused, it does help in a significant way to show why formular phrases were of certain lengths and how they were combined into verses and sentences.

(i) Word-groups and rhythmical cola

It is well known that the overwhelming majority of Homeric verses are divided by word-break in the third foot at the so-called central caesura, either after the first longum of that foot ('masculine' caesura) or after its first trochee, supposing the foot to be dactylic and not spondaic (the even commoner 'feminine' caesura). Thus the dactylic hexameter verse is regularly divided (although not quite invariably, cf. e.g. διογενὲς Λαερτιάδη πολυμήχαν' 'Οδυσσεῦ (7x *Il.*, 13x *Od.*), where an exceptionally 'heavy' word bridges over the central caesura) by word-break into two nearly equal halves, the first being slightly the shorter. Each of these 'halves' then tends to fall into two smaller word-groups because of the prevalence of word-break after one or one-and-a-half feet in the first 'half', and before the fifth foot (and occasionally the fourth) in the second. Thus the whole verse tends to be divided by prevalent word-breaks as follows:

$$\text{A}^1\text{A}^2 \quad \text{M} \quad \text{F} \qquad \text{B}$$
$$- \cup \cup \vdots - \vdots \cup \cup - | \cup | \cup - \vdots \cup \cup \vdots - \cup \cup - \circleddash$$

(in which of course the double-shorts can be replaced by metrically equivalent long syllables). Here A^1 and A^2 mark the alternative positions of prevalent word-break within the first half of the verse, M and F those of the 'main' or 'central' word-break, masculine or feminine, and B the position of the 'bucolic' caesura, or rather diaeresis, within the second half of the verse.

Sometimes the subsidiary word-breaks are overrun or displaced, but, even so, many Homeric verses fall into the following 'ideal' pattern, represented by three verses drawn at random:

1.29	τὴν δ' ἐγὼ	οὐ λύσω·	πρίν μιν καὶ	γῆρας ἔπεισιν
2.46	εἵλετο δὲ	σκῆπτρον	πατρώϊον	ἄφθιτον αἰεί
3.398	θάμβησέν τ'	ἄρ' ἔπειτα	ἔπος τ' ἔφατ'	ἔκ τ' ὀνόμαζε

Of these the first also illustrates the normative effect of a standard verse-pattern, since in terms of sense καί is more closely attached to the fourth colon (the name given to such a rhythmical word-group) than to the third. Perhaps it would be more correct to treat it so, but the well-defined word-group after the bucolic diaeresis asks to be taken on its own. That reminds us that the central caesura is, after all, the most important one. Often the subsidiary ones depend on personal interpretations, and in each of the three instances above it could be argued that the first half-verse runs virtually continuously, with word-break at A^1 or A^2 being more or less accidental, the result perhaps of word-length probabilities, and not representing any real division in phrasing.

There has been much discussion of the significance of these metrical cola since Hermann Fränkel drew attention to them in a fundamental article over fifty years ago ('Der kallimachische und der homerische Hexameter', *GGN* (1926) 197–229). At their least intentional they simply reflect (i) the necessary avoidance of any division of the verse exactly in the middle (or rather at the end of its third foot), which entails establishing normative articulation near but not at that point; (ii) a tendency to subdivide the two resulting near-halves at favoured points in accordance with (a) the commonest lengths of words and short phrases, and (b) the avoidance of certain positions where word-break could be as distracting, for different reasons, as a conspicuous one at the end of the third foot. The main positions to be avoided here, unless there is also word-break at the regular positions, are after the first trochees of the second and the fourth foot ('Meyer's Law' and 'Hermann's Bridge' respectively); these are not arbitrary inhibitions, but are primarily perhaps due to the desire to avoid sequences of trochaic breaks which give a bouncing effect (see G. S. Kirk, 'The structure of the Homeric hexameter', *YCS* 20 (1966) 76–104 and especially 95–9).

Fränkel had argued, not exactly that the cola are units of meaning, but that the word-breaks which limit them are *Sinneseinschnitte*. That is not always the case, as H. N. Porter observed in 'The early Greek hexameter', *YCS* 12 (1951) 3–63; they are, according to him, simply rhythmical units in origin, each of which is 'an expected sequence of syllables produced by a brief rhythmical impulse' (p. 17), that impulse having a normative effect and affecting the semantic articulation of the verse. The cola are not therefore units of meaning, although they tend to comprise organic word-groups; they are not units of composition exactly (since the singer does not compose by marshalling first the first colon, then the second, and so on), although they are very much bound up with the act of composition and reproduction; still less are they reflections of shorter archaic verse-forms. Rather they are a reflection of sentence-articulation as predisposed by a permanent rhythmical pattern – perhaps little more than that. This is why arguments about precisely where substitute colon-divisions are to be placed if the usual word-breaks are missing (for example, if not at A^1 or A^2, then after the first longum? Or, if no B and no fourth-foot caesura, then is a substitute to be found after the first longum of the fifth foot?), tend to be self-defeating. Much of Fränkel's and Porter's work was concerned with a search for detailed formalistic rules which are simply not inherent in the material, and it is perhaps the 'ideal' four-colon verse itself that is chiefly to blame. The analysis has nevertheless been a productive one, since many Homeric verses do naturally fall into those cola, fairly strictly defined; but a considerable minority are best or inevitably treated as two-colon in the traditional and obvious way, while another important minority – and this time a drastically neglected one – fall into three cola instead.

Concentration on the four-colon verse (or on its two-colon 'ancestor') has diverted attention from a notable factor in Homeric metrics to which constant reference will be made in the Commentary: that is, the substantial minority of Homeric verses which have either no 'main' caesura or a semantically bridged one, and then have a strong *fourth-foot* caesura, here designated as R, after the first longum – the B caesura tends to be absent from such verses, or semantically irrelevant, also. The result is what for lack of a better term I have named a 'rising threefold verse' or 'rising threefolder', containing three cola of increasing length as follows:

$$- \overline{\cup\cup} - \qquad \overline{\cup\cup} - \overline{\cup\cup} - \qquad \overset{\text{R}}{\overline{\cup\cup}} - \cup\cup - \overline{\cup}.$$

Thus e.g. 2.173:

$$\text{διογενὲς} \qquad \text{Λαερτιάδη} \qquad \text{πολυμήχαν' Ὀδυσσεῦ}$$

where the third-foot caesura is completely bridged by a long, 'heavy' and necessary word. That this verse-pattern is not just due to an exceptional licence allowing such words to be accommodated is shown by the much greater frequency of rising threefolders with semantic but not literal bridging of the central caesura, for example:

1.48   ἕζετ' ἔπειτ' $\overset{\text{A}^2}{ }$ ἀπάνευθε νεῶν $\overset{\text{R}}{ }$ μετὰ δ' ἰὸν ἕηκε

1.61   εἰ δὴ ὁμοῦ   πόλεμός τε δαμᾷ   καὶ λοιμὸς Ἀχαιούς

In each of these there *is* word-break at F (and indeed at B), but it would be absurd to phrase the verses so, that is, by separating ἀπάνευθε from νεῶν and πόλεμος from δαμᾷ. Similarly, and especially in 1.48, the bucolic diaeresis is scarcely felt (since μετά belongs closely with ἕηκε and καί with λοιμός), and in both cases it is the fourth-foot word-break R which counts, and which balances the A break.

The pronunciation and phrasing of Homeric verses cannot be accurately reconstructed, mainly because of uncertainties over the effects of tonic accent, elision and correption, and musical accompaniment; but one can be reasonably sure that the rhythmical and musical effect of four-colon verses (or two-colon ones in which subsidiary word-breaks are hardly noticed) was very different from that of the three-colon 'rising threefolder', which has a more urgent, progressive or flowing effect. Often the latter is deliberately placed for climax or contrast at the end of a speech or a long passage of narrative; and it is important to identify and sense such cases (ignored by the commentators) both as an aspect of Homeric artistry and as part of the rhythmical, musical and semantic counterpoint of the verse. That also requires the modern reader to read aloud, whether literally or in the mind, in order not to miss completely the complex interplay of verse and meaning.

Needless to say there are other possible combinations of cola. For example if there is no real break within one or other 'half' of a verse with the main M or F caesura, that gives a three-colon verse which is not, however, a 'rising' one:

4.235   οὐ γὰρ ἐπὶ ψευδέσσι   πατὴρ Ζεὺς   ἔσσετ' ἀρωγός

(where it is better to treat the first four words as constituting a single rhythmical unit than to posit an alternative A break after οὐ γάρ). A commoner occurrence is of verses without any noticeable phrasing-pause at either A or B (even though there may be word-break there), which are therefore best treated as two-colon; for example

1.486   ὑψοῦ ἐπὶ ψαμάθοις,   ὑπὸ δ' ἔρματα μακρὰ τάνυσσαν
4.250   ὣς ὁ γε κοιρανέων   ἐπεπωλεῖτο στίχας ἀνδρῶν

of which the former has word-break at A^2 and B and yet the close grammatical link between ἐπί and ψαμάθοις and ἔρματα and μακρά shows that there is no real pause, either expressed or felt, in phrasing. It is probably the presence of many verses of this type, and the excessively formalistic reluctance of colometrists to allow for ambiguous cases, that has caused the four-colon observation to be still generally disregarded. But there are of course thousands (literally) of cases in the *Iliad* and *Odyssey* where the verse can be seen to fall into those four rhythmical word-groups, most clearly perhaps where modern punctuation emphasizes the breaks; for example

1.282   'Ατρείδη,   σὺ δὲ παῦε   τεὸν μένος,   αὐτὰρ ἔγωγε
1.334   χαίρετε,   κήρυκες,   Διὸς ἄγγελοι   ἠδὲ καὶ ἀνδρῶν,
1.335   ἆσσον ἴτ'·   οὔ τί μοι ὔμμες   ἐπαίτιοι,   ἀλλ' 'Αγαμέμνων.

The strengthening of colon-breaks by the syntax of a sentence can result in a dramatically staccato aural effect, especially in contrast with a preceding verse in which the colon pattern is not so strongly emphasized. Thus at 1.156ff. Akhilleus interrupts his bitter attack on Agamemnon by the thought that the Trojans had done him no particular harm, since many shadowy mountains and the echoing sea lie between:

1.156   ἐπεὶ ἦ μάλα πολλὰ μεταξὺ
157   οὔρεά τε σκιόεντα   θάλασσά τε ἠχήεσσα·

– a wonderfully flowing description in which each half-verse, whatever word-breaks it may contain, is a colon in itself. But now comes the abuse again:

1.158   ἀλλὰ σοί, ὦ μέγ' ἀναιδές,   ἅμ' ἑσπόμεθ',   ὄφρα σὺ χαίρῃς,
159   τιμὴν ἀρνύμενοι   Μενελάῳ   σοί τε, κυνῶπα,

in which 158, with its heavy internal punctuation, hammers home the four colon-divisions; or, to express it differently, divides the constituent word-groups of the sentence into rigidly rhythmical units. That is the dramatic staccato effect, which might become oppressive if it lasted for more than a single verse. Here a certain progressive relaxation follows immediately in 159 (where the theoretically possible colon-separation in τιμὴν ἀρνύμενοι is surely overridden by sense).

That colon-structure is concerned with aural effect is obvious enough; sometimes it combines with different mechanisms of versification to achieve an especially striking result. Here (printed neutrally) is the conclusion of Agamemnon's unfavourable comparison of Diomedes with his father Tudeus at 4.399f.:

τοῖος ἔην Τυδεὺς Αἰτώλιος· ἀλλὰ τὸν υἱὸν
γείνατο εἷο χέρεια μάχῃ, ἀγορῇ δέ τ' ἀμείνω.

The former verse has word-break at the four regular points of colon-division, but clearly τοῖος ἔην Τυδεύς makes a continuous semantic and auditory unit, and the verse is in effect a three-colon one with a (relatively rare) shorter central colon. Αἰτώλιος receives surprising emphasis from this arrangement; then after strong bucolic diaeresis a new sentence begins, running over the verse-end in integral enjambment into a conclusion remarkable not only for its running dactyls but also for its uninterrupted series of ει/η sounds, always at the arsis, the naturally stressed first syllable of every metrical foot:

γείνατο εἷο χέρεια μάχῃ ἀγορῇ δέ τ' ἀμείνω.

Colon-structure goes underground in the face of this kind of competition; the rhythms of word-grouping, of phrasing, are overlaid by the most formal and concrete rhythms of the verse, accentuated as they are here by this remarkable and insistent repetition of a single vowel sound. Positively, the effect is to lead the singer straight on and across the central caesura to the fourth-foot word-break after μάχῃ. Negatively, it may tend to reduce the rhetoric of this heavily chiastic sentence by stressing a phonetic similarity between μάχη and ἀγορῇ at the expense of their semantic contrast. Yet the normative effect of the final, third colon after a fourth-foot word-break (most conspicuous in rising threefolders) helps to save the day – together, perhaps, with the closing spondee and contrasting long o-sound of ἀμείνω. The result, in any case, is to place additional emphasis on this 'better at speaking' idea, which, like that on 'Aetolian' in the previous verse, may be surprising in relation to Agamemnon's general line of argument but makes a powerful-*sounding* end to his whole address..

That was an exceptional case, but often a sequence of verses can display subtle and complicated variations of colon-structure (or, in more straight-forward language, of rhythm and phrasing) without any such extreme effects or the intervention of other, and more plainly rhetorical, techniques. Here is an instance from book 1:

1.568   ὣς ἔφατ', ἔδεισεν δὲ βοῶπις πότνια Ἥρη,
569   καί ῥ' ἀκέουσα καθῆστο, ἐπιγνάμψασα φίλον κῆρ·
570   ὄχθησαν δ' ἀνὰ δῶμα Διὸς θεοὶ Οὐρανίωνες·
571   τοῖσιν δ' Ἥφαιστος κλυτοτέχνης ἦρχ' ἀγορεύειν,
572   μητρὶ φίλῃ ἐπὶ ἦρα φέρων, λευκωλένῳ Ἥρῃ

Of these only 571 is an 'ideal' four-colon verse; 568 might look like one, but it is hard to imagine that in singing there would have been any audible break (greater than that between single words within the phrase, that is) between βοῶπις and πότνια Ἥρη. Verse 569 is best regarded as two-colon; and both 570 and 572 are emphatic rising threefolders (in both cases with semantic, not literal, bridging of the central caesura: ἀνὰ δῶμα Διός must cohere, and ἐπὶ ἦρα φέρων likewise – it would be absurd to phrase 570 as a four-colon verse, which would leave one with Διὸς θεοί, 'the gods of Zeus'!).

Caution is always needed in interpreting colometry – that is exemplified once again just six verses later:

1.578   πατρὶ φίλῳ ἐπὶ ἦρα φέρειν Διί, ὄφρα μὴ αὖτε
579   νεικείῃσι πατήρ, σὺν δ' ἡμῖν δαῖτα ταράξῃ.

Of these the former is clearly an adaptation of 572 (rather than both drawing differently on a formular prototype), but the colometry is completely altered by the addition of Διί to φέρειν/-ων and the consequent establishment of a valid bucolic caesura. The main caesura is still semantically bridged, so that with A² and B breaks operating we are left with a distinctly awkward, quite uncommon and definitely non-rising threefolder, with the central colon outweighing those that surround it. Then 579: the first 'half' of the verse is a single colon, technically breaching 'Meyer's Law' by having word-break after the second-foot trochee with no preceding A breaks, but

actually causing no offence because of the following м caesura (and therefore
no consecutive trochaic break). In the second 'half' normative colometry
would cause us to observe the bucolic diaeresis as significant, especially since
δαῖτα ταράξῃ makes a neat word-group of a common type, i.e. object + verb,
at the verse-end; but syntax shows this to be misleading, since σύν would
then be separated from ταράξῃ, with which it goes in tmesis, and appear
to govern ἡμῖν, the other main term in its deceptive colon. That would make
nonsense: Zeus is not going to break up the feast σὺν ἡμῖν, with our help,
he is going to con-found (σὺν...ταράξῃ) our feast, i.e. ἡμῖν, for us.
Therefore this verse consists of two indivisible cola: an object-lesson in the
complex interplay between rhythm and meaning, and the need (as some
would say) to keep colometry in its place.

Despite that last warning, it is clear that close attention to colometry, but
always in relation to sense and syntax, can give important insights into the
rhythmical structure of the individual verse and the phrasing of the
individual sentence (altered, in the case of long sentences, by variations in
enjambment, on which see pp. 31ff.), including its adaptation to the
hexameter verse-rhythm itself. To the question 'Why concern ourselves with
such details?' the answer is that Homeric poetry was composed to be *heard*,
and that hearing it more or less aright is a precondition of *understanding* it,
in a way that does not depend on gross distortions of sound and language
at the most basic levels. The Commentary will not always pause to point
out such details of colon-structure, which can be wearying and irrelevant
and detract from other kinds of information or judgement; nor will it do
so in the related matter of formular structure, to which we may now turn.

(ii) The formular style and its operation

It is now generally agreed that oral poetry tends to develop a conventional
phraseology, amounting in many cases to a systematic corpus of phrases for
different characters, objects and functions, much more markedly than
literate poetry or ordinary speech; and that a highly developed system like
the Homeric one maintains both remarkable coverage ('scope') and
remarkable avoidance of duplication ('economy' or 'thrift') in the creation,
preservation and deployment of these fixed, traditional or conventional
phrases known as formulas. There is a wider dimension of the formular style
which includes traditional verses and even passages, or, more loosely,
conventional motifs and themes; and a narrower one which occasionally
affects even single words; but the fixed phrases or word-groups are the most
revealing in the first instance.

The conventional nature of much Homeric phraseology has been observed
and to some extent understood at least from the time of H. Düntzer in the

middle of the last century, with Witte, Meister and Meillet contributing important insights in the early part of the present one; but it was the publication in 1928 of Milman Parry's Paris dissertation *L'Épithète traditionnelle dans Homère* that first made almost complete sense of this aspect of Homeric style. Milman Parry both demonstrated in detail the systematic nature of an important part of Homeric phraseology, and drew the convincing if not wholly provable conclusion that such a system could only be developed for the purposes of specifically oral poetry. That is common knowledge by now, and there is neither need nor opportunity for a complete re-exposition here of the whole Parry concept; his collected works are published (translated where necessary) in the volume edited by his son Adam Parry, who also contributed a brilliant introductory survey, and entitled *The Making of Homeric Verse* (Oxford 1971) – here, *MHV*. Nevertheless many scholars have been reluctant to come to terms with Milman Parry's ideas, modified and extended as they now need to be. At first an Anglo-Saxon prerogative, the 'oral theory' (to use one of its grander titles) has now at length been absorbed by many other European scholars, especially in Germany, and has tended to moderate (as it did earlier in Britain and the United States) that excessively 'analytical' criticism and its excessively 'unitarian' counterpart which had been established in the nineteenth century and then subjected to new and unsatisfying refinements, 'neo-analysis' and the like, during the present one. At the same time some scholars in Britain and Germany, at least, have grown disenchanted with the mechanical extremes of the oral–formular approach at its most technical and doctrinaire (with 'hard-line Milman Parryism', as the saying goes); and, instead of accepting it in a generalized and moderated form as an essential but not exclusive tool of stylistic analysis, have reverted to highly personal modes of response more in tune with traditional, a-historical literary criticism on the one hand and structuralist-based approaches, including the idea of the sanctity of the text, on the other. It need hardly be stated that the present Commentary, concerned as it is with Homeric style at the microscopic as well as the macroscopic level, will often have occasion to draw attention to these formular elements and their implications, although not (it is hoped) in an excessive and ultimately too indigestible way.

The name–epithet formulas (ἄναξ ἀνδρῶν ᾿Αγαμέμνων, πολύμητις ᾿Οδυσσεύς, etc.) provide the most complete system and are therefore often chosen to illustrate the working of formulas in general. That can be misleading, but it is reasonable to start from them. They cover four main sections of the verse: three of increasing length from the verse-end back toward the main caesura (nearly always the feminine one, as it happens), and one from the beginning of the verse to the main caesura (usually the

masculine one in this case). The purpose clearly is to enable the singer to
deploy a particular idea at varying length and in different parts of the verse
according to the requirements of the rest of the sentence he has in mind.
With Hektor (in the nominative) it works as follows, moving from the
verse-end backwards:

(a)	[B] φαίδιμος Ἕκτωρ|	(29x)
(b)	[R] κορυθαίολος Ἕκτωρ|	(25x)
(c)	[F] μέγας κορυθαίολος Ἕκτωρ|	(12x)
(d)	|Ἕκτωρ Πριαμίδης [M]	(6x)

where B, R, F and M stand for the various regular word-breaks already
discussed. It is plain that filling the second half of the verse, and especially
perhaps the adonic verse-end 'signature' – ∪ ∪ – ○, if possible with
ready-made material, was the singer's initial concern in versifying; that is
why there are alternative formulas for the complete range of permissible
word-group-gaps from verse-end to feminine caesura. These naturally
correspond with the prominent rhythmical cola in this part of the verse;
thus (a) runs from B to verse-end and fills the last colon in the four-colon
verse; (b) runs from R, the fourth-foot caesura, to verse-end and thus fills
the third and last colon in a rising threefolder (also in other verse-patterns,
e.g. those with main caesura and a quasi-colon, only a single iamb,
between F and R); (c) fills the long final colon in a two-colon verse or a
non-rising threefolder. Here it is simply achieved by adding μέγας to the
next shortest version, but often it accommodates a new epithet, e.g. Γερήνιος
(ἱππότα Νέστωρ), which incidentally entails both F and B and so fills the
last two cola in a four-colon pattern. As for (d), the need for established
noun–epithet groups to fill the whole of the first part of the verse is evidently
not so great (although names by themselves are common enough as first
word, e.g. Ἰδομενεύς, Χαλκίδα, Κήρινθον, Αἴας, Τυδείδης, filling the first
colon); more than half of the main gods and heroes lack such a formula
(see *MHV*, table 1 on p. 39).

Now it is useful to look beyond the diverse but restricted name–epithet
formulas at some more obviously functional ones. At the beginning of the
verse, in the *first colon*, we find scores of short standard expressions containing
conjunctions, pronouns and connecting or adversative particles. These tend
to fill the shorter or longer initial colon, that is, the first foot or foot-and-a-half.
For example:

to A^1	to A^2
αὐτὰρ ὁ	αὐτὰρ ἐπεί
δὴ τότε	τοὶ μὲν ἔπειτ'
ὡς τότε	τίφθ' οὕτως

καὶ τότε	ἀλλ' ὅτε δή
ὡς ὁ μέν	οἱ δ' ὅτε δή
ὡς ὁ γε	οἱ δ' ἐπεὶ οὖν
ἢ καί	εἴ κέν πως
ἦμος δ'	ἔνθ' ἄλλοι
οἱ δ' ἐπεί	ὑμῖν μέν

Sometimes the formulas in the first colon will be verbal, rather:

ἀλλ' ἴθι	βῆ δ' ἀκέων
βῆ δὲ κατ'	βὰν δ' ἰέναι
ὡς φάτο	ὡς εἰπών
εἰ δ' ἄγε	ὡς ἄρ' ἔφη
ἔμμεναι	εἴθ' ὄφελες

In the longer form of the colon participles or other verbal forms abound:

οὐλομένην
λισσομένη
χωόμενον
εὐχόμενος
ἔκπερσαι
αἰδεῖσθαι
ῥίγησεν
μίστυλλον

These represent only a small selection of the phrases repeatedly found in the first colon of the verse.

In the *second colon* we shall not expect to find introductory phrases (even though some sentences will begin there after enjambment), but rather subject and object words, verbs and short adverbial phrases; in fact most of these are fitted into the gaps between A^1 and M and A^2 and F, since A^2 to M is very short and A^1 to F is largely confined to – – – ∪ (since – ∪ ∪ – ∪ tends to move to the verse-end):

A^1 to M	A^2 to M
φωνήσας	[only ∪ ∪ –, too short,
εὐχόμενος	perhaps, to take seriously
κεκληγώς	as a colon]
ἱπποδάμους	
Πριαμίδης	
εἰς ἀγορήν	
ἐς πόλεμον	

The structural elements of Homeric verse

A¹ to F	A² to F
φωνήσασα	πρόπαν ἦμαρ
ἔδεισεν δέ	κλέος εὐρύ
κοιμήσαντο	μέγα τεῖχος
Πηλείωνος	παρὰ νηυσίν
Πάτροκλος δέ	κατὰ δαῖτα
	κατὰ κῦμα
	δ' ἄρα πᾶσιν
	προσέειπε

The fact is that the second colon is not very conspicuous for its formular content, and is a part of the verse in which the singer makes less use of pre-formed phraseology than in the first and the fourth. Much the same is true of the third colon. To use a different way of showing this, here are the words or expressions which fill the *third colon* (both from M and from F) in the first 22 verses of *Iliad* book 2 (with a few omissions where there is no B, and taking no account of semantic bridging):

verse 1	καὶ ἀνέρες	12	ἕλοι πόλιν
2	Δία δ' οὐκ ἔχε	13	Ὀλύμπια
3	κατὰ φρένα	15	Τρώεσσι δέ
4	πολέας ἐπί	16	ἐπεὶ τόν
5	ἀρίστη	17	θοὰς ἐπί
6	Ἀγαμέμνονι	18	Ἀγαμέμνονα
8	θοὰς ἐπί	20	Νηληΐῳ
9	Ἀγαμέμνονος	21	γερόντων
10	ἀγορευέμεν	22	προσεφώνεε

Apart from κατὰ φρένα (17x *Il.*, 12x *Od.*, mostly as part of the longer formula κατὰ φρένα καὶ κατὰ θυμόν|) and Ἀγαμέμνονα -ος -ι (he being subject of the passage), there is no marked formular quality to most of these expressions, which cover most grammatical functions including verbal.

However, even a very short form of the third colon, between M or F and R, can be shown to be an important place for verbs, many of which are formular; so most clearly in verses introducing speech, e.g.

τὸν δ' ἀπαμειβόμενος	προσέφη	νεφεληγερέτα Ζεύς
τοῖσι δ' ἀνιστάμενος	μετέφη	πόδας ὠκὺς Ἀχιλλεύς
τὸν δὲ μέγ' ὀχθήσας	προσέφη	ξανθὸς Μενέλαος

(see Hainsworth, *Flexibility*, 14f.). Here and in many other such formular verses, R to verse-end is filled with a name–epithet formula, the first half-verse (sometimes divisible into two cola, sometimes not) consists of various arrangements of pronoun (as direct object), particle and participle, and the link is provided by a verb of address, προσέφη or μετέφη, filling that short medial colon, where in other types of verse one finds μετὰ δέ, παρὰ δέ, or short verbs like βάλε, ἕλε, ἀπέβη. Where there is a B break, rather, the third colon is longer and often again contains the main verb; thus within 5.59–100 we find it filled by ἐνήρατο, ἐπίστατο, ἐφίλατο, τεκτήνατο, ἀπὸ δ' ἔξεσε, ἐτιταίνετο, διὰ δ' ἔπτατο, παλάσσετο δ'. Clearly these compose a loose formular system in which a word-type takes the place of an exactly repeated word; a different instance of the same tendency is provided by the occurrence of similar prepositional phrases in that same space, e.g. within 5.64–118 θεῶν ἐκ, κατὰ δεξιόν, ὑπ' ὀστέον, κατὰ ἰνίον, καθ' ἵππων, ἐς ὁρμήν.

The *fourth colon* is a conspicuous receptacle of formular phrases, mostly of course of two words, of which noun–epithet groups are among the most prominent – not merely the name–epithet ones already mentioned, but conventional descriptions of many common nouns (which are not so often extended backwards toward the central caesura as the name–epithet ones). J. B. Hainsworth's tables II–VII (*Flexibility*, 132ff.) show very clearly how heavily the – ∪ ∪ – – and – ∪ ∪ – ∪ noun–epithet groups in the *Iliad* and *Odyssey* together are concentrated in the last two feet of the verse. Many of them are not provable formulas (that is, occurring at least twice) but are 'unique expressions', some of which nevertheless look like formulas (for example θέσφατος ἀήρ, ἀνδρὶ δικαίῳ, φήγινος ἄξων, ἄφρονι θυμῷ, ἄγγελος ὠκύς, πικρὰ βέλεμνα, δείελον ἦμαρ, ὥρια πάντα, from tables II and VI) – and may indeed be so, although not represented more than once, as it happens, in Homer; others in any case exemplify the common formular pattern and naturally gravitate to this colon.

These noun–epithet groups also provide a clear indication of the fixity of formulas in certain positions in the verse – or, as I prefer to stress, in certain cola. Their location is of course conditioned by their metrical length and shape as well as by their syntactical function, but it is interesting that Hainsworth finds 106 regular noun–epithet formulas of – ∪ ∪ – – shape, and 72 of – ∪ ∪ – ∪ shape, exclusively confined to the fourth colon. Most of them occur just 2 or 3 times, but these occur 10 times or more in the *Iliad* and *Odyssey* together:

πατρίδος αἴης (16x)	ἰσόθεος φώς (14)
θουρίδος ἀλκῆς (22)	αἴθοπι χαλκῷ (11)
πάντες ἄριστοι (etc.) (16)	νηλέϊ χαλκῷ (19)
δαῖτος ἐΐσης (11)	ὀξέϊ χαλκῷ (37)
δουρὶ φαεινῷ (22)	χεῖρες ἄαπτοι (etc.) (13)
πάντες ἑταῖροι (etc.) (16)	χειρὶ παχείη (18)
θυμὸς ἀγήνωρ (24)	ὄβριμον ἔγχος (13)
μώνυχες ἵπποι (etc.) (34)	κῆρα μέλαιναν (17)

πότνια μήτηρ (33)   πικρὸς ὀϊστός (etc.) (11)
νηὸς ἐΐσης (19)   νήπια τέκνα (14)
νηΐ μελαίνῃ (29)   ἄλκιμος υἱός (etc.) (15)
φύλοπις αἰνή (12)

Some of them obviously form parts of formular systems, e.g. νηλέϊ/ὀξέϊ χαλκῷ (cf. also ἤνοπι/νώροπι χαλκῷ, 3x each).

Hainsworth's book argues that the Homeric formulas are more flexible than Milman Parry had suggested, and that is true: they are open to modification, development and movement within the verse. This is not a completely closed mechanical system; the ability to alter the nuances of formular language is an important part of the good singer's equipment, as will often appear in the Commentary; but here the main intention is to illustrate the fundamentals of formular composition and in particular its close connexion with the rhythmical impulses determining the hexameter verse. In fact even the – ∪ ∪ – ⊻ noun–epithet word-groups show a degree of flexibility; seventeen such formulas (and rather more unique expressions) appear in the second colon (A¹ to F) and not elsewhere (Hainsworth's table IV), and nearly a hundred more are found *either* in the second *or* in the fourth colon (with occasional appearances in other parts of the verse), nearly always more frequently in the latter.

The noun–epithet groups make a useful case-study, but it is important to remember that they are only one kind of formula, numerically outweighed by other types even after the bucolic diaeresis. In the first 100 verses of *Iliad* book 3, for instance, there are, remarkably enough, only *six* real noun– (including name–) epithet groups in the fourth colon, the average being closer to twice that. Other word-groups there (most of them formular or potentially so) are adverbial (like οὐρανόθι πρό), or particles or conjunctions (like ἤ τέ κεν ἤδη), or, much the commonest, verbal phrases (like ἆλτο χαμᾶζε, οἴκάδ' ἀγέσθω, ἠδὲ μάχεσθαι, μακρὰ βιβάντα, μῦθον ἀκούσας, ἄλγος ἱκάνει, πολλὰ πέπασθε), or adjectival (like καλλιγύναικα, νυκτὸς ἀμείνων), or other noun-phrases (like ἀνδρὸς ἐρωήν, ὄρνιθες ὥς). That demonstrates once again the possible complexity, formular or near-formular, of these colon-receptacles.

(iii) From verse to sentence

The preceding sections have briefly indicated how the Homeric verse falls into rhythmical cola into which word-groups are slotted; and how many of these groups become conventional phrases or formulas, a basic element in the processes of composition and reproduction. In its simplest form the

Homeric sentence fills a whole verse with 2, 4 or sometimes 3 such word-groups, and it is a reasonable guess that in the early stages of the poetical heroic tradition nearly every verse would be of this kind, not unlike those of the unsophisticated South Slavic singers studied in modern Yugoslavia by Milman Parry and A. B. Lord. By the time of the composition of the two great epics a major, almost revolutionary development in sentence-length and rhythmical complexity had been completed; whole-sentence verses are now in a minority of one in six or more, and most sentences overrun the verse-end to a greater or lesser extent in what is known as enjambment. It is almost as important for the connoisseur of Homer to appreciate the various ways in which sentences can run from verse to verse, with all the implications that has for sound and rhythm, as it is to know what exactly is happening within the verse itself.

The development of the sentence is controlled by a fundamental rule of Homeric style, which is that thought together with expression is always or for the most part *linear* and *progressive*; it does not turn back on itself or delay, or artificially rearrange, important elements of meaning. The heavily periodic sentence in which (as in literary Latin) the resolution of the sense tends to be left until the end and to be preceded by balanced subsidiary clauses is alien to the style and technique of most oral poetry, which could not, indeed, easily function under such limitations. The idea of the oral singer as improviser has been much exaggerated by classical scholars, in particular: rather the singer tends to develop his songs gradually, by assimilation and careful practice. There is nevertheless an *element* of improvisation in any oral performance, and to a lesser degree in the process of preparation itself. That requires the singer to proceed from one point to another in a sequence that is progressive and, in a simple way, logical; it allows him to develop long sentences only if they are free of involution and reversal. His thoughts tend to emerge one after the other and to find expression in what Aristotle termed the running style (εἰρομένη λέξις, literally diction that is strung together like beads in a necklace) as opposed to the turning or periodic style (λέξις κατεστραμμένη: *Rhet.* Γ 9.1409 a 26–9). It is a paratactic rather than a syntactic mode of expression, in which thoughts, or the elements of sentences, are set out side by side, as it were, rather than being built into a kind of pyramid.

It would be wrong to exaggerate this aspect of Homeric style, which is of course periodic in some degree and in which elaborate syntax can be found from time to time; but it remains true that a simple and progressive accumulation of ideas underlies most of the narrative and even the speeches. That affects the ways in which sentences are lengthened from the basic whole-verse type so as to spill over into a subsequent verse or verses. One of the commonest forms of enjambment is best described as 'progressive'

The structural elements of Homeric verse

(Milman Parry called it 'unperiodic'; see *MHV* 252f., and my *Homer and the Oral Tradition* (Cambridge 1976) ch. 7), and occurs when a sentence which could be regarded as grammatically complete at the verse-end (which contains a whole thought, as Parry expressed it) is extended by the addition of adjectival, adverbial or verbal ideas (e.g. in a participial phrase), or by an 'and' or 'but' addition. The poet simply adds another idea, and so lengthens and elaborates a thought that could have stood by itself. Such an extension can be confined to a single 'runover' word, or to a phrase lasting to the main caesura, or to a longer clause, and it may itself be succeeded by, or actually generate, a further extension. That can be seen quite clearly in the opening verses of the *Iliad*:

1.1 Μῆνιν ἄειδε, θεά, Πηληϊάδεω 'Αχιλῆος
2 οὐλομένην, ἣ μυρί' 'Αχαιοῖς ἄλγε' ἔθηκε,
3 πολλὰς δ' ἰφθίμους ψυχὰς "Αϊδι προΐαψεν
4 ἡρώων, αὐτοὺς δὲ...

in which 1 is potentially complete in itself but is extended by progressive enjambment through the runover-word participle οὐλομένην – a word which is not in itself essential (although it expands the implication of μῆνιν) but which generates the subsequent relative clause ἣ μυρί'...ἔθηκε. Next follows a second progressive enjambment through the addition of a parallel main clause filling the whole of the next verse, πολλὰς δ'...προΐαψεν. Then there is yet a third progressive enjambment, again through the use of a runover-word, ἡρώων – this allows a subsidiary idea to be developed ('made them prey for dogs'), with a further runover-phrase ('and all birds', not quoted above) carrying the enjambment into verse 5 and the new idea of the plan of Zeus.

Although this protracted opening sentence contains some subordination (for example the relative clause in 2), it is completely linear and progressive in its development of ideas:

1.1 Sing, Muse, of Akhilleus' wrath
2 – destructive wrath, which brought grief to the Achaeans
3 and cost many lives
4 of heroes, and made them prey for dogs
5 and all birds; and (so) the plan of Zeus was fulfilled...

One idea, that is, leads to another; the linear style with its progressive enjambment (in particular) is also a generative style, in which one idea or expression leads on to the next. That is what convinced Victorian critics of the 'plainness' and 'directness' of Homeric diction (so Matthew Arnold, *On Translating Homer*); but it is not so simple, plain and direct as at first appears, since it contains a great deal of sheer artistry (rather than being the unaffected mode of expression of natural man...), using as it does conventional decorative expressions as a means of advancing inconspicuously to fresh ideas. The directness with which it carries the hearer forward is sometimes deceptive; and by allowing him a certain freedom to regroup ideas with which he has been presented (and that is easier to do when many of them are expressed in conventional and recognizable phrases), it manifests a dimension which determinedly periodic diction may be said to lack.

Progressive enjambment is the.least drastic kind; slightly commoner is that in which the sentence is definitely incomplete at the verse-end and has to be carried on into the succeeding verse. There are two grades here. The first, which I call 'periodic' (it is Milman Parry's 'necessary' type 1), is not very frequent: a subordinate clause (for example a temporal one, or the protasis of a conditional sentence) fills the first verse, to be followed by the main clause in the next. There is a slight notional pause (which might be represented by a comma) at the point of enjambment, which also marks the completion of a word-group although not of a whole thought. The second and more frequent grade represents greater continuity and closer enjambment; this 'integral' kind (Parry's 'necessary' type 2) allows no such pause or possible punctuation, but leads straight from one verse into the next, for example from subject or object before the verse-end to verb in the next verse. All three types are illustrated in the following passage from book 4:

4.446 οἱ δ' ὅτε δή ῥ' ἐς χῶρον ἕνα ξυνιόντες ἵκοντο,
447 σύν ῥ' ἔβαλον ῥινούς, σὺν δ' ἔγχεα καὶ μένε' ἀνδρῶν
448 χαλκεοθωρήκων· ἀτὰρ ἀσπίδες ὀμφαλόεσσαι
449 ἔπληντ' ἀλλήλῃσι, πολὺς δ' ὀρυμαγδὸς ὀρώρει.

Here 446/7 exemplifies *periodic* enjambment, 447/8 *progressive* (with the decorative runover-word leading into a fresh accession of meaning), 448/9 *integral*. In terms of possible punctuation 446 could end with a comma, 447 with a full stop – but it is resuscitated, as it were, by a runover-word. Verse 448 could tolerate no such punctuation, and sense and sound run on with minimal interruption into the next verse, which brings the series to a conclusion with some formality here, emphasized by the less concrete final statement 'much din arose'. The 'minimal interruption' just mentioned is what is provided not only by the completion of a word-group, ἀσπίδες ὀμφαλόεσσαι, but also by the normative effect of the verse-end and by the completion of the hexameter pattern itself. Only very rarely is that almost completely obliterated in violent enjambments like that involved in the separation of an epithet from its (following) noun, as for example at 16.104/5, δεινὴν δὲ περὶ κροτάφοισι φαεινή | πήληξ βαλλομένη καναχὴν ἔχε.

As Parry commented (*MHV* 264), such cases tend to be caused by 'a chance interplay of formulas'.

(iv) The cumulative technique

The progressive form of enjambment, in particular, encourages the building up of longer sentences in a linear mode. Sometimes one can almost hear the components of a sentence being cumulated one upon another in an accretive technique that can be prolonged or curtailed by the singer at will. Together with the normative rhythmical units into which formular phrases can be easily fitted, this provides the oral composer with a means of composition and versification that allows the formation not only of relatively long sentences but also of a relatively complicated narrative. For cumulation is a principle of composition which applies not only to the accretion of terms and ideas in the sentence, but also to that of sentences and passages in the development of motifs and themes in the episodic structure. On both scales one finds the addition of decorative (and often highly traditional) material not only for its own sake but also as a means of transition to new expressions and ideas.

The cumulative style is seen at its barest and most obvious in lists of various kinds, for instance in the details of the arming of Paris at 3.330–8. Thus to each of the first two items of armament the poet adds further description in a separate, cumulated verse (here preceded by a dash):

3.330 κνημῖδας μὲν πρῶτα περὶ κνήμῃσιν ἔθηκε
  331 – καλάς, ἀργυρέοισιν ἐπισφυρίοις ἀραρυίας·
  332 δεύτερον αὖ θώρηκα περὶ στήθεσσιν ἔδυνεν
  333 – οἶο κασιγνήτοιο Λυκάονος· ἥρμοσε δ' αὐτῷ.

Next comes the sword, which is also elaborated in progressive enjambment, but by a runover epithet whose main purpose seems to be to lead to another item, the shield, which clearly had to be mentioned and is not a merely decorative addition:

334 ἀμφὶ δ' ἄρ' ὤμοισιν βάλετο ξίφος ἀργυρόηλον
335 – χάλκεον, αὐτὰρ ἔπειτα σάκος μέγα τε στιβαρόν τε·

For the next item the singer reverts to purely decorative cumulation in a couplet which balances the preceding one in its runover epithet:

336 κρατὶ δ' ἐπ' ἰφθίμῳ κυνέην εὔτυκτον ἔθηκεν
337 – ἵππουριν· δεινὸν δὲ λόφος καθύπερθεν ἔνευεν·

Finally a single verse provides contrast for the last item of armament, in which the descriptive cumulation is differently achieved by a simple relative clause:

338 εἵλετο δ' ἄλκιμον ἔγχος ὅ οἱ παλάμηφιν ἀρήρει.

Another subject which invites a simple kind of cumulation is the simile in its specially Homeric form, in which details of the scene evoked are dropped into the listener's mind one after the other, as for example in the famous comparison of the stained ivory cheek-piece at 4.141–7:

As when a woman stains ivory with purple dye,
a Maeonian or Carian woman, to be a cheek-piece for horses;
and it lies in a chamber, and many horsemen
have longed to carry it; and it lies as a king's precious possession,
both ornament for his horse and glory for its charioteer;
so, Menelaos, your thighs were stained with blood,
your handsome ones, and shins and fair ankles beneath.

Here the parataxis and the prominent cumulation, sometimes functional and sometimes purely decorative, have a typically moving and pathetic effect (see on 4.143–5). Elsewhere a similar way of building up long sentences can lead to a different result; here, from earlier in the same fourth Book, is Here's reply to Zeus at 51ff., this time in a verse-by-verse paraphrase in which each cumulation, necessary or not, is marked by a dash:

4.51 Three towns are my favourites,
52 – Argos and Sparte and Mukenai.
53 You can destroy *them* when they offend you;
54 – I do not try to defend them, or grudge you that.
55 – For even if I tried to prevent you
56 I could not succeed, since you are much stronger.
57 – But you should not bring my efforts to nothing
58 – for I too am a god, of the same race as you,
59 – senior daughter of Kronos, indeed,
60 – both by birth and because
61 I am your wife, and you are highest god.

This quite condensed argument contains almost nothing in the way of decorative progression and runover-word cumulation; rather the flow of ideas is transmitted in a series of apparent afterthoughts (almost), each of which, however, arises as a kind of gloss on its predecessor. Thus 52 is a necessary specification of 51, and 54 a desirable one (in the statement of Here's position) of 53; furthermore 55/6 (in periodic enjambment) explains her attitude as expressed in 54. Then 57 limits the apparent concession by

35

adding that, even so, she deserves some respect (i.e. she is reinforcing her claim to continue her enmity against Troy); 58 shows why, and 59 adds another reason, itself developed in 60/1 (in integral enjambment) by a further twofold justification.

The very next sentence (4.62ff.) works somewhat differently, but still the progressive and cumulative method is manifest:

> 4.62 ἀλλ' ἤτοι μὲν ταῦθ' ὑποείξομεν ἀλλήλοισι,
> 63 σοὶ μὲν ἐγώ, σὺ δ' ἐμοί· ἐπὶ δ' ἔψονται θεοὶ ἄλλοι
> 64 ἀθάνατοι· σὺ δὲ θᾶσσον 'Αθηναίη ἐπιτεῖλαι
> 65 ἐλθεῖν ἐς Τρώων καὶ 'Αχαιῶν φύλοπιν αἰνήν,
> 66 πειρᾶν δ' ὥς κε Τρῶες ὑπερκύδαντας 'Αχαιοὺς
> 67 ἄρξωσι πρότεροι ὑπὲρ ὅρκια δηλήσασθαι.

This long sentence is formed by alternating progressive and integral enjambments (progressive in 62/3 and 63/4, integral in 64/5, progressive in 65/6, integral in 66/7), with elaborative half-verse cumulation in 63 and runover-epithet cumulation in 64 – producing internal stops and a parenthesis, in effect, about the other gods. In these initial three verses the elaborative cumulations generate related ideas by contrast:

> 62 let us yield to each other
> 63 – you to me, I to you; the other gods will follow,
> 64 – immortal gods; but tell Athene...

If we then apply the earlier types of analysis by colon-structure and formular content, the construction of this same sentence becomes even plainer. Verses 64 and 67 are 'ideal' 4-colon verses; 63, 65 and perhaps 66 are 3-colon (not 'rising') in different ways; 62 may be seen as 2-colon, rather. The first and last verses seem to frame the sentence with their spondaic fifth feet. Formular elements include |ἀλλ' ἤτοι μέν, ἀλλήλοισι|, θεοὶ ἄλλοι|, |ἀθάνατοι, θᾶσσον *sic*, ἐπιτεῖλαι|, |ἐλθεῖν, Τρώων καὶ 'Αχαιῶν *sic*, φύλοπιν αἰνήν|, 'Αχαιούς|, πρότεροι *sic*, ὑπὲρ ὅρκια δηλήσασθαι|. These, of course, fit into the cola, or in other words conform to the basic rhythmical structure of the hexameter verse.

It needs to be emphasized in conclusion that this illustration and its predecessors have been chosen for the clear way in which they exemplify certain specific points about verse and sentence, not because they are necessarily wholly representative. Homeric sentences vary enormously in length, complexity and periodicity; some will respond better than the last illustration, for example, both to colon-identification and to formular analysis. It is important in any case not to infer that these basic analyses of verse- and sentence-construction will disclose the full essence of any particular passage. That, after all, will be conveyed as much by its meaning as by anything else; and meaning has not been much emphasized so far, in what is intended as a preliminary examination of some of the more fundamental characteristics of Homeric craftsmanship. Further and less tangible aspects of the epic style will be examined in subsequent volumes.

3. Aristarchus and the scholia

The kind of scholarship which entails a thorough and unprejudiced study of a work of literature in all its aspects was not one of antiquity's strongest points. Yet Hellenistic Alexandria produced one such scholar of undoubted genius – Aristarchus of Samothrace, head of the Library there in the first half of the second century B.C. He worked on several authors, but it was his editions of and commentaries on the *Iliad* and *Odyssey* that were his highest achievement. Much of the critical work on the *Iliad* in recent times has been rendered obsolete and can reasonably be passed by in silence; neglecting Aristarchus is another matter, for reasons already outlined on pp. xxiiif. Not only is he an influential part of the history of the poems and their transmission, but his opinions on literally hundreds of problems arising out of the text deserve serious consideration. It is the main purpose of this short chapter to indicate how he worked, and in particular how his ideas have been reconstructed from the medieval scholia, an unusually complicated matter.

The earlier stages of transmission of the text of the *Iliad* are a subject for speculation; for a fuller account see e.g. my *The Songs of Homer*, ch. 14. The Homerids of Khios have already been mentioned (pp. 2f.); they are one factor in the oral transmission of the epic down to the time of its first full recording in writing, which may have coincided with the making of an official text, for the purpose of controlling rhapsodic competitions in the Panathenaia at Athens, at some time during the sixth century B.C. By the following century a crude kind of scholarship had been carried further, not only into the extent of the Homeric canon (whether it included the poems of the Cycle and some of the Hymns, for example) but also into the appropriateness or otherwise of certain Homeric descriptions and episodes, not least about the gods. The latter topic already interested Theagenes of Rhegion in the late sixth century B.C., and by the middle of the fifth the Sophists had taken up the study both of Homeric vocabulary and of Homeric morality, which they manipulated to support their own concern with contemporary ethics. Toward the end of the century the prolific scholar and Atomist Democritus of Abdera wrote a treatise on the meaning of obscure words in Homer, and this kind of work was continued in the Lyceum, where non-linguistic Homeric 'problems' were also studied. Recensions of the actual text of the *Iliad* were undertaken by Antimachus of Colophon in the late fifth century as well as by Euripides' nephew and namesake. Judging by surviving fragments and testimonies, all these different kinds of work on Homer, including even that produced under the aegis of Aristotle, tended to be slipshod, arbitrary and dogmatic; moreover special kinds of distortion were now being fostered both by moralists of the Platonic school and by allegorists who found support among the Stoics.

A more scientific approach to the preservation and study of the *Iliad* was introduced with the establishment early in the third century B.C. of the libraries and associated research institutes at Alexandria and Pergamon, which gave new life to the collection, recording and text-based interpretation of archaic and classical Greek literature. Little about the Pergamene tradition has survived, but the editions and treatises of the great sequence of Alexandrian librarians, from Zenodotus of Ephesus in the first half of the third century B.C. to Aristophanes of Byzantium and then Aristarchus in the following century, made an enormous impression. Aristarchus was clearly the greatest of the three, and the work of his predecessors has survived for the most part only through his comments on or disagreements with them. He founded a school of Homeric criticism which was still influential in the Roman era, and it is through four Greek scholars of the period extending from Augustus to Marcus Aurelius that much of his own specific criticism descended to the Middle Ages and so to us.

These four scholars are best known through the scholia, or marginal comments, in the greatest of all medieval Greek manuscripts, Venetus Graecus 822 (once Marcianus 454) of the *Iliad*, a prized possession of the library of St Mark's in Venice; it was written in the tenth century and is known as Venetus A or simply A. At the end of each Iliadic Book in this luxury edition is the following subscription: 'Set out beside the text (παρακεῖται) are the *Critical Signs* of Aristonicus, Didymus' remarks *On the Aristarchan Recension*, and extracts from Herodian's *Iliadic Prosody* and Nicanor's *On Homeric Punctuation*'. The last two of these scholars worked in the first century A.D. and dealt, as their titles show, with the effects of accentuation and punctuation on the Iliadic text. The first two were more important. Didymus was a scholar of prodigious energy and little originality who summarized Aristarchus' readings and comments, sometimes quoting his words and on occasion misunderstanding them, and adding sporadic references of his own to post-Aristarchan scholars. Aristonicus summarized, with a certain amount of his own interpretation, the comments by Aristarchus which related to the critical signs in his recension of the text (chiefly the horizontal stroke or obelus, signifying athetesis or suspect authenticity; the diple referring to a critical note, sometimes registering disagreement with Zenodotus; the antisigma marking a displaced verse, and the asterisk marking one wrongly repeated from elsewhere). The scholia based on these four works, which fill most of the generous margins of each page of the great codex, permit the reconstruction of a good part, at least, of what was in effect a full-scale edition and commentary by Aristarchus on the *Iliad*.

If the only Iliadic scholia to have survived had been these main ones from the margins of Venetus A, life for the Homerist would be somewhat poorer but undoubtedly simpler. As it is, certain other manuscripts of the *Iliad* are also equipped with scholia – chief among them T, the 'Townleianus' or codex Burney 86 in the British Museum, and B, another codex in the library of St Mark's, once Marcianus 453 but now catalogued as Venetus Graecus 821; both are of the eleventh century. These contain scholia which had descended in a different and less pure tradition than those of A, but one which still incorporates comments going back to the Aristarchan school as well as others from grammarians and lexicographers of the Roman and early Byzantine eras. They are known as the *exegetical scholia*; often naive, they sometimes, too, contain insights, or neat summations of a particular point of view, which are well worth taking into account. Recently their contribution to the literary criticism of the *Iliad* has been reviewed in a useful article by N. J. Richardson (*Classical Quarterly* N.S. 30 (1980) 265–87), from which the following introductory remarks, among much else, deserve quotation:

the majority of the exegetical Scholia...derive from scholars at the end of the Hellenistic and the beginning of the Roman period, who were consolidating the work of earlier critics. They contain some later material, notably extracts from the work on Homeric problems by Porphyry...But in general they seem to reflect the critical terminology and views of the first century B.C. and the first two centuries A.D. These have their limitations, and one may feel that the vocabulary of critical terms which the Scholia use lack flexibility and at times verge on the naive: but within their limits they nevertheless show a lively appreciation of some fundamental aspects of Homer's art.

Together with the main scholia in A which depend on Didymus, Aristonicus, Herodian and Nicanor (or rather on a later summary compilation known to scholars as the 'four-man commentary'), these exegetical scholia comprise the scholia vetera or scholia maiora. This is to distinguish them from a third class, the so-called scholia minora or D-scholia (so named by error after Didymus, who had nothing to do with them). These D-scholia are not always confined to special manuscripts, but have become conflated with the scholia vetera in, for example, B – even, sometimes, in A. Their special contribution takes two main forms: either brief notes on single words, which sometimes seem to go back to school-text glossaries of the classical period (see Erbse I, p. xi), or long and often rambling ἱστορίαι from much later sources, not without signs of Aristarchan influence here and there, on matters of history, mythology and geography. It is fashionable to claim that the D-scholia are neglected, but in my experience they only rarely offer anything that is both new and valuable to the modern commentator.

The reader will already have noticed, perhaps with a certain displeasure, that the assessment of the scholia is a highly complicated and specialized affair. Its foundations were laid by the publication of Venetus A by de Villoison in 1788, and then in the last century by F. A. Wolf, K. Lehrs and A. Ludwich. In this century further progress has been made by T. W. Allen, A. R. Roemer and M. H. A. L. H. van der Valk; but the greatest gift for the modern scholar, and one which simplifies the task of commentator and reader alike, is the exemplary 5-volume edition (+ index volumes) by Hartmut Erbse, entitled *Scholia Graeca in Homeri Iliadem* (Berlin 1969–), in which the scholia vetera are collected, edited, explained, and assigned between Didymus, Aristonicus, Herodian and Nicanor on the one hand, and the exegetical tradition, and other sources including D, on the other. The following paragraphs will summarize the relationship of the manuscripts involved and the scholia themselves; and will then explain the method of referring to them in the present Commentary. In conclusion I shall revert to Aristarchus and consider very briefly the basis of his criticisms and readings.

First, it is clear from the twelfth-century scholar Eustathius, bishop of Thessalonica, who used the same source as A for certain of his comments, that A depends on a summary ascribed to an otherwise unknown pair called Apion and Herodorus, who themselves depended on a compilation of the 'four-man commentary' by one Nemesion in the fifth or sixth century. Ap.H. (i.e. Apion and Herodorus) is therefore the lost archetype of A which Erbse tries to reconstruct. The exegetical scholia, by contrast, are represented by T on the one hand, and somewhat less accurately by a group of manuscripts including B on the other. This group comprises BCE³E⁴ (on which see Erbse I, p. il), and is called b; therefore the exegetical class as a whole is represented by bT, which depend on a lost archetype, parallel with but earlier than Ap.H., which Erbse terms c, a very mixed compilation of early Byzantine times.

The exact relations between A and its lost archetype Ap.H., and between bT and their lost archetype c, are discussed at some length (in Latin) by Erbse in the prolegomena to his first volume. Here it is necessary to say no more than that Didymus and Aristonicus are known mainly through A, and the exegetical scholia sometimes through A but mainly through b or T or both. Erbse edits A, b and T, and prints in the margin against each scholium an indication of its type, i.e. *Did.* for Didymus-based, *Ariston.* for Aristonicus-based (and similarly for *Nic.* and *Hrd.*, i.e. Nicanor and Herodian), and *ex.* for exegetical. It is important to note that D in his margins stands for influence from the D-scholium tradition and not for Didymus. In the present

Commentary I have cited the scholia using Erbse's categories, but have abbreviated 'Aristonicus' still further to Arn; thus 'Arn/A' means 'according to the A-scholium, which here, according to Erbse, is ultimately derived from Aristonicus'; similarly with 'Did/A'. I have gone still further – perhaps too far – in the direction of simplification by assuming that Did and Arn directly represent Aristarchus (thus the usual form of reference is simply e.g. 'Aristarchus (Arn/A) athetized, thought that, etc.'), although it has been seen that they were simply reporting him, not always completely accurately, and with their own views sometimes intruding. Naturally I have tried to note cases where the latter affects the issue, but for further information recourse must be had to Erbse. As for the exegetical scholia, I have referred to them occasionally as just that, especially to begin with, but normally as T, b or, most frequently, bT (since b usually confirms T, if less accurately). Thus 'bT say that...' means that the (complex and mixed) exegetical tradition advanced the view or views which follow.

Finally, since the opinions of Aristarchus are by far the most important aspect of ancient Homeric criticism and indirectly of the study of the medieval scholia, one must give some consideration to the question of how those opinions were formed. In particular, since so many of them were concerned with the authenticity or otherwise of whole verses (and it was in this respect that his criticisms had the greatest effect on the vulgate), and with particular readings of words or phrases, did he have access to special copies of the *Iliad* on which his judgements were based, or were those judgements purely intuitive, or were they a mixture of the two? This is a key question which applies not only to Aristarchus but also to Zenodotus, and modern Homerists have argued strongly on one side or the other. The first point is that Aristarchus often cited particular editions, usually divided into the πολιτικαί or 'city' texts and the individual or κατ' ἄνδρα ones. Of the former, the Massiliotic, the Sinopic, the Cyprian, the Argolic and the Chian are conspicuous; of the latter, those of Antimachus, Euripides the younger and Rhianus. Thus on *Iliad* 1.423–4 the main scholium in A, obviously by Didymus (Did/A), begins by quoting directly from Aristarchus, who read κατὰ δαῖτα not μετὰ δαῖτα and cited the Massiliotic, Sinopic and Cyprian editions in support, as well as those of Antimachus and Aristophanes (i.e. his teacher and predecessor), to which Didymus adds Callistratus, Sidonius and Ixion: οὕτως δὲ εὕρομεν καὶ ἐν τῇ Μασσιλιωτικῇ καὶ Σινωπικῇ καὶ Κυπρίᾳ καὶ Ἀντιμαχείῳ καὶ Ἀριστοφανείῳ. Καλλίστρατος δὲ ἐν τῷ Πρὸς τὰς ἀθετήσεις ὁμοίως, καὶ ὁ Σιδώνιος καὶ ὁ Ἰξίων ἐν τῷ ἕκτῳ Πρὸς τὰς ἐξηγήσεις. Here it is obvious that Aristarchus sometimes, at least, consulted different recensions; but it is only rarely that such a full statement of his supporting sources is provided. The questions still remain, how accurate were those sources, and how great a part did they play in making up

Aristarchus' mind for him? Aristarchus himself sometimes classifies other texts in general terms, citing either 'common', 'popular', 'worse' or 'more casual' ones (κοινότερα, δημώδεις, φαυλότερα, εἰκαιότεραι, [ἀντίγραφα or ἐκδόσεις as the case may be]), or 'ancient', 'more accurate', 'more refined' ones (ἀρχαῖα, παλαιά, ἀκριβέστερα, χαριέστερα) – sometimes too 'all' or 'most' editions, αἱ πᾶσαι or πλείους. That suggests at first sight that he not only consulted many different texts of Homer but also divided them into categories of reliability, and himself relied on the higher categories. Yet closer study of his methods and criteria as revealed in the vast majority of Didymus' and Aristonicus' reports (most of them not citing these other texts and editions) suggests, on the contrary, that his judgements were generally made on the basis of his own opinions and rules, and that he cited those other authorities mainly when they supported him.

Moreover the city and individual texts, when their readings are taken as a whole, seem to be very erratic and to possess no special ancient authority; indeed the 'common' or 'worse' ones often appear, by modern criteria, more reliable than the 'ancient' or 'more refined' ones! Obviously this is a large and difficult topic; most scholars from Nauck and Wilamowitz on have held that Aristarchus sometimes made conjectures and on other occasions relied on earlier texts. That seems like a reasonable view on *a priori* grounds, but on the whole I side with van der Valk, who in *Researches* II, 86 records his opinion, reached after astute if sometimes arcane studies, that 'Aristarchus' readings are nearly always subjective and personal conjectures', and that the cited texts, whatever their description, are comparatively recent products of Hellenistic and especially Alexandrian criticism. That applies *a fortiori* to Zenodotus also, whose distinctly shorter text, in particular, is clearly the result of his applying stringent and sometimes foolish standards of τὸ πρέπον, 'what is appropriate' in Homer, rather than being due to any authoritative special sources which modern criticism can discern.

4. The first four Books of the *Iliad* in context

Some preliminary consideration of the nature of each of the Books to be treated in this volume, and of their relation to the *Iliad* as a whole, may be found useful. That in turn requires a brief examination of the structural principles and literary unity of the complete poem; although the fuller assessment of its ultimate aims and concerns will be deferred until a later volume, when the Commentary is further on its way and when important details like the Meleagros-*exemplum* in book 9 have been properly examined.

The division of the *Iliad* into four-book segments is mainly a matter of editorial convenience; but, for the first half of the poem in particular, the segments do have some organic character. Thus books 1–4 culminate in the first engagement in battle to be described in the poem; books 5–8 see further delays and diversions, among which the Troy-scenes of 6 serve a special purpose after the exploits of Diomedes in 5; books 9–12 begin with a major attempt to conciliate Akhilleus, the failure of which, after the digression of the night-expedition in 10, leads to the serious fighting of 11 and 12 and Hektor's breaking into the Achaean camp. In the second half of the epic the pressure mounts as fighting continues relentlessly, with Zeus's support of the Trojans (in accordance with his promise to Thetis to avenge Agamemnon's slight on her son) leading finally to the death of Patroklos at the end of 16.

The struggle for Patroklos' body fills the whole of book 17 (which should not really be strongly separated from 16 by the accident of sixfold division, although 17 is in a sense a self-contained episode); the next three Books are focused on Akhilleus, in despair at his friend's death, complaining to Thetis, having new armour made for him by Hephaistos, then in 19 formally reconciled with Agamemnon and in 20 beginning to wreak havoc on the Trojans. The division between 20 and 21 is again an artificial one, although the interruption of the Theomachy (parts of which fall in each Book) is not in itself serious, since the episode is somewhat incoherent in any case. Book 21 shows Akhilleus as utterly formidable, irresistible once the fight with the river is resolved, and ends with Hektor remaining outside the walls as his defeated troops stream into the city. Book 22 describes his death at the hand of Akhilleus, the last and most profound martial event of the poem; the maltreatment of his body leads directly into the cremation of Patroklos in 23, followed by his funeral games. Finally in 24 the special misery caused by Akhilleus' wrath and rejection of the traditional laws of heroic behaviour is allayed, in part at least, by his divinely-inspired return of Hektor's body to Priam for burial.

It can sometimes be revealing to look at the poem through such artificial groupings as this, as one means of discovering where its true organic transitions and boundaries lie – always remembering that the division into twenty-four Books (on which more will be said in a subsequent volume) is probably itself, to some extent at least, a product of post-Homeric activity over the presentation and storage of the text. Thus dividing it into four segments of six Books each (rather than six of four) makes a slightly artificial break at the end of the great Troy-scenes of 6, since Hektor is still returning to battle, together with Paris, at the beginning of 7. The end of 12 remains a major and organic division, with Hektor breaking into the camp followed at the start of 13 by the diversion of Poseidon's deceit of Zeus; but the division between books 18 and 19, despite the latter beginning with a new day, is not a particularly strong one, with Thetis bearing Akhilleus' new armour at the end of the former and handing it over in the opening verses of the latter. Nevertheless the last six Books have a certain unity as a whole, containing as they do Akhilleus' formal reconcilation with king Agamemnon, then his return to battle and slaying of Hektor in revenge for Patroklos, with the funerals first of the one and then, after Akhilleus' own return to heroic nobility, of the other.

The break between books 12 and 13 halfway through the poem is the only one revealed by such divisions into four or six or any other number of blocks which has strong organic authority. This opinion derives some support from the *Odyssey*, which undergoes a major change in scene and feeling as the sleeping Odysseus is landed by the Phaeacians back in Ithake, with a deliberate echo of the proem itself at 13.89–92. That comes not at the exact point of division between Books, but about halfway through the poem nevertheless. There is no obvious functional reason for such a break around the midway mark, and it should not divert us from the conclusion that the *Iliad* does not, in general, fall into large formal segments, either as indicated by Book-divisions (which may nevertheless sometimes reflect more ancient points of pause or transition), or by major episodes, or even by the passage in the action from one day to the next – which undeniably can, as between books 7 and 8, mark a change of scene or tempo. Indeed the most natural division of the *Iliad*, despite the midway climax of Hektor breaking into the camp at the end of book 12, might be into three 'movements', the first of which describes the wrath and its early consequences, then the delays before the battle moves decisively against the Achaeans; the second the severe fighting in the central part of the poem, ending with the disaster of the death of Patroklos; and the third Akhilleus' re-entry into the action, with the death of Hektor, regeneration of Akhilleus and implied doom of Troy as its main focus.

For it is worth remembering that, if any very formal divisions *were* to be strongly marked and clearly felt, that would hardly help the unity of the epic as a whole. And yet, on the contrary, the more one examines the minor breaks and transitions of the *Iliad*, the more one comes to feel the overriding cohesion of the whole structure. The dominant theme of the wrath of Akhilleus is clearly and powerfully established in book 1; thereafter the Achaeans are gradually and with many interruptions led toward the battle that will show Akhilleus and Agamemnon the destructive futility of internecine strife. That battle begins at the end of book 4 and is represented in a special and untypical way by the fighting dominated by Diomedes in 5. It does not reveal itself as the poet's main material until the vast block of battle-poetry which begins with book 11 and soon leads to the wounding of important Achaean warriors. By now the wrath-theme has been dramatically reaffirmed by the embassy to Akhilleus in 9. Once Agamemnon, Odysseus and Diomedes are out of action, Zeus's plan of letting the Achaeans be driven back on the ships can be painfully and thoroughly brought into effect. Occasional diversions like the attempt by Here and Poseidon to deceive Zeus in books 14 and 15 can still take place, but in the main it is the singer's skill in varying the pace and quality of fighting itself that carries the audience onward through almost endless martial encounters. Because the fighting is now taking place inside the Achaean defences, contacts between those waiting and those in action increase; and at last, as fire blazes from the stern of one of the ships, Akhilleus allows Patroklos and the Myrmidons to bring relief, with Patroklos in Akhilleus' own armour. His killing of Zeus's son Sarpedon is the prelude to his own death at the hands of Hektor and Apollo; and leads on, in the culminating one of three special death-scenes which reveal the creative taste and genius of Homer himself, to the destruction of Hektor in 22. This seals the fate of Troy and allows Akhilleus, at last, to be drawn back from the berserk madness into which the loss of Patroklos had propelled him.

All through those last Books the major themes and lesser motifs of the poem are linked with uncommon deliberateness and effect: the loan of the armour, which justifies the extraordinary description of the Shield of Akhilleus – a symbolic representation, simile-like but on a larger scale, of the scenes and values of peace and war; the death of Patroklos which prefigures that of Hektor, and causes Akhilleus to elicit his mother Thetis in a scene parallel to, and ironically consequent upon, that in book 1; the distortion of roles and relationships between Priam and Akhilleus as they meet at last under divinely mysterious and tragic circumstances. Something similar happens, too, with the progress of the narrative through the central (and on one level fundamental) scenes of war, deprived as the Achaeans now are of Akhilleus, which occupy the whole central section from books 11 to 18. It would be surprising if the opening events of the poem were to be less closely and significantly interwoven than that; and it is to their unfolding that these concluding pages of introduction are addressed.

Books 1 to 4, on which the detailed commentary follows, describe the progress of events from the beginning of the quarrel between Akhilleus and Agamemnon to the very first encounters on the battlefield – encounters such as had not occurred, or so it is implied, for some considerable time, and certainly never before on such a scale even though the siege is now in its tenth year. The quarrel itself is treated in book 1 with extreme brilliance, through a careful and deeply dramatic presentation of the speeches and counter-speeches in which the two protagonists drive themselves into destructive bitterness and blindness to others. The movement from the brief and selective proem, through the initial exchanges between Agamemnon and Khruses (which already establish the king as a man likely to be at fault) and then Apollo's anger and the plague he sends, leads naturally and with increasing detail to the Achaean assembly, to Kalkhas' involvement of Akhilleus, and to the clash over the two young women – or rather over the pride and honour of the two heroes who think they own them. Akhilleus declares he will take no further part in the fighting; Agamemnon sends his heralds to remove Briseis, and Akhilleus, inspired, no doubt, by Athene's intervention a little earlier, swallows the insult and calls in agony of heart on his mother Thetis. She comes from the depths of the sea to comfort him, and promises to intercede with Zeus for the Achaean reverses which Akhilleus considers necessary to restore his pride. After an interlude describing the delivery by Odysseus of Khruseis back to her father and the remission of Apollo's anger, the singer moves to Olumpos for the remainder of the Book. There he describes Zeus's reluctant but powerful oath to do as Thetis asks, followed by the perturbed interference of Here, leader of the pro-Achaean deities, and his affirmation of authority despite wifely pressure. The Book ends with the gods feasting; it has established them, and Zeus, Athene and Here above all, as crucial and even humane elements in the drama to be unfolded. It is a wonderfully coherent presentation of the issues of the tale as a whole, with only the realities of war left almost unnoticed so far; and free from structural difficulties except over Agamemnon's claim to remove Briseis in person, and the curious summary of events given by Akhilleus to Thetis. Both of these will be considered in the Commentary as they arise; they may well indicate relics of different versions, imperfectly assimilated in the slow and progressive formation of a monumental poem, but are minor factors, in any case, in the deeply impressive opening to the epic as a whole.

The second Book is less straightforward and, despite its great interest and several dramatic scenes and episodes, contains two major structural difficulties: Agamemnon's testing of morale, then the catalogues of the two armies. The former raises questions similar to those about the removal of Briseis in book 1; probably the reasons are analogous, namely the imperfect incorporation of different versions and additional themes pre-existing in the oral tradition. The difficulties will be fully discussed in the Commentary; what needs to be stressed here is that it would be a mistake on the reader's part either to overlook those difficulties completely or to exaggerate their effects on a listening audience.

With the catalogues the matter is different; for the truth is that almost exactly half of this very long Book (if we include the preliminaries from 455 on) is devoted to a detailed listing of the separate contingents on each side, with the Achaeans treated at far the greater length; together with the places from which they came, the names of their commanders, and the numbers of ships that brought the Achaeans to Troy. All this detailed information must have required close attention on the part of any audience for over an hour at the very least. That does not sound too demanding, perhaps, given the abnormal powers of endurance presupposed by the monumental *Iliad* as a whole – and given, too, the interest that many details both of political geography and of heroic ancestors must have had. Yet the latter, at least, are not beyond dispute; many of the named leaders are poetic inventions, and many legendary ancestors are omitted who could have been included. Even so, the Achaean catalogue in particular might have presented far less trouble to an ancient audience, particularly once the *Iliad* had been accepted as a kind of national epic, than it does to some modern readers.

It is here that a commentary can be of special help; for the truth is that the catalogues are fascinating enough, provided one knows something about the people and places concerned and about what, in general, is happening. In any event it is obvious that the whole *Iliad* should be read, unless any particular portion of it can be shown to be spurious – and that is not the case with the catalogues. Their problem, rather, is the nature of Homer's particular sources for them, since, despite the fascination with lists and genealogies evinced by many singers and tellers of tales, their detail and scale transcend those probable in any ordinary Greek oral repertoire.

Book 2 can be seen as a whole as an elaborate and interrupted description of the process of carrying Zeus's oath into effect, at least to the extent of bringing the forces on either side to the point of engagement. They will be prevented from joining battle, at the last moment, by Paris' challenge to a duel early in book 3 and then by further distractions and diversions. This constant series of delays can be seen as the result of a fundamental compositional technique applied to these first four Books and several of their successors. The technique is not solely a device to create suspense, although suspense is certainly created thereby; for the argument that the audience knows roughly what is to happen, and therefore that no suspense is involved, is obviously insufficient. The delays are also designed to characterize the whole action which follows from Akhilleus' wrath as of unusual importance. The clash of armies, when once it is fully established in the central portion of the poem, is of monumental scale and profound consequences – therefore the preliminary assembling of the armies, the Achaeans in particular, deserves the fullest poetical treatment. Something like that must have seemed to justify, for the monumental poet, his decision to include the catalogues, despite the risk that, after massive preparations for the march-out itself, the detailed listing of participants and places of origin would be something of an anticlimax. Admittedly, one becomes involved in it almost without warning. Perhaps, too, it was indirectly needed to re-establish the grand theme of Akhilleus' wrath, since the earlier part of book 2, through Agamemnon's paradoxical behaviour and the Thersites revolt, had shown the Achaean side as too riddled by uncertainty to be capable of that truly magnificent failure which Homer and Akhilleus equally required.

The third Book, like the first, is wonderfully coherent and dramatic. It explores, with many echoes and overtones, three main themes: first the duel between Paris and Menelaos, which is arranged just as the armies are about to engage; then the Viewing from the Walls, through which, as the duel is being prepared, Helen identifies for king Priam some of the main Achaean warriors on the plain below; finally the manœuvring by Aphrodite of Paris and Helen, as she rescues Paris from certain defeat and sets him in his bedchamber, then forces the reluctant Helen to make love with him. Each of these themes is brilliantly handled in itself (with only the Viewing containing minor difficulties, again through the selective deployment of traditional material); but each, in addition, fulfils different and less direct purposes. Bringing Paris and then Helen into the limelight reminds the audience of the whole cause of the war, not only Helen's weakness and Paris' vanity and lust but also the power of the goddess who caused it all; it reminds them, too, that trampling on the laws of hospitality and marriage must be paid for. The first glimpse of life inside this beleaguered but sociable town, to be developed in book 6, is given here, as also of the qualities, not so much of the Achaeans, whose description, except with Odysseus, is almost a formality, as of Hektor and Helen and the rather charmless love-goddess herself. Above all, if the audience has had to draw on its reserves to follow the long catalogues of the previous Book, it is now carried along in episodes that are both absorbing in themselves and deeply illuminating over persons and scenes that will be crucial later.

The fourth Book maintains the same level of concentration, given that its purpose is still to delay, until its end at least, the final clash of forces.

For mass fighting to become once again possible, the truce made for the formal duel of book 3 has to be terminated. That is achieved through the intervention of Athene at Here's behest, and she descends like a meteor, taking the form of a warrior who persuades the archer Pandaros to shoot at Menelaos and so violate the truce. The Achaeans and king Agamemnon are outraged, their moral commitment to capturing Troy correspondingly strengthened. In an episode parallel with that of the Viewing from the Walls in the preceding Book Agamemnon reviews his contingents, distributing praise and blame in a manner which raises a few difficulties (like why Odysseus and Diomedes are singled out for rebuke, and why the former is linked with Menestheus and the Athenians) but serves to give substance to some of these great warriors and emphasize the contradictory qualities of the commander-in-chief himself. At last the conflict of the two armies can be delayed no longer; it is heightened by general descriptions of noise and motion and by developed similes which echo each other and provide a referential substructure for the concrete action. The concluding ninety or so verses describe the first encounters of what will later become an almost endless series; early among them, the death of young Simoeisios exemplifies the pathetic qualities which Homer always sees, and often lets his audience perceive, in war even of the most heroic kind.

It is not the purpose of these preliminary remarks to solve in advance the particular problems which arise in the first four Books, or to condition the reader in his response to them. The work of the Commentary can therefore now begin.

COMMENTARY

BOOK ONE

1–7   Proem: invocation of the Muse and statement of the poet's theme – Akhilleus' wrath and its disastrous consequences

1   The goddess of 1 is the Muse; so also in the opening of the *Odyssey*, ἄνδρα μοι ἔννεπε, Μοῦσα – 'Tell, me, Muse, of the man...' (similarly at *HyAphr* 1, *HyHerm* 1). Muse or Muses are used with little distinction in such cases, compare the invocation at the beginning of the Catalogue of Ships at 2.484 (and 3x elsewhere), ἔσπετε νῦν μοι Μοῦσαι 'Ολύμπια δώματ' ἔχουσαι; also the opening verses of Hesiod's *Theogony* and *Works and Days*. An initial invocation to the Muse or Muses is conventional for epic poems and for the literary kind of hymn, as is the request to 'sing of' – that means, through the poet – the main theme which is to be outlined. ἀοιδοί, singers, regularly claimed to be inspired and taught by the Muses, the goddesses of music, dance and song who were imagined as daughters of Zeus and Mnemosune, Memory, and as dwelling on Mt Helikon or in Pieria close to Mt Olumpos. Hesiod's account of his own inspiration by them as he herded sheep on Mt Helikon is the fullest evidence (see *Theog.* 22–34), but Homer in the *Odyssey* shows Demodokos the Phaeacian singer and Phemios, court singer in Ithake, as similarly inspired. The former is a singer 'whom the Muses loved above others...and gave (him) the gift of sweet song' (*Od.* 8.62–4); he must have been taught (as Odysseus says at *Od.* 8.488) 'either by the Muses...or by Apollo'. Phemios claims to be αὐτοδίδακτος, literally 'self-taught', but the meaning is that he had no human teachers, for 'the god engendered all sorts of themes [literally, 'paths'; i.e. of song] in my heart' (*Od.* 22.347f.). Similarly to Demodokos the god 'gave in abundance the gift of song, to bring delight in whatever way his spirit bids him sing', ὅππη θυμὸς ἐποτρύνῃσιν ἀείδειν (*Od.* 8.44f.).

The 'wrath' of which the goddess is to sing will persist throughout the entire poem and is to determine, in a sense, the fate of Troy; it is caused by king Agamemnon who needlessly slights Akhilleus, but also by Akhilleus himself who shows himself to be tactless in handling his commanding general, and, more important, over-obsessive in defence of his own honour at the expense of his comrades with whom he has no quarrel. How far the

51

wrath-theme might be derived from earlier poetry, and how fundamental and far-reaching it is in the construction and purpose of the *Iliad* as a whole, will be considered from time to time as the Commentary develops; something has been said in chapter 4 of the Introduction, pp. 46f. Meanwhile its immediate beginning is the subject of book 1 which follows.

Usually a heroic song would have a specially composed proem like those of the *Iliad* and *Odyssey*. So much is suggested, among other evidence, by the opening of Pindar's second Nemean ode (the Homeridai most often begin from Zeus as proem, Διὸς ἐκ προοιμίου). But the 'Homeric' Hymns were sometimes themselves called proems, as for example by Thucydides (3.104.4, of *HyAp*), and some of the shorter ones were clearly designed as preludes to a longer epic piece; see N. J. Richardson, *The Homeric Hymn to Demeter* (Oxford 1974) 4f. Moreover a proem could easily be varied from time to time, especially perhaps to suit a special audience or to accord with longer or shorter versions of what was to follow. Thus some (rather unsatisfactory) variants of the *Iliad*-proem are reported. According to Nicanor and Crates as cited by the Anecdotum Romanum (1, p. 3 Erbse), the bibliophile Apellicon owned a text with a single-verse proem, Μούσας ἀείδω καὶ 'Απόλλωνα κλυτότοξον, whereas Aristoxenus claimed that some texts had these three verses in place of 1–9:

> ἔσπετε νῦν μοι, Μοῦσαι, 'Ολύμπια δώματ' ἔχουσαι
> ὅππως δὴ μῆνίς τε χόλος θ' ἕλε Πηλείωνα
> Λητοῦς τ' ἀγλαὸν υἱόν· ὁ γὰρ βασιλῆϊ χολωθεὶς

The first of these verses is Iliadic (4x, see above), but the others show signs of inept condensation, and in particular the linking of Akhilleus' and Apollo's wrath does justice to neither (cf. van der Valk, *Researches* II, 365f.). By contrast the style of the full proem as it appears in the ancient vulgate (i.e. vv. 1–9) is typically Homeric in its forceful conciseness, its cumulative expression with runover in 2 and 4, its verse-pattern climax (7 is a rising threefolder after mainly twofolders, see pp. 20ff.) and its rhetorical transition to the main narrative in 8f. One cannot be absolutely sure that as it stands it *was* by the monumental composer, Homer, but there is nothing against the idea and the tradition is in favour of it.

Had this proem not existed, modern arguments about the exact subject of the poem would be even more diffuse than they are. The ancient critics gave vent to a mass of not very pertinent preliminary questions, preserved in the exegetical scholia AbT on 1: why begin from such a dispiriting concept as wrath? Why describe just the end of a war and not its earlier stages? Why call the poem *Ilias* and not *Akhilleia*, to match *Odusseia*? Why command, rather than request, the goddess to sing? The truth is that Homer provides his audiences with just so much information as they need at this point; the epic is to be set around the central theme of Akhilleus' anger, and this anger had disastrous consequences for the Achaean army. That is enough to highlight the singer's evident purpose of creating a monumental poem out of a profusion of traditional war-poetry, by relating the fighting to a single dramatic event which alters the fortunes of war and encourages the beleaguered Trojans to fight in the open plain.

2 οὐλομένην: '"accursed"...that of which we say ὄλοιο', Leaf; an emphatic runover-word cumulation developed in what follows, 'which put countless griefs on the Achaeans'. On the cumulative technique of this and the next three verses see also pp. 32f.

3 Apollonius of Rhodes evidently read κεφαλάς for ψυχάς in his copy (so bT); this finds some support in 11.55, which has κεφαλάς in a verse which is otherwise identical with 3 (except for minor adjustments). But the contrast implied by αὐτούς in 4 will be clearer if that word implies dead bodies – as opposed to living souls, and therefore ψυχάς, in 3. The implications of the two terms are fractionally different, and Homer chooses each of them according to context. Oral poets can be loose in their deployment of traditional, formular material, but they can also be very precise, as here.

4–5 These verses were athetized by Zenodotus according to Aristarchus (Arn/A on 4); Zenodotus nevertheless read δαῖτα for πᾶσι in 5, a fussy change of the vulgate which Aristarchus (who is evidently Athenaeus' source, through Aristonicus, at 1.12e–13a, cf. Erbse 1, 9) tried to refute on the erroneous ground that Homer never uses δαίς of animal food – as he in fact does at 24.43.

5 A half-verse cumulation, in itself decorative rather than essential for its information, but nevertheless leading to an important new comment. What is this plan of Zeus? Probably, as Aristarchus seems to have argued (Arn/A supplemented by D), that implied by Zeus's promise to Thetis at 1.524–30 to avenge the slight on her son Akhilleus by favouring the Trojans. Aristarchus (Arn/A) also criticized the 'fictions' of recent critics, οἱ νεώτεροι, chiefly perhaps the idea that Zeus's plan in the *Iliad* was identical with that signified by the same phrase in the post-Homeric *Cypria*, frag. 1.7, namely to lighten the over-burdened earth by means of heavy casualties at Troy (this tale is also summarized in the D-scholium on vv. 5f. here).

6–7 ἐξ οὗ: either 'from the time when', giving the starting-point of Zeus's plan, or 'from the point at which', depending on 'Sing, Muse' in 1 and giving a delimitation of the theme; compare *Od.* 8.499f., where the singer Demodokos 'revealed his song, taking it from where, ἔνθεν ἑλών...' The latter is probably correct, despite Aristarchus' support of the former (Arn/A); the poet is implicitly telling himself to sing (with the Muse's help) of the wrath of Akhilleus, from the point at which he and Agamemnon first quarrelled.

8–21   Transition to the main narrative, and the priest Khruses' request to Agamemnon for the return of his daughter Khruseis

8   A rhetorical question designed to highlight the answer, as well as in this case to lead on to the beginning of the story itself. An elaborated form of the expression ἔριδι ξυνέηκε μάχεσθαι occurs at 7.210.

9   It was *Apollo* who started the dispute; an action that is to be so portentous deserves a divine cause. The circumlocution 'son of Leto and Zeus' happens to be unique in Homer, since he did not elsewhere need to be named in such a way as to fill the verse down to the main caesura; although cf. 16.849 Λητοῦς ἔκτανεν υἱός|. The contracted form Λητοῦς is required by metre here and at 14.327, although not at 16.849 which could have read Λητόος (although the vulgate still has the contracted form).

10–11   These verses lack rhythmical fluidity, either because of the difficulties of condensation or through corruption of what must have been an especially frequently-sung passage. In 10 ἀνὰ στρατόν is a common formula, but one which elsewhere, like κατὰ στρατόν, almost always falls before the bucolic caesura – 53 is an exception, but cf. 384, another slightly awkward verse. ὦρσε is also unusually placed (only here in this position out of 17 Iliadic uses and similarly with ὦρσεν; 2/11x *Od.*); ὀλέκοντο δὲ λαοί|, on the other hand, represents an established formula-pattern, cf. στείνοντο δὲ λαοί| etc. The verse-pattern of 10 is also unusual; it is a threefolder with short central colon and rare word-division (in these circumstances) after the second foot: νοῦσον ἀνὰ στρατὸν ὦρσε κακήν ὀλέκοντο δὲ λαοί. In 11 the repeated pattern of dactyl followed by two spondees is also uncommon, although emphatic enough; and τὸν Χρύσην is an exceptionally developed use of the demonstrative ὁ on its way to becoming the Attic-Ionic definite article (although Chantraine, *GH* II, 163–5 usefully underlines the role of emphasis as well as of contrariety in many Homeric uses, differing here from M. Leumann, *HW* 12 n. 1).

ἠτίμασεν and other forms of ἀτιμάζειν are otherwise Odyssean (15x); admittedly the great majority of mss have ἠτίμησ' (although A, B and the fifth-century Ambrosian Codex have ἠτίμασεν, normally printed in modern texts), but this makes the verse unusually and apparently pointlessly spondaic.

12–16   Now the transition from proem to narrative is complete, and the condensed style gives way to a smoothly formular sequence leading to a minor climax in the rising threefold 16 after the preceding twofold verses.

12   The runover-word followed by a strong stop is emphatic, but the consequent harshness of the integral enjambment is unusual; so M. W. Edwards, *TAPA* 97 (1966) 135.

13   ἀπερείσι' ἄποινα, with ἄποινα δέχεσθαι in 20 and δέχθαι ἄποινα in

23, shows that the poet could draw on a developed formula-system based on the idea of ransom.

14–15 The half-verse cumulation in 15 (repeated at 1.374) alters the picture a little harshly; 14 has clearly stated that Khruses is holding garlands in his hands, but 15 reveals that the στέμματα must be fillets (probably of wool) tied to his priestly staff or sceptre – it is *that* which he holds – as a sign of holiness. This is not rhapsodic elaboration, but rather an example of typical, if rare, oral imprecision arising out of the cumulative style.

16 The dual form ᾿Ατρεΐδα is regular and correct (although it is only found once elsewhere, at 19.310, apart from the exact recurrence of this verse at 1.375); it was supported by Aristarchus (Arn/A) against Zenodotus' fussy alteration to ᾿Ατρεΐδας, and is the reading of the medieval mss. It balances κοσμήτορε λαῶν, a development of the common formula ποιμένα -ι λαῶν (44x *Il.*) which must be in the dual, for metrical reasons, if it is to be used in the plural.

17–21 Khruses makes the opening speech of the poem; it is short and carefully composed, mainly out of formular phrases. The ordered variation in verse-pattern is the first thing to be noticed; 17 and 18 are twofold (17 with only the lightest of central caesuras); 19 and 20 are rising threefolders, their formal parallelism accentuated by the -σθαι at their ending:

ἐκπέρσαι   Πριάμοιο πόλιν   εὖ δ᾽ οἴκαδ᾽ ἱκέσθαι·
παῖδα δ᾽ ἐμοὶ   λύσαιτε φίλην   τὰ δ᾽ ἄποινα δέχεσθαι

Then 21 reverts to the calmer twofold pattern. Secondly, the nuances of meaning are quite subtle despite the heavily formular components. The priest's apparently mild request contains a hint of trouble to come – a prayer for Achaean success (obviously a mere formality from a dweller in the Troad) leads to a succinct request for his daughter's release for ransom; then in the closing verse he gently points out that this would be no more than showing due respect for Apollo (for he has held back until now the name of his god and protector). In other words, rebuffing Khruses will mean offending the god himself, a message Agamemnon fails to grasp.

18 Out of 88 Iliadic and 94 Odyssean occurrences of θεοί in the nominative this is the only one in which it is scanned as a monosyllable by synizesis (though cf. θεοῖσιν at *Od.* 14.251). It is certain that the poets were capable of expressing this kind of simple thought without the use of such a rare pronunciation (it became commoner later) and the abandonment of such an extensive and strict formular system. Bentley's ὔμμι θεοὶ μὲν δοῖεν is the best emendation proposed so far, the postponement of μέν being unusual but not impossible.

22–42 Agamemnon's insulting reply, followed by Khruses' departure and prayer to Apollo for revenge

22 ἐπευφήμησαν: 'approved', simply, without the post-Homeric connotation of 'in silence'.

23 On αἰδεῖσθαι see 4.401–2n. *fin.*

25 κακῶς and κρατερόν make a strong impression after the deceptive mildness of the preceding verse: 'this did not please him, but he dismissed him unkindly and gave him the following harsh command'.

26–32 Again, Agamemnon's reply begins with a smooth and indirect (but sinister) recommendation consisting of three cumulative verses; then comes the abrupt and categorical 'I shall not release her', followed by a cumulative sentence of corresponding length to the first and culminating in the malicious detail of 31; finally a single-verse injunction, it too moving from staccato beginning to apparently relaxed end.

26–8 Complicated in meaning if apparently straightforward in form (see the preceding comment): first the indirect prohibition ('let me not find you here', meaning 'do not stay'), then the legalistic and almost gloating amplification, by polar disjunction, of 27 ('either now or later') with its derogatory δηθύνοντ' ('hanging about'), leading to the menacing and blasphemous 28.

29–31 The threats against the girl Khruseis are, by contrast, openly expressed, ungainly (in the sound of πρίν μιν) and pathetic ('far from home') by turns, and leading to the tasteless summation of household duties, from weaving to concubinage, in 31. The sentence is a powerful one typical of Agamemnon at his nastiest; it is not surprising that it offended Aristarchus' over-sensitive ideas of what was 'seemly' in Homer, and he athetized the three verses 'because they undermined the point and the threat, since even Khruses would have been pleased to have her associate with the king; moreover it is unfitting, ἀπρεπές, that Agamemnon should say such things': so Aristonicus in A, although 'even Khruses...with the king' may seem unlikely to derive from Aristarchus himself.

33 ὁ γέρων, like ὁ γεραιός in 35, comes close to the developed definite article; see comment on 10–11.

34 Is there an intended contrast between the priest's silence (ἀκέων) and the roar of the sea (πολυφλοίσβοιο)? Ostensibly not, since he is silent because he decides to obey and not reply, and the sea is roaring because that is what it typically does, at least in the genitive – πολυφλοίσβοιο is a standard epithet and fills the necessary part of the verse, given that the poet chooses to emphasize the idea of the sea at this point. Yet the overtones of θῖνα...θαλάσσης and so on are often of tension or sadness (e.g. of the heralds going unwillingly at 327; the embassy at 9.182; Akhilleus' mourning at 23.59, cf. his sadness at 1.350) and this perhaps colours Khruses' temporary silence, making it ominous.

35–6 Compare *Od.* 2.260, where Telemakhos goes aside to pray, ἀπάνευθε κιών ἐπὶ θῖνα θαλάσσης (cf. *Od.* 6.236). The participial phrase belongs to an interesting formular system that is aurally generated:

ἀπάνευθε θεῶν	(3× *Il.*)
ἀπάνευθε νεῶν	(4× *Il.*)
ἀπάνευθε κιών	(1× *Il.*, 2× *Od.*).

'Going apart' is presumably to increase the ritual effectiveness of the prayer and the personal claim upon the god (not so that the enemy cannot overhear, as bT suggest!). The rising threefold verse 35 is a solemn one, and the solemnity is increased by the formal mention of the god's parentage in 36.

37–42 Khruses' prayer follows the regular religious pattern: initial listing of the god's titles and local associations; then the special claims on his favour; finally, and quite briefly, the request itself.

37–8 Khruse is the priest's home town, and his name is taken from it. It probably lay on the west coast of the Troad some five miles north of Cape Lekton, near the site of the later city of Hamaxitos, where there are slight remains of a temple of Apollo Smintheus; see Cook, *Troad* 232–5. Strabo (13.612f.) objected that this temple was too far from the sea to fit the Homeric description (cf. 34–6 and 430–41); that seems rather pedantic since the later Smintheum (surely a crucial factor in the case) is only a kilometre or so from the coast. He placed it south of Mt Ida in the plain of Adramuttion, with Thebe and Killa in the same area. Thebe at least probably did lie there (cf. Cook, *Troad* 267), and Killa may have done; in any case Khruseis must have been on a visit away from home when she was captured at Thebe, 1.366–9 – see the third paragraph of the comment on 366–92.

39 Σμινθεῦ: according to Apollonius Sophistes (Erbse I, 20) Aristarchus insisted that the epithet was derived from a city in the Troad called Sminthe, against those who thought 'unfittingly' that it came directly from σμίνθος = 'mouse' (in Mysian) and therefore meant 'mouse-god' or protector against mice; for in Rhodes at least there was a festival called Smintheia for Apollo and Dionusos, because they killed the mice who were destroying the young vines.

ἔρεψα is from ἐρέφω or ἐρέπτω, 'I roof', implying perhaps *completion* of a temple rather than a simple type of building in which the roof was the main part, i.e. on posts. Early (ninth-century B.C.) temple-models, like house-models, show complete walls (some of apsidal type), cf. e.g. Lorimer, *HM* pl. XXXII.

40–1 For the burning of thigh-bones in sacrifice see the comments on 447–68 and 462–3.

42 The prayer itself is brief, epigrammatic almost, and comprehensive. Δαναοί is another Homeric name for the 'Αχαιοί (who are also called 'Αργεῖοι, Argives, see also on 2.333–5); it implies descent from the mythical king Danaos who took refuge in Argos with his daughters the Danaids.

43–52 *A plague is sent by Apollo upon the Achaean army*

44–7 Apollo manifests himself directly – as archer-god he sometimes needs to be on or near the spot, not on Olumpos. He is equipped with quiver and arrows which clatter as he rushes down, emphatically enraged (44 χωόμενος, 46 χωομένοιο). Zenodotus athetized 46f. for reasons unspecified, οὐ καλῶς according to Aristarchus (so Arn/A). Verse 47 does indeed arouse some suspicion of rhapsodic interference, since αὐτοῦ thus (not in contrast with anything else) is weak, and the very mention of the god's movement unnecessary after what has preceded. Has χωομένοιο displaced an original κινυμένοιο (cf. |τοῦ καὶ κινυμένοιο at 14.173), then developed in 47? But 'like night', at least, is effective; surprisingly it is not found elsewhere in the *Iliad*, although recurring in the perhaps rhapsodic expansion about Herakles with his bow in the underworld at *Od.* 11.606 (κλαγγή also appears there in the preceding verse, although of the dead not of arrows).

50 The exegetical commentators (AbT) made some odd suggestions about why mules and dogs were the first victims: to give men due warning, since Apollo was a humanitarian god? Or because these animals are notorious sniffers and therefore likely to pick up diseases quickly – mules especially so because of their mixed nature? Yet the animal victims *are* remarkable, and could be a reminiscence of a real plague, cf. Thucydides II.50.1. Apollo's arrows usually signify sudden death for men, generally from disease, just as Artemis kills women, often in childbirth.

51 βέλος ἐχεπευκές (also at 4.129) is an unusually violent case of metrical lengthening. The epithet means 'pointed', cf. πεύκη, πευκεδανός, Chantraine, *Dict.* s.v.

53–120 *Summoning of the assembly, and beginning of the quarrel between Akhilleus and Agamemnon*

53–4 ἐννῆμαρ, 'for nine days', according to a scholium of Erbse's class h, 'because the poet is inclined to the number nine', which is true; we should say rather that it is a conventional interval in the oral tradition. Several other and less probable explanations were considered, for example that it is the time taken for a fever to reach its climax (for a similar medical concern in the exegetical tradition see 2.20–1n. *init.*). Note the unusual rhythm of 53, where ἀνὰ στρατόν (on which see also 10n.) in effect bridges the third-foot caesura and there is no fourth-foot break.

55–6 Why was it Akhilleus who summoned the assembly? Because he was the greatest of the warrior-captains, and (as bT say on 54) up to a point anyone could call an assembly; but also, for the poet, because this action draws him into the necessary quarrel with Agamemnon. Herē gives him the idea of doing so, which has the added advantage of identifying her early in the poem as sympathetic to the Achaean side. She works from afar, which also emphasizes her divine power; where the intervention has to be more concrete and immediate (as with Apollo and the plague, or with Athene at 194f.) the deity must be present in person, fully or partly materialized. The exegetical scholiasts (bT) worried over 56: how could Here be concerned for the Danaans if she was about to encompass the wrath of Akhilleus? Their answer, correct in its way, was that, despite early casualties, his withdrawal from fighting would bring the Trojans into the open and so shorten the war.

57 ἤγερθεν ὁμηγερέες τ' ἐγένοντο|: typical epic redundance, and traditional, since this is a formular expression (2x *Il.*, 3x *Od.*); compare e.g. ἀγορήσατο καὶ μετέειπεν (9x *Il.* including 73, 15x *Od.*). ὁμηγερέες is also formular before the masculine caesura, 4x *Il.*

58 On the apparently otiose, 'apodotic', δ' see 194n.

59–67 It is worth noticing that Akhilleus' opening remarks to Aga-memnon are perfectly unprovocative.

59 Aristarchus (Arn/A, Hdn/bT) rightly disagreed with those who wished to separate πάλιν from πλαγχθέντας so as to give it a temporal sense, 'again', which is non-Homeric, and make it allude to the tale of an earlier false landing at Teuthrania in Mysia, cf. Proclus' summary of the *Cypria*, OCT v, 104.

59–61 εἴ κεν with the optative in 60 is a remoter condition than εἰ with the future indicative in 61 (so Leaf). Here it represents a parenthetical correction: 'now we shall be driven back home (if we escape death at all), if we are to contend with plague as well as war'.

63 Zenodotus athetized this verse, evidently because dream-interpreters, not otherwise mentioned in the *Iliad*, belong to a different category from prophets and priests. Aristarchus replied (Arn, Hdn, Nic/A) that the punctuation in 62 should follow ἐρείομεν and not ἱερῆα, so that μάντις is the genus, ἱερεύς and ὀνειροπόλος are the species. The first is the prophet in general (with bird-flight as a special province, see on 69–70), the second prophesies from sacrifices, the third from dreams. That may be too subtle; it reduces the afterthought-effect of 63, although it is true that the cumulative style enjoys afterthoughts.

65 Aristarchus (Hdn/A) supported an enclitic particle ταρ here, εἴ ταρ rather than εἴτ' ἄρ'; admittedly εἴτε...εἴτε is a relatively new development (so Chantraine, *GH* ii, 293f.), but the vulgate εἴτ' ἄρ'...εἴθ' is probably correct, nevertheless.

Akhilleus here categorizes certain ritual errors quite carefully – divine displeasure could arise over either prayers or sacrifices, omitted or wrongly performed; but he does not mention, perhaps deliberately, other possible offences, such as the one Agamemnon might have committed against Apollo's priest.

ἑκατόμβη was generally derived from ἑκατὸν βοῦς (so e.g. bT), although in 66 it is sheep and goats, not cattle, that are its constituents, and elsewhere the number of animals involved is less than a hundred; cf. 6.93 and 115, 23.146f. To doubt the etymology (as e.g. Leaf does) is probably superfluous, since the term may well have become generalized over the course of time.

66–7 It is worth looking back at the elegant variations in colometry: 62 and 63 twofold with strong central caesura, 64 and 65 fourfold with light semantic bridging of the main caesura but no fourth-foot break. Then comes contrast as the sentence closes, with 66 most naturally sung as a rising threefolder (αἵ κέν πως ἀρνῶν κνίσης αἰγῶν τε τελείων), leading through integral enjambment into the completive and restful twofold 67.

ἀντιάσας with the genitive means 'come to meet' (and therefore accept) sacrifices, cf. *Od.* 1.25. βούλεται must be subjunctive after αἵ κεν, and is therefore irregular in form – perhaps read βούλητ' with Payne Knight and Curtius (Chantraine, *GH* i, 458).

68 A formular verse, occurring 5x *Il.* including 101, 1x *Od.* κατ' ἄρ' ἕζετο: on what? the ground? seats? Presumably the former, since the Achaean assembly would normally be held, by force of circumstance, somewhere near the ships – at 7.382f. it is close to the stern of Agamemnon's ship. At 2.99 and 211, after coming to assembly from the ships and huts, 'they sat down and were marshalled into (or according to, κατά) their places', ἐρήτυθεν δὲ καθ' ἕδρας. At 18.246f. the Trojans *stand* in assembly because of their panic. Probably the terminology and the assumption of seating in phrases like καθ' ἕδρας are derived from settled peacetime conditions; for example at *Od.* 8.16. the Phaeacians flock to the ἀγοραί τε καὶ ἕδραι. Homer evidently did not pay close attention to this relatively minor matter.

69–70 Kalkhas is unlikely to be a Homeric invention, if only because of his close connexion with events at Aulis; although his father Thestor is unknown and looks fictitious. The minor Trojan Alkmaon is also 'son of Thestor' at 12.394, and a third Thestor is Patroklos' victim at 16.401. This suggests that Thestor for Homer is a general-purpose name devoid of very specific associations – although θεσ- may have useful divine echoes in the present instance, cf. θέσπις, θεσπέσιος. Kalkhas is a diviner by bird-flight

(69 οἰωνοπόλος), but also a μάντις in the broad sense (see on 63) – priest and prophet of Apollo (72) who thus accurately understands past and present as well as foreseeing the future (70, and cf. Hesiod, *Theog.* 31f., where the poet, like the prophet, needs divine inspiration for his all-embracing knowledge).

71 Is this an implicit reference to the otherwise non-Homeric tale of the expedition's earlier navigational error that brought it to Mysia (59n.) – or simply to Kalkhas' favourable interpretation of the portent at Aulis, recalled at length by Odysseus at 2.300–2, which set the fleet on its way to Troy?

74–83 Kalkhas' opening speech (its cautious, not to say devious, tone contrasting piquantly with ἐΰφρονέων in 73) is designed to protect him against the king's probable annoyance at what he will say, namely that Agamemnon must surrender his own prize. The dangerous wrath of kings against bearers of bad news was a commonplace later, for example in Sophocles' *Oedipus Tyrannus* and Euripides' *Bacchae*, and was probably so already in the epic tradition before Homer's time. Kings were also prone to be angry at mere disagreement, cf. 2.195–7, 9.32f.

74 μυθήσασθαι: 'to declare ⟨the meaning of ⟩' Apollo's wrath.

76 Typical formular variation of the verb, with μοι ὄμοσσον (4× *Il.*) for μευ ἄκουσον (2× *Il.*, 4× *Od.*). σύνθεο, something like Leaf's 'mark my words', is redundant in the standard form of the verse (e.g. ἐκ γάρ τοι ἐρέω, σὺ δὲ σύνθεο καί μευ ἄκουσον) but useful in the variant form.

bT comment that Akhilleus does not resent Kalkhas' demand for an oath because he knows it is designed to protect himself against the king.

77 μήν (Ionic) becomes μέν (Attic).

78 ἄνδρα is direct object of χολωσέμεν: 'that I shall anger the man who...'

80 χέρηϊ: more correctly χέρεϊ (a contracted form of χερείονι) according to Herodian in A. Zenodotus is said to have athetized the verse (so bT), which is in fact harmless, a typical heroic *sententia*; but since he also read κρείσσω not κρείσσων (that is, to be taken with κότον in 82), Erbse is right to suspect that it was really 81 he objected to – no more enlighteningly, if so.

82 κότον: 'resentment' in contrast with 81 χόλον, '(immediate) anger'. ὄφρα τελέσσῃ: 'until he brings it to fulfilment'.

85–91 Akhilleus' response to Kalkhas: he swears an oath to protect him, as requested, and by Kalkhas' tutelary god Apollo (whom he describes as 'dear to Zeus' at 86, as he himself had been described by Kalkhas at 74). No one will lay hands on the prophet, not even Agamemnon – a gratuitous addition, this, and mildly insulting, the beginning of trouble. The comprehensiveness of Akhilleus' guarantee was plain enough without directly mentioning the king again.

85 θεοπρόπιον here and θεοπροπίας in 87 are variant forms used as convenient to the singer. The -προπ- component has no connexion with *prec-* = 'pray' as LSJ and others claim, but rather with πρέπω; a θεοπρόπος is one who 'makes the god, or the divine thought, *known*', Chantraine, *Dict.* s.v.

88–9 The oath itself is couched in solemn terms, helped by the solemn expansion of ζῶντος, 'living', into 'and seeing the light upon earth', a regular expression in later poetry; and by the progression from the routine epithet 'hollow' to the more significant 'heavy', of hands (T is unwise here in claiming that this is because they are holding weapons).

There is an interesting variation of this couplet at *Od.* 16.438f.: (the man does not exist)

> ὅς κεν Τηλεμάχῳ σῷ υἱέϊ χεῖρας ἐποίσει
> ζώοντός γ' ἐμέθεν καὶ ἐπὶ χθονὶ δερκομένοιο

in which the latter verse has the advantage over the Iliadic version of avoiding the contracted forms ἐμεῦ and ζῶντος, a relatively 'late' feature (indeed the latter contraction is unparalleled in Homer); the short dative plural κοίλης is a similar development (of -ῃσι) which Homer avoided where possible. In fact 88–9 could be re-cast as follows:

> οὔ τις σοὶ παρὰ νηυσὶ βαρείας χεῖρας ἐποίσει
> ζώοντός γ' ἐμέθεν καὶ ἐπὶ χθονὶ δερκομένοιο

There is no sign of this in the tradition, but one is tempted to wonder whether oral economy would have been abandoned so lightly.

90–1 Now comes the cumulative addition in which insult lies: not only the specifying of Agamemnon (see on 85–91) but also the ambiguous description in 91; for εὔχεται, although it usually implies a justified claim (made in accordance with what Leaf termed 'a naive consciousness of position'), as in Nestor's flattering reference to Agamemnon at 2.82, can also suggest a dubious boast as at e.g. 20.102, 'would not easily win, even if he claims to be all of bronze'.

91 The MS tradition is unanimous for ἐνὶ στρατῷ (or ἀνὰ στρατόν) as at 15.296, despite the unusual agreement of the ancient critics – Zenodotus, Aristarchus, Sosigenes, Aristophanes, so Did/A – that 'Αχαιῶν, viz. ἄριστος 'Αχαιῶν, is correct. Both are formular variants, but the former is obviously preferable for specifically martial or tactical contexts, as indeed at 15.296, the latter for more general ones. What Agamemnon claimed was to be 'by far the best of (all) the Achaeans', that is, as overall king. It is odd that the scholars had so little effect, even though they were probably right; but that sometimes happened. The irony suggested by εὔχεται (on which see the previous comment) is all the heavier since Akhilleus assumes himself to be 'best of the Achaeans', ἄριστον 'Αχαιῶν, at 244.

92–100 Kalkhas is emboldened to disclose the cause of the plague in no uncertain terms: Agamemnon has dishonoured, ἠτίμησ' (94), Khruses, and must return his daughter without ransom.

93 The wording of Akhilleus' question at 65 is exactly repeated in this categorical negative response.

96 Aristarchus athetized (Arn/AbT) 'because superfluous', ὅτι περισσός. This refers to the way in which τοὔνεκ' takes up ἕνεκ' ἀρητῆρος in 74. There may be some minor looseness here, but it does nothing to cast doubt on a verse which is forceful and, in ἠδ' ἔτι δώσει, brilliantly disquieting in its implications for the future.

97 Yet another case, hard on 91 but more serious, in which the medieval MSS ignored the majority advice of the ancient critical tradition; for they accepted Zenodotus' inelegant λοιμοῖο βαρείας χεῖρας ἀφέξει despite Aristarchus with the support of Rhianus and the Massiliotic 'city' text (so Did/A, with T adding 'and almost all the editions', καὶ σχεδὸν πᾶσαι). It is not often that a city text was cited for a correct reading, Δαναοῖσιν ἀεικέα λοιγὸν ἀπώσει, which despite the MSS has become the modern vulgate.

98 πρίν γ' ἀπὸ πατρὶ φίλῳ δόμεναι ἑλικώπιδα κούρην: a good instance of the combination of simplicity and ornateness (including alliteration here) in Homeric expression. πρίν γ' has been neatly prepared for by πρίν in the preceding verse; the tmesis of ἀπό...δόμεναι is effective since it encloses πατρὶ φίλῳ, and stresses his importance as recipient – the epithet φίλῳ, although a standard one, still has emotive force, especially when set against ἑλικώπιδα of the daughter. This is a unique description of a girl in Homer, although formular in ἑλίκωπες 'Αχαιοί (etc.), 6x *Il.*; perhaps, therefore, dignity rather than charm is implied. The meaning of the ἑλικ- element has been much debated; ancient critics and lexicographers varied between 'black' (citing an unidentified dialect-form as well as Callimachus, cf. frag. 299.1 Pfeiffer) and the more obvious 'swivelling' in various more or less improbable applications. In modern times Leaf has supported 'with rolling eyes', implying animation, while Page, *HHI* 244f., revived 'black-eyed'; Chantraine, *Dict.* s.v. remains cautious.

99 ἀπριάτην is an adverb at *Od.* 14.317 and was so taken by Aristarchus here (Arn/A), but the parallelism with ἀνάποινον suggests rather that it is adjectival here.

99–100 As often, the conclusion of a sentence or short speech in Homer is slightly different in rhythm so as to provide climax or contrast. Kalkhas' speech from 93 on consists of a pair of 4-verse sentences, each lightly enjambed in periodic, progressive and cumulative style. All 8 verses are two- or fourfold, with strong central caesura in all except the opening and closing ones, 93 and 100, where there is light semantic bridging. But only 99 and 100 have true runover cumulation, grammatically inessential but contrived to lead on to fresh information; in addition 100 alone has a strong stop after the runover (ἐς Χρύσην), followed by a short summarizing statement. The effect of the whole speech is of straightforward and comprehensive, but not banal, assertion, combining formular elements and repetitive references to previous speakers' words (e.g. 93, 95) with individual touches (e.g. 96 ἔτι δώσει, 98 ἑλικώπιδα).

101 On the question of seating see 68n.

103 The strong stop after the runover-word sharpens its impact: '– annoyed he was; and his black φρένες were greatly filled all round with might [i.e. rage]'. Anatomically the φρένες are the midriff, but commonly in Homer imply 'heart' or 'mind' in a general sense. They are in any case the seat of passion, whether courage, confidence, anger or love. It is tempting to take ἀμφὶ μέλαιναι as one word (as most MSS did against the scholiasts, cf. AbT), 'black all over', especially perhaps in view of 17.499, ἀλκῆς καὶ σθένεος πλῆτο φρένας ἀμφὶ μελαίνας (cf. also 17.83 and 573). Yet it is unambiguously stated elsewhere that emotion *surrounds* the φρένες; love φρένας ἀμφεκάλυψεν at 3.442 and 14.294, and, of desire for food, περὶ φρένας ἵμερος αἱρεῖ at 11.89. The φρένες are black probably because suffused with blood, which is regularly so described, as μέλαν αἷμα, in Homer.

104–5 His eyes, ὄσσε, shine like fire, a sign of μένος in general – compare Hektor's at 12.466; and as he begins, πρώτιστα, to speak he gazes upon Kalkhas in an evil fashion, κάκ' ὀσσόμενος, confirming by this slightly awkward repetition that his μένος is anger, not 'good' martial might.

106–20 Agamemnon directs his remarks first at the seer and then at the Achaeans in general (he is using the plural imperative by 118). His anger comes out in three different and successive ways: (i) by the biased denigration of Kalkhas as prophet; (ii) by the uncontrolled central sentence (109–15) which turns to a frank and even brutal comparison of Khruseis with Klutaimestre; (iii) by the unreasonable closing demand for the immediate production of an equivalent prize.

106 A verse with a powerful beginning, 'prophet of evils', and a puzzling end; for κρήγυον is not found elsewhere in Homer, and presents other difficulties too. It obviously means 'good' rather than 'true' here, see on 116–17; its later uses are mainly Hellenistic and might be derived from this very passage, although occurrence in an early Hippocratic treatise (*Coan Prognoses* 31) suggests that it could be an old vernacular term. Moreover τὸ κρήγυον εἶπας is curious; this Book has other relatively developed uses of the definite article (see on 11), but the article with a neuter adjective, as here, almost looks post-Homeric; it is more extreme than at *Od.* 14.12. The neglect of digamma can be paralleled, of course, and in any case εἶπας can be easily restored to the regular form εἶπες. Perhaps Attic modernization of the phrase should be assumed, in which case Leaf's suggestion κρήγυον ἔειπες, with metrical lengthening of the upsilon, might be envisaged as the Homeric form. Most MSS do in fact have ἔειπες or ἔειπας (which is not recorded in e.g. OCT precisely because of incompatibility with κρήγυον); although that could be under the influence of common verse-endings like μῦθον ἔειπεν, κατὰ μοῖραν ἔειπες.

108 Probably οὔτε...οὔτ' (rather than οὐδὲ...οὐδ') is correct, and Aristarchus and Aristophanes (Did/A) preferred it as more emphatic. The exegetical scholia (AbT) show that there was probably much ancient discussion about Agamemnon's motives for blackguarding Kalkhas, especially in view of the latter's helpful divination at Aulis (71n.). At the time he may have thought the prospect of a ten-year war, even if ultimately successful, bad rather than good – and then there was the matter of his having to sacrifice his daughter on Kalkhas' advice. Homer does not mention Iphigeneia by that name, but that does not mean that the tale was post-Homeric, as T on 106 suggests; see on 2.101–8.

110 Aristarchus athetized this verse (Arn/A) because that makes the expression more concise, σύντομος; but brevity was not often what an oral singer wanted. For τοῦδ' ἕνεκα foreshadowing οὕνεκ' in 111 cf. πρίν...πρίν in 97f.

112 Leaf says βούλομαι here means 'prefer', as in 117 and also 11.319, 23.594 etc.; but in those passages the verb is followed by ἤ, which makes all the difference. Agamemnon simply says 'I want to have her at home', and then goes on to explain that he prefers her, προβέβουλα, to Klutaimestre.

113 Klutaimestre is correctly so written, without an 'n'. This is now accepted as the correct version of her name (though with -α for -η) in Attic tragedy; A alone of Homeric MSS gives a slight sign of that by writing a diaeresis over the ν in this, her solitary Iliadic mention, and a single papyrus and scholium omit the letter. The derivation is agreed to be from κλυτός (see Chantraine, *Dict.* s.v. κλέος) and μήδομαι, cf. μήστωρ: 'famous counsellor' (and not from μνάομαι in the sense of 'woo', cf. μνηστήρ).

114–15 The formula κουριδίην ἄλοχον etc. usually has an affectionate and pathetic ring, as in 'young bride'; so at 11.243, and also of the husband, κουρίδιον, at 5.414 and 15.40. Here, on the other hand, those overtones are not present, and it means little more than 'wedded wife' in the legal sense, as perhaps at 7.392 and 13.626. Agamemnon prefers Khruseis because she is 'no worse' (i.e. better) than Klutaimestre in three respects: physically (δέμας ἠδὲ φυήν, 'body and stature', a rather formal phrase which may be designed to play down for the occasion any element of what the scholia called πόθος, that sexual desirability to which the king had already alluded at 31); in intelligence or perhaps disposition, rather (φρένας); and in accomplishments (ἔργα, i.e. weaving and other household duties). The whole rhetorical list of female qualities could be worse – that is, even more heroic; but it has a suggestion of the cattle-market all the same. That suits Agamemnon's temperament.

116–17 From Agamemnon's reluctant agreement to accept Kalkhas' diagnosis of the trouble it appears that his criticism in 106–8 had been that the seer's earlier prophecies had been unpalatable rather than untrue – unless his anger has made him quite inconsequential. In any case he seems just to have thought of a face-saving device: he will surrender his own prize provided another just as good is substituted without delay (118).

In 117 the vulgate reading is σόον, but Aristarchus (Did/A) argued for σῶν here in accordance with *Od.* 5.305 (and *Il.* 22.332), despite accepting σόον at 16.252. In fact the correct uncontracted form is σάον. Zenodotus athetized 117 as 'foolish', but Aristarchus (Arn/A) justly replied that it must be taken in context and is quite in character. It is indeed typical of the king's rather unctuous manner when he remembers his duties.

119 All the Argives receive a γέρας, a prize, when booty has been captured; the present consignment has come from raids on other cities of the Troad. As commander-in-chief Agamemnon has first claim.

121–87 The quarrel develops: Akhilleus threatens to go home, and Agamemnon to take Briseis

122–9 Apart from the gratuitous φιλοκτεανώτατε (which in any case may have been a little less insulting in an acquisitive heroic society than we should profess to find it), Akhilleus' response is calmly stated and not overtly provocative. It begins with a careful reply, in three whole-verse sentences, to the question in 123; and even the interrupted and integrally enjambed closing statement, 127–9, is not exactly excitable. His analysis of the position seems logical enough: (i) There is no unused stock of prizes. (ii) What has already been distributed cannot reasonably be recalled. (iii) The king will be recompensed three- and fourfold if and when Troy is captured. But this does leave the supreme commander without a female captive for the time being (for if he has others at his disposal, as Akhilleus certainly does at 9.664f., this is not mentioned); and from the standpoint of τιμή, 'honour', that is the important thing.

124 For ἴδμεν followed by a participle see on 4.356–7 *fin.*

126 Is the meaning 'it is not fitting for the army to gather these things up again', or 'it is not fitting to gather these things up again from the army' (with λαούς as second object of ἐπαγείρειν)? The run of the sentence slightly favours the former, but the emphasis on λαούς as first word perhaps swings the balance to the latter; Akhilleus would be pointing out that any redistribution would affect the army as a whole, not just the leaders, which is an effective debating-point. That would depend on whether the ordinary soldiers got a share of the booty; presumably they did, and 119 if anything suggests it.

128 'Three- and fourfold' as might be legally due to a creditor, as AbT astutely comment.

129 Aristarchus (Arn/A) criticized Zenodotus for reading Tροίην, and argued for trisyllabic and adjectival Tροΐην, meaning 'a Trojan city' rather than the city Troy itself; 'for it was unclear' (he adds) 'whether they would capture it'. Precisely; that is what αἴ κέ ποθι Ζεύς in 128 says, whereas further captures in the Troad would be easier to predict. Thus Zenodotus on this occasion was right.

131–47 Agamemnon now lets his feelings show more clearly. ἀγαθός in 131 is not necessarily flattery (see also on 275–6), and indeed bT are probably right in claiming it as an ironical counterpart to Akhilleus' κύδιστε at 122. But then in 132 he openly accuses Akhilleus of deceit – by which he presumably means that the result of his supposedly close reasoning is intolerable, and the reasoning itself therefore specious.

133–4 Aristarchus (Arn/A) athetized, on the ground that the verses are weak in content and composition as well as unfitting for Agamemnon. This shows how erratic a judge of style Aristarchus can be on occasion. First, they are necessary to the context since 132 could not lead directly to 135. Secondly, they are perfectly in character. Thirdly, their subtle complexity of expression (especially in ὄφρ' αὐτός..., in contrast with the pathetic but falsely-echoing αὔτως...δευόμενον), combined with the supposedly naive and resumptive parataxis of κέλεαι δέ..., are typical of Homer at his brilliant best.

136 A difficult verse: ὅπως ἀντάξιον ἔσται cannot mean 'see to it that...', or at least this construction is not paralleled in Homer. Rather '(let them give it) fitting it to my wishes, in such a way that it will be a just equivalent'.

138 The increase in syllabic weight from τεόν to Αἴαντος to 'Οδυσῆος is paralleled in 145 (δῖος 'Οδυσσεύς being taken together).

139 Aristarchus (Arn/A) athetized the verse as unnecessary after 137, and because ὁ δέ κεν...is foolishly obvious. The run of the sentence does indeed suggest a time when 138 was its completion; but the elaboration in 139, aoidic rather than rhapsodic in character, is effective precisely because of what Aristarchus found silly, namely the sinister and·dramatic 'he will be angry, will the man I come to'. Its paratactic and false-naive quality resembles that of κέλεαι δέ με...in 134, which Aristarchus also found objectionable. Note that ἵκωμαι implies that Agamemnon will take the prize in person, see on 185.

141–7 In the latter part of his reply Agamemnon reverts to his better kind of royal demeanour, in ordering preparations to be made for the girl's prompt return to her father. The balanced pairs of imperatives (141f. ἐρύσσομεν and ἀγείρομεν, 143f. θείομεν and βήσομεν) express the workmanlike nature of his injunctions; somehow, however, an unctuous note is heard, to which the gratuitous ἐπιτηδές (only here and at *Od.* 15.28 in Homer), as well as the frequent use of the first person plural ('let's all do this together...'), contribute. The profusion of epithets is conventional enough, but nevertheless *divine* sea and *fair-cheeked* Khruseis add, in the circumstances, to the bland and devious impression (ἅλα δῖαν 6x *Il.*, but 14x without that epithet).

145–6 The final sting is the addition of Akhilleus to the list of possible delegates (on which compare 138, with comment, as well as on 308–11) as an apparent afterthought, and then with the ambivalent address as πάντων ἐκπαγλότατ' ἀνδρῶν. How insulting is this term ἔκπαγλος? Iris addresses Akhilleus so when she bids him go to the rescue of Patroklos' corpse at 18.170, and Akhilleus himself addresses a Trojan victim likewise at 20.389. No particular insult can be intended in the former at least; indeed the range of ἔκπαγλος in general is from 'amazing' to 'vehement' to 'excessive' according to context – it does not simply mean 'terrible' or 'violent' as LSJ assert; see also on 3.415. Yet it does not in any event suggest qualities desirable in the leader of a mission of expiation and reconciliation (or for that matter in a man of counsel, 144), and its choice by Agamemnon is certainly malicious.

148–71 The expressions introducing the speeches on either side (121, 130) have been neutral so far, as 172 will be; but now Akhilleus speaks ὑπόδρα ἰδών, 'with frowning look', from root *δρακ-, cf. δέρκομαι; that is, from under lowered brow (or as Chantraine says, *Dict.* s.v. δέρκομαι, 'regardant de bas en haut'), a formula associated with speech and expressing extreme displeasure and rebuke; see also on 2.245. The speech that follows is both passionate and rhetorical, as in its initial question (150f.). At times like this (compare especially 9.308ff.) Akhilleus thinks and speaks like no one else in Homer, mainly because of his unique vision of what war really means and what draws men to it.

149 'Clothed in shamelessness' (cf. 'utterly shameless' in 158) because he exploits the τιμή of others in favour of his own. κερδαλεόφρον is 'crafty' (as of Odysseus at 4.339) rather than 'avaricious' – κερδαλέος can signify both.

151 ὁδὸν ἐλθέμεναι: a specific reference to the journey to Khruse proposed by Agamemnon, with the rest of the verse as transition to the idea Akhilleus wants to develop, namely the reasons for fighting.

154–6 The suggested motives for fighting – to avenge cattle- or horse-rustling or the destruction of crops – are distinctly over-simplified, since the heroic code of gift-obligations must often have compelled one chieftain to take up arms in another's quarrel.

156–9 See pp. 21f. for the relation between sense and colon-structure in these four verses.

157 A fluid and emotive verse, with its pattern of long, short, and long vowel-sounds; see also Griffin, *HLD* 75.

158–60 The style becomes breathless, with a sporadic interjection of pure abuse ('utterly shameless one...dog-face').

161 'You threaten to take away my prize in person': see on 185.

162 Are the two separate points made here a mere accident of the paratactic style, so that the real meaning is no more than 'I worked hard to get the prize the Achaeans gave me'? Probably not; the careful argumentation (despite flashes of passion) suggests that Akhilleus feels he has two separate claims on Briseis: (i) he suffered much in order to win her, and (ii) he was formally awarded her as prize. πολλὰ μόγησα -ας is repeated at 2.690, and the whole theme will be developed at length by Akhilleus at 9.325–32 and 341–4.

165 The alliteration, prefigured in 164, is part of the rhetorical style, and here expresses one of Akhilleus' bursts of indignation.

167–8 The note of pathos, prominent from 161 on, continues in the proverbial 'little but loved' (cf. *Od.* 6.208) as well as in 'when I have worn myself out fighting'.

169–71 The conclusion is surprising, since we expect Akhilleus simply to announce his withdrawal from the fighting. It is all the more dramatic for being stated in such a matter-of-fact way: 'Now I shall go to Phthie, since it is obviously much better to return home with my curved ships, nor do I mean to continue dredging up wealth for you here [σ' elided for σοι, 170] when I am being dishonoured'. Here the paratactic style does some odd but effective things with the logic of the sentence: the ἐπεί-clause professes to give a reason, but is really no more than a parenthetical supplement; the true reason, that he is being dishonoured, is given in a paratactic addition, 'and I do not propose to...' ὀίω (with either long or short iota in Homer) and ὀίομαι (always with long iota for obvious metrical reasons) mean something like 'have the impression that' (so Chantraine, *Dict.* s.v. οἴομαι), with the idea of personal prediction (amounting sometimes, as here, almost to intention), as distinct from νομίζω ('believe on the basis of accepted truth') and ἡγέομαι ('judge after careful consideration'). On 169 φέρτερον see 186n.

172–7 Agamemnon begins calmly, by contrast, and is both sarcastic and complacent.

173 φεῦγε μάλ': 'run away by all means' (Leaf); the irony continues in the clause that follows, 'if that is what your heart is set on' – similarly

Diomedes to Agamemnon at 9.42. θυμὸς ἐπέσσυται is lightly formular, 3×
Il., not *Od.*

175–6 Here the idea of τιμή, which underlies the whole dispute between
the two men, is more openly expressed. The addition of Zeus to those who
will honour Agamemnon constitutes a startling claim. One reason for
Agamemnon's confidence must be that kings are 'Zeus-reared', διοτρεφέες
(8× *Il.*, 4× *Od.*); his own title to respect is fully set out at 2.100–8 (see
comments there), where his royal sceptre is said to have been given to
Pelops by Zeus and then to have descended in the male line. But then the
recognition in 176 that Akhilleus, too, is one of these Zeus-reared kings, and
that they can nevertheless be hateful and behave badly, seems to under-
mine the whole argument. At this point Agamemnon must have it in mind
that he is commander-in-chief, and therefore especially entitled to Zeus's
protection. Moreover the other leaders have sworn allegiance to him, and
that involves Zeus as ὅρκιος, protector of oaths.

177 Aristarchus evidently athetized here (Arn/A), thinking the verse
to belong more properly at 5.891 (Zeus to Ares). It is indeed used a little
loosely here; as the scholiast on Dionysius Thrax 13.1 (1, 60 Erbse) observed,
a love of fighting and battles is no bad thing in a general. Yet 178 follows
better on 177 than on 176, and doubtless the verse – a formular one which
could be applied either more or less aptly in different contexts – should be
kept. αἰεί in any event makes a typical start to a rebuke, cf. 541.

178–80 The asyndeton of 178 and 179, the rising threefolder 179 and
the sigmatic stress of 180 all indicate Agamemnon's growing excitement.

179–80 The 'companions' are, of course, some of the same Myrmidons
he will rule over (180; as prince, at least, since his father Peleus still lives)
back home in Phthie. It is a border region in a sense, or at least one that
had seen certain shifts in population (pp. 186f.), and there may be a sneer
at Akhilleus' provinciality.

181 The threat is formally stated as though it were an oath or a prayer.
It is thus no idle one, nor will Akhilleus take it as such.

182–4 As bT pertinently observe, Agamemnon manages to imply that
he is as superior to Akhilleus as Apollo (who has taken *his* prize) is to himself.

183 Agamemnon stresses that the ship (141–6) is to be *his* ship manned
by *his* companions, i.e. that his action is voluntary and not forced on him
by Akhilleus. The verse is similar in pattern and formular composition to
179:

| 179 | οἴκαδ' ἰών | σὺν νηυσί τε σῆς | καὶ σοῖς ἑτάροισι |
| 183 | τὴν μὲν ἐγώ | σὺν νηΐ τ' ἐμῇ | καὶ ἐμοῖς ἑτάροισι |

Part of the same formula-system has appeared already in 170:

| 170 | οἴκαδ' ἴμεν | σὺν νηυσὶ | κορωνίσιν, | οὐδέ σ' ὀΐω... |

This verse, however, is a fourfolder, that is, there is no strong semantic bridging of the central caesura (for although 'curved' goes with 'ships', the connexion is not so close as effectively to override the caesura – nor is there a fourth-foot word-break to provide a substitute). Verses 179 and 183, on the other hand, are rising threefolders, with virtual bridging of the central caesura (since the possessive pronoun goes very closely with its noun) and substitution of a fourth-foot caesura instead, balancing the second-foot one and so dividing the verse into three increasing rhythmical units.

185 αὐτὸς ἰὼν κλισίηνδε: now Agamemnon tries to make it clear that the appropriation of Briseis (who is named in 184 for the first time) is to be credited to him and no one else. It is that which makes him say he will go *in person* to Akhilleus' hut and take her. He does not, in the event, do so, but sends two heralds instead (320–48). Why? Perhaps because he is a natural boaster – bT compare his emphatic but unfulfilled assertion about Khruseis at 29, τὴν δ' ἐγὼ οὐ λύσω, which is not entirely fair because the plague intervened to change his mind. Or perhaps because a little tact and royal prudence intervene? That is possible; in any case Akhilleus for his part, in his eventual reply at 225ff., does not refer specifically to this obviously sensitive detail but merely in general terms to δῶρ' ἀποαιρεῖσθαι, 230; and in his final great oath at 297–303 he contents himself with saying that he will not fight over Briseis, but will kill anyone who tries to take anything else of his.

So far the apparent discrepancies over whether Agamemnon will remove Briseis in person can be explained as psychological subtleties, and do nothing to justify Analytical speculation about the possible conflation of divergent accounts. Thus at 137f. the king had threatened to take either Akhilleus' prize or that of Aias or Odysseus – if, that is, no other adequate prize could be provided. At 161 Akhilleus reports this as a threat by Agamemnon to remove *his* prize αὐτός, for which, in that particular context, 'in person' may be too definite a translation. Then in the present passage Agamemnon in his rage escalates his threat in three ways: (i) he drops any reference to the possibility of a substitute prize from some common stock (perhaps because Akhilleus has pointed out at 124 that there is no such thing); (ii) he omits Aias and Odysseus as possible donors and concentrates on Akhilleus; (iii) he makes αὐτός (cf. 137 and 161) unambiguous by expanding it to αὐτὸς ἰὼν κλισίηνδε. When it comes to instructing the heralds at 322ff. he says that *if* Akhilleus refuses to surrender the girl to them, *then* he will go and take her in person 'accompanied by many more'. All this may well reflect, and probably does so, a close observation on Homer's part of the vagaries of human character and behaviour; but soon things will become more difficult. In reporting events to his mother Thetis, Akhilleus will first of all say that Agamemnon took the girl away himself, ἑλὼν γὰρ ἔχει γέρας, αὐτὸς ἀπούρας (356); then, that the heralds took her

(391f.). There is a contradiction here, and it cannot be explained away by arguing that αὐτὸς ἀπούρας implies no more than that it was Agamemnon's wilful decision; αὐτὸς ἰὼν κλισίηνδε here makes that virtually impossible. Admittedly, when Thetis prefers the former version in supplicating Zeus she may be choosing the one likely to affect him most; but that kind of motive cannot be assumed when Thersites, also, in addressing the whole Achaean assembly at 2.240, uses that same unambiguous description: 'because he took his prize and keeps her, having removed her himself'. That is malicious, like everything else Thersites says – but could he have said it if part of it could be immediately controverted by practically everyone present?

The possibility begins to present itself that what began as a mere threat is becoming established in the minds of some of the characters – and, at odd moments, of the poet himself? – as what actually happened. There is still no compelling need to presuppose two clearly distinct versions, in one of which the king removed the girl in person, in the other of which he did not; but by now one may be more inclined to accept, as well as the certainty of much psychological insight, the possibility of a degree of oral inconsistency and imprecision.

186 φέρτερος, 'superior': there is an implied contrast with καρτερός in 178. Akhilleus may be stronger in battle, but Agamemnon is his superior overall, and that is what counts. Attempts to give φέρτερος a more specific meaning (let alone make out that φέρτερον meaning 'better' at 169 and 4.307 is an 'abnormal feature', Shipp, *Studies* 229) are misguided.

187 A sense of completion at the end of the speech is given both by the (inevitable) end-stopping after four preceding enjambments and by the restoration of the regular twofold pattern after the intermittent threefolders in the speech as a whole, at 174, 177, 179, 183 (q.v. with comment) and 186. The speech began with light enjambment and comparatively frequent end-stopping (especially in the sequence of whole-sentence verses at 176–8); it ends with a long six-verse statement containing one periodic, one progressive and three integral enjambments. The effect is of unshakeable intention rather than uncontrollable passion.

The content of the verse is remarkable too, since Agamemnon concludes by in effect denying the right of free speech in assembly and claiming that his opinion must prevail in any dispute. That is contrary to the accepted practice, emphatically stated (with this episode in mind?) by Diomedes later in the poem when at 9.32f. he tells the king 'I shall fight (μαχήσομαι) with you over your wrong-headedness, as is the established custom in assembly – and do not be angry about it': ἢ θέμις ἐστίν, ἄναξ, ἀγορῇ· σὺ δὲ μή τι χολωθῇς. That is, others have the right to put forward their opinion in assembly just as much as the presiding king, and he must not lose his temper thereat (cf. 74–83), let alone threaten reprisals. Normally, no doubt, in the case of a disagreement between the king and a single other chieftain the rest would tend to support the king. In the present instance Akhilleus will take no notice of the king's threats but will abuse him even more strongly (225ff.), and after an attempt at mediation by Nestor the assembly will be dissolved in deadlock.

188–222   Akhilleus is tempted to kill Agamemnon on the spot, but Athene intervenes in person and dissuades him

188   The affront to his honour contained in the king's last words turns Akhilleus' growing anger into ἄχος, mental anguish.

188–92   His heart is divided over whether to draw his sword and kill Agamemnon, or not; the description of his internal struggle is made more graphic by the addition that it took place within his 'shaggy chest' (στῆθος can be used either in the singular or in the plural, for a single chest). The φρήν, which often as here is simply the seat of emotions, also has in Homer a more technical sense of diaphragm or lungs (see further R. B. Onians, *The Origins of European Thought*[2] (Cambridge 1954) 23ff.; Chantraine, *Dict.* s.v.).

Aristarchus (Arn/A) felt that 192 'undermines the idea of his anger' and athetized it, implausibly, arguing that what Akhilleus was trying to decide was whether to rouse up the others or to kill Agamemnon himself.

193–4   The traditional vocabulary for expressing inner conflict is limited; even the vocabulary for the organs of thought and feeling is imprecise. θυμός, in origin 'breath' and so 'anger' as in 192, is more or less equivalent to φρήν in the formular phrase κατὰ φρένα καὶ κατὰ θυμόν (10x *Il.*, 11x *Od.*; the whole of 193 is found 4x *Il.*, 3x *Od.*), simply as 'heart' or 'mind' in a loose sense. Here 193 perhaps suggests too deliberate a consideration, and his simultaneous and impulsive drawing of his sword from its scabbard suggests more accurately what is likely to happen.

In a way, Athene may be said to represent, or embody, his ultimate decision to go no further – see 3.396–8n., on Aphrodite as a partial embodiment of Helen's emotions – although it is to her divinity rather than her arguments that he accedes at 216–18. His violent and confused emotions are reduced to something like a formal debate, although in his own heart and mind. The goddess no doubt represents, to some degree, the orthodox code of behaviour – the principle of order which the gods encourage and support in men – to which he eventually adheres; but she also acts as an individual caught up in the actual course of events.

194   ἦλθε δ᾽ ᾽Αθήνη: the δ᾽ is 'apodotic' and apparently otiose (so Aristarchus according to Arn/A), as commonly in the language of epic; it 'underlines the correspondence between subordinate and main clause' in the paratactic style (Chantraine, *GH* 11, 356f.). So also in a temporal sentence (for example) at 57f., οἱ δ' ἐπεὶ οὖν ἤγερθεν... τοῖσι δ' ἀνιστάμενος μετέφη (also 4.210f.), and in a conditional one at 137, εἰ δέ κε μὴ δώωσιν, ἐγὼ δέ κεν αὐτὸς ἕλωμαι.

195–6 Aristarchus (Arn/A) athetized here, obviously wrongly, on the grounds that the poet could not have intuited these divine matters, and probably, also, that the verses are correctly in place at 208f. The ancient critics did not in any event properly understand the use of repetition in the oral style, but, even apart from that, the poet as narrator often ascribes divine motives without hesitation. In fact the language is slightly better fitted to this initial context, since ἄμφω at 209 (revealing to Akhilleus that Here likes him no better than Agamemnon) might be regarded as rather tactless.

197 Athene 'took [*or* seized] him by his brown hair': she gave it a good tug is the implied meaning, to gain his attention without delay. This is perhaps the most remarkable of all corporeal interventions by a god or goddess in the *Iliad*. Aphrodite picks up a chair at 3.424 (see comment there), Ares kills and strips a warrior at 5.841–4, Apollo knocks Patroklos' armour off him at 16.791ff., and so on – but Apollo, at least, is concealed in mist, invisible, and Aphrodite is disguised, even if only partially so. Here Athene appears in her own presence, even if to Akhilleus alone, and that makes her simple and material action all the more striking.

198 The verse is a little casual in expression, with Athene 'appearing' to Akhilleus (in the sense that he saw her, ὁρᾶτο) although she is behind him and he has not yet turned round (199). It could be a singer's afterthought to increase the power or intimacy of the theophany by restricting it to a private audience, or perhaps even to limit the departure from realism; bT suggest that it is to spare Akhilleus' pride.

200 Her terrible eyes shine forth – she is a goddess, and in an urgent mood. But she is also Athene, who is conventionally γλαυκῶπις in Homer (as indeed shortly at 206); whether that means 'blue-grey-eyed' or 'owl-eyed', it still makes her remarkable for her gaze, and Akhilleus recognizes her at once. The exact reference of γλαυκῶπις cannot be determined, but see Leumann, *HW* 148ff.; βοῶπις of Here suggests there may be a relic of theriomorphic forms in each case, but see further on 551.

201 This is the first occurrence in the poem of a very common formular verse (14× *Il.*, 15× *Od.*) and its even commoner component ἔπεα πτερόεντα προσηύδα (55× *Il.*, 60× *Od.*, + variants). Words are 'winged' because they fly through the air rapidly, like birds.

202–5 He expresses no surprise, but bursts into an indignant little speech (two short related questions, two abrupt assertions) which characteristically assumes that it is the king's outrageous behaviour rather than any fault of his own that has caused Athene's appearance.

203 ὕβριν: G. P. Shipp incorrectly classed the use of this word as 'late' ('one of the many features that suggest that A [i.e. book 1] is not old' (!), *Studies* 199) on the grounds that it is common in the *Odyssey* and only appears, with its derivatives, five times in the *Iliad*. But arrogant behaviour is, of course, characteristic of the suitors, and that is why it is so frequent in the probably later poem. It is repeated here at 214, where it is implied by 213 to be a legal offence, see on 213–14.

205 As often, the gist of the oath or threat is contained in an epigrammatic concluding verse. τάχα means 'soon' in Homer; ἄν with the subjunctive is an emphatic future, Chantraine, *GH* II, 212.

207–14 Athene says briefly why she has come and that Here has sent her (see also on 195–6). The short sentences with twofold verses, sometimes progressively enjambed or internally interrupted, suit the urgency of the occasion but also suggest an effortless confidence.

207 αἴ κε πίθηαι -ηται: a formula (5× *Il.*, 1× *Od.*) presumably designed in the first instance for mortal rather than divine persuasion; although even the gods can use coaxing language to mortals, and Athene is being tactful here, especially at 211–14 as the scholiasts noted. The αἴ κεν...locution does not in any case necessarily imply serious doubt about the outcome, see on 408 and 2.72.

212 A formular verse, 6× *Il.*, 3× *Od.* (including minor variations).

213–14 Actually Akhilleus will receive far more than the value of Briseis, if she can be so valued; 24.686 suggests that 'three times' is a conventional factor, which also has legal overtones (cf. 128 and comment, also on 203), as well as reinforcing the passionate sibilation. The resumptive σὺ δ' ἴσχεο...provides typical closing contrast after the more leisurely pace and discursive tone of the preceding verse-and-a-half.

215–18 Akhilleus' three-verse reply maintains the small scale and low key of Athene's 8-verse speech of advice which precedes it. The whole episode, indeed, after Akhilleus' initial violent impulse, is kept severely in place, presumably so as not to detract from the dramatic force of the main argument between the two leaders. Akhilleus' uncharacteristic reasonableness perhaps prefigures his more important change of heart over the mutilation of Hektor's body in book 24. It begins in 216 with an almost sycophantic tone, but quickly reverts to heroic values of indignation and calculation.

218 A rising, climactic threefolder, proverbial and epigrammatic in expression, with gnomic τε in its second part as often in generalizations (including similes).

219–22 A serviceable conclusion to the episode, framed by two/threefolders (219 and 222) with fourth-foot caesuras. ἦ = 'he spoke', and ἦ καί normally indicates that the action about to be described accords with the words just reported. Zenodotus for some reason (Arn/A on 219f.) compressed 219f. into a single verse, ὡς εἰπὼν πάλιν ὦσε μέγα ξίφος οὐδ' ἀπίθησε, thus doing away with a graphic counterpoint to 194 – perhaps because he thought hands were properly heavy because loaded with weapons, cf. comment on 88–9.

221 βεβήκει: 'was in the act of going'.

222 Aristarchus (Did?/A) wondered whether the verse should be athetized, since it will transpire at 423f. that the gods had departed on the previous day on an 11-day visit to the Aithiopes. But in that case it would be not only this verse but the whole intervention of Athene (who had come 'from the sky', 194f.) that would be in doubt. In fact there *is* a mild oral inconsistency, arising not so much here as when the poet comes to develop the Thetis scene later in the Book; see on 423–5.

223–305   The quarrel continues; Nestor's attempt at conciliation fails, and the assembly is dissolved

223 ἀταρτηροῖς: a word of unknown derivation according to Chantraine, *Dict.* s.v.; yet context here and at *Od.* 2.243, as well as Hesiod, *Theog.* 610, compels something like 'mischievous' or 'harmful' as the meaning, and so does not preclude the obvious connexion with √αρ = 'join', and so 'discordant'.

225–33 Aristarchus (Arn/A) was clearly right to reject Zenodotus' attempt to athetize this whole passage, presumably because of its violent abuse of Agamemnon. The exegetical scholia in T show that there was a lively ancient debate on how justified Akhilleus' accusations (of drunkenness, shamelessness, cowardice and greed) might be. The pro-Agamemnon party regarded the criticisms as malicious distortions of necessary kingly qualities, such as having wine available for official entertaining, remaining somewhat inaccessible and avoiding being a conspicuous target in battle. That is clearly rather absurd, but the question remains a difficult one. The representation of Agamemnon in the epic as a whole is complex and variable, emphasizing now his generic royal qualities, now his genuine difficulties as commander of such a diverse and temperamental force, now his special personal weaknesses. For he was often undeniably irresolute (as in his repeated suggestions that the expedition should give up and go home, which begin in the next Book), although not actually cowardly; he put the blame on others when he could; and his demeanour toward Akhilleus and concern with his own possessions, as indicated in preceding comments, has been less than admirable.

225 Akhilleus has already called Agamemnon 'dog-eyed' or 'dog-faced', κυνῶπα, at 159, in connexion with the idea of his shamelessness (μέγ' ἀναιδές, 158). Fawning gaze combined with unabashed sexual and excremental interests probably accounts for the choice of dogs; but the term can also be used of women – or goddesses – and Helen describes herself so at 3.180 (q.v. with comment) and *Od.* 4.145. Cf. Hesiod, *Erga* 67, with M. L. West's comment.

226–7 Akhilleus' next insult depends on an interesting contrast between ordinary warfare, with the whole λαός ('host' or army) involved, and the λόχος composed only of nobles, σὺν ἀριστήεσσιν 'Αχαιῶν. The λόχος is the small raiding or ambushing party which calls for the highest daring and endurance, as is most explictly described at 13.275–86; at 13.277 the λόχος is where 'true value, ἀρετή, is most clearly discerned'. See also on 275–6.

228 τὸ δέ τοι κῆρ εἴδεται εἶναι: '*that* appears to you as death itself', i.e. as a mortal danger to be avoided.

229–30 A brilliant and stylish summation of Akhilleus' previous complaints: Agamemnon prefers to remove the property of ⟨anyone⟩ whoever disagrees with him.

231–2 Another passionately compressed accusation: Agamemnon is δημοβόρος, 'devourer of the people', that is, of their property, because they are weak and let him get away with it; otherwise his latest affront would have been his last. There is a marked similarity in tone to Hesiod's criticism of 'gift-eating kings' at *Erga* 260–4; no doubt it was something of a commonplace.

233–44 Now Akhilleus turns from abuse to a more positive and even more impressive kind of rhetoric; he swears a solemn oath by the staff he holds in token of his right to address the assembly. This is the oath: that the Achaeans will miss him sorely, and that Agamemnon will be helpless as they fall at Hektor's hands, and will bitterly regret dishonouring the 'best of the Achaeans' (cf. 91n.). Shipp's suspicions of 'lateness' (*Studies* 226), based primarily on ναὶ μά in 234 and Attic παλάμαις (invariably corrected to -ῃς) in the mss at 238, are not compelling.

234–9 The staff or σκῆπτρον belongs to the heralds who control the assembly; they give it to the speaker whom they recognize as having the floor. It is therefore a particularly solemn object, symbol of royal and indeed divine authority – Agamemnon's own staff or sceptre at 2.100–8 has descended to him through the rulers of Argos from Zeus himself, and here at 237–9 the staff Akhilleus is holding is one habitually held by the law-makers who guard the divine ordinances laid down by Zeus; see also on 2.109. The oath is made even more impressive by associating the staff with the idea of inevitability: just as it will never sprout leaves again, so will this oath be fulfilled. The development of detail in 235–7 (its being cut in the mountains, the bronze axe that trimmed it) resembles that of similes, and for some of the same reasons, for example emphasis and emotional force – but also to make the oath more impressive and exotic, and therefore more effective.

239 A particularly solemn verse, beginning with the name and authority of Zeus and ending with an emphatic reaffirmation of the power of the oath that will follow.

240–4 The oath turns out to be quite indirect in its formulation, almost riddling to begin with (240), then dwelling on Agamemnon's helplessness against Hektor in the closely enjambed verses which follow (241–4). The effect is sinister and the upshot unmistakable: that his withdrawal from the fighting is seriously meant, and that the king will come to rue the day he caused it. The verse-structure in this whole speech is marked by frequent internal punctuation combined with severely regular colon-pattern – there is not a single threefolder after the initial verse of abuse at 225.

242 ἀνδροφόνοιο: a powerful, almost shocking (πρὸς...κατάπληξιν, T) first use in the poem of this epithet, although it is formular for Hektor (11x).

243–4 ἀμύξεις: literally 'lacerate', another strong word, the more so for not being fully formular (although ἄμυσσε occurs once elsewhere at the verse-end at 19.284): 'you will lacerate your spirit within you | in anger because...' On ἄριστον Ἀχαιῶν see 91n.

245–52 The language of this short narrative interlude, with its strong internal stops, runover, cumulation and integral enjambments, is much tenser than that of Nestor's speech which follows at 254–84, where whole-verse patterns will predominate. Note the symmetrical arrangement of 245–9: strong bucolic diaereses at 246 and 247 are flanked by verses with heavily marked central caesura, while the uninterrupted and indeed almost honey-sweet flow of 249 marks the conclusion.

245–6 Flinging the staff to the ground expresses Akhilleus' frustration (Telemakhos does the same, and bursts into tears, at *Od.* 2.80f.); but it is also a dramatic confirmation of his oath.

246 A cumulative verse which serves the purpose of stressing the staff's special status through its exceptional decoration (on which see 2.45n.), but also of getting Akhilleus seated as Agamemnon is.

247 For the king rages ἑτέρωθεν, 'from the other side'; the poet evokes a tableau which symbolizes the fixed opposition of the two men. The scene could almost have ended here, and the assembly have been dissolved, but Nestor is introduced without delay and within 247 itself, so that his intervention is unlikely to have been an afterthought or subsequent elaboration. Thus Nestor's role as counsellor and mediator is established early in the poem, the quarrel is given even more weight, and the inflexibility of the two contenders – who at 285–303 will reject his reasonable proposals – is demonstrated in a new light.

247–52 Nestor is described quite fully here at his first mention in the poem, unlike Akhilleus and Agamemnon who were assumed to be well known. Perhaps he was unfamiliar to many of the audience, or perhaps the singer just wants to emphasize his persuasiveness and venerability so as to give greater force to his advice. He is also 'one of Homer's favourite characters' (Willcock).

Anything that is γλυκύς, sweet, to men can be described by an obvious exaggeration as 'sweeter than honey' – even war and anger, in Homer; but because honey tastes sweet on the tongue it was especially appropriate to sweet words, and became a commonplace, notably in Pindar, for the poet's words.

250–2 A neatly constructed sentence beginning with a rising threefolder and passing from integral enjambment to the relaxed cumulation of the final verse. Nestor rules over the third generation in Pulos (the important Achaean kingdom in the south-western Peloponnese, see on 2.591–4) and is unusually old to be present on the field of battle; hence his role of counsellor and his garrulous reminiscences. But what did Homer mean by saying that 'two generations...had already perished...and he ruled among the third'? bT, partly dependent here on Porphyry's commentary, insisted that since his father Neleus had perished, and his brothers too (at the hands of Herakles, 11.690–3), Nestor as survivor must be ruling over a third generation of subjects; therefore, assuming thirty years to a generation, he must be over sixty and perhaps around seventy. At *Od.* 3.245, however, Telemakhos comments of Nestor that 'they say he has thrice reigned over generations of men'; he is admittedly ten years older now, but there may be a misunderstanding of the distinction between ruling *among* the third generation (252 μετὰ δὲ τριτάτοισιν ἄνασσεν) and ruling *over* three generations (*Od.* 3.245 τρίς...ἀνάξασθαι γένε', where the language is ambiguous).

250 μερόπων ἀνθρώπων: 7x *Il.*, 2x *Od.* The formula must have been long established, not only because no one later could say precisely what it meant but also because it had had time to generate an unmetrical adaptation into the nominative, μέροπες ἄνθρωποι, at 18.288. Later poets occasionally used μέροπες to mean 'mortal' or suchlike; the commonest explanation of the word was that it was a compound of √μερ meaning 'share' or 'divide up', cf. μείρομαι, and ὄψ, 'voice', therefore 'dividing up one's speech into separate words', 'articulate'. This is unlikely to be correct since, as Leaf long ago observed, if the word is an ancient one the digamma of Ϝόψ could not have been neglected, and therefore μερ- would have been scanned as long. Merops is a prophet and Trojan ally at 2.831 and 11.329; more to the point may be that the early inhabitants of Kos were called Μέροπες according to Pindar (e.g. *Nem.* 6.31) and others, and that μέροψ is also the name of a bird (the Bee-eater). The tribal names Druopes and

Aeropes, too, are apparently based on bird-names, which has led to the speculation that Meropes could be a tribal name of that kind (cf. Chantraine, *Dict.* s.v.); which still leaves the problem of why men in general should be called by that tribal name. For other theories, none compelling, see Frisk s.v.; H. Koller, *Glotta* 46 (1968) 18–26.

254–84 Nestor's intervention is straightforward and expressive, with predominantly end-stopped verses; internal interruption is conspicuous only at 270f., and integral enjambment only in the conclusion, at 282–4. The speech is pointed and persuasive, and even the autobiographical central section is a purposeful *exemplum* which does something to reinforce the old man's role as conciliator.

258 The rising threefolder neatly defines this rare combination of qualities, on which see 2.201–2n.

259 A practised transition into one of Nestor's reminiscences, which will become even longer as the epic proceeds.

260 Aristarchus (Arn/A) argued for ἡμῖν, not ὑμῖν as supported by Zenodotus, in order to soften the criticism: 'better than us', not 'better than you'. Most medieval MSS sided with Zenodotus, and indeed Nestor is not usually too delicate in his references to modern decadence; but Aristarchus may be right in view of 262.

263–5 These are Lapiths from Thessaly, famous in myth and art for the fight that broke out when the Centaurs became drunk at king Peirithoos' wedding to Hippodameia and tried to rape her and the other women. Theseus of Athens, an old friend and ally, helped Peirithoos against them; the basic story, without this Athenian detail, is attested also at 2.742–4 and *Od.* 21.295–304, and ends in the Centaurs being driven out of their home on Mt Pelion and across to the Pindos region. The verse concerning Theseus recurs in the sub-epic and pseudo-Hesiodic *Shield of Herakles*, 182; it is not discussed in the scholia, is quoted as Homeric by Dio and Pausanias, but survives in only a minority of medieval MSS. It is probably correct to see it as a post-Homeric embroidery, probably of Athenian origin in the sixth century B.C. when Theseus-propaganda was at its height. As for Nestor's involvement with the war between Lapiths and Centaurs, that may be Homer's own idea (so Willcock), based on the tradition that his father Neleus was Thessalian by birth and only moved down to Pulos later.

266–7 The dramatic repetition κάρτιστοι...κάρτιστοι...καρτίστοις is an entirely successful piece of rhetoric, archaic and almost hieratic in feeling – although not of course necessarily archaic in composition.

268 φηρσίν: it is quixotic to deny, like Leaf citing Meister, that φήρ is the Aeolic form of Ionic θήρ. These 'wild animals' are the Centaurs, shaggy creatures who are half man and half horse (Homer does not need to say that explicitly) and dwell on the slopes of Mt Pelion in Aeolic-speaking

Book One

Magnesia. It is quite probable that there were earlier hexameter poems about them, Aeolic rather than Ionic in colouring and origin, from which phrases like φηρσὶν ὀρεσκῴοισι were derived. The latter word recurs only once in Homer, at *Od.* 9.155, and then of goats; probably therefore it means something close to 'mountain-dwelling', with its second element connected with κοῖτος, κεῖμαι, 'lying'.

271 κατ' ἔμ' αὐτόν: 'by myself', not because he was unwilling to fight among the Lapiths (since he had accepted their invitation to help them), but rather as a boast: he fought without a chariot or charioteer to back him up, as he also claims to have done at 11.720.

272 μαχέοιτο: 'late' according to Shipp, *Studies* 226; 'exceptional' but not necessarily post-Homeric according to Chantraine, *GH* I, 351. μαχέοιντο at 344 is another matter, and either μαχέονται or μαχέωνται should probably be restored there.

273–4 The message of the *exemplum* is that strong fighters follow Nestor's advice and obey him; and the word 'obey' rings out three times as past and present are reconnected.

275–6 σύ: Nestor does not address Agamemnon by name but can be imagined as turning to him first; despite his distinction (ἀγαθός περ ἐών) he should not remove the girl – not because Akhilleus says so, but in order not to upset the original distribution of booty. ἀγαθός does not ever mean 'strong', quite, in Homer (as Griffin, *HLD* 53, assumes); it is the adjective of which ἀρετή, aristocratic excellence in general, is the equivalent noun. At 131 the same qualification, ἀγαθός περ ἐών, was applied by Agamemnon himself to Akhilleus; it covers both martial and social distinction, indeed the two go together – see also the next comment.

276–81 Now Nestor turns to Akhilleus: he should avoid quarrelling with Agamemnon, who is φέρτερος, 'superior', in so far as he rules over more people – and that outweighs Akhilleus' own superiority as fighter (καρτερός, 280) and son of a goddess. The argument depends on the idea of kings as protected by Zeus, and therefore of the greatest of kings as more protected than others. 278ff. admittedly does not state this very clearly, but there is no reason therefore to count it as post-Homeric elaboration, as Von der Mühll and others have done. Agamemnon is accepted by the other βασιλῆες as overall leader, and we know moreover that they were bound to him by oath, which involves Zeus once again as ὅρκιος.

282–4 At this point Nestor turns back emphatically to Agamemnon, completing the ring of argument and the A–B–A pattern with a very direct injunction (σὺ δὲ παῦε) backed by a personal request (αὐτὰρ ἔγωγε| λίσσομ') based on Akhilleus' key role in Achaean defence.

286–91 Agamemnon pays enthusiastic lip-service (ναὶ δὴ ταῦτά γε πάντα...) to what Nestor has said, but obviously has not heeded a word

81

of it. He completely ignores the practical suggestion that he should give up the idea of taking Briseis, and harps obsessively on Akhilleus' domineering behaviour instead of abandoning his own μένος as Nestor had asked at 282. In particular, at 290f. he specifically sidesteps the old man's soothing distinction between φέρτερος and κάρτερος. In short, every single part of Nestor's speech is studiously ignored.

291 Aristarchus (Arn/A) took ὀνείδεα as subject of προθέουσιν, literally 'insults run forward' for him to utter them, an odd and difficult expression which also fails to contribute to a strong statement overall. He was doubtless persuaded by the difficulty of προθέουσιν if its subject is to be θεοί; that would, however, give a far stronger sense, something like 'if the gods have made him a powerful fighter, do they for that reason put it before him [i.e. encourage him] to speak only in insults?' The difficulty is in taking -θέουσιν as a part of τίθημι. Chantraine, *GH* I, 459 n. 1, who describes the form as 'extrêmement déconcertante', rejects the possibility of its being a present indicative, preferring the idea that it might be an aorist subjunctive with short vowel to e.g. Schwyzer's conjecture that it comes from προθήμι, i.e. προσίημι. The difficulty remains, but does not in my opinion justify Leaf's conclusion 'I see no choice but to regard the passage as hopelessly corrupt.'

292 ὑποβλήδην: literally 'interruptingly' ('it is a sign of anger not to tolerate a detailed accusation', bT). The term is used only here in Homer (but cf. 19.80 ὑββάλλειν), who normally lets his characters have their say. Even here, indeed, Agamemnon's point as expressed in 287–91 seems complete in itself; it is only the present verse that suggests he was intending to continue.

293 Agamemnon has complained that Akhilleus wishes to be in command, and the latter's interruption is designed to show that this is not so, but rather that he refuses to yield to the king in doing everything he says (that is, however wrong it might be – he is obviously thinking of the order to surrender Briseis). This is, in fact, a reasonable defence of Akhilleus' position. A king does not have to be obeyed when he is patently wrong, or wrong by general consent.

294 ὑπείξομαι is from ὑπο-ϝείκω; the original digamma is ignored, but such cases of this in a compound verb (as e.g. in ἀπειπόντος, 19.75) are too widespread in Homer to be regarded as exceptionally late, let alone post-Homeric.

295–6 Aristarchus athetized 296 (Arn/A on 295), believing that μὴ γάρ ἔμοιγε does not need another verb but depends on ἐπιτέλλεο; 296 is therefore a feeble supplement by someone who failed to understand this. Similar arguments are applied by Aristarchus elsewhere, sometimes more justifiably as at e.g. 21.570; but in the oral cumulative style such explanatory additions can be made by a singer even when they are not necessary. In the present case γάρ in 295 implies that the sentence will continue; moreover there is nothing un-Homeric in 296, indeed the deceptively mild 'I don't believe I shall obey you' (which Aristarchus probably judged to be unacceptably weak) is highly effective as well as typical of Homer.

297 A formular verse (7× *Il.*, 6× *Od.*), often used in tense and excited utterances to introduce a new consideration or a drastic conclusion. Here the new thought, at 298–303, will be expressed coherently and with apparent calm, whatever the passion behind it – at least until 303 itself. See also on 4.39.

298–301 This clarifies Akhilleus' position but also introduces one important change in it, which turns out to be a brilliant device for avoiding an immediate physical confrontation (and so observing the spirit of Athene's advice at 206ff.) at the same time as preserving his own honour apparently intact. It is not quite the case that he 'yields in a noble-natured way', μεγαλοφυῶς εἴκει, as bT put it; rather he makes the honourable counter-threat that is required by Agamemnon's threat to take Briseis in person, but restricts it to any further aggressive act by Agamemnon, not to the girl's removal itself. It is, of course, highly unlikely that the king will consider seizing any further possession of Akhilleus; the imagined case is an artificial one which allows the latter to sound threatening without actually involving himself in a possibly dangerous situation. But that is not all, for in 299 he contrives to implicate the Achaeans in general, not just the king, in the removal of Briseis, and thus distracts attention, to some extent, from Agamemnon's particular crime against himself. He does this both in the first and in the second part of the verse: '(I shall fight) (a) neither with you, Agamemnon, nor with anyone else...(b) since you [in the plural] have taken her away, after giving her to me'; the implication perhaps being that the Achaeans as donors (see on 162) have more right to take her back.

302–3 The threat is rephrased as a challenge made in public – ἵνα γνώωσι καὶ οἵδε –which culminates in a sinister and typically epigrammatic conclusion: try it, and blood will. flow – or rather, since Homer's language, formular though it may be, is more vivid than any modern cliché, 'straightway will your black blood spurt around my spear'. For ἐρωέω (and ἐρωή) in Homer see Chantraine, *Dict.* s.v.; the basic meaning seems to be 'withdraw from', sometimes with the added connotation of haste, including both 'rush out' as here and 'draw back' as at 13.776, 14.101.

305 λῦσαν: their both rising to their feet, ἀνστήτην, indicates that the assembly is over; there is no formal dissolution, as normally, by the king or his agents the heralds.

Book One

306–48   Khruseis is sent home by ship, and Briseis is removed from Akhilleus' hut by Agamemnon's heralds

307   This is the poem's first mention of Patroklos, as 'son of Menoitios' simply – an allusive reference which suggests (proves, indeed, unless it be the result of minor oral insouciance) that the audience was already familiar with him. That does not necessarily mean that he was an important figure in the heroic tradition (like e.g. Agamemnon, who was introduced solely by patronymic at 7; see also on 247–52), or that his role before Troy was not greatly expanded by the monumental composer. Admittedly, Μενοιτι-άδη is Homer's formular way of denoting Patroklos in the dative case in the central part of the verse (4× *Il.*); but the poet could easily have recast the verse to give his name directly had he thought it necessary to do so. As it is, the bridging of the main caesura by the heavy patronymic gives the effect of a third successive rising threefolder, after 305 and 306, and thus helps to constitute an especially forceful and emphatic conclusion to Akhilleus' part in the great debate. The highly unusual run of threefold verses will continue, however, with 308.

308–11   Akhilleus returns to his hut by the ships, and Agamemnon begins to carry out the intention expressed at 141f.; a ship is launched, then his captive Khruseis is led on board for return to her father Khruses. A sacrificial hecatomb (see on 65) is also embarked, as well as twenty rowers and Odysseus as captain. At 145f. Agamemnon had named him or Aias or Idomeneus as possible candidates for this office (as well as Akhilleus himself, presumably to annoy), but Odysseus with his knowledge and resourcefulness (πολύμητις in 311 is admittedly the standard epithet for him in this position in the verse) was the obvious choice when it came to the point. On 311 εἶσεν ἄγων see 4.392n.

312   ὑγρὰ κέλευθα: an otherwise Odyssean formula (4×), with the whole phrase ἀναβάντες...κέλευθα recurring at *Od.* 4.842 and 15.474. The complete description of the journey to Khruse will follow at 430–87 and is full of Odyssean language. That is mainly, no doubt, because the *Odyssey* has much occasion to describe seafaring, the *Iliad* little; there is no need to regard the voyage as an intrusion into the *Iliad* by a singer primarily concerned with the other epic.

313–14   Once the ship has sailed, Agamemnon instructs the army to purify itself by washing. The epic often describes simultaneous actions as happening consecutively; that was an accepted convention which made for simplicity of presentation in the narrative and maintained the linearity of the oral style (pp. 31f.). Here, nevertheless, it is clear that the crew leave without purifying themselves, and this led to some complicated explanations by ancient critics. But the crew do purify themselves by ritually washing their hands, 449 χερνίψαντο, before sacrificing once they have arrived at Khruse. The army, on the other hand, proceed immediately to sacrifice hecatombs of bulls and goats to Apollo (315–17); and before that they purify themselves at the earliest opportunity. Theirs is, admittedly, an unusual cleansing, more than a token washing of hands, presumably so as to rid their whole bodies of pollution. As often, symbolic and hygienic require-ments overlap; their whole bodies have been exposed to danger from the plague, and so the cleansing is unusually thorough. Clearly, too, there is ordinary dirt to be removed, and the epic did not wholly ignore that; Here cleans the dirt, λύματα as here, from her skin with ambrosia (en-visaged as an ointment) at 14.170, whereas Odysseus and Diomedes paddle in the sea to wash off the sweat (and then have a proper bath afterwards) after their night expedition at 10.572–6, cf. 11.621f. The troops do roughly the same here. They throw the dirty water, the λύματα, into the sea, which is a purifying agent; see Parker, *Miasma* 210, 229n. 130. A compared Euripides, *IT* 1193, but *Il*. 19.266–8 is also relevant, for there the carcase of a boar used in an oath-sacrifice is thrown into the sea to be consumed by fishes.

315–17 On hecatombs see 65n. κνίση in 317 is the smoke and savour of burnt fat, from the fat-encased thighbones that were the gods' special portion; see on 447–68. This happens to be the only place in Homer where the savour is specifically described as rising, together with the smoke of the altar fire, to the sky where the gods are conceived as dwelling. Seven times in the *Iliad* gods (including Athene at 194f.) are said to come down to earth οὐρανόθεν, from the sky; that is not meant to contradict the idea of their dwelling on Mt Olumpos, since its peaks were above the clouds and therefore in the αἰθήρ, the upper air which was sometimes described as the sky itself.

320 Talthubios and Eurubates: in Sparta the Talthubiadai were the family or guild of heralds, presumably from pre-Homeric times on; and there is a second herald called Eurubates among the Achaeans in Homer (he is Odysseus' herald at 2.184). Thus both names seem to be generic ones for heralds. In the *Iliad* Talthubios is more frequently cited than Eurubates; he goes on various errands (the two heralds are described as ὀτρηρὼ θεράποντε, busy helpers, in 321), as well as performing sacred and other public duties; but it is Eurubates who accompanies the embassy to Akhilleus at 9.170. There he is partnered by Odios, a third Achaean herald who receives no other mention (he has a Trojan ally as namesake, one of the two Halizonian leaders, 2.856 and 5.39).

322–5 A compact and urgent instruction: the first two verses are each crisp, whole-verse imperatives; the next two are more hypothetical and syntactic, balancing each other in their strong central caesuras. This is where

Agamemnon makes his threat unmistakably plain, yet at the same time prudently modifies it a little: if Akhilleus refuses to surrender the girl, then he will come in person, but with a posse (σὺν πλεόνεσσιν) that will make Akhilleus' personal strength irrelevant.

326 κρατερὸν δ' ἐπὶ μῦθον ἔτελλε: 'and enjoined upon them a strong word', that is, of command – in fact the command he has just given in his short speech.

327–47 The use of the dual for the two heralds, already established in 321, continues predominantly throughout the episode down to 347, with occasional lapses in 329 and 332 (also in 334, although χαίρετε there is a formula of greeting which hardly needs subjecting to further refinement or specification; however, cf. χαίρετον at 9.197). Heralds often worked in pairs, and stressing this tends to emphasize their authority.

327 For the 'shore of the loud-roaring sea' see on 34.

328 This verse recurs as 9.185, cf. 652. The Murmidones are Akhilleus' troops from Phthie, see on 2.683–4; their name was probably something of a mystery even to the singers of the oral heroic tradition, as 2.684 may suggest. Their ships, with their huts directly on the landward side of them, are drawn up at one end of the Achaean line, with the greater Aias' at the other and those of Odysseus in the middle, as 8.222–7 = 11.5–9 specifically state.

331 ταρβήσαντε καὶ αἰδομένω: the combination of aorist and present tenses may be explained by their alarm being temporary, whereas their respect for a king is permanent. Fear and respect are naturally connected, especially toward a king; bT cite Helen's remark to Priam at 3.172, αἰδοῖός τέ μοί ἐσσι, φίλε ἑκυρέ, δεινός τε.

334–5 The heralds are 'messengers of gods and men'; bT suggest that Akhilleus is here tactfully suppressing their connexion with Agamemnon, and that their divine association lies in preparing sacrifices – but they do of course also serve Zeus-reared kings, see on 175f. They have come unwillingly and stand afraid and in silence; Akhilleus, despite his sorrow at their arrival ('he did not rejoice to see them', 330), greets them in an open and friendly way and shows without delay that he understands them to be merely carrying out orders. The poet clearly thinks it important to reveal Akhilleus' human side early in the poem, especially in contrast with the frightening aspect he had displayed in the quarrel in assembly. Similar courtesy to visitors on Akhilleus' part is conspicuous in book 9.

337–9 He extends the same courtesy to Patroklos, now directly named for the first time (see on 307). Akhilleus' speech is regular and relaxed in its construction so far, with mainly two/fourfold verses, progressive enjambment and the hieratic balance of 339, appropriate to a solemn call to witness ('before blessed gods and before mortal men').

Book One

340–2 Mention of the king, tense and emphatic in its strongly demonstrative τοῦ and the blunt ἀπηνέος, brings a corresponding change of style: strong integral enjambment at 340/1, made harsh by the awkward synizesis of δὴ αὖτε and the jingling χρειώ ἐμεῖο γένηται. Then 342, with its strong stop after the emphatic runover phrase τοῖς ἄλλοις, is rough but effective: *he* will not need my help, because he is out of his mind with rage – but the others will.

343–4 These two verses are cumulative, each designed to explain and expand its predecessor. For ἅμα πρόσσω καὶ ὀπίσσω cf. 3.109f. and (without ἅμα) 18.250, both with verbs of seeing; here νοῆσαι means 'perceive', as regularly in Homer. οἶδε νοῆσαι, strange at first appearance, is in fact logical enough (in contrast with the bizarre περίοιδε νοῆσαι, of Odysseus, at 10.247): 'he does not know how to perceive [i.e. look] both forward and backward at the same time', which implies using experience of the past to predict what will happen in the future. At 18.250 'saw forward and backward' is used absolutely, and one suspects this was the phrase's earliest application; here and at 3.109f., however, it is followed by a ὅπως-clause, 'perceive...how to'. In the whole context even 343 by itself seems a little too elaborate, but now 344 makes a strangely awkward addition, not so much because of the probably Attic form μαχέοιντο with its unusual hiatus, since that is probably a surface corruption (see on 272), but rather because fighting *in safety* among the ships is a needless paradox. In short, both these verses are untypically heavy-handed, and even suggest a rare possibility of rhapsodic expansion. For Akhilleus' words could have ended at 341 ἀμῦναι – but they would then allow, and might seem to some to require, further expansion. The Homeric singers themselves, and certainly the monumental composer, can often be seen elaborating by progressive cumulation in such circumstances; but occasionally, and perhaps here, a forced quality in diction and thought suggests that possibility of less skilled attention.

345 = 9.205 and 11.616; on all three occasions Patroklos obeys Akhilleus without comment. That is standard epic practice where no particular reaction to an instruction, other than carrying it out, is needed, and bT are wrong to make Patroklos' silence here a particular indication of his mild and tactful nature. That is not to deny that he is Akhilleus' wholly obedient friend and subordinate (which makes the strong pressure he will apply at the beginning of book 16 all the more pointed).

346–7 ἐκ δ' ἄγαγε...δῶκε δ' ἄγειν: the language of Akhilleus' instruction at 337f. is adjusted for the description of the event itself, in a characteristically oral manner.

348 Briseis' attachment to her captor is suggested here by her unwillingness, ἀέκουσ', to go. She was also fond of the gentle (within limits)

Patroklos, as she will reveal in her lament over his body at 19.287–300. Whether Akhilleus would really have taken her back to Phthie as his wife, as she there recalls Patroklos as having told her when she was first captured, is another matter. Akhilleus himself is in tears at 349, but that is surely because of the affront to his honour more than through losing Briseis; later, at 19.59f., and admittedly because he sees her as indirect cause of Patroklos' death, he is to wish that she had somehow died in the sack of Lurnessos.

348–430   Akhilleus calls on his mother, the sea-goddess Thetis, to help him avenge the insult to his honour; she promises to ask Zeus to favour the Trojans

348–57   E. A. Havelock ('The alphabetization of Homer', in *Communication Arts in the Ancient World* (New York 1978), 14) detects an 'echo-principle' at work between this scene, in which Akhilleus goes aside on the sea-shore and prays to Thetis, and 34–6 where the priest Khruses went along the sea-shore and prayed to Apollo. There is, indeed, a degree of both thematic parallelism and verbal repetition:

349 ἑτάρων...νόσφι λιασθείς   35 ἀπάνευθε κιών
350 θῖν' ἐφ' ἁλὸς πολιῆς   34 παρὰ θῖνα πολυφλοίσβοιο θαλάσσης
351 πολλὰ δὲ...ἠρήσατο   35 πολλὰ δ' ἔπειτ'...ἠρᾶθ'
357 ὡς φᾶτο...τοῦ δ' ἔκλυε   43 ὡς ἔφατ'...τοῦ δ' ἔκλυε

How far the singer's listeners are intended by him to feel, less than fully consciously perhaps, a significant parallelism and contrast, and how far this is due rather to the oral poet's technique of working with a limited range of themes and phrases, is a difficult question to answer, especially since for the oral composer theme (or motif) and language are often closely interwoven.

349   δακρύσας: see the previous comment. The components of this verse are formular, but with one or two untypical elements nevertheless: thus ἕζετο occurs 18x *Il.*, including 10x in this position in the verse, and λιασθείς 5x, always last word as here (it is also preceded by νόσφι at 11.80); but ἑτάρων, 13x *Il.*, is only 3x in this position, and ἄφαρ (= 'forthwith', cf. ἄψ), although common enough, is normally placed elsewhere in the verse and scanned as an iamb not two shorts. The resulting word-order is harsh, especially in the separation of ἑτάρων from νόσφι on which it depends – one suspects that νόσφι λιασθείς was normally absolute. Naber's ἄτερ for ἄφαρ is attractive (cf. 498 ἄτερ ἥμενον ἄλλων and 5.753 θεῶν ἄτερ ἥμενον ἄλλων), despite the doubts of van Herwerden and van Leeuwen; although ἄφαρ was obviously the accepted Alexandrian reading, as e.g. bT confirm.

350   The grey salt sea (see also on 359), the repetition inherent in ἁλός and πόντον, Akhilleus' gazing over the sea, the shore itself (see on 34), all intensify the pathos of events and develop the loneliness and despair of the preceding verse; compare Odysseus on Kalupso's shore at *Od.* 5.82–4. Aristarchus (Did/A) wrote ἀπείρονα, not οἴνοπα, πόντον, and that would increase the pathetic effect (so Ameis, unjustly reprehended by Leaf for 'a German rather than a Greek idea'!); but, of the two, πόντον at the verse-end is always οἴνοπα elsewhere (5× *Il.*, 5× *Od.*), and ἀπείρονα is confined to γαῖαν (2× *Il.*, 5× *Od.*) except for *Od.* 4.510, κατὰ πόντον ἀπείρονα κυμαίνοντα. OCT and most modern editors have sided with Aristarchus (whose view did not affect the Alexandrine tradition or the medieval vulgate); but the established formular usage, although it might not be so effective in this verse, may nevertheless be correct.

351　Problems over formular usage continue: Zenodotus according to Aristarchus (Arn/A) read χεῖρας ἀναπτάς, although this form would be unique in Homer. Others according to (?Didymus in) T read χεῖρας ἀνασχών. This is a more serious contender against the vulgate's ὀρεγνύς; it is perhaps related to 450 where Khruses prays thus to Apollo, and the formula recurs in four other Iliadic passages, always with an Olympian as recipient of the invocation. Holding up one's arms in prayer to a god in the sky (or on Olumpos) is reasonable enough – but doing so in invoking a goddess beneath the sea is probably not. *Stretching out* one's arms, ὀρεγνύς, possibly with a downward inclination, would be more appropriate here, and it is no objection that the phrase recurs in the *Iliad* only of Priam imploring Hektor in the plain below at 22.37. Matters are rarely that simple, however, for at *Od.* 9.527 χεῖρ᾽ ὀρέγων is in prayer to an Olympian, while at *Od.* 13.355 ἀνασχών is used of prayer to the Nymphs. Yet on the argument adduced at the end of the preceding comment, formular consistency and economy sometimes seem to outweigh differences of detail in subject-matter, and ἀνασχών could have been Homer's choice even despite Aristarchus, the MSS and the particular nuance of meaning. But obviously ὀρεγνύς should occur in any printed text, and, after all, there was probably no complete consistency of practice in such matters even in Homer's time.

352–6　Akhilleus' prayer (ἠρήσατο, 351) turns out to be a statement of complaint, rather, although a request for help is also implicit. It is fluently composed, with initial periodic enjambment (352) and runover-phrase supplementation (354), then integral enjambment (355) leading to typical verse-pattern contrast in conclusion.

352–3　The disposition of γε and περ suggests the meaning to be as follows: 'since you, a goddess, bore me, Zeus ought to have guaranteed me honour – especially since my life is short', rather than simply '...since you have borne me to have a short life'. At 9.410–16 Akhilleus will reveal that Thetis had told him of a choice, either of a short life but a glorious one if he remained at Troy or of a long life without glory if he abandoned the expedition and returned home. We hear nothing of this elsewhere in Homer, but there is no real discrepancy with the present passage, or with 169–71 where the idea of leaving is first mentioned by Akhilleus.

356 This verse recurs in Thetis' report to Zeus at 507, in Thersites' speech at 2.240 and, with adaptation, in Nestor's at 9.111. The rhythm is unusual as A noticed, in that word-end after the second trochee without any preceding break, |ἠτίμησεν·:ἑλών, is in breach of 'Meyer's Law'. However, the result sounds inoffensive here (and that is the real test) – either because the spondaic first foot avoids the undesirable verse-end echo that might otherwise be produced, or because there is no emphatic following sequence of trochaic cuts to cause offence (cf. my remarks in *YCS* 20 (1966) 78f. and 97–9). The verse-rhythm overall is three/fourfold with diminished main caesura, and contrasts well with the more straightforward twofold rhythm of its predecessors in this short speech. On the claim that Agamemnon has taken away (ἀπούρας < ἀπόϝρας) his prize in person, see the discussion on 185.

358 πατρὶ γέροντι: she is sitting by her father 'the old man of the sea'; the verse is repeated at 18.36, the context of which shows her father to be Nereus (who is not directly named in Homer), since her sisters there are Nereids (18.52). The ancient sea-god has other names and aspects, Proteus at *Od.* 4.365 and 385, Phorkus at *Od.* 1.72, 13.96 and 345.

359 πολιῆς ἁλός echoes not only ἁλός in the preceding verse but also ἁλὸς πολιῆς, lightly adapted to a different position in the verse, in 350. Thetis rises out of the sea 'like a mist'; does that mean that she has the actual appearance of a mist, and therefore only assumes anthropomorphic shape when she appears before her son and strokes him in 361? Perhaps so; one thinks of Athene descending like a meteor at 4.75–8 (see the comment there, also on 4.78–84) or like a rainbow at 17.547–52, or disappearing like a bird at *Od.* 1.319f., respectively before or after assuming human disguise. The present case is slightly different, in that mist is a natural form for the manifestation of a sea-goddess; other poets independent of the Homeric tradition have seen spirits of sea, lake or river in the form of the mists that appear to rise from them.

361 A formular verse (4× *Il.*, 2× *Od.*) applied to deities as well as humans; κατέρεξεν is from an epic verb καταρρέζω, evidently 'pat' or 'stroke'.

362–3 Thetis' urgent enquiry culminates in an emotional rising three-folder: ἐξαύδα, μὴ κεῦθε νόῳ, ἵνα εἴδομεν ἄμφω.

365 It is an epic convention that one can relate one's ancestry, or recent events, even after firmly telling one's interlocutor that such a thing is unnecessary; so Glaukos to Diomedes at 6.145ff. and Aineias to Akhilleus at 20.203ff.

366–92 This earlier part, over half, of Akhilleus' reply to Thetis' enquiry is a long summary, without the all-important speeches, of the events dramatically described so far, and which have led to Akhilleus' present distress. It is surprising to find such a summary so close to the beginning of the whole poem and so soon after the extremely full description of arguments and events. Thetis does not need it (but cf. the previous note), nor does the singer or his audience at this point – although sometimes such a résumé can be helpful to both.

Aristarchus (Arn/A on 365) evidently athetized all 27 verses, which are obelized in A; 372–5 (= 13–16) and 376–9 (= 22–5) are in addition asterisked as being exact repetitions of the earlier descriptions; see also Arn/A on 18.444–56, where Aristarchus is implied to have similarly disapproved of another summary involving Thetis, this time given by her to Hephaistos; reference is made there to the present passage. All this does not amount to much. Aristarchus evidently noticed, as he would, that neither the summary as a whole nor the exact repetitions it contained are strictly necessary, and athetized on that account alone. But we know (a) that repetitions are part of the oral style, and (b) that so too, on occasion, are summaries or résumés. Admittedly Thetis' report in book 18 is better motivated than the present one; nevertheless there is much to suggest, especially in the language itself, that this is no low-grade or wholly mechanical affair, as the following survey will make clear.

It is perhaps significant that **366–9** goes beyond what has been revealed in either speech or narrative; there has been no mention of Thebe or its king Eetion so far, and it takes special knowledge (or untypical carelessness) on the part of the composer of these verses to have Khruseis captured at Thebe whereas her home is at Khruse. According to 6.395–7 and 425–8 Thebe is where Andromakhe's mother, too, was captured, Eetion being her father. bT on 1.366 explain that Akhilleus was deterred by Athene from attacking Khruse, and went on to sack Thebe, where Khruseis happened to be visiting Eetion's wife for some religious function. This could be a later invention, but our poet must have known something about Khruseis' visit. His general competence is suggested by his skill at précis-making, demonstrated in what follows, in which he can often be seen drawing on Homeric language not used so far in this Book, or even occasionally innovating, in a minor way, in a reasonable epic style.

Thus **366** ἱερὴν πόλιν is an unusual phrase, but cf. ἱερήν of Ilios at 7.20 or Zeleia as ἱερῆς at 4.103 and 121; Ἴλιος ἱρή (etc.) | is a common formula, see on 4.164. διεπράθομεν in **367** is not exactly used elsewhere, although other parts of the compound are found four times subsequently and ἐξεπράθομεν occurred at 125; similarly with **368** δάσσαντο, cf. 22.354 δάσονται and δέδασται at 125. In **369** ἐκ δ' ἕλον for selecting a prize is

paralleled by ἔξελον at 16.56 and 18.444 (the latter being the opening verse
of Thetis' résumé for Hephaistos), but is unparalleled in the previous
narrative of book 1. Such variations of terminology are necessitated by the
omission of speeches that occurred in the original, or the abbreviating of
other material there; thus Χρύσην...ἀρητῆρα in 11 becomes Χρύσης...
ἱερεύς in 370, and he is angry, χωόμενος, in 380 rather than afraid and silent
as at 33f.; Apollo's hearing his prayer is expressed differently (43 τοῦ δ'
ἔκλυε, 381 ἤκουσεν), and the explanation that Khruses was 'dear to Apollo'
in 381 is new (and not exactly repeated elsewhere in Homer, as it happens).
Then the shooting of the god's arrows is differently expressed, the κακὸν
βέλος of 382 being not exactly paralleled, although dramatic in its own
right; so is the victims' death, where 382–3 is good (on ἐπασσύτεροι see
4.42n.), although not the equal of the original at 52. At 383–4 the words
of the original (53) are quite ingeniously expanded and fitted into the
required new grammatical sequence; at 385 εὖ εἰδώς may echo 73 ἐϋφρονέων;
at 387 ἀναστάς is formular in this position (5× *Il.*), but did not occur in
the fuller account; 388 ἠπείλησεν μῦθον is awkward in construction and
rhythm (being a different kind of breach of Meyer's Law from 356, see
comment there), not otherwise paralleled in Homer – the only harsh feature
in this whole summary. Verse 389 is a rising threefolder with σὺν νηΐ θοῇ
reminiscent of 179 and 183 (see on 183), although the reference is to
Akhilleus' ship and not the one bringing back Khruseis; while ἑλίκωπες
'Αχαιοί (etc.) is a formula (6× *Il.*), here for the first time in the poem; see on
98. The δῶρα of 390 represent a different way of referring to what was
earlier (99, 142, 309) described as a hecatomb; 391 is competently adjusted
to the event seen in retrospect, with κλισίηθεν and not κλισίηνδε (185) or
κλισίην (322); finally 392 directly recalls the words of 162, although with
the necessary adjustment in word-order neatly executed.

Such a survey demonstrates that the whole passage is far from being a
mere mechanical summary of what has preceded; it naturally makes
extensive use of the earlier language, but often departs from it in order to
bypass the omitted speeches or make the condensation more fluent. This
is not the work of a rhapsode or decadent singer, but of a singer working
within the living oral tradition. There is no obvious reason for denying that
he is the main composer himself, although the initial puzzle would remain;
why did he find a summary of this length necessary so soon after the events
and arguments had been set out *in extenso*? Competent and fluent though
it may be within its chosen limitations, it is not, after all, very dramatic or
interesting, at least compared with the fuller version. One possibility is that
it was composed as a shorter alternative to the whole quarrel-scene, one that
could be used when mood and circumstances required (although it is not
so easy to see when such a successful episode could have seemed superfluous);

another is that it was the original version, or at least an earlier one, of the Khruseis story, on the basis of which the main composer then developed the fuller and dramatic version complete with speeches. Subsequently the shorter version might have been incorporated in the complete poem, after slight adaptation, as an *aide-mémoire* to Thetis – the difficulty here being that the language of the two versions suggests that the longer is being abbreviated rather than the shorter expanded. Neither of these explanations is particularly attractive, and the puzzle remains; although its impact on the unity and effect of the whole Book should not be exaggerated.

[*See the bold-type verse-numbers in the preceding note for detailed comments from 366 to 392.*]

393–412 The second part of Akhilleus' address to Thetis turns from the summary of past events to his specific request, preceded by the argument that Thetis is in a position to grant it.

395 ὤνησας κραδίην: a non-formular expression not found elsewhere in Homer, with ὀνίνημι bearing its occasional meaning of 'delight' rather than its commoner one of 'help'.

396–406 Zenodotus athetized these verses according to Aristarchus (Arn/A); one can see why, since the tale of Thetis' past interventions is a peculiar one (as will emerge in the comments which follow), and might conceivably have been a subsequent elaboration stimulated by ἠὲ καὶ ἔργῳ in 395 – in which case 408 might follow on from 395 more naturally than 407 does. But the probability is, in the absence of other evidence, that the digression is Homeric.

399 There is no other reference either in Homer or in later poets to this particular act of *lèse-majesté*, which has one or two points in common with the tale of Ares being tied up in a jar for thirteen months (although by mortals) at 5.385–91. Disobedience by Here and other deities is alluded to several times by Zeus, but in order to show that he always comes out easily on top, which did not happen here; so later in this Book at 565–7, where he encourages Here to obey him with the threat that the other Olympians will be unable to save her from his physical violence if she refuses. Then at 15.18–24 he reminds her how he had once suspended her in the air with anvils tied to her feet, and the other gods could not release her but were flung to the earth below if they tried – as Hephaistos was (as he tells her at 1.587–94) when he once tried to save her from a beating by Zeus and was hurled off Olumpos, to land in Lemnos, for his pains; or like Ἄτη at 19.130f. Zeus's confidence is shown by his threatening speech to the assembled Olympians at 8.5–27: he will hurl anyone who disobeys him into Tartaros, and challenges the lot of them to a divine tug-of-war in which he claims that he could pull them up, with earth and sea as well, and hang them in mid-air from Olumpos. It was a main theme of Hesiod's *Theogony* that Zeus had had to overcome serious rebellions, especially from the Titans and then Tuphoeus, in his rise to supremacy. There, too, Briareos the hundred-handed giant (joined in Hesiod with his brothers Kottos and Guges) enables him to overcome an act of revolt, although not by other Olympians but by the Titans (see M. L. West on Hesiod, *Theog.* 149 and 617–719). Homer, naturally, concentrates on Zeus's eventual supremacy rather than on the details of his early struggles; even so Thetis' reminiscence is unusual, and there is no hint in Zeus's confident remarks elsewhere that the gods had ever presented a real threat to him, as the present passage suggests.

400 Poseidon, Here and Athene are the divine supporters of the Achaeans in the *Iliad,* and their being cast as protagonists in the attack on Zeus is another sign that the whole episode (which caused much agitated discussion among the exegetes, cf. bT on 399–406) has been adapted to a specifically Iliadic context.

403–4 Βριάρεως is the divine name, men call him Αἰγαίων. There are three further cases of alternative human and divine names in the *Iliad,* and two instances of divine terminology, but without human equivalent, in the *Odyssey*:

	subject	divine name	human name
(i) *Il.* 2.813f.	mound near Troy	σῆμα πολυσκάρθ- μοιο Μυρίνης	Βατίεια (i.e. 'brambly'?)
(ii) *Il.* 14.290f.	bird	χαλκίς	κύμινδις
(iii) *Il.* 20.74	river	Ξάνθος	Σκάμανδρος
(iv) *Od.* 10.305	magic plant	μῶλυ	
(v) *Od.* 12.61	clashing rocks	Πλαγκταί	

No principle to account for these peculiarities of name has been satisfactorily proposed; neither that the 'divine' name is an older linguistic form (untrue of (i) and (ii), where κύμινδις is presumably pre-Greek); nor that the 'divine' name is non-Greek (untrue of (i), (ii) and (v)); nor that it is, on the contrary, Greek (untrue of (iii), where both names are presumably non-Greek in origin, and (iv)).

These other instances cannot, therefore, be expected to shed light on Briareos/Aigaion here, which has in any case a special characteristic: that this giant existed before men were created, and his name was therefore assigned by primeval gods. Men would come to hear of him later, when they might have given him their own special name to describe his developed sphere or function. Both names, in fact, are probably Greek, βρι- implying 'strong' as in ὄβριμος and αἰγ- being probably connected with 'goat'. The rest of 404 looks at first as though it offers an explanation of the name

Aigaion – '(he is called that) because he is stronger than his father'; but even if Αἰγαίων is a patronymic (as e.g. Lattimore and Willcock suggest, comparing Κρονίων as a patronymic form from Κρόνος), and if Αἰγαῖος was an epithet of Poseidon as is sometimes held, the form Αἰγαίων still does not contain the required implication of comparison or superiority. If that is the case, then ὁ γὰρ αὖτε βίην οὗ πατρὸς ἀμείνων refers to the whole context: '(you secured Zeus's release by calling on Briareos/Aigaion) because he was stronger than his father', who in that case must be envisaged as Poseidon, the strongest of the three rebel deities. But this is rather uncertain; Leaf's statement that 'the father of Briareos was, according to the legend, Poseidon' is not entirely true, since he was son of Ouranos and Gaia according to Hesiod, *Theog.* 147–9. The *Theogony* added at 816–18 that Poseidon eventually gave Briareos his daughter Kumopoleia (a sea-nymph, to judge by her name) in marriage; could πατρός be used to denote the father-in-law? The short answer is No, and difficulties remain. Zenodotus according to Aristarchus (Arn/A) attempted to meet them by substituting a different (defective) couplet in place of 404:

Αἰγαίων'· ὁ γὰρ αὖτε βίη πολὺ φέρτατος ἄλλων
ὁππόσοι ναίουσ' ὑπὸ Τάρταρον εὐρώεντα

in which ἄλλων is Düntzer's emendation of corrupt ms ἁπάντων. Aristarchus objected that Aigaion was not a Titan but a sea-creature – erroneously in that Briareos was confined beneath the earth (just as the Titans were) at *Theog.* 617–20, but rightly, perhaps, in emphasizing a probable connexion between Aigaion and the Aegean sea, and therefore Poseidon.

Much remains obscure, and the expression at this point is a little awkward – although rendered the more so by the punctuation in e.g. OCT; the parenthesis, if any, is ὅν...Αἰγαίων' rather than ὁ γὰρ...ἀμείνων. Yet the awkwardness can be paralleled in other abbreviated references to legendary occurrences outside the normal Homeric ambit, for example in Glaukos' genealogy at 6.145–211 or the Meleagros tale at 9.527–99.

405 γαίω is related to γάνυμαι, 'I am radiant (with joy)'; κῦδος also is a kind of emanation, of power, confidence and renown. καθέζετο occurs 11x *Il.*, 3x *Od.*, always in this position before the bucolic caesura; κύδεϊ γαίων, 4x *Il.*, is always preceded by it and was devised probably in the first instance for Zeus (2x), then applied to lesser beings (Ares at 5.906) sitting by his side and basking almost comically in his aura.

407 On 'grasping by the knees' see the discussion of the supplication when it actually occurs, on 512–13.

408 For the αἴ κέν πως idiom and its implications see on 207 and 2.72; here, unlike the other contexts cited, Zeus's reactions cannot be a foregone conclusion and the expression conveys more of its literal meaning.

409 For the Achaeans to be driven back to the ships and penned in there (ἕλσαι from εἰλέω or Ἴλλω, here meaning 'confine' or 'compress' but sometimes, perhaps from another root, meaning 'turn round') is what Akhilleus wants; but when Thetis relays his needs to Zeus at 503–10 she will do so in more general terms, just naming the required end (that they shall honour him once again) and leaving the means to his divine intuition.

410 κτεινομένους is a powerful runover-word; Akhilleus knows that they must suffer heavy casualties before his honour is restored, and accepts the possible sacrifice of friends and allies without evident distress.

ἐπαύρωνται from ἐπαυρίσκομαι, perhaps associated with εὑρίσκω (Chantraine, *Dict.* s.v.): 'touch', 'reach', 'enjoy', sometimes in an ironical sense as here.

412 The result of fulfilling Akhilleus' wishes for the restoration of his τιμή is to be that Agamemnon recognizes his ἄτη, that fatal infatuation with his own supposed rights that has led to all the insults and injustice and the consequent quarrel. Agamemnon himself will admit to ἄτη at 2.111, where – as later in the poem also – he will blame it on Zeus.

414 Thetis meets her son's complaints with mournful resignation, but concedes that he deserves something better. τί νύ σ' ἔτρεφον αἰνὰ τεκοῦσα; she asks: literally 'why did I bring you up, having given birth to you terribly?' (*sc.* in view of your evil destiny, cf. 416 and 418) – it is a kind of hendiadys, 'why did I bear-and-raise such an unfortunate son?' αἰνὰ τεκοῦσα is unique in Homer, but cf. 22.431 αἰνὰ παθοῦσα, likewise in a lament; the phrase may have been part of the special vocabulary of dirges.

415–16 'Would that you had been sitting among the ships without tears and grief': ὄφελλον (etc.), imperfect, and ὄφελον (etc.), aorist, express regret and are intensified by the addition of the particle αἴθε or ὥς, cf. e.g. 3.40 αἴθ' ὄφελές τ' ἀγονός τ' ἔμεναι...and Chantraine, *GH* II, 228. The thought here is loosely expressed; Akhilleus' 'sitting among the ships' is solely because of the quarrel, and he could hardly be free from grief in such circumstances; had he been griefless, he would have been out there fighting as usual.

416 The junction of αἶσα with the adverbial formula μίνυνθά περ, οὔ τι μάλα δήν, without a verb, is strained and difficult. Understanding ἐστί does not help (despite van Leeuwen, Leaf and others), since μίνυνθα...should qualify a verb expressing action or duration as at 13.573, ὥς...ἤσπαιρε μίνυνθά περ, οὔ τι μάλα δήν. At 11.317f. ἀλλὰ μίνυνθα| ἡμέων ἔσσεται ἦδος the meaning is equivalent to '*we shall rejoice* for a short while'; αἶσα ⟨ἐστί/ἔσσεται⟩ here could not be similarly understood. What should really be understood is something like ζῆν: 'it is your destiny ⟨to live⟩ for only a short while, not at all for long'; but Greek would not permit that kind of omission. Otherwise we have to assume that αἶσα itself contained a verbal idea, 'destiny of living', although its application at 418, just two verses below, is against that. On μίνυνθα see also on 4.446.

417–18 This couplet matches its predecessor in its integral enjambment with runover-word, followed by a concise causal summary; the start of Thetis' speech is carefully composed in sentence-structure if not in detailed syntax. Ring-composition is obvious here: τῶ σε κακῆ αἴση τέκον in 418 takes up the initial rhetorical question in 414 (τί... τεκοῦσα) by way of the mediating αἶσα of 416. Akhilleus is especially ill-fated because he is *both* short-lived *and* unhappy.

419–22 Thetis turns to the practical part of her reply: she will go to intercede with Zeus, while Akhilleus is to maintain his wrath (against all the Achaeans now, 422, not just Agamemnon) and abstain from fighting. On 420 αἴ κε πίθηται see 207n.

423–5 The news that Zeus is away from Olumpos and will not be back for a further eleven days comes as something of a surprise, to the audience at least; Akhilleus himself offers no comment. Thetis' words at 420 had suggested that she would proceed directly to Olumpos, and earlier, at 221f., it was clearly stated that Athene had returned from earth to join the other gods on Olumpos on this very day; see on 222, where I suggested a 'mild oral inconsistency' when the Thetis-episode came to be developed here. Probably the poet decides at this point, rather suddenly, to establish an eleven-day interval. One point of this might be to allow time for the return of Khruseis to her father in the episode that is to follow; although usually in the epic such chronological niceties are not observed, and the singer moves directly and without comment from one action-sequence to another, even if it is in a different locale; see the comments on 313–14 *init.* and on 430–1. That is the case even if the actions are in fact simultaneous. Alternatively it has sometimes been suggested (most recently by Macleod, *Iliad XXIV* 32) that the eleven-day interval here is planned to correspond with the eleven days of divine concern over Akhilleus' treatment of Hektor's body, at 24.23–32. That possibility may be reduced by a consideration adduced in 493–4n.; and would it really have the effect, at such a distance in the text, of 'isolating the action of the *Iliad* from the continuum of the Trojan War' as Willcock claims? Perhaps so, a little – after all, the isolation would be achieved by each interval separately, even if the audience did not connect them. Moreover the imposition of the interval of inaction would increase the length and perhaps also the impact of Akhilleus' wrath itself. It remains mildly surprising, nevertheless, that such a device should be introduced so suddenly and without special comment; but the fluent management of the gods' return home at 493f. speaks against any possibility of post-Homeric elaboration.

Aristarchus (Did/A on 423f., on which see also p. 42) cited strong ancient authority – the Marseilles, Sinope and Cypriot texts as well as Antimachus' and Aristophanes' commentaries, to which Didymus added Callistratus, Sidonius and Ixion – for κατὰ δαῖτα rather than μετὰ δαῖτα in 424, in spite of which the vulgate retained the latter. Similarly elsewhere he argued for κατά rather than μετά when the connotation is of moving to become involved with something (e.g. κατὰ στρατόν at 484, κατὰ λαόν at 2.163 and 179). He extended his restriction of μετά by reading ἐπ' ἀμύμονας in 423, surely without justification. Didymus also implies that he read ἕπονται, not ἕποντο, in 424; that would be an attempt to resolve the inconsistency noted above by suggesting that while Zeus left yesterday, the other gods (including Athene) are following today. Such a complication is improbable in itself, and as e.g. van Leeuwen and Leaf noted, ἕπεσθαι does not mean 'follow at an interval'; moreover ἅμα probably connotes 'in company (with him)' rather than merely intensifying πάντες.

425–7 Thetis offsets her frustrating news of delay with some nicely persuasive expressions, especially in the intimately reassuring and emphatically balanced τοι of 425 δωδεκάτη δέ τοι αὖτις and 426 καὶ τότ' ἔπειτά τοι εἶμι; also in the confident spondaic repetitions of 427, καί μιν γουνάσομαι καί μιν πείθεσθαι ὀίω, including as it does the understated 'I believe I shall persuade him' (after the αἴ κε πίθηται of 420, on which see 207n.).

ποτὶ χαλκοβατὲς δῶ is formular, 4x *Il.* (always with Διός), 2x *Od.*; Chantraine (*Dict.* s.v.) is doubtful whether δῶ is related to δῶμα or is an adverb of motion like -δε, then misunderstood; I greatly prefer the former and simpler explanation.

429–30 Akhilleus is angry 'because of the woman', Briseis that is – primarily, we should understand, because of the affront to his honour. It is *his* unwillingness, 430 βίῃ ἀέκοντος, not hers (cf. 348 ἀέκουσ') that is stressed here.

430–87 Odysseus delivers Khruseis to her father Khruses and, after propitiating Apollo with prayer and sacrifice, returns with his ship to the Achaean camp near Troy

430–1 At 308–12 a ship was launched for Odysseus' voyage to Khruse; now he arrives there. Notice, once again, the ease and simplicity of the transition from one scene of action to another, quite different one. It is achieved in mid-verse here, and with no special preparation (... αὐτὰρ 'Οδυσσεύς), in contrast with e.g. 314, where οἱ δ'... had been prepared for by οἱ μέν... in 312.

432–9 This description of the ship's arrival, like that of its return home at 475–87, is full of 'Odyssean' language; see the notes on 312 and 434 and the conclusions there outlined, especially that this is primarily because seafaring occurs often in the *Odyssey* but almost nowhere else in the *Iliad*. G. P. Shipp (*Studies* 229f.) observed that the whole Khruse episode is grammatically 'pure' in the sense of containing few unusual forms; that is because it is exceptionally formular and traditional in expression, with a high concentration of typical scenes and motifs.

432 This verse recurs as *Od.* 16.324. bT comment that πολυβενθέος, 'of great depths', gives the character of harbours in a single word. That is a poet's or a scholar's rather than a seaman's view – although the implied observation about standard epithets is correct: a harbour in the genitive is always 'of great depths' when an epithet of this metrical value is required. In realistic terms a harbour needs to be neither very deep nor very shallow if ships are to anchor in it in safety: not so shallow that they run aground, but not so deep that they cannot anchor in a convenient depth – 5 or 6 metres would do for most ancient ships. Strictly that applies to the ὅρμος, the place of anchorage as distinguished at 435. According to the present account they enter the outer harbour, take down mast and sails, and row to a no doubt sheltered corner which might be difficult (as AbT say, more pertinently this time) to reach under sail. Aristarchus' reading ἐγγύς for ἐντός (Did/A) is therefore misconceived.

433 ἱστία μὲν στείλαντο, 'they gathered up the sails': the middle form does not recur in Homer except in the rather different 23.285, and Wakefield's στεῖλάν τε θέσαν τ' is an obvious correction if one is needed. The *Odyssey* has 16.353 |ἱστία τε στέλλοντας and 3.10f. ἱστία νηὸς ἐΐσης| στεῖλαν, but the middle form may have been adopted, imprecisely no doubt, when the metrical context called for the extra short syllable.

434 ἱστοδόκῃ means literally 'mast-receiver', being a crutch at the stern onto which the mast was lowered. Zenodotus and the MSS are probably right with ὑφέντες, 'letting down', against Aristarchus' ἐφέντες (rather than ἀφέντες, Did/bT and A). The whole verse recurs, not in the *Odyssey* this time (where πρότονοι, forestays, happen to be mentioned only in mast-*raising* scenes, 2.425 = 15.290), but at *HyAp* 504, in the scene where the Cretan ship arrives at Krisa; 437 also occurs there (as 505), but it is also formular in the *Odyssey* (4×). The arrival-scene in the Hymn, only 5 verses in all, shares some of its nautical phraseology with the *Odyssey*, some with the *Iliad* here, and has some of its own. This suggests that there was a wide range of seafaring poetry on which all these poets could draw; thus 'Odyssean' language (see on 432–9) here does not entail direct dependence on the *Odyssey* at all points. It is worth observing that Odysseus' ship carries out distinct manœuvres in its two landfalls: here at Khruse it is anchored and then secured with stern-lines to the shore, later at the Achaean camp (484–6) it will be beached and then supported upright with props.

435 Confusion between the two processes just mentioned may indirectly account for the vulgate's προέρυσσαν ('drew forward' rather than προέρεσσαν, 'rowed forward', which is obviously correct), despite Aristarchus (Did/A) who cited the Argolic and Sinopic texts as well as Sosigenes in favour of the latter.

435–7 These three verses recur as *Od.* 15.497–9; for 436 cf. also *Od.* 9.137. εὐναί are anchor-stones, probably flat and so bed-like (as the Greek term suggests) to minimize dragging – although many of the pierced anchor-stones found by underwater exploration are not notably flat. A pair of anchors are evidently dropped, one from each side of the bow, and stern-lines from each quarter hold the ship in to the shore – a method of mooring still widely practised in the tideless and often steep-to Mediterranean.

436–9 Initial and emphatic ἐκ is not merely repeated, but is used for a third and a fourth time. The effect of this exaggerated epanaphora is remarkable; it is purely rhetorical, to convey urgency, speed and orderly progress rather than the idea of 'out' itself; there is no real connexion between throwing out anchors and taking themselves, the cattle and the girl out of the ship. The figure works better, perhaps, in its regular two-verse form (as it would in 436f. taken by themselves) than in exaggerated applications as here; although the threefold version at 2.382–4 succeeds because of the genuine semantic force of the repeated εὖ.

437 This verse, but with βῆμεν for βαῖνον, is found 4x in the *Odyssey*; here the imperfect βαῖνον is unnatural, but the provision of an aorist, e.g. βάν, would require a kind of remodelling which was evidently not considered worthwhile.

440–1 The preceding four verses have been structurally similar, both through their initial ἐκ and because of their twofold pattern; the last of them, 439, also provides a certain contrast and climax through its heavily spondaic rhythm. Now the mood changes as the men proceed rapidly to hand back the girl and begin the sacrifice, and urgency and excitement are well expressed in this striking pair of rising threefolders.

442–5 Odysseus' words are compact and to the point; as often the concluding verse is more relaxed (lacking as it does internal breaks, in contrast with its three predecessors) and discursive. Aristarchus (Arn/A) athetized 444 as grammatically superfluous, which is true but irrelevant.

446 Another rising threefolder, matching 441 not only in this respect but also in its identical central element ἐν χερσὶ τίθει. The verse is formular in itself (3x *Il.*, if the slight variant at 23.565 is included, of handing over prizes at the funeral games in book 23, and 1x *Od.*); but the central element is the basis of the system and occurs independently (3x *Il.*, including χείρεσσι for χερσί, 4x *Od.*). The poet forgoes any attempt to put the priest's presumably mixed feelings into words, and concentrates on his joy at receiving his daughter back.

447–68 This description of animal sacrifice is a 'typical scene' with many standard verses. The language is fluent and clear with a number of technical ritual terms; it is not noticeably archaic, except conceivably in the rarity of integral enjambment (only at 462/3) and the regularity of verse-pattern (although there are rising threefolders at 464 and 466). This is the fullest description in the *Iliad* of this fundamental ritual act

(Agamemnon's sacrifice and prayer for victory at 2.410ff. being similar but lacking some details), only surpassed by Nestor's elaborate sacrifice on the sea-shore near Pulos at *Od.* 4.321ff. For further description and summary of the not wholly consistent Homeric evidence see my discussion in *Entretiens Hardt* xxvii (Vandoeuvres–Genèves 1981) 62–8, and especially the comparative table of detailed actions on p. 64.

The main points of the present description are as follows. First the cattle comprising the hecatomb (on which see 65n.) are stationed round the altar (447f.; no doubt in as regular a fashion, ἑξείης, as could be achieved quickly, ὦκα); the circle is sacred, and at 2.410 the sacrificers themselves surround the single victim. They purify themselves symbolically by washing their hands (449) – someone would have brought a bowl of water for that as at *Od.* 3.440f. – then take up the οὐλοχύται, barley-groats that were to be scattered over the victims, obviously from a basket which is specifically mentioned at *Od.* 3.442; as they hold the grain the prayer is spoken (see on 451–6). At 458 they throw the grain 'forward', προβάλοντο, onto the victims (rather than the altar as bT suggest), then draw back (αὐέρυσαν) the victims' heads so as to expose their necks and turn them toward the sky (459). They slaughter and skin them (still 459), then cut out the thigh-bones and wrap them in fat (460 κνίσῃ ἐκάλυψαν), making two folds – that is, a kind of sandwich with the bones in the middle (461 δίπτυχα). Then they put on bits of raw meat (461 ὠμοθέτησαν) which, as we learn from *Od.* 14.427f., were taken from all the limbs so as to symbolize the offering of the whole animal (so AbT). Then Khruses the priest burns them on a wooden spit and pours a libation of wine over them (462f.). When the god's portion has been consumed by fire they all eat the innards (σπλάγχνα, 464), which, as 2.426 shows, have been roasted meanwhile; then they carve up, μίστυλλον, the rest of the carcase(s) and roast the pieces on five-pronged forks (465, where the ὀβελοί, spits, are presumably the πεμπώβολα of 463 = *Od.* 3.460); they withdraw, ἐρύσαντο, the pieces when cooked and prepare the feast (466f.). By this point the secular meal is under way and the sacrificial ritual in the strict sense has been completed.

A few ritual actions have been omitted in this particular passage (as at 2.410ff.) but occur elsewhere in Homer: gilding the victim's horns (as at *Od.* 3.436–8), paralysing it with an axe-blow, accompanied where appropriate by the ritual female shriek, before slitting its throat (*Od.* 3.449f.), cutting hair from its head (*Il.* 3.273) and throwing this on the fire (*Od.* 3.446, 14.442). Some of these further actions belong to any formal sacrifice but happen not to be mentioned in our passage, or in other particular versions of the typical scene; others belong to especially elaborate and peacetime circumstances (notably Nestor's sacrifice in *Od.* 3) or to a special application like the oath-sacrifice at *Il.* 3.268ff.

451–6 Khruses' prayer reverses his earlier one at 37–42 in which he called on Apollo to punish the Achaeans. The invocation in the opening two verses is identical in each case, as might be expected; the next three verses, setting out his special claim on the god's attention, differ – here it is that Apollo had granted Khruses' previous prayer and so should also grant the present one (453–5). Finally in each case the request itself is confined to a succinct closing verse; here, that the plague should be ended.

In 454 τίμησας is rightly so accented, i.e. as main verb and not as participle, because of the μέν...δέ balance of the verse as a whole.

458–69 These verses recur in the description of Agamemnon's sacrifice and feast for the chieftains at 2.421–32 (see on 447–68 for the 'typical scene' of sacrifice and preparation of a meal) – all except for 462f., for which the book 2 version has a different pair of verses and which recur, on the other hand, in the description of Nestor's sacrifice as *Od.* 3.459f. For the reasons for this switch, see the next comment.

462–3 The version represented by book 2 is departed from at this point, probably for two reasons: (i) if the sacrifice is being performed by a priest, or by a king in his priestly function, then the main act of offering should be performed by him and not (as elsewhere on less official occasions) by the participants at large. Thus Nestor in *Od.* 3 personally burns the fat-encased thigh-bones and also pours a libation, and Khruses must do the same here; Agamemnon in *Il.* 2 leaves the burning of the sacred portion, like that of the secular portions that follow, to the others. (ii) The *Odyssey* version has the additional slight advantage of referring to the sacrificer as old, γέρων, suitable both to Nestor and to Khruses here. The distinction of the two versions is a fine one, from which it might be inferred, not that the whole scene is a carelessly-organised *cento* of formular verses and motifs (as Leaf and others have thought), but that it shows signs of careful adjustment to particular circumstances; but see also on 470–1.

467–8 = 2.403f., 7.319f. (also 2× *Od.*, with trivial variations). In addition 468 recurs alone at 602 and 23.56.

469 An even commoner verse than its predecessors, since it applies to any meal, not just to one following a sacrifice (7× *Il.*, 14× *Od.*).

470–1 The young men ἐπεστέψαντο, 'crowned', that is, filled to the brim, the mixing-bowls (which were used for mixing the wine with water in the usual Greek manner). They then distributed the mixture to all present, making a ritual beginning (ἐπαρξάμενοι) with a few drops in each cup for a libation, after which the cup would be filled for ordinary drinking; cf. 9.176 and *Od.* 3.340–2, also 21.271f. It is odd that this is done when they have already been drinking, as in 469, and it is possible that these two verses, which were part of the formular stock of descriptions of various moments in this whole typical scene of eating and drinking, were incorrectly applied here, either by the monumental poet or by a subsequent elaborator; they are of course inorganic. Düntzer went so far as to omit the whole of 469–74, which was certainly excessive; see on 474.

473 παιήονα here is the song, the 'paean', not the name of the healer-god Paian who was equated with Apollo (so Aristarchus (Arn/A), who also noted that καλόν is adverbial with ἀείδοντες). The epic and Ionic form Παιήων and the contracted Doric and tragic Παιάν, also Lesbian Πάων, are based on earlier Παιάϝων, cf. the Mycenaean dative *pa-ja-wo-ne* (Chantraine, *Dict.*, s.v. παιάν, with references). The etymology of the divinity (which resembles 'Ιά(ϝ)ονες in its termination) is obscure; he gave his name to the particular shout or song of praise addressed to him by his worshippers (rather than *vice versa* as with Ἴακχος as a name for Dionusos; but cf. Burkert, *Griechische Religion* 127), probably by way of the invocation 'Ιὴ Παια(ϝ)ών; his Cretan priests sing the Iepaieon for Apollo, ἰηπαιήον' ἄειδον, at *HyAp* 517. Here and at 22.391f. it is a song of rejoicing; in the latter Apollo is not mentioned, but here the rejoicing is clearly coupled with praise of the god. It is also accompanied by dance in the μολπή; compare the processional hymn led by Apollo himself in the *Hymn to Apollo* passage (514–19).

474 Here Aristarchus athetized (Arn/A) on entirely inadequate grounds (repetition of the idea of μολπῇ, 472, in μέλποντες, and of the god in ἑκάεργον); Leaf commented (on 471) that the participles in 473 and 474 separated by κοῦροι 'Αχαιῶν 'are awkward', although this seems, rather, a case of typically Homeric cumulation.

475–87 The return home of Odysseus and his crew: they sleep on the beach in readiness for an early start, sail at dawn with a favourable wind, then draw up the ship on shore on arrival back at the Achaean camp. Here too, and not unexpectedly, there is much phraseology of Odyssean type.

475 The verse occurs 6x *Od.* (and twice more with trivial variations); not exactly elsewhere in *Il.*, but 4x similarly, especially δύῃ τ' ἠέλιος καὶ ἐπὶ κνέφας ἱερὸν ἔλθῃ (3x).

476 Almost identical with *Od.* 12.32; bT comment that they slept by the stern-lines so that they would know from the ship's movement if a favourable breeze sprang up – almost an excess of nautical realism, this (were they using the taut lines as pillows?). The point surely is that they were as close to the ship's stern as possible, ready for boarding at first light.

477 A familiar verse in the *Odyssey*, 20x as opposed to only 2x *Il.*, here and at 24.788 (with (ἐ)φάνη ῥοδοδάκτυλος 'Ηώς twice elsewhere and one further variant). Book 24 likewise has much phraseology in common with the *Odyssey*, and for a similar reason: that part of its content is Odyssean, rather than typically Iliadic, in character. There are of course many more individual dawns to be noted in the later poem (see also on 2.48–9). Macleod, *Iliad XXIV* 47, noted that dawns tended to be mere time-markers

there, whereas they often serve special purposes in the *Iliad*. His further claim
(p. 32) that the present verse and 24.788 are significantly related because
they follow events involving Khruseis and Hektor who had 'aroused such
damaging passions in Achilles' is harder to support.

M. L. West has a good note on ῥοδοδάκτυλος at Hesiod, *Erga* 610,
pointing out that it might refer either to a pattern of rays like spread fingers
or to a 'single sliver of red light at the horizon', cf. Alcaeus frag. 346.1 L–P.

479 The favourable breeze (ἵκμενον οὖρον, not elsewhere *Il.* but 4× *Od.*,
again presumably because of the frequency of sea-journeys there) is a
conclusive sign that the propitiation of the god (472 ἱλάσκοντο) has been
successful; Homer has no need to say that the plague ceases forthwith.
ἵκμενον is probably connected with ἱκνέομαι (so Chantraine, *Dict.*), and is
a breeze that goes with them, rather than making them arrive; the
D-scholium in A is correct here against the exegetical one in AbT, which
absurdly connects the term with ἰκμάς.

481–3 = *Od.* 2.427–9 (except for the slight variant ἔπρησεν δ' ἄνεμος;
the *Iliad*'s ἐν δ' ἄνεμος πρῆσεν is better).

483 διαπρήσσουσα κέλευθον is formular, cf. *Od.* 2.213 and 429:
'accomplishes its course', with traces of the derivation of πράσσω from
περάω, 'pass over'.

484 On κατά see 423–5n., second paragraph.

485–6 They draw up the ship on the beach (485 = *Od.* 16.325, cf. 359)
and fix (literally 'stretch') tall props, obviously of wood, against it to hold
it upright. Verse 486 is not an Odyssean one but recurs at *HyAp* 507 (its
predecessor 485 being close to *HyAp* 488, see on 434). Once again this
suggests the existence of a body of technical ship-poetry on which the *Odyssey*
draws frequently, the *Iliad* and even the longer Hymns occasionally. That
the Achaean ships were shored up with ἕρματα is mentioned elsewhere only
at 2.154.

487 They disperse without reporting to Agamemnon, which might have
been dramatically something of an anticlimax (in the narrative, that is, not
in life); bT comment that the plague must have ended, and that in itself
would show the success of their mission.

*488–92 Akhilleus meanwhile has withdrawn from the fighting and stays in anger
by the ships*

488–92 Zenodotus athetized these five verses (Arn/A), omitting 491
altogether. But the glimpse of Akhilleus putting his wrath into action (or
frustrated inaction, rather) is a necessary reminder after the voyage-
to-Khruse interlude and before the long scene on Olumpos which now
follows.

Book One

488-9 The language of Thetis' instruction at 421f., ἀλλὰ σὺ μὲν νῦν νηυσὶ παρήμενος ὠκυπόροισι| μῆνι' Ἀχαιοῖσιν, is adjusted as necessary to the narrative context. For Πηλῆος υἱός compare Πηλῆος υἱέ, similarly positioned, at 16.21, 19.216.

490 κυδιάνειραν is found elsewhere only in the formula μάχην ἄνα κυδιάνειραν (etc.) (8x Il., not Od.); for the present adaptation bT compare 9.440f., where the conjunction of war and assembly also occurs, with the latter as 'where men are very conspicuous', ἀριπρεπέες.

492 After the formal balance of the οὔτε...οὔτε verses preceding, this concluding verse stands out not, as often, by a difference in verse-rhythm or type of enjambment (progressive here as in its predecessor) but by developing the pathetic phrase 'eating his heart out' in the second part of 491 into an almost paradoxical *deep longing* (ποθέεσκε) for the turmoil of war.

493–611 Thetis goes to Zeus on Olumpos; he reluctantly grants her request, which causes him to be upbraided by Here. Hephaistos mediates and the evening ends in feasting and music

493-611 This scene on Olumpos has three phases of roughly equal length: (1) Thetis supplicates Zeus (493–533); (2) Zeus and Here quarrel (533–69); (3) Hephaistos re-establishes harmony (570–611).

493-4 The gods return from their visit to the Aithiopes, cf. 423–5 and comment. These two verses (of which 493 = 24.31, see on 477) are emphatically related by their initial cola, ἀλλ' ὅτε δή and καὶ τότε δή, and are strongly formular in their components. The time-interval is conventionally expressed; ἠώς occurs 27x Il., 15x at the verse-end as here (as against 40x and 35x Od.). Eleven-day intervals are convenient because of the formula-system developed around δυωδεκάτη γένετ' Ἠώς| and |ἦδε δυωδεκάτη...and so on. There are not one but two such intervals in book 24: Akhilleus defiles Hektor's body for eleven days (31) (i.e. it lies for eleven nights in Akhilleus' hut (413)), and an eleven-day truce for its burial is envisaged by Priam (667). These intervals, both closely concerned with the treatment of Hektor's body, might be deliberately similar (which is not discussed by Macleod in his commentary); that reduces, if anything, the likelihood of an intentional connexion between this eleven-day divine absence in book 1 and one particular member of the pair of interrelated intervals of book 24; see on 423–5. Different intervals are also possible, for example nine- and ten-day ones as at e.g. 21.155f., 24.107f., 6.175 – sometimes with similar wording based on ἐνδεκάτη, δεκάτη in place of δυωδεκάτη etc.

495 An effective half-verse cumulation, leading from the resumptive and almost otiose πάντες ἅμα to the more pointed Ζεὺς δ' ἦρχε; he in turn generates the contrasting Thetis and so introduces the scene between them which follows.

496 The complicated pattern of cumulation and enjambment continues. This verse with its predecessor 495 is packed with meaning, entailing internal stops, as against the almost frigid balance and flow of the preceding pair, 493f. For ἀνεδύσετο κῦμα θαλάσσης compare Thetis' earlier emergence at 359, ἀνέδυ πολιῆς ἁλὸς ἠΰτ' ὀμίχλη, where the genitive 'out of the sea' is more to be expected than the accusative here. The latter is more appropriate with the other meaning of the verb, 'draw back from', as in e.g. 13.225 ἀνδύεται πόλεμον, where the sense of the preverb is different. Van Herwerden conjectured ῥίμφα for κῦμα which is a bare possibility, although ῥίμφα does not fall into this position in the verse in its 13 other Iliadic occurrences, whereas κῦμα θαλάσσης| occurs 3x elsewhere in the poem.

497 ἠερίη: 'like mist', or 'early in the morning'? The first is tempting because of 359 ἠΰτ' ὀμίχλη, but must be rejected because Here will shortly tell Zeus at 557 that Thetis ἠερίη γὰρ σοί γε παρέζετο, and she can hardly have been mist-like when she sat down. Moreover ἠέριοι must mean 'early in the morning' or something similar when applied to the Kikones at *Od.* 9.52. Chantraine, *Dict.* s.v., distinguishes two words, one connected with ἀήρ and the other with ἦρι as in ἠριγένεια, 'early-born', and opts for the second here.

Thetis 'ascended the great sky', according to Aristarchus (Arn/A), because the peaks of Olumpos were above the clouds.

498-9 Zeus is apart from the other gods to emphasize his independence and superiority as well as to make it easy for Thetis to approach him. He is seated at the highest point of Olumpos, presumably on a throne in his sanctuary there. He is εὐρύοπα, 'loud-sounding' (from ϝόψ = 'voice') not 'far-seeing' (cf. ὄψις, ὄπωπα), as is appropriate to the god of thunder.

500-1 These are standard gestures of supplication (see on 512-13), graphically described – 'as in a picture', bT. She grasps his chin ὑπ', from below.

502 Δία Κρονίωνα ἄνακτα: the titles present Zeus in his most august aspect.

503-10 Thetis' prayer proceeds as quickly as possible to a relatively full statement of the request and the circumstances causing it; title and sanction are less conspicuously dealt with than in e.g. Khruses' prayers to Apollo at 37-42 and 451-6, for Thetis is a goddess herself.

505 Nauck's υἱέα μοι τίμησον would neatly avoid the hiatus of μοι υἱόν, if that is found offensive; see also on 532-3. The superlative followed by ἄλλων is idiomatic, cf. 6.295, 23.532, *Od.* 5.105. Chantraine (*GH* II, 60) debates whether the genitive is partitive or ablatival, i.e. 'in distinction from others'; but ἄλλων, because of its separative meaning, must surely be the latter, as against πάντων etc. in similar constructions, which are partitive. On Akhilleus as ὠκυμορώτατος see on 352–3.

507 See on 356, an identical verse.

509 'And set domination upon the Trojans [i.e. make them dominant] until such time as...'

511–12 Zeus responds to her prayer with a long and dramatic silence...

512–13 ...during which Thetis does not relax her hold upon his knees: 'as she had clasped [literally, touched] them, so did she hold on to them, clinging to them'. ἐμπεφυυῖα is from ἐμφῦναι, literally 'grow into'; compare the formula of supplication and address, ἐν δ' ἄρα οἱ φῦ χειρὶ ἔπος τ' ἔφατ' ἔκ τ' ὀνόμαζε (5× *Il.*, 4× *Od.*). Grasping the knees and touching the chin, as at 500f., are the two main ritual gestures of supplication, supplemented where possible by kissing the knees or hands. Thus at 8.370–2 Thetis here will be reported as having kissed Zeus's knees and grasped his chin in supplication; at 10.454f. Dolon is trying to touch Diomedes' chin just before he is cut down; at 21.67–75 Lukaon clutches Akhilleus' knees with one hand, his spear with the other, as he asks him to show reverence (αἰδώς) and pity to him as a suppliant; and at 24.477–9 Priam grasps Akhilleus' knees and kisses his hands. A certain amount of flexibility is allowed, according to the posture, behaviour and exact status (e.g. threatening immediate violence or not) of the person supplicated; knees and chin are important places to touch since they symbolize special concentrations of that person's life-force and power, and physical contact is in any case essential – as also, for example, with a deity's altar when the appeal is less direct. See further J. P. Gould, *JHS* 93 (1973) 74ff., and J. B. Hainsworth in *Odissea* II, 196.

514–16 She reinforces her supplication not, as might be expected, by setting out the particular ἔργον (504) that according to Akhilleus, at least, would constitute her claim to a counter-benefit from Zeus – that is, her having got Briareos to protect him (396–406); but rather by dwelling in general terms on how he must despise her if he does not definitely accede to her request. This might be relevant to the status of the Briareos episode, on which see 396–406n.

These three verses are carefully balanced, 514 and 516 being two/fourfold and end-stopped, and the intervening 515 three/fourfold, internally punctuated and leading into its successor by fluent integral enjambment.

514 She requires not merely a breaking of the silence with some possibly non-committal reply, but a direct promise confirmed by a positive gesture – a telling hint of the awesome oath that is to follow.

515 ἐπεὶ οὔ τοι ἔπι δέος: the meaning is 'since you can do as you like and need have no fear of anyone'.

518–19 Aristarchus (Did/A) was certainly wrong to read Ἥρη in the nominative, but the syntax remains puzzling: 'Destructive work indeed, your inciting me to enter into hostilities with Here, whenever she provokes me with insulting words.' The difficulty lies with ὅτ' ἄν, 'whenever'; Thetis is only inciting him on this one occasion, therefore the indefinite construction is out of place. The underlying meaning is probably intended to be that whenever Here provokes and insults him, it is because someone like Thetis has first incited him. A loose combination of formular elements is the likeliest culprit, rather than textual corruption as van Leeuwen suspected. ἐχθοδοπῆσαι occurs only here, although ἐχθοδοπός is found in Attic, presumably formed like e.g. ἀλλοδαπός.

520 καὶ αὕτως: 'even as it is' (Leaf).

522 ἀπόστιχε: aorist imperative of ἀποστείχω (2x *Od.*, not otherwise *Il.*, but the simple form στείχω occurs 4x *Il.*); it has a distinctly colloquial ring, 'march off home', 'be off with you'.

522–3 The verse-end cola correspond in rhythm and partly in sound, ὄφρα τελέσσω : ὄφρα πεποίθῃς. The latter is a simple purpose-clause (Chantraine, *GH* II, 266), the former a completive clause also expressing purpose (*ibid.* 297), as in 6.361 θυμὸς ἐπέσσυται ὄφρ' ἐπαμύνω. 'These things shall be my concern, for me to bring them to accomplishment.'

525–7 A rhythmically varied trio of verses after the repetitive adonic clausulae (i.e. after strong bucolic diaereses) of the three preceding ones. Verse 525 is twofold but leads into violent enjambment (violent, because it separates adjacent epithet and noun) with the single runover-word, presumably to place heavy emphasis on τέκμωρ. It is followed by mildly progressive enjambment and half-verse cumulation from 526 to 527, where οὐδ' ἀτελεύτητον is not so much plethoric as legalistic in its logical completeness: 'this is an affirmation which is irrevocable, truthful and certain of fulfilment'. It is tempting to read ἐμοί for ἐμόν in 526; the latter is intelligible ('my ⟨word⟩'; hardly 'my τέκμωρ', exactly, after ἐξ ἐμέθεν in 525) but not very precise, since it is only on special occasions like this that Zeus's decisions are irrevocable. τέκμωρ itself is an old word for πέρας, 'goal' or 'end', according to Aristotle; 'a fixed mark or boundary', LSJ; here it is rather the *determination* of a resolve (see also Chantraine, *Dict.* s.v. τέκμαρ). The nodding of the head as a normal sign of assent or approval is elevated by Zeus into an irreversible ritual commitment.

528–30 The solemn affirmation is described in Homer's grandest style, aided by the use of splendid and sonorous words and phrases – κυανέῃσιν, ἀμβρόσιαι, ἐπερρώσαντο, κρατὸς ἀπ' ἀθανάτοιο.

528 The verse recurs at 17.209, where Zeus, this time in private, nods to confirm his resolve about Patroklos. There is no difference in implication between ἐπινεύω here (in tmesis) and κατανεύω at 527; he nods his head forward, including his dark brow – κύανος is a kind of enamel shown by later references to be dark blue, but at 24.94 κυάνεος clearly means blue-*black* since nothing can be blacker than it. Zeus's brows are blue-black presumably because they are shaded by, but also reflect, his hair, the 'ambrosial locks'. It seems to me unlikely that, as Willcock suggests *ad loc.* in the tradition of nineteenth-century nature-myth addicts (cf. e.g. my *The Nature of Greek Myths* (Harmondsworth 1974) 43f.), the description here is based on thunder-cloud imagery.

529-30 'The lord's ambrosial [that is, divine] locks ἐπερρώσαντο, moved quickly forward, from his immortal head'; ῥώομαι is an epic verb meaning 'rush on', as for example at 11.50. According to AbT the 'swiftness of the syllables' of ἐλέλιξεν, presumably the reduplication of ἐλ-, evoke the shaking of the mountain and the swiftness of the movement; more important, perhaps, is the observation that these verses inspired Pheidias in the design of his great statue of Zeus at Olumpia. There is a reduced version of the episode at 8.199, where *Here* shakes on her throne and causes great Olumpos to tremble, and it may be that what is to be understood as agitating Olumpos here – if one is to insist on some specific physical cause for what is primarily intended as a metaphorical effect – is Zeus moving in his throne rather than the act of nodding his head.

532-3 Objection has been taken to the hiatus both of ἅλα ἄλτο (532) and of δέ ἑόν (533). The former is not a serious difficulty, since hiatus at the end of the first foot, although not common, is not especially rare either. In this case some sense may have been retained of the initial sigma concealed in ἅλλομαι, 'I leap', cf. Latin *salio*, of which ἄλτο is the athematic aorist with psilosis, cf. Chantraine, *GH* 1, 383. The latter instance is more surprising (although hardly 'inexcusable', Leaf); it might even be correct – after all, no one in antiquity took exception to it; although emendations like Brandreth's Ζεύς δ' ἷε ὅν πρός δῶμα have the added advantage of removing a slightly inelegant zeugma (Thetis leapt into the sea, Zeus into his palace).

533-4 The other gods' respect – fear, almost – for Zeus is shown by their rising to their feet when he enters his house where they have been waiting; compare their rising to Here at 15.84-6. This became a common motif in the hymnodic tradition, and is almost parodied in the divine terror at Apollo's approach in *HyAp* 2-4. οὐδέ τις ἔτλη| is a formula (8x *Il.*), closely paralleled, with μεῖναι ἐπερχόμενον following, when Hektor fears Akhilleus at 22.251f.

536 The bouncing rhythm is caused not so much by uninterrupted dactyls as by the trochaic word-breaks in the second and third feet; it is a faintly undesirable accident, unrelated to meaning.

537 ἰδοῦσα shows that Here saw something suspicious in his manner despite all the precautions, and the double negative οὐδέ...ἠγνοίησεν confirms the indirectness of the scene.

539 κερτομίοισι, 'with jeers': a syncopated expression, 2x *Od.*, for κερτομίοις ἐπέεσσι (etc.) as at 4.6, 5.419, *Od.* 24.240; cf. on μειλιχίοισιν at

4.256, although perhaps we should read κερτομίαισι after κερτομίας at 20.202 = 433 and *Od.* 20.263. The etymology of the word is in any case unknown.

540–3 The goddess's jeers (539) are overtly confined to the term δολομῆτα, 'deviser of deceit'; the rest of her remarks suggest no more than pained surprise and a degree of hypocrisy. It is a wonderfully devious little speech; she knows perfectly well who has been with Zeus, and will say so at 555–7. She also manages to imply, with no justification, that Zeus ought not to make decisions, δικαζέμεν, on his own, and that his never willingly telling her of his intentions amounts to some kind of failure on his part, οὐδέ...τέτληκας. bT commented that 'wives are angry if their husbands do not tell them everything'; part of Homer's characterization of Here is indeed that of an interfering wife, but her passionate support for the Achaeans, combined with Zeus's regard for Hektor, requires her to be constantly alert.

544 Zeus is πατὴρ ἀνδρῶν τε θεῶν τε 12x *Il.*, 3x *Od.* (a considerable but not necessarily significant difference of vocabulary-preference between the two poems). It is the regular way of describing him after τὴν (etc.) δ' ἡμείβετ' ἔπειτα; but the choice of this particular formula of address as against that represented in 560, for example, is especially suitable here, stressing as it does his august and autocratic side against Here's insinuation that he is just an ordinary husband. 'Father of men and gods' is more than just a 'polar' expression (cf. on 548), and marks his pre-eminence over everything divine and human. The listing of various offspring of both classes, as is done by AbT, is beside the point; his 'fatherhood' is no more literally meant than 'Our Father, which art in heaven'.

545–50 Zeus replies in the same apparently calm style, insisting on his power of private decision; his conclusion is distinguished by the rising threefolder 549.

546 The Ionic future εἰδήσειν occurs 2x *Od.* (as well as in Herodotus), although εἴσεται as in 548 is commoner.

548 'None of gods...or men' is a true polar expression; that is, wholly rhetorical, since there is no likelihood of men being involved – compare Heraclitus frag. 30, κόσμον τόνδε...οὔτε τις θεῶν οὔτε ἀνθρώπων ἐποίησεν..., and Xenophanes frag. 23.1, εἷς θεὸς ἔν τε θεοῖσι καὶ ἀνθρώποισι μέγιστος.

551 βοῶπις πότνια Ἥρη: 14x *Il.*, not *Od.* (where Here occurs only three times in the nominative). It is customary to say that βοῶπις (which, however, is also applied to a mortal woman, Phulomedousa, at 7.10) may be a relic of a time when Here was envisaged as theriomorphic. That seems doubtful, especially since no properly theriomorphic stage can be traced in Greek or pre-Greek religion. Athene is similarly and quite regularly 'owl-eyed' – or 'blue-grey-eyed', since γλαυκ- can mean either. The owl is her special attribute, just as the cow is associated with Here (for example through Io), but 'blue-grey-eyed' might nevertheless be the intended meaning, and 'with placid gaze', like that of a cow, that in Here's case.

552–9 The game of half-truths continues: Here, after expressing indignation at the idea that she has ever been unduly inquisitive, decides the time has come to reveal much of what she knows – not only that Thetis has entreated Zeus early that morning (on ἠερίη see 497n.), but also, as a strong suspicion (ὀίω, 558), exactly what he has pledged.

552 Herē has occasion to address Zeus in these terms no less than six times in the poem; no other deity would address him so strongly (although Menelaos calls him 'most destructive' of gods at 3.365) – αἰνότατε is not used elsewhere, except that Iris calls Athene αἰνοτάτη at 8.423, where she also calls her a bitch. The verse-end formula μῦθον ἔειπες (etc.) is in itself quite common, 32× *Il.*

553–4 The indignation is cleverly maintained in the assertive long syllables of καὶ λίην, the careful placing of σε and γ', and the rhetorical redundance (reinforced by οὔτε…οὔτε) of εἴρομαι and μεταλλῶ. Verse 554 almost mocks Zeus's complete freedom to make up his own mind; ἀλλὰ μάλ' εὔκηλος is phonetically emphatic with αλλ-, -αλ-, -ηλ-, and φράζεαι ἅσσα θέληοθα with -αз-, -ασσ-, -ησθ-: 'but in full freedom work out just whatever you wish'. αἴ κ' ἐθέληοθα (etc.) occurs 6× *Il.* at the verse-end, but generally these two verses are non-formular, and seem carefully shaped for the context.

557 On ἠερίη see 497n.

558–9 Once again the conclusion of a short speech is marked by a different verse-pattern: in this case, strong enjambment with emphatic runover-word after a sequence of end-stopped or lightly enjambed verses that suggested something of Here's self-imposed calm.

561–7 Zeus's reply is less relaxed; a passionate firmness is conveyed by the interrupted verses, closed off by the continuous flow of 566f. at the end.

561 δαιμονίη expresses affectionate remonstrance here, as it does when Andromakhe and Hektor use the term to address each other at 6.407 and 486; often it implies a stronger rebuke, as at 4.31. Derivation from δαίμων is obvious, but the precise development of different nuances of meaning, as with many colloquialisms, is not. αἰεὶ μὲν ὀίεαι, 'you are for ever making suppositions', takes up ὀίω in 558.

564 After the thinly-veiled threat of 562f., here is a lofty and evasive concession that her suspicions are well-founded: 'if the situation is as you say, then it must be because I wish it so' ('you may be sure it is my good pleasure', Leaf); compare 2.116, a more straightforward use of μέλλει…φίλον εἶναι.

566–7 Finally comes the direct threat of unpreventable physical violence (see on 399), developed by Hephaistos in what follows. ἰόνθ' in 567 represents ἰόντα, although one might expect a genitive absolute, ἰόντος, rather (so Aristarchus, Arn/A): 'lest none of them can help you when I come closer to you', the last words being a nice piece of understatement.

568–72 The colometry of these verses is discussed on p. 23.

569 καί ῥ' ἀκέουσα καθῆστο: the formula is simply and neatly adapted from 565.

571 Hephaistos plays a major role, from here to 600, in restoring divine harmony. That could have been concisely stated in two or three verses, but the singer clearly wishes to elaborate the motif of Zeus's supremacy and concealed violence, as well as the character of the pacific Hephaistos himself.

573 Hephaistos begins with the same words as Zeus had used at 518, ἦ δὴ λοίγια ἔργα.

574 A rising threefolder, in which σφώ (4x *Il.*, cf. νώ 2x *Il.*), which was later the Attic form, should perhaps be σφῶ' (for σφῶι): Chantraine, *GH* I, 266. Quarrelling because of mortals must have been particularly galling to those gods who were not deeply committed on either side; and Hephaistos was devoted to pleasant living, see also 579.

578–9 On the colometry, and the adaptation of 578 and 572, see also pp. 23f. In 579 σύν goes with ταράξῃ not ἡμῖν.

578 Another rising threefolder, with light formular variation of 572:

572 μητρὶ φίλῃ ἐπὶ ἦρα φέρων
578 πατρὶ φίλῳ ἐπὶ ἦρα φέρειν

both being developed out of simpler formular elements: μητρί and πατρί are often 'dear', as in the rather similar rising threefolders

441 πατρὶ φίλῳ ἐν χερσὶ τίθει, καί μιν προσέειπε(ν)
585 μητρὶ φίλῃ ἐν χερσὶ τίθει... (see on 584–5)

and other traces of an ἦρα φέροντες (etc.) system are found elsewhere (1x *Il.*, 3x *Od.*). The etymology of ἦρα is debated, but it is perhaps related to Old Icelandic *voevr*, 'friendly': so Frisk.

580–1 The incomplete conditional statement can be treated either as an aposiopesis or more probably, with Leaf, as a form of exclamation: 'Suppose he should wish...! ⟨He would be able to⟩ , for he is much the strongest.'

582 καθάπτεσθαι is also used of engaging someone with hostile words, not 'gentle' ones as here; so at 15.127 and (without ἐπέεσσι) 16.421. It does not of itself imply hostility, but rather a direct effort to engage someone in speech for an important reason – more than simply to address them.

583 ἵλαος with metrical lengthening.

584–5 A pair of rising threefolders; see on 578 for the second of them. The δέπας of 584 is a two-handled cup, ἀμφικύπελλον, and obviously easier to hold in both hands when full. Aristarchus (Did/A) read χειρί nevertheless, and was supported by the Marseilles text as well as Aristophanes and Sosigenes; his reason was presumably χειρί in 596. The vulgate retained the plural form, which may well be correct, especially in view of 23.565 Εὐμήλῳ δ' ἐν χερσὶ τίθει (of a piece of armour).

586–94 Hephaistos now addresses Here directly, repeating the gist of his appeal but reinforcing it with a reminder of what had happened to himself when he once tried to protect her against Zeus. He is presumably referring to the incident described at 15.18–24, in which Zeus, enraged with Here for driving his son Herakles down to Kos in a storm, had hung her from Mt Olumpos with a pair of anvils tied to her feet, and then thrown anyone he caught trying to release her down to earth, half-conscious. The exegetical scholium in A reminds us that there were 'two throwings of Hephaistos', since at 18.394–9 he thanks Thetis for saving him when his mother Here (whom he there describes as a bitch) threw him out of Olumpos because he was lame. There were presumably two variant and in fact contradictory stories to account for his lameness; the monumental composer uses both of them, at a long interval in the poem, to motivate first Hephaistos' role as mediator between Here and Zeus, and then his special gratitude to Thetis.

592–4 The description is full of charm and subtle meaning, and it is a sign of Milton's genius that he could even improve on it (*Paradise Lost* 1.740–6). The day-long descent emphasizes the lofty remoteness of the divine mountain, the little breath that was left in him (cf. ὀλιγηπελέων at 15.24) and his own immortal resistance to such violence. Lemnos was Hephaistos' main cult-centre in the Greek world, because of its natural gas rather than as an active volcano – but also because it was close to the Asiatic region from which the idea of a divine smith was drawn. The island's pre-Greek inhabitants (it was not colonized before the ninth century B.C.) were called Sinties according to Homer here. They were 'of wild speech', ἀγριόφωνοι, at *Od.* 8.294, being Pelasgians according to Philochorus; bT tell us that he, Eratosthenes and Porphyrius tried to derive their name from σίνεσθαι, 'to harm', clearly a mere conjecture.

597 ἐνδέξια, 'from left to right', which was the propitious direction.

598 οἰνοχόει was the correct Ionic form according to a galaxy of texts and critics including Aristarchus (Did/A); the medieval texts wrongly kept the Attic form ᾠνοχόει, but cf. on 4.2–3. The divine nectar is described as though it were wine, and is drawn from a mixing-bowl – was it, too, mixed with water?

599–600 Why do the gods burst out laughing at the sight of Hephaistos? Not just because he is ποιπνύοντα, 'bustling'; bT on 584 are probably correct that part of the comic effect lay in the lame god (on whom see further on 607) performing the role of wine-pourer, properly the duty of the comely Hebe or Ganumedes, and in such a bustling (and perhaps even deliberately parodying) way. Whether the cripple's 'leaping up' at 584 was part of the humour, as the scholiasts thought, is more doubtful; but the anecdote about his own fall among the Sinties may have been designed by this amiable god to provide light relief as well as deterrent example. At least it made Here smile (595 and 596), and in general that was not easy to do.

601–2 A formular description of feasting; 601 occurs 6x *Od.*, and, from πρόπαν on, 2x elsewhere *Il.*; 602 occurs 5x *Il.* (including 468 in the present Book), 2x *Od.*

603–4 The rather awkward addition about Apollo and the Muses is unparalleled in Homer, although a similar but more elaborate picture is drawn at *HyAp* 182–206, where they are accompanied in the dance by the Graces and Hours, Harmonie, Aphrodite and Artemis – even by Hermes and Ares for good measure. That development is the certain result of rhapsodic taste; the present pair of verses, with their rather awkward progression '(did not lack feast) or lyre...or Muses', could conceivably be a late-aoidic elaboration. ὀπὶ καλῇ occurs 3x *Od.*, including ἀμειβόμεναι ὀπὶ καλῇ at *Od.* 24.60, itself a probably rhapsodic excursus in which there are nine Muses (unique in Homer), as at Hesiod, *Theog.* 60. At all events it is the first surviving reference to 'amoebean' verse.

605–8 The sun sets and the gods depart for bed, just like mortals, each to his or her own house which the craftsman Hephaistos has built (cf. 11.76f., 14.166f. ~ 338f., 18.369–71). Zeus's palace where they had been celebrating was probably higher up than any of them, although not necessarily on the topmost peak of Olumpos, cf. 498f.

607 ἀμφιγυήεις: there has been much debate about this word; Chantraine, *Dict.* s.v. *γύη regards it as an expanded form of ἀμφίγυος, used of spears in the *Iliad* and itself rather mysterious, although probably meaning 'flexible'. It is undeniable that (as bT on 607 probably had in mind) γυιώσω at 8.402 and 416 means 'make lame' – but is this itself perhaps derived from the assumption that the ancient description of Hephaistos, ἀμφιγυήεις, must mean 'crippled' in some sense? He is χωλόν at 18.397, which does not however state, as is said of Thersites at 2.217, that he was χωλὸς ἕτερον πόδα, that is, lame in one leg only. Could he have been no more than 'curved [the root meaning of γυ-] on both sides', that is, severely bow-legged?

609–11 'Very much a rhapsodist's tag' (Leaf): surely not – these verses make a satisfying close to the Book, and it strengthens both the force and the irony of the encounter between them to show Zeus and Here in the other side of their relationship, as real spouses. It is true that the compound καθεῦδ', as opposed to the simple verb, occurs only here in the *Iliad* but six times in the *Odyssey*; but that is not significant either of 'lateness' or of 'Odyssean' composition.

BOOK TWO

1–34 Zeus cannot sleep; he summons destructive Dream and bids it appear to Agamemnon and tell him to attack the Trojans without delay. Dream stands over the king's head as he sleeps and, in the guise of Nestor, passes on Zeus's message

1–2 = 24.667f. (down to παννύχιοι), the only other place in Homer where men in general are ἱπποκορυσταί, 'equippers of chariots', an epithet applied elsewhere to the Paeonians and Maeonians. Both ancient and modern critics have shown concern over an apparent contradiction between the end of book 1, where Zeus went to sleep with Here beside him, and the statement here that 'sweet sleep did not hold him'; but οὐκ ἔχε(ν) (epic imperfect) clearly means 'did not continue to hold him' in contrast with the others who slept παννύχιοι, 'all night through'. Exactly the same contrast in much the same terms occurs at 10.1–4, between Agamemnon and the other Achaean chieftains; again the motif makes a useful way of beginning a new Book. Another apparent discrepancy is the disregard here of Here – but that is understandable if book-division implies, as it surely must, a pause considerably greater than that involved, for example, in modern paragraphing. The break between the two Books is a good and a natural one: 1.611 brought that day and that particular scene on Olumpos to a close, whereas 2.1 begins a new day with Zeus deciding how to bring about what he has promised.

According to Leumann, *HW* 44f. and Chantraine, *Dict.* s.v. ἥδομαι, νήδυμος is a false reading for ἥδυμος (cf. ἡδύς), through mistaken word-division: not ἔχε νήδυμος but ἔχεν ἥδυμος. That may be so, despite Aristarchus (Arn/A); but *Od.* 12.366 and 13.79 do not allow such a word-division (i.e. after ephelcystic nu), even if other Homeric uses (6x *Il.*, 2x *Od.*) do.

4 τιμήσῃ is probably correct, parallel as it is with ὀλέσῃ; AbT have the optative, τιμήσει', which is possible.

5–7 Zeus's tactics are swiftly conceived and executed, as befits a supreme god; he gets destructive Dream into his presence with great abruptness – 'destructive' because dangerously misleading. The division of dreams into true and false is most clearly made by Penelope at *Od.* 19.560–7; for failures in interpretation cf. also *Il.* 5.150, but for the deceptive dream as such this is the *locus classicus*; see also on 20–1.

8–15 The first four verses of this speech of instruction are quietly

115

authoritative; the remainder, which include what is to be told by Agamemnon himself, are made more dramatic by internal stops, runover-words
and phrases and integral enjambments. Verses 12 and 13, with runover-word
cumulation, are particularly stark, whereas the two concluding verses
provide some easing of the tension, especially in the summarizing half-verse
at the end.

8 βάσκ᾽ ἴθι: this is how Zeus regularly begins his instructions to Iris when
he is sending her to carry a message. βάσκω, virtually confined to this
formula, is a rare form of βαίνω, 'go'. On the hiatus in οὖλε Ὄνειρε see
on 3.46.

15 Τρώεσσι δὲ κήδε᾽ ἐφῆπται: a lapidary summary. As a consequence
of Here's wearing down of the other gods, the Trojans are in trouble – cares
are literally 'fastened to them' (so also, apart from in repetitions of this
speech, at 6.241). Aristotle evidently read a different expression here,
δίδομεν δέ οἱ εὖχος ἀρέσθαι, as at 21.297 (*Poetics* 25.1461a22; *Soph. el.*
4.166b6). His comments show that this was an old reading favoured by those
who were pedantically worried by attributing a false statement directly to
Zeus; see also on 38.

19 ἀμβρόσιος...ὕπνος, literally 'immortal sleep' (not 'fragrant' as
Leaf and others have supposed). ἀμβρόσιος is presumably formed from the
privative prefix and a word related to βροτός, 'mortal', and based (as
Chantraine says, *Dict.* s.v.) on an Indo-European root *mer (cf. Latin *morior*),
meaning death. The term is applied in Homer to anything divine – hair,
sandals, clothes, and, especially in the noun-form ἀμβροσίη, to the special
food of the gods; also to a divine unguent. Here, sleep is ambrosial
metaphorically, because it is as sweet as the kind the gods have. At 57 and
elsewhere even night can be so described.

20–1 The Dream stands 'above his head', like the evil dream over
Rhesos' head at 10.496, because that is where it can best penetrate both
eyes and ears (rather than because the senses were rooted at the base of the
brain as AbT pedantically asserted). It assumes Nestor's likeness in order,
presumably, to give itself credibility – but also, perhaps, as Shipp suggests
(*Studies* 232, after Von der Mühll), to anticipate and help establish Nestor's
emphatic role in this Book; the formular description 'Neleus' son' adds both
information and importance. A more interesting complexity lies in the
Dream taking the appearance of Nestor but at the same time telling
Agamemnon at 26 that it is a messenger from Zeus. One would suppose that
Agamemnon might dream *either* of Nestor advising him *or* of a truly divine
messenger doing so; Nestor himself in the role of the latter might seem to
break the Dream's verisimilitude. The poet appears to be abbreviating a
longer description such as that of *Od.* 4.795–841, where Athene sends an
image of a mortal woman-friend to Penelope; the image advises her, and

Book Two

Penelope even joins in the conversation as she sleeps. Finally the image reveals herself as a divine messenger, but when Penelope wakes up she merely rejoices at how clear the dream had been.

22 μιν is direct object of the verb of address in the formular verse-type τῷ/τῇ μιν ἐεισάμενος/-η προσέφη/προσεφώνεε/μετέφη (∪∪) – ∪∪ – ū̆| (7× *Il.*, 1× *Od.*).

23–34 All of this speech except for the last verse-and-a-third, down to 33 φρεσί, will be exactly reported by Agamemnon to the assembly at 60–70; but only its central section, 28–32, directly reproduces Zeus's instructions at 11–15 (with necessary minor adjustments of number, person and so on). Expansion by a messenger is the exception in Homer, but the added verses 23–7 contain a necessary address to the sleeping king, as well as desirable identification and an appeal to his credulity.

23–4 εὕδεις: so also, as opening word, in the reproach by Patroklos' ghost to the sleeping Akhilleus at 23.69, and similarly Athene to Penelope at *Od.* 4.804. οὐ χρὴ παννύχιον εὕδειν is part of a formula-cluster to which εὗδον παννύχιοι in 2 also belongs.

25 This has the appearance of a formular verse, but does not in fact reappear in Homer except for its repetition at 62. μέμηλε (etc.) in this position is, however, formular: 11× *Il.*, 4× *Od.*

26–7 Διός...ἐλεαίρει: as Iris tells Priam at 24.173f. in a scene that is quite similar in structure and expression. Aristarchus (Arn/A) athetized 27 on the ground that Zeus has a real reason for pitying Priam in book 24, whereas here he is only feigning concern. This ignores formular practice, and in any event the divine messenger tries to establish credibility in both cases alike.

28 θωρῆξαί σε κέλευσε is a simple but neat adaptation of Zeus's words θωρῆξαί ἐ κέλευε in 11, cf. also λύσασθαί σε κέλευσεν at 24.175.

33–4 The evil Dream had a strong motive for adding to Zeus's words at the beginning (see on 23–34), but this expansion at the end seems a little gratuitous – the runover cumulation 'from Zeus' might be held to weaken the gnomic force of what had been Zeus's own closing words, 'and upon the Trojans are troubles fixed'. The first part of the addition, from ἐκ Διός to φρεσί, is predictably repeated by Agamemnon to the assembly at 70, and he also paraphrases 34: εὖτ' ἄν σε μελίφρων ὕπνος ἀνήῃ becomes in 71 ἐμὲ δὲ γλυκὺς ὕπνος ἀνῆκεν. The intervening phrase (33f.), μηδέ σε λήθη | αἱρείτω, in which λήθη is a Homeric *hapax legomenon*, is replaced by the functional ὡς ὁ μὲν εἰπὼν | ᾤχετ' ἀποπτάμενος in 70f. These variations are cleverly accomplished, although with occasional slight signs of roughness – much in the manner of the oral and not the literate composer.

35–83 Agamemnon awakes and reports his dream to the other leaders. He proposes making ready for a general attack on Troy after an initial testing of morale, and Nestor expresses cautious agreement

35–40 Direct narrative is resumed after the conclusion of the Dream's speech, and the style becomes simpler, with frequent verse-end stops. Agamemnon, not yet awake, is filled with confidence by the Dream's words (36f.); the poet, in commenting on his delusion, takes the opportunity of moderating the implications of Zeus's plan so as to foretell sufferings for both sides alike – a device which reminds the audience that no swift Achaean defeat will follow.

38 νήπιος: a typical Homeric expression, literally 'childish', but often (as LSJ remark on 22.445) indicating no more than lack of complete knowledge. νήπιος etc. comes as first word in the verse 21x *Il.*, 9x *Od.* (out of totals of 33x and 21x respectively); in nine of the Iliadic uses it is followed after a stop by οὐδέ as here. The comment is ironical and general: 'fool he was (since he did not know how things were to turn out)'; bT, pursuing the egregious critical notion of trying to exonerate Zeus from total deceit (see on 15), claimed that Agamemnon's folly lay in taking 'now' in 12 and 29 as indicating victory that very day.

41 'The divine voice was poured around him', that is, it was as though still present, he remembered it – a vivid and imaginative expression. ὀμφή (2x *Il.*, 2x *Od.*) always refers in Homer, and often later, to the voice of a god.

42 ἕζετο δ' ὀρθωθείς: strictly 'sat upright', as apparently at 23.235; but the idea may be that he first sat up, then stood up. At 10.21 Agamemnon similarly wakes up and then, ὀρθωθείς, puts on his tunic, and afterwards (at 10.22 = 44 here) his shoes. The order in which clothing and accoutrements are donned is quite logical: tunic, coat, shoes, sword (on its baldric round the shoulders), then staff (see on 46).

45 ξίφος ἀργυρόηλον, 'silver-studded sword': probably a very old formula, since its three component terms are all found in the Linear B tablets (*qi-si-pe-e, a-ku-ro, wa-o* ? = *wa-lo*), and such swords, in which the bronze blade is joined to the handle with silver-headed rivets, are Mycenaean (but also later: see St. Foltiny, *Arch. Hom.* E 237). When Agamemnon arms for his *aristeia* in book 11 his sword is described as having golden, not silver studs (11.29f.). Aristarchus (Arn/A) justifiably commented that such details depend on the poet's feelings at the time, and it is certainly true that the more precious metals are associated with the most important occasions. It is also relevant that the standard long epithet for a sword at the verse-end, as here, is 'silver-studded' (9x *Il.*, including 2x with φάσγανον not ξίφος;

Book Two

4× *Od.*). For a shorter formula the epithet was ὀξύ, 'sharp' (5× *Il.*, 15× *Od.*), and occasionally a sword could also be κωπήεντα -ι, 'hilted' (3× *Il.*), or ἄμφηκες, 'two-edged' (2× *Il.*, 2× *Od.*). These are the details of a typical formular system; there was no regular epithet for a *gold*-studded sword, and one must conclude that such an object, although not unknown, was primarily a poetical exaggeration. There was, however, a standard phrase 'pierced with golden studs', χρυσείοις ἥλοισι πεπαρμένον, used of Akhilleus' staff at 1.246 and Nestor's cup at 11.633 – but 'pierced' would be even more difficult of a sword. Therefore at 11.29f. the poet has to devise a unique phrase, ἐν δέ οἱ ἧλοι | χρύσειοι πάμφαινον, for a very special object and occasion.

46 Staff not spear is taken for this peaceful mission; or perhaps 'sceptre' rather than 'staff' is the *mot juste* here, since this is no ordinary staff, not even a heraldic one, but the ancestral (πατρώϊον) sceptre of the house of Atreus, descended from Zeus himself and so ἄφθιτον. It is shortly to be described at 100–8, see on 109.

48–52 The lightly-enjambed and relaxed narrative style continues.

48–9 Homer has a number of different expressions for the onset of dawn, and it is interesting that they have not been reduced to a compact formular system. Admittedly the *Odyssey* makes heavy use of ἦμος δ' ἠριγένεια φάνη ῥοδοδάκτυλος Ἠώς (no less than 20×, against only 2× *Il.*); but it also has Ἠώς δ' ἐκ λεχέων παρ' ἀγαυοῦ Τιθωνοῖο | ὄρνυθ' (at 5.1f.) and ὡς ἔφατ', αὐτίκα δὲ χρυσόθρονος ἤλυθεν Ἠώς (4× + 2 variants). The *Iliad*, apart from its two uses (in books 1 and 24) of the 'early-born rosy-fingered Dawn' verse, has Ἠὼς μὲν (δὲ) κροκόπεπλος ἐκίδνατο πᾶσαν ἐπ' αἶαν (2×, + variants like κροκόπεπλος ὑπεὶρ ἅλα κίδναται Ἠώς (23.227)) and Ἠὼς μὲν κροκόπεπλος ἀπ' Ὠκεανοῖο ῥοάων | ὄρνυθ' (19.1f.); also, at 11.1f., the rising-from-beside-Tithonos verse as quoted above from the *Odyssey*, as well of course as the present instance, when Dawn comes to Olumpos to announce daylight to Zeus and the other gods. Here the second verse (49) is loosely paralleled by the complement of the Tithonos-version, ἵν' ἀθανάτοισι φόως φέροι ἠδὲ βροτοῖσι (*Il.* 11.2; *Od.* 5.2), as well as by the remarkable variant of 23.226, ἦμος δ' ἑωσφόρος εἶσι φόως ἐρέων ἐπὶ γαῖαν. There are also, of course, several less emphatic references in either poem to dawn unpersonified: when it was still dawn, the twelfth dawn came, etc. These, too, display less formular economy than might be expected, but it is with the highly artistic variations of dawn appearing (or spreading, rising, or bringing light) over hills or sea that a departure from normal oral economy of means can be most clearly detected. Several such verses occur at the beginning of an important new episode, sometimes (as with *Iliad* books 8, 11 and 19 and *Odyssey* book 5) of a new Book. In these circumstances the singer can be seen seeking both colour and drama in his expression, and a special kind of poetical deliberation and effort is apparent; see also Macleod, *Iliad XXIV* 47f.

51–2 Verse 51, except for πόλεμόνδε in place of ἀγορήνδε, occurs also at 443 (with 50 ~ 442 and 52 = 444), the passage in which the chieftains at last begin marshalling the army for the march-out. Traditional analytical scholars, dismayed at apparent inconsistencies in Agamemnon's testing of morale (to be discussed on 73–5 below), were often persuaded that an 'original' version continued directly from 52 to 445. In other words, Agamemnon immediately accepts the Dream and proceeds to marshal the army without delay; all the rest (his reporting of the Dream to the other leaders, the testing of the troops, their restraining by Athene and Odysseus, the fresh assembly with the Thersites episode, followed by speeches by Odysseus and Nestor) accrued subsequently, incorporated by some 'diasceuast' to develop the separate motif of the testing. This, in short, was what Leaf believed. We shall see as the scene develops that there are indeed some harshnesses of sequence and a few unexpected details, and shall have to ask whether they could perhaps have served an artistic purpose – or whether they suggest, rather, an assemblage of different versions and motifs such as might be carried out by an oral singer. That kind of possibility was considered as a way of accounting for apparent inconsistencies about whether or not Agamemnon removed Briseis in person in book 1, although in the end it was accepted only in a very modified form (see on 1.185) or not at all. Such a process certainly had something in common with the separate stages of composition envisaged by the old Analysts, and its assumption rests on some of the same criteria of consistency as were invoked by them – although it would allow far more for psychological and artistic subtleties. It has, however, much greater plausibility in the context of an oral tradition under manipulation by a monumental composer than in that of an accumulation of fixed versions conjoined with each other by an improbably incompetent literate co-ordinator.

53 That Agamemnon should call a meeting of the council of 'elders' (that is, senior commanders) πρῶτον, first, while the army was being assembled, is not in itself surprising; as bT put it, 'he fills the interval while the army assembles'. Aristarchus (Did/A) read βουλή in the nominative, making ἷζε intransitive, as usually although not invariably in Homer. Zenodotus and the 'common texts' were probably right for once in preferring the accusative, not only because of the run of the narrative but also because 55 shows that the king did in fact call the session.

54 Why by Nestor's ship and not Agamemnon's? Presumably because the latter had left his part of the lines in order to find the heralds (50), and also because 'it was in Nestor's likeness that the Dream appeared' (bT, cf. 57f.), and the singer wants to build up his role here.

The best MSS, as well as bT, have Πυλοιγενέος as against Πυληγενέος in the ancient vulgate. The epithet occurs once else at 23.303 (but of Antilokhos' horses); again the reason for the unusual description seems to be the poet's wish to prepare for Nestor's important role in the poem – see also 77 and the notes on 20–1 and 1.247–52.

55 Usually Zenodotus' text is shorter, but he substituted a couplet for this particular verse: 'but when they were assembled and gathered | strong Agamemnon stood up and addressed them'. These are themselves formular verses, cf. 1.57–8 and note. Aristarchus (Arn/A) objected that 'he is unlikely to have stood, to address seven people', and the two verses do indeed clearly belong to an assembly-scene, not to one describing a small group. Zenodotus' motives are unknown, but he may have found πυκινὴν ἀρτύνετο βουλήν puzzling. The phrase is better in place at 10.302, where Hektor also summons his leaders but has a specific idea to propose, that of sending out a spy. Here, however, the expression must refer to the appended test of morale rather than to the Dream itself. Note ἀρτύνετο in comparison with ἤρτυνον, ἤρτυε (with temporal augment) at 15.303 and 18.379; Homeric practice varied over the augment, and Aristarchus tended to omit it when it was metrically indifferent, with the MSS tending to retain it: see further Chantraine, *GH* I, 479ff.

56–9 These verses vary somewhat the language of the narrative at 18–21 (although the first halves of 59 and 20 are identical), partly because Nestor was there given a description designed to introduce him to the audience (20–1n.) rather than for ordinary use by Agamemnon; also 'ambrosial' is transferred from Agamemnon's sleep (19) to the night itself (57). Once again Zenodotus (Arn/A) gets a detail wrong: θεῖος...ὄνειρος is virtually guaranteed by 22, but he read θεῖον, and took it with ἐνύπνιον as a noun; yet this is clearly adverbial, 'in sleep'.

57 ἀμβροσίην διὰ νύκτα, in that order, occurs only here, to create a trochaic main caesura; the common formula is νύκτα δι' ἀμβροσίην (3x *Il.*, 2x *Od.*).

60–70 This passage (to φρεσίν) exactly reproduces 23–33 (to φρεσί), which itself included a more or less verbatim repetition of Zeus's instructions at 11–15; see the comments *ad loc*. Leaf commented that 'the third repetition of the message is really too much' (actually it is only 65–9 that occurs for a third time), and approved Zenodotus' two-verse condensation (Arn/A), an abrupt 'the father who rules on high, dwelling in the upper air, bids you fight with the Trojans toward Ilion'. But Zenodotus was almost certainly wrong: the oral style maintained the exact words in divine instructions and in messenger speeches, even up to three times and at relatively close intervals as here. The Dream's address and instructions, with the addition about Here having persuaded the other gods, are concise and interesting and thus easily stand repetition, especially since they are part of an emphatic development in the action.

64 This was athetized by Aristarchus (Arn/A), consistently with his athetesis of 27, cf. comment on 26–7.

70 Agamemnon omits the Dream's final instruction (33f.) not to forget his words when he awakes – it is in any case only an elaboration of the order to 'keep them in mind' – for the simple reason that he has obviously not done so, or he would not now be reporting the Dream to the others.

72 αἴ κέν πως θωρήξομεν: a manner of speaking which does not necessarily imply any real doubt about their ability to do so (despite the idea of testing the troops' morale which is immediately to follow), as when Iris at 18.199 tells Akhilleus to show himself at the trench to the Trojans αἴ κε...ἀπόσχωνται πολεμοῖο (which is the inevitable consequence); similarly 1.207 (cf. also 1.420), where Athene tells him that she has come to stop his violence αἴ κε πίθηαι, 'in case you may obey me', there being little doubt that he will do so. See further the comments on 1.207 and 408, and Chantraine, *GH* II, 282f.

73–5 The proposal to 'test them with words', which turns out to mean ordering their immediate return home, is introduced quite unexpectedly. It is not suggested by the Dream, nor is it a regular device for getting the troops into action; in fact there is nothing really similar anywhere else in the *Iliad* – the closest is the disguised Odysseus' 'testing' of his father Laertes in *Odyssey* book 24, which has aroused a degree of critical suspicion. Agamemnon's addition of the phrase ἥ θέμις ἐστί, 'which is customary (or lawful)', seems designed to counter any feeling of surprise or sense of the unusual by the council-members – for his words must refer to his idea of testing, and not to his own rights as supreme commander. It is possible that the poet also found them useful as a means of disguising an awkward sequence of ideas or conjunction of themes. ἥ θέμις ἐστί is a formular expression (6x *Il.*, 4x *Od.* in this exact form), coming either at the beginning or at the end of the verse (except only at *Od.* 3.187) to designate proper behaviour, including that of a ritual and family kind: for example it is customary and right to pour libations and offer prayer at a religious feast; to embrace one's father; to swear an oath that one has obeyed the rules in a contest; to disagree with the king in assembly if necessary. It can also serve, vague as it is, to justify a kind of behaviour which a character – or the poet himself – does not wish to spend time in elaborating further. This is best exemplified by 9.276 = 19.177, of Agamemnon swearing that he has not lain with Briseis, 'which is the custom, lord, of men and women' – see also his own version of this at 9.134 where a variant of the formula is used. What is laid down (the literal meaning of θέμις) by custom is probably the swearing of an oath in such circumstances, rather than refraining from sleeping with a war-captive as such. There is a certain ambiguity here, perhaps intentional; something similar may be seen in the phrase found at 4.398 and 6.183, θεῶν τεράεσσι πιθήσας, 'obeying the portents of the gods', where these are not further specified or (one conjectures) precisely identified by the audience, and where the poet is in any case presenting a heavily summarized version of the tales of Tudeus and Bellerophon. On the testing see further on 86.

75 Agamemnon's instructions are crystal clear: when he has urged the troops to take flight, the other commanders are to dissuade them from following his advice. In the event only Odysseus will do so, and then only on instruction from Athene. Note the prominence hereabouts of ἐρητύειν and its forms, not only of restraining the troops from flight (164, 180, 189) but also of heralds marshalling them for assembly (97, 99).

76–83 These verses were athetized by Aristarchus (Arn/A) on several grounds: that the mention in 76 of sitting down is inappropriate (see on 55); that Nestor had nothing really to say; that dreams are not made true or false by the status of the dreamer – a false dream can come to anyone and in any guise; and that the omission of these verses allows 84f. to refer to Agamemnon, since it is he rather than Nestor who should lead the way and be called 'shepherd of the peoples' (see on 84–5). Leaf adds that the speech is 'jejune' and not in Nestor's usual style, also that 81 is more in place in book 24 (on which see 80–1n.). None of these criticisms is decisive and some are little more than pedantic. Nestor has little to say, admittedly, but then someone has to express agreement or disagreement with Agamemnon, and Nestor is the obvious person to do so; nor is it true that he is always prolix. The surprising thing is that he makes no reference to the peculiar idea of a test of morale – indeed his concluding remark at 83, which is an exact repetition of Agamemnon's words at 72 ('but come, let us arm the Achaeans'), is most appropriate to a version in which that idea was never mentioned.

77 Again the deliberate 'placing' of Nestor (see on 20–1 and 54); routine descriptions do not usually take the form of a relative clause as with ὅς ῥα... here.

78 A formular verse (9× *Il.*, not *Od.*), four times of Nestor, once each of five other characters. It suits him particularly well because of his role as adviser, since ἐΰφρονέων, which can imply either good sense or benevolence, presumably means the former here.

80–1 These verses are closely similar in content to 24.220–2, indeed 81 = 222. There Priam says that if any other mortal, whether priest or prophet, had instructed him, he would reject the instruction as false. This is in fact a little confused, because, as he goes on to say at 223, he accepts it because he heard it in person and not from a mortal but from a god. In short, τις...ἄλλος in the phrase 'any *other* mortal' is illogical in 24.220, which is therefore not the model on which 80 here was based, *contra* Leaf. Probably neither is the model, but each is a particular application (in the case of 24.220 a misused one) of a loose formular pattern 'if anyone else, εἰ...τις...ἄλλος, had said/done, then...' In 81 νοσφιζοίμεθα means 'keep apart from it [i.e. the Dream]', that is, have nothing to do with it, reject it as false.

84-210 Agamemnon addresses the assembled army, and carries out his plan of suggesting flight as a test of morale. As a consequence they rush for the ships, and Athene spurs Odysseus to restrain them and make them return to assembly

84-5 Aristarchus was surely right (see on 76-83) that we should normally expect Agamemnon to be the first to leave, and also expect ποιμένι λαῶν to refer to him (as 6x elsewhere by name, including 254) rather than to Nestor, who receives this appellation only once and then in the untypical circumstances of the chariot race, at 23.411.

86 ἐπεσσεύοντο δὲ λαοί: more fully at 207f., οἱ δ' ἀγορήνδε | αὖτις ἐπεσσεύοντο, i.e. from the ships and huts, again followed by a simile, compare also 147-50. Here the statement is rather abrupt, introduced as it is by the half-verse cumulation about 'sceptre-bearing kings' (in which the formular epithet σκηπτοῦχοι, without the rho, recalls the etymology of σκῆπτρον as that on which one σκήπτει, 'leans'), and especially as an introduction to the elaborate description in 87-100. The phrase refers back to 50-2, where Agamemnon told the heralds to summon the Achaeans to assembly; but 87 would follow on better after 52 itself, quite apart from the merits or otherwise of the council and the idea of testing morale. There is of course no support for this in the MSS or the ancient critics – even Zenodotus did not doubt the whole of the council scene; but it would undoubtedly avoid several serious problems if Agamemnon's urging the troops to give up and go home at 139-41 arose out of his own indecisiveness, much as in book 9 where the same three verses recur (9.26-8). That, of course, would itself ignore the tonic effects of the Dream, and there are indeed later references to the council meeting, at 143 and 194. Such attempts at mechanical solutions by the excision of large areas of text nearly always run into trouble; even so, the observation of different possible sequences of thought and language can be useful in reminding us of the complex ways in which such apparently inconsistent episodes are likely to have arisen in an oral tradition. Behind the paradoxes and confusions of the testing-motif in its present form one is probably right to detect other versions, in the earlier tradition or in the monumental poet's own repertoire, which omitted the test, or the test together with the council, or even the deceitful Dream itself.

87–93 The first extended simile in the whole poem, also the first of three imaginative diversions (with Agamemnon's sceptre and the counting of the armies) in a long stretch, from 76 to 133, that is serviceable rather than exciting in rhythm and diction; for example rising threefolders are absent until 135, 136 and 139. In the simile itself the races, ἔθνεα, of bees are particularly apt to the various tribal contingents; they will recur, of birds and of flies, in two of the march-out similes at 459 and 469, on which see the comments *ad loc.* Homer has one further bee (or wasp) simile at 12.167–72, but in a very different capacity as they lie in wait in their 'hollow (κοῖλον) home', 169, which is similar to their 'hollow (γλαφυρῆς) rock' here, in image if not in language – for in this case there is no formularity of language for similar concepts. Three distinct aspects of the bees are observed here: (i) they keep on issuing from the rock (88); (ii) they fly close-packed like a bunch of grapes (βοτρυδόν, 89), onto spring flowers; (iii) they fly here and there in different groups (αἱ μὲν...αἱ δέ, 90). Of these (iii) may be held to develop the implications of (i), but (ii) presents a slightly different picture, unless each group is imagined as flying in its own cluster. It is possible that the bunch-of-grapes idea is derived from swarming rather than gathering honey; although one need not emulate those ancient scholiasts (AbT on 88 and 89) who brought current theories on bee-keeping to bear.

87 ἀδινάων is connected with ἄδην, connoting satiety; the adjectival form came to mean 'at close intervals', either spatially or temporally – here, 'close-packed'.

91 If the parallel between simile and narrative situation were exact, then ἔθνεα would simply be the masses of troops, like the bees; but the additional meaning of 'races' or 'tribes', referring to the different contingents coming from different parts of the naval lines, is surely present.

92–3 'In front of the deep shore': seen from the plain, that is – the ships are drawn up in ranks next to the sea, with the huts, κλισίαι, among them or close to them. The contingents must emerge from these on to the flat ground on the landward side, and proceed along it to the ἀγορή, the 'place of gathering' literally, by Odusseus' ships according to 11.806f. ἐστιχόωντο in 92 (it is the only form of στιχάομαι in Homer, 9x *Il.*) strictly means 'went in columns [or ranks]', since *στίξ (later στίχος) is a row or rank. The four uses in the Catalogue of Ships later in this Book have that literal sense, but at 3.341, where Paris and Menelaos advance against each other from opposite sides, the meaning is clearly much looser. Here, therefore, the verb itself fails to make it plain whether the contingents marched in columns toward the place of assembly or simply 'advanced' in a less regular fashion, indeed like the bees. That would accord with the difficulty the heralds have in marshalling them into their seats when they arrive (96–9); but the issue is settled the other way by ἱλαδόν in 93, which must mean 'in troops' (rather than 'in a troop'), since ἴλη – only the adverbial form occurs in Homer, and then only here – regularly signifies a company of soldiers in later Greek. Therefore the separate contingents are envisaged as advancing in companies to the assembly in a more or less purposeful way.

93–8 The half-verse cumulation of 93 leads almost imperceptibly into a sequence of more urgent and interrupted verses.

93–4 Ὄσσα is 'Voice', or rather 'Rumour', which 'blazed', δεδήει (intransitive pluperfect of δαίω), among them – it is Zeus's messenger, an embodiment perhaps of the role of the heralds from whom the order to assemble had emanated back at 52. The idea is dramatic in itself and appropriately high-flown in its expression, emphasizing, like the bee-simile beforehand and the metaphorical language that is to follow, both the great numbers and the urgent response of the Achaean host.

95–6 The assembly was in turmoil (τετρήχει is epic intransitive pluperfect of ταράσσω, 'disturb'), similarly to the Trojan one at 7.346 (τετρηχυῖα); and the earth groaned as they sat down, presumably at their weight and haste rather than at the din, ὅμαδος, they were making – the phrase recurs in a more natural context as the whole Achaean army advances at 784.

96–7 The nine heralds were shouting to marshal them into their places and make them keep silence. For the idiom of εἴ ποτ'...σχοίατ' see on 72; it implies difficulty rather than any real doubt over the outcome. The exegetical scholiasts tried to name the nine heralds but had to resort to the *Odyssey* to fill out the number – the *Iliad* has only Talthubios, two Eurubates's, Odios, Thootes and perhaps Stentor.

100–1 The relapse into silence adds to the solemnity (for the time being at least) of Agamemnon's rising to his feet holding the ancestral staff or sceptre.

101–8 The description of the descent of the royal sceptre of Mukenai is stylized but not, as it seems, very archaic. Each verse, a plain twofolder, briefly records a succeeding stage in the transmission, until 108 brings a sense of emphasis and completion by turning to the extent of Agamemnon's kingdom. Verses 102–5 each repeat the same basic grammatical structure and the same central theme: 'A gave it (δῶκε, δῶκεν, δῶκ') to B'; then 106 and 107 slightly elaborate the pattern (by adding θνῄσκων and φορῆναι repectively) and substitute 'left' (ἔλιπεν, λεῖπε) for 'gave'. Two connected problems arise: (i) what exactly is Hermes' role? The exegetical scholia (AbT) on 101–7 imply that he received the sceptre as token of his heraldic function – but in the rest of the account it is the emblem of kingship, rather, and it is probable, although not stated, that Hephaistos made it and gave it to Zeus for that reason, after Zeus's deposition of Kronos. In that case Hermes is a mere messenger carrying the sceptre from Zeus to Pelops, and δῶκε in 103 has a different implication from its other uses in the passage. But Hermes also played a special role in the Pelops myth, since as father of Murtilos, the charioteer first suborned and then betrayed by Pelops, he brought about the famous quarrel between Atreus and his brother Thuestes as a punishment on the house. Could this have anything to do with Zeus's employment of him as intermediary here? (ii) But in any case this quarrel seems to be totally ignored by Homer; Atreus and Thuestes are implied by 106f. to be on good terms, since the latter becomes regent (presumably) and in due course hands back the power to Atreus' elder son Agamemnon. How different from the myth exploited in tragedy and known at least since the sub-epic poem *Alcmaeonis* (according to the scholium on Euripides, *Orestes* 995), whereby Thuestes gets the golden ram, and hence the kingship, by immoral means and is later served by Atreus with his own children for dinner! Aristarchus (Arn/A on 106) stated that Homer did not know this version; the probability is, rather, that it was available to him, but that he preferred on occasion (as also over the circumstances of Oidipous' death at 23.679f.) to use a less elaborate version. The *Odyssey*, however, knows of Aigisthos' treachery and probably, therefore, of the whole story of the curse on the house of Atreus (1.35–41 and 3.304–10); perhaps the poet's choice here in the *Iliad* is dictated by the wish to avoid distracting detail. For it is the passage of kingship by regular stages from Zeus to Agamemnon that is important here; Thuestes could hardly be omitted completely, since his rule over Mukenai for a time must have been well known, but the quarrel itself might be glossed or suppressed. The choice in 107 of the term 'left' (instead of the more intentional 'gave') might have something to do with this, as indeed the scholia suggest.

103 This is the first use in the *Iliad* of these formular and apparently ancient epithets for Hermes. διάκτορος could mean 'guide' (since the Homeric name Aktor is *nomen agentis* of ἄγω, and Hesychius glossed διάκτωρ as ἡγεμών). ἀργεϊφόντης was most commonly explained as 'slayer of Argos'. The -φόντης component is relatively certain; the reference to Argos, the giant charged by Here with guarding Io against the attentions of Zeus, is less so – although the assertion of bT that Homer did not know the Io story is merely based on his lack of reference to it elsewhere. West, *Works and Days* 368f., has revived the 'dog-slayer' interpretation favoured by J. Chittenden and Rhys Carpenter, but without much plausibility. In any event the titles are traditional and could originally have borne quite different meanings, or have been assimilated to popular etymology.

104 ἄναξ is applied only here to Hermes, in a rather forced and wholly untraditional way; usually among gods it is used of Apollo or Zeus himself. πληξίππῳ may be connected (as T suggested) with Pelops' role as chariot-driver, for it was thus that he won his bride Hippodameia – whose name also means something similar.

106 Similarly the scholiast (b on 104–6) suggested that πολύαρνι of Thuestes recalls the tale of the golden ram whose possession conferred kingship.

108 'To be lord over many islands and all Argos': Ἄργος in Homer can connote the city of Argos in the north-east corner of the Peloponnese, or the whole Argolis including Argos, Tiruns and Mukenai, or the whole Mycenaean world with the Peloponnese as its main focus, or (on easily identifiable occasions, cf. e.g. 681) the region of 'Pelasgian' Argos in northern Greece from which Akhilleus came. Here the context shows it to refer to Agamemnon's special kingdom, and not for example to his leadership of all the Achaean contingents at Troy; presumably the Argolis, therefore (although there are complications, as will be seen when his domain and Diomedes' are defined in the Catalogue of Ships at 559–80 below). The 'many islands' are surprising, but are presumably those of the Saronic gulf, Aigina, Kalaureia and Hudrea in particular – although only the first of these can have been of much importance in the late Bronze Age or for that matter later. The exegetical tradition as represented by b had to resort to the idea of his overall leadership in order to extend the reference to important islands like Rhodes, which is of course out of the question; it recorded an even more outlandish idea that 'islands' was a name given to nine Argive villages. It remains true that 'many islands' in the Hellenic context naturally makes one think of the Aegean islands generally – which, however, except for those off the south-west Asiatic coast in the Catalogue of Ships, are for the most part ignored by Homer.

109 Ancient and hallowed as it is, the royal sceptre is merely leant on when the king begins to speak – rather, for instance, than being wielded to and fro to point up his argument, which is what a good speaker normally did according to Antenor at 3.218f. But it is soon to be used in an even more mundane way by Odysseus, first to restrain the troops at 199 and then for belabouring Thersites at 265f.

No doubt a staff *was* put to different uses at different times, being a utilitarian as well as a symbolic object, but the epic tradition also tended to become imprecise over its different special functions, which are as follows: (1) as symbol of kingship, as in the present passage, cf. also 46 and 206, 6.159, 9.38, 9.156, 9.298, 18.556f., *Od.* 3.412, also the formula σκηπτοῦχος βασιλεύς (etc.) as e.g. at 1.279. (2) As symbol of priesthood, 1.14f. and 28 (when decorated with woollen fillets); or of prophethood, *Od.* 11.91. (3) As symbol of the right to speak in assembly, e.g. at 279, sometimes specifically described as being given to the speaker by a herald (cf. (5)), as e.g. at 23.567–9 and *Od.* 2.37f.; or as being flung down as accompaniment of an oath or impassioned statement, as at 1.245f. and *Od.* 2.80; or as being held up in the air for an oath, 7.412 and 10.321 and 328. (4) As held by law-givers in session (cf. (1)), as at 1.237–9, cf. 2.206, 9.99, *Od.* 11.569. (5) As symbol of the office of herald, as at 7.277, 18.505, 23.567f. (as respectively intervening in a duel, giving sceptres to law-making elders, giving a sceptre as right to speak in assembly). (6) As means of divine inspiration, cf. 13.59 (martial inspiration by touching with Poseidon's σκηπανίῳ), or, with the ῥάβδος rather, of magical transformation, cf. 24.343, *Od.* 5.47 etc.; compare the Muses' σκῆπτρον at Hesiod, *Theog.* 30. (7) As accompaniment of declamation, 3.218f., as in its post-Homeric use by rhapsodes. (8) To lean on, as an aid to walking, e.g. 18.416 (and compare the present verse); in the *Odyssey*, especially for beggars, at 13.437, 14.31, 17.199, 18.103. (9) To push or beat people with, at 199 and 265 in the present Book, cf. 24.247.

These may be divided into broadly sacred and institutional uses (1 to 6) and broadly secular ones (7 to 9), although, as already remarked, even a gold-encrusted sceptre of divine origin, like Agamemnon's, can be used as a secular staff on occasion. But there is also a probable degree of confusion in the tradition over the overlaps between (1), (3) and (5) in particular (cf. comment on 278–82); for example, how was the herald's staff or sceptre related to the king's? Which one was given to a speaker in assembly? Did the kings sitting in assembly all have special staffs? Griffin, *HLD* 9–12, has useful comments and further bibliography; the royal sceptre, like kingship from the gods, is derived from the Near East (*ibid.*, n. 25), but his idea of the sceptre as representing 'the authority of the community' is more doubtful, and probably results from modern confusions of functions (3), (4) and (5) above.

110–41 Agamemnon's speech might appear at first hearing as curiously indirect, inconsequential even, typical perhaps of his deviousness or contradictory position or of the ambiguous role assigned him in the epic as a whole. Yet closer attention shows it to be relatively straightforward once the parenthetical explanations and elaborations are registered: 'Zeus has broken his promise that I would take Troy – it was a deceit, and now he bids me return home in failure and dishonour (111–15). This must be his inclination, since he can easily otherthrow a city when he wants to (114–18). [Taking up 'in dishonour' in 115] For it is disgraceful for such a large army to have fought with a smaller one, and for so long, without success (119–22). [Taking up 'so large' in 120] For the Trojans are less than a tenth of our number (123–30); except for their allies; it is they that frustrate me (130–3). [Taking up 'and no conclusion has yet appeared' in 122] It is nine years that have passed, rotting the ships, and our wives still wait, and we achieve nothing (134–8). So let us go home, since we shall not take Troy (139–41).' Thus there is overall ring-composition ('I/we shall not take Troy'), with various excursuses within the speech arising out of the concept of dishonour, and a progression of the argument from 'Zeus must be telling me to go' to 'Let us therefore all go, now.' Under the surface, moreover, lies the irony that Agamemnon is hypocritically accusing Zeus of deceit and yet does not understand that the Dream was a trick. Early in book 9, at 18–28, Agamemnon will make a similar suggestion of retreat in identical terms, except for the omission of 119–38 (the excursus, that is, on the Achaean disgrace in having fought for so long against lesser numbers and achieved nothing). Perhaps that elaborate central section is included here to make his 'testing' more thorough, by throwing the army's failure into an even clearer light; perhaps it would be otiose in book 9, where the king's attitude of despair is perfectly sincere, so that such rhetorical embellishments might seem less appropriate; perhaps, finally, the poet felt that repeating the whole long speech might remind the army that they had heard it somewhere before, and that it was not serious.

Zenodotus (Arn/A) substituted a single Odyssean verse (24.433) for 112–19 inclusive, presumably to avoid repetition and because he thought most of the passage fitted better in book 9 (as 18–25).

111 Agamemnon is especially prone to invoke Ἄτη, Zeus-sent infatuation, to excuse his own shortcomings, cf. comment on 1.412, so also at 9.18, cf. 19.87. Didymus in A reports a complicated scholarly wrangle (involving Dionysius Thrax, Dionysodorus, Ammonius and Callistratus as well as Zenodotus and Aristarchus) over whether μέγας or μέγα should be read; the latter, with adverbial sense, is clearly right.

112 Blaming Zeus for sending Ἄτη is one thing, calling him σχέτλιος, consistently wicked, is quite another. Diomedes uses the term humorously of Nestor at 10.164, but there is no humour here. Hekabe uses it in deadly earnest of Hektor at 22.86, but she means that Hektor is obstinate, not wicked, for remaining outside the walls. But Agamemnon means more than that Zeus is obstinate; he is σχέτλιος because (ὅς, 112) he has deceived him, therefore the term must carry its common Iliadic hostile sense (see e.g. on 3.414). Akhilleus at 22.15 addresses Apollo as ὀλοώτατε, but no mortal elsewhere addresses the highest god in such strong terms (Kalupso as a goddess can call all the other gods σχέτλιοι at *Od.* 5.118). Perhaps Agamemnon is allowed to do so because he is not meant to be speaking quite sincerely.

The promise that he would destroy Troy was 'before', πρίν, and must refer to indications like the portent at Aulis – not, of course, to the deceitful Dream itself.

114 Similarly the 'evil deceit' devised by Zeus must refer to the non-fulfilment of Zeus's earlier indications (as Agamemnon chooses to present it), and not to the actual deceit from which the king is suffering through the Dream. The confusion of real and professed deceit is effectively ironical.

121–2 Alliteration, already present in 117f., becomes especially prominent here. Assonance and alliteration are a spasmodic feature of the epic style, often with no determinable purpose, although rhetoric like Agamemnon's here naturally tends to encourage them.

123–8 Until now the speech has been undramatic and routinely cumulative in expression, with conventional verse-structure and moderate enjambment. The present graphic and hypothetical calculation, set out in a single long and progressively-enjambed sentence and brought to an epigrammatic climax in 128, noticeably elevates the style.

124–6 On the 'cutting' of oaths see on 3.73–5. Aristarchus (Arn/A) athetized 124 because oaths would be out of place in an obviously exaggerated calculation, but this misunderstands the Homeric style. The hypothetical counting could in any case only have been done under truce, and the μέν...δέ clauses after the ἄμφω of 124, with the change of construction in 126, emphasize the involvement of both sides: 'If we both wished to be numbered, namely to count the Trojans...and for us to be split up into tens...'

130–3 Aristarchus (Arn/A) athetized these verses also, on the stronger but still insufficient ground that elsewhere in the poem (including 122, one might add) it is implied that the Achaeans outnumber the enemy in general. Pointing out that the allies are so numerous does weaken Agamemnon's point, but he is presumably made to do so because the contrast between Trojans and their allies is sometimes important, for example in Glaukos' rebuke to Hektor at 17.140ff.

132–3 πλάζουσι, 'knock me off course'. The idiom which follows might look self-pitying, even humorously so, but is not: 'they do not let me sack Troy, eager though I am to do so'.

135 Nothing is said elsewhere about the poor condition of the ships; it is a well-observed detail which might be distracting in other contexts but is a forceful illustration here of the lapse of time with nothing accomplished.

137 εἴατ'(αι), 'are sitting', from ἧμαι. On the epic third person plural see Chantraine, *GH* I, 475f.; it is properly so spelled, rather than as ἧατ', by the MSS, cf. M. L. West on Hesiod, *Theog.* 257 and 622. The pathos of the waiting wives and children is stressed by the heavy word ποτιδέγμεναι and its postponement in the sentence.

139–40 After the frustrated complexity of Agamemnon's preceding thoughts, the concise decision of these two whole-sentence verses stands in persuasive contrast.

143 All were stirred by Agamemnon's words – save those who had been at the council meeting and knew them to be false; this addition was athetized by Aristarchus (Arn/A) as superfluous. It could indeed be an afterthought, but in the oral cumulative style many verses were that, in a sense. While not incompatible with the idea of a version in which (as at 9.17ff.) the king's suggestion was seriously meant, it does nothing in particular to support it.

144–6 The second developed simile of the poem (after 87–93) and the first of many sea-images; it is carefully matched by a second wave-simile at 209f. marking the army's return to the place of assembly after this confused withdrawal from it. The crowd ripples, or surges rather, like the waters south of the island of Ikaria (and north of Samos) in a south-easterly gale – or as Homer puts it more dramatically 'east wind and south rushing on out of father Zeus's clouds', in which the hendiadys of east and south is confirmed by the singular verb and participle. The detailed local knowledge has often been taken as confirmation of Ionian authorship, and so in its limited way it is. That stretch of sea *is* especially rough, although particularly in northerly gales, rather, when the winds rush down off the steep lee side of Ikaria.

None of the language of the simile is 'abnormal' as Shipp implies (*Studies* 231), although it is true that ἐπαίξας usually comes in martial contexts. ὡς is the MS reading in 144; φή was supported by Zenodotus but opposed by Aristarchus (Arn/A), who claims that Homer never uses the word; but cf. 14.499.

147–8 Now a supplementary comparison is added to reinforce the effect of disturbance and rapid movement; again a harsh wind sweeps down, but this time it is a west wind which bends a deep crop of corn.

149–54 The urgency as they rush for the ships, telling each other to drag them down to the sea and beginning to clear the runways, is enhanced by a sequence of broken verses and strong enjambment in 149, 150, 151 and 153. Only 152 proceeds, by contrast, with an uninterrupted sweep, which might be felt as expressive of smooth launching. There is a careful alternation of impressionistic general touches (the noise of the rush to the ships, the shouting to each other, the din ascending to the sky) and closely observed practical matters (the rising dust, the need to clear the runways, the props supporting the ships). These last are mentioned elsewhere only at 1.486, and the runways not at all – in fact οὐροί in such a sense is found only here in surviving Greek.

155 With ὑπέρμορα compare 20.30 and *Od.* 1.35 ὑπὲρ μόρον; *Il.* 20.336 ὑπὲρ μοῖραν; 16.780 ὑπὲρ αἶσαν; 17.327 ὑπὲρ θεόν. These are metrical variants which make up a loose formular system. For the difficulty of contravening μοῖρα, apportioned destiny, see Here's protest to Zeus at 16.433ff. It is the destiny of the Achaeans *not* to have a premature and fruitless return home, not only because the eventual fall of Troy was a familiar part of the mythical tradition but also because, in particular, it had been foretold in the portent at Aulis and in Kalkhas' interpretation of it, soon to be recalled at 299–332.

156–68 The poet could have made Odysseus intervene directly of his own volition, and without the mechanism of divine instruction – it might have rendered his attitude more comprehensible at little cost in dramatic effect. On the other hand it may have seemed important to the poet to establish the Olympian part in the proceedings by repeated divine interventions early in the poem. Zenodotus (Arn/A) omitted the whole of Here's speech, reading εἰ μὴ ᾿Αθηναίη λαοσσόος ἦλθ᾿ ἀπ᾿ ᾿Ολύμπου as 156 and continuing with 169 εὖρεν ἔπειτ᾿ ᾿Οδυσσῆα...Here's instructions do indeed give an odd effect when they are repeated complete to Odysseus, since it is he and not Athene who 'restrains each man with gentle words' (164 = 180); given his nature and his knowledge of events he could and would have done this without exceptional stimulus from a goddess. Aristarchus evidently felt much the same, but met the difficulty less drastically by athetizing 164 only (as well as, less understandably, 160–2), see on 180.

157 ἀτρυτώνη occurs 5× *Il.*, 3× *Od.* as an epithet for Athene and as part of the formula (αἰγιόχοιο) Διὸς τέκος, ἀτρυτώνη, as here. Derivation is uncertain, but probably from τρύω, cf. τείρω, 'wear out', and therefore 'unwearied' as in Aeschylus, *Eum.* 403, ἄτρυτον πόδα; in which case the capital letter adopted in many modern texts is unjustified. There is nothing to be said for association with Τριτογένεια (on which see 4.313–15n.), ἀτρύγετος or ὀτρύνω.

163 According to Aristarchus (Did/A) 'all' the ancient texts, ἅπασαι, had κατὰ λαόν not μετὰ λαόν; some medieval MSS did not agree, but the former is correct – see on 1.423–5 (second para.).

164 Aristarchus (Arn/A) athetized the verse here: see on 156–68 *fin.*

165 = 181 ἀμφιελίσσας (etc.) is the standard epithet for ships when they occur in the nominative or accusative plural or the genitive singular. It probably means 'curved at both ends', like ἐΐση and κορωνίς, *contra* Leaf (and S. West on *Od.* 3.162).

170–1 Odysseus, unlike the others, had not laid hand on his ship in readiness to launch it 'since great grief was coming upon his heart and spirit' (171). That he should be upset by the turn of events is understandable, but surely there was no question of him (or any of the others who had attended the council) joining in the active preparations for flight, knowing as he did Agamemnon's by now obviously mistaken purpose in proposing it? bT tried to reduce the anomaly by taking οὐδ᾿ ὅ γε to imply 'nor did he (or any other of the chieftains)...'; but the real problem lies in the causal clause which follows: 'he (or they) did not do so *because of great grief*' – the only logical reason for holding back being his knowledge that Agamemnon's proposal of flight was a trick. An even less likely suggestion is recorded in Eustathius, 197.4 (Erbse I, 218), that not touching his ship was a sign to the others to desist.

174–5 However that may be, these words of Athene do not necessarily prove that Odysseus is being shown to be unaware of Agamemnon's plan; for the goddess might be lightly taunting him into action, professing to base her words on his actual quiescence rather than on its possible motives – much as Agamemnon does with Diomedes at 4.365ff.

180 The key to this verse (which also occurred as 164) is probably ἀγανοῖς, meaning 'gentle' or 'kindly'. That term is wholly inappropriate to Here's instructions to Athene at 164; there was no reason for the goddess to be gentle, nor are her instructions to mortals typically so (it is Apollo's or Artemis' arrows, bringing a swift death, that are typically so described in a similar phrase at 24.759 and 5× *Od.*). With Odysseus the case is different, for it turns out that he adopts two quite different tactics with two different groups: he will be gentle with the leaders (189), brusque with the troops (199). It is in relation to this contrast that the idea of 'gentle' has real point. Thus it is from verse 189 that 'gentle words' seem to be transferred back to, or foreshadowed in, Athene's instructions at 180. Perhaps it was the main poet himself who also transferred the concept to Here's orders at 164, where it was essentially out of place; but the logic of the whole passage is improved, as Aristarchus probably saw, by omitting it there.

184 Odysseus' herald (only here, and presumably at 9.170, in the *Iliad*) has the same name as Agamemnon's at 1.320. He is described in personal detail at *Od.* 19.244–8, and is probably not just an *ad hoc* invention – although Eurubates, 'broad-ranger', might be a traditional name for a herald, or at least for a fictitious one. At any rate Odysseus' throwing off of his cloak and its gathering up by the herald provide a vivid detail to illustrate the hero's swift and purposeful response.

186 This is almost identical with 46, which confirms what ἄφθιτον αἰεί anyhow suggests, namely that the sceptre which Odysseus here receives from Agamemnon is the Zeus-descended one described at 101–8. It is therefore a particularly potent symbol of authority, and of Odysseus' acting in Agamemnon's interests despite appearances.

188–210 Odysseus persuades the Achaeans to stop their flight and return to assembly. He uses very different arguments, and a different tone, to the leaders on the one hand and the troops on the other, but the two speeches are carefully balanced, so much so as to remind one of later rhetorical exercises. In neither case, however, is the sequence of thought quite straightforward. The argument is repetitious in places, and one or two sentiments in either address might seem marginally more appropriate to the other. It is tempting to play with possible transpositions as Aristarchus did, see on 193–7; but no rearrangement, even if it could be justified on general grounds, leads to a wholly coherent result. Concise and closely-packed speeches in Homer quite often have their loose connexions of thought – that is one result of the paratactic style, among other causes; and the probability is that both the present speeches have been accurately enough transmitted. Note the successive whole-verse sentences, the absence of strong enjambment until 205/6 and the rarity of even mild cumulation, especially in the first speech.

190–1 On δαιμόνι' see on 200 and 3.399. The initial address looks clear enough at first sight: 'you should not be showing fear like a coward'; but δειδίσσεσθαι is transitive, not intransitive, in its other four Iliadic occurrences, and Leaf and Monro must be right in claiming the meaning here as 'it is not fitting to try and terrify you as though you were a coward'. That is certainly more conciliatory (cf. ἀγανοῖς in 189) than implying that each king really *was* behaving like a coward. More important, perhaps, it accords with the other application of this evidently formular phrase at 15.196, χερσὶ δὲ μή τί με πάγχυ κακὸν ὡς δειδισσέσθω: 'let him not try to terrify me as though I were a coward'. The marked antithetical quality of the speeches shows up again in 191 αὐτός...ἄλλους, as well as in 193, 201 and 204.

192 Didymus in A records impressive support for 'Ατρείωνος as against 'Ατρείδαο (despite which, and perhaps through Zenodotus' support, the latter appears in the medieval mss); Aristarchus evidently cited it as the reading of the majority of the 'elegant' ancient texts to which he had access (αἱ πλείους δὲ τῶν χαριεστάτων), as well as of Aristophanes. Formular usage, however, suggests that in this instance Zenodotus was right: 'Ατρείωνος never recurs (although the dative form appears once), whereas 'Ατρείδαο comes 9x *Il.*, 9x *Od.* at the verse-end as here. A more important difficulty (on which see also the next two notes) is that in a way the kings do know Agamemnon's intentions up to this point – to attack Troy, ultimately, in accordance with the Zeus-sent dream. What they do not know is how he will react to the failure of the testing of morale.

193–7 Aristarchus (Arn/AT on 192) argued for moving 203–5 ('the rule of many is not good' etc.) to follow 192, as being more relevant to kings than to populace; and he athetized 193–7 as ineffectual in a speech urging restraint. That is clearly wrong – Aristarchus at his weakest and most subjective. Some reference to the council meeting, and to the plan of testing the army by urging flight, is clearly needed, and it is made in 194 which is obviously authentic (unless one supposes the whole testing to be some kind of addition, which Aristarchus did not). The sequence of ideas can be justified as it stands if we allow for a degree of rhetorical licence:

191 Stop the flight and return to assembly
192 because you do not know what Agamemnon is going to do
193 – he is testing them (and will soon punish them for failing the test)
194 as we learned at the council.
195 [restating the second part of 193] You should beware of his punishing the Achaeans
196 because kings are naturally prone to anger
197 and are able to exercise it, because they are supported by Zeus.

194 Were all those who are here addressed by Odysseus present at the council? The 'kings and prominent men' of 188, that is? At first sight it appears so: those who attended were described as 'the elders' at 53, they summoned the troops to arms at 72 and 83, and Nestor addressed them as 'leaders and councillors of the Argives' at 79. But 'elders', at least, γέροντες, is less clear than one might expect; at 404–9 they are named as just seven, not counting Agamemnon himself. Some ancient texts made this verse a statement, not a question: not all those addressed by Odysseus were at the council (and so Agamemnon's intentions were unknown to them, cf. 192) – which is ingenious rather than probable.

195–6 For royal anger compare 1.78–83, also concerning Agamemnon.

198–9 See on 188–210; the correspondence of the two speeches extends to the frequentative verbs of 199, cf. 189 ἐρητύσασκε.

The 'men of the community' in 198, the ordinary soldiers, that is, had been creating a great din (153) and shouting to each other to launch the ships (151f.); that is what βοόωντα refers to. The form is an instance of epic *diectasis*, the artificial re-distension of a contracted verb with assimilation of the original stem-vowel.

The use of the royal sceptre of the house of Atreus as an instrument for pushing the troops around is a little surprising, although understandable in the circumstances – see also on 109. At its least physical interpretation ἐλάσασκεν might mean little more than 'steered them', i.e. back toward the place of assembly.

200 δαιμόνι' maintains the correspondence of the parallel speeches, cf. 190; it is a traditional and formal mode of address, purporting to assume that the person addressed has some relic of heroic connexion with the gods, usually as a form of exaggerated (and here definitely ironical) politeness: 'my good Sir' *vel sim.*

Book Two

The 'sit down' instruction of 191 is repeated here; it implies returning to the assembly (as they do at 207, ἀγορήνδε) and resuming their seats there.

201–2 Heroic rebuke tends to be exaggerated, even unfair; compare Agamemnon's unjustified words to Menestheus and Odysseus at 4.338–48 and to Diomedes at 4.370ff., and see also on 207. Being good both at fighting and in council is relatively rare among the senior commanders – Akhilleus and Agamemnon are at 1.258, and Agamemnon again at 3.179; so also Diomedes at 9.53f. The ordinary troops are good at neither.

ἐναρίθμιος looks like an unusually useful word for epic verse, but although forms of ἀριθμός occur six times in the *Odyssey* it is only paralleled in the *Iliad* by 124 ἀριθμηθήμεναι. This does not necessarily make it a 'late feature' (Shipp, *Studies* 232); it may equally well suggest that this whole passage is by Homer, and traditional in only some of its component terms and phrases.

203–5 The troops have, in fact, simply been obeying their commander, but Odysseus cleverly implies, first, that they have pre-empted the right of decision (203), and that this amounts to taking over the role of the kings themselves. This in turn leads to the noble-sounding generalization of 204 (οὐκ ἀγαθὸν πολυκοιρανίη), perhaps a traditional poetic epigram suitable for several different kinds of occasion.

204 κοίρανος is an evidently ancient word, occurring only occasionally in Homer and later poetry, for a leader in war (usually) or peace. It was probably superseded in general use by ἄναξ and βασιλεύς, both common in the Linear B tablets, as they became more and less specialized respectively.

206 Many MSS omit this verse; those that have it read βασιλεύῃ, which is metrically impossible. Monro and Allen retain it in OCT, but with Dio Chrysostom's βουλεύῃσι; but many editors have regarded it as an unnecessary addition based on 9.99 and designed to supply an object for δῶκε in 205 – 'which does not need one', Leaf. But surely δῶκε *does* need an object, and the retention of σφίσι, which has no specific point of reference in this context, suggests strongly that 9.98f. (or its prototype) is indeed the model, which is deployed here very much in the oral style. The solecism βασιλεύῃ is irrelevant, and is due to βασιλεύς in the preceding verse.

207–10 After the unusually simple verse-structure of the two balanced speeches (see on 188–210), the return to narrative restores a more regular level of enjambment (integral at 207 and 209) and cumulation (209).

207 The choice of κοιρανέων is partly determined by 204, but it is no accident that the verb is used of Agamemnon in its only other Iliadic occurrence, at 4.250 (apart from the god Ares at 5.824), as he carries out his morale-raising tour of inspection, the so-called *Epipolesis*. There are strong formal correspondences between the beginning of that episode and

Odysseus' actions here, especially in the two short speeches of encouragement and rebuke addressed by the king to two contrasted groups, the eager and the apparently remiss. Compare 4.232f. with 2.188f. and 4.240f. with 2.198f. – also the balanced pairs of speeches themselves (although the language and style of these differ considerably in the two contexts). Immediately after the second speech in each case there occurs a resumptive verse with κοιρανέων; at 4.250 it takes the form ὣς ὁ γε κοιρανέων ἐπεπωλεῖτο στίχας ἀνδρῶν. Obviously each passage is due to the same poet, Homer rather than a predecessor, developing a standard theme in ways that are similar in outline and structure but distinct in detail.

208–10 The return of the army to the place of assembly is described in terms that recall, although more briefly, its rush from the assembly to the ships at 142ff., by a form of ring-composition: αὖτις ἐπεσσεύοντο in 208 takes up νῆας ἐπ' ἐσσεύοντο in 150, ἠχῇ in 209 corresponds with ἀλαλητῷ in 149, and the simile of the roar of the swell as it pounds on a long beach at 209f. recalls the rough waves of the Icarian sea shortly before 144–6 (although that simile, like its complement at 147–9, illustrates movement rather than noise). On the wave-simile itself see further on 394–7.

209–10 Strong onomatopoeic effects of pounding and surging echo the breaking of the waves, not only in πολυφλοίσβοιο but also in the unusual sequence of anapaestic words, with rhyme or near-rhyme before a word-break, in 210: αἰγιαλῷ μεγάλῳ βρέμεται σμαραγεῖ. On σμαραγεῖ see 462–3n.

211–393 The army settles down in assembly once again, only for Thersites to rail against the leaders and repeat the call for retreat; he is chastised by Odysseus, who then restores morale with a long speech, followed by others from Nestor and Agamemnon himself

211 Corresponds closely with 99, which described the initial marshalling of the troops in assembly before Agamemnon addressed them and caused their panic retreat to the ships. ἐρήτυθεν δὲ καθ' ἕδρας occurs in both; but this verse contains in addition a second formular motif, namely ἄλλοι as first word contrasted with an individual who behaves differently, sometimes (as here) to initiate a fresh scene, as also at 2.1 = 24.677 and following, 'other gods and men slept, but not X'; cf. also 5.877–9.

212 Thersites is a 'speaking' name formed from θέρσος, the Aeolic form of Ionic θάρσος, implying either boldness or rashness – in his case, obviously the latter. He is the only character in the *Iliad* to lack both patronymic and place of origin – some minor characters are given only the one or the other, but he, who is not exactly minor, receives neither. This is usually taken to mean that he is a common soldier, a member of the πληθύς, 'multitude' (143), or δῆμος, 'people' (198), who are left unnamed by the poet. But that is not what Thersites himself claims at 231, for example, where he says he has captured Trojan prisoners and brought them back for ransoming, which is surely a feat for the 'front fighters' or (named) nobility, with whom the poet is chiefly concerned. The division into aristocrats (or 'outstanding men', cf. 188) and the rest is in any case a rather loose one, and it seems more probable that the omission of both patronymic and city or region is intended, rather, to distinguish this outrageous person – who would not be permitted to open his mouth ῖ. assembly if he were a common soldier, except to roar approval or occasional dissent – from his noble and more fortunate peers. It is true that the Trojan Dolon, who is also ugly and evidently somewhat despised, is given a father by name, and is also said to be rich (10.314–16); but then Thersites is worse than him, for he is 'unmeasured in speech'. That is a term used only here in Homer, though cf. ἀφαμαρτοεπής at 3.215; it is equivalent in sense but not metre to ἀκριτόμυθος, also of Thersites, at 246. For the expansion of the meaning of ἀμετροεπής in the next verse cf. 5.63 and 9.124.

214 οὐ κατὰ κόσμον develops ἄκοσμα in the preceding verse, and ἐριζέμεναι is an explanatory ('epexegetic') infinitive: '(who was adept at disorderly words) for wrangling with the kings, recklessly and in no orderly fashion'. οὐ κατὰ κόσμον is a formula (4x *Il.*, 4x *Od.*, cf. εὖ κατὰ κόσμον, with mobility within the verse, another 4x *Il.*), preceded by μάψ ἀτάρ at 5.759 and *Od.* 3.138.

215–16 'But he used to say whatever seemed to him likely to raise a laugh among the Achaeans'; εἴσαιτο, 'seemed', is aorist optative middle of *εἴδω. The harsh enjambment leading to runover ἔμμεναι introduces a compressed and staccato description of Thersites that might seem deliberately to echo his distorted physical appearance.

216 αἴσχιστος (etc.) occurs only here of physical ugliness rather than moral turpitude. These two qualities clearly tend to coincide in the heroic scale of values – although good looks, at the other extreme, do not necessarily entail courage or ἀρετή. That is shown by the case of Nireus of Sume, who at 673 is 'the fairest man to come to Troy' (after Akhilleus, of course, who himself finds Priam fine-looking at 24.632), but is otherwise insignificant.

217–18 φολκός comes only here in surviving Greek; its meaning is unclear but presumably it refers to the lower limbs, since the description seems to pass on to the upper body with τὼ δέ οἱ ὤμω later in the verse. LSJ conjecture 'bandy-legged', but 'dragging the feet (or one foot)', cf. ἐφέλκεσθαι (so Lobeck, see Chantraine, *Dict.*) is better – because he was lame in one leg, χωλός etc. As for his shoulders, they are round or 'curved', κυρτώ, in a very marked way, hunched or literally 'holding together', συνοχωκότε, over his chest.

219 φοξός, etymology unknown, almost certainly means 'pointed' here – ὀξυκέφαλος, 'with pointed head', according to the grammarians Apollonius Sophistes and Pollux, rather than (by another ancient suggestion recorded in A) 'over-baked' as of a pot. ψεδνή means 'sparse', and ἐπενήνοθε is perhaps related to ἄνθος, 'flowered upon'(cf. 10.134), though cf. Chantraine, *Dict.* s.v. ἀνήνοθεν. The shambling, limping gait, the hunched back and shoulders and the pointed, balding cranium combine to make Thersites a monstrosity by heroic standards.

220–3 After the restful and informative whole-verse sentence of 220 the interrupted, staccato style briefly continues. Akhilleus and Odysseus were Thersites' usual targets; now it is Agamemnon. The army resents his criticism, overlooking (as it seems) the king's unpredictable behaviour and puzzling advice. That is the case if τῷ in 222 refers to Thersites rather than to Agamemnon himself, as it grammatically could do and as Leaf (for example) thought to be the case. But the language of 223, where the army is 'horribly enraged and resentful' against this person, surely points to Thersites. That they must have been confused by Agamemnon and doubtful of his intentions and reactions is beyond argument, but the violence of the language is excessive for what they might have felt for their commanding general, whereas it would have been entirely justified in relation to someone already described as Thersites has been.

222 λέγ' comes close to the later meaning 'said' or 'spoke', but still retains much of its original sense of 'counted out' or 'enumerated'; see also on 435, and 125 λέξασθαι.

224 'Shouting loudly', literally 'a long way': the established formular use of μακρά to refer to distance is with βιβάς, βιβῶντα, etc., 'long-striding', 7× *Il.*, 2× *Od.* The present use is a formular adaptation or extension, as is 18.580 μακρὰ μεμυκώς.

225–42 Thersites' speech is a polished piece of invective. An apparently harmless initial question allows him to point out, in a smooth and carefully subordinated three-verse sentence (226–8), that Agamemnon gets more than his share of booty in the form of bronze and women. Or is it more gold he needs, ransom-money for Trojans captured not by the king himself but by Thersites and his like – or a young woman to make love to? This explicit and insulting enquiry (229–33), again with elaborate syntax and careful enjambment and subordination, leads to a sharp change of tone and style, for now Agamemnon is briskly told that rebuking the army does not become the man who started it all. Then Thersites turns with bitter sarcasm on the assembly at large. After initial insults (235) the expansive style returns: they should indeed retreat with their ships, leaving the king to digest his rights and learn whether the army is important or not. Finally the sneers are turned against Akhilleus, as Thersites ingeniously drags in the quarrel over Briseis.

Literal-minded critics have objected that Agamemnon himself had proposed retreat, therefore it is a serious inconsistency for Thersites to talk as though he had opposed it; but it is not hard to understand Thersites as inferring, from Odysseus and the other kings having prevented the launching of the ships, that Agamemnon had in fact been deceiving the troops. It is not necessarily an inconsistency, therefore, and in itself may not be serious enough to warrant the assumption of drastic thematic conflation. At the same time the possibility of a progressive build-up in the aoidic tradition of this whole episode, with gradual oral expansion of the assembly through the addition of motifs of testing and rebellion, cannot be completely discounted (see also on 86); and such a process might well have produced the occasional sequential harshness.

225 Compare 1.65, of Apollo, εἴτ' ἄρ' ὅ γ' εὐχωλῆς ἐπιμέμφεται εἴθ' ἑκατόμβης, in which ἐπιμέμφεται stands in the same (formular) position in the verse. Here the idea of 'lack', which has to be understood in 1.65, is explicitly stated by χατίζεις: 'for the lack of what do you blame us?', with αὖτ' neatly reinforcing the idea of Agamemnon as insatiable.

226–31 Bronze (no doubt mainly in the form of armour, tripod-cauldrons and ingots) as well as women suitable to be servants are the normal loot from small towns like the twenty-three around the Troad captured by Akhilleus (9.328–32; they include Lurnessos, cf. 19.60). Gold, on the other hand, is likely to come mainly from wealthy Troy itself, obviously not by capture at this stage but as ransom. Akhilleus (at 1.166f. and 9.331–3) confirms that Agamemnon stayed in camp and kept the best part of the spoils; Willcock well comments that 'Thersites' arguments are like a parody of those of Achilles in Book 1.'

231–4 Zenodotus (Arn/A) omitted these verses because of their sarcastic quality, but they are powerful and obviously authentic. He had also omitted 227f., adjusting 226, neatly enough, to read πλεῖαι δὲ γυναικῶν.

232–3 Just as gold is more valuable than bronze, so a young concubine is more valuable – or more suitable to Agamemnon's greed – than an ordinary female captive. Possession of a concubine was no doubt the regular thing for a chieftain in time of war, but Thersites implies that just having Khruseis (or her presumed substitute Briseis) is not good enough for king Agamemnon. The phrase μίσγεαι (etc.) ἐν φιλότητι is formular, but the addition of γυναῖκα νέην and the ἵνα construction give it an almost pornographic flavour. Thetis' practical words to her son Akhilleus on sexual needs, at 24.130f., suggest a different scale of values and taste, but they are exceptional.

233–4 A final insult before Thersites turns his attention to the army: as king, Agamemnon should not lead his troops in the direction of evil (literally 'make them go toward', βασκέμεν being a causal form of βαίνειν). It is not entirely clear what Agamemnon is being blamed for – for the plague and the quarrel according to bT, but also, certainly, for keeping them all at Troy.

235 πέπονες: elsewhere in the plural, and used as a rebuke or sarcastically, only at 13.120. In the singular it is a polite form of address. Calling them Achaean *women* (so also 7.96) is an ingenious piece of rhetoric – it is cowardly *not* to flee.

237 γέρα πεσσέμεν: 'to digest [i.e. enjoy] his rights'; but Akhilleus 'digesting' his wrath at 4.513 (cf. 24.617) suggests this may be an unpalatable business.

239 Akhilleus is briefly praised, but only for malicious reasons, and criticism will quickly follow at 241.

240 The verse repeats 1.356 and 507, see on 1.185 and 356; this attempt to renew the provocations of the quarrel in book 1 has caused some critics to wonder whether Thersites' intervention did not belong, in some earlier version, to that quarrel itself. νῦν in 239 does not argue either way, *contra* Leaf, since it can mean 'just recently' as easily as 'a moment ago'. Yet all the points raised by Thersites are valid in retrospect, and 236–8 suit an occasion on which the suggestion of mass withdrawal has already been made (as it is not made in book 1, for 169f. applies only to Akhilleus himself). It seems that Homer's intention was to make the repeated assembly here into a strong episode in its own right, and Thersites' accusations, which justify the replies by Odysseus and Nestor, are a natural and successful way of doing so.

245 ὑπόδρα ἰδών is a well-established formula, 17x *Il.*, 9x *Od.*, usually in the formular verse-type τὸν δ' ἄρ' ὑπόδρα ἰδὼν προσέφη + name–epithet group (∪∪–∪∪–⏑). On ὑπόδρα see on 1.148–71; ἠνίπαπε is a strange reduplicated form from ἐνίπτειν, 'to rebuke'.

246–64 Odysseus' words to Thersites are dangerously measured in tone, with much periodic and progressive enjambment especially in the formal, oath-like threat at the end (258–64).

246 λιγύς περ ἐὼν ἀγορητής (also at 19.82; cf. 1.248, 3.214) is sarcastic: Thersites is a ready talker but devoid of judgement (ἀκριτόμυθε, cf. 212 ἀμετροεπής).

247 Disagreeing with the leaders is bad enough, but Thersites is οἶος, alone, and does not even have popular support.

248–50 For he is the worst man in the army, therefore he may not (optative with ἄν) hold forth (ἀγορεύοις) 'with kings on his tongue [literally, in his mouth]', βασιλῆας ἀνὰ στόμ' ἔχων, i.e. daring to criticize kings. This last is a unique locution, and cannot mean (as bT suggest as an alternative) 'holding up your face against royal authority'; for βασιλῆας must be direct object of ἔχων, which leaves ἀνὰ στόμ' as an adverbial phrase.

251 φυλάσσοις: 'watch out for the opportunity for', bT.

252–6 These verses were athetized by Aristarchus (Arn/A) as 'pedestrian in composition' and because Thersites must have been standing, not sitting (255 ἧσαι, cf. 211f.). It is true that they are both inessential and loosely phrased, also that Odysseus will be more optimistic at 295ff. about the eventual outcome. Yet the style is still Homeric, and ἧσαι may convey the idea of continuously doing something (cf. 1.134, 2.137, and especially Diomedes to Sthenelos at 4.412) rather than of literally sitting. There is, nevertheless, a slight awkwardness here, but not one an imitator would be likely to perpetrate; and the resumptive σὺ δὲ κερτομέων ἀγορεύεις of 256 is an effective piece of rhetoric.

257 This emphatic formular verse, with slight variations at its beginning, occurs 8x *Il.* (with 3 further variants), 6x *Od.*

258–64 The elaborate threat ('*if* I find you repeating this folly, *then* may Odysseus' head no longer be on his shoulders, *nor* may I be called Telemakhos' father, *if* I do not strip off your clothes... and drive you out of the assembly back to the ships') derives its force from its content and elaborate syntax rather than from any apparent urgency in delivery, for it is contained in whole-verse clauses with only slight enjambment and internal punctuation. Something similar can be seen in Akhilleus' threatening oath to Agamemnon at 1.234–44, although that is far more interrupted.

258 An unusual, not a formular, expression, although elsewhere, also, the head stands for the man himself, cf. 18.114, 23.94, 24.276, *Od.* 1.343.

260 On Odysseus as father of Telemakhos see also on 4.354.

261–4 The leisurely expression continues, giving the impression that Odysseus is calmly, decisively and almost lovingly detailing the degrading treatment he would be prepared to dispense. The exposure of a man's genitals (262) (except in the case of a young man slain in battle as Priam says at 22.71f.) is shameful, as the word αἰδῶ or αἰδοῖα itself suggests. That would be even more so, no doubt, in the case of a deformed person like Thersites. Odysseus' threat is violent and unusual; the epic tradition generally avoided genitals, and even among the multifarious wounds in battle they occur only once in the *Iliad*, when Adamas is hit by Meriones 'between genitals and navel, most painful of all places' (13.568f.; see the note which will appear there for Cretans as inflicters of especially unpleasant wounds).

265–6 The integral enjambment with runover-verb sounds temporarily harsh and suits the action. πλῆξεν recalls the threat of 'unseemly blows' at 264; the actual beating is a cruel one, although less drastic than the threat of stripping naked.

265–9 These verses contain many vivid details, alternating between the physical effects of the blows and Thersites' reactions, which are horrifying and pathetic: he bends away from them and weeps (266), sits down in fear (268), is in pain (ἀλγήσας), looks helpless (ἀχρεῖον ἰδών) and wipes away a tear (269).

270 Why are the troops 'grieved', ἀχνύμενοι? Presumably because of all the recent confusion as well as the bad taste left by Thersites' harangue (cf. comment on 220–3) – not because of his present sufferings, which they find amusing. These are tough soldiers and that is natural enough, but the heroic sense of humour inclined that way in any case. The same 'sweet laughter' is elicited when the lesser Aias trips in the foot-race and fills his mouth and nostrils with dung (23.784), or from Zeus when he sees Artemis after she has been beaten by Here (21.508, cf. 408). One is reminded, too, of the 'unquenchable laughter' of the gods on Olumpos when the crippled Hephaistos hobbles round pouring their wine (see 1.599f. and comment). Misfortune and undignified appearance are the two things that normally seem to cause heroic – and divine – amusement in the *Iliad*; in the *Odyssey* laughter usually comes from the suitors, and is of the derisive kind.

271 A common formular verse for introducing a general comment from onlookers; it occurs as a whole 3x *Il.*, 6x *Od.*, and its first half an additional 5x *Il.*, 6x *Od.* (with another 3x each with ὡς ἄρα for ὧδε δέ). εἴπεσκε is an iterative form of the aorist, used in the extended sense 'frequent individuals said' rather than, as normally, 'each individual said frequently', i.e. on different occasions.

272–7 This typical comment is carefully constructed and consists of three two-verse statements. The first of them leads by rhetorical contrast into the second, each with progressive enjambment; and the third, with integral enjambment, draws the conclusion. (i) Odysseus has done many good things; (ii) but this is the best yet; (iii) so Thersites will not criticize the leaders again.

ὢ πόποι (272) is common in the *Iliad* (29x); it usually expresses alarm or pained surprise, only occasionally in a sarcastic or light-hearted way as here (cf. e.g. 16.745).

At least one of the six verses is distinctly abnormal in language: in 273 βουλάς as first word (never elsewhere with an epithet in the plural) normally depends on βουλεύειν or the like; ἐξάρχων elsewhere has the special meaning of leading a dirge, dance or song; πόλεμόν τε κορύσσων is a bold metaphor, 'bringing war to a head' (cf. 21.306), although usually the verb is used in the middle voice to mean 'put on a helmet' or more generally 'equip oneself'; see on 4.274 and 424–6, and Leumann, *HW* 210. Verse 275 has some unusual elements too: ἐπεσβόλος occurs only here and means 'flinging words about' (i.e. from ἔπος and βάλλειν), although the noun-form occurs at *Od.* 4.159; and the closest parallel to plural ἀγοράων, 'assemblies', or rather 'talking in assembly', is again from the fourth book of the *Odyssey*, 4.818. The closing couplet reverts to standard formular language.

278–82 Eustathius 220.18 (see Erbse I, 244f.) reflected some concern over why Odysseus should be said to stand up, when he had not been described as sitting down after beating Thersites and would not naturally have done so. But the poet needs to re-establish the normal conditions of debate in assembly after the interruptions and the fracas; the would-be speaker's rising to his feet is regular procedure (e.g. 1.58, 68 and 101 in the opening assembly), and the formula here used to describe the action, including the mention of the staff, was applied to Agamemnon at 100f. The herald (or heralds) normally calls for silence before the debate begins, not as the first speaker rises (as with Athene here) and standing by his side; so e.g. at 96–8. At 23.567–9, however, in the funeral games, the procedure is exactly as here; and at *Od.* 2.37f. the herald hands the staff to the speaker but without the call for silence (for the functions of the staff see on 109). Yet this is obviously, in any event, a special case, since the herald is a disguised goddess. It is a logical complement to Athene's foiling the rush to the ships – for which she had descended from Olumpos, cf. 163–7 – that the Achaeans should completely abandon the idea of retreat; that she achieves by making sure that Odysseus has an immediate hearing and persuades the army of the need to continue fighting. She could have obtained the same result by stimulating a mortal herald into action (as Iris could have with the Trojan Polites at 791), rather than by disguising herself; but her direct action provides an emphatic introduction to an unusually crucial speech, as well as rounding off the whole theme of her personal intervention.

278–9 Some old texts (and a small minority of medieval ones) read δέ for δ' ὁ, wrongly (κακῶς) according to (Didymus in) bT. Aristarchus is probably correct, despite the unusual occurrence of two near-definite-articles in the same verse. Each of these, in its own way, has some emphatic or demonstrative force: (i) ἡ πληθύς, the multitude, i.e. that one sitting there; (ii) ὁ πτολίπορθος Ὀδυσσεύς, 'the [i.e. that famous] ravager-of-cities Odysseus'. In addition the quasi-demonstratives contribute to the antithesis between the two parties: *here* the multitude, *there* Odysseus. The careful balance continues in the phrasing both of this and of the following verse; each has a strong stop at the central caesura and continues with ἀνά/παρά and a name–epithet formula in the nominative, leading on by integral enjambment to the main verb in the next verse. πτολίπορθος is applied to Odysseus only once else in the *Iliad*, at 10.363, again preceded by ὁ (although it is attached 4x to Akhilleus without it, also 4x to others). In the *Odyssey*, where his part in the sack of Troy is of course well known, he alone has this epithet, although without the article (6x + 2 similar).

281 πρῶτοί τε καὶ ὗστατοι is a unique phrase in Homer. It appears to be formally based on τίνα πρῶτον, τίνα δ᾽ ὗστατον at e.g. 5.703 = 11.299; but Leaf notices that here it has a local sense and means 'those in front and those behind'.

283 An Iliadic formular verse (9×), not an Odyssean one. On ἐϋφρονέων see also 78n.

284–332 Odysseus' speech at this ·critical juncture must be specially persuasive, and it is important to notice that it is very carefully composed yet at the same time presupposes the whole testing-motif. It makes five separate points, of which the fourth is elaborated in conspicuous detail: (i) the army, not Agamemnon, is to blame, since it had promised not to return home until Troy had fallen (284–8); (ii) their moaning about going home is like that of widows or young children (289f.); (iii) admittedly being delayed by bad weather even for a month is frustrating, and they have been away for nine years – even so, returning with nothing accomplished is a disgrace (291–8); (iv) therefore they should be patient, and wait to see if Kalkhas was right in his interpretation of the portent they all witnessed nine years ago at Aulis (and which is described in full), namely that Troy would fall in the tenth year (299–329); (v) nothing has happened to controvert this, so they should stay until Troy falls (330–2). Thus Odysseus begins by distracting attention from Agamemnon's peculiar behaviour by accusing the rest of them of disloyalty (i) and infantile behaviour (ii). Then he softens the criticism a little by sympathizing with the hardship of being away from home for so long, only to continue by saying that nothing is worse than failure (iii). So far the arguments are about how the army *ought* to behave; now in (iv) comes the elaborate and practical argument that, questions of duty apart, Zeus had revealed that Troy would in fact fall within the year, and (v) nothing had happened to cast that into doubt. There is a marked and appropriate stylistic difference between the first part of the speech (points i–iii) and the second (points iv–v), the former containing many integrally-enjambed verses making complicated sentences, the latter, especially from 308 on, being more straightforward in expression, with many whole-verse sentences and elaboration of detail through cumulation and progressive enjambment.

285–6 A paratactic sequence: 'they want to make you a reproach among men, and do not fulfil their promise...'; that is, '...by not fulfilling...'

286–8 The 'promise' was presumably a general commitment by the army to carry the expedition to a successful conclusion, made 'as they were leaving Argos' (i.e. mainland Greece, 287), rather than the earlier and famous vow of Helen's suitors, never directly alluded to by Homer, to come to the aid of the successful candidate if the need ever arose. Idomeneus' reference at 4.267 (q.v. with note) is no more specific than here.

290 'They lament to each other about going home'; for the construction compare *Od.* 5.153, νόστον ὀδυρομένῳ.

291 The sense is difficult and much debated. πόνος almost certainly means 'toil', 'labour' rather than 'grief', as indeed Aristarchus argued (Arn/A); it nearly always does so in Homer, although 6.355 at least is an exception. The literal meaning seems to be, therefore, 'truly it is also a labour to depart in distress'. Fighting before Troy is often described as a labour – the paradox is that going home (for that is the meaning of 'depart', as the previous verse shows) can involve equal hardship. The conditions in which this would be so are presumably implied by ἀνιηθέντα (perfect passive participle of ἀνιάω, 'cause distress or annoyance to'); this particular form recurs only once in Homer at *Od.* 3.117, where Nestor tells Telemakhos that to describe all the sufferings of the Achaeans at Troy would take more than five or six years, and that he would have returned home ἀνιηθείς long before that. There 'in distress' implies 'because of the long lapse of time', but also 'because the end did not seem to be in sight'. If that nuance were applied to the present verse the following argument would emerge: 'truly it would be a labour [i.e. as much as toiling on the battlefield] to return home in frustration with nothing accomplished'. That suits quite well the general development of Odysseus' argument in the verses that follow, and would be repeated by ring-composition in the conclusion at 297f. The only difficulty is καὶ γάρ at the start of the very next verse, 292, which could not offer a direct explanation of the point being made (according to the present interpretation) in 291, but would rather look forward to the reservation expressed in 297f. Thus the sequence of thought would be 'Going home in frustration would be as bad as toiling on the battlefield, because, although even a month's delay away from home is bad (and we have had nine years!), it is nevertheless disgraceful to wait for a very long time and then return with nothing to show for it.' This is preferable to Lehrs' interpretation (favoured by Leaf short of resort to emendation), 'truly here is toil to make a man return disheartened'. Some looseness in the run of the argument may in any case be expected in view of the proverbial colouring of 291, since proverbs tend to be rather roughly adapted to context in the *Iliad* as a whole, cf. e.g. 20.246–50. Perhaps such a proverbial use was triggered by νέεσθαι, which likewise ends the preceding verse. The infinitive of this verb is in any case a common formula at the verse-end (20x *Il.* out of a total of 22 uses, and 32x *Od.* out of 33), especially after οἴκόνδε as in 290 (6x *Il.* including 3x in this Book, where of course the idea of returning home is an important theme).

295 Not 'it is the ninth revolving year', for according to 134 nine years have already elapsed; but rather 'it is the ninth year that is turning, i.e. at an end', cf. τροπή = 'solstice'.

299–300 The tone becomes even more accommodating. Odysseus urges them directly now, addressing them as 'friends'; and through the first person plural of δαῶμεν (a unique but not really surprising syncopation of δαείωμεν, 'learn') he claims to share their feelings. In 300 most MSS, but not A, have εἰ not ἤ; nevertheless Aristarchus (Did/A) opted for the latter, which is probably correct. The proper form of disjunction in indirect questions in Homer, and the commonest form in the vulgate (even though εἰ is universally supported at 6.367) appears to be ἠέ (elided as ἤ)...ἦε (ἤ); see Chantraine, *GH* II, 293f., and on 346–9 *fin.*

301–2 Again the persuasive complicity: we all know what happened at Aulis, and you yourselves witnessed it. It is important that Odysseus should continue by vividly recalling this portent to their minds. The undeniable reality of the portent itself is made to spread over into Kalkhas' interpretation of it.

Aristarchus (Arn/A) and nearly all the MSS read the adjectival form μάρτυροι (cf. 7.76 ἐπιμάρτυρος) against Zenodotus' μάρτυρες, but the latter may well be correct.

303 'Yesterday and the day before', so to speak – an idiom not elsewhere found in Homer, but relatively common in classical Greek in the form πρώην τε καὶ χθές, e.g. Hdt. 2.53.1; 'it seems just like yesterday' (Willcock). This kind of interpretation is probably correct against attempts to link the expression closely with ἠγερέθοντο in the next verse (as by Lehrs followed by Leaf): χθίζα τε καὶ πρωΐζ', ὅτ' ἐς Αὐλίδα νῆες Ἀχαιῶν | ἠγερέθοντο, 'when the Achaeans' ships had gathered yesterday or the day before', that is, the portent occurred a day or two after the ships had assembled. But the word-order is strongly against this.

305–7 The *holy* altars around the spring with its *shining* waters under the *fine* plane-tree are all formular epithets, but their aggregation (together with the regularly *perfect* hecatombs) deliberately stresses the authenticity of the reminiscence and, by implication, of the religious experience itself. Pausanias (as Leaf observed) noted at 9.19.7 that the spring was still shown in his day and that part of the plane-tree was still preserved in Artemis' temple at Aulis; that is probably sheer antiquarianism, since there is no reason for believing that Homer's description was based on special local knowledge. There had to be water at Aulis, otherwise the fleet would not have assembled there; and plane-trees grew around springs then, as now.

305 ἀμφὶ περί looks odd, but the former word is adverbial and to be taken closely with ἔρδομεν, whereas the latter is an ordinary preposition governing κρήνην.

307–18 Fables of a contest between a snake and a bird in a tree, which end with one of them devouring the other's young, were of high antiquity and had various morals. In the Accadian myth of Etana it is an eagle that devours the snake's offspring (*ANET* 114f.; on Mesopotamian and Greek

Book Two

fables in general see West, *Works and Days* 204f.). In the present case there is no special moral and it is merely the devouring of a particular number of victims that is important – the birds are equivalent to years. The snake is described in portentous detail; his back is dark and blood-coloured, ἐπὶ νῶτα δαφοινός (308), and he is σμερδαλέος, huge and terrible (309). The young birds are pathetically described as νεοσσοί, νήπια τέκνα (311), as they crouch under the leaves of the highest branch (312). There were eight of them and the mother made nine, which increases the pathos, as perhaps does the deliberate *naïveté* of the jingling ἣ τέκε τέκνα in 313. The snake emerging from beneath the altar (or rather one of the altars, cf. 305) adds to the religious aura; it is Zeus that sends him (cf. also 318), not Artemis the special deity of Aulis, since only he could determine or recognize in advance the outcome of the war.

314 τετριγῶτας is perfect participle of τρίζω, an established epic term for whining or squeaking (being onomatopoeic in its present stem at least, cf. τρίζουσαι at *Od.* 24.5 and 7): of birds (as here) or bats, of souls going down to Hades, even of a wrestler's back under strain at 23.714. Zenodotus (Arn/A) rather typically read τιτίζοντας, an otherwise unattested verb evidently meaning 'twittering'.

315 τέκνα comes at the verse-end for the third time in five verses. The epic singers evidently did not object (any more than Euripides, for example, later) to this kind of repetition, occasionally at least; it is accentuated here by the -ῶτες -ῶτας near-rhyming of the intervening endings. Such effects are often fortuitous, but the pathetic tone discussed in the note on 307–18 shows that it is almost certainly deliberate here.

317 A rising threefolder, the only one in the plain narrative of the portent (compared with the rather frequent instances at 289, 290, 292, 298, and possibly 284, 302 and 304, in the earlier part of Odysseus' speech; and 324, 326 (~ 317), 328 and possibly 332 in the latter part).

318–19 A well-known crux. The mss give ἀρίζηλον (= 'very conspicuous', ἀρι- being the intensive prefix, ἐρι- in Aeolic, cf. ἐριούνιος), which was probably the reading favoured by Zenodotus (although Aristonicus in A attributed ἀρίδηλον to him, the same word in a later and unmetrical form). The meaning would then be that Zeus made the serpent 'very conspicuous' by turning it into stone. Aristarchus, on the other hand (Arn/AT), evidently read ἀίζηλον = 'invisible' and athetized 319 (so Lehrs, cf. Erbse 1, 254). This is probably correct – although many commentators have thought otherwise – for two reasons, of which the first is the more important: (i) it makes a significant contrast with ὅς περ ἔφηνε, which is otherwise rather pointless: 'the snake was made invisible by the god who had made it visible' (so Aristarchus, Arn/T); (ii) the content of 319 is in any case difficult to envisage precisely: where was the stone snake? Still in the tree? Turning

149

something portentous into stone is far more plausible in the case of the Phaeacian ship so turned by Poseidon at *Od.* 13.161–4 (163, ὅς μιν λᾶαν θῆκε), which was probably the model for whoever provided 319 as a supplementary explanation for texts in which 'very conspicuous' was read in 318. On ἀίζηλον, presumably ά-privative + root of ἰδεῖν = 'see' + -ηλος as suffix, see Chantraine, *GH* I, 169 (who supports this reading), also *Dict.* s.v. ἀίδηλος.

321 ὡς is temporal: 'So when the dread beasts had intruded on the hecatombs for the gods...'; the innocent sparrows join the snake as terrible monsters because of their role in the portent.

322 ἀγόρευε, imperfect, 'began to speak'.

323–32 Odysseus recalls Kalkhas' exact words, which will themselves repeat where possible the terms of Odysseus' previous narration of events; thus 326 ~ 317, 327 = 313. This is oral economy, or artifice based thereon.

323 ἄνεῳ or ἄνεω, 'in silence', see 3.84n.

325 'Late in arriving, late in fulfilment'; both words are unique in Homer but appropriately prophetic in tone, an effect to which the repeated o-sounds somehow contribute.

328–9 The actual interpretation of the omen is baldly stated, and Kalkhas does not try to explain it further – compare Theoklymenos' even more arbitrary interpretation of a portent at *Od.* 15.531–4. One might have expected the meaning to be that eight years had passed and Troy would fall in the ninth – that is, the fledglings would represent the years so far, the mother the fateful year to come. We know that nine years had already elapsed (see on 295); the poet could in theory have said at 313 ἐννέ', ἀτὰρ μητήρ δεκάτη ἦν (although admittedly ἐννέα is not elided elsewhere in Homer), but did not choose to do so. Therefore the fledglings must symbolize the years already past, the mother the present year.

330 All that has happened so far is that nine years have passed with no result; at least that does not conflict with Kalkhas' interpretation, so that Odysseus can claim, somewhat speciously, that the whole of it is being brought to pass.

333–5 They are called Ἀργεῖοι ('Argives') first, then Ἀχαιοί ('Achaeans'), apparently indifferently; the latter is nearly always used as last word in the verse.

334 = 16.277, also of the ships resounding. σμερδαλέον (etc.) always occurs as first word in the verse, as here (27x *Il.*, 9x *Od.*); σμερδαλέον κονάβησε -ιзε etc. is also well established in the poetical vocabulary (7x *Il.*, 1x *Od.*). It is a bold and dramatic application of the phrase, none the less, to the ships echoing the din of the army.

336–68 Nestor's speech here, like all his interventions, has its idiosyncratic side. It begins with an apparently ill-timed rebuke which ignores

Odysseus' elaborate, well-planned and evidently effective (cf. 335) address. Its outline is as follows: (i) you (we) are wasting time in childish disputes, forgetting our pledges to fight (337–43); (ii) Agamemnon should stick to his resolve and lead the army in battle, ignoring the odd dissenter (344–9); (iii) for Zeus sent a favourable omen, lightning on the right, on the day the Argives left Aulis for Troy (350–3); (iv) therefore let no one attempt to leave for home before Helen has been avenged – if anyone does, he will be killed (354–9); (v) Agamemnon should marshal the troops tribe by tribe so that cowards can be easily distinguished (360–8). Of these points the first, third and fifth all create difficulties: (i) for the reason mentioned, that the rebuke is out of place after Odysseus' speech and its favourable reception, (iii) because it ignores Odysseus' reference to a different omen at Aulis, and (v) because the tactical advice is inconsistent with the remainder of the poem, in which tribes and phratries are virtually unmentioned. It is conceivable that earlier versions of the tale had either a speech by Odysseus or one by Nestor, not both, but that the monumental composer decided to have both together. Odysseus' speech, as we saw, is constructed with great care and even brilliance; Nestor's has the advantage of eliciting an enthusiastic response from Agamemnon, and this, with the army's equally keen reaction at 394ff., may be needed to restore the king's authority. Extreme unitarians, who refuse to accept the slight anomalies that can arise out of the progressive accumulation of oral materials, would have to argue that Nestor deliberately ignores Odysseus for some personal or psychological reason. Willcock (who is not extreme) comments that 'Nestor, building on the good effect of Odysseus' speech, takes a much tougher line'; whereas bT on 337 suggested that Nestor ignored him through disapproval of his conciliatory tone at 296.

336 Γερήνιος ἱππότα Νέστωρ: the first occurrence out of twenty-one in the *Iliad* of this standard phrase for Nestor. Nothing is known about 'Gerenian'; ancient speculation ranged from an otherwise unknown people (so Hesiod, *Ehoiai*, frag. 35, 6–8 M–W) to a connexion with γέρων, 'old', or γέρας, 'privilege', both unlikely. ἱππότα, 'horseman', significantly occurs of other heroes only five times in the poem – of Phuleus, Tudeus, Oineus and Peleus (twice), each with the all-purpose name-suffix in -ευς (see von Kamptz, *Personennamen* 122–6) and belonging to an earlier generation (although Peleus is conceived in the *Iliad* as being still alive). For this reason, and because the meaning of Γερήνιος had apparently been forgotten, the whole formular phrase is probably an ancient one, going back some generations (at least three?) in the oral poetical tradition.

337 ᾱγοράασθε by metrical lengthening.

340 Literally 'may all counsels...be in the fire', i.e. if we are to squabble like children (337f., 342) then all agreements may just as well be abandoned. For the use of the optative see Chantraine, *GH* II, 215 *fin.*

341 The most solemn libations were of unmixed wine; Aristarchus (Arn/T) observed that when Achaeans and Trojans 'mixed wine in a mixing-bowl' at 3.269f. they were not mixing it with water, but were mixing different portions of wine contributed by each side, for symbolic purposes. On δεξιαί see 4.158–9n.

344 ἀστεμφέα: the general meaning is 'fixed, unmoving', cf. 3.219; whether the ἀ- is privative or copulative is uncertain (στέμφυλον = 'compressed olives'; στέμβω apparently means 'agitate', cf. Frisk).

346–9 A loosely constructed and rather confusing sentence: 'Let *these* perish, the one or two [i.e. Thersites and anyone like him] among the Achaeans who have different ideas – which they will not bring to completion – before they get back to Argos [i.e. Greece], before they even know whether the promise of Zeus is false or not.' The threat is that they will perish before ever they get back home, which is what they are 'separately planning', νόσφιν βουλεύωσ'. The appended πρίν...πρίν καί is a rhetorical addition developing the idea of their planning, not of their perishing – they are planning to return home before they even know about Zeus's promise (which is doubly foolish). This leads on to Nestor's description of the omen at 350–3, just as φθινύθειν is developed, in a chiastic arrangement, shortly afterwards at 357–9: they will perish because they will be struck down as soon as they lay hand on a ship. In 349 we should probably read ἤ τε... ἠὲ καὶ οὐκί as in a few MSS, cf. on 299f.; although Shipp, *Studies* 142 and 233f., maintains that this part of Nestor's speech is linguistically late and abnormal and therefore that the unique εἴτε...εἴτε should be retained. That may be going too far, although there certainly are some relatively late forms hereabouts, see on 360–8 *fin.*

348–50 Nestor's emphatic declaration that Zeus has given his approval shows the 'falsehood' idea in 349 to be ironical.

351 This omen evidently occurred later than that described by Odysseus, on the very day the fleet sailed from Aulis (compared with 303f., 'when the ships had gathered at Aulis'). Later tradition, represented for example in Aeschylus, *Ag.* 188–99, suggests that a long interval elapsed between arrival and departure – the delay in fact which led to the sacrifice of Iphigeneia. Even so, Nestor's failure to refer to the earlier and certainly more striking portent, and to the graphic account of it by Odysseus, is remarkable; the difficulty cannot be removed by omitting 351f. as e.g. Leaf suggested, since that would create a new contradiction over the occasion of the snake-portent.

353 ἀστράπτων should strictly be ἀστράπτοντ', since it refers to Κρονίωνα in 350: so Aristarchus (Arn/AbT), but it is an easy *ad sensum* lapse. For the phrasing of the verse compare the similar language of 9.236f. ἐπιδέξι', 'on the right', indicates the favourable side.

354-6 A powerful exhortation with its initial rising threefolder followed by the three/fourfold 355 and ending with 356, in which each of the four main words constitutes a separate rhythmical colon, to give a decisive, almost a pounding effect.

355 The recommendation of mass rape (which is what it amounts to) is phrased in a typically epic – that is, bowdlerized – way, almost as if one were simply to take one's place in the marital bed for a long night's rest.

356 By sleeping with a Trojan wife they will be taking revenge for all the sufferings caused on Helen's account – that is, because of Paris having unlawfully slept with an Achaean one. The verse recurs almost exactly at 590, which however casts little light on the present meaning. Aristarchus (Arn/A) rejected the opinion of contemporary χωρίʒοντες, 'Separatists', that the *Iliad* and *Odyssey* took a wholly different view of Helen: in the latter she was clearly guilty of leaving voluntarily with Paris, whereas here, they claimed, the 'struggles and groans' are her own; that is, she was forcibly abducted. Admittedly the grammar is ambiguous, in that the struggles, ὁρμήματα (rather than 'cares' as the exegetical scholiasts thought), could in theory either *belong to* Helen or be hers in an objective sense, that is, *be about* her or be undergone by others *because of* her; but the whole subsequent tradition portrayed her as running off willingly (even if it was her wraith that did so!), and there would have been little point in Priam telling her 'I hold not you, but the gods, responsible' at 3.164 if she had been obviously innocent. The *Odyssey* makes it plain, for example at 4.261-3, that she left home out of love for Paris, and the two poems are unlikely to have diverged on this central issue.

357-9 Another 3-verse exhortation, of a more sinister kind, to balance 354-6. ἐκπάγλως, 'astoundingly' (connected with ἐκπλήσσω, cf. Chantraine, *Dict.* s.v.), increases the irony: 'if you have an astounding urge to go home, just lay a hand on your ship – and you will be dead', in front of (i.e. in the sight of) the rest.

360-8 The first of several pieces of very specific tactical advice offered by Nestor, mostly in the first half of the poem, in his role of trusted counsellor. Like some although not all of the others, this has an unusual and faintly anachronistic flavour, being more appropriate to the kind of fighting he describes in his reminiscences of past conflicts between the Pylians on the one side and the Arcadians or Epeans on the other, than to that before Troy. Compare his advice at 4.297-309 (cowards to be stationed in the middle, charioteers to stay in close formation like the men of old); 6.67-71 (no interruption of the advance in order to plunder the dead); 7.327-43 (Achaeans to build a defensive wall and trench after burning their dead); 9.65-8 (guards to be stationed at night outside wall and trench); 10.204-17 (a spy to be sent among the Trojans to discover their plans); 11.796-803

(Akhilleus should let Patroklos wear Akhilleus' armour so as to frighten the Trojans); 14.62f. (useless for the wounded leaders to try and fight); 23.306–48 (detailed tactical instructions to his son Antilokhos for the chariot-race). Nestor's advice also tends to be expressed in untraditional language: 'No portion of either poem is richer in notable features than 362–8' (Shipp, *Studies* 233). That is not beyond argument, but φρήτρηφιν in 363 and κατὰ σφέας and μαχέονται in 366 are surprising; see on those verses.

361 Nestor's advice is preceded by a solemn introduction, as at 9.60–2. This verse is not exactly repeated elsewhere but its components are formular: οὐδ' ἅλιον ἔπος ἔσσεται ὅττι κεν εἴπῃ, 24.92, cf. 24.224; ὅττι κεν εἴπω etc., 5× *Il.*, 9× *Od.*

362–3 The emphatic asyndeton of κατὰ φῦλα, κατὰ φρήτρας (with the anaphora of κατά and lengthening of its final syllable in the second instance), followed by the marked rhetorical repetitions of 363, is typical of Nestor's didactic and gnomic style. The advice to marshal men by contingents (or tribes – see below) and phratries or brotherhoods looks almost too obvious; surely that would have been done at the beginning of the campaign, not after nine years? Moreover it includes a kinship term, 'brotherhoods', which is paralleled only in another of Nestor's idiosyncratic comments at 9.63f., where he asserts that the man who likes civil dispute is ἀφρήτωρ. Phratries were important in Athens before Kleisthenes, and Leaf among others saw a reference here to the social organization of the seventh or sixth century B.C. φῦλα in this context looks as though it should mean 'tribes' in a political sense rather than merely 'contingents' or, loosely, 'races', as elsewhere in Homer, e.g. at 840; but the proper term for clan or tribe is φυλή not φῦλον, and that leaves its trace only once in the *Iliad*, in the puzzling καταφυλαδόν applied to the Rhodians at 2.668. Perhaps, as N. G. L. Hammond comments on this passage (*A History of Greece* (Oxford 1959) 67), 'The commoners, rather than the princes, were loyal members of these "brotherhoods" (phratries), which were based on kinship and formed together into tribes'; the nobles on the other hand were ἑταῖροι under their leader. According to A. Andrewes in his fundamental article 'Phratries in Homer', 'the tribes and phratries are an intrusion from [Homer's] own time: not an interpolation but...a lapse from consistency' (*Hermes* 89 (1961) 132). He also observed (129f.) that many organizational details throughout the epic, not only those suggested by Nestor, are mentioned in order to make the particular occasion an impressive one, and are thereafter wholly neglected – so for example of the Myrmidons being divided into five groups at 16.168ff., or the Trojans at 12.86f. That is what happens here, for although Agamemnon is enthusiastic about the proposed division by tribes and phratries the proposal is never actually carried out, not even in Nestor's own contingent according to the evidence of 4.293–300. The closest to it is when Iris disguised as Polites tells Hektor at 2.803–6 (and as a means of introducing the Trojan catalogue, just as Nestor's advice here leads to the Achaean) to ensure that each contingent of the polyglot allies is led by a man of its own speech (cf. Andrewes, *op. cit.*, 132).

φρήτρηφιν in 363 is a directly datival use of the case-ending -φι, which is normally locative, instrumental (as in Mycenaean) or ablative; it has the advantage here of increasing still further the emphatic alliteration of φ.

365–8 Nestor is concerned to discourage cowards, as he also will be at 4.299f. The rising threefolder at 365 is balanced by that at 367, and the balance is emphasized by the corresponding γνώση and γνώσεαι as first word in each couplet; see also on 391–3.

366 κατὰ σφέας, 'by themselves', cf. 1.271 κατ' ἔμ' αὐτόν (also spoken by Nestor). μαχέονται is conceivably an Atticism, μαχήσομαι (etc.) being the regular Homeric form of the future tense of this verb; in that case the verse would probably have been a supplement by a rhapsode who felt 365 to be incomplete in itself. But the balanced couplets (see the previous comment) suggest if anything that the present arrangement is original.

370–6 Agamemnon is always appreciative of Nestor's advice; here he is ecstatic about it. The thought that Troy would fall if he had ten such counsellors turns his attention back to his actual and very different circumstances.

377–8 He blames Zeus first and foremost (a motif to be developed when he finally renounces the quarrel with Akhilleus, at 19.86ff.) but concedes in 378 that he himself began the provocation. In other words he has already partly recovered from his excess of kingly arrogance in book 1.

379–80 Agamemnon's mind turns to the future again: what would *really* cause Troy's fall (for 371–4 had been, after all, a mere flight of fancy) would be the termination of his quarrel with Akhilleus. The tone of 380 is emphatic, sinister and ironical, especially in the abstract ἀνάβλησις and the poetical but still almost colloquial οὐδ' ἡβαιόν. The former recurs at 24.655 (where C. W. Macleod in his commentary described the effect as euphemistic – much as it is here). ἡβαιόν is the epic form of the later βαιός etc., 'little', and Chantraine, *Dict.* accepts Leumann's suggestion (*HW* 50) that it results from the false division of οὐ δὴ βαιόν; see also on 386.

381 This verse recurs as 19.275. δεῖπνον is the main Homeric meal, dinner, as distinct from ἄριστον, breakfast, and δόρπον, supper. It is normally taken at midday, but can imply, as it does here, simply a substantial meal without too careful a specification of the hour at which it is to be eaten.

Ἄρηα connoting war in general is formular at the verse-end (11× *Il.*, not

Od.), as object of ἐγείρειν, φέρειν, μένειν as well as of ξυνάγειν. The dative is used similarly, e.g. at 385.

382-4 An example (as AbT commented on 382) not only of *epanaphora* (εὖ μέν τις...εὖ δέ τις...εὖ δέ τις) but also, in the first and third of the three verses, of *homoioteleuton* or similar (rhyming) ending, in θέσθω and μεδέσθω. Agamemnon's instruction to the troops is thus both rhetorical and highly emphatic; as often in such cases there is a rising threefolder involved, here at 382. Its concreteness and detail are worthy of Nestor himself, with a touch of his eccentricity: were they really likely to forget to feed the horses (although I suppose spear-points did need sharpening from time to time)? The epic tradition is usually quite vague about such details.

386 The rhetorical style continues; this verse is very similar to 380, not only in its formular ending οὐδ᾽· ἡβαιόν -αι (6x *Il.*, 3x *Od.*) preceded by (μετ)έσσεται, but also in the choice of an unusual verbal abstract as subject, here παυσωλή, there ἀνάβλησις, on which see 379-80n.

387 'Unless night separates' is tantamount to 'until...'

388-90 Another rhetorical and carefully balanced sentence, different in arrangement from 382-4 but repeating many of its elements; there is *anaphora* again, with prominent μέν...δέ, also indefinite τις in the form τευ...τευ. Chest sweating under shield-strap is another graphic detail, and shield, spear, horse and chariot all reappear.

391-3 Once again a rising threefolder, 391, introduces the climax, which is a repetition of Nestor's warning against shirkers (357-9) in different terms. The sinister tone is maintained both by the stark contrast between the innocent-sounding 'staying by the curved ships' and the brutal implication of the dogs and birds, and by the circumlocution of οὗ οἱ ἔπειτα | ἄρκιον ἐσσεῖται, in which ἄρκιον means something like 'reliable' – 'he will not be able to rely on escaping the dogs and birds' (i.e. those that will devour his corpse). ἐσσεῖται is an artificial form of regular ἔσσεται or ἔσται, only elsewhere at 13.317.

394-483 The troops return to the ships and prepare a meal before going into battle; the chieftains dine with Agamemnon, who sacrifices an ox. Then the heralds give the order to form up; an unparalleled sequence of similes marks the march-out of the troops onto the plain

394-7 The army gives a great shout, presumably of excitement and approval, after Agamemnon's speech just as it had done (and in the same formular language, Ἀργεῖοι δὲ μέγ᾽ ἴαχον) at 333 after that of Odysseus. The noise is compared with the roar of the waves as the south wind (the violent scirocco, that implies) drives them against the cliffs of a promontory. This is the third wave-simile in this Book, cf. 144-6 and 208-10 with comments. In 209f. the surf breaks on a long beach, whereas here the waves pound against projecting cliffs; there is little essential difference, but the description of the former is clearer and more straightforward; here the effort to suggest the projection of the cliffy headland, in the first half of both 395 and 396, is almost laboured. Similarly the poet finds it necessary to reinforce his initial south wind with 'winds of all kinds' blown from all directions (for Aristarchus, quoted by Didymus in A on 397, is clearly wrong in taking κύματα as subject of γένωνται). ἔνθ' ἢ ἔνθα in 397 recalls similar (but not formulaically identical) language in the bee-simile at 90. For the relation of all this to previous similes in book 2 see Moulton, *Similes* 38–42 and especially 41, where the argument about the implied direction of motion calls for some caution.

399 κάπνισσαν, 'made smoke' – that is, by lighting fires; a compact expression, only here in Homer, and one that presents a lively picture of the scene.

400–1 Another unusual detail; sacrifices accompanied by prayer, apart from public occasions, are regularly confined to aristocratic, heroic dinners (compare the description of the army making supper at the end of book 7). The ordinary troops must of course have sacrificed and prayed from time to time – ἔρεζε can also include the making of bloodless offerings as at 9.534f. – but the poetical tradition was not much interested in that. bT noted that each man praying to his own particular deity emphasizes the diversity of the contingents, also that the troops pray for self-preservation, the leaders for success – for example Agamemnon at 413–18 will pray for the fall of Troy and the death of Hektor. A closer look at 401 shows that self-preservation may involve keeping clear of the real fighting altogether, for μῶλον Ἄρηος is a formular phrase that means simply 'the tumult of battle' (so in its other three Iliadic uses) and not some especially dangerous and legitimately avoidable encounter. Reading κατὰ μῶλον for καὶ μῶλον would avoid this implication, but has no manuscript warrant.

402–3 Agamemnon's provision of an ox for sacrifice (and one in prime condition as is appropriate to Zeus), in contrast with the common man's unspecified meal and sacrifice at 399f., calls to mind the scene, almost a caricature, on the Shield of Akhilleus at 18.556–60, where an ox is sacrificed for the royal luncheon while porridge is prepared for the harvesters.

404–9 The order of those invited to the chieftains' dinner has a certain logic, in parts at least: Nestor and Idomeneus come first in age, Aias and Diomedes may be mentioned next because of their superior fighting qualities after Akhilleus (and on the lesser Aias see 406n.). bT offered various explanations, none particularly persuasive, for the postponement of Odysseus until sixth. As for Menelaos, he came αὐτόματος, of his own accord. Verse 409 was considered by many in antiquity (according to Athenaeus

5.177C), including Demetrius of Phalerum (frag. 190 Wehrli), to be an addition; see Erbse on 405–9 and van der Valk, *Researches* II, 499. It is indeed inorganic and, more serious, slightly awkward in expression: 'for he knew in his heart how his brother was labouring' (ἀδελφεός being the regular epic form of later ἀδελφός). That is, he came without invitation to save his brother the trouble, occupied as the latter was with inviting the others and arranging for the sacrifice and subsequent feast. Without this verse we should certainly take the reason for Menelaos' coming unbid to be slightly different, namely that as Agamemnon's brother, as well as inspirer of the whole expedition, he would appear as of right, irrespective of how busy Agamemnon might be. But 408 is just the kind of condensed and allusive statement that tended to attract further explanation, either in the cumulative oral tradition or, occasionally, in the subsequent phase of rhapsodic transmission and sporadic elaboration. It is often impossible, as here, to distinguish the two; only when there is real absurdity in the expansion can we be sure that post-Homeric agents were involved.

404 This is the first occurrence in the poem of the verse-end formula ἀριστῆες -ας Παναχαιῶν (8x *Il.*; Παναχαιοί by itself 1x *Il.*, 3x *Od.*). Παναχαιοί is a logical enough form for the united Achaeans, cf. Πανέλληνας at 530 (which may well, however, be a rhapsodic addition, see on 529–30); its use in apposition to γέροντας is paralleled only by the rather odd κουρῆτας ἀριστῆας Παναχαιῶν at 19.193.

406 Αἴαντε δύω: presumably the great, Salaminian Aias is accompanied, as often, by the lesser Locrian one (so bT), with whom he is especially associated because of his shared name. But one has to remain aware that occasionally, and evidently through retention in the poetical tradition of an early use of the dual, Αἴαντε and Αἴαντ' as well as Αἴαντες -ας -εσσι(ν) (34x *Il.* in all) can refer instead to the greater Aias *and his half-brother Teukros*; so definitely at 4.273 (and 280) – see on 4.272–3; and also 13.197 (despite 13.203). This intriguing fact was first observed by J. A. Wackernagel (*Kuhns Zeitschrift* 23 (1877) 302ff.) and is clearly and fully discussed by Page, *HHI* 235–8 and n. 52 on pp. 272f.; see also on 527.

408 Menelaos like Diomedes is βοὴν ἀγαθός, 'good at shouting' or, in the traditional translation, 'good at the war-cry'. There is no need to argue whether or not the trumpet had been invented (cf. bT) to understand that a loud voice and an ability to use it for rallying one's troops would be a useful characteristic in a leader. Menelaos is a lesser fighter than Diomedes, but his sharing this prestigious description is probably mainly due to his name being metrically equivalent – that is often the salient consideration, real unsuitability apart, in an oral tradition. At all events Menelaos is so described 17x against Diomedes' 21x; the phrase is very occasionally transferred to others (Hektor, Aias, Polites).

Book Two

410–31 On the dedication of the animal victim, the prayer, the slaughtering, the preparation and burning of the divine portions and the roasting of the other meat see on 1.447–68, a closely similar version of this typical scene of sacrifice (in particular 421–4 = 1.458–61 and 427–32 = 1.464–9). The main differences are that in book 1 there are several victims (a hecatomb), and they are stationed round the altar – here the sacred circle is composed by the sacrificers themselves who surround the single animal; there is no formal altar in Agamemnon's hut, as there obviously had been in Apollo's precinct at Khruse. The washing of hands is omitted in this version of the scene (the description of which in any case tends to vary slightly on each occasion); there is no mention of the sacrificer pouring wine on the divine portion as at 1.462f.; the σπλάγχνα, the sacred bits of the entrails that were eaten as part of the sacrifice and before the secular meal, are explicitly described here at 426 as being roasted, although that is merely assumed in the book 1 version. Finally the acts of spitting and roasting are here carried out by all present – Agamemnon is not singled out as the priest Khruses obviously needed to be in the hecatomb-sacrifice of book 1; on this point see on 1.462–3.

412–18 Agamemnon's prayer is thoroughly heroic in tone, rather than pious, tactful or even practical; he wants victory now, with Priam's palace ablaze and Hektor dead, all before dusk. Compared with Khruses' prayer to Apollo at 1.451–6 it is also perfunctory in its failure to cite the local affiliations and special functions of the god and to show reason why he should grant the present request. But perhaps the matter of local epithets is not so simple; Aristarchus (Arn/A) defended the titles given to Zeus in 412 against the version of 3.276 which some critics evidently preferred here, namely Ζεῦ πάτερ Ἴδηθεν μεδέων κύδιστε μέγιστε, on the ground that it would be unsuitable to mention the god's connexion with Mt Ida and the Troad when he was being asked to destroy Troy itself. It might be added that 'of black clouds' here may be held to give a sinister foretaste of αἰθαλόεν in 415; see also on 4.166–8.

415 αἰθαλόεν, 'smoky' or 'sooty', is descriptive of a palace's *megaron* or main room at *Od.* 22.239 – that is, as blackened by the smoke of the central hearth. Here, however, both position and context show the epithet to have a different and special reference: the palace will be smoky because it is being burned down (so also bT). As for the vulgate reading πρῆσαι, Aristarchus (Did/A) wrote πλῆσαι in his editions, and this was the commonest reading in antiquity. πρῆσαι (from πρήθω = 'blow' or 'blaze', although only the former meaning is found elsewhere in Homer) is possible as Didymus observed, but πλῆσαι, 'fill', seems preferable and is indeed quite brilliant: 'fill the doorways with blazing fire'.

417 χαλκῷ ῥωγαλέον: '(making it) in tatters [literally, broken, cf.

ῥήγ-νυμι] with the bronze (spear-head)', a half-verse cumulation that renders the envisaged spearing of Hektor even more vivid – and even more extravagant, perhaps, as a wish.

419–20 This is the only place in Homer where a god refuses a prayer but 'accepts' the sacrifice in some way, and it worried Aristarchus (whose comment is preserved in full by Didymus in A), always anxious as he was to absolve Zeus from the suspicion of double-dealing (see on 1.15 and 35). Aristarchus therefore took δέκτο μὲν ἱρά to imply the sending of some favourable sign enabling prophets to declare that the offerings had been received: οἷον αἴσια ἐσήμαινεν ὥστε λέγειν τοὺς μάντεις ὅτι δέδεκται. This seems implausibly complicated, and reads too much in the way of behind-the-scenes action into a short phrase. More probably the purpose of 'accepting' was to show Zeus as still deceiving Agamemnon, in a way; there was no real dishonesty, as πώ in 419 shows: Zeus did not yet fulfil this kind of prayer (but would ultimately do so). To reject it openly would therefore have been misleading (and probably fatal to the insecure Achaean morale), and was in any case unnecessary; for Homeric gods did not invariably or even frequently give any specific indication of their reaction, favourable or otherwise, to prayer or sacrifice or both combined.

421–9 For the details of sacrifice see on 410–31.

425–6 The description of putting the divine portions on spits differs slightly from that of 1.462–3 (see the comment there), mainly, it seems, to make the ritual act into one performed by all those present rather than by a single officiant like the priest Khruses, or Nestor at *Od.* 3.459f. The portions are of two kinds: the fat-encased thigh-bones, which are placed in the fire on wooden spits (425) and wholly consumed by the flames, giving off savour for the gods; and selected innards, σπλάγχνα, which are spitted on iron spits and toasted before being eaten as part of the sacred ritual by the main participants (426f.).

427–8 The first of these formular verses (2× *Il.*, 2× *Od.*) is a rising threefolder; the second falls firmly into two parts, but there is an alternative version found elsewhere (2× *Il.*, 1× *Od.*), μίστυλλόν τ' ἄρ' ἐπισταμένως πεῖράν τ' ὀβελοῖσιν, which is also threefold and might seem an effective substitute here. But, although the sense of the two versions is very similar, there is a difference which affects the choice of one or the other; for the second version, which does not mention τἆλλα, the rest of the meat, is appropriate to condensed descriptions of the preparation of meals in which, for one reason or another, the divine portion is not specifically mentioned, as it is here. In either case the secular portion of the slaughtered animal is cut up and grilled on iron spits (which may or may not have been the same as those used for the entrail-tasting, see the end of the preceding comment).

430–2 430f., striking for their alliteration and assonance and consequent emphasis on δαῖτα, δαίνυντ', δαιτός – that is, on the shared meal – occur twice each in the *Iliad* and *Odyssey*; but 'when the meal was over' was evidently an even more useful idea (and one subject to less variation), and 432 αὐτὰρ ἐπεὶ πόσιος καὶ ἐδητύος ἐξ ἔρον ἕντο is a very common formula (7× *Il.*, 14× *Od.*).

434–40 Once the meal is finished, Nestor is the natural member of the group to propose what should be done next. After all the diversions and delays the army is ready for action, and, as Nestor says, it is time for the heralds and commanders to reorganise it.

434 Agamemnon lord of men shares the laudatory epithet κύδιστε with Zeus alone: 10× *Il.*, 2× *Od.* (Agamemnon), 5× *Il.* including 412 (Zeus).

435 μηκέτι νῦν δήθ' αὖθι λεγώμεθα literally means 'let us now no longer *be collected* here for a long time' according to Aristarchus in his second volume of *Iliad*-commentaries (as directly quoted by Didymus in A), against Zenodotus' text μηκέτι νῦν δὴ ταῦτα λεγώμεθα, 'let us now no longer *talk of* these things'. λέγειν, λέγεσθαι can have either meaning in Homer (see on 222); for the latter, which is a development of the former, cf. in particular 13.292 = 20.244, ἀλλ' ἄγε μηκέτι ταῦτα λεγώμεθα νηπύτιοι ὥς. Aristarchus' difficulty according to Leaf and others was that no conversation had been specifically mentioned as taking place at the preceding meal; there must obviously have been some, but whether the need to assume such conversation is 'contrary to epic practice' as Leaf claims is debatable. Nevertheless, and in the light of the established formula μηκέτι ταῦτα λεγώμεθα (also 2× *Od.*), it looks as though Zenodotus was right in both interpretation and text on this occasion, and Aristarchus wrong. The contrast then established with ἔργον in 436 may provide slight further support for this view.

436 Somehow the future tense ἐγγυαλίξει became the medieval vulgate reading; the present -ίζει had, however, strong ancient support (from Aristarchus, Apollonius of Rhodes, Aristophanes and αἱ πᾶσαι, 'all the versions', according to Didymus in AT – it also occurs in the margin of a second-century A.D. papyrus and a few MSS, cf. the *apparatus criticus* in OCT *ad loc.*). The present tense is probably correct: the god is already guaranteeing the outcome of the enterprise (and had probably done so, it might be added, by the portent at Aulis, cf. 301ff.).

437–44 The role of the heralds in marshalling the army is underlined by the closely-packed repetitions κήρυκες...κηρύσσοντες...ἀγειρόντων... κηρύκεσσι...κηρύσσειν...ἐκήρυσσον...ἐγείροντο.

446–51 The poet stresses the importance of the occasion by another intervention on the part of Athene, designed to lift morale still further. This is the first of a sequence of special effects (the series of five similes at 459ff., the invocation of the Muses at 484ff., the catalogues themselves from 494 on) to presage the beginning of the battle that forms the heart of the whole epic. The divine intervention is in one respect metaphorical, since Athene did not take human appearance, or say anything, nor did the troops actually see her – they just seem to have felt her presence as she filled them with strength, σθένος, at 451. Yet the vivid description of the αἰγίς, the aegis, that she has or holds (ἔχουσ᾽, 447) gives her a certain visual impact too. Exactly how the poets of the epic tradition imagined the aegis is a difficult question. It is deployed by Zeus (4.167 and 17.593) and Apollo (15.229, 308, 318, 361; 24.20) as well as Athene (here and at 5.738; 18.204; 21.400; *Od.* 22.297). It is probably a goat-skin in some form, for that is its obvious etymology (so e.g. Chantraine, *Dict.* s.v.); it is put around the shoulders at 5.738 and 18.204 (that is, presumably, like a sword (-strap), 5× *Il.*, or shield (-strap), 1× *Il.*). This suggests that it may be thought of as a shield covered with goat-skin, although in classical art Athene's aegis is a skin thrown over the shoulders like a small shawl; see also *Arch. Hom.* E 53–6. No less interesting than the object itself is the nature of its quite intricate description here, which can be compared with the very different account at 5.738–42, where it is decorated with a Gorgon's head, Rout, Strife and so on. The present passage shows signs of careful elaboration on the basis of occasional formular elements, in a manner that in itself is not typically oral. The commonest noun-epithet formula for the aegis is αἰγίδα θυσαν-όεσσαν (5× *Il.*), which seems to have generated the description of its hundred golden tassels in 448f., like those on Here's girdle at 14.181; it is replaced here by another formula, 'ageless and deathless', perhaps because αἰγίδ᾽ needs to be first word in the verse for emphasis, not near the verse-end as in the tassel formula. But παγχρύσεοι, 'all-golden', is unique here as a term if not as a concept, and ἠερέθονται ('dangle' or 'float', an epic form of ἀείρω) is hardly formular, although see on 3.108. Similarly in 449 both ἐϋπλεκέες and ἑκατόμβοιος belong to the Homeric vocabulary but are not used here in any established formular way, and in 450 παιφάσσουσα (implying darting rather than dazzling, see Chantraine, *Dict.* s.v.) is paralleled only by ἐκ-παιφάσσειν at 5.803. The phraseology seems therefore to have been developed and adapted for the occasion; there is none of the awkwardness that seems to characterize specifically post-Homeric development, for example by rhapsodes, and we might therefore see here the work of the main composer himself.

451–4 The singer reverts to less individual and more heavily formular language, in which 453f., to the effect that war became sweeter to them than returning in their hollow ships to their dear native land, effectively rounds off the whole episode of the testing of morale and the debate on whether or not they should give up and return home.

455–83 The sequence of five developed similes, which includes two further minor comparisons, is unique in Homer, and makes a suitably majestic prelude (together with the invocation of the Muses that will immediately follow) to the elaborate Achaean catalogue. The possibility of doublets or alternative versions being accidentally incorporated, or of rhapsodic elaboration in the manner of the variants in Hesiod, *Theog.* 734ff., obviously presents itself but does not stand up to close examination. Each simile arises naturally enough out of its predecessor and either supplements an existing point of comparison or introduces a new one. Moreover there is no sign – except conceivably for 478f. – of typical rhapsodic taste and ambition. The progression (with careful alternation of ἠΰτε... τῶν δ' ὡς τ'... ἠΰτε... τοὺς δ' ὡς τ'... ἠΰτε as means of introducing the comparison) is as follows:

455–8 The gleam of armour as they advance is like that of a forest fire in the mountains.

459–66 The races of Achaeans resemble those of birds flocking in the meadow round the Kaüstrios river, both in numbers and in noise; the ground rings with the noise of feet and horses' hooves.

467–8 They stand in the Scamandrian meadow as numerous as spring leaves and flowers.

469–73 They are as numerous as they stand in the plain as the races of flies round milk-pails in springtime.

474–7 Their leaders marshal them like goatherds dividing up their flocks.

477–9 Among them is Agamemnon, like Zeus, Ares or Poseidon.

480–3 He stands out like a bull in a flock of cattle – Zeus has made him no less conspicuous.

Moulton, *Similes* 27–33, well observes that the movement is from broad panoramic scenes of nature to detailed pastoral ones.

455–6 AbT rightly drew attention to the grandeur of conception and language: the fire is ἀΐδηλον (destructive, that which makes something disappear from sight, ἀ-ἰδεῖν), it burns up the ἄσπετον (immense, indescribable, privative ἀ- + the root found in ἐνισπεῖν) forest on the mountain peaks. This is the first of the developed fire-similes in the poem, only preceded by the short comparison at 1.104.

457–8 ἐρχομένων takes up the ἰέναι of 451; they are pouring out of the camp and gathering on the plain. The gleam and flash of polished bronze are a recurrent image in the *Iliad*, a symbol of martial power and valour. Here the gleam penetrates the upper air to the sky itself (like the noise of battle at 17.425); the language, especially in θεσπεσίοιο and παμφανόωσα, remains elevated.

459–66 This famous simile illustrates both the numbers and movement of the troops on the one hand and the noise of their marching on the other.

459 'Winged' is an otiose epithet for birds in one way, but these are large birds and their wings (πτερύγεσσι) are relevant in 462. ἔθνεα, 'races', is a term already applied to bees in the rather similar comparison at 2.87 (see on 87–93 and 91), and the concluding verse mentioning the 'races' of Achaeans is the same in each case (91 = 464). Moreover ἔθνεα πολλά will be applied in the very next developed simile to flies, at 469; perhaps the one use of the formular phrase helped to suggest the other.

460 'Of geese or cranes or long-necked swans'; cranes recur in another simile at the beginning of the next Book (3.3–8), where it is their honking as they fly (against the Pygmies – there is a special mythological reference there, see on 3.5–6) that is the point of comparison.

461 Most ancient critics (so probably Aristarchus, Hdn/bT) read ᾿Ασίω without a second iota, as genitive of a proper name Asias (a Lydian king according to Herodotus 4.45.3); but 'Asia' seems to have been used of this part of the coastal region until it was applied more widely, and the 'Asian meadow' – which is certainly how Vergil understood Homer at *Georgics* 1.383f. and *Aeneid* 7.701f. – is probably correct. The Kaüstrios (later Kaüstros) flowed into the sea at Ephesos, and Homer as an Ionian may well have known it; Leaf noted that this is the only detailed reference in Homer to this east Aegean coast outside the Troad, although cf. 144–6n.

462–3 The bees at 90 likewise flew 'here and there', although without the spasmodic effect of the successive trochaic word-breaks as in 462 here. The birds are 'exulting in their wings', swooping about perhaps as they look for a spot to land. In 463 they have landed, one in front of another with a great cawing, and the whole meadow σμαραγεῖ, 'resounds', an onomatopoeic term which certainly implies noise (as in 210) and not flashing or gleaming – that is a confusion with the different (oriental) root of σμάραγδος, 'emerald'. Aristarchus (Did/A) supported ἀγαλλόμενα (against -αι, which is highly unlikely in view of 463 προκαθιζόντων but nevertheless retained in most mss).

465–6 They 'poured forth' into the plain; that, with the 'many races' of 464, makes it appear that the poet is thinking of their multitude rather than their noise. However, the noise element, prominent of the birds in 463, is now singled out – but has to be redefined, for it is not their shouting that makes the noise (that would contradict the contrast emphasized at 3.2–8 between the disciplined Achaeans and the noisy, disparate Trojans) but rather the echoing of the ground under their marching feet and their horses' hooves, a rather forced conception perhaps.

467–8 Lest there should be any remaining confusion the idea of multitude is now specifically stated as the Achaeans take station in the plain beyond the ships. The 'Scamandrian plain' of 465 has become the 'Scamandrian meadow' now, not only to echo the Asian meadow of 461 but also to allow it to be ἀνθεμόεντι, 'flowered', and so foreshadow the leaves and flowers of 468; these images are woven into one another with extraordinary virtuosity. ὥρη in its three other Iliadic uses is supported by a word for spring (including 471); here and in the similar *Od.* 9.51 it may imply either that or simply 'due season', which amounts to much the same.

469–73 The idea of the great numbers of the Achaeans, suggested by the massed birds and then more explicitly stated in the short leaves-and-flowers comparison, is now developed by a more homely simile: they are like flies swarming in springtime round the full milk-pails in a sheepfold; compare the simile of the ewes being milked at 4.433–5.

469 Similar to the first verse of the bee-simile at 87, ἠΰτε ἔθνεα εἶσι μελισσάων ἀδινάων; on ἔθνεα see 91n., on ἀδινάων 87n.

470 ποιμήν in Homer is the guardian of sheep or cattle; here, the ποιμνήϊον is the sheepfold, since cattle seem to have been kept for draught or meat rather than for milking (so e.g. M. L. West on Hesiod, *Erga* 590). ἠλάσκουσιν is a frequentative form of ἀλάομαι, 'wander', with metrical lengthening of the initial vowel: 'fly around'. Neither buzzing (see on 465–6) nor interest in blood, as bT asserted, is in question here.

471 Springtime links this simile with the immediately preceding one; it is now that the milk is most prolific (so the D-scholium, *contra* Leaf). δεύει means 'drench', 'make wet', probably meaning simply that the pails are full to overflowing.

473 διαρραῖσαι μεμαῶτες, 'eager to shatter (the enemy)', a deliberately harsh formula (twice elsewhere in *Il.*) in contrast with the pastoral scene, to remind the audience of martial qualities (cf. 451–4) as well as sheer numbers.

474–6 After the sheepfold, the goatherds – the herdsmen themselves, for now, after concentrating on the army *en masse*, the poet turns to its commanders.

474 An αἰπόλος is a goatherd, αἰπόλια are things he has to do with, i.e. herds; they are πλατέ(α), broad or flat (a formula, 2x *Il.*, 2x *Od.*, 1x Hesiod, *Theog.*), perhaps because they are wide-ranging rather than close-packed like a flock of sheep.

475 The goats have come to their pasture and the herdsmen easily divide them into groups; the idea to be conveyed is of skilled leaders rather than inherently disciplined charges.

476 Again the 'here and there' phrase, almost a leitmotiv of these similes (cf. 462 and 90).

477–8 Agamemnon stands out among the leaders, he is like a Zeus among them. It is a powerful and extravagant idea that he resembles the god in 'eyes and head', literally: a unique phrase, more likely to imply 'in his gaze and by his height' (cf. 3.193 and comment, where Odysseus is μείων μὲν κεφαλῇ than Agamemnon) than any specific facial resemblance.

479 No doubt is cast on this verse either in the ancient tradition (AbT admired it) or by modern editors, but it ought to raise an initial suspicion. It might be a simple oral cumulation, but is an anticlimax after the unusual comparison with Zeus. The king's *waist* is like Ares'; normally ζώνη applies to a woman's waist, and it needs a slight mistranslation like 'girth' to make it seem natural here. His chest is like Poseidon's – again the only parallel is Odysseus at 3.193f., where he is shorter than Agamemnon but broader in shoulders and chest. ἴσος Ἄρηϊ is a common general expression (5× *Il.*) of comparison with the war-god, and may be the model here; there is no other case of a specific comparison with Poseidon (see the useful conspectus in Anne Amory Parry, *Blameless Aegisthus* (Leiden 1973) 218–23).

480–2 The focus on Agamemnon continues; after the sheepfold and goatherds, now cattle – he stands out among the others like a bull among a herd of cows. The comparison is a simple one, in which 482 is a slightly repetitive addition for emphasis rather than to add any new visual detail.

482 As supreme commander Agamemnon is favoured by Zeus even among the other 'Zeus-reared kings'.

483 'Conspicuous among men and outstanding among heroes' is an awkward expression most closely paralleled by Agamemnon's entry in the ensuing catalogue, where at 579 πᾶσιν δὲ μετέπρεπεν ἡρώεσσιν – a more natural phrase in which ἡρώεσσιν is not totally deprived, as it is here, of the preposition it needs (especially after ἐν πολλοῖσι). ἔξοχον ἄλλων is common at the verse-end (6× *Il.*, 4× *Od.*) and ἔξοχον ἡρώων occurs twice in book 18 at the beginning of the verse; ἔξοχον ἡρώεσσιν| looks like a strained adaptation of the two.

484–760   The poet calls on the Muses to list, through him, the Achaean leaders and their ships. There follows the famous 'Catalogue of Ships', recording in nearly four hundred verses the twenty-nine constituent contingents of the army with their leaders, towns and ships

484–93 The poet summons the Muses to help him in his task of recording the leaders and their ships, and incidentally points out the impracticality of naming the ordinary troops in detail. The catalogue is to be a major episode, as this solemn invocation, following hard on the long string of similes, makes plain.

484 'Tell me [who were the leaders]'; they are to tell the poet, and he must relay the information to his listeners. Alternatively, 'tell *for* me', that is, use me as your instrument – the sense is almost the same; compare *Od.* 1.1, ἄνδρα μοι ἔννεπε Μοῦσα...The present verse recurs three times in the

Iliad: at 11.218, before a list of Agamemnon's victims; at 14.508, before another list of victims after Poseidon has inspired the Achaeans; and at 16.112, where the Muses are to tell (or make the poet tell) how fire fell on the Achaean ships. In other words, the verse is always used to mark a solemn moment (or one that needs to be made solemn), usually involving a list of some kind. The Ὀλύμπια δώματ' ἔχουσαι -οντες formula occurs 10x *Il.* in all (including 2.67) and 10x *Od.*

485–6 These two verses are parenthetical: the Muses know everything and are present everywhere (note the emphatic sound-effects of ἐστε... πάρεστέ...ἴστε), men can only repeat hearsay. Μοῦσαι is of uncertain etymology, but in the post-Homeric period the Muses were made daughters of Memory, Μνημοσύνη. The contrast between divine omniscience and human ignorance is of course a common one (and is put in a typically odd way by Hesiod at *Theog.* 22ff.).

487 This verse is repeated, with slight necessary change, at the conclusion of the Achaean list at 760.

488 With the Muses' help he can manage to deal with the leaders, but the troops lie beyond his powers – not beyond the Muses', presumably, but their instrument is too fragile, the sheer numbers are too large. μυθήσομαι is probably aorist subjunctive (rather than future indicative), like ὀνομήνω; for ἄν + aor. subj. with εἰ + opt. in the protasis compare 11.386f.

489–90 Aristarchus (Arn/A) judged the hyperbole to be typically Homeric and compared *Od.* 12.78, where Scylla's cliff is unclimbable 'even if a man had twenty hands and feet'.

491–3 These three verses, which look almost like an afterthought, are at first sight puzzling. The poet has declared that he can deal with the leaders, provided the Muses help him; the troops would be beyond his powers even if he had ten tongues, and so on – *unless the Muses reminded him of how many came to Troy.* In other words, it is not after all the sheer size of the task (requiring ten tongues), it is lack of knowledge that is the impediment. However, the sequence of thought is made clearer (as Aristarchus seems to have proposed, Nic/A on 488–92) if 489f., like 485f., are treated as firmly parenthetical. That leaves a chiastic statement which can be summarized as follows:

> 484 Tell me, Muses,
> 487 who were the leaders;
> 488 the troops I could not recount
> 491f. unless the Muses reminded me.

Close attention to the wording can now suggest how the 'reminding' (492 μνησαίαθ') can be reconciled with the poet's professed physical inability to deal with such large numbers: he is not about to tell *who* were the troops, as he had with the leaders (οἵ τινες at 487 implying family and place of origin as well as name: so bT on 488 [comment *a* in Erbse]), but rather *how many* they were, 492 ὅσοι. That may be confirmed in the final summarizing verse, 493: 'so I shall tell of the ships' commanders and of all the ships together'. The last phrase, νῆάς τε προπάσας, obviously refers in the first instance to the number of ships given for each contingent, but the total number of troops is roughly implied by the only two indications that will be given of a ship's complement – 120 for the Boiotoi (at verse 510) and 50 for Philoktetes' ships (at 719). Thucydides, who studied the catalogue very closely, at 1.10.4 took these as maximum and minimum numbers, with the implication that the average lay between the two. Actually the Boeotian number is likely to be as exceptional as their other statistics, and fifty is a more realistic ship's complement. Be that as it may, the catalogue at last begins.

The commentary is temporarily interrupted at this point, and will be again, for the insertion of introductions to, and conclusions on, first the Achaean catalogue (the 'Catalogue of Ships') and then that of the Trojans and their allies. It may be helpful to give a brief Index of these interruptions and resumptions:

Introduction to the Achaean catalogue

Preliminary remarks

The catalogue lists 29 Achaean contingents covering most of the Greek world of Homer's time, or earlier; although it neglects the central Aegean islands, the whole of the Aegean coastline of western Asia Minor with its large off-lying islands of Samos, Khios and Lesbos, also the Megarid and much

Book Two

of the Thessalian plain. It accords closely with the rest of the *Iliad* in language and style (on which see pp. 170f., 173 below), and to a lesser degree in content. No major warriors or places from the bulk of the poem are omitted here, and the regions it neglects are also absent from the poem at large; there are however three major discrepancies over the areas ruled by Agamemnon, Odysseus and Akhilleus, and these will be discussed on pp. 180ff. The effect of the catalogue as a whole is somewhat daunting for most modern readers, or for all in fact who are not connoisseurs of ancient political geography; but ancient audiences and readers must have been fascinated in different ways by the document's coverage, conciseness and virtuosity of expression, quite apart from its mythical and patriotic relevance. Several medieval manuscripts and at least one papyrus omitted the whole thing (see on 496), but it certainly formed part of the epic as early as the late seventh century B.C.; indeed it is too skilfully attached and developed to be any kind of post-Homeric addition. Quite apart from its technical interest, moreover, it forms an imposing introduction to the march-out of troops and the gradual long process by which Zeus's promise to Akhilleus at the end of book 1 is brought into effect. G. P. Shipp has shown (*Studies*, 235-7) that it contains a number of 'late' linguistic features – as indeed any other equally long segment of the poem might do; at most that would put it in the same position as the developed similes, that is, as especially associated with Homer and the act of monumental composition. It might be felt that the catalogue, or anything resembling it, could only be accommodated in such a monumental epic, and cannot have been part of the regular oral tradition about the heroic past, the Troy saga in particular; for it would swamp any normal short song, and could not stand as such a song on its own. Similarly it is extremely unlikely to have been composed *ex nihilo* for its present place. These are important factors in the debate over whether its source was ultimately a 'real' list, versified or not, which originated close to the time of the Trojan War itself (and when we use that phrase we have to remember the possibility that the expedition might have been very seriously exaggerated, created almost, in the poetical tradition).

Literature

The following modern critical treatments are relevant:

1 B. Niese, *Der homerische Schiffskatalog* (Kiel 1873)
2 T. W. Allen, *The Homeric Catalogue of Ships* (Oxford 1921)
3 V. Burr, ΝΕΩΝ ΚΑΤΑΛΟΓΟΣ (Leipzig 1944)
4 G. Jachmann, *Der homerische Schiffskatalog und die Ilias* (Köln 1958)
5 D. L. Page, *History and the Homeric Iliad* (Berkeley 1959)
6 A. Giovannini, *Étude historique sur les origines du catalogue des vaisseaux* (Berne 1969)

Book Two

7 R. Hope Simpson and J. F. Lazenby, *The Catalogue of Ships in Homer's Iliad* (Oxford 1970)
8 Robert G. Buck, *A History of Boeotia* (Edmonton 1979)

Of these, 1 and 6 regard the catalogue as reflecting the political state of Greece in the seventh (or arguably the eighth) century B.C.; 4 (which has won little support) regards it as a post-Homeric pastiche; 2, 3, 5 and 7 apply archaeological and other considerations to show that it is based on a detailed source not much later than the time of the expedition against Troy (that is, probably, the mid to late thirteenth century B.C.).

Typical elements in the catalogue-entries

(1) *General syntactical structure of leader(s)/places statement*
There are three different modes, sometimes carefully varied for successive entries, sometimes not (an analogy is the way of introducing similes, e.g. ἠΰτε...or τῶν δ', ὡς...). They are here called A, B and C:

A 'Of the X's...Y (and Z) was/were leader(s), (of them) who dwelt in/possessed (etc.) D, E, F...' So the first entry (Boiotoi) and 5 others.
B 'Those who dwelt in/possessed (etc.) D, E, F...of them Y (and Z) was/were leader(s).' This is much the commonest mode, embracing the entries for Argos, Mukenai, Pulos and 14 others, with the Murmidones as a variant in addition.
C 'Y led (brought) (so many) ships from D (E, F...).' Four small contingents are described in this mode (which includes the ship-numbers, cf. F below), including that of (Salaminian) Aias. Somewhat similarly Odysseus led the Kephallenes, but the ship-number is postponed and expressed in a variant of the D-mode below.

Obviously this formal variation helps to avoid monotony in the listing, but it is also partly determined by other factors. Thus A seems to be chosen for contingents designated by an ethnic that can be placed emphatically as first word (and has either two or three long syllables in every case); thus Βοιωτῶν, Φωκήων, Λοκρῶν, Αἰτωλῶν, Κρητῶν, Μαγνήτων. Ethnics used for other contingents (Ἄβαντες, Ἀθηναῖοι, Ἀρκάδες, Ἐπειοί, Κεφαλλῆνες, Ἐνιῆνες) do not meet the metrical conditions (except for Μυρμίδονες, who are, however, conjoined at 684 with Ἕλληνες and Ἀχαιοί), and so are introduced in mode B. B in fact accounts for 18 out of the 29 entries and covers most of the really important contingents, with heavy concentration from Abantes at 536 to Doulikhion at 625 and also among the minor contingents toward the end. Mode C emphasizes a single leader, albeit of a small contingent, by placing his name as first word (although after αὐτάρ, as a necessary metrical concession, in the case of Odysseus). It also allows the ships to be mentioned at the beginning of the entry and in the same single verse, in 4 cases out of 5, aiding conciseness in 3 of those cases at least.

The upshot of these observations is (i) that the ultimate composer of the catalogue proceeded in accordance with the developed rules and tendencies of oral poetry, with formal variation kept to a functional minimum; and (ii) that there is no difference between the treatment of important (and in some sense 'archaic', even 'Mycenaean') contingents and minor ones which may seem intrusive or appended on other grounds, like several of those from northern Greece toward the end of the list.

(2) Expression of ship-numbers

D The commonest mode is 'together with them/him 40 black ships followed', τοῖς/τῷ δ' ἅμα τεσσαράκοντα μέλαιναι νῆες ἕποντο. This occurs 9 times, plus 3 variants in which 50 (πεντήκοντα) or 80 (τοῖσι δ' ἅμ' ὀγδώκοντα, 2x) replace the 40 ships. Thus this formular verse-form accounts for 12 out of the 29 contingents, with a considerable range of importance even over those that each bring 40 ships; generally, however, these are fairly minor in the *Iliad* as a whole, from Phocians, Locrians and Abantes to Aetolians, Eurupulos' contingent, Polupoites' contingent, Magnesians. Two of the three variants with higher ship-numbers apply to more important contingents (Argives and Cretans, with Athenians (50) making the third).

E Four more entries have a different formular verse, 'with (or for) them/him 30 hollow ships lined up', τοῖς/τῷ δὲ τριήκοντα γλαφυραὶ νέες ἐστιχόωντο (with 90, ἐνενήκοντα, substituted for 30 in the case of the Pylians). Here, typically of the metrical resourcefulness of oral poetry, 'hollow' replaces the 'black' of mode D and the 'relatively late but authentically Homeric' (Chantraine, *GH* I, 225) Ionian form νέες, with epsilon in the stem, is used rather than νῆες. The main verb is also varied, and it is notable that both 'followed' (as in D) and 'lined up', as here, describe sailing *to* Troy (i.e. from Aulis) and not being drawn up on the beach once there, as they are during the action of the poem as a whole.

F 'Y led (brought) (so many) ships from D (E, F...)' accounts for 4 more contingents, cf. mode C in the leader-entries above. The ship-number differs in 3 of the 4 cases in which this mode is used; it is always small, with the (totally unimportant) Enienes having the largest number, 22; then (Salaminian) Aias 12, Tlepolemos (Rhodes) 9 and Nireus (Sume) 3. (Odysseus also brought 12 ships, see under C.) It is noteworthy that all these are non-decimal numbers, i.e. not a 'round' 30, 40 etc.

G 'Of them Y was in command of (so many) ships', with varying numbers; for example 576 τῶν ἑκατὸν νηῶν ἦρχε κρείων Ἀγαμέμνων. There are

5 such entries, with contingents varying greatly in size and importance (Mukenai (100 ships), Lakedaimon (60), Arcadians (60), Eumelos (11), (Philoktetes) (7)); the main verb ἦρχ'/ε/εν is the common element, with no fixed position in the verse but some formular character (see below).

D, E, F and G account for 12, 4, 5 and 5 entries respectively; of the remaining 3, one is a variant of A (Boeotians, 'of them...50 ships went, κίον'), one of G (Murmidones, 'of them of 50 ships Akhilleus was leader, ἦν ἀρχός'), and the third is the unique Epeans (4 leaders each with 10 ships, 'ten swift ships followed each man', δέκα δ' ἀνδρὶ ἑκάστῳ|νῆες ἕποντο θοαί, 618f., in which verb and epithet correspond with D and the Boeotian variant respectively).

The D entries are bunched near the beginning of the catalogue (with 5 out of 6 from Phocians to Argives) and near its end (with 3 out of the last 4). The E's and F's are well distributed. The G-mode seems to be established by the important and closely-related group formed by the contingents of Agamemnon, Menelaos and the Arcadians (for whom Agamemnon supplied the ships), and then emulated near the end by the Eumelos and (Philoktetes) entries. The formular verses involved in D and E have already been observed; incidentally the former has feminine, the latter masculine main caesura – in other words they fulfil different metrical functions. The G entries are also interesting in this respect, since they make up a small formular system in which each verse is different but overlaps at least one other of the group in some aspect of phraseology and arrangement:

Mukenai:	τῶν ἑκατὸν νηῶν	ἦρχε κρείων 'Αγαμέμνων
	'Ατρεΐδης	(576f.)
Lakedaimon:	τῶν οἱ ἀδελφεὸς ἦρχε	βοὴν ἀγαθὸς Μενέλαος
	ἑξήκοντα νεῶν	(586f.)
Arcadians:	τῶν ἦρχ' 'Αγκαίοιο πάϊς	κρείων 'Αγαπήνωρ
	ἑξήκοντα νεῶν	(609f.)
Eumelos:	τῶν ἦρχ' 'Αδμήτοιο	φίλος πάϊς ἕνδεκα νηῶν
	Εὔμηλος	(713f.)
(Philoktetes):	τῶν δὲ Φιλοκτήτης	ἦρχεν τόξων ἐὺ εἰδώς
	ἑπτὰ νεῶν	(718f.)

Finally a note on the non-decimal ship-numbers (of which 22 is the largest, i.e. they are confined to small contingents). Twelve is useful because of its two possible forms, δυοκαίδεκα and δυώδεκα; 3 is a useful monosyllable if leader, place, ships and epithet are to be confined to a single verse, as with Nireus of Sume, and 9 serves an almost similar function with the Rhodians (as well as being a multiple of three for the assumed tripartite division of their fleet). Eleven produces a useful formula for after the bucolic diaeresis, ἕνδεκα νηῶν|, and 7 does something similar at the beginning of the verse,

|ἕπτα νεῶν. Gouneus' 22 ships are inexplicable (except as based on fact, which seems particularly unlikely in his case), especially since simple 20 is missing; but that may be just a question of how much of the verse needs to be filled. All the other multiples of 10 are there up to 100, with the exception only of the metrically intractable 70, ἑβδομήκοντα – a number which could nevertheless have been managed less directly, had the poet been more bound by hard information and less by conventional phrasing than he appears to be.

The conclusions to be drawn from all this correspond closely with those of the leader-entries, section (1): (i) that there is a degree of conventionality and indeed arbitrariness in the numbers assigned to many contingentś, especially of the 40-ship type, although important contingents tend to get larger numbers and unimportant ones smaller ones; and (ii) that the assignment of ships is handled in a developed formular manner and shows no trace of earlier technique or the survival of particularly archaic language or style.

(3) *Epithets for, and arrangement of, place-names*

Chapter IV of D. L. Page's *History and the Homeric Iliad* is entitled 'The Homeric description of Mycenaean Greece' and contains arguments in support of his own conclusion that 'the Catalogue is substantially a Mycenaean composition' (p. 124). Some of these arguments are, however, debatable, including that which concerns the epithets for places in the catalogue. There are about 180 places named there, divided between the 29 different contingents (with towns, which form the vast majority, are included a few regions, mountains, rivers or other landmarks). Most of these do not have any descriptive epithet, but about 62 do (sometimes the 'epithet' will be a formular phrase like ἐϋκτίμενον πτολίεθρον), or about 70 if we include looser geographical phrases like πηγῇς ἐπὶ Κηφισοῖο. A few of these epithets are applied to more than one place, e.g. ἐρατεινήν -άς, ἐϋκτίμενον πτολίεθρον, or even more specific ones like πολυστάφυλον or πολυτρήρωνα. Before discussing Page's conclusions it may be helpful to list the epithets under five general headings descriptive of their broad meaning or application (see Table 1 on p. 174).

The geographical phrases, as distinct from simple epithets or epithets + noun, are below the dotted line and are obviously fairly specific, describing such-and-such a place as 'under (Mt) Kullene' or 'around the streams of (river) Boagrios' or 'by the Boebean lake'. Even so, only a general indication of region or landscape is given. The epithets themselves are potentially more interesting. The question is, are they (like most epithets in the rest of the *Iliad*) conventional and standardized, moderately detailed perhaps but even then applicable to many or most subjects – people, objects

Table 1. Epithets for place-names.

well-built town	rocky, steep, high	fertile, broad, by sea/river	lovely, holy, rich	others
ἐϋκτίμενον πτολίεθρον	πετρήεσσαν	ἐϋαλον πτολίεθρον	ἱερόν	ἐσχατόωσαν
(αἰπύ) πτολίεθρον	αἰπύ/Αἰπύ	ἀγχίαλον	ἱεράων νησῶν	ἀργινόεντα
(ἐραλον) πτολίεθρον	αἰπεινήν	πολυστάφυλον	ζαθέην	λευκήν
πόλεις εὖ ναιεταόσας	τρηχεῖαν	ἀμπελόεντ'	δῖαν	(λευκὰ κάρηνα)
ἐϋκτιμένης -ην	πολύκνημον	ἀνθεμόεντ'	ἐρατεινάς -ήν	κοίλην
ἐΰκτιτον	κλωμακόεσσαν	εὐρεῖα	ἱμερτόν	κητώεσσαν
τειχιόεσσαν	ἠνεμόεσσαν	εὐρύχορον?	ἄφνειον	καλλιγύναικα
	πολυτρήρωνα	ποιήενθ'		ἑκατόμπολιν
	δυσχείμερον	λεχεποίην		
	λευκὰ κάρηνα?	πολύμηλον		
	εἰνοσίφυλλον	μητέρα μήλων		
πόλιν Εὐρύτου	ὑπὸ Κυλλήνης	πηγῇς ἐπὶ Κηφισοῖο	Ποσιδήϊον ἀγλαὸν ἄλσος	
		Βοαγρίου ἀμφὶ ῥέεθρα	Δήμητρος τέμενος	
		βαθὺν κατὰ κόλπον		
		ἐχούσας		
		Ἀλφειοῦ πόρον		
		παρὰ Βοιβηΐδα λίμνην		
		κρήνην (Ὑπέρειαν)		
		νησούς τε (Καλύδνας)		

or places as the case may be? Or are they different in kind? Page has maintained the latter: that many or most of the epithets are in fact very specific, like πολύκνημον, 'much-ridged', ἀγχίαλον, 'close to the sea', ἀργινόεντα, 'gleaming white', πολυτρήρωνα, 'with many doves'; and that, since these epithets are not normal Iliadic ones, this indicates a special knowledge of many of these catalogue towns – one that entered the heroic tradition from a special source, itself concerned with the accurate description and listing of places. Whether or not that source was a Mycenaean poem listing the Achaean ships and contingents at Aulis is not at present important; the question is, *are* these epithets, taken overall, so specific, and so different from the ordinary Iliadic range? It is my conclusion that they are not, and the tabulation opposite shows one of the reasons why. For the truth is that all the epithets (and other descriptive phrases) save about eight can be divided into one or other of four general categories of meaning. That a town is 'well-built' or 'walled', or 'rocky' or 'steep' in some sense, or 'fertile' or 'grassy' or 'with many flocks' on the other hand, does not presuppose any meticulous classification of particular places, since most ancient towns in Greece fitted easily under one or more of these headings. Some epithets, admittedly, are more specific in themselves, that is, add something to these general meanings: 'walled' perhaps implies 'with remarkable walls', and certainly Tiruns, which receives this epithet, was that, and so perhaps too Gortus in Crete which is so described – naturally, they are metrically equivalent, and perhaps if Mukenai had been so it, too, would have had its walls singled out for special mention.

Similarly J. G. Frazer among others found many pigeons in the cliffs near the site of Thisbe, which might give special force to the epithet πολυτρήρωνα (although Strabo, 9.411, found them near the port not the main town). Aulis is certainly 'rocky', and so is Puthon–Delphoi which shares the epithet – but so too are at least half the habitation-sites in Greece. Lukastos in Crete and Kameiros in Rhodes (in adjacent contingents, be it noted, at 647 and 656) share the description ἀργινόεντα, 'gleaming white'; the soil of the latter, at least, is sandy (rather than chalky), and the epithet might be carefully chosen – there are certainly many sites it would *not* suit – but then again it might not.

In the long and informative n. 22 on pp. 159f. of his book Page lists, in addition to some 30 places-name epithets common to both the catalogue and the rest of Homer, a dozen or so that come only in the former (including, indeed, πολυτρήρωνα, πολυστάφυλον, τειχιόεσσαν and ἀργινόεντα; also the two 'by the sea' epithets, ἔφαλον and ἀγχίαλον). Considering the catalogue's intention of recording in detail not merely the kingdoms but also the many specific towns, some obviously quite small, that the Achaean troops came from – as compared with the rest of the *Iliad*'s concern with families and regions, rather – I do not find this at all surprising. Page also remarks on several metrical equivalents both in the catalogue and in the remainder of the *Iliad*: for example πετρήεσσαν, τειχιόεσσαν, κητώεσσαν, καλλιγύναικα, κλωμακόεσσαν, μητέρα μήλων in the former, ποιήεσσα, παιπαλόεσσα, βωτιάνειρα in the latter. But this lack of 'thrift' does not necessarily show that these epithets must be specific to different places or, if so, that they are accurately assigned to these particular places listed in the catalogue; moreover it makes the degree of specificity no different from that of the *Iliad* at large, which makes no claim to be based upon a historical document. As for the Iliadic epithets whose omission in the catalogue might seem significant, several (πιδήεσσα, παιπαλόεσσα, βωτιάνειρα, ἐριβώλακα, ὑλήεσσα) refer to mountains, other natural features, or whole regions, and are generic. Of the rest only ἠμαθόεντος 'sandy' (4x of Pulos), πολυχρύσοιο 'of much gold' (2x of Mukenai, cf. 18.289 of Troy) and the two epithets about horses (εὔπωλον 2x of Troy, ἱπποβότοιο -ον 7x of Argos and once of Trikke) are at all striking at first sight – but then one realizes that 'sandy' and 'of much gold' are designed for formulas in the genitive case and near the verse-end, whereas the catalogue needs to place both Pulos and Mukenai, for emphasis, at the head of the verse. Somewhat similarly, if the catalogist had had occasion to mention the *region* Argos more than once in this list, the omission of 'horse-rearing' (which refers in the rest of the *Iliad* to the region not the town) would have been remarkable; but in fact he does not refer to the region at all. Moreover Argos, like the others, comes as first word in the verse and in the accusative, and is therefore not suited by an epithet designed for a different case and position. This is not a cast-iron argument, but it probably does much to dispose of a possible anomaly.

Whoever provided the basic materials of the catalogue obviously knew the Greece of his day (or the preceding generation, at least) quite well: well enough to recognize that Helos (wherever it was, exactly, in southern Laconia) was by the sea, that Anthedon was on the borders of Boeotia, that Dodone was in the mountains and had hard winters. Some of the epithets used are appropriate to particular places – Mukenai is known to be a 'well-built town', but what of the obscure Medeon, which rates the same description but must always have been a small site, one that is ignored by Pausanias and had changed its name by Strabo's time? Other descriptions are much vaguer, 'holy' or 'lovely' or 'flowering' or 'grassy' on the one hand, 'rocky' or 'rough' or 'steep' on the other. In short, the knowledge embodied in this catalogue tradition cannot be shown to be so detailed and specific in its use of epithets, at least, as to presuppose a purposeful source-document like a muster-list, let alone a Mycenaean one.

Finally in relation to the catalogue's epithets it is important to recognize that their use is much affected by the limited and conventionalized structure of the many verses whose primary purpose is to contain place-names. The first contingent to be listed, that of the Boeotians, is typical of the rest in this respect (except that it has a higher than usual proportion of epithets):

> 496 those who dwelt in Hurie and *rocky* Aulis
> and Skhoinos and Skolos and *many-ridged* Eteonos,
> and Thespeia and Graia and Mukalessos *with broad dancing-floors*
> and those who dwelt around Harma and Eilesion and Eruthrai
> 500 and possessed Eleon and Hule and Peteon
> and Okalee and Medeon, *well-built city,*
> and Kopai and Eutresis and Thisbe *of many doves,*
> and who (possessed) Koroneia and *grassy* Haliartos
> and who possessed Plataia and dwelt in Glisas
> 505 and who possessed Hypothebai, *well-built city,*
> and *sacred* Onkhestos, *Poseidon's lovely grove,*
> and who possessed Arne *of many vines,* and Mideia
> and *holy* Nisa and *remote* Anthedon
> – of them went fifty ships...

The italicizing points to the salient fact, that most of the epithets come in the second half of the verse; that is so with descriptive epithets in the oral hexameter style in general and has functional causes, but here in the catalogue it also provides a dramatic climax to many of these otherwise potentially monotonous verses, especially in the tripartite form 'X and Y and (epithet) Z' (like 497, 498, 502 in the sample). ἐϋκτίμενον πτολίεθρον, 'well-built city', is a valuable filler for the second half of the verse, which may explain the sublimation of Medeon in 501 and the anachronism in 505 (for Hupothebai was presumably a relatively humble suburb adjoining the Kadmeia, ruined or not). Only six epithets in the whole catalogue (sacred, holy, rich, hollow, by-the-sea, grapey), with two or three descriptive phrases like 'Demeter's shrine', are found in the first half of the verse. That, as noted, has its reasons, but here it produces the special consequence that many place-names are automatically deprived of any possible further description – because they fit best, for various other reasons, into the first half of the verse. Among these are important places like Argos, Mukenai and Pulos which evidently needed to be placed at the beginning of the verse for emphatic reasons.

The upshot of this is that the catalogue's place-name epithets, already seen to be for the most part very general in meaning, are also usually arbitrary in distribution, depending as they do to some considerable extent on the rigid and conventionalized arrangement of these particular verses.

Book Two

Special problems of the Achaean catalogue

Consideration of leaders, places mentioned and the order in which they are named is best remitted to the comments on individual contingents, but meanwhile these special topics deserve preliminary attention:

  (i)   the special prominence given to the Boeotians and their neighbours
 (ii)   the status of the Athenians and their relation to Salaminian Aias
(iii)   the kingdoms of Diomedes and Agamemnon
 (iv)   the extent of Nestor's domain
  (v)   the relation of Meges' kingdom to that of Odysseus
 (vi)   the switches, first to Crete and the south-eastern islands, then to central and northern Greece
(vii)   the kingdom of Akhilleus and the plausibility or otherwise of the other northern contingents.

(i) That the BOEOTIANS should be placed at the head of the list, and be given the highest number of leaders, places and troops, is remarkable in view of their minor role in the rest of the poem. The usual explanation, which clearly deserves serious consideration, is that this is somehow connected with the expedition having been assembled at Aulis in Boeotia before crossing the Aegean sea to Troy. The emphasis on the ships, the verbs applied to them (for example they 'followed', ἕποντο, the leader or leaders in the commonest, 40-ship formulation), and the initial description of the contingents of Protesilaos and Philoktetes as though they were still present, all make it probable that the catalogue at some earlier stage was conceived as a list of ships and battalions as they assembled at Aulis, and was then lightly adapted to make a list of contingents in the tenth year at Troy. In that case the Boeotian prominence must be the result either of Boeotian patriotism – or of non-Boeotian tact toward a temporary host, which seems rather far-fetched. The Boeotian colouring extends to surrounding contingents, too, in successive entries; for the Phocians, Locrians and Abantes (Euboeans) are all assigned numbers of ships and places that greatly exceed their minor importance in the *Iliad* as a whole; so e.g. Page, *HHI* 125. At the same time the list's systematic regional basis makes it natural that, once the Boeotians had been named at the beginning, their immediate neighbours (including of course Orkhomenos) should be mentioned next and perhaps in proportionate strength.

Modern scholars have been tempted to assign the unadjusted form of the catalogue to a supposed Boeotian 'school' of catalogue-poetry, and they rely on two supporting factors: the catalogue-oriented work of Boeotian Hesiod shortly after Homer (especially in his *Ehoiai* or Catalogue of Women, but also, to a considerable extent, in the *Theogony* and *Erga*), and the marked

178

Theban and Minyan associations of the list of heroines encountered by Odysseus in his descent to the underworld at *Od.* 11.235–330 (except for Lede at 298–304 and Phaidre etc. at 321–5). That might be so, but it would not particularly indicate a Mycenaean or near-Mycenaean date for the composition of the catalogue – rather a later period, if anything, closer to that of Homer and Hesiod themselves. According to Thucydides 1.12.3 the Boiotoi entered the region later to be called after them no earlier than sixty years after the Trojan war (for his afterthought to the effect that a group of them were there earlier is clearly a concession to the Homeric catalogue itself); but strictly that affects only their initial naming at verse 494, itself a rising threefolder and therefore perhaps a product of developed Homeric style. Other factors, especially the mention of *Hupo*thebai and the absence of the Kadmeioi, might seem to suggest an accurate knowledge of Theban affairs in the Late Bronze Age; but the truth is that this knowledge was available throughout the whole period of the mythological tradition and was not necessarily contemporary, or nearly so, with the geographical and political conditions of the Trojan War. The reduction of once-powerful Orkhomenos to a minor kingdom (it was subsequently to become part of Boeotia itself) again seems to reflect a genuine historical process, but one that could be elicited from the oral tradition at almost any time. For further conclusions about the twenty-nine recorded Boeotian towns (including one sanctuary) see on 494–510 below.

(ii) The ATHENIAN entry mentions no other place save Athens itself, characterized as 'well-built city' (546) and then given further detail through the description of Athene's protection of its early king Erekhtheus and the cult of him in her temple there – a ritual comment which could have been cumulated at almost any date. The failure to mention Marathon, Aphidna, Eleusis and Thorikos (for the last cf. *HyDem* 126) suggests strongly that synoecism (the incorporation of other towns and demes under Athens), credited in the mythical tradition to Theseus, is envisaged as having already taken place. It is doubly surprising in that case that Theseus is not even mentioned and that the Athenian commander is the otherwise obscure Menestheus son of Peteos. Page, *HHI* 145f., argues that this is an indication of the antiquity of the reference: Ionian poets would have opted for Theseus or one of his sons as leader, and Menestheus' very obscurity shows him to be a genuine early reminiscence. Giovannini (*Étude* 26) does not accept this reasoning; for him the substantial number, fifty, of Athenian ships and the comparatively elaborate Erekhtheus digression show that the composer knew Athens to be already important. One has to remember that the Mycenaean fortifications of the Acropolis would have continued to look imposing even through the Dark Age; even so, the Giovannini argument could well point to a date of composition after the city's strong economic recovery in the ninth century B.C. Menestheus remains difficult (his role in the rest of the poem is relatively minor), but at least he tends to guarantee the genuineness of the Aias entry which followed. This became a *cause célèbre* when the Megarians asserted that the Athenians had added the entry (in which Aias is said to have stationed his ships next to the Athenians) in order to bolster their claim to Salamis; but if they had interfered with this part of the text, they might reasonably have been expected to improve the Athenian role in the poem generally, not least through Menestheus. See further on 552–8.

(iii) The domains of DIOMEDES and AGAMEMNON, especially the exclusion of the latter from the Argive plain and the extension of his kingdom northward from Mukenai and along the Gulf of Corinth as far west as Aigion, are surprising to say the least. Agamemnon's realm appears incompatible with 108, where he is said to rule (in succession to Atreus and Thuestes) over 'many islands and all Argos' – what are these islands, if he is to be deprived of those of the Saronic gulf? Equally difficult is the idea that Mukenai and Argos, a mere eight miles apart, are to be treated as independent political units, and that Mukenai itself is to be cut off from the rich Argive plain which it must have been founded to exploit and protect. In the mythical tradition as a whole Mukenai is closely linked with Argos, in fact it is often difficult to tell which was the main seat of the family of Atreus. On the other hand the tale of the war between Argos and Thebes makes Adrastos king of Argos and treats him as independent of Mukenai; a trace of this shows in the *Iliad* itself, since at 4.376 (as T. W. Allen observed, *Catalogue* 66) Tudeus comes as an envoy to Mukenai from Argos as though to a foreign state. That Diomedes' father Tudeus had fled from his native Aetolia and joined the expedition of the Seven against Thebes is part of this whole tradition; his son Diomedes had been a member of the Epigonoi, the successors, who in the next generation captured Thebes where their parents had failed. Diomedes had returned to Argos, married Adrastos' daughter (cf. 5.412–15; his father had married her elder sister!), and evidently inherited the kingdom, so that his place in the catalogue is not in itself surprising. In the rest of the poem the question of his contingent, exactly whom he commands, is kept strangely silent (especially so in the fifth book which he dominates), except only at 23.471 where he is alluded to by Idomeneus as 'Aetolian by race, but he rules among Argives'.

As for Agamemnon, his separation from the Argive plain is only one of the difficulties; it also cuts him off from his brother Menelaos' kingdom of Lakedaimon and makes his own possession of seven towns in the southwestern Peloponnese (9.149–56) even more puzzling. Page (*HHI* 130–2) avoids the whole problem by concluding that Diomedes must have been a subordinate ally of Agamemnon, who chose to live in Mukenai rather than

Argos because of 'precedent and prestige'; but that is not what the separate catalogue entries suggest. Moreover there is one passage in the remainder of the poem which may show *Sikuon* as coming under Agamemnon's control, and therefore confirm the catalogue's version of his sphere of authority; that is 23.296–9, where we are told that Ekhepolos of Sikuon had given a mare to Agamemnon in order not to have to accompany him to Troy. That is not absolutely watertight, for others, not direct subjects, tried to buy themselves out of joining the expedition; but it slightly strengthens the possibility that the catalogue is here reflecting a real state of affairs (incidentally Adrastos of Argos had himself been a refugee at Sikuon, where he also had a cult: Herodotus 5.67.1). That implies a different period from that of the poem at large, and one in which Mukenai had been forced to look northward to maintain its wealth. In fact the Corinthian plain is almost as rich as the Argive, and Mukenai's position gave it access across the low range of hills it controlled. If such a shift in the politics and economics of the north-eastern Peloponnese ever occurred it is likely to have been in the period of decline at the very end of the Bronze Age and not before, when Mukenai's political and cultural supremacy seems to have been unshaken.

(iv) All the earlier groups of contingents in the catalogue have had their problems (Boeotians and their neighbours; Athens and Aias; Argos and Mukenai); the next group, at 581–624, consists of the contingents of Menelaos, of Nestor, of the Arcadians and of the Epeans, and here it is the kingdom of NESTOR that causes certain difficulties. Menelaos' towns are obviously set in the Eurotas valley and the Tainaron peninsula – it is a narrow Lakedaimon, but a geographically possible one either for the Mycenaean period or for somewhat later. On the other hand Nestor's realm (on which see 591–4n.) does not really correspond, except for Pulos itself and perhaps Kuparisseis and (unknown) Aipu, with that of the Linear B tablets from Pulos; indeed only Pulos and probably Arene = classical Samikon can be given a definite location. Dorion = Malthi is usually accepted but is far from certain. At least Pulos receives some confirmation from the tablets as being the Messenian one, since the palace at Ano Englianos is almost certainly 'Nestor's'. Otherwise Nestor's contingent does not look strongly Mycenaean in character, so far at least. Moreover the seven cities offered by Agamemnon to Akhilleus in book 9 (149–56 = 291–8) lie νέαται Πύλου ἠμαθόεντος (153 = 295) – strictly this means 'at the lowest part of sandy Pulos' (cf. Chantraine, *Dict.* s.v. νειός), but 'below Pulos', i.e. just outside its borders, is a permissible extension of meaning. They are dotted round the Messenian Gulf on either side of Pherai = modern Kalamata; this is a region that falls between Nestor's kingdom and that of Menelaos, in a reference that is just as likely to be a Mycenaean reminiscence as anything in the catalogue itself. Therefore the omission of these seven towns, at least most of which were on Mycenaean sites, does nothing to support the idea of the catalogue as in essence a Mycenaean document. Finally there is a marked overlap of place-names between Nestor's reminiscences of local wars with northern and north-eastern neighbours, at 7.132ff. and 11.670ff., and the catalogue entries for Pulos, Arcadians and Epeans – the latter group being slightly the fuller. Imitation one way or the other is improbable, and a common tradition must be assumed. Page (*HHI* 254f., supported with greater caution by Hope Simpson and Lazenby (henceforth HSL) 87) is confident that this tradition goes back to two generations before the Trojan War (because Nestor is a very old man then); but there is no hard evidence to suggest this rather than the possibility of development in the early Dark Age – as other scholars (references in Page, n. 116 on p. 295) have urged.

(v) Two contingents from the North-West of Greece, particularly its offshore islands, are puzzling. At 631–7 ODYSSEUS leads the Kephallenes, who are said to possess Ithake, Neritos with shaking leaves, Krokuleia and rough Aigilips, Zakunthos and Samos, and 'the mainland and parts across the water'. Neritos is suggested to be a mountain by its epithet, and indeed *Od.* 9.21f. and 13.351 show it to be in Ithake: I agree with HSL 103f. that Krokuleia and Aigilips are likely to be other Ithacan natural features, although they are not mentioned in the *Odyssey*. Zakunthos is indubitably the island of that name, and the facing part of the mainland is either part of Elis (the Ithacan Noemon keeps horses there according to *Od.* 4.634–7) or part of Acarnania. Samos must be either the whole of the island later known as Kephallenia, or the northern part of it; at *Od.* 4.671 the suitors are to lie in wait for Telemakhos 'in the strait between Ithake and rugged Samos', and it is highly probable that the whole island was originally called Samos (or Same), and was later known as Kephallenia after its inhabitants the Kephallenes.

That is Odysseus' kingdom, logical so far as it goes although surprisingly small for one who is a major commander in the rest of the poem. The surprise is greater because of the immediately preceding contingent, that of MEGES at 625–30. He leads forty ships 'from Doulikhion and the holy Ekhinaes islands which are dwelt in across the sea facing Elis'. He himself had come to Doulikhion as a refugee, presumably from Elis (since he is counted as an Epean leader at *Il.* 13.691f.). In classical times the Ekhinades islands were the small group in the northern approaches to the Corinthian Gulf, and they included a long narrow island called Doulikhion, which means 'long'; Strabo 10.458 identifies it with the one mentioned here in the catalogue. The trouble is that the Ekhinades group and its Doulikhion are virtually barren ('rough living for a goat', Page commented of the latter, *HHI* 163), whereas Meges leads 40 ships against Odysseus' mere 12. It is not as though Meges were a well-known character who has to be provided with a home somehow; rather Doulikhion seems to have been a place that deserved to be mentioned, and the somewhat obscure Meges is found to command it – although that leaves the problem of why it was not simply assigned to Odysseus. Where is the Homeric Doulikhion? Leukas is one possibility, favoured by HSL 101 after T. W. Allen (whether or not it could be regarded as an island is irrelevant here, since 625 does not necessarily categorize Doulikhion as such). Admittedly it is longer than it is broad, fertile in parts and close to Ithake; on the other hand Kerkura–Corfu, though further to the north and identified from at least the time of Thucydides with the Odyssean Skherie, is quite notably long and narrow and exceptionally fertile; it is relevant that according to *Od.* 16.247–51 Doulikhion supplied 52 suitors, Same 24, Zakunthos 20 and Ithake 12. Yet too much weight should not, perhaps, be attached to these considerations; the probability is that Odysseus was a folk-hero of western Greece who was drawn into the Ionian heroic tradition somewhat erratically. That accounts both for the Homeric vagueness and inconsistencies over geography in that relatively distant part of the world, and for the discrepancy between Odysseus as a minor leader in the catalogue and as one of the most important of all (although still with certain limitations) in the rest of the poem.

(vi) Although the places named for each contingent are usually in no particular logical order, the contingents themselves are presented, for the most part, in a conspicuous geographical sequence. Page (*HHI* 134f.) was emphatic that the catalogue is 'a list of participants in a military campaign' and not 'a sort of topographical survey'; but one cannot overlook the careful geographical progress that is maintained, with two breaks, in the order of contingents; G. Jachmann, *Schiffskatalog* 183, is right about that. The catalogue is based neither on a *periplous* (since it describes regions in the interior as well as round the coast) nor on a *periegesis* (since that kind of literary tour is hardly known before the second century B.C.): so Giovannini, *Étude* 52. Yet it reveals a distinct interest in the political geography of Greece and is quite certainly not a direct relic of a muster-list at Aulis – unless the contingents are supposed to have arrived there, and to have stationed themselves on arrival, in the exact order of their regions of origin! What seems to have happened is that the compiler or composer of the catalogue (whoever that was), having decided to start from Boeotia and indeed from Aulis, moved round the borders of Boeotia so as to take in (and give special prominence to, in most cases) its immediate neighbours: Orkhomenos, the Phocians, the (eastern) Locrians, the Abantes in Euboea, finally the Athenians with Salamis appended. From Salamis the list moves onward, skipping Megara and the Megarid, into the north-eastern Peloponnese. Now starts another, clockwise sweep from the Argolid and Mukenai (with Corinthia, Sikuon and eastern Achaea intervening) down to Lakedaimon, Pulos, the Arcadians and finally the Epeans in the later Elis. From there in the north-west Peloponnese we move to the realms of Meges and Odysseus (see (v) above), then back across to the Aetolians on the facing mainland. There the circuit abruptly stops and a new start is made with the central Cretans a couple of hundred miles to the south. The second 'tour' moves from Crete to Rhodes and then to the small and unimportant island kingdoms of Sume and Kos (the latter including Kasos and Karpathos which actually lie on the route from eastern Crete to Rhodes). Here, once again, the geographical progress is interrupted; an even more abrupt switch is made back across the Aegean and up to Akhilleus' Myrmidon contingent from the Sperkheios valley on the southern borders of the later Thessaly. The third and final 'tour' now moves round the edge of Thessaly (as we call it; the Thessaloi, who entered the area after the Trojan War, are ignored by Homer), more or less anti-clockwise this time, making a brief excursion across the Pindus to Dodone and ending with the Magnetes back in the east.

The question arises why the catalogue does not maintain its progress through Greece continuously, or nearly so, and without the two major interruptions and restarts. Two possible explanations, not necessarily mutually exclusive, seem to me worth considering. (1) Giovannini (*Étude* 53ff.) has made the valuable observation that various lists of political units were made in geographical order and recorded in inscriptions of the classical and Hellenistic periods. The Athenian tribute-list is an obvious example, and it may have had earlier precedents. But there was another well-known genre of inscriptions, whose origins might be traced up to the early years of the Olympic games at least, which could be more significant. That is the list of θεωροδόκοι or 'receivers of sacred envoys'; cities responsible for the administration of international religious festivals would record the names of officials in other cities throughout Greece with whom their envoys had made contact and who would ensure that the sacred truce was observed and the proper delegations sent. The fullest evidence comes from a Delphic inscription of around 200 B.C. (*BCH* 45 (1921) 4–31; further references in Giovannini, 55 n. 6). As it happens this records five or six itineraries followed by the θεωροί or sacred envoys, of which three are remarkably similar to, although more extensive than, the three 'tours' of the catalogue; for one is to 'Boeotia and the Peloponnese', another to 'Thessaly and Macedonia' and a third 'to Crete'. It is clear that envoys were despatched simultaneously in different directions, along different traditional routes which would also, no doubt, be practical ones in geographical terms. This is interesting, for it offers a possible kind of explanation for why the catalogue falls into three separate 'tours'; but I find it hard to accept Giovannini's further conclusion that it must be specifically based on a seventh-century B.C. predecessor of the surviving Delphic list. I continue, for example, to believe that the Boeotian focus of our catalogue is probably due to the tradition of the expedition's assembly at Aulis (and not to the proximity of Boeotia to Delphi). Yet Giovannini deserves great credit for drawing attention to an important possibility: that there was a long-standing tradition of the simultaneous despatch of sacred envoys along traditional routes covering all the Greek cities, and that the structure of the catalogue, whatever special information may be derived from Mycenaean times, is modelled on such a tradition.

There is, however (2), a second kind of consideration which is relevant to the first, and might complement, amend or even possibly replace it as an explanation of the form of the Homeric list. It is quite simply that the three routes of the catalogue, once it chose to start from Boeotia, are natural ones in terms of the political and physical geography of Greece, whether in the Late Bronze Age or in the Dark Age or indeed in Homer's own period. (It is worth noting, in passing, that Pausanias, too, made a clockwise tour through Greece, starting from Athens.) Given that the survey of the Peloponnese starts from the Isthmus of Corinth and takes in part of Achaea in its first stage, it will then either have to stop there, or continue across the Corinthian gulf to Aetolia and western Locris, or move to the offshore islands. The need to mention Odysseus, if nothing else, ensures that it will do the last of these three. After Ithake and thereabouts it has no alternative to moving across to Aetolia, given that Thesprotia and Acarnania are relatively unimportant, that the Pindos mountains block any move to the north-east, and that Aetolia must be included if only for the legendary importance of Kaludon. Having reached Aetolia this particular circuit has to be interrupted, otherwise it would complete itself by reaching Phocis again (and thus bring a false conclusion to the catalogue as a whole) – it would also entail traversing the unimportant western Locris, which as things are is omitted both from the catalogue and from the rest of the poem. The result is that the compiler started on a wholly new area. Central Crete and Rhodes (at least) had to be covered, the former because of Idomeneus quite apart from political geography; the movement is now from Crete to Rhodes (via Kasos and Karpathos, although these are slightly displaced) and ends with Kos and Kalumnos. What is also surprising here is that the route is not extended either northward to Samos and Khios, or westward to take in the Cyclades at least. Such omissions constitute an independent puzzle, and one that cannot be solved in the present instance by postulating the loss of a complete itinerary. In any event the progress simply stops once again, and the catalogue continues directly with its third and final area. Beginning with Akhilleus' contingent from around the Sperkheios valley, it proceeds up to the north side of Mt Othrus (Protesilaos' contingent), then to Pherai and Iolkos (Eumelos' contingent, with Philoktetes' somewhere beyond), then to three realms in the northern and central reaches of the Thessalian plain, finally across to the Pindus again and then back to the Magnetes. That makes a slightly erratic but at least reasonably complete tour of most parts of north-central Greece as far up as Mt Olumpos; a tour that could have started from eastern Locris had the composer or compiler not been deflected southward by the need to complete the inner circle of Boeotia's immediate neighbours.

The above general consideration shows that the arrangement of the catalogue and its two major changes of direction could be the result, not of particular precedents in the routes taken by e.g. religious ambassadors, but of inevitable facts in the geography of Greece itself, and the way that anyone, particularly without modern maps, might respond to them. More could be made of such an argument – which for present purposes, however, may help to remove one of the catalogue's many complications.

(vii) Page, *HHI* 126, makes two points very emphatically: (1) that AKHILLEUS, the greatest hero in the *Iliad*, 'is being confined to a relatively obscure and insignificant territory'; (2) that in the rest of the *Iliad* 'the dominions of his father Peleus... extend to Iolkos and Mount Pelion'. Hope Simpson and Lazenby (HSL 129) have dealt very neatly with both of these assertions. (1) is correct as far as it goes, but there is nothing to show that Akhilleus' homeland was, or even should be, of great political or military importance. He was a well-known individual fighter in the poetical tradition, but that does not mean that like Agamemnon he had to be a great ruler back on the Greek mainland. (2) is incorrect; both Page and Leaf, whom Page cites on this point, had falsely assumed that dealings between Akhilleus' father Peleus and the Centaur Kheiron (cf. *Il.* 16.143f.) showed Peleus' kingdom to extend to the Pelion area. That Peleus had some historical associations with Pelion is shown by his name, but there is nothing in the *Iliad* as a whole to suggest anything more than that; rather the poem confirms the catalogue at this point by emphasizing Akhilleus' connexions with the river Sperkheios (e.g. 23.141f.).

The kingdoms to the north of Mt Othrus, those which roughly surround the plain of the later Thessaly, vary greatly in their inherent plausibility. (a) The kingdom of Protesilaos (its contingent commanded by Podarkes after Protesilaos' death on arrival at Troy) extended inland from the whole western shore of the Pagasitic Gulf; only Pteleon in the south and Purasos in the north can be located with virtual certainty, although Strabo (9.435) was sure that Antron lay close to the south of Pteleon, also on the coast. (b) Eumelos was the legendary ruler of Pherai, which like Iaolkos (Iolkos) became an important city and can be securely located (although see on 711–12); presumably his kingdom included the whole of Lake Boibe. (c) Philoktetes' kingdom, which comes next at 716ff., is harder. It is marked by four place-names, of which two can only be set somewhere on the coast and neither Olizon nor Meliboia are 'established' as HSL indicate on their map 7. The contingent of Magnetes under Prothoos came from 'around Peneios and Pelion with shaking leaves' according to 757; the only way to allow that is to give them the region north of Mt Pelion, and confine Philoktetes to a small kingdom south of it, albeit one containing the eastern shore of the Pagasitic Gulf. The whole peninsula was of course part of Magnesia by historical times. (d) The sons of Asklepios ruled those from Trikke, Ithome and Oikhalie (729ff.); at least the first of these can be fixed, in the modern Trikala, and the kingdom seems to have occupied the north-western corner of the Thessalian plain. Eurupulos' kingdom (734ff.) is harder; neither Ormenion nor Asterion can be securely located, and Titanos may be a mountain, a town, or the acropolis of Asterion. HSL 143 conclude that it lies 'in the south-eastern part of the western plain of Thessaly'. (e) The Lapith kingdom of Polupoites (738ff.) has one reasonably identified place, Argissa = historic Argura (so Strabo 9.440, who is probably correct here although erratic in several of his other identifications around Thessaly); Oloosson = historic Elasson is more speculative. That places it in the northern part of the Thessalian plain and the southern foothills of Mt Olumpos. Gouneus' kingdom (748ff.) is a far more tenuous affair, but Dodone brings it into Epirus (which did indeed have its Mycenaean settlements), unless like Strabo we discover a Thessalian place of that name (cf. HSL 149). Finally Prothoos' Magnetes have been discussed under (c) above. Further discussion of locations will be found under each contingent.

There is a degree of vagueness over some, at least, of these northern contingents. That is not surprising, perhaps, considering that the Thessalian region lacked the strong natural boundaries, on all sides, of many Greek states, apart from the plain itself in the centre and the mountains surrounding it. Parts of the region were, nevertheless, quite fully settled during the Late Bronze Age, and some of this settlement is ignored by the catalogue. During the subsequent 'Dark Age' there was a drastic regrouping of political units, initiated no doubt by the incursion of the Thessaloi (ignored, as already noted, by Homer) some two generations after the end of the Trojan War: cf. Thucydides 1.12.3. Any lacunae in this part of the catalogue are as likely to emerge from that period or its immediate successor as from any other.

Now, after two pages of maps, the detailed Commentary can continue.

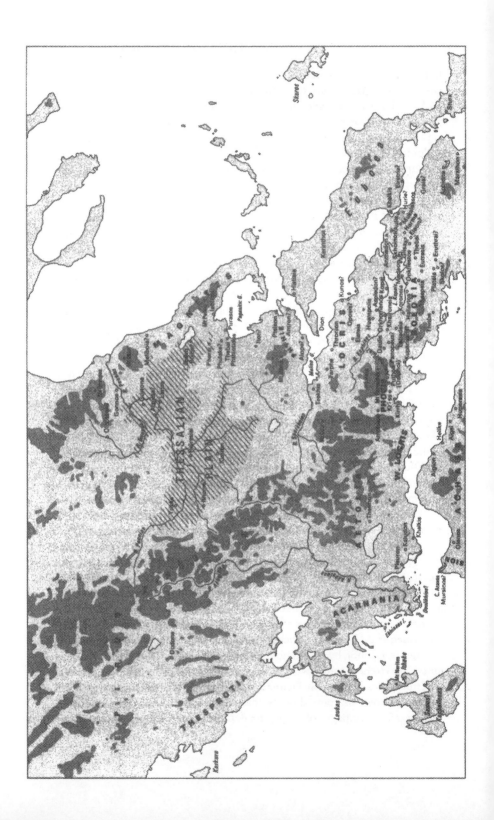

I Mainland Greece

Book Two

494–510 THE BOEOTIAN CONTINGENT. (See also pp. 178f. and 194f. for general discussions of the problems raised by this untypical entry.) As well as being first to be listed, this is also by far the largest in the number of places named, largest in number of leaders and presumably second largest after Agamemnon's contingent (cf. 580) in number of troops (only fifty ships, not exceptional, but with the unique detail that 120 went in each ship; the complement is specified in only one other entry, at 719, where Philoktetes' seven ships each had 50 rowers; see also on 491–3 and 509–10). Introductory syntax is mode A (see p. 170 above: 'of the X's...Y and Z...were leaders...(of those) who dwelt in A, B, C...'). Ship-number expression at 509f. is unique in the verb used (κίον for ἕποντο or ἐστιχόωντο), and paralleled only by the equally untypical Myrmidon entry at 685, τῶν αὖ πεντήκοντα νεῶν ἦν ἀρχὸς Ἀχιλλεύς; it is nevertheless traditional in some of its components (e.g. κίον – ∪ ∪ – ∪ |; ἑκάστη(-η) etc. at the verse-end). The departure from the usual modes D, E, F and G (pp. 171f.) must be in order to compress the statement of actual ship-numbers so as to accommodate the relatively complex detail about 120 men in each into little more than a single verse. If so, that is a very deliberate appendage.

494–5 Three of the five commanders are obscure: Klonios and Arkesilaos occur only once in the main body of the poem, when they are killed by Hektor in the same group of victims at 15.329–42; Prothoenor is killed at 14.450 (where his father is said to be Areilukos, likely to be a cardboard figure since another Areilukos is killed at 16.308). The two main leaders are obviously mentioned first; they are somewhat more prominent, although by no means conspicuous, in the rest of the poem. There they are mentioned together on two separate occasions, and that is important – it means that the catalogue and the *Iliad* at large are not entirely independent creations. Page (*HHI* 136) thought that this and similar associations prove 'that both have ultimately a common origin in poetry about the Trojan War', but that does not follow. It is quite possible, for example, that the Boeotian entry – which certainly contains much non-Iliadic detail – was elaborated by the main composer, Homer, to fit in with, and make use of, details from the rest of the poem; and it is interesting that Peneleos and Leitos are named in the rising threefold type of verse of which the monumental composer was evidently a master. Both these heroes are exhorted by Poseidon at 13.91f., both are wounded at 17.597–604; otherwise Peneleos is mentioned independently twice, Leitos once. The Boiotoi as a fighting group make one further appearance in the unusual small catalogue (together with Ionians and Phthians) at 13.685–700.

496–508 The 29 places named are as follows (with brief notes on location and finds, in which HSL refers to Hope Simpson–Lazenby, Giov to Giovannini, B to Buck):

HURIE (496)   Close to Aulis according to Strabo 9.404; usually identified with the Mycenaean mound-site at Dramesi, where a prehistoric stele with engravings of ships was found (cf. C. W. Blegen, *Hesperia* Suppl. 8 (1949) 39–42), but B prefers another site closer to Khalkis. HSL 19 note that no Protogeometric (hereafter PG) or Geometric (hereafter G) pottery has been found at Dramesi, and imply that this supports a Mycenaean origin for the reference to Hurie; but Hesiod refers to it in a context quite independent of Homer's catalogue, and that proves that it was known in the mythological tradition and available to a catalogist at any time (frags. 181 and 253 M–W).

AULIS (496)   Location not in doubt; continuously occupied into the early Iron Age, and politically independent until the fifth century B.C. (Giov 24). Epithet πετρήεσσαν, 'rocky', is suitable for the Aulis site – and many others, of course.

SKHOINOS (497)   Likewise independent until the fifth century B.C. (Giov 24); Strabo 9.408 placed it a few miles out of Thebes on the Anthedon road (and so perhaps near Lake Hulike/Likeri, HSL 21).

SKOLOS (497)   Its ruins were placed by Pausanias, 9.4.4, in the territory of Plataia, but cannot be securely identified with any particular Mycenaean or other ancient sites, although there are several small ones in the area.

ETEONOS (497)   Position unknown; in the Parasopia according to Strabo 9.408, though he assumed it had changed its name to Skarphe. Epithet πολύκνημον, 'many-spurred', suits many sites in Boeotia, but not for example those round Lake Kopais.

THESPEIA (498)   Presumably at or near the site of classical Thespiai, where some Mycenean pottery has been found (HSL 22).

GRAIA (498)   Probably a *kome* of Oropos in the fifth century (cf. Thucydides 2.23.3; Giov 25); a possible Mycenaean site is mentioned by HSL 22, but B prefers the Dramesi site usually allotted to Hurie. According to Pausanias 9.20.2 the inhabitants of Tanagra (omitted by the catalogue) claimed that its early name was Graia; there is at least some phonetic similarity. See also J. M. Fossey in *Euphrosyne* 4 (1970) 3–22.

MUKALESSOS (498)   Its ruins were known to Pausanias (9.19.4) and are probably to be identified with an ancient site near the modern village of Rhitsona; a little Mycenaean pottery has been found there, but the cemetery dates back to the mid-eighth century B.C. (HSL 22f.); it is also mentioned in *HyAp* 224. Epithet εὐρύχορον, 'with broad dancing-floor(s)', which does not necessarily have a geographical implication.

HARMA (499)   Was near Mukalessos, and its ruins were seen by Pausanias (9.19.4) and Strabo (9.404), who connect its name with Amphiaraos being engulfed by the earth with his chariot, ἅρμα, as he fled from Thebes. It is usually located at an ancient site (with Mycenaean and classical sherds, but no PG or G so far) commanding the pass on the road from Thebes to Khalkis. The lack of Dark Age and ninth-/eighth-century pottery does not mean that knowledge of Harma must be Mycenaean in immediate origin, since the Amphiaraos connexion might have been a long-standing one (and enabled an otherwise inconspicuous place called 'Harma' to have survived in the legendary tradition).

EILESION (499)   Location 'quite uncertain', HSL 23.

ERUTHRAI (499)   The classical town was absorbed by Thebes in the fifth century (Giov 24); it was in the region of Plataia but its exact location is unknown, and there is little point in trying to choose between various Mycenaean hill-tops in the neighbourhood, if only because that assumes that it (and the catalogue's reference to it) must have originated in the Late Bronze Age.

ELEON (500)   Was a political unit, and shared a border with Tanagra, in the fifth century according to Pausanias 1.29.6; it is usually identified with an extensive Mycenaean site (also classical, but no PG or G so far) near the modern village which has been so renamed, 'overlooking the eastern part of the Theban plain...a settlement second only to Thebes in the Theban plain' (HSL 24f.).

HULE (500)   Is mentioned elsewhere in the *Iliad* (at 5.708f.) as bordering the 'Kephisian lake', i.e. Lake Kopais, but nothing else is known.

PETEON (500)   In Theban territory and near the road to Anthedon according to Strabo 9.410, but nothing else is known and there is no obviously suitable site.

OKALEE (501)   At *HyAp* 239–43 the god crosses the Kephisos river and passes 'Ὠκαλέην πολύπυργον ('with many towers') before reaching Haliartos, but no suitable site is known. The information in the Hymn seems independent of the catalogue.

MEDEON (501)   Near Onkhestos according to Strabo 9.410; it is usually identified with a small Mycenaean acropolis at Kastraki west of Davlosis on the south-eastern shore of Lake Kopais (HSL 26; they say that no PG or G has been found there, but B 12 mentions Dark Age remains). The conventional description ἐϋκτίμενον πτολίεθρον, 'well-built town', does not suit this small site well.

KOPAI (502)   Was on Lake Kopais (Pausanias 9.24.1) and can be identified by inscriptions with a site at modern Topolia (B 8); some PG sherds have now been found, as well as sparse Mycenaean.

EUTRESIS (502)   Is firmly identified by an inscription with a site at the north end of the Leuktra plain, some 8 miles south-west of Thebes. There are traces of Mycenaean circuit-walls; it seems to have been abandoned at the end of the Bronze Age and not properly resettled until the sixth century B.C. This is important, since Eutresis has no strong legendary associations to guarantee it a place in the oral tradition (in contrast with e.g. Harma). It is also unusual in having been scientifically excavated and published (H. Goldman, *Excavations at Eutresis in Boeotia* (Cambridge, Mass. 1931)). That gives special significance to the evidence of desertion, although even that is uncertain since 'two small fragments of geometric pottery were picked up on the site' (p. 8), and the sixth-century town was not built precisely over the prehistoric one. Yet the absence of PG and G is still striking in the new ploughing around the low hill-top, as I noticed in January 1984.

THISBE (502) Location is confirmed by inscriptions near the modern town so named, 'about four kilometres from the sea in the Permessus valley' (B 11). The Mycenaean and the classical (and possibly earlier) towns occupied different hills, so the absence of PG and G sherds so far is not necessarily significant. Epithet πολυτρήρωνα, 'with many doves'; modern pigeons have been observed in profusion in the neighbourhood, see p. 175.

KORONEIA (503) The location on a hill overlooking the south-western part of Lake Kopais is certain, and there was a polis there by the end of the ninth century at least (B 9of.). PG and G are still missing from the long record of habitation (B 6, based on more recent information than HSL 28). According to Strabo 9.411 Koroneia was taken by the Boiotoi after the Trojan War – in other words he connected it especially with the tradition recorded by Thucydides (1.12.3) that the Boiotoi entered Boeotia only sixty years after Troy fell.

HALIARTOS (503) Mentioned in *HyAp* 243, it was a large settlement on the southern shore of Lake Kopais from Mycenaean times on (PG is lacking so far, but G has been found). Its epithet ποιήενθ', 'grassy', is not really appropriate to its location.

PLATAIA (504) The classical city is identified, and the early habitation area seems to have been north-west of it, where Mycenaean, Geometric and Early Corinthian sherds provide 'some evidence of continuity at the site' (HSL 29).

GLISAS (504) Was probably a polis in the fifth century, and is mentioned by Herodotus at 9.43.2; Strabo 9.412 described it as on Mt Hupatos, modern Sagmatas, and it is usually placed at a small acropolis (Mycenaean and classical sherds) near Syrtzi. Teumessos, which is mentioned in *HyAp* at 224, was only a mile away according to Pausanias 9.19.1, but is ignored by the catalogue.

HUPOTHEBAI (505) Excavation has shown that the fortified Mycenaean palace, the Kadmeia, was destroyed before the burning of Troy VIIa, which accords with the Homeric tradition (4.406) for what that is worth. The name *Under*-Thebes was presumably given to the surviving settlement round the acropolis; how long can it have retained that name before 'Thebes' was restored? Not very long, one might imagine, which would confirm a late- or Sub-Mycenaean origin for this detail. The descriptive formula 'well-built town' does not accord with a particularly lowly status for Hupothebai, but seems to be applied somewhat arbitrarily (see on Medeon, for example).

ONKHESTOS (506)   Is specified here as the sanctuary, not the nearby town; its probable site is known (HSL 30f.), but the absence of PG or G sherds is probably accidental, since the description of the curious ritual there at *HyAp* 230–8 shows that the sanctuary was well established (and presumably ancient) in the late seventh or early sixth century B.C. That is confirmed by Hesiod frag. 219 M–W.

ARNE (507)   Its location was and is unknown; Strabo 9.413 asserted that, like Mideia, it had been swallowed by Lake Kopais, whereas Pausanias 9.40.5f. said that it was the old name of Khaironeia (a conspicuous omission from the catalogue) – a claim which has less plausibility than that Graia (q.v.) was Tanagra. Attempts to connect it with the huge Mycenaean *enceinte* at Gla have little to be said for them. Its epithet πολυστάφυλον, 'of many vines', is conventional and probably unspecific.

MIDEIA (507)   Was treated very much like Arne; Strabo said it had been engulfed, Pausanias (9.39.1) claimed it as the ancient name of Lebadeia, another conspicuous absentee. It is utterly unknown.

NISA (508)   Strabo, citing Apollodorus, who wrote a treatise on the places in the catalogue, said that no sign of it was to be found in Boeotia (9.405). Some in antiquity tried to identify it with Nisaia in the Megarid, a region otherwise ignored in the catalogue, but this looks like a counsel of despair. Its epithet is ζαθέην, 'holy', which, if it is not just a metrical convenience, might tend to associate it with the ubiquitous Nusa that was claimed as a haunt of Dionusos.

ANTHEDON (508)   A certainly identified site (through inscriptions) at modern Mandraki on the coast north of the Euripos. Mycenaean and Geometric (down to Hellenistic) sherds were found on the acropolis overlooking the harbour, the only one apart from Aulis and probably Hurie to be mentioned. Its epithet ἐσχατόωσαν presumably means 'on the borders', which is true; see on 507–8.

The places omitted are important, in a survey which obviously set out to be comprehensive and included several which must have been relatively minor at any period. Apart from the huge fortress-site at Gla in Lake Kopais (unless that was Arne, Mideia or Nisa, which is unlikely), they are above all Tanagra, Khaironeia and Lebadeia – important cities in the Archaic and classical periods, and with a proved Mycenaean background in the first two cases at least. Teumessos and Alalkomenai should probably also be added; for the former see under Glisas above, while Alalkomeneis is an epithet of Athena at *Il.* 4.8 and 5.908 – both were known in the legendary and/or cultic tradition. Finally one would expect Kreusis, the port of Thebes on the Corinthian Gulf (at modern Livadhostro) and with Mycenaean and Archaic remains, to have been included. Khaironeia and Lebadeia are in western Boeotia close to the border with Phocis, but should that excuse their omission? Tanagra, on the other hand, was in the important eastern region not far from Aulis, and its absence is a major anomaly. As with Khaironeia (and Kreusis) there is a gap in the evidence of settlement, covering PG and G; are we therefore to use the Burr/Page/Hope Simpson–Lazenby argument in reverse and say that any ignoring of Tanagra must have been done not in the Mycenaean period but in the Dark Age? A more sensible conclusion might be that the list of Boeotian towns is a somewhat hit-or-miss affair, the product not of any single and systematic listing (such as the imagined Mycenaean muster-list) but of various pieces of information culled from the diverse oral tradition, whether cultic, mythological, political or genealogical in character. There may be a degree of misunderstanding or even sheer fiction, too; I am suspicious of the trio Arne, Mideia and Nisa in particular, the first being the place in Thessaly from which the Boiotoi left for Boeotia according to Thucydides 1.12.3 (there is an Arne mentioned elsewhere in the *Iliad* (at 7.9) as home of one Menesthios son of Areithoos, but where it was is uncertain); for the other two see under their entries on p. 194, as well as on 507–8.

The absence of Protogeometric (in particular) pottery from several of the probable sites is not altogether unexpected, since the serious depopulation and reduction of town-sites that is characteristic of the Dark Age in Greece, especially the later eleventh and early tenth century B.C., obviously applied to Boeotia too. At the same time the absence of PG and G sherds should not be taken as hard evidence of total abandonment during this period; HSL are suitably cautious over this, unlike Page. For many of these sites the Mycenaean evidence is very sparse – many are weather-beaten hill-tops. where surface material is swept away or too badly worn to be identifiable, and almost none of them have been systematically explored let alone scientifically excavated. It is highly probable that further excavation would show total depopulation to be very rare; in any case nearly all these places were resuscitated by the classical period, which (except with a natural all-purpose settlement-site, which would in any event be unlikely to be abandoned) presupposes *either* some form of physical survival *or* retention in the oral tradition. One or the other may well have happened even in the case of Eutresis.

496 Despite the initial rising threefolder of 494, the catalogue now establishes its predominant pattern of strongly two/fourfold verses, into which the place-names most conveniently fit. Exceptions are 558, 572, 592, 609, 653, 673, 677, 685, 691, 703 = 726, 714, and perhaps 542, 618, 654, 671.

Incidentally the scholia for both the catalogues are relatively unhelpful, often giving no more than the fictitious name of a place's founder; yet Aristarchus and the other ancient critics evidently accepted both the Achaean and the Trojan catalogues as substantially authentic, and admired their thoroughness, variety and ingenuity (cf. e.g. b on 494–877, Arn/A on 681 and 718). A small minority of MSS (but including T, with scholia, and its relative Ge) and at least one papyrus omitted them, and three MSS placed them after the end of book 24; cf. OCT and Erbse 1, 288.

ἐνέμοντο is one of three verbs used to express the concept of 'dwelling in', the others being εἶχον (e.g. 500) and ἔναιον (e.g. 522). This was not only for variety and decoration (as b on 494–877 suggests) but also for metrical flexibility. The basic connotation of νέμω -ομαι is of habitual use, and 'inhabit' is one of its specific applications (Chantraine, *Dict.* s.v.); another is 'cultivate' as at 751.

497–8 Each of these verses names three places, the last of which is given an epithet; the two bare names fill the first half of the verse, the third with its epithet fills the last half. The effect is pleasing, but we should not expect the epithet to be particularly informative or necessarily appropriate.

499–500 Again there are three places in each verse, but with construction and arrangement varied from the preceding couplet so as to avoid monotony. Aristarchus (Arn/A) maintained that the upsilon in Hule is metrically lengthened (as compared with 7.221 or, more to the point – since this is definitely the Boeotian Hule – 5.708f.); but the common noun ὕλη (etc.) is regularly spondaic in Homer and later Greek (e.g. 30x *Il.*).

501 As a fresh variation a formular phrase, ἐϋκτίμενον πτολίεθρον, fills the second half of the verse. It is not particularly appropriate to what looks like a relatively confined site (see under Medeon on p. 192).

502 Back to the pattern of 497–8. Zenodotus (Arn/A) evidently read Messe for Thisbe by confusion with 582, where πολυτρήρωνα occurs for a second time. Thisbe is of course a good Boeotian site, and Messe a relatively unknown Lacedaemonian one.

504 Two different 'dwelling in' verbs, ἔχον and ἐνέμοντο, occur here in the same verse.

505 Another 'well-built town', no more appropriate than in the case of Medeon in 501; for Hupothebai must refer to the settlement below the Kadmeia, and which must have survived the destruction by the Epigonoi (successors to the Seven against Thebes); see also pp. 193f. It suggests a suburb, or the relic of a ravaged city, not an especially well-built one; b recognized the difficulty but offers no real help.

506   The sanctuary of Poseidon at Onkhestos was famous for a curious ritual described in the (Homeric) *Hymn to Apollo* (where the same formula occurs at 230, Ποσιδήϊον ἀγλαὸν ἄλσος). Newly-trained foals had to draw empty chariots through the sacred grove; if one crashed, the chariot was left there and dedicated to the god. The form Ποσιδήϊον with an η is an Ionic adaptation of the Aeolic possessive adjective (Shipp, *Studies* 17; it is hard to see why he classes this on p. 235 as a possibly 'late' feature).

507–8   Zenodotus read Askre for Arne, presumably because of the difficulty of precisely locating the latter; see also p. 194. Aristarchus (Arn/A) dismissed this on the ground that Hesiod's miserable home-town (*Erga* 640) is hardly a likely candidate, cf. M. L. West *ad loc.* This may be right, although *Erga* 609–14 suggests that vines were grown at Askre, cf. 507 πολυστάφυλον; moreover the 1982 survey of the Cambridge–Bradford Boeotian Expedition has revealed a 'huge' Archaic and classical site, at least; anything seems possible! As for Mideia and Nisa, I have expressed my suspicions about these particular places on p. 195. There was a Nisaia in the Megarid, an area otherwise apparently deliberately neglected in the catalogue; it is unlikely to be referred to by Nisa here, a place on which Strabo 9.405 quoted Apollodorus (in his treatise Περὶ Νεῶν, 'On the Ships') as saying that it οὐδαμοῦ φαίνεται τῆς Βοιωτίας. Anthedon, by contrast, certainly existed; it was a harbour-town a few miles north of the Euripos. Its epithet ἐσχατόωσαν, literally 'being last' (as at 10.206, as well as of Epean Mursinos at 616), is a typical example of epic *diectasis*; the verbal form based on ἔσχατος is also artificial, but that does not make it a new formation (Shipp, *Studies* 97) in the sense of being post-Homeric. Its meaning is probably specific, since Anthedon lay on the borders with Locris (i.e. it was 'last' in Boeotia, e.g. for a ship proceeding up the coast).

509–10   The Boeotians had 50 ships, a standard number (see p. 171) surpassed by Argos, Mukenai, Lakedaimon, Pulos, the Arcadians even (note that these are successive entries) and the Cretans. What distinguishes them in this respect is that each of their ships carried no less than 120 men; only one other such statistic is mentioned in the catalogue, that Philoktetes' ships carried 50 men each (Akhilleus' ships are also said to have a complement of 50 at 16.169f.). Thucydides 1.10.4 suggested that the intention was to indicate the maximum and minimum complement; admittedly Philoktetes had one of the smallest numbers of actual ships (only seven), but it seems far more likely that 50 was a standard complement (compare the ubiquitous later *penteconter* or 50-oared ship), with 120 as yet another honorific exaggeration on behalf of the Boeotians. Ancient commentators confined themselves to citing Thucydides' guess or to a brief reference to the Boeotians' Phoenician ancestry, since the Phoenicians were famous for their seamanship. Even so, total Boeotian numbers ($50 \times 120 = 6,000$) were evidently exceeded by Agamemnon's contingent at least. His men at 577f.

are 'much the most numerous'; he had 100 ships, so each of them must have held 'much more' than sixty men. Such calculations are, needless to say, of very little relevance.

511–16 THE ORKHOMENOS CONTINGENT.

511 ORKHOMENOS was one of the most powerful of all Achaean cities at the height of the Mycenaean age in the early thirteenth century B.C., with a royal tholos-tomb as splendid as (although now less well preserved than) the 'Treasury of Atreus' at Mukenai. It was cited for its wealth along with Egyptian Thebes by Akhilleus at 9.381, and its legendary status is stressed by its epithet Μινύειον here – the tribe of Minyans being descended from the eponymous king Minuas and also prominent in the Argonautic expedition from Iolkos. Here in the catalogue its territory is drastically reduced; even Kopai along the north shore of Lake Kopais, once controlled by Orkhomenos, has come into the Boeotian sphere. That proves an origin for this reference not earlier than the LHIIIC (Late Helladic III c) period, when the political geography of the Mycenaean world was falling apart – at a time, indeed, after the Boiotoi had entered Boeotia from Thessaly. Since there may have been continuous habitation at Orkhomenos, however much reduced, into the Early Iron Age (HSL 38f.), the information implicit in this entry could belong to the Dark Age, rather. ASPLEDON was probably but not certainly at modern Pyrgos, between Orkhomenos and Kopai overlooking the north shore of the lake; there was a Mycenaean settlement there, with no indication so far of later occupation.

512 Ialmenos is only mentioned once in the whole of the rest of the *Iliad*, at 9.82 where he goes on guard-duty with his twin brother Askalaphos among others. The latter is somewhat more prominent; he meets a heroic death at 13.518–26 and is mourned by his father Ares at 15.111–16. That the two leaders should be associated in the rest of the poem, also, is perhaps significant as Page noted at *HHI* 136; even more important, however (and not mentioned by Page), is that the two verses in question, one in the catalogue and one in book 9, are almost identical: | – – 'Ασκάλαφος -ν καὶ 'Ιάλμενος -ν υἷες -ας "Αρηος. This constitutes a quite elaborate formula, therefore, common to the final composer of the catalogue and to Homer in book 9. Obviously that formula has not descended in two separate streams of tradition about the Trojan War, as Page thought; rather Homer (or a close predecessor in the central heroic tradition) either copied from the catalogue or, more probably, expanded an earlier form of catalogue in his own (traditional) language. Adaptation can be proved in the cases of Philoktetes and Protesilaos (see below); here it is not essential, and suggests a considerable degree of Homeric influence on this supposedly authentic earlier list.

513–15 The birth of the twin commanders as the result of Ares' secret union with Astuokhe, the daughter (rather than wife) of Aktor (son of Azeus, of whom nothing is heard elsewhere), is elaborated in a typically Homeric manner. Another Aktor was father of Menoitios and grandfather of Patroklos (11.785 and 16.14, Menoitios being a Locrian by origin, cf. 18.324–7); a third was father of the Molione (who were probably envisaged as Siamese twins, see on 620–1), and a fourth, father of the Myrmidon leader Ekhekles according to 16.189. The repeated use of the same name for a stock paternal figure is eased by the different forms of patronymic: Ἄκτορος υἱός, Ἀκτορίωνε, Ἀκτορίδαο.

514–15 παρθένος αἰδοίη looks like a common formula, but the two component terms are not found conjoined elsewhere (as it happens?). ὑπερώϊον εἰσαναβᾶσα *is* a formula, but primarily in the *Odyssey*, where it bears an innocent sense (2x, of Penelope going upstairs to her chamber; so too with 14 other variations, with ἀναβᾶσα, ὑπερῷ', ὑπερώϊα σιγαλόεντα etc.). Something similar is found in the *Iliad* only at 16.184, a description very reminiscent of the present one (by which I do not mean that it is copied from it); Hermes had fallen for Polumele at a dance, taken her upstairs and impregnated her with the Myrmidon leader Eudoros (Polumele then married Ekheklos son of Aktor, see the preceding comment): αὐτίκα δ' ἐς ὑπερῷ' ἀναβὰς παρελέξατο λάθρῃ. The last two words constitute another formula, which recurs here in 515; there are two not dissimilar expressions in the *Odyssey*. This brief vignette describing the birth of the twins is a charming and typically Homeric one, which also serves the purpose of stressing their close connexion with the Minyan tribal deity.

517–26 THE PHOCIAN CONTINGENT. This entry is weak on personnel but strong on political geography – the eight places and one district named are for the most part clearly identifiable, and cover most of the main towns of the region in historical times (but not Amphissa and Elateia).

517 The Phokees, Phocians, are described by an ethnic name as are e.g. the Boiotoi at 494 and the Lokroi at 527, and not simply as inhabitants of a group of towns like the Orkhomenos–Aspledon contingent at 511; Phokis was a clear geographical and political unit. The leaders are Skhedios and Epistrophos. The latter is not mentioned elsewhere in the poem and is presumably a fiction, since two other men of the same name are briefly mentioned on the Trojan side later in this same Book, at 692 and 856. Skhedios is also confusing; he will be killed by Hektor in the struggle for Patroklos' body, at 17.306–11, with the added details that he was 'far the best' of the Phocians, lived in famous Panopeus and ruled over many men: but at 15.515 Hektor had killed another Skhedios, also a Phocian commander but 'son of Perimedes'. This was of course noted by Aristarchus (Arn/A), who could not explain the anomaly. A possible conclusion is that the oral tradition knew vaguely of a Phocian king called Skhedios in the past but was uncertain about his parentage.

518 An earlier form of this verse must have been υἷες (*or* υἱέες) Ἰφίτοο μεγαθύμοο Ναυβολίδαο. It is one of the few cases in which an uncontracted genitive singular in -οο can be guaranteed in Homer, since the second iota of Iphitos is naturally short as at 17.306 and *Od.* 21.14. Aristarchus (Hdn/A) judged this to be a case of artificial metrical lengthening, i.e. as Ἰφίτου, but that is surely wrong; see Chantraine, *GH* I, 44f. (and for lengthening of omicron before (σ)μεγα-, I, 176f.). Either υἱέες (Aristarchus) or υἷες (the medieval vulgate) is possible, the latter being technically correct since Ἰφίτοο originally began with a digamma, consciousness of which would lengthen the preceding short syllable.

519–23 KUPARISSOS may have been the earlier name of Antikura, at the head of the gulf of that name to the east of the gulf of Itea; at least Pausanias (10.36.5) thought so. PUTHON is certainly the later Delphi, and is indeed 'rocky' (or perhaps 'cliffy' because of the Phaidriades). There was continuity of settlement there, in all probability, from the Late Bronze Age on; the evidence presented in Desborough, *Last Mycenaeans* 123–5, requires very careful consideration, and even he (who was exceptionally cautious) accepted that 'we have continuity of memory' of a cult near the site of the later great altar of Apollo; moreover PG sherds as well as the latest IIIC have been found (pp. 124 and 125 n. 2). KRISA is confused with Puthon itself at *HyAp* 282–5; it is usually identified with the strongly fortified Mycenaean acropolis at Agios Giorgios below Delphi on a spur commanding the Pleistos valley just south of the modern village of Khryso, but that is unconfirmed. Its description as ζαθέην, 'holy', is uninformative and may be simply conventional. There may also have been confusion between Krisa and Kirrha, the harbour-settlement near the modern Itea. DAULIS and PANOPEUS are close to each other near the Boeotian border among the eastern foothills of Parnassos, each of them a Hellenic city with Mycenaean traces on the acropolis but no Protogeometric or Geometric so far. Panopeus is Skhedios' home at 17.307f. (cf. 517n.); that being so, its fifth position in the list of Phocian towns confirms the often arbitrary order of places named in the catalogue. It is described as καλλίχορον (compare εὐρύχορον of Mukalessos in 498) at *Od.* 11.581. ANEMOREIA, probably implying 'windy', is of uncertain location; HSL 43 favour the site of modern Arakhova above and to the east of Delphi. Classical HUAMPOLIS lies across the river Kephisos from Daulis and Panopeus; a few Late Bronze Age fragments have been noticed there, and its strategic position is likely to have been continuously occupied. Hellenic LILAIA lay on the north side of Mt Parnassos and just south of the Kephisos river, near one of its sources as 523 suggests. HSL 44 are probably right in taking 522 to refer to several different places along the river and not specifically to Parapotamioi as Pausanias claimed at 10.33.7f.

525–6 Only here and with Salamis (558) and Lakedaimon (587) is anything said about where a contingent stationed itself. The intention is presumably to stress the Phocian connexion with the Boiotoi as neighbours; otherwise the Phocians are wholly unimportant in the rest of the poem.

527–35 THE LOCRIAN CONTINGENT. A concise and symmetrical entry for an unusual contingent of light-armed troops, with three verses (or possibly only two or one, see on 529–30) describing Aias as commander, then three listing eight places, most of them obscure, then a standard ship-number verse, finally a resumptive verse which in describing the position of Locris also leads on to the next, Euboean entry.

527 Locrian Aias, 'the lesser' (so 528, by comparison with the 'great' Aias, μέγας Τελαμώνιος Αἴας), is named as sole commander; he is a prominent figure in the *Iliad* at large. His father Oïleus (later misspelt Ileus according to Aristarchus, so Arn/A) is πτολίπορθος, 'sacker of towns', at 727f., where a bastard son Medon is mentioned; according to 13.694–7 Medon had escaped to Phulake after killing a male relative of Aias' mother Eriopis. The Locrian contingent is unique according to 13.712–22 (following on from the peculiar 'little catalogue' of Boeotians, Ionians, Locrians, Phthians and Epeans at 13.685–700): their general has taken his stand close to his greater namesake at 701–8; the latter's troops are in close support, but the Locrians, by contrast, have no heavy armour but have come to Troy equipped only with bows and slings, which they now discharge from the rear. Aias himself is a swift runner (his commonest formular description is Ὀϊλῆος ταχὺς Αἴας, 9x *Il.*), and he is especially devastating in pursuit of the fleeing enemy, 14.520–2. According to 529f. he wore special armour, but usually in the *Iliad* he fights in the conventional way. That is almost certainly because he is closely associated with the greater Aias, as for example at 13.46–75 where they are filled with might by Poseidon and the Oïlean Aias comments on the fact; here and often they are described as Αἴαντε, the two Aias's – a term which had earlier referred to the great Aias and his brother Teukros but was applied later, and evidently by the monumental composer himself, to the Telamonian and Oïlean Aias together: see 406n. and Page, *HHI* 235–8. Despite that association, the Locrian Aias was not greatly admired in the heroic tradition, a reflection perhaps of his light-armed, unheroic and provincial (rather than 'semi-savage', Page 237) side. Thus in the funeral games for Patroklos he will pick a stupid quarrel with the respected Idomeneus (23.473–98) and then fall down in a patch of dung, to everyone's amusement, in the foot-race he should have won (23.773–84). When Troy is finally sacked he drags Kassandra with Athene's sacred image away from the altar – that was described in the Cyclic *Iliou Persis*, but was known to Homer and his audience; even so he might have escaped from shipwreck on the way home, but a stupid boast put an end to him (*Od.* 4.499–511).

528 Was athetized by Zenodotus (who must also therefore have athetized the following two verses, although that is not specifically said) but defended by Aristarchus (Arn/A) as 'necessary'. That is correct, since some distinction between this Aias and his namesake would be expected; the difference here is merely in height and may depend primarily on the formula μέγας Τελαμώνιος Αἴας (12× *Il.*).

529–30 Aristarchus (Arn/A) athetized these verses for three reasons: as a redundant expansion, especially in the repetition ἀλλὰ πολὺ μείων in 529; because of the oddity of his linen corslet; and because of the misapplication of Πανέλληνας. (1) Actually the cumulative development is quite Homeric, and ἀλλὰ πολὺ μείων effectively emphatic: he was not only 'lesser', he was much less, a slight man (ὀλίγος), different also in his lighter equipment. (2) λινοθώρηξ equates him with his light-armed Locrian troops; the same epithet is applied to one Amphios in the Trojan catalogue at 830, but otherwise such corslets are not mentioned elsewhere in Homer – heavy bronze armour is proper for heroes, and the Achaeans in particular are Ἀχαιῶν χαλκοχιτώνων (24× *Il.*). Yet Alcaeus (frag. 357.6 L–P) grouped linen corslets with other (bronze) armour, and they are not unexpected for mobile troops like the Locrians, on which see 527n. Usually, however, their commander Aias behaves as though he were regularly armoured, and even here in 530 his skill with the spear (although consonant with his performance at 14.520–2) does not completely accord with Locrian slings and arrows. (3) Moreover Πανέλληνας does constitute a difficulty, as Aristarchus noted: it is not used elsewhere in Homer (although cf. Παναχαιοί, especially in the verse-end formula ἀριστῆες -ας Παναχαιῶν, 8× *Il.*), and, still more important, Ἕλληνες itself occurs only once (in the Myrmidon entry at 684) and then in the special sense of inhabitants of the region of Hellas close to Phthie, a sense present in all the five uses of Hellas in the *Iliad*. On four occasions the *Odyssey* extends this use somewhat in the formula καθ'/ἀν' Ἑλλάδα καὶ μέσον Ἄργος, in which Hellas probably represents central and northern Greece as distinct from the Peloponnese. Here the form Πανέλληνας shows that the meaning has been extended still further to cover the Greeks at large, much as Ἀργεῖοι and Δαναοί did; this is certainly a 'late' development – the question is whether it is a post-Homeric one. On the whole I am inclined to conjecture that it is, and that this verse is due to a rhapsode; 529, of course, could still be Homeric.

531–3 OPOEIS is the most important place in this Locrian list; it was Patroklos' birthplace according to 23.85f. (and Akhilleus expected him to return there, 18.326) and, as Opous, the chief city of the region in historical times. It was either at modern Kyparissi or at Atalanti; its port according to Strabo 9.425 was KUNOS, for which there is a possible site north of modern Livanates, with Myc (= Mycenaean), G, Archaic and classical sherds (HSL 47), but this is really quite uncertain. KALLIAROS and BESSA were a

mystery to Strabo; SKARPHE was presumably at the site of the later
Skarpheia somewhere near the southern shore of the Malian gulf. No
Locrian AUGEIAI is known, but the recurrence of another 'lovely Augeiai'
in Lakedaimon at 583 does not make it any more or less probably fictitious
than Kalliaros and Bessa, at least. TARPHE was located by Strabo 9.426 at
the classical Pharugai, which may be the medieval Boudonitsa (HSL 49).
With THRONION we are on stronger ground; the catalogist allows himself
a definite local indication, 'around the streams of Boagrios', and an
inscription shows that the later city at least was just south of its mouth near
the modern Pikraki. No pre-classical sherds seem to have been found there
so far, and HSL 49 are properly cautious, but in view of the Boagrios detail
I think it unlikely that the Homeric Thronion should be sought elsewhere.

Eastern Locris was always a backwater (and western Locris, ignored in
the *Iliad*, even more so); it has been relatively little explored, and
consequently the accuracy or otherwise of this entry is impossible to assess.
The omission of the port of Larumna is odd, and Alos and Alope seems to
have been pushed into Akhilleus' territory, see on 682. The evident
obscurity of at least half the places listed suggests that the catalogist is doing
his best to magnify a small and peculiar contingent.

534-5 A standard ship-number verse, with 40 ships assigned to the
Locrians as likewise to their neighbours the Phocians and Abantes/
Euboeans, leads by an easy cumulation to a summary of their general
position opposite 'holy' (for no special reason?) Euboea.

536-45 THE EUBOEAN CONTINGENT (THE ABANTES).

536 This is the second mode B entry (see p. 170), and the first in which,
now the pattern has been established by 511, the leaders are postponed for
some verses. As in the case of e.g. Lakedaimon (see on 581), the entry begins
with the name of the general region, in this case of the whole island, then
lists the towns within it. The inhabitants of Euboea are called Abantes, a
tribal name (cf. Epeioi, Kephallenes, Murmidones, Enienes), supposedly
after a mythical ancestor Abas. They 'breathe might', a formula applied
twice to the Achaeans but which may have special relevance here in the
light of 542-4, where they are swift, long-haired behind (ὄπιθεν κομόωντες,
see on 542), spearmen eager to pierce their enemies' corslets. During the
Lelantine war Khalkis and Eretria (see the next comment) made an
agreement to ban long-distance weapons and fight only at close range (cf.
Strabo 10.449), and that might reflect a martial tradition also referred to
here.

537-9 The variety of arrangement in listing the seven towns deserves
notice: 537 has 'D and E and epithet + F' (like 497, 498 and 502 in the
Boeotian entry); 538 has 'D + epithet and E + descriptive phrase', and 539
'who possessed D and dwelt in E'. The two most important towns in the

island are placed first. KHALKIS, at the northern end of the Euripos narrows, has been continuously inhabited from Neolithic times to the present day. Around 700 B.C. it became locked in struggle with EIRETRIA (Eretria), ostensibly for possession of the fertile Lelantine plain. Strabo (9.403; 10.448) referred to an old and a new Eretria, which has caused much confusion, not resolved so far by the important discoveries at Xeropolis/Lefkandi; the excavators are no longer convinced this was the old site (cf. Popham, Sackett and Themelis, *Levkandi* 1 (London 1979), 423f.), and there is still much to be said for the view of e.g. HSL 51f. that the general position of the classical city near Nea Psara was also that of its predecessors, although Mycenaean and PG traces are slight so far. HISTIAIA (in which -ιαι- is scanned as one long syllable by synizesis) was presumably at Oreos (so b; the ancient commentators are not usually much help over these identifications), where PG is lacking so far. KERINTHOS is ἔφαλον, 'by the sea', and Strabo 10.446 placed it by the river Boudoros on the eastern shore; different parts of a curving low hill just south of the river-mouth were inhabited from the Neolithic period onward, with many PG sherds and some Mycenaean. DION was near Histiaia according to Strabo 10.446, and is usually placed at Kastri near modern Likhas, close to Cape Kenaion in the north-west corner of the island. Sherds indicate continuous settlement there from the Middle Bronze Age on; it is a 'flat-topped hill' (HSL 53), 'about 60 metres above the sea' (*BSA* 61 (1966) 37), in a position which suggests that αἰπὺ πτολίεθρον should not be taken too literally. KARUSTOS and the whole of the southern part of the island are remarkably lacking in signs of prehistoric or Early Iron Age habitation (*BSA* 61 (1966) 83), which is surprising in view of Karustos' fertile plain. That may reflect heavier connexions with Boeotia from the centre and north of the island; but there must have been a considerable settlement at or near the modern Karustos, even before the Archaic and classical age. STURA must have been at the site of the classical town on the coast some 15 miles north-west of Karustos; neither Late Helladic nor Early Iron Age pottery has yet been found there, but the Styrans were said to have been Druopes (cf. Pausanias 4.34.11) and so had ancient mythological connexions.

540–1 Elephenor is described as ὄζος Ἄρηος, a relatively common formula (10x *Il.*) which seems to mean 'companion' rather than 'offshoot' of Ares: see Chantraine, *Dict.* s.v. 2. ὄζος. He and his father Khalkodon are known to the rest of the *Iliad*, although only by a single mention since he succumbs to Agenor at 4.463–9, where 464 = 541 here; he is described there as 'leader of the great-hearted Abantes', cf. 15.519 μεγαθύμων ἀρχὸν Ἐπειῶν, and is a surprisingly early casualty (see on 4.464).

542 According to Strabo 10.445, Aristotle had said that the Abantes had originally come from Thrace; and at *Il.* 4.533 the Thracians are described as ἀκρόκομοι, 'top-knotted'. Since the Achaeans as a whole grew their hair long (κάρη κομόωντες -ας, 26x *Il.*; see on 3.43), this suggests that ὄπιθεν κομόωντες distinguishes the Abantes as leaving their hair long at the back and cutting or shaving it in front – in order to stop the enemy grabbing it, according to Arkhemakhos, a local historian cited by Strabo 10.465!

543–4 See also on 536. αἰχμητής by itself is an honorific term, also at 7.281, and for ἀμφὶ στήθεσσι cf. 2.388; but in general the phraseology here is not formular, although the individual words are familiar enough.

545 Again the 40-ship verse, cf. 534. The Abantes entry as a whole has been elegantly executed. The places listed suggest an Iron-Age as much as a Mycenaean original, and the omission of Amarunthos and the conspicuous Dustos is surprising in any event; the interest in the martial habits of the Abantes could reflect the impending conflict between Khalkis and Eretria in Homer's own time.

546–56 THE ATHENIAN CONTINGENT.

546 The form of this entry is similar to that of the Euboean one (see on 536), i.e. mode B with postponement of the leader. Here there is only one city to be named, Athens itself, although with much elaborative detail; on the omission of other towns in Attica, and whether or not this reflects synoecism under Theseus, see also pp. 179f. Here the conventional description ἐϋκτίμενον πτολίεθρον is appropriate (cf. 501 and 505 with notes) since the fortified Acropolis must always have been conspicuous from Mycenaean times on.

547–51 Athens is the δῆμος or 'community' of Erekhtheus, its mythical early king who according to this passage was born from the soil itself, nurtured by Athene and established in her own temple. This account of his birth (which is hardly mentioned in later mythographers) symbolized the Athenians' claim to be autochthonous, not to have entered their land from elsewhere like the Boiotoi or Abantes or to have been displaced by people like the Dorians. At *Od.* 7.80f. Athene came to Marathon and Athens and entered 'the compact house of Erekhtheus'; that is a rather different conception from the catalogist's, both in the mention of Marathon alongside Athens and in the implication that the building she and the king shared was his palace rather than her temple. The palace idea stems from an earlier stage, since shrines in the Late Bronze Age were in, or closely associated with, the royal house. The king dwelling in some precursor of the classical Erechtheum represents a later development of that symbiosis, but it is, of course, the heroized king that dwells there, not the living one, and that is confirmed by 550 (see on 549–51).

548 ζείδωρος -ν ἄρουρα -ν, 3x *Il.*, 9x *Od.*, 'the ploughland with its gift of wheat', is a general formula for earth or soil, although the exegetical scholiast in A maintained that it was especially appropriate to Attica where, in the Rarian plain near Eleusis, crops were supposed to have first emerged.

549–51 ἑῷ ἐν πίονι νηῷ, 'in her own rich temple'. πίων is connected with πῖαρ, 'richness' or 'fat' even, and is a favourite epic term with a varied formular system at the verse-end, e.g. πίονα μῆλα (1x *Il.*, 5x *Od.*), πίονας αἶγας (5x *Od.*). For ἐν πίονι νηῷ| cf. especially ἐν πίονι δήμῳ 'in the rich community' (5x *Il.*), which has a typical oral echo in πίονα -ι δημόν -ῳ, 'rich *fat*' (2x *Il.*, 3x *Od.*). Athene's temple is fat because of the offerings made there – to Erekhtheus not herself in this instance, since μιν in 550 must refer to him, not only because of the run of the sentence but also because (as b noted) victims sacrificed to her were properly female, whereas these are bulls and rams. It was in Erekhtheus' reign, according to a tale reported in Pausanias 1.28.10f., that animal sacrifices were initiated at the Bouphonia. The 'revolving year (*or* seasons)' of 551 suggests an annual festival; there may or may not be some idea of an early form of the Panathenaia, which was held in the month of Hekatombaion.

552 On Menestheus son of Peteos see also pp. 179f.; references to him in the post-Homeric tradition, which strove to justify his somewhat mysterious appearance here, are well summarized by Page, *HHI* 145–7 and n. 79 on pp. 173–5. His role in the *Iliad* is inconspicuous, even undistinguished; and nothing else about him that was not obviously invented was known in the historical period. In company with Odysseus he is reproved by Agamemnon in the inspection of troops at 4.327–48 (but then even Diomedes will be reproved, and keeps silence as Menestheus does here); he becomes isolated in the fighting (a typical motif) and sends for Aias to help him at 12.331–77; at 13.190–7 they are fighting in close proximity, obviously with Aias in the more prominent role; in the 'little catalogue' at 13.689–91 he appears with some otherwise unknown lieutenants, of which one is killed at Menestheus' last mention at 15.329–31. To describe this as a 'dismal record' (Page, *op. cit.* 145) is perhaps to exaggerate – at the same time it is not what one would expect of the leader of an Athenian contingent, given that Athens was of some importance in the Mycenaean world and came through the Dark Age relatively well, to recover strongly by Homer's time. Yet the fact remains that Menestheus *does* appear in the rest of the *Iliad*, and the association with the greater Aias in books 12 and 13 is apparently organic. He also appears, almost certainly, as Helen's Athenian suitor in Hesiod's *Ehoiai* or *Catalogue of Women* (frag. 200.3 M–W). He must have been known to the general heroic tradition, as well as to any special tradition of catalogue poetry, for generations. That does not necessarily make him, as Page argued, a specifically Mycenaean relic, although he may have been one. The temptation to oust him in favour of one of Theseus' sons, as happened in the Cyclic tradition, was evidently resisted even when the text was under strong Athenian control during the sixth century B.C. through rhapsodic contests at the Panathenaia (see p. 12 and Shipp, *Studies* 56).

553–5 These verses were athetized by Zenodotus (Arn/A), presumably because nothing is said later of Menestheus' skill at marshalling troops and chariots; as the exegetical scholiast comments in b, Homer 'grants him this since he will not distinguish himself in the fighting'. Aristarchus evidently replied to Zenodotus, correctly, that Homer often does not follow up such general characterizations; and he took the verses to be authentic. But they are, nevertheless, open to some doubt. The praise is overdone even granted that some elaboration is in order, and the apparent afterthought about Nestor, although it follows a Homeric pattern (cf. e.g. Nireus of Sume at 673f.), is a little crude, not least in adducing his age as the reason. The expression throughout is unremarkable (except that ἐπιχθόνιος...ἀνήρ in 553 is again over-emphatic) and uses some typical formular elements. κοσμῆσαι is a favourite catalogue verb for obvious reasons, but it is more significant that, although ἀσπιδιώτας (etc.) appears nowhere else in Homer, verse 554 (with ὀτρύνων not κοσμῆσαι) occurs at 16.167 of Akhilleus and the Myrmidons – that is, in a key Iliadic context. I draw the conclusion that these verses are not pre-Homeric or dependent on some special catalogue-tradition; they are the work *either* of the monumental composer *or* of a relatively skilled rhapsodic elaborator, even conceivably a Panathenaic competitor. Verse 555 could be an independent addition, but seems to belong stylistically with the others.

556 The common 40-ship verse (the D-mode, see p. 171) has been amended by substituting the metrically equivalent πεντήκοντα for τεσσαράκοντα. That this could be so easily done, yet was not done elsewhere, implies some special motive – perhaps Athenian pride – rather than any desire for variation. The Boeotians and Myrmidons also had fifty ships (some contingents had more), yet not in this formular verse-type.

557–8 THE SALAMIS CONTINGENT. See pp. 170 and 171 for the leader and ship-number modes (C and F), used also for three other small contingents. The other 12-ship fleet is Odysseus' at 637.

558 This positioning detail finds some parallel at 526 and 587; the motive was obviously to associate the Salaminians closely with the Athenians, much as the Phocians are implied to be closely allied with the Boeotians at 526. Why? This became a matter for warm debate in antiquity and is still puzzling. Aristarchus is known to have athetized the verse (through the Aristonicus-based comments in A on 3.230 and 4.273), on the strong ground that in the rest of the poem the Salaminian contingent was *not* closely associated with the Athenians: cf. 3.225 and 229f., where Aias stands between Odysseus and Idomeneus, and 4.273 and 327 (which admittedly contradicts 8.224–6 = 11.7–9, where Aias' ships are at one end of the line), where he and Athenian Menestheus are quite separate from each other when Agamemnon inspects the troops. Another reason for suspicion is that it is extraordinary for so important a warrior (however small his homeland and contingent – compare Odysseus) to be dismissed so summarily; as Willcock comments on this verse, he is not even given his usual epithet Τελαμώνιος or Τελαμωνιάδης to distinguish him from his lesser namesake. Admittedly something not dissimilar happens to him even outside the catalogue, in book 3, where Helen as she identifies the Achaean leaders for Priam dismisses him in a single verse, 229, before passing on to a more elaborate four-verse description of Idomeneus. It is possible that this is a piece of psychological subtlety (see on 3.229 and 230–3) – or is the explanation a different one which applies in both cases, namely that (as Page declared, *HHI* 147 and 233–5) the great Aias belongs to a generation of heroes earlier than the Trojan War, and is only inserted into the late-Mycenaean original of the catalogue, at 557, at some subsequent stage, with 558 being added later still? Page's evidence is mainly Aias' great tower-like shield with its seven ox-hides, which he constantly uses and is virtually absent elsewhere – a type known from artefacts of the Shaft-grave period and a little later but not from LHIIIB, which covered much of the thirteenth century B.C. and included the fall of Troy VIIa (see H. Borchhardt, *Arch. Hom.* E 1of. and 46–8; A. M. Snodgrass, *Arms and Armour of the Greeks* (London 1967) 19f.). In assessing this suggestion it is important to remember that Aias is a major force in the poem as a whole and therefore well rooted in the heroic tradition; it is conceivable that Patroklos, say, or even Nestor, was heavily developed by the monumental composer for the special purposes of a monumental *Iliad*, but Aias is so ubiquitous that this can hardly be so in his case. Therefore if he belonged originally to a pre-Trojan heroic ambience, he must at least have passed down through later Mycenaean memory so as to enter the developing Early Iron Age tradition along with the rest – and so might well have been amalgamated with the Achaeans against Troy even in an early catalogue-tradition.

That leaves the well-known story referred to by Aristotle (*Rhet.* A 15.1375 b 30), that in the quarrel between Athens and Megara over possession of Salamis in the sixth century B.C. the Megarians claimed that the Athenians had inserted this couplet in their own interest into the text of Homer, and proposed another version:

Αἴας δ' ἐκ Σαλαμῖνος ἄγεν νέας ἔκ τε Πολίχνης
ἔκ τ' Αἰγειρούσσης Νισαίης τε Τριπόδων τε

– these obviously being places in the Megarid. The substituted couplet is clearly inauthentic if only because it records no specific number of ships, and the whole story, although interesting for the light it sheds on the status of the *Iliad* and its supposed historicity at that time, suggests rather (and despite 553–5n. *fin.*) that Athenian interference at this point is unlikely.

Verse 558 is a rising threefolder very much in the Homeric style, and its relaxed use of the verse-end formula-type ἵσταντο φάλαγγες (so also at 13.126; 14X with other verbs ending -ντο) slightly supports its pre-rhapsodic status. That still leaves a problem about why Homer might have dealt with Aias in this abrupt and peculiar way; one suspects that it may be because his Aeacid genealogy – so prominent in Pindar, for example, but ignored by Homer – was still under dispute that further details about his family and background were suppressed. The epithet Αἰακίδης is reserved in the *Iliad* (24X) for Akhilleus; Peleus and Telamon were both, of course, sons of Aiakos.

559–68 THE ARGOS CONTINGENT. This B-mode entry is also discussed under 'Special Problems', pp. 180ff. Diomedes is found ruling cities in the Argolid which might be expected to fall within the realm of Agamemnon and Mukenai; but he is well established in Argos itself, as indeed his father Tudeus had been since leaving Aetolia, and had fought for Adrastos against Thebes and married his daughter. He is now king of Argos, and therefore of other places in the southern Argive plain and the Akte peninsula which stretches away to the south-east.

559–62 The position of ARGOS itself is in no doubt. The Larisa hill dominated the rich plain below, and the city at its foot was continuously inhabited from the Bronze Age onward; unlike Mukenai and Tiruns it suffered no detectable damage at the end of LHIIIB, i.e. soon after the presumed date of the Trojan expedition. TIRUNS (Tiryns) was built on and around a low, strongly fortified rock a few miles to the south-east and on the (ancient) coast near Nauplion. Its massive Cyclopean walls, noted in the epithet τειχιόεσσαν, were first built around 1400 B.C.; the citadel was burnt around 1200, but reoccupied and then inhabited more or less continuously until its decline in the historical period. Herakles, Proitos and Perseus were all legendary kings of Tiruns (with Proitos' brother Akrisios remaining as king of Argos). HERMIONE is connected with ASINE as 'possessing (*or* controlling) a deep gulf'; the latter lies near the head of the Argolic gulf just south of Nauplion, but the site of Hermione is on the south coast of the Akte peninsula facing Hudrea. Their gulfs are different ones, therefore; any impression to the contrary is probably due to the gulf-possessing formula having been loosely converted to the plural. Both places had flourishing Mycenaean settlements and with good natural positions were probably never completely depopulated; Hermione was known as a small harbour-town in the classical era. TROIZEN lay across the hills to the north of Hermione, overlooking a small but fertile plain which ran down towards Kalaureia (modern Poros) and Methana. It was settled both in Mycenaean and in classical times, and probably in between, but in any event its mythological connexions, especially with Theseus and Athens, would ensure its retention in the heroic tradition even during the Dark Age. The location of EÏONES, on the other hand, is unknown, although an ancient conjecture identified it with Methana. EPIDAUROS was presumably at the Mycenaean and later site near the modern small harbour of Palaia Epidauros, with the sanctuary a few miles inland; the cult of Apollo Maleatas near the sanctuary there was early, even if Asklepios was a relative late-comer. AIGINA was obviously the island, continuously inhabited from the Neolithic age onward, and not a place of the same name mentioned by Strabo (8.375) in the territory of Epidauros. MASES, finally, was a little port used by the people of Hermione in Pausanias' day (2.36.2); a possible LHIIIB site has been found for it (HSL 63). All these places (except for the unknown Eïones) could have figured as elements of an Argive kingdom at almost any period. Geographically there is a certain logic to them, confined as they are to the southern part of the Argive plain and to the Akte peninsula (to which access is conveniently gained from Tiruns, and of which Aigina is evidently regarded as an appendage). Apparent omissions round the plain are Lerna and the great fortress of Mideia; the former was known in myths because of the Hudra and Herakles, but was not an important settlement after the Early Bronze Age, whereas Mideia (whose importance is confirmed by the rich and extensive cemetery at Dendra) does not seem to have survived the Mycenaean era. See also on Agamemnon's kingdom, 569–80.

563 The catalogue creates a little formula-system around ἡγεμόνευε(ν): |τῶν (δ') αὖθ' ἡγεμόνευ'(ε), as here, 6x; |τῶν αὖ (μὲν)...ἡγεμόνευε| 2x; |Τρῶσι μὲν ἡγεμόνευε, |Λοκρῶν δ' ἡγεμόνευεν and 3 other variants.

564 Sthenelos like Diomedes was one of the Epigonoi, the Successors of the Seven against Thebes; his father Kapaneus had been one of the Seven, as Tudeus had. He often accompanies Diomedes in the rest of the poem.

565–6 Mekisteus had been another of the Seven, and his son Eurualos was the third Argive Epigonos (cf. e.g. Apollodorus 3.7.2); he naturally joins Diomedes and Sthenelos as a commander of the Argive contingent against Troy. He plays some part in the rest of the poem, killing four Trojans at 6.20–8, perhaps in close company with Diomedes (6.12–19), and unsuccessfully opposing Epeios, with Diomedes as his second, in the boxing-match at 23.677–99. His father Mekisteus is said there (at 679f.) to have beaten all the Cadmeans in the funeral games for Oidipous – suspiciously like Tudeus at 4.385–90. His grandfather Talaos (who is here given the double form of patronymic, Ταλαϊών becoming Ταλαϊονίδης, cf. Πηληϊάδης and the Hesiodic Ἰαπετιονίδης) was son of Pero and Bias (who had become joint king of Argos) according to the Hesiodic *Ehoiai*, frag. 37.8ff. M–W; it is clear that this whole complicated Argive genealogy was established long before Homer's time.

The medieval vulgate had Μηκιστέος ὗἶος, with synizesis, but it is clear that Μηκιστῆος υἱός, with the latter word, as often, scanned as an iamb, is correct, cf. Chantraine, *GH* I, 223f. and Leaf on 1.489.

568 τοῖσι δ᾽ ἄμ᾽ ὀγδώκοντα is substituted for τοῖς δ᾽ ἄμα τεσσαράκοντα in the common 40-ship formular verse; the Argos contingent has to be given exceptional importance, although less than Agamemnon's.

569–80 THE MUKENAI CONTINGENT is introduced in the common B-mode in a verse exactly matching 546, of Athens, including 'well-built city'. For the surprising diversion of Agamemnon's direct political power away from the Argive plain and into Corinthia and Achaea to the north, see 'Special Problems' (iii) on pp. 180f., as well as the Argos entry above. That was just possible, in political and geographical terms, at the very end of the Bronze Age or in the early Dark Age – that is, it must reflect a radical development in the power-structure of the Argolid and its encircling fortresses, one that can only have been produced by the revolutionary changes that led to the burning of Mukenai and Tiruns at the end of LHIIIB and of Mukenai again in IIIC. Mukenai was far enough up in the northern corner of the Argive plain, and in control of the pass that led over toward Corinth, to be able to isolate itself from the south and concentrate on the different sources of agricultural wealth that lay toward the Isthmus and the north-west. The immediate causes of this radical realignment (which is suggested here and there in the rest of the poem) are unknown.

570–5 KORINTHOS (in which by the accidents of excavation substantial, although still not prolific, Mycenaean relics have only been found fairly recently) must always have been 'prosperous', commanding as it does, from its site at the foot of Acrocorinth, the fertile plain toward the Isthmus and running in a narrow band westward along the coast. KLEONAI (whose epithet ἐὐκτίμενον is surprising immediately after ἐὐκτίμενον πτολίεθρον in the preceding verse) had a strategic position linking Mukenai with Korinthos, on the northern side of the low hills separating the two. It was 'an important Mycenaean settlement' (HSL 66), as well as a classical polis. ORNEAI cannot be firmly located, although Pausanias (2.25.5f.) provides some support for placing it in the Leondi valley near modern Gymno (HSL 66f.); if so, its position corresponds in a way with that of Mukenai itself, since it would lie on the Argolid side of the passes into Phliasia and Corinthia. ARAITHURIE (which is 'lovely' like Arene and the two Augeiai elsewhere) was the earlier name of Phlious according to Strabo 8.782 and Pausanias 2.12.4f. SIKUON lay some 4 miles back from the Gulf shore near modern Vasiliko, with a harbour-town below. Adrastos 'first ruled there' because he came as an exile from Argos, married king Polybos' daughter, and later returned to Argos after the attack on Thebes; Herodotus (5.67.1) mentions his hero-shrine at Sikuon in the time of Kleisthenes. HUPERESIA was the earlier name of historical Aigeira (overlooking the Corinthian gulf roughly half-way

between Sikuon and Aigion) according to Pausanias 7.26.2. 'Steep' GONOESSA
is unknown. Historical PELLENE lay up in the hills between Sikuon and
Aigeira, overlooking the gulf; no Mycenaean relics have been detected there
so far (HSL 69). AIGION lies under the modern town on the plateau above
the sea; it is the furthest westward point of Agamemnon's domain, unless
AIGIALON (Αἰγιαλόν τ' ἀνὰ πάντα), which surely refers to this whole coast,
extends further westward as Pausanias (7.1.1) says. Finally classical HELIKE
was destroyed by earthquake in 373 B.C., and its flat surrounding lands (it
is described as 'broad' here) were engulfed by the sea, as Pausanias (7.24.5f.
and 12f.) vividly describes; its earlier site (notice here that they live 'around'
it, ἀμφ') must have been nearby, a few miles to the south-east of Aigion.
Both cities had famous shrines of Poseidon; at 8.203 Here reminds the god
of how the Achaeans 'bring him gifts to Helike and Aigion'.

This entry leaves no doubt about Agamemnon's surprising realm; it
unambiguously extends right along the fertile coastal strip bordering the
south shore of the Corinthian gulf, at least as far as Aigion, and 8 out of
the 12 places mentioned belong to that region. It may be significant that
Achaea (especially its western end around Patrai) appears to have remained
unscathed in the latest Mycenaean era, LHIIIC, and to have received
refugees from other parts, especially perhaps the heavily disrupted Argolid;
see A. M. Snodgrass, *The Dark Age of Greece* (Edinburgh 1971), especially
29, 86f., 170f. Protogeometric relics, by contrast, are very thin there so far;
there must have been a steep decline in population after *c.* 1100 B.C., but
tradition would survive – including perhaps that of some kind of influx from
the direction of Mukenai!

576–8   The ship-entry is in the G mode, see pp. 171f.; Agamemnon's 100
ships constitute the largest fleet of all (and if their numbers were to be taken
very strictly, which they should not be, there would have to be more than
60 men to a ship in order to exceed the Boiotoi at 509f.). That suits his
position as supreme commander, whatever might have happened to his
special domain, and accords with the rest of the *Iliad* (see on 100–8).

577–80   'Ατρεΐδης makes a convenient runover-word, and these verses
could have been cumulated by the monumental composer as part of the
adjustment most clearly exemplified (although for slightly different reasons)
at 699–709 and 721–8.

578   νώροπα, only of bronze and in this formula (6x *Il.*, 2x *Od.* in either
accusative or dative), is of unknown derivation, although probably 'bright'
or 'blinding' rather than 'resounding' (of Hesychius' three glosses), cf. the
gleam of bronze as e.g. in the simile at 455–8.

579–80   Athetized by Zenodotus (Arn/A) because at 768 Aias is said to
be 'best', ἄριστος, after Akhilleus. That is wrong, as Aristarchus evidently
observed, because they were best in different respects: Agamemnon in

wealth and position, Aias in martial skill and courage. Didymus in A noted that in his second edition Aristarchus (like Zenodotus, indeed) read πᾶσιν δέ in 579 instead of ὅτι πᾶσι, which nevertheless passed into the medieval vulgate; the paratactic construction of the former is indeed preferable. Agamemnon's 'standing out' among the heroes is a more elegant use of the kind of language applied to him at 483, q.v. with comment.

581–90 THE LAKEDAIMON CONTINGENT follows naturally upon that led by Agamemnon, for family reasons if not for geographical ones (given that Agamemnon has been cut off from the Argive plain); that is emphasized by calling Menelaos 'his brother' at 586. The run of B-mode entries continues.

581 LAKEDAIMON is the whole region, κοίλην, 'hollow', because enclosed by the high ranges of Parnon and Taügetos. κητώεσσαν occurs only here and in the same phrase at *Od.* 4.1, where the scholiast states that Zenodotus read καιετάεσσαν, a word applied by Callimachus to the Eurotas river in frag. 224; see Stephanie West on *Od.* 3.158 and 4.1. Either reading could be right; the choice of meaning lies between an ancestor of κῆτος = marine monster, implying perhaps 'gulf' or 'belly', and καιέτας or καιάδας = 'fissure' (being the later name of the underground prison in Sparta, cf. Thucydides 1.134.4) or καιέτα = 'catmint' in Hesychius.

582–5 PHARIS was on the route past Amuklai straight to the sea according to Pausanias 3.20.3; that is not enough to locate it. SPARTE was probably at the site of the historical city, although the later Menelaion at Therapnai across the Eurotas river was important in the Mycenaean era and early Dark Age and should be considered; it is, however, three miles from Archaic and classical Sparte. MESSE 'of many pigeons' is usually identified with Pausanias' Messa (3.25.9f.) on the west coast of the Tainaron peninsula, and that with the site of the Frankish Castle of Maina on the Tigani promontory, where there are some possibly Mycenaean remains – and some pigeons nearby (HSL 77), as on many Greek cliffs. BRUSEIAI was in the Taügetos foothills according to Pausanias 3.20.3f., but cannot be precisely located. AUGEIAI can hardly have turned into classical Aigiai as Strabo 8.364 thought, nor should it be suspected as a doublet of the other, Locrian Augeiai, similarly 'lovely'; it is simply unknown, unless Stephanus of Byzantium was right to equate it (perhaps) with Therapnai: see HSL 78. AMUKLAI is some five miles down the Eurotas from Sparte; it was continuously settled from the Early Bronze Age to the Hellenistic period (for the absence of Sub-Mycenaean sherds is probably without significance), and according to Ephorus as reported by Strabo 8.364 it remained in native hands after the 'Return of the Herakleidai'. HELOS, 'seaside town', was somewhere round the Helos bay or marsh (it is now a fertile plain); there were several Mycenaean sites there, most of them apparently abandoned between the

Late Bronze Age and classical times, although Asteri (see R. Hope Simpson, *Mycenaean Greece* E 21 on p. 106) has probable Dark Age pottery. LAAS must have been on the site of classical Las, also occupied by the Frankish Castle of Passava some five miles towards Areopolis from Gutheion/Yithion. No Mycenaean or Dark Age remains have been found there, but Gutheion itself claimed the islet of Kranae on which according to *Il.* 3.443–5 (q.v. with note) Paris made love to Helen when abducting her from Lakedaimon, and there is a rich Mycenaean cemetery at Mavrovouni nearby, with some PG sherds found there too; see Hope Simpson, *op. cit.* E 41 and 42 on p. 109. Classical OITULOS lay beyond Las overlooking the small harbour now called Limeni on the west coast of the Tainaron peninsula, and the catalogue-site must be somewhere nearby.

The Lacedaemonian towns listed here are confined to the Eurotas valley and Helos bay, with a south-western extension to Laas and Oitulos. They form a reasonable geographical unit, more restricted than that of historic Lakedaimon, and cannot be more probably assigned to one pre-Homeric era rather than another – although the omission of places down the west coast of the Malea peninsula, certainly connected with the Helos region in the Late Bronze Age, is suggestive. Kuthera is not mentioned, although it occurs twice in the rest of the poem as a homeland of warriors; but then the catalogue ignores many islands.

586–7 The G-mode ship-entry is similar to that of the Arcadians, likewise special allies of Agamemnon, also with 60 ships, at 609f. Menelaos' close relationship to Agamemnon is stressed here, but his troops are arming ἀπάτερθε, 'apart', no doubt to emphasize his partial independence (rather than the separation of their realms by that of Diomedes).

588 ᾗσι προθυμίῃσι πεποιθώς is a slightly strained application, not found elsewhere, of the formula-pattern -ῃσι/-ηφι πεποιθώς | (4x *Il.*), itself probably developed from the older ἀλκὶ πεποιθώς | (5x *Il.*, 1x *Od.*; πεποιθώς itself only 2x *Od.* against 15x *Il.*, a significant instance of the slight but real difference in formular vocabulary between the two poems).

590 See on 356, where the verse has already occurred; the struggles and groans are at least as likely to be those caused by Helen in others (including Menelaos) as those undergone by herself.

591–602 THE PULOS CONTINGENT; see also 'Special Problems' (iv), pp. 181f., and pp. 215f. below.

591–4 PULOS was presumably in Messenia rather than in Triphylia or Elis, although that was much disputed in antiquity. The Mycenaean Pulos is now known to have been at Ano Englianos, where the 'Palace of Nestor' has been unearthed on the edge of the hills overlooking the northern part of Navarino bay. Classical Pulos was at Koruphasion down below (cf. Strabo 8.359), its acropolis later occupied by a Venetian castle. ARENE, described in Nestor's account of a war with the Epeans at 11.722–4, is at classical Samikon in Triphylia, where there was a substantial Mycenaean fortified settlement (HSL 83). Its epithet, 'lovely', is given to four other places and is clearly conventional. THRUON 'ford of the Alpheios' is clearly identical with Nestor's Thruoessa at 11.711f., described as 'a town, a steep hill, far off on the Alpheios, on the borders of sandy Pulos' (νεάτη Πύλου ἠμαθόεντος). Strabo 8.349 placed it at the later Epitalion. AIPU is ἐΰκτιτον, which like ἐϋκτίμενον and ἐΰκτίμενον πτολίεθρον seems to be applied where convenient for metrical and stylistic reasons. Its position is unknown. KUPARISSEEIS, according to Strabo 8.349 (whose identifications in this part of the world are for the most part clearly speculative), was north of the river Nedon and not the Messenian Kuparissia on the coast, by which he probably meant the site of the modern town so renamed, where there was some kind of Mycenaean settlement. AMPHIGENEIA according to the same source lay in the same district (Makistia) as Kuparisseeis. PTELEON is unknown and HELOS likewise. DORION has commonly been identified with the Mycenaean hill-site at Malthi, and according to Pausanias 4.33.7 is by a spring on the road from Megalopolis toward Kuparissia. Some doubt remains, although the general region of the Soulima valley is beyond dispute; Malthi = Dorion depends on identifying the spring at the modern village of Kokla with that called 'Akhaiia' by Pausanias.

Nestor's realm as indicated here extends northwards from Pulos itself as far as the Alpheios river at Thruon, taking in Dorion in the Soulima valley which runs eastward into the upper Pamisos valley. This is very different from the area controlled from Pu-ro according to the Linear B tablets from Ano Englianos. Much of course is obscure there, but the 'hither province' and the 'further province' seem to extend from Methone to the Neda river up the east coast, and also across from Pulos to the Messenian gulf around Kalamata and up the Pamisos valley, which is ignored in the catalogue; they certainly do not reach into Triphylia. Names common to the two sources are only Pulos/Pu-ro itself and Kuparisseeis/Ku-pa-ri-so, but that (as Hope Simpson, *Mycenaean Greece* 151, points out) is at least partly because the tablets were primarily listing districts, whereas the places in the catalogue are mostly towns. Yet the two kingdoms obviously do not coincide; are we therefore to denounce the Homeric account, here and. elsewhere, as mere poetic fiction, as John Chadwick does in the tenth chapter of his *The Mycenaean World* (Cambridge 1976)? Surely not; there is enough hard geographical detail in the catalogue at large to show that this is an inadequate approach. Rather the two versions are likely to reflect two different periods. The tablets were written in the late thirteenth century B.C.; the Homeric version probably reflects a state of affairs later than that (*contra* Hope Simpson, *op. cit.* 151), if only because Nestor's reminiscences of wars against the Epeans and Arcadians, which are generally consistent with the catalogue kingdom, are likely to reflect post-Bronze-Age conditions. For the towns of the lower Pamisos valley, including Pherai, see also on 9.149–53, where they lie in Agamemnon's gift; if Pulos somehow lost control of this area at the end of the Bronze Age, then it might well have pushed up into Triphylia to compensate.

594–600 Dorion leads to an elaboration by the main composer, which raises two separate problems. (i) Where exactly was Oikhalie, city of Eurutos and his son Iphitos who was murdered by Herakles? At 730 the catalogue places it firmly in Thessaly, in the realm of the Asklepiadai. That implies that the Thracian singer Thamuris (who has something in common with Thracian Orpheus) has here wandered down from Thessaly into Messenia, where he meets the Muses – rather than meeting them near Thessalian Oikhalie itself. Wandering singers are ignored elsewhere in Homer, but were a probable fact of life. Yet at *Od.* 21.15 Iphitos and Odysseus met 'in Messene', and in the post-Homeric tradition Oikhalia was placed as often in Messenia (or Euboea, indeed) as in Thessaly. That may, of course, have developed from confusion engendered by this very passage; Hesiod at any rate seems to have set Thamuris' encounter 'in the Dotion plain' near the Boebean lake in Thessaly (*Ehoiai* frags. 65 and 59.2f. M–W), and that is a more likely place for bumping into the Muses than the south-western Peloponnese. The resemblance between Δώτιον and Δώριον is probably irrelevant, especially since it is visual rather than aural/oral, but it may be significant that Nestor himself, as a grandson of Kretheus king of Iolkos, had come down into Messenia from close to the Boebean lake, which together with Iolkos comes under Eumelos of Pherai later in the catalogue at 711f.

(ii) But why in any case did Homer choose to introduce this diversion here? It serves no purpose beyond that of attaching some elaboration to Dorion, which could have been done with a simple epithet. Other expansions in the catalogue have some distinct purpose; for example at 699ff. and 721ff. to explain the absence of Protesilaos and Philoktetes. The closest parallel is the Tlepolemos story at 658ff., but he at least is an important person in the fifth Book, rather than one of a string of places. Pointless challenges to deities – this is a particularly foolish one – leading to dire punishment were admittedly a favourite folk-tale or mythical motif. The closest Homeric parallel is the tale of Niobe at 24.602–9, with Meleagros as another improving example at 9.527ff.; but these and other such allusions had some special relevance to their context. Perhaps it was professional singer's pride, more conspicuous in the *Odyssey* than the *Iliad*, that motivated an otherwise rather gratuitous elaboration; Thamuris went too far, but at least an almost divine power in song is suggested by his story.

597 στεῦτο is an old epic verb meaning 'declared solemnly, promised', see Chantraine, *Dict.* s.v. στεῦται.

599–600 πηρός evidently implies 'damaged' or 'mutilated', with respect to speech, hearing, sight perhaps, or other bodily organs or functions. It cannot mean 'blind' here, since that was traditionally no handicap to a singer; Demodokos in the *Odyssey* was blind, and Homer himself was probably supposed to be so at least as early as *HyAp* 172. 'Paralysed' is implied here rather than 'dumb', since the Muses took away not only his power of song but also his ability to play the *kitharis* or lyre.

601–2 An E-mode ship-entry (see p. 171) with 90 replacing the regular 30.

603–14 THE ARCADIAN CONTINGENT is chiefly remarkable for its contrast with the rest of the poem, where it is completely ignored.

603–4 Mt Kullene dominates western Arcadia from the north-east. Aiputos is described as son of Elatos by Pausanias 8.16.1–3, who says that he was killed by a snake near Kullene. He is not, therefore, the better-known Messenian Aiputos who was Hippothoos' son; he is probably mentioned precisely because of his tomb, which must have been a landmark in these barren uplands – something was still visible in Pausanias' day. The 'close fighters' of 604 are either from this region or are the Arcadians in general, although nothing is heard about their fighting qualities elsewhere, except by implication in Nestor's reminiscences of border-warfare at 7.133ff.

The conjunction of αἰπύ| and |Αἰπύτιον is remarkable, but probably not significant; although the singer may have liked it when it occurred to him, cf. Πρόθοος θοός at 758. ὄρος αἰπύ| recurs at 829.

605–8 Classical PHENEOS was in that same region under Mt Kullene (on Pyrgos hill near Kalyvia), and Mycenaean sherds were found on the slopes of its acropolis (including LHIIIC according to HSL 91 although not Hope Simpson, *Mycenaean Greece* D 20 on p. 89). ORKHOMENOS 'of many flocks' was another classical polis and controlled another upland plain to the south, overlooking Lake Pedhios Khotoussis. RHIPE, STRATIE and windy ENISPE are all unknown, and called forth Strabo's ironic comment that they are 'hard to find and no use when found, because abandoned'; in his Augustan era even Pheneos, Orkhomenos and Mantinea were non-existent or in ruins (8.388). TEGEE must have been on or near the scattered site of the historical city a few miles SSE of modern Tripolis; excavation at the temple of Athena Alea revealed Mycenaean traces and there may have been continuity of cult. 'Lovely' (again: see e.g. on Arene, 591–4n.) MANTINEE was probably on and around the Gourtsouli hill just north of the classical city (HSL 92f.), where a few Mycenaean sherds, although not LHIIIC so far, as well as ?PG have been noticed. STUMPHELOS was on the north-west side of the Stymphalian lake; nothing has been found between LHIIIB and Archaic, but the presumably ancient tale of Herakles and the Stymphalian birds would suffice to mark this place at any period. PARRHASIE was the district of western Arcadia (all identifiable sites so far have been in the east) to the west and north-west of later Megalopolis; a few Mycenaean relics have been found in this part, although exploration has been slight.

609–10 A G-mode ship-entry (pp. 171f.), as with Mukenai, Lakedaimon and the Eumelos and Philoktetes contingents; the Lakedaimonian entry at 586f. is closely similar: τῶν οἱ ἀδελφεὸς ἦρχε... ἑξήκοντα νεῶν, followed by further information (the Lacedaemonians armed apart from Agamemnon's troops; the Arcadians were many to a ship). For crew-numbers, ἐν νηΐ ἑκάστη..., cf. the Boiotoi at 509f. (ἐν δὲ ἑκάστῃ | ...ἑκατὸν καὶ εἴκοσι βαῖνον), also the Epeans (619, πολέες δ' ἔμβαινον Ἐπειοί) and Philoktetes (719f., ἐρέται δ' ἐν ἑκάστῃ | πεντήκοντα...).

Agapenor will not be mentioned again in the *Iliad*; an Ankaios from Pleuron in Aetolia had wrestled with Nestor in his youth according to 23.635 and could conceivably be Agapenor's father, but the truth is that the catalogist knows a certain amount about (eastern) Arcadian towns but nothing whatever about Arcadian warriors, of this generation at least. Nestor at 7.132–56 (cf. 4.319) recalls a clash between Pylians and Arcadians in his youth when he killed their leader Ereuthalion, the huge squire (θεράπων) of Lukoorgos (from Arne according to the implication of 7.8f.), who had earlier deprived Areithoos of his famous mace; but these were presumably western Arcadians if they extended to Pheia and the Iardanos river (see 7.135).

611 ἐπιστάμενοι πολεμίζειν does not recur exactly elsewhere, although cf. 16.243 ἐπίστηται πολεμίζειν and another variant at 13.223. It is a weak phrase here, perhaps designed to reinforce the 'close fighters' of 604 and lend these ghostly Arkades a little substance.

612–14 Athetized by Zenodotus but 'necessary' according to Aristarchus (Arn/A) to explain how these inlanders could have ships. Leaf observed that no similar explanation would be deemed necessary for the inland Thessalian contingents. At all events the supplement is neatly executed in typically formular language (even θαλάσσια ἔργα μεμήλει -εν recurs, although of sea-birds, at *Od* 5.67, although that could be the model of the present use rather tha· an independent proof of formularity). Its content is not as realistic as it pretends to be, since the Arcadians would need special crews, apart from the ships themselves, who *did* know about seafaring; as for explaining the Arcadians' absence from the rest of the poem, that was perhaps beyond human ingenuity.

615–24 THE EPEAN CONTINGENT.

615–17 BOUPRASION was the name of the region between Capes Araxos and Khelonatas (cf. Strabo 8.340), and there may also have been a town of that name as 23.631 suggests (the Epeans buried Amarunkeus Βουπρασίῳ, 'at Bouprasion' simply). At 11.756f. Nestor reminisces about bringing chariots ἐπὶ Βουπρασίου πολυπύρου (also to πέτρης...'Ωλενίης and 'where it is called the hill of Alesion'), which is compatible with either town or region. ELIS (it is 'noble', δῖαν, like Arisbe, dawn, the sea, and Lakedaimon in *Il.* but not *Od.*) could also be either a region (that one later known as 'hollow Elis') or the city, inhabited in Mycenaean times and, with short interruptions, probably continuously thereafter. That both Elis and Bouprasion here are meant as regions, comprising between them the whole territory occupied by Epeans, is suggested by the four names that follow, which are said to enclose them. Of these HURMINE is almost certainly the site later occupied by the conspicuous medieval castle of Khlemoutsi on the Khelonatas promontory, with LHIIIB–C and Geometric found so far: see HSL 97–9, who have a particularly good discussion of these Epean sites. MURSINOS ('last' or 'furthest', see on 507–8) is likely to be the stronghold at Kastro tis Kalogrias on the Araxos promontory, settled from Neolithic times more or less continuously and matching Hurmine to its south-west. Classical Olenos lay on the north-facing coast some twenty miles eastward, and the OLENIAN ROCK, whether town or just natural feature, must be thereabouts. Three corners of a rough rectangle enclosing western Elis have now been defined, and the fourth, ALESION, would be expected to be somewhere east of Hurmine and south of Petre Olenie – although not so far south, perhaps, as the Alpheios river.

618–19 The Epeans have the largest number of leaders, four, after the Boeotians' five; each of them has ten ships, a unique arrangement suggesting that the country was divided into four regions; but that can hardly depend on the four places just named, which seem to mark the corners of the whole territory; see the previous comment. This leadership arrangement is in any case not maintained in the rest of the *Iliad*, from which Thalpios and Poluxeinos are absent and which has Cyllenian Otos, a companion of Meges, as leader of the great-hearted Epeans at 15.518f., not to mention the ambivalent Meges himself, for whom see on 627–30.

620–1 Of the four leaders *Amphimakhos* and *Thalpios* are called 'Ακτορίωνε (the improbable vulgate reading is 'Ακτορίωνος), which must imply grandsons of Aktor as e.g. Akhilleus is Αἰακίδης, grandson of Aiakos. Their more famous fathers were the Aktorione or sons of Aktor (621), Kteatos and Eurutos (nothing to do with the Eurutos of 596), also called Aktorione Molione (11.750) or just Molione, presumably a metronymic, at 11.709. These were eventually killed by Herakles while they were helping Augeias (Pindar, *Ol.* 10. 26f.), but had come up against Nestor in his youth on two occasions: at 11.750 (cf. 11.709f.) he says he would have killed them in the Pylian–Epean border war had not their father Poseidon saved them, and at 23.638–42 he was beaten only in the chariot-race, in the funeral games for Amarunkeus at Bouprasion, because the Aktorione were twins, and that helped their management of their chariot. It cannot only be for this reason that they were regarded in the post-Homeric tradition, at least, as Siamese twins, cf. e.g. Ibycus, frag. 285 Page; conjoined warriors appear in at least three warrior-scenes on Attic Geometric pots – see further on 23.638ff. Of their sons, Amphimakhos will be slain by Hektor, and his body retrieved by the Athenian leaders, at 13.185–96; Thalpios does not recur. The former is son of Kteatos, the latter of Eurutos, in the reverse of the usual epic and later practice whereby ὁ μέν refers to the last of a preceding pair, ὁ δέ to the first.

622–3 *Diores*, son of the famous Amarunkeus whose funeral games were recalled by Nestor at 23.631ff., meets a dramatic and painful death at 4.517–26. *Poluxeinos*, the fourth leader, is son of Agasthenes and grandson of Augeias; he is not mentioned again in the poem. Eustathius 303.5 (reproduced at Erbse I, 314) gives an impressive-looking genealogy whereby Epeios of Elis and Phorbas of Olenos united against Pelops; each married the other's sister (Epeios' was called Hurmine!). Epeios' son was Alektor, his grandson Amarunkeus, his great-grandson Diores. Phorbas had Augeias and Aktor as sons; the former had Agasthenes (and a selfless brother, Phuleus, on whom see 627–30n.), and Poluxeinos as grandson; the latter had Kteatos and Eurutos, and Amphimakhos and Thalpios as grandsons. Very neat, but it says nothing about Poseidon's paternity of the Aktorione–Molione.

625–30 THE DOULIKHION CONTINGENT.

625–6 Aristarchus commented (Arn/A) that the form of words does not necessarily distinguish DOULIKHION from the Ekhinaes islands – it could be one of them, or it could be separate. Its identity, discussed under 'Special Problems' (v) on pp. 182f., is uncertain. The EKHINAES themselves (they are 'holy' for unknown, or probably no particular, reason) are 'across the sea from Elis' and are presumably the small group of barren islands off the mouth of the Akheloos river. One was called Doulikhion according to Strabo 10.458, but could hardly be the centre of a kingdom as suggested here. Still less could it have supplied almost half the total number of suitors in the *Odyssey* (16.247–51), where it is named with Same (probably all or part of Kephallenia) and Zakunthos as grouped round Ithake (*Od.* 9.22–4). This contingent is an artificial one, its geography as confused as much of that of western Greece in both poems, and its leader's affinities are themselves in doubt: see the next comment.

627–30 Meges is leader in this B-mode entry, with (at 630) the common 40-ship contingent – as against Odysseus' mere 12! He plays a moderate role in the rest of the poem, certainly not an insignificant one as Page, *HHI* 163 claimed (quoted with approval by HSL 102, who overlook many of Meges' appearances). He appears briefly at 5.69–75; he is described as an Epean at 13.691f.; at 15.302 (where the ἀτάλαντος "Αρηϊ formula of 627 is repeated) he is grouped with Aias and Teukros, Idomeneus and Meriones; at 15.518ff. he attacks the slayer of his Epean comrade Otos of Kullene, and his corslet (brought by his father Phuleus from Ephure) saves him in further fighting (15.529ff.). As 'son of Phuleus' simply he appears at 10.110 and 175 and 16.313; his final appearance is at 19.239. There is thus some doubt over whether Meges is an Epean or not. On this point the catalogist, at least, is consistent enough; Meges' father Phuleus had moved to Doulikhion because of a quarrel with *his* father (629), and we know from later sources (e.g. Strabo 10.459; see also on 622–3) that this was the Epean Augeias, whom Phuleus blamed for cheating Herakles.

631–7 THE KEPHALLENES CONTINGENT.

631 A C-mode entry (p. 170), emphasizing the leader's name by placing it at or near the start of the opening verse. Odysseus' troops bear their tribal name of Kephallenes; for the form cf. the Enienes at 749. They evidently gave their name to the island here called Samos (634), later Kephallenia.

632–4 ITHAKE is Odysseus' own island, the modern Ithaca. For NERITOS 'with quivering leaves', one of its mountains (*contra* Strabo 10.452), KROKULEIA and 'rough' AIGILIPS (probably other parts or natural features of Ithake), see also under 'Special Problems' (v) on pp. 182f. ZAKUNTHOS and SAMOS (Kephallenia, perhaps primarily its northern part), like Ithake itself, were settled in the Mycenaean period, Kephallenia quite extensively so, down into the twelfth century B.C. Continuity into the Early Iron Age is probable here and there in Ithake and western Kephallenia at least – Zakunthos has been little explored. The date of origin of such a description of islands and places is impossible to determine, especially since there was some obvious confusion, so far as Ionian singers on the other side of Greece were concerned, about these distant western and north-western regions.

635 'The mainland and the facing parts' could be either Acarnania or Elis. At *Od.* 4.634–7 Noemon of Ithake wants to fetch his mules and twelve mares from Elis, where he seems to have been grazing them; that is firmly in favour of the latter. On the other hand that north-west facing coastal strip is precisely the part occupied by the Epeans, with whom Meges but not· Odysseus has special connexions. Acarnania is quite feasible; the description is intentionally, perhaps, vague (ἤπειρος and ἀντιπέραια are from different roots but amount to the same thing here).

637 Odysseus' 12 ships (the same number as Aias' from Salamis, incidentally) are described in an adaptation of the D mode (p. 171). They alone of all the ships are μιλτοπάρῃοι, 'scarlet-cheeked' (not elsewhere in *Il.*, IX *Od.*), μίλτος being red ochre. The cheeks may simply be a metaphor for the curving bows, and not imply that a face was represented or even that eyes were suggested, as often in Geometric and later vase-paintings. According to Herodotus 3.58.2, 'in the old days all ships were coated with red'.

638–44 THE AETOLIAN CONTINGENT (AITOLOI).

638 The A-mode introduction is expanded at 641f., after the list of places, by further explanation of why Thoas is leader. He is moderately prominent in the rest of the poem, occurring in six different episodes. At 13.216–18 Poseidon disguised himself as 'Andraimon's son Thoas|who in all Pleuron and steep Kaludon|ruled over the Aitoloi and was honoured like a god by the people', and at 15.282–4 he is 'by far the best of the Aitoloi, skilled with the throwing-spear,|good in the standing fight, and in assembly few of the Akhaioi|excelled him', as he rallied the Greek forces.

639–40 The site of Hellenistic PLEURON is known, some ten miles west of ancient Kaludon; the Archaic and classical town lay nearby, and there were probably earlier settlements in the near neighbourhood. OLENOS is unknown, but was placed by Strabo 10.451 near Pleuron; PULENE was probably in the same general region. KHALKIS 'next the sea' was probably at modern Kruoneri at the foot of Mt Varassova, which dominates the north shore of the entrance to the Corinthian Gulf; once again Mycenaean and later settlements seem to have been on distinct although neighbouring sites. 'Rocky' KALUDON (also 'steep' and 'lovely', twice each in other parts of the *Iliad*) is firmly located, with a conspicuous acropolis used in the Mycenaean period and the later town and sanctuary below. It was famous in myth and legend, not least for the Calydonian boar and the war of the Aitoloi and Kouretes alluded to in the tale of Meleagros at 9.529ff.; for this reason if for no other it could never have been forgotten, but in fact the remains suggest that it was continuously inhabited. So too, probably, was ancient Thermon, just north of Lake Trikhonis, whose omission from this list of Aetolian towns is surprising; in fact Thoas' contingent is confined to a relatively small part of south-western Aetolia.

641–2 These verses explain why the best-known Aetolian royal family does not provide the leader at Troy: Oineus' sons no longer live, nor does he himself, and Meleagros (in particular) is dead. The tale of Meleagros' wrath is told by Phoinix as an example to Akhilleus at 9.529ff., but that says nothing about his death, which is perhaps why it has to be specially mentioned here. Hesiod, *Ehoiai*, frag. 25.12f. M–W, says that he was killed near Pleuron in the fighting against the Kouretes; that must be after he had ended his wrath and saved Kaludon from siege in Homer's version, and is perfectly plausible. Oineus had presumably died in Kaludon from old age, despite his offence to Artemis which had started the trouble with the boar (9.534–6). He is specifically said to have remained at home when Tudeus went to live in Argos (14.119f.); the latter, of course, joined the Seven against Thebes and was killed and buried there (14.114). Nothing is said here about the descendants of Oineus' brothers Agrios and Melas (14.117), and Thoas' father Andraimon must have belonged to a different family.

The two verses were athetized by Zenodotus (Arn/A), perhaps as a result of their slightly awkward expression – it is not at first sight clear that Meleagros was one of the sons, and one might have expected a specific mention of his brother Tudeus. Aristarchus also commented (Nic/A) that αὐτός in 642 refers to Meleagros and not Oineus if there is no strong pause before θάνε δέ: 'nor was brown-haired Meleagros himself still alive, but he had died'. That might seem more natural in content, since Oineus would in any case be old to go to Troy; but it is less natural in expression, despite ἄρ' (in its primary use 'expressing a lively feeling of interest', Denniston, *Particles* 33f.), and there is no good parallel in Homer to θάνε used in just that way.

644 The standard 40-ship verse ends this first 'tour' (see 'Special Problems' (vi), pp. 183ff.), in which there is nowhere left to go except across the Pindus or into unimportant western Locris, which would lead back into Phocis and necessitate a new start in any case.

645–52 THE CRETAN CONTINGENT (KRETES): a fresh start is made for a brief and selective island tour of the southern and south-eastern Aegean.

645 An A-mode entry (p. 170); Idomeneus, together with his second-in-command Meriones (to be described in the resumptive verses 650f.) are of course major figures in the rest of the poem.

646–8 All seven cities named seem to be located in central Crete. KNOSOS (Knossos) is Idomeneus' own town (and that of his father Deukalion and his grandfather Minos) according to Odysseus' false tale to Penelope at *Od.* 19.172–81, which gives a more detailed description of Crete than this one. The 'palace of Minos' was destroyed around 1400 B.C. but reoccupied, and Knossos and its region probably continued to be inhabited into the Iron Age. There is evidence of continuity at GORTUS too (HSL 111f.); its acropolis was fortified in late Minoan times, and the powerful walls reflected in its epithet τειχιόεσσαν (as of Tiruns at 559) and still visible in places probably belong to the later part of LMIIIC (and can even be described as Sub-Minoan). From there one might expect to move to Phaistos, but, as often, some of the places are taken out of any logical order and we move back across the mountains to LUKTOS and MILETOS near the northern coast – that is, if the former is equivalent to the later Luttos and the latter to the later Milatos, which seems especially probable (despite Strabo 10.479; it has also been identified with Minoan Mallia). LUKASTOS is hard to locate; Sir Arthur Evans placed it not very persuasively at the Minoan site of Visala (HSL 113f.). Its epithet ἀργινόεντα, 'gleaming', may refer to whitish soil or cliffs and is not entirely inappropriate to Kameiros, at least, to which it is also applied in a rhythmically almost identical 3-place verse at 656. PHAISTOS is certainly known, being one of the most important Minoan palaces and towns and 'clearly also an important place in the Early Iron Age' (HSL 114, who have a not very convincing argument, partly based on *Od.* 3.293–6, about its relations with Knossos and Gortus). RHUTIOS has been associated with the Late Minoan and Archaic and classical remains (Early Iron Age relics seem lacking, HSL 115) on the Kephala ridge above Rotasi, at the eastern end of the Mesara plain and some 10 miles east of Gortus.

According to Desborough, *Last Mycenaeans* 229 and 236, Crete suffered stagnation after the destruction of the palaces and during the fourteenth and thirteenth centuries B.C.; links were maintained after 1200 with the Dodecanese, Melos and perhaps Argos; there were further disturbances a generation or so later, when some of the population took to the hills and the east of Crete became isolated from the centre, which 'remained in touch with the Aegean, and adopted certain features of the Protogeometric style' (236). These conclusions, based on the evidence of pottery, have some weight. Their relevance to the catalogue is that its concentration on central Crete could well derive from that period in the Early Iron Age when the east, at least, was out of touch and could be neglected. For the evidence of the *Odyssey* see the next comment.

649   Crete has 90 towns, not 100, at *Od.* 19.174–7, where it is also said to contain Akhaioi, Eteokretes ('genuine Cretans') and Kudones, agreed to be from central, eastern and western Crete respectively, as well as more mysterious Dorians and Pelasgians. The present verse need not imply that Idomeneus' troops came from all over Crete – rather than, like the others, its central part.

652   The standard 40-ship verse is converted to 80 ships, one of the largest contingents, probably in view of Crete's reputedly large number of towns.

653–70   THE RHODIAN CONTINGENT.

653   Tlepolemos is a son, not just a descendant, of Herakles, see 658–9 below and 5.638f.; the rising threefolder, due to the heavy patronymic though it may be, gives him a touch of class.

654   His small number of ships, according to this F-mode entry (pp. 171f.), might seem to be explained by the haste with which he had to prepare for his escape according to 664f. – but since then Zeus had poured wealth on him and his people, 670. At least the number is divisible by three to match the three cities, but then the common 30-ship number would serve just as well (although its whole-verse format would have to be changed from the F-mode entry). Yet he himself only reappears – conspicuously, it is true – in his fatal encounter with Sarpedon in book 5, where Rhodes is not mentioned; and the Rhodians in general (their epithet ἀγερώχων, of uncertain derivation, is usually applied to the Trojans, 5× *Il.*) do not appear in the rest of the poem.

655–6 RHODOS here and elsewhere is the island, the town of that name not being founded until 408 B.C. The Rhodians are 'triple-arranged', and the addition of 656 strongly suggests that this is because they are in three groups, each from one of these cities; although see 668 with comment for another possibility. LINDOS, IELUSOS (Ialusos) and KAMEIROS are the three independent *poleis* of the island, at least after the Dorians arrived probably in the tenth or early ninth century B.C.; they became members of the 'Dorian Hexapolis' together with Kos, Knidos and Halikarnassos. But were these towns, as e.g. Willcock says *ad loc.*, 'already there in Mycenaean times'? There is no doubt that the island was quite extensively settled in the Late Bronze Age, but the question is whether these three places were the inevitable foci of such settlement. Few Mycenaean sherds have been found at Lindos itself, and none on the acropolis at Ialusos; although an extensive Mycenaean cemetery on two hills just to the east of it contained around 150 chamber tombs, at least 17 of them from LHIIIC (Desborough, *Last Mycenaeans* 152f.). There is also a Myc cemetery a few miles west of Lindos. At Kameiros, again, there are 5 Myc chamber-tombs a couple of miles to the east, but nothing certain from the site itself; on these data, but not the conclusions drawn from them, see Hope Simpson, *Mycenaean Greece* 192–8. Lindos and Ialusos, at least, are natural sites, but Siana/Agios Phokas (Hope Simpson, *op. cit.* 197, with references), some 15 miles down the coast from Kameiros, has at least as strong a claim to be an important Mycenaean settlement; on the other hand, after the Dorian immigration there were three political units and three only, precisely those named here. Even apart from Tlepolemos being a Heraclid (and the Dorian 'invasion' being called the 'Return of the Herakleidai' in historical times), and from the τριχθά...καταφυλαδόν of 668 (q.v.), the prima-facie evidence of the places named and the historical and archaeological facts at our disposal point to the Iron Age and not the Late Bronze Age as the background of this entry. Incidentally according to Desborough (*op. cit.* 157f.; his sensible comment is that 'It can hardly be supposed that there was a complete depopulation'), there seems to have been a gap in the archaeological record of Kos after the end of LHIIIC (perhaps as late as 1050 B.C.), whereas at Rhodes 'the next available material is Late Protogeometric', i.e. from around 900 B.C., suggesting some discontinuity.

658–60 About Astuokheia (Pindar, *Ol.* 7.23 calls her Astudameia) little is known; the Ephura from which she was taken as a war-captive was in Thesprotia according to Aristarchus (Arn/A), the river Selleeis being connected with the Selloi who dwelt around Dodone according to 16.234f. Eustathius 315.44 (perhaps following a lost scholium as Erbse suggests, 1, 318f.) added that Herakles was helping the Aitoloi and killed Astuokheia's husband Phulas.

βίη Ἡρακληείη (etc.) occurs six times in the *Iliad*; in five of those it makes a convenient formula to fill the second half of the verse. βίη with the genitive of the name, e.g. Πατρόκλοιο βίη, is also a well-established locution meaning 'strong Patroklos' and so on; it is used of Helenos (three times), Huperenor, Herakles himself, Teukros, Priam and Diomedes as well as Patroklos (twice). This degree of development suggests that the idiom is an ancient one, which its naive quality may confirm.

661-6 It was in Tiruns that Tlepolemos killed his grandfather Likumnios, Alkmene's bastard brother, according to Pindar, *Ol.* 7.27-9 – unintentionally as is usually the case in this standard folk-tale motif. That he built ships (literally 'fastened' them, ἔπηξε) is mildly surprising since a hurried retreat is implied. In 665 Aristarchus (Hdn/A) took οἱ as pronoun and not definite article, and that is accepted in e.g. OCT; but Leaf points out that οἱ ἄλλοι, τῶν ἄλλων is common in Homer.

667 ἄλγεα πάσχων (etc.), 4x *Il.*, 9x *Od.*, cf. other verse-end formulas with ἄλγεα, e.g. ἄλγεα θυμῷ (5x *Il.*, 5x *Od.*). That the journey should be a difficult one is again typical of this standard narrative theme, embodied in a sense even in Odysseus' return in the *Odyssey*.

668-70 τριχθὰ δὲ ᾤκηθεν καταφυλαδόν recalls διὰ τρίχα κοσμηθέντες in 655. That clearly refers to their division among the three cities of 656, and the present phrase would do the same were it not for καταφυλαδόν. Tribes, φῦλα in a technical sense, are rarely considered in Homer, see on 362-3, and the division into three tribes inevitably raises the question whether these might be the three Dorian tribes, especially in view of Tlepolemos as Heraclid and the three cities' later Dorian status. In Odysseus' description of Crete (see on 649) the Δωριέες τε τριχάϊκες are mentioned at *Od.* 19.177 – a puzzling reference in itself, but one which would prove that the epic tradition took cognizance of the three Dorian tribes *if* τριχάϊκες were certainly a compound of τριχά = 'threefold'. However, a formidable battery of philologists including Leumann, Frisk, Risch and Chantraine (*Dict.* s.v.) opt for a different meaning, 'with waving horsehair plumes', cf. κορυθάϊκι etc., derived from θρίξ and ἀΐσσω. On the other hand Bechtel, Meillet, Schwyzer and Benveniste had supported the τριχά derivation; some reserve on the matter is still permissible, especially since Hesiod, frag. 233 M-W supports the second interpretation.

Page, *HHI* n. 86 on p. 176, conceded that 'No doubt the Dorian tribes are meant by καταφυλαδόν in 668', but then claimed that 668-70 'are a later addition'. This is because Aristarchus (Arn/A) athetized 669 on the ground that it represents an unnecessary gloss on ἐφίληθεν by someone who did not see that 668 is self-contained: 'they dwelt in three divisions by tribes, *but in amity with each other*' – surely an impossible interpretation. Page also objects that ἐφίληθεν| ἐκ Διός is not 'an old Epic combination' and that πλοῦτον is Ionian and 'not included in the traditional formular vocabulary', neither point being convincing once one sees that these diversions or expansions in the catalogue are unlikely to be much if at all older in their expression than Homer. Page in short makes the common confusion between 'relatively late in the oral tradition' and 'post-Homeric' or 'interpolated'. In fact πλοῦτος (etc.) is found five times elsewhere in the *Iliad* and is certainly not post-Homeric; it is incorporated quite naturally in the formula θεσπέσιον -ην...κατέχευε -εν, cf. e.g. *Od.* 8.19.

The matter is a complicated one and has been much discussed, and there are other possible factors in the argument: for example that Tlepolemos is in any case not said to have been the first Achaean to settle in Rhodes, and that his conflict with Lycian Sarpedon in book 5 might be a reflection of actual warfare with the mainland in the Late Bronze Age. Nevertheless καταφυλαδόν in particular is difficult to ignore, and my provisional conclusion is that some reference *is* intended to the notion, surely widely diffused by Homer's time, that the Dorians were somehow descended from Herakles and were divided into three tribes. Be that as it may, the introduction of Tlepolemos makes a pleasant and relaxed narrative diversion from the severer lists that surround it.

671–5 THE SUME CONTINGENT. It is hard to imagine this small and poor island, between Rhodes and the Knidos peninsula, as having ever been an independent state, even to the extent of providing three ships. Nor would sheer good looks, in a heroic society, make up for a man being 'weak...and with few troops' (675). Neither Nireus nor his troops are heard of again, nor of course are his parents; his mother Aglaie has the same name as one of the Graces. Verse 674 recurs as 17.280, where it is used of the greater Aias who was second only to Akhilleus in appearance and deeds, εἶδος and ἔργα. The triple epanaphora of Nireus' name is remarkably effective (although Zenodotus evidently did not think so, since he athetized 673 and 675 and omitted 674 altogether, Arn/A). Indeed this brief C-mode entry is well composed and quietly memorable; it is unlikely to be pure invention, although the obscure person who nevertheless has some special gift or skill is a typical narrative motif.

676–80 THE KOS CONTINGENT.

676–7 The placing of the small and obscure NISUROS at the head of this island group is perhaps fortuitous, or perhaps determined by metre or even alliteration (to keep the four places with initial kappa together). As at Sume, the Kastro above the main harbour has signs of ancient settlement.

KRAPATHOS and KASOS are more important; they form an island bridge between the southern tip of Rhodes and the eastern tip of Crete. The former was quite heavily settled in the Mycenaean period, especially around the classical town of Potidaion, modern Pighadia, in the south-east. KOS is altogether more fertile, in its north-eastern half at least, and important Mycenaean (LHIIIA–C) and PG and G remains have been found in excavations at the Seraglio hill just outside the modern (and Hellenistic/Roman) town; occupation was perhaps continuous (HSL 123f.), although see on 655–6 *fin.* Kos was probably the leader of this island group – for king Eurupulos see the next comment. The KALUDNAI islands are presumably Kalumnos (where the Perakastro hill above the harbour of modern Pothia was occupied down to the end of the Mycenaean period and then has PG and G as in Kos) together with Pserimos and conceivably Leros.

678–9 About Pheidippos and Antiphos nothing more will be heard; as sons of the Heraclid Thessalos they are likely to be kings of Kos and descendants of Eurupulos, said to have possessed Kos at 677. Kos maintained the tradition that it was founded in some way by Thessalos and from Thessaly (indeed the elder son of its most famous citizen in later times, Hippocrates, was also called Thessalos). Eurupulos was grandfather of the Heraclid Thessalos according to some sources; a different version is given by b on 677, that Herakles captured Kos and became father of Thessalos by Eurupulos' wife Khalkiope. Herakles' connexion with the island is borne out by Homeric references at 14.254f. and 15.24–30, as well as by later ritual; other genealogical speculations are relatively worthless. The Heraclid connexion parallels that of Tlepolemos of Rhodes and can hardly be accidental; it confirms the faintly Dorian colouring of these island entries, which are likely to have originated no earlier than the end of the Dark Age. The brief island 'tour' ends at this point, and no attempt is made to extend beyond the Dorian group either northward to Samos or westward to Naxos and the Cyclades.

680 An E-mode ship-entry after the B-mode introduction at 676.

681–94 THE MURMIDONES CONTINGENT.

681 A fresh start is made, for the last time (see pp. 184–6), with the contingents from around the later Thessaly; that is emphasized by νῦν αὖ. The following word, τούς, suggests that a different type of entry with a verb like ἦγε, 'led' or 'brought', was envisaged (rather than ἔσπετε or ἐρέω, cf. 484 and 493, as Aristarchus (Nic/A) supposed); the construction in fact reverts to the ordinary B-mode with τῶν αὖ at 685.

'Pelasgic' Argos must be the region of the Sperkheios river and the Malian plain. The Pelasgoi were thought of as prehistoric inhabitants of Greece; Akhilleus addresses Zeus as Δωδωναῖε, Πελασγικέ at 16.233 and there were Πελασγοί in Crete according to *Od.* 19.177; there were Pelasgoi in Asia

Minor too (see 2.840). Pelasgiotis in historical times was the whole of the east-central Thessalian plain around Larisa, some way north of here beyond Mt Othrus.

682 Only TREKHIS can be identified – it is presumably close to historical Trakhis, renamed Herakleia, south of the Sperkheios delta. A few Mycenaean sherds, but nothing then until classical, have been found there; Dark Age occupation in this whole region looks very thin. ALOS is quite unknown, and ALOPE was placed by Stephanus of Byzantium on the north shore of the Malian gulf; but there were towns of those names in (eastern) Locris, not mentioned in the Locrian catalogue-entry, and some confusion is possible.

683–4 Akhilleus claims Phthie and Hellas as his home elsewhere also (9.395, which also does something to substantiate the 'fair women' epithet here; cf. *Od.* 11.495f., also 16.595f. for Hellas and 1.155 and 9.363 for Phthie). The tribal name Ἕλληνες was extended to the Greeks in general (although not by Homer, as Aristarchus remarked, Arn/A), for reasons we do not understand. The addition of καὶ Ἀχαιοί in 684 is surprising; it may be based on misunderstanding of 530 Πανέλληνας καὶ Ἀχαιούς *vel sim.*, although that verse itself is under suspicion, see on 529–30. Phthie is implied to have extended beyond the Sperkheios region by 13.693, where Phthians are led (in that admittedly eccentric list) by leaders of the Protesilaos and Philoktetes contingents, which came from further north and as far as Magnesia.

685 A variant of a G-mode ship-entry, see p. 172; it has the advantage of placing the emphasis heavily on the leader's name, ἦν ἀρχὸς Ἀχιλλεύς|.

686–94 Now comes the explanation that the Myrmidons were not at present involved in the war, which means, in effect, in the march-out (686). It is less essential than the similarly appended explanations about Protesilaos (699ff.) and Philoktetes (721ff.), since Akhilleus was there at Troy, whereas they were not. Perhaps that is why Zenodotus athetized them (Arn/A), to which Aristarchus replied that they were 'necessary'. The poet (and that means the monumental poet) intends by this device to emphasize still further Akhilleus' withdrawal from active participation on behalf of the Achaeans, and to remind the audience yet again (after all the detail about other contingents which must, to an extent at least, have been distracting) of the great quarrel that is to determine future events.

686 πολέμοιο δυσηχέος, 7x *Il.*; it is uncertain whether the epithet is formed from ἄχος, 'pain', with metrical lengthening of the alpha, or from ἠχή, 'sound', 'reputation', with suppression of its original initial digamma. ἐμνώοντο from μνάομαι is found only here and 2x *Od.* meaning 'remembered'.

687 Patroklos is ignored here (largely for dramatic reasons, no doubt) as a possible substitute for Akhilleus, which he is to become in book 16. It is Akhilleus himself that counts.

689–90 Now Akhilleus' wrath is recalled, but Agamemnon is not directly mentioned; rather attention is focused on Briseis and his winning of her at Lurnessos. The toils he underwent, πολλὰ μογήσας, reflect his words to Agamemnon in the quarrel-scene and the prize ᾧ ἔπι πολλὰ μόγησα (1.162); he will develop the idea at greater length in his indignant speech to the embassy in book 9 – the sleepless nights and bloody days in which he captured twenty-three cities and gave the spoils to Agamemnon (9.325–32), who then took away the woman he cared for, captive though she was (9.341–4).

690–1 At 19.59f. Akhilleus will tell Agamemnon that he wished Briseis had dropped dead on the day he captured Lurnessos. This town lay below Mt Ida, and Aineias had nearly been caught when herding cattle there before the attack (20.90–2 and 188–90). At 1.366ff. Akhilleus recalled the attack on Thebe (described as Ὑποπλακίη at 6.397), the city of Eetion from which Khruseis was captured in the same raid as Briseis.

The formula τείχεα Θήβης is applied to Boeotian Thebes (before it was destroyed by the Successors) at 4.378; διαπορθήσας is not found elsewhere as a compound in Homer, and the simple form πορθέω 'replaces πέρθω in Attic and Ionic' (Shipp, *Studies* 199) and occurs 1x *Il.*, 2x *Od.* It belongs to the latest stage of the oral vocabulary, no doubt, but cannot confidently be said to be post-Homeric. The verse (691) is a rising threefolder.

692–3 Munes was king of Lurnessos, cf. 19.296, Epistrophos evidently his younger brother. The latter name, together with that of his father and grandfather in 693, goes beyond information supplied elsewhere in the poem and confirms that the expansion is not merely rhapsodic.

694 κεῖτ' takes up the κεῖτο of 688 by ring-composition, a potentially insipid formal device which here serves to sharpen the contrast with the powerful and ironical τάχα δ' ἀνστήσεσθαι ἔμελλεν, 'but he was soon about to rise up' ('not in the Homeric style', Leaf!), which plays on the literal meaning, 'lie down', of κεῖτο.

695–710 THE PHULAKE CONTINGENT.

695–7 PHULAKE is shown by 700 (as well as by 13.696 = 15.335) to have been Protesilaos' home and therefore the capital. Its exact location is nevertheless unknown; Strabo 9.435 says it was near (Phthiotic) Thebes, and so in the north-west corner of the Pagasitic gulf. 'Flowering' PURASOS was the later Demetrion, according to the same source, and is probably the mound-site above the harbour at Nea Ankhialos, where Myc and G sherds have been found (HSL 132). Strabo also says there was a grove of Demeter close by, which must be the Δήμητρος τέμενος of 696. ITON 'mother of flocks' has been provisionally placed 'in the foothills to the south-west of the

Krokian plain' (HSL 133). ANTRON 'next the sea' was south of Pteleon and had an off-lying submarine reef known as 'Antron's donkey' according to Strabo 9.435; it is probably directly across the strait from Histiaia. 'Grassy' PTELEON – epithets come thick and fast here, and this one at least does not look particularly appropriate for another harbour site – lies on the hill called Gritsa at the head of Pteleon bay; the contents of tholos tombs there suggest continuous habitation from the Late Bronze into the Dark Age (HSL 133). Thus Protesilaos' kingdom runs down the west side of the Pagasitic gulf to meet Akhilleus' along the north shore of the Malian gulf to the south, and abuts Eumelos' kingdom centred on Pherai to the north. No particular date can be conjectured for the original source of the entry.

698–709 The statement that Protesilaos was leader is in the standard form of a B-mode entry and, like other expressions for leaders and ship-numbers, has no especially archaic characteristics. Consideration has now to be given to whether such forms of expression might not have originated before the time of monumental composition – otherwise, it might be asked, what is the point of creating something that has to be immediately corrected in the case of Protesilaos and (shortly) Philoktetes? Probably there *is* point and purpose enough, in both historical and dramatic terms: Protesilaos and Philoktetes were well-known figures, their substitutes Podarkes and Medon were not; they were remembered to have no part in the developed fighting before Troy, but yet to have been members of the expedition when it first left Greece. It is rhetorically effective, therefore, to name them as leaders, especially since the catalogue is allowed to maintain its archaic naval format, and only then to amend the picture. Both entries look homogeneous, afterthoughts and all.

699–702 This amendment begins emotionally: the black earth already held him, his wife was left with cheeks lacerated (ἀμφιδρυφής) by mourning and with the house in Phulake half-finished, a unique detail in which δόμος must have a concrete sense. It was a 'Dardanian man' who slew him – that has a timeless ring – as he leapt ashore by far the first of the Achaeans.

703 This verse, to be repeated at 726, is in strong stylistic contrast; the rising threefolder provides an epigrammatic summary of their pathetic longing as well as neatly leading on to present realities.

704–9 The sequence of cumulated twofold verses, the first three of them quite strongly spondaic, introduces yet another tone, of deliberateness and order; but with rising emotion again, to round off the passage, in the interrupted and integrally enjambed couplet 708f. Podarkes is the younger brother, a lesser man than Protesilaos; accepted as leader all the same, but they still missed Protesilaos (in a neat reversion to the πόθεον of 703). He will recur only once in the poem, when like Medon (another replacement, see on 726) he appears surprisingly as a Phthian leader at 13.693 (and at

13.698 will be remembered to be son of Iphiklos son of Phulakos, as at 705 here).

ἀρείων...ἀρήϊος in 707f. is perhaps rather weak, especially with ἥρως intervening.

710 The conventional ship-number verse helps to emphasize the restored regularity of the contingent.

711–15 THE PHERAI CONTINGENT.

711–12 Can PHERAI be at the site of the classical polis, some seven miles from Lake Boibeis, and still be described as παραί, 'by', the lake? Yet this high mound-site near modern Velestino was part of an extensive settlement from Mycenaean times, at least, to Hellenistic and beyond. BOIBE is usually identified with the remarkable site at Petra on the lake's western shore (with an outer circuit of Cyclopean walls almost 5 kilometres long) – unless it was Mycenaean Pherai itself. No Iron-Age pottery earlier than classical has been found there. GLAPHURAI is quite unknown and its name (*pace* HSL 136) does nothing to suggest a sea-port. IAOLKOS (Iolkos) is firmly located on the edge of modern Volos; it was the home of king Pelias in the Argonaut myth, and its Mycenaean palace, burned during LHIIIC, was soon reoccupied. If there was a gap in occupation outside the palace it 'cannot have been much more than a generation' (Desborough, *Last Mycenaeans* 234), and the new stone buildings in PG, which might of themselves justify the epithet 'well-built', were a rarity at that time (Desborough, *op. cit.* 31f.).

712–15 Eumelos' father Admetos, son of Pheres according to 763, was most famous for having employed Apollo for a year – it was this that led to his possession of marvellous horses, 763ff. – and, later at least, for his shabby treatment of his wife Alkestis, daughter of King Pelias of Iolkos. His is an ancient and well-known kingdom containing, in Pherai and Iolkos, two of the most important cities in Thessaly; even so, Eumelos himself will be completely neglected after this Book until the chariot-race in book 23, and is only given eleven ships.

716–28 PHILOKTETES' CONTINGENT.

716–17 None of the four places can be identified with any confidence, and that makes understanding this contingent particularly hard; see also p. 187. HSL 138 place METHONE on a hill at the edge of the Lechonian plain overlooking the bay of Volos. Strabo's account (9.436) of THAUMAKIE, OLIZON and MELIBOIA has a gap in it, but probably said little more than that they lay on the coast. An inscription may suggest that Meliboia (Philoktetes' home according to a later tradition) lay near Thanatou (or Athanati) north-east of modern Ayia and on the south-east flank of Mt Ossa. 'Rough' OLIZON could be anywhere on the coast, and it is hard to see why people have been so ready to identify it with a little acropolis-site at Palaiokastro on the neck of the Trikeri peninsula.

718–20 Philoktetes was an archer, and so were his men; it may be to accommodate this description of them that the unusual detail is added (in this G-mode ship-entry, cf. pp. 171f.) that they went fifty to a ship; of course they acted as oarsmen, ἐρέται, as the troops in other contingents must have done. It is a small contingent in any case, with only seven ships, and perhaps suggests a narrow territory.

721–3 The story of Philoktetes' snake-bite and his sojourn on Lemnos (the version by which it was on some other, barren island was later, according to Aristarchus, Arn/A) is obviously well known to the epic audience. This brief summary is fluently composed for the occasion rather than being an extract from, or condensation of, a longer account, as on a larger scale Nestor's reminiscences or the tales of Bellerophon in book 6 and Meleagros in book 9 give the impression of being. Verse 723 is a powerful one, a rising threefolder in effect, with κακῷ (rarely a weak term in Homer) emphasizing, as b remarks, the hero's sufferings, and ὕδρου – strictly a water-snake – 'baleful' like the lion at 15.630 (a simile) or the boar at 17.21 (simile-like).

724–5 ἔνθ' ὅ γε κεῖτ' ἀχέων echoes τῆς ὅ γε κεῖτ' ἀχέων of Akhilleus at 694. Both phrases pick up an earlier κεῖτο (at 688 and 721); the meaning of the verb is metaphorical in Akhilleus' case, literal in Philoktetes' – the former was just sitting around, the latter is lying in agony, but the adaptation is typical of the formular style. The direct echo, again with ingenious adaptation one way or the other, is continued in the second part of each verse:

694 τῆς ὅ γε κεῖτ' ἀχέων, τάχα δ' ἀνστήσεσθαι ἔμελλεν
724f. ἔνθ' ὅ γε κεῖτ' ἀχέων, τάχα δὲ μνήσεσθαι ἔμελλον
'Αργεῖοι

Zenodotus athetized 724–5 (Arn/A) and probably 726 as well, as Leaf suggested in his apparatus, since he also adjusted 727 to begin τοὺς δὲ Μέδων. Aristarchus countered this with his 'argument from necessity': 'it is necessary to know that Philoktetes was afterwards brought back from Lemnos'. But that is simply incorrect; the audience must have known that in any case, and it is a matter for the composer's taste and judgement how much of the story he includes here. What shows the verses to be authentic is precisely their ingenious overlap with the Akhilleus passage, which would be beyond the capacity, or indeed the intentions, of any rhapsodic or later developer. The elaborations of Akhilleus, Protesilaos and Philoktetes have much in common stylistically, and many points of contact with the rest of the poem; they are in all probability by the monumental composer, Homer himself.

726 = 703 (of Protesilaos' contingent), followed in each case by

|ἀλλά...κόσμησε(ν). Here the substitute commander is Medon, a more interesting figure than Podarkes; he is bastard son of Oïleus of Locris, and therefore half-brother of the lesser Aias. At 13.694–7 = 15.333–6 we learn that he had fled to Phulake from his native land, where he had killed an older relative (just as Tlepolemos had, cf. 661–6), a male relation of his step-mother Eriopis, Oïleus' wife. It is strange, none the less, that he should inherit the command of his adopted country's contingent, and no less so that with Podarkes he should be found leading Epeans at 13.693. He will be slain by Aineias at 15.332.

729–33 THE CONTINGENT OF THE ASKLEPIADAI.

729–30 TRIKKE is presumably the modern Trikala, where there are signs of continuity of settlement from the Mycenaean into the Early Iron Age. ITHOME is κλωμακόεσσαν, a word understood as meaning 'rocky' by Lycophron 653; Strabo (9.437) placed this Ithome in the territory of Metropolis, at the foot of the Pindos mountains and overlooking the south-western edge of the western Thessalian plain. Mycenaean and later relics are sparse in this region. The OIKHALIE of king Eurutos cannot be specifically located in these parts; for the confusion over this place see also on 594–600. At least it can be deduced that the contingent comes from the later Histiaiotis.

731–2 The leaders are the 'good healers' Podaleirios and Makhaon, Asklepios' sons. The former is only mentioned once in the rest of the poem, fighting at 11.833; the latter several times, when he treats the wounded Menelaos in book 4 and especially when his own wound (11.506f.) is a matter for concern – Akhilles sees him being brought back to the camp and sends Patroklos to confirm who it is (11.599ff.). It is as an army doctor that he is most important – the contingent as a whole is not otherwise mentioned; Trikke was the centre of the earliest cult of Asklepios, who is, however, described simply as 'blameless healer', and probably as an ordinary mortal therefore, at 11.518. See also on 4.193–4.

733 Four out of five of these last contingents have standard ship-numbers, with either 40 or (as here) 30 ships. The poet does not worry about how these inlanders obtained their ships, as he had done with the Arcadians (612–4).

734–7 THE CONTINGENT OF EURUPULOS.

734–5 ORMENION cannot be precisely located, neither can the spring HUPEREIA (whether it is at Ormenion or a separate place). Strabo (9.438) knew an Ormenion over near Mt Pelion and a Hupereia spring in Pherai, but admits that this is strange. ASTERION and the 'white summits' (which could refer to a town, cf. 117, or a mountain) of TITANOS are equally obscure, although the Argonaut Asterion according to Apollonius, *Argonautica* 1.35–9 came from Peiresiai at the confluence of the Apidanos and

Enipeus rivers, that is, in the north-eastern part of the western Thessalian plain. Strabo placed Titanos near Arne, the later Kierion, some 15 miles to the south. τίτανος, 'white earth', is probably named after the place.

736 However vague his realm, Eurupulos occurs frequently in the rest of the poem, and seems to be a well-known figure in the epic tradition.

738–47 THE CONTINGENT OF POLUPOITES AND LEONTEUS.

738–9 Strabo (9.440) equated ARGISSA with the later Argura on the river Peneios just west of Larisa; much Myc and some PG pottery was found in the Gremnos mound there (HSL 145). GURTONE lies further down the Peneios, but ORTHE is unknown. ELONE according to Strabo (9.441) was near the Europos river which he took to be the Homeric Titaressos (751n.); HSL identify it with an important Mycenaean site at Karatsoli, with no PG or G observed; this is possible but quite speculative. OLOOSSON is usually identified with classical Elasson (complete with 'white' cliffs) in the foothills of Mt Olumpos up the Meluna pass; but the similarity of name is superficial and this again is speculative. Nevertheless Polupoites' realm can be fairly securely placed in the northern part of the eastern Thessalian plain.

741 ἀθάνατος is only rarely applied as an attribute of a god, for obvious reasons; nevertheless the formula ἀθάνατος τέκετο Ζεύς occurs 4× *Il.* Zenodotus had the brilliant idea of reading ἀθάνατον in each case: 'false!' as Aristarchus remarked (Arn/A), since most of Zeus' children by mortal women, including Peirithoos, were of course mortal.

742–4 The fight of the Lapiths and Centaurs is alluded to at 1.262–8 and *Od.* 21.295–304. Here the tribal name Λαπίθαι is not mentioned (although Polupoites and Leonteus are so described at 12.181f.), presumably because the audience knew the story so well. Again, 'Centaurs' is not used; they are φῆρες, 'beasts' (on which see 1.268, where they are 'mountain-dwelling', and comment). For κλυτός with a feminine noun in 742 compare *Od.* 5.422, κλυτὸς ᾿Αμφιτρίτη; also, more generally, 19.88, ἄγριον ἄτην; 20.229, ἁλὸς πολιοῖο; *Od.* 4.406, πικρὸν...ὀδμήν – rare cases which are presumably a concession to the pressure of metre. In 743 ἤματι τῷ is a usefully expanded phrase (21× *Il.*, usually followed by ὅτε, 4× *Od.* – a significant difference) for the general idea of 'when'; sometimes, as here, it imports a kind of fairy-tale precision. τεκέσθαι usually means 'engender' of the father, as in 741, but 'gave birth to' of the mother; in 742, however, the day meant is probably Hippodameia's wedding-day; Peirithoos is envisaged as taking immediate vengeance on the Centaurs, whom he drove back to their haunts on Pelion and then across to the Pindos mountains (which is where the Aithikes lived according to Strabo 9.430).

745–6 οὐκ οἶος, as Aristarchus noted (Arn/A), refers back to 740; for the ἅμα τῷ γε locution see on 822–3. Leonteus was probably younger than Polupoites, since his grandfather Kaineus had been Peirithoos' contemporary (1.263f.) and was killed in the brawl at the wedding (being invulnerable, he was driven into the ground by the Centaurs' branches): see Apollonius, *Argonautica* 1.57–64, who adds that his father Koronos was from Gurtone. Both leaders will recur later in the poem, bearing the same formular descriptions as they have here (that is, Polupoites will be μενέπτολεμος twice, and Leonteus ὄζος Ἄρηος twice). Their most prominent action is their heroic defence of the gate attacked by Asios, in an extensive and effective episode at 12.127–94; but they also take part in the weight-put at 23.836ff., which Polupoites wins.

748–55 GOUNEUS' CONTINGENT.

748 Gouneus brings 22 ships in this C-mode entry (p. 173), an eccentric number perhaps designed to give him some individuality. This contingent and the next (and final one) make an odd conclusion to a list which, even in some of its Thessalian coverage, is impressive for its sheer information. Not only is KUPHOS unknown, but so is Gouneus too; he has no patronymic, unusually, and will not recur in the poem.

749–51 The use of tribal names reflects the remote and lightly-settled terrain; there is no need to go so far as b, who concludes that these are βάρβαροι, non-Greeks (see N. G. L. Hammond, *Epirus* (Oxford 1967) 395). The Enienes and to a lesser extent the Peraiboi were tribes associated, at different periods, with many parts of Thessaly and its surrounding mountains; see HSL 149. DODONE must surely be the famous seat of the oracle of Zeus on the far (western) side of the Pindus; although Strabo (7, frag. 1 Meineke, cf. 9.441 *fin.*) claimed after Kineas that it was originally in Thessaly near Skotoussa. The TITARESSOS river is here said to join the Peneios (752), which runs right across northern Thessaly after rising in the Pindus. Strabo (9.441) must be wrong in equating the Titaressos with the Europos, which joins the Peneios (with a mild demonstration of non-mingling waters over a short stretch, cf. 753–4) right over in the east, near the entrance to the vale of Tempe; he is probably taking into account the proximity of Gonnos, the classical city to which Gouneus' name may be related (cf. H. von Kamptz, *Personennamen*, 289). Hammond, *op. cit.* 393, concludes that the Enienes (Ainianes) were 'washed up on the side of the upper Spercheius valley' by the invasion from north-western Greece which brought the Thessaloi into Thessaly at the end of the Bronze Age. If it is implied by 750 that the Enienes, rather than the Peraiboi alone, came from around Dodone, then that may be evidence for a Late-Bronze-Age, rather than a Dark-Age, origin for some of the information in this entry.

755 According to 15.37f. the Stux is 'the greatest and most terrible oath [*sc.* to swear by] for the immortal gods'; cf. Hesiod, *Theog.* 775, where it is στυγερὴ θεὸς ἀθανάτοισι. Another infernal river, the Kokutos, is said to be an offshoot of the Stux at *Od.* 10.514, in the same words Στυγὸς ὕδατός ἐστιν ἀπορρώξ; that may be the source and inspiration of the present verse, which looks like a learned afterthought on the incompatible waters of the two rivers. A third infernal river, the Akheron, rose on the west side of the Pindus and was associated with the Thesprotian entrance to the underworld; it looks as though the Stux also, although usually located in Arcadia, had connexions with this part of the world and so with the Peneios which also rose in the Pindus, although on its eastern side.

756–9 THE MAGNETES CONTINGENT.

756–8 Nothing further will be heard of Prothoos (or his unusually-named father); on -θοος θοός cf. 603–4n. *fin.* As for the Magnetes themselves, they were a tribe which eventually gave its name to the whole mountainous coast from the mouth of the Peneios down to Pelion and the rugged peninsula to the south of it. This is compatible with 757 but not with the apparent realm of Philoktetes, on which see 716–17n. The least doubtful of the fixed points in his realm is Meliboia, which seems to lie on or near the coast on the southern slopes of Mt Ossa; that would cut right into a people who dwell 'around Peneios and Pelion with quivering leaves'. It is tempting to solve the problem by assuming that Pelion here really refers to Ossa, considering these as two parts of a continuous mountain chain; modern maps have even been adjusted in favour of that interpretation (as HSL 151 observe). But the mountains are quite distinct, and were always so regarded by the Greeks; the solution must lie elsewhere, perhaps in a genuine confusion on the part of the composer at this point. But why in any case does he name a separate contingent of Magnetes? That is a question we may never be able to answer, except perhaps by the general observation that documents, including oral ones, are prone to corruption in their final sections.

760 This verse rounds off the Achaean catalogue by repeating 487 with minor adaptation. 44 (living) leaders have been named, of whom 10 will be killed later in the poem; the ships number 1,186 in all, which at an average complement of roughly 50 gives a force of some 60,000 – hardly what the later descriptions of fighting (not to mention supplies) suggest! It is, of course, legitimate poetical exaggeration, and it has been noted (p. 173) how arbitrary the ship-numbers are.

Conclusions on the Achaean catalogue

The commentary on the detailed catalogue-entries has been written as far as possible without prejudice, except perhaps against the extreme forms of the 'Mycenaean origin' theory (as exemplified in places by V. Burr and by D. L. Page in the works cited on p. 169). It has also tried to avoid the temptation, exemplified here and there in HSL, of looking round for

Mycenaean sites (in which Greece was extraordinarily rich) to identify at almost all costs with otherwise speculative place-names in the catalogue. It has likewise been unsympathetic to the idea (most seriously advanced by B. Niese and A. Giovannini) that the main content of the catalogue derives from the state of Greece in the eighth or even the seventh century B.C.; although some details from close to Homer's own time are obviously to be expected. A detailed survey of the catalogue suggests different dates of origin for various pieces of information over the long span of the heroic oral tradition, from the time of the historical siege of Troy or even earlier down to the latest stages of monumental composition. The following, in brief, are some of the points which have emerged. It must be stressed that they are not adequate in themselves to give a definite and complete picture of the nature and origins of the catalogue, on which reserve is still necessary.

(1) From the form, mainly, of the leadership and ship-number entries (on which see pp. 170 to 173) it is clear that the ultimate composer of the catalogue consistently followed the developed rules of the Homeric formular style, with no trace either of earlier (or archaic) descriptive technique – except for what might inhere in the concept of such a long list in the first place – or of the survival of especially archaic language.

(2) The special treatment of the Boeotians may indeed suggest a contribution, at some stage in the tradition, by Boeotian singers both expert in catalogue-poetry and having access to reminiscences of Aulis as place of assembly for the Achaean fleet. The catalogue-elements in the Nekuia in book 11 of the *Odyssey*, as well as in Hesiod, *Theogony* and *Ehoiai*, show that such Boeotian interests need not have been particularly early in relation to Homer.

(3) The argument which has been so important to proponents of a Mycenaean catalogue in some form, that nearly a quarter of the place-names were not certainly identifiable in the historical period with specific geographical locations, and so offer 'proof positive and unrefuted that the Catalogue offers a truthful, though selective, description of Mycenaean Greece' (D. L. Page, *HHI* 122), is not really tenable. Many or most of these names could have been retained in an oral tradition, not necessarily always a poetical one, even when the original places to which they had been attached had become depopulated. Clearly, of course, the main reason for such retention would be association with great historical or mythical events in the past, and this is where the Trojan War comes in.

(4) Details of particular contingents occasionally suggest Mycenaean information the transmission of which must depend on some such unknown tradition; but many Mycenaean elements derive from places like Argos, Mukenai or Tiruns whose connexion with the tale of the Trojan War was maintained by monuments like the Lion Gate or Cyclopean walls as well

as by continuity of habitation. Even places like Harma in Boeotia or Stumphelos in Arcadia might retain a mythical aura capable of surviving destruction or abandonment at the end of the Bronze Age. Eutresis presents greater difficulties, but even there depopulation may not have been total (see p. 195) and the memory of the name could have survived.

(5) Several striking assertions or omissions are more likely to depend on conditions of the Dark Age than of its Mycenaean predecessor: the omission of Tanagra, Khaironeia and Mideia (see pp. 194f., 210); the reduced importance of Orkhomenos; the description and distribution of the Abantes in Euboea; the separation of Agamemnon's realm from that of Diomedes; Nestor's wars against Arcadians and Epeans; the restriction of the Aetolian contingent to south-western Aetolia and the omission of Thermon (see p. 222); the concentration on central Crete and neglect of the eastern part of the island in particular; the account of Rhodes and its three settlements, and also of Kos and neighbouring islands. These matters are all discussed under the separate entries.

(6) Careful thought has been applied at a relatively late stage to the omission of elements that would be clearly anachronistic, especially Dorian regions and places like Messenia, Doris, Acarnania or Megara (so Burr 110). Similarly the 'afterthoughts' about Protesilaos and Philoktetes are just as likely to be dramatically motivated as to be a clumsy attempt to bring an Aulis-bound document up to date.

(7) There remain many reminiscences of people and places that go back ultimately to the state of affairs obtaining in LHIIIC; as well as much that reflects the more confused political geography of the Early Iron Age (primarily from *c.* 1025 to 900 or 850 B.C.). But nothing suggests the survival of a specific document like an actual Linear B muster-list, or any poeticized version of one. That such documents, in a simple form, were possible is shown by the clay tablet of the fifteenth or fourteenth century B.C. from Ras Shamra (ancient Ugarit), no. 8279, described with justifiable enthusiasm by Burr, *op. cit.* 121ff., on which three ships, with their commanders' names and places of origin, are listed as they leave on some naval occasion; or by the famous Pylos tablet An12 with its ἐρέται Πλευρωνάδε ἰόντες, *e-re-ta pe-re-u-ro-na-de i-jo-te*: 30 men in all, probably (as Ventris and Chadwick comment, *Documents* 183) the complement of a single ship. Such lists may have acted as a practical stimulus to the composition, at some time in the Dark Age most probably, of a proto-catalogue perhaps Boeotian in origin; anything more than that seems, at present, implausible.

(8) Such a conclusion departs significantly from that of e.g. D. L. Page, that the Achaean catalogue is 'substantially a Mycenaean composition' (*HHI* 124), 'substantially an inheritance from the Mycenaean era...rather carelessly inserted into the Iliad after the composition of the Iliad in

something like its present form' (134); and that 'both Catalogues are, and so far as we can tell have always been, Orders of Battle...and their connexion with an overseas expedition must have been historically true' (154). One can, of course, see why Page reached his conclusions, which are presented in the most forceful and picturesque of all modern discussions of the matter; but the evidence is not so clear and one-sided as he supposed, and points to a more gradual and a more complex progression of information and memories through a long and diverse oral tradition.

The Commentary can now continue.

761–79   A short statement, as some kind of afterthought, about the outstanding warrior and horses

761–2   487 = 760 came in the invocation of the Muses as prelude to the catalogue, and this may help the transition to another call upon the Muse (in the singular now, as at *Od.* 1.1 which also has μοι ἔννεπε Μοῦσα) to tell the poet who was 'by far the best of them', that is, of all the leaders just mentioned; to which their horses (of which there was no mention in the catalogue) are awkwardly and gratuitously appended. By itself the new invocation suggests that a considerable list is to follow; in fact it is hardly a list at all, just one person, one set of horses, and an expanded description (after 686ff.) of the Myrmidons' enforced leisure. For conclusions about the authenticity of this episode see after 779n.

763–7   By a chiastic arrangement after 762 the horses are specified first: by far the best were the two mares belonging to Eumelos of Pherai, son of Admetos and grandson of Pheres. They had been bred by Apollo and, we may infer, given by Apollo to Admetos at the end of the god's year of servitude to the mortal prince, then by Admetos to Eumelos. They are the fastest horses in the chariot-race, cf. 23.375f., although Eumelos comes to grief with them.

765   ὄτριχας: 'similar (ὁ- as in ὁ-πατρος, cf. ὁμο-) in the length of their coats'. οἰέτεας: from *ὁ-ϝέτεας with metrical lengthening of ὁ-, i.e. 'similar in years', of the same age. σταφυλῆ so accented (as distinct from σταφύλη = bunch of grapes) is, as Ab reveal, a stonemason's rule: 'equal over their backs (when measured) by the rule', i.e. of exactly equal height.

766   Πιερίη is the medieval vulgate reading, but there was obviously argument about this in antiquity – although not, it seems, by Aristarchus, since the regular scholia remain silent. A scholium in a first-century B.C. papyrus (P. Oxy. 1086) says 'some ignorantly write Πιερίη', and Πηρείη is attested in other papyri and in Stephanus of Byzantium, who claimed to know of a place of that name in Thessaly. Other minority readings are Πιρείη, Φηρίη. The choice seems to lie between accepting Pieria, which although north of Mt Olumpos was a haunt of the Muses and therefore of Apollo, and reading Φηρείη, that is, the region of Pherai, Eumelos' capital. Admittedly Pherai is spelled with an epsilon in the catalogue-entry at 711, but the name of Eumelos' grandfather (cf. Φηρητιάδαο at 763) suggests that an eta is possible. That would allow the natural inference that Apollo bred the mares while serving Admetos at Pherai.

767 φόβον Ἄρηος φορεούσας is an unparalleled and inelegant phrase (although φορέω of horses carrying a charioteer is found at 770, 8.89 and 10.323; Shipp, *Studies* 237 is surely wrong in claiming 770 as 'rather unnatural' on this account). Perhaps Phobos as son of Ares should be understood, see on 4.440–1; but even that is awkward.

768–70 Of men, Telamonian Aias was far the best – so long as Akhilleus raged (and Akhilleus' horses were likewise best, 770, on which see also the previous comment). The choice of Aias might not seem automatic – what about Diomedes, for instance? – but Odysseus is of the same opinion at *Od.* 11.550f. It is fair to assume that Akhilleus' two semi-divine horses at least (Xanthos and Balios, children of the Harpy Podarge by the west wind), who also 'flew with the winds' (16.149), would outdo even those bred by Apollo. Nevertheless there is something to be said for Schulze's idea, approved by Leaf and by Bolling, *External Evidence* 76, (who exaggerate, however, the irregularity of μήνιεν with metrical lengthening of iota), of replacing Τελαμώνιος Αἴας in 768 by πόδας ὠκὺς Ἀχιλλεύς and omitting 769–70 as a gloss.

771–2 These verses recur at 7.229f. as part of Aias' boast at the beginning of his duel with Hektor, where they are perfectly in place.

773 The runover-word Ἀτρείδη is a little awkward, although more or less exactly paralleled at 9.332; it obviously helps the singer to turn to how the Myrmidons are engaged. ῥηγμῖνι θαλάσσης| is found 4x *Il.*, 10x *Od.*

774 Recurs at *Od.* 4.626 and 17.168, of the suitors at leisure.

775 Again the runover-word (see on 773). In the two *Odyssey* passages the runover into the following verse explains that the suitors were playing 'on a levelled pitch', ἐν τυκτῷ δαπέδῳ, which would presumably be inappropriate here. The addition of bows, or bows and arrows, is not altogether smooth, since one does not 'throw' or 'release', 774 ἱέντες, an arrow quite as one does a discus or a javelin. In general, runover-words or phrases are often unnecessary but rarely inconsistent. The second half of the verse recurs at 8.544, where οἶσιν suits the owners better than the horses as here; the ancient critics passed over this difficulty, together with most others in this whole passage.

776 λωτὸν ἐρεπτόμενοι occurs at *Od.* 9.97 of the companions munching lotus among the Lotus-eaters. Lotus is mentioned twice elsewhere in the *Iliad*, not as fodder but as exotic ground-cover; σέλινος, parsley, has that role in its single other Homeric occurrence, growing outside Kalupso's cave at *Od.* 5.72. 'Marsh-reared parsley' here is none the less a wonderful phrase; Ab explain that it is different from rock-parsley and inhibits strangury in horses deprived of exercise – an idea they may well have derived from the whole Homeric context.

777–8 For the chariots closely wrapped and stored in the huts see 5.193–5, where Pandaros' eleven chariots are said to have been left at home indoors, ἐν μεγάροισι, with sheets, πέπλοι, thrown over them. πεπυκασμένα (etc.), 'closely covered', is formular (3x *Il.*, 1x *Od.*) in this position; at 23.503 Diomedes' chariot is closely covered with gold and tin. The singer has ingeniously rephrased an Iliadic idea, although a certain doubt is left about the practicality of storing a whole contingent's chariots under cover, in huts, on campaign; although Akhilleus' κλισίη, at least, will be termed an οἶκος at 24.471 and thereafter described as a palace or μέγαρον rather than a hut.

οἱ δ' ἀρχόν... ποθέοντες in 778 appears to be modelled on 703 = 726, of Protesilaos and Philoktetes, οὐδὲ μὲν οὐδ' οἳ ἄναρχοι ἔσαν, πόθεόν γε μὲν ἀρχόν. There is a slight roughness, once again, in the adaptation, since the Myrmidons were not 'longing for' Akhilleus, who was still alive and close by, in the sense in which the two other leaders, long dead or absent, were missed. Another small anomaly is the use of ἀρηΐφιλον (etc.) as attribute of a common noun; elsewhere it is predominantly applied to Menelaos (19x), then twice to others and 4x to the Akhaioi; it occurs only once in the *Odyssey*.

779 |φοίτων 2x *Od.*, including 10.119 φοίτων ἴφθιμοι Λαιστρυγόνες ἄλλοθεν ἄλλος, cf. ἔνθα καὶ ἔνθα here; |φοίτα -ᾳ 5x *Il.* The verse is made up of formular components, including also κατὰ στρατόν (see on 1.10–11) and μάχοντο -αι| (18x *Il.*, including 14.132 οὐδὲ μάχονται). There remains some slight inconsistency with 774f.; are the Myrmidons enjoying themselves with discuses and so on, or are they wandering around the army at large with nothing to do? Presumably they are doing both at different times, and each description brings out another facet of their enforced idleness.

Individually, the main items of this whole passage (from 761 to 779) are unobjectionable: Eumelos' horses must have been the best, after Akhilleus' indeed, and will be implied to be so in the games for Patroklos. The greater Aias may be the next best warrior after Akhilleus, and fulfils that role as Achaean champion against Hektor in book 7 (from which 771–2 may well be derived, see comment there). The description of how the Myrmidons occupied themselves expands the bare statement of 686 and helps to emphasize Akhilleus' withdrawal. Two or three details do not seem quite right, especially in 775–9 (the horses' exotic fodder, the storage of the chariots, the longing for Akhilleus). As for the language, it depends to an unusual degree on phrases and verses culled from elsewhere, with a few strains and infelicities (see especially on 767, 775, 778) but also, in 765, a good and unique description of a pair of horses. There is some 'Odyssean' language, but then the idle Myrmidons *are* in something like the position of the leisured suitors. The least satisfactory aspect of the whole passage is its sheer inappropriateness, its needlessly abrupt change of ethos and its effect of anticlimax after the great Achaean catalogue itself. The invocation to the Muse at 761 may be designed to reduce that effect, but turns out to be inappropriate to what will follow. This is not in any case a rhapsode's elaboration – the formular adaptation is too skilful at the technical level but it could be a singer's expansion, and not by Homer himself.

780–815 While the Achaeans advance Iris is sent by Zeus to the Trojans; she takes the form of the look-out Polites and reports the approach of a great army. Hektor dismisses the assembly and the Trojan forces issue from the city and form up in the plain

780 ἴσαν of advancing troops is frequent; οἱ δ’ ἄρ’ ἴσαν, also of the Achaeans, recurs at 3.8. The advance is characterized by a pair of similes, one very brief, the other somewhat longer, that in a small way balance the great sequence before the catalogue begins (see on 455–83). In fact 780 would follow well upon 760. There will be further and related similes immediately after the Trojan catalogue, that is, at the beginning of book 3.

The fire-simile here ('as if the whole earth were grazed upon by fire') is dramatic and rhetorical; it may be based on 455–8, which is in a lower key and more exact in its point of reference – the brightness of the gleam of a forest fire, whereas here it must be the speed and comprehensiveness of a fire's advance that is intended (which is why I feel that 'grazed on' rather than 'inhabited' must be the implication of νέμοιτο, only here in the passive).

781–4 Just as the brief fire-simile may be based on 455–8, so this simile seems to be a development of the metaphor at 95f., ὑπὸ δὲ στεναχίζετο γαῖα| λαῶν ἰζόντων. Here the earth groans as when Zeus lashes it in anger around Tuphoeus, which probably implies in an earthquake: so M. L. West on Hesiod, *Theog.* 858. Tuphoeus is the monster created by Gaia as a final challenge to Zeus and thunderbolted by him and cast beneath the earth, as described at *Theog.* 820–68 (and with interesting additional details provided uniquely by b on 783 here). For εἰν Ἀρίμοις see West on *Theog.* 304; it is clear that ancient critics did not know which particular region this signified, and that local claims were made on behalf of several different apparently lightning-blasted or generally volcanic areas. Strabo 13.626 (perhaps partly from Apollodorus according to Erbse 1, 337 who quotes the passage) mentions various suggested locations: near Sardis, in Mysia, in Cilicia or Syria, or in the west near Mt Etna (where Pindar, *Py.* 1.15ff. placed Tuphos and the Corycian cave) or in Pithekoussai (modern Ischia). 'They say that Tuphoeus' bed is there' in 783 means that he lies there in captivity, weighed down by the earth; West on *Theog.* 304 *fin.* is unlikely to be right that it also implies 'where he keeps his spouse'.

785–9 The composer allows, or enjoys, a temporary spate of verbal echoes: ὦκα/ὠκέα, ἄγγελος/ἀγγελίη/ἀλεγεινῇ, ἀγοράς/ἀγόρευον, ὁμηγερέες/γέροντες.

785 785 will shortly be repeated at 3.14, where it is the dust raised by, not the noise of, their feet that will be the point of comparison.

786–7 An abrupt change of scene: Zeus sends Iris to the Trojans with, σύν, a grievous message (Greek is as concrete as English in this construction). ἀλεγεινῇ (etc.) has a strong inclination in the *Iliad* to be last word in the verse (17/21x).

788–9 ἀγοράς ἀγόρευον comes only here; see also on 4.1 as well as on 785–9 above. |πάντες ὁμηγερέες occurs also at 7.415, preceded by a verse of similar general import, οἱ δ' ἔατ' εἰν ἀγορῇ Τρῶες καὶ Δαρδανίωνες, which would however have omitted the graphic detail 'by Priam's gates'. Justice may have been dispensed, as b remarks, outside the palace, but that does not mean that assemblies were held there; in cramped Troy as in most ancient Near Eastern cities that would have been impossible. The poet is not concerned with such matters, and he needs Priam to be available as well as Hektor. νέοι ἠδὲ γέροντες is a formula (2x elsewhere, in book 9); cf. νέοι ἠδὲ παλαιοί, 2x *Od.*

791–5 Iris resembles Polites in voice, and also, it goes without saying, in appearance; compare 13.216 where Poseidon resembles Thoas in voice, εἰσάμενος φθογγήν, and is taken as Thoas by Idomeneus. Willcock *ad loc.* considers what relation Iris might have to the 'real' Polites, who, after all, was posted as look-out and would naturally rush back to report what he had seen. It is, he thinks, the real Polites who speaks here, but the vividness of his words makes him seem like the divine messenger Iris. Athene taking the appearance of a herald at Odysseus' side at 279f. is a close parallel – see on 278–82, where it was remarked that Athene 'could have obtained the same result by stimulating a mortal herald into action (as Iris could have with the Trojan Polites at 791), rather than by disguising herself; but her direct action provides an emphatic introduction to an unusually crucial speech...' In any case Zeus must be seen to be in control of events since he has agreed that the slight on Akhilleus shall be paid for, which requires a general battle. But once the poetical tradition had accepted the idea of anthropomorphic gods intervening in person, whether or not in disguise, it becomes difficult and largely pointless to seek a specific recipe ('how far is it the "real" man?') on any particular occasion.

Aristarchus (Arn/A) athetized these 5 verses on various unconvincing grounds arising out of this merging of roles, for example that 802 sounds as though it should come directly from the goddess rather than from a younger brother of Hektor.

793 The 'tomb of old man Aisuetes' will not be heard of again, but various landmarks were created as required, for example the hill called Batieia at 811–14 below.

796–806 This speech of Iris/Polites is quite brief, persuasive rather than urgent in style (except for 797 with its strong internal stop and striking πόλεμος...ὄρωρεν), and carefully put together. It begins, like e.g. Nestor's at 337ff., with a rebuke: Priam is always talking (ἄκριτοι here implies 'numberless' words rather than ill-judged ones as in ἀκριτόμυθε of Thersites at 246), as though it were still peacetime; but now it is war indeed. Next comes an emphatic and rhetorical statement (he has been in many battles, but never seen so big an army) illustrated at 800 by a somewhat routine comparison and culminating, by effective contrast, in what he has actually witnessed: they are coming over the plain toward the city. Finally he turns to Hektor as army commander, with specific tactical advice very much in Nestor's style – see on 336–68 and 802–6.

797 ἀλίαστος occurs in its literal meaning, 'from which one cannot withdraw' (λιάζομαι). For the phrase cf. πόλεμον δ' ἀλίαστον ἔγειρε at 20.31; ὄρωρεν (etc.) is formular at the verse-end, 2x *Il.*, 5x *Od.*

798 Aristarchus (Did/A) read ἤδη μέν for ἦ μὲν δή, the latter preferred by Herodian and most MSS and almost certainly correct.

800 |λίην γάρ: so at 19.226, 21.566. Leaves in Homer are usually a symbol of self-renewing rather than of multitude; for sand in this latter sense cf. 9.385.

801 ἔρχονται πεδίοιο, 'they are coming across the plain', cf. ἐρχομένων·...διέπρησσον πεδίοιο in 785. Aristarchus (with Zenodotus and Aristophanes, so Did/A) read προτὶ ἄστυ, not περὶ ἄστυ which became the medieval vulgate reading nevertheless. προτί is probably correct, maintaining as it does the idea of the army approaching; in this case μαχησόμενοι might be taken absolutely, 'they are coming toward the city with warlike intent'.

802–6 The advice concerns an organisational matter which in real terms would have been dealt with years ago – if it had ever been necessary; for the truth is that the idea of contingents led by officers speaking a different language from their own is quite fantastic. Leaf's cure for the anomaly was to excise 803f., but it is probably just due to oral carelessness. The different languages of the Trojan allies is a motif occurring elsewhere, at 4.437f.; it is used here to give a superficial correspondence with Nestor's advice to Agamemnon at 362f. to divide his troops by tribe and phratry. In each case the purpose is to motivate a catalogue of the contingents.

802 An idiomatic verse but not a formular one on Homeric evidence.

804 πολυσπερέων: literally 'much-sown', i.e. scattered. The verse looks like a proverb.

806 πολιήτας: 'his fellow-citizens', a developed Ionic dialect-form not found elsewhere in Homer, who uses πολῖται etc. (2x Il., 2x Od., with of course the proper name like Polites here). Again, neither ἐξηγείσθω nor κοσμησάμενος are exactly paralleled elsewhere.

807–8 Aristarchus (Arn/A) explained οὐκ ἠγνοίησεν as οὐκ ἀπίθησεν, that is, Hektor 'did not fail to recognize' the message and accordingly dissolved the assembly. But there is a hint, too, that he realized that Polites was divinely inspired or even a goddess in disguise. For ἐσσεύοντο cf. 150, where after the dissolution of *their* assembly the Achaeans rushed, ἐσσεύοντο, for their ships.

809 Here Aristarchus (Arn/A) was surely wrong in claiming πᾶσαι to be equivalent to ὅλαι, meaning that the (single pair of) gates were opened wide, on the ground that only the Scaean gate is specifically mentioned in the *Iliad* (in fact the Dardanian gate should probably be added, see on 3.145). Normally the poet does not have occasion to refer to other gates; but the historical Troy ('like all great towns', Leaf, but that is not entirely true, e.g. in the case of Mukenai itself) with its great walls surviving from the sixth city *did* have several gates, and would in any case tend to be classed with seven-gated Thebes as object of a famous siege. The purpose is to emphasize that they streamed out of the city *en masse*.

810 This verse recurs at 8.59 and *Od.* 24.70, with its first half probably also at 11.529 (where the mss read ἱππῆες πεζοί τε) and its second, πολὺς δ' ὀρυμαγδὸς ὀρώρει, an additional 2x *Il.* (+3 variations).

811–15 Earlier, the Achaeans had poured out of their camp (464f.), stopped in the Scamandrian meadow (467), were marshalled for war (476f.) and marched towards Troy (780–5). For the Trojans, a fixed point not far from the city is named as the place of marshalling, corresponding roughly with the 'Scamandrian meadow'; that gives some emphasis to their formation, although nothing to match the simile-sequence which marked the Achaean march-out. It also adds to the landmarks round the city which the poet seems anxious to develop for the sake of realism, like the tomb of Aisuetes at 793.

811–12 This 'steep hill' is ἀπάνευθε, 'apart', only to the extent that it is περίδρομος, i.e. with room all round it for the troops to be assembled.

813–14 For human and divine names in the *Iliad* and *Odyssey* (there are three other cases in *Il.*, +2 in *Od.* with divine names only), see the first part of 1.403–4n., where the conclusion was reached that 'No principle to account for these differences [*sc.* of names] has been satisfactorily proposed'. Each instance, therefore, has to be assessed independently. Here, Batieia is almost certainly based on βάτος = bramble (*Od.* 24.230 and later Greek); 'Bramble Hill' is the workaday descriptive name of the hill, but it had another name also, 'tomb of bounding Murine', πολυσκάρθμοιο being probably related to σκαίρω = leap or dance. The scholia offer no help except that Murine was an Amazon's name (so D). The main town of the nearby island of Lemnos was also called Murine in classical times – perhaps that is also related to the supposed Amazon princess; Priam at 3.187–9 recalls how he helped the Phrygians fight against the Amazons at the river Sangarios away to the east. The question of tumuli or tumulus-like hills around Troy is a complicated one; there are prominent ones on the skyline (looking from near Hissarlik itself) just south of the Sigeion headland, modern Kum Kale, and they were identified from antiquity on with the tombs of Akhilleus, Patroklos and Antilokhos; any burials there are almost certainly post-Homeric, see Cook, *Troad* 159–65. The Murine tomb was identified by Schliemann with 'the notable mound of Pasa Tepe' (Cook, *op. cit.* 107) nearly a mile south of Troy; Mme Schliemann found supposedly prehistoric as well as Archaic sherds there, but Cook (108) is cautiously more inclined to an Archaic date for the mound and its burial. It is quite probable, however, that there *were* prominent tumuli built in the country-side around Troy in the third and second millennium B.C. (especially perhaps in the periods of Troy II and Troy VI Besik Tepe at the southern end of the Sigeion ridge is the best candidate, cf. Cook 173f., and a cemetery of Mycenaean date has recently been found near there, see vol. II, intro.), and that these, sometimes confused no doubt with natural hillocks, could be recalled, and perhaps given exotic names, at any period down to that of the composition of the *Iliad* and after. Ancient tombs, especially when associated with so exotic a character as 'bounding' Murine (which sounds like some ritual action rather than that of a female warrior, as such), would be regarded as holy places, and their specific names might well be regarded as 'divine' in contrast with their common descriptive ones.

815 A specially composed verse (for it had to include both the Trojans and their allies) corresponding roughly with 474–6, where as goatherds διακρίνωσιν their flocks the Achaean leaders διεκόσμεον the Achaeans. Where exactly the allies emerge from is left vague – they cannot have been at the assembly within the city, and formally it is those who were that rushed for their armour in 808.

Book Two

Introduction to the Trojan catalogue

This is a far sketchier list than that of the Achaeans, and displays only an erratic knowledge of western Asia Minor beyond the Troad, not only the hinterland (which is largely ignored) but even the coast. The sizes of contingents are not indicated; there are of course no ships involved, such as gave at least arbitrary numbers to the Achaean units. In the 62 verses (against 226 for the Achaean catalogue), 16 contingents (against 29) are listed. Relatively few towns are mentioned, and most of the entries are distinguished by tribal names; a relatively large number of natural features (rivers, mountains, a lake) occur, most of them on or near the coast. Twenty-six leaders are recorded, of whom most succumb later in the poem and as many as 8 are not subsequently mentioned at all. There are also specific inconsistencies with the rest of the poem; they will be mentioned as they arise, but they exceed those of the Achaean list.

The question has often been raised, and usually answered rather dogmatically, whether this cursory and patchy quality is the product of what Greeks knew about these parts in the Late Bronze Age, or whether it reflects some later era. My own judgement will be given on pp. 262f. after further consideration of the facts, but meanwhile it is important to remember that deliberate archaizing may have been a contributory factor; thus J. M. Cook (cited by HSL 179) was right to stress that Greek settlement in western Asia Minor was widely known to have been subsequent to the Trojan War, and that may have been taken into account. D. L. Page was less cautious; he began by asking whether the Trojan catalogue was 'substantially of Mycenaean origin' (*HHI* 137) and replied that it was, so much so that it supported his doubtful case for a similar view about the Achaean list.

The Achaean catalogue was both extensive and systematic, relying heavily on certain typical patterns for the arrangement of each entry. It is useful to establish whether the Trojan list adheres to the general economy, at least, of the leader(s)/places patterns summarized on pp. 170f. The answer is that the three different modes there called A, B and C are all represented, but in markedly different proportions from the Achaean list, where B ('those who dwelt in (etc.)...of them Y was leader') was much the commonest (18 of 29 entries); here, on the contrary, it applies to only 3 of the 16 entries. The A mode ('of the X's...Y was leader, (of them) who dwelt in (etc.)...') occurs 4 times, the C mode ('Y led (so many ships) from...'), as many as 6 times here (as opposed to 6 and 4 times respectively in the longer list), but in impure forms even apart from the necessary absence of the ship-element. There are in addition 3 entries which cannot be assigned to any of the three modes. Finally it is to be observed that ἡγεμόνευε(ν), a frequent verb for the idea of 'led' in the Achaean list and

248

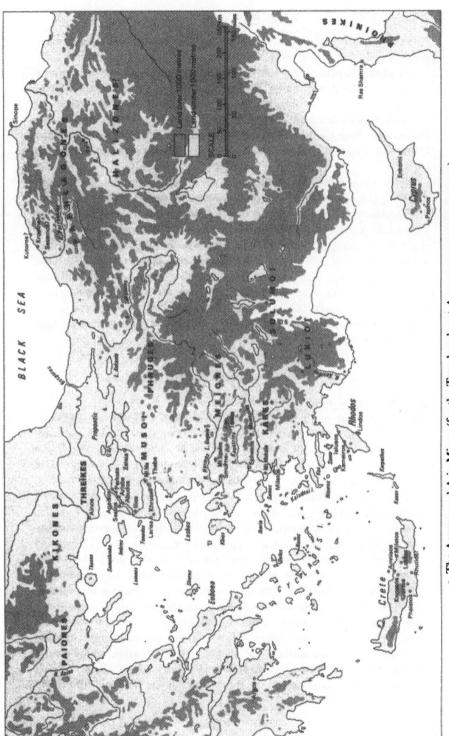

2 The Aegean and Asia Minor (for the Troad and east Aegean see map 3 on p. 251)

especially in the B mode, is here used only once, and then in a peculiar way – see on 816.

On a broader matter of organisation there is some similarity between the two lists; for the three 'routes' of the Achaean one (pp. 183ff.) find a pale analogue in the Trojan one, which, once the contingents from around the Troad have been described, appear to follow four radii (Thracians, Kikones, Paeonians; Paphlagones, Halizones; Mysians, Phrygians; Maeonians, Carians, Lycians), the last place along each radius being described as 'far off'.

So far it seems that the composer of the Trojan list, although obviously following the general pattern of the Achaean one, departed from it in syntax and structure. That is consistent with his use of conventional phrases and epithets for places and natural features; they were a marked characteristic of the Achaean list (pp. 173ff.), but are far less noticeable, and mainly different where they do occur, here (where admittedly place-names are in short supply). Thus the only place-name epithets in common are 836 δῖαν Ἀρίσβην and 841 Λάρισαν ἐριβώλακα; 855 ὑψηλοὺς Ἐρυθίνους is a probable interpolation. Of mountains, 824, 829, 868 and 869 provide two or three loose parallels, but as with rivers (849, 869, 877) the rest of the *Iliad* provides the main model.

816-77   The catalogue of Trojan contingents and those of their allies

816–18 THE TROY CONTINGENT.

The Trojan catalogue starts logically enough from the main city involved; it then passes to other contingents from the Troad, then radiates outwards in four different directions to take in the allies. As a result Hektor, the Trojan military leader, is named first – a less puzzling beginning that that provided for the Achaean list by the numerous but unimportant Boeotians.

816   This is the first occurrence in the poem of κορυθαίολος Ἕκτωρ|, which occurs no less than 38 times. It is likely to be an ancient formula, long established in the heroic tradition; both elements of κορυθαίολος are found in Mycenaean Greek, κόρυς e.g. in the genitive singular as *koruto* and αἰόλος probably as an ox's name, *aiworo* (Chantraine, *Dict.* svv.). The former means 'helmet', the latter implies either 'quick-moving' or 'gleaming' – Page, *HHI* 249ff. has little difficulty in disposing of 'shaking the helmet' and the like and showing that the meaning must be 'with gleaming helmet'. That means a bronze helmet; Page thinks that since the epithet is virtually confined to Hektor, and other helmet-epithets do not imply metallic qualities, that entails actual Late Bronze-Age information about special Trojan armour. Obviously this over-simplifies the issue, in which Hektor's scansion as well as the need for differentiation are factors. Admittedly

3 The east Aegean coast

neither Aias, for example (to take a metrically similar name) is 'gleaming-helmeted', but that is because they have other special qualities to be remarked.

Hektor commands the Τρῶες, here the inhabitants of Τροίη/Ἴλιος itself (see 819–20n.), but used also of those of Zeleia in the Troad at 826, see also on 826–7. ἡγεμόνευε is a common 'leadership' verb in the Achaean list but occurs only here in the Trojan one, and then followed by the dative Τρῶσι and not the normal genitive. This is an Odyssean usage, rather, and means 'acted as guide (for them)' rather than 'was their commander'. Its irregular adoption here seems to be determined by the need for μέν (cf. 494 Βοιωτῶν μέν at the start of the Achaean list); otherwise we should find Τρώων δ' (as at 527 Λοκρῶν δ' ἡγεμόνευε...), quite regularly. The use of a different leadership verb, e.g. ἦρχε, could have avoided this, and with a certain recasting the verse could have retained both Τρώων as emphatic first word and μέν; the composer of the Achaean list, at least, would surely have acted accordingly.

817–18 Another example of the present composer's less than meticulous adaptation of locutions derived from the Achaean catalogue; Hektor's Achaean counterpart Agamemnon seems to provide the model for these verses at 577f., Ἀτρεΐδης· ἅμα τῷ γε πολὺ πλεῖστοι καὶ ἄριστοι| λαοὶ ἕποντ'. The continuation, which glorified Agamemnon, is dropped as perhaps being excessive for Hektor, and is replaced (after θωρήσσοντ' for ἕποντ') with the unparalleled and unsatisfactory half-verse μεμαότες ἐγχείῃσι. The use of μεμαώς, -ῶτες, -υῖα (etc.) is extremely frequent and generated many formular sub-systems, but nowhere among its 87 Iliadic and 14 Odyssean instances is it accompanied by a dative as here, 'eager *with* spears'; it is either absolute or followed by an infinitive ('eager to...') (except only for 13.197 where it takes a surprising genitive). Could the reason for this aberration be found in the Achaean list, once again, where at 543 the Abantes are described as αἰχμηταὶ μεμαῶτες ὀρεκτῇσιν μελίῃσι, 'eager with forward-thrust ash-spears'? But the usage there turns out to be absolutely regular, since the following verse supplies the infinitive, θώρηκας ῥήξειν δηΐων '(eager with...ash-spears) to break the corslets of the enemy'. This is the kind of misunderstanding that was extensively considered by Leumann in *HW*, although this passage is not included by him.

819–23 THE DARDANIAN CONTINGENT.

819–20 The second contingent is led by Aineias (and two others, 822f.), representing the junior branch of the house of Dardanos. The history of the royal family is given by Aineias himself at 20.215ff.: Dardanos, son of Zeus, founded Dardanie on the slopes of Mt Ida before Ilios had been established in the plain (216f.). His son was Erikhthonios, and *his* son Tros, who had three sons (231f.), Ilos, Assarakos and Ganumedes (Ganymede, who was abducted by Zeus, see on 4.2–3). Ilos' son was Laomedon who fathered Tithonos and Priamos (Priam), the father of Hektor and others; Assarakos' son was Kapus who fathered Ankhises the father of Aineias (by Aphrodite, 820f.). It was obviously Ilos that founded the city in the plain, named Ilios after him but also called Troie after the Troes, the descendants of Tros in general. Assarakos and his descendants must have stayed on in Dardanie, probably a rural area or group of villages rather than a town – in 'the middle valley of the Scamander' according to H. Thomas and F. H. Stubbings in their valuable short survey, *Companion* 301. Thus the Dardanioi of 819 are from the foothills of Ida, where indeed Aineias was herding cattle when he was nearly caught by Akhilleus in the course of his raids on Lurnessos and Pedasos at 20.89–92. The form Dardanoi is also used, in the formular verses of address κέκλυτε μευ Τρῶες καὶ Δάρδανοι ἠδ' ἐπίκουροι (4× *Il.*) and Τρῶες καὶ Λύκιοι καὶ Δάρδανοι ἀγχιμαχηταί (6× *Il.*). Thus the poetical tradition remained conscious that the whole Trojan force consisted of three elements: (i) the Troes proper, from the city of Ilios and perhaps a few other places in the vicinity; (ii) the Dardanoi or Dardanioi, from the foothills of Ida; (iii) the allies, ἐπίκουροι, from farther afield. Occasionally Δάρδανος -οι can be applied to the Trojans in general (as in the two uses of Δάρδανος ἀνήρ; at 701 the man who killed Protesilaos as he leapt ashore was probably a Trojan in the general sense rather than specifically a Dardanian; on Euphorbos see 872n.), cf. also 11.285f. (in which Τρῶες...καὶ Δάρδανοι in 286 are subsumed under Τρωσί in 285).

820–1 The tale of the love of Aphrodite and Ankhises and of Aineias' birth is developed in the pseudo-Homeric *Hymn to Aphrodite*, whose composition is placed by R. Janko, *HHH* 180, before 650 B.C., although a slightly later date may be preferable in certain respects.

822–3 οὐκ οἶος/-η/-ην, ἅμα τῷ/τῇ γε is a cumulative formula which occurs 4× *Il.*, 6× *Od.*; see on 3.143. The pattern for the present use could be set by the Lapith entry in the Achaean list, where Polupoites is named as leader at 740 but then Leonteus is added at 745, οὐκ οἶος, ἅμα τῷ γε Λεοντεύς...Aineias is joined as leader of the Dardanians by two sons of Antenor, Priam's chief counsellor at Troy. Why? Because Priam did not trust Aineias, as b suggests? Or because the two branches of the family remained to some extent intermingled (cf. 819–20n.)? Or is it rather because· this pair of verses is borrowed from 12.99f., where they exactly recur in a short and compressed list of Trojan and allied units? Arkhelokhos will be killed by Aias at 14.463–74, where his physical resemblance to Antenor is mockingly remarked; his death is avenged by Akamas (14.475–85), who himself dies at 16.342f.

824–7 THE ZELEIA CONTINGENT.

824 The people of Zeleia are called Τρῶες in 826, yet their town is 'under the furthest foot of Ida' on the river AISEPOS, which runs into the Propontis some miles to the west of the later Kuzikos (Cyzicus); that they came from by the Aisepos is also stated in the main body of the poem, at 4.91. This puts ZELEIA some 70 miles ENE of Troy as the crow flies, on the edge of foothills which can only be called those of Mt Ida in a fairly loose sense.

825 They are prosperous, ἀφνειοί, perhaps *because* they 'drink the black water of Aisepos', for that implies that they live in its relatively fertile valley. πίνοντες...Αἰσήποιο is a delightful description which finds no exact counterpart in Homer; μέλαν ὕδωρ| (in which 'black' implies 'dark') is a formula (2x *Il.*, 4x *Od.*), not so common as μέλαν αἷμα|; here the order is reversed and ὕδωρ assumes its naturally short upsilon as elsewhere within the verse. The Aisepos is one of the eight rivers listed at 12.20–2 as flowing into the sea from the Idaean hills.

826–7 They are Trojans in a sense, just as Aineias' Dardanians were. The Dardanians belonged to the junior branch of the royal family, these do not; yet these first contingents from around the Troad have close associations with the Trojans in Troy (see on 819–20). Their leader is Pandaros, the famous archer who is to wound Menelaos in book 4 and be killed by Diomedes in book 5, where he is said to come from Lukie (5.105 and 173) – although his troops are still called Troes there, most plainly at 200. It is clear that this is not the historical Lycia, from which indeed, from the region round the Xanthos river, Sarpedon and Glaukos led the Lycian contingent at 876f.; Pandaros is never closely associated with them. It is sometimes assumed that he was originally Lycian and was transferred to the region of Troy by a confusion in the tradition (as e.g. by M. P. Nilsson, *The Mycenaean Origin of Greek Mythology* (Berkeley 1932) 57f.), but there is no other evidence to support such an assumption; if there was confusion, it was more probably caused by his connexion with Apollo Λυκηγενής (4.101) as archer-god. And as T. W. Allen observed (*Catalogue* 151 n. 1), Lukos is a common Asiatic river-name, at least.

827 Apollo's giving Pandaros his bow in person implies little or nothing more than that he was a famous archer; see the preceding note.

828–34 THE ADRESTEIA CONTINGENT.

828–9 Strabo's geography of the Troad was sometimes erratic, but he is the best guide we have (at 13.587–9) to the location of these places overlooking the upper Hellespont and south-western shore of the Propontis (Sea of Marmara). Taking them from west to east, PITUEIE was the predecessor of the later Lampsakos, near the point where the Hellespont broadens out; and MT TEREIA was probably close by (although it could have been near Zeleia). APAISOS (which is called Paisos when an Amphios succumbs at 5.612) was between Pitueie and the later Parion, which lay some 20 miles east of Lampsakos. ADRESTEIA was the easternmost of the group, between Parion and the later Priapos (which lay some 12 miles east of Parion, still to the west of the river Granikos).

Τηρείης ὄρος αἰπύ corresponds with 603 Κυλλήνης ὄρος αἰπύ, and for δῆμον Ἀπαίσου| cf. 547 |δῆμον Ἐρεχθῆος.

830 Adrestos (presumably of Adresteia and a descendant of the eponymous founder) and Amphios are the two leaders; *an* Adrestos is captured, then killed, by Menelaos at 6.37ff., and yet another is killed by Patroklos at 16.694. Amphios has a linen tunic, he is λινοθώρηξ, like the Locrian Aias at 529; but when someone called Amphios who dwelt in Paisos but was son of Selagos is killed by the greater Aias at 5.612f. he obviously has normal armour – he is struck in the ζωστήρ at 615, and then at 621f. Aias is prevented by enemy pressure from 'removing his fine armour from his shoulders'. Aristarchus (Arn/A) dealt summarily with any possible confusion by asserting that there was another Amphios, of Perkote, son of Elatos (which is probably a MS error for Selagos). The reference must be to the passage in book 5, which does not in fact call that Amphios a Percosian (although Merops, the father of this one, is). 5.613f. adds that Amphios was rich in possessions and harvests, but that destiny led him to help the Trojans – a phrase which corresponds strikingly with 834, κῆρες γὰρ ἄγον μέλανος θανάτοιο. This recurs at 11.332; in fact the entire four verses 831–4 recur as 11.329–32, where Merops' two sons are killed in their chariot by Diomedes and Odysseus. This, then, is where the two sons of Merops as described in the catalogue are unambiguously killed (and that one of them is λινοθώρηξ and yet in a chariot can just be accepted); but there seems to be some confusion, nevertheless. My own conjecture is that it lies in the catalogue and not in the rest of the poem; the catalogue entry looks unimpeachable in itself, of quite high quality – but probably because much of it is derived from the encounter in book 11. That part, 2.831–4, could have been brought in to replace some simpler statement about Merops and his sons; but this would not remove the other problems. One would really like to put Merops where in an obvious sense he belongs, that is, with the Perkote contingent; but then the two sons killed at 11.328f. would be nameless, which is not Homeric.

835–9 THE PERKOTE CONTINGENT.

835–6 ABUDOS and SESTOS controlled the Hellespont at its narrowest point, the former on its southern, the latter on its northern shore. The site of historical Abudos, a Milesian colony, lies just north-east of modern Kanakkale, with Sestos, always closely associated with it, opposite. PERKOTE, PRAKTIOS (also a river) and ARISBE had disappeared by Strabo's time (13.590), but he reasonably placed them between Abudos and Lampsakos;

thus Merops' affiliation with Perkote at 831 is helped by physical proximity (though see the preceding note). These places therefore lie along the Hellespont, closer to Troy than those of the previous contingent.

837–9 Their leader is Asios son of Hurtakos. His son Phainops was Hektor's dearest guest-friend and lived in Abudos according to 17.583f., but Asios himself comes from Arisbe and the river SELLEEIS, a relatively common river-name; he is to be distinguished from Hekabe's brother Asios who lived in Phrygia (16.717–19). It was suggested by b on 838 (perhaps after Aristonicus according to Erbse) that his horses are mentioned because they were concerned with his death at 13.384–93, where he comes to a painful end when attacking Idomeneus on foot, with his horses and chariot close behind him. That is made more likely when one observes that 838f., describing the horses, are identical with 12.96f., the beginning of Asios' imprudent venture in which he disobeys Poludamas' advice and takes his chariot into the thick of the fighting; in short, his chariot and horses are very much part of his quite considerable role in the central part of the *Iliad*. The author of this entry seems to know this.

Perkote and Abudos were evidently in especially close touch with Hektor and the Trojans, judging by this and other references. Thus Melanippos was a cousin who herded his cattle at Perkote and came to help defend Troy, living in Priam's palace there (15.546–51); Iphidamas son of Antenor was raised by his grandfather in Thrace and came with twelve ships, which he left at Perkote, to fight at Troy (11.221–30); a half-brother of Hektor (one of Priam's illegitimate sons), Demokoon, came from Abudos for the same purpose (4.499f.).

The repetition of Asios' name and patronymic, with reversal of their order, is elegantly done, although the composer of book 12 (from which 838f. are probably derived, see above) deserves most of the credit, just as he does for 837 (with its rare but effective formula ὄρχαμος ἀνδρῶν) which is evidently derived from 12.110. Yet similar epanalepsis is found later in this Trojan list at 849f. and especially 870f. For the former, again, there is a model elsewhere: 849f., of the river Axios, is closely similar to 21.157f. (although with οὔ...ἐπικίδναται αἶαν for ὅς...ἐπὶ γαῖαν ἵησιν). But the latter is unparalleled: Ἀμφίμαχος καὶ Νάστης ἡγησάσθην, | Νάστης Ἀμφίμαχός τε...The virtuosity of these repetitions and reversals should not be exaggerated, but it remains clear, nevertheless, both that the composer of the Trojan list knew the rest of the poem very well indeed (including the Achaean list) and that he was in addition a reasonably accomplished poet.

840–3 THE CONTINGENT OF PELASGOI.

840–1 φῦλα of a particular tribe or people is not so used elsewhere in the *Iliad* (see also on 362–3). The Pelasgoi are ἐγχεσίμωροι, an epithet which recurs twice in the *Iliad* and once in the *Odyssey*, and the second element of which (etymology unknown, probably meaning something like 'glorying in', cf. Chantraine, *Dict.* s.v. ἔγχος) is found in Ιόμωροι, 2x *Il.*; see on 4.242. LARISA was a place-name particularly associated with the Pelasgoi, ancient inhabitants of Greece (cf. Πελασγικὸν Ἄργος, the homeland of Akhilleus, at 681, also Apollodorus II.4.4). Strabo (9.440) mentions no less than eleven Larisas; one was north of the later Hamaxitos on the west coast of the Troad (Strabo 13.620; Cook, *Troad* 219–21), which would suit the proximity of this contingent to the preceding ones from in and around the Troad – although when Hippothoos dies before Troy at 17.301 it is said to be 'far from Larisa'. That caused Strabo to opt for the Larisa near Kume, further south, but he was probably wrong. The Pelasgoi are stationed near the Leleges at 10.429, and the Leleges lived in Pedasos in the Troad according to 21.86f.

842–3 For the naming of one leader first, as though he were the only one, then adding another (or others), cf. 822f., 870 (after 867), and, in the Achaean list, 651. Pulaios is a nobody, but Hippothoos was unwise enough to grab the foot of the dead Patroklos at 17.288ff. and be slain on top of him by Aias at 298–303. His grandfather Teutamos has a name which is Illyrian rather than Asiatic (von Kamptz, *Personennamen* 345f.), although a Teutamos was king of Assyria at this time according to an extravagant account in Diodorus 2.22.1. Allen noted (*Catalogue* 153) that the *Iliad* gives some Trojans or allies, usually minor ones, Greek names, as with Hippothoos; others have clearly Asiatic names like Priamos himself; others have probably Asiatic names disguised as Greek, like Astuanax and Kassandra. In the present Trojan list nearly all the personal names are Greek, which emphasizes their fictitious origins.

844–50 THE CONTINGENTS OF THRACIANS, KIKONES AND PAEONIANS.

844–5 The THREIKES are the first of the three contingents of European allies, moving from east to west; the Hellespont 'fences them in' in the sense of providing a southern boundary for them, as it also provides a northern one, in the same phrase (used also at 617 in the Achaean list), for Priam's kingdom at 24.544f. Akamas is no more conspicuous than his Dardanian homonym (there are others, too) of 823 – Ares takes his likeness at 5.462, then he is killed at 6.7f., where his father is given as Eussoros. His colleague Peiroos is successful against Diores at 4.517–20, where his name is contracted as Peiros, his father is Imbrasos and he comes from Ainos; his son Rhigmos is killed by Akhilleus in the river, but he himself appears to have survived.

846–7 The KIKONES have another leader, Mentes, at 17.73, Euphemos here being distinguished by nothing except his unusually-named father and grandfather. They are more conspicuous in the *Odyssey*, where their town Ismaros was attacked by Odysseus and his companions according to *Od.* 9.39ff.

Book Two

848–50 The PAIONES come τηλόθεν, 'from afar' (as similarly for the last of each of the following main groups of allies), from AMUDON on the river AXIOS (modern Vardar) which flows into the Thermaic gulf right across in Macedonia. The Paeonians are archers here but spearmen at 21.155; their leader Puraikhmes is killed by Patroklos in book 16, where 288 is closely similar to 849 here. The most distinguished Paeonian is Asteropaios, not mentioned here since at 21.155f. he says that he has only been at Troy for ten days. He claims the river Axios as his grandfather and describes it in similar terms to 849f., cf. 21.158 ὃς κάλλιστον ὕδωρ ἐπὶ γαῖαν ἵησιν – this being part of a complex of overlapping formular systems, e.g. dawn ἐκίδνατο πᾶσαν ἐπ' αἶαν etc., Nireus is ὃς κάλλιστος ἀνὴρ ὑπὸ ῎Ιλιον ἦλθε, 673. The Axios was well known to be muddy, in fact (Strabo 7, frag. 23 quoted by Erbse I, 346), and Paeonian devotion to it may have come into the tradition from some patriotic source.

851–7 THE CONTINGENTS OF PAPHLAGONES AND HALIZONES.

851 The leader of the PAPHLAGONES is Pulaimenes, who became notorious in the critical tradition for being killed at 5.576 and still alive at 13.658. The 'shaggy heart of so-and-so' (on the lines of βίη 'Ηρακληείη and so on) is used only once else in the *Iliad*, of Patroklos at 16.554.

852 This verse is a not very elegant rising threefolder. The Enetoi in historical times were settled in Illyria and famous for horses; nothing else (cf. Strabo 12.543) is known about these supposed Asiatic forebears. The 'wild mules' have caused much zoological dismay (cf. e.g. G. Devereux, *JHS* 85 (1965) 29–32, who excludes the possibility of wild asses from this region), since mules cannot propagate themselves; but Priam's at 24.278 were a gift from the Mysians, who came from the same general area (see 858–61, where nothing is said about mules). Probably ἀγροτεράων is used loosely, meaning that these mules were allowed to run wild after they had been bred, or (as Ab suggested) that they were suitable for work in the fields.

853–5 These verses were perhaps not read by Apollodorus in the second book of his treatise on the catalogues, Περὶ νηῶν; nor by Eratosthenes who was his main source there. The matter is not so clear as the *apparatus criticus* of OCT *ad loc.* suggests; the argument depends solely on Strabo (7.298 and 12.553), who did not accept their criticisms of Homer's Asiatic geography, in particular that Homer 'did not know the coastline' of Paphlagonia (since KUTOROS, SESAMOS, KROMNA, AIGIALOS and ERUTHINOI were agreed by Strabo himself to be ranged along the southern shore of the Black Sea; e.g. Kutoros was an emporium of Sinope according to Strabo 12.544, and Aigialos reveals its position by its name). Nevertheless Apollodorus' criticism of 'not knowing the coastline' probably *does* imply a text which lacked Kutoros and the rest, although that is not absolutely certain. That would accord with

Pompey later placing the inland Paphlagonians under the rule of Pulaimenes' descendants (Strabo 12.541), suggesting an inland origin for the family. Finally Callisthenes, according to Strabo 12.542, added an implausible verse about the Kaukones (not otherwise located despite a couple of mentions in the rest of the poem) after 855, and transposed 854 to apply to them; that is, he did not read 854 (which there carries 853 and 855 with it) under the Paphlagonian entry. In any case the listing of so many as five towns is unparalleled for a single contingent in this Trojan list; taking all things together these verses do look like a learned interpolation of the post-Homeric era of Black-Sea colonization. Allen, *Catalogue* 157, suggested that they might have come from a Trojan catalogue which is known to have been included in the *Cypria*.

856–7 The HALIZONES are briefly mentioned again only when their leader Odios is killed by Agamemnon at 5.39; his colleague Epistrophos does not even achieve that (he has namesakes at 2.517 and 692). This whole contingent seems unreal; τῆλε merely makes it furthest from Troy in its group, but 'ALUBE where is the birth of silver' (γενέθλη only here in Homer) cannot be located, although Strabo 12.549 followed others in connecting it with Khalube home of the Khalubes, famous miners of iron. Similar and equally specious attempts were made to connect the Halizones themselves with the Amazones. There is more to be said for the suggestion that Alube recalls the Halus river, which runs mainly through Paphlagonian territory; Halus was a Hittite name and the Hittites were major suppliers of silver to the Greek world in the 2nd millennium B.C.

858–63 THE MYSIAN AND PHRYGIAN CONTINGENTS.

858 T. W. Allen was too severe when he wrote that 'The Musoi might be in the moon' (*Catalogue* 161); the historical MUSOI are firmly located to the south-east of the Troad, with Phrygia further away in the same direction, which perfectly suits this new radius; see also Strabo 12.564. The Musoi who are linked with the Thracians at 13.4–6 must be a different branch. Ennomos and Khromis took part in the fight for Patroklos' body (17.218, where Khromis becomes Khromios); the former is said at 860f. to have succumbed to Akhilleus in the fight in the river, but is not specifically mentioned in book 21.

859–61 Aristarchus (Arn/A) athetized 860f. on that ground, without clear justification. For the motif of the seer who tries to prevent his sons' death, or fails to foresee his own, cf., most immediately, Merops at 831–4.

862–3 We learn more about the PHRUGES from the rest of the poem than we do here: that Priam served with their huge army under Otreus and Mugdon against the Amazons, close to the Sangarios river (3.184–90); and that Hekabe's brother Asios came from Phrygia (16.718f.). Here they are led by Phorkus and Askanios (who at 13.792ff., however, is said to be a recent replacement at that point); they come from ASKANIE, hardly a lake since it would typically be identified as such in Homer, but a region which gave its name to the large lake near the later Nicaea, some 20 miles south of the extreme eastern arm of Propontis.

864–77 THE MAEONIAN, CARIAN AND LYCIAN CONTINGENTS.

864–6 The leaders of the MEÏONES, Mesthles and Antiphos, are sons of Talaimenes and the 'GYGAEAN LAKE' under Mt Tmolos. Nymphs give birth to mortals in the epic tradition, usually Naiads of river rather than lake as here; indeed at 20.384f. a Naiad gave birth to Iphition, whose father was Otrunteus, in this very region, 'under snowy Tmolos in the rich community of Hude'. The Gygaean lake, said to be near the tomb of Aluattes (north of Sardis) by Herodotus, 1.93.5, was presumably named after an ancestor of the famous Guges. Mesthles makes one other brief appearance; Antiphos (who has an Achaean homonym at 678 and a Trojan one at 4.489) does not even do that. At 5.43f. another Maeonian, Phaistos, comes from Tarne (which it is probably wrong to identify with Atarneus facing Lesbos); at 20.390–2 Iphition (mentioned just above) is further said to have been born ἐπὶ λίμνῃ | Γυγαίῃ by the Hullos and Hermos rivers. One cannot help wondering whether this assertion is not the source of the somewhat stark and surprising statement of the catalogue here, that the Gygaean lake gave birth to the two (other) leaders. The rest of the poem adds the river Kaüstrios and Mt Sipulos (2.461 and 24.615) to the description of this Maeonian region, which is surprisingly detailed considering that it lies – exceptionally for this whole list – some way inland. Was this why some people named Homer's father as Maion at least as early as Hellanicus in the fifth century B.C., according to *Certamen* 20?

867–9 The KARES (who according to 10.428f. were stationed close to the Paiones, Pelasgoi, Leleges and Kaukones) are βαρβαροφώνων, which means on any interpretation of βάρβαρος that they do not speak Greek – which is surprising since MILETOS was a Minoan foundation certainly inhabited by Mycenaean Greeks toward the end of the Bronze Age. Their homeland is further identified here by the river MAIANDROS and MT MUKALE, well-known landmarks at any period, but also by MT PHTHIRES which became a source of controversy in the later scholarly tradition. Too much can perhaps be made of this; Hecataeus of Miletos, the first great geographer, according to Strabo 14.635 identified it with Mt Latmos, which directly overlooks Miletos and is the third conspicuous natural feature of this whole region. Others disagreed, but Hecataeus was after all a native Milesian who worked no more than a couple of centuries or so after Homer; he was in a good position to identify an archaic local name correctly. Page, *HHI* 142f., made much of the difficulty, and assumed that because in Strabo's words

Book Two

Hecataeus *thought* Latmos was Homer's Phthires, this was a mere conjecture on his part. That does not follow – Strabo simply gives Hecataeus' opinion. We cannot safely conclude, as Page does, that Phthires was a prehistoric name, and therefore the Trojan catalogue a prehistoric document. According to the b scholiast, Φθεῖρες (*sic*) got its name from small pine-cones being called 'lice', which is not impossible; other less probable solutions are recorded by Eustathius, 368.13. That the mountain was closely forested is suggested by its epithet ἀκριτόφυλλον, a term unique in Homer (although cf. ἀκριτόμυθε of Thersites at 246) but which must mean 'with dense leaves' (so that you could not distinguish them).

870–1 For the repetition with reversal of word-order cf. 837f. ('Υρτακίδης ἦρχ' Άσιος... | Άσιος 'Υρτακίδης) and 849f.; for the mention of one leader alone (Nastes at 867), then with another, a brother, added, cf. 840–2. The present instance is discussed, and its considerable skill noted, in the last paragraph of the comment on 837–9.

Neither Nastes nor this Amphimakhos (there is another one, a leader of the Epeans, at 620 and elsewhere) will be mentioned outside this passage; in particular the latter is not named as a victim of Akhilleus in the river, as 874ff. suggests he will be; but the same is so with the Mysian Ennomos, see on 858.

872 One of the brothers has golden ornaments like a girl; according to Aristarchus (Arn/A) it is Amphimakhos, which is grammatically more likely since his was the last name to be mentioned. Simonides had evidently taken it to be Nastes, but also mistook the gold for golden armour – it is hard to credit that he made this mistake in view of ἠύτε κούρη, and Aristarchus was certainly right that the gold must have been in the form of brooches in the hair, if wrong to characterize this as a non-Greek custom. Indeed he correctly compared Amphimakhos with Euphorbos at 17.51f., whose 'hair like the Graces' was wet with blood|and his locks which were fastened in wasp-brooches [ἐσφήκωντο] with silver and gold'. But Euphorbos, who is probably the model here, was not a barbarian in any sense (nor are his girlish tastes exactly a 'mark of outlandishness' as stated in *Companion* 305f.); he is a Δάρδανος ἀνήρ at 16.807f., and that means a real Trojan since his father Panthoos is one of Priam's trusted senior councillors, δημογέροντες, at 3.146–9.

873 This verse is close to 20.296, νήπιος· οὐδέ τί οἱ χραισμήσει λυγρὸν ὄλεθρον (in which the last noun–epithet phrase occurs 6× *Il.*). ἐπήρκεσε is paralleled in Homer only at *Od.* 17.568, so the substitution is quite a sophisticated one.

874–5 Down to ἐν ποταμῷ repeats 86of., with the rest of 875 describing quite effectively what happened to the gold. δαΐφρων is used of Akhilleus several times, and is perhaps especially appropriate to his sharpness here

261

in detecting and stripping off the unusual articles of value; but see on 5.181. In short the whole description of the Carian leaders is well composed, making use of motifs and turns of phrase from elsewhere, but with a difference.

876–7 THE LYCIAN CONTINGENT.

876–7 It is remarkable that the Lukioi, Lycians, who are the most important allies in the rest of the poem, are confined to these two closing verses, which sound almost like an afterthought. Yet their position is logical enough, depending on their being at the end (as 877 τηλόθεν confirms) of this final chain of allies. One might, nevertheless, have expected some further development and detail to round off the whole list and give weight to this important contingent; in addition, a resumptive verse (at least), like 760 for the Achaean list, has probably been lost. Sarpedon and Glaukos are the most prominent individuals after Hektor himself to be mentioned in the whole Trojan list, the latter especially in his encounter with Diomedes in book 6 (in which the migration to Lycia of his grandfather Bellerophon is recounted), the former at many points until his death at Patroklos' hands in book 16; moreover Lukie and the Lukioi are mentioned independently on several occasions. Lycia, in the south-western corner of Asia Minor, was indeed remote and relatively inaccessible even in historical times; but the Xanthos river valley was its most fertile stretch, and it is a mistake to be concerned (like *HSL* 179) because no pottery earlier than Late Geometric has been found from the historical city-site there. That reveals nothing whatever about the probable date of this entry, since this historical site is not a typical Mycenaean one, and little exploration for early settlement-sites in other parts of the valley has been carried out so far.

Conclusions on the Trojan catalogue

The following factors are relevant.

(1) The scantiness of the Trojan catalogue compared with the Achaean might make it look like an afterthought, but it has quite an elaborate and well-composed introductory scene, 780–815. Moreover its brevity may be deliberate, so as to throw more emphasis on the Achaeans.

(2) The three features often said to indicate an origin in the Late Bronze Age (and certainly before the Ionian migration to the Asia Minor coast), namely the references to Alube, Mt Phthires and the barbarophone Carians of Miletos, actually do nothing of the sort. The first is semi-mythical in any event, and, if it is a memory of Hittites, that could have survived for centuries into the Iron Age. That Phthires was so ancient a name that it could not be identified later is disproved by Hecataeus. Miletos had been inhabited

by Greek-speakers since at least the fourteenth century B.C., and the reference to non-Greek-speaking Carians must be deliberately archaizing.

(3) The list is relatively detailed for the northern Troad, the Hellespont and southern Propontis, and reveals more than one might expect about Maeonia (around Sardis) and Caria. The gaps are primarily the western Black Sea and Bosporos, and the central Aegean coast. Knowledge of the Troad and Hellespont was available quite early through sporadic trade, but the Black Sea was not fully penetrated until after 900. The southern Troad was perhaps omitted because of Akhilleus' attacks there in the rest of the poem; the omission of the whole coast (including Ephesos and Smurne) down to Miletos must be due to archaizing, and Maeonian knowledge may be the result of personal interest in the region by a member of the poetical tradition. Smurne was, of course, one of the strongest contenders to be the birthplace of Homer himself.

(4) There are obvious differences from the Achaean catalogue (especially in the leader-modes, the number of towns, the epithets), but also similarities: common motifs or manners of speaking, e.g. the seer who mistakes the future; the 'not alone but...' addition; carefully developed epanalepsis; the idea of 'routes' or 'radii' as organizing principle (see p. 250 above).

(5) The list contains important passages and details apparently derived from other parts of the *Iliad*: 831 the sons of Merops, 865 the Gygaean lake, 872 golden ornaments. The first two of these may show some distortion or misunderstanding in the process.

(6) But the rest of the poem has additional information about some regions and contingents which could have been borrowed, but is not; e.g. about Paiones, Phruges, Kaukones. There is no such careful process of up-dating as there was in the Achaean list, e.g. over Protesilaos, to account for late arrivals like Asteropaios.

(7) The list contains a few felicitous ideas or expressions which are not exactly paralleled elsewhere, including 825 'drinking the black water', 870ff. the Carian leaders.

These factors do not lead to a firm conclusion, and it would be foolish to press for one on the present state of the evidence. But they seem to me to suggest that the Trojan list is not, and is not strictly based on, a pre-historic document; that the omission of facts known to Ionian settlers is more probably the result of conscious archaizing than of temporal priority; that composition was the work of a singer, perhaps indeed Homer himself, who knew both the Achaean catalogue and the details of the whole poem, but selected from them erratically at times, and perhaps at a relatively late stage of adjustment and refinement.

BOOK THREE

1–14   The two armies advance against each other across the plain

1   The forces on each side have been described, together with their leaders, in book 2; this verse provides a brief resumption and leads to further images of the armies as they advance. ἁμ' ἡγεμόνεσσιν ∪ – ∪| is a formula, 4× *Il.*, and the whole verse has much in common with 12.87 πένταχα κοσμηθέντες ἁμ' ἡγεμόνεσσιν ἔποντο.

2–14   The language and ideas of the assembling of the two armies in the previous Book are repeatedly evoked: the noise of the Trojans (2.803f. and 810), the comparison with clangorous birds (2.459ff.), οἱ δ' ἄρ' ἴσαν of the Achaeans (at 8 and 2.780), the mountain peaks which blaze with fire at 2.456 but are shrouded in mist at 10, in both cases to illustrate an aspect of a marching army, with the same final verse ἐρχόμενον...πεδίοιο (14 = 2.785). The repetitions and overlapping imagery serve to link the elaborate scenes of preparation with the actual advance of each army, and further to integrate the catalogues into the whole scene.

3–5   The simile is closely related to 2.459–65, one of the set introducing the Achaean catalogue. There the birds were geese, cranes or swans in the Asian meadow by the river Kaüstrios, settling in front of each other with loud cries, 463 κλαγγηδὸν προκαθιζόντων. Here, they are cranes taking off for their migration from the darkness of winter to the streams of Okeanos (which indicates the ends of the earth rather than specifically the south). The common elements are the cranes, their noise (κλαγγή, κλαγγηδόν), and more loosely their landing or taking off and their association with rivers. For the noise made by the Trojans cf. 2. 803f. and 810, and for an explicit contrast with the silent Achaeans cf. 4.428–36, where they are compared with bleating sheep. κλαγγή, 'strident noise' (of birds, warriors, a bowstring), is from κλάζω, from which κεκληγώς -οντες (10× *Il.*), also ἔκλαγξαν at 1.46 of Apollo's arrows. The noun is emphatically repeated twice within the simile; of the Trojans it is reinforced by ἐνοπή, a more general term for 'voice' or 'shout', especially of the battle-cry but also of birds. With οὐρανόθι πρό| compare Ἰλιόθι πρό| (3× *Il.*, 1× *Od.*) and ἠῶθι πρό| (1× *Il.*, 2× *Od.*); the adverbial locative suffix -θι (cf. Chantraine, *GH* I, 244–6) is used in a special way mainly for metrical convenience, although οὐρανόο πρό is possible. The meaning is 'in front of heaven', that is, up in the air, with the vault of sky as background.

4   'And they when they come to flee from winter and boundless rain', a brilliant and unusual description (with formular elements, e.g. ὄμβρος| etc. 4× *Il.*, 3× *Od.*, ἀθέσφατος οἶνος| *Od.* 11.61), in which ἀθέσφατος as well as the hendiadys seems to convey something of the birds' horror of winter. It means 'immense', 'unnatural' almost, because 'not decreed by the gods', ἀ-θεσ-φατος (unless the ἀ- is not strictly privative, a possibility considered by Chantraine, *Dict.* s.v. θέσφατος).

5–6 The war of the cranes and Pygmies ('fist-like men', from πυγ-μή = fist) is not elsewhere referred to by Homer, but was a popular theme later, first on the foot of the Attic black-figure François vase painted by Kleitias of about 570 B.C. (and on at least three other black-figure pots), then in Hecataeus (AbT on 6). Herodotus 3.37.2 alludes to a pygmy-like cult-statue in upper Egypt, and at 2.32.6 had heard of little men in the heart of Africa; the idea of pygmies may have been based on fact – Aristotle thought so too, and that they lived in caves (*Hist. An.* 8.597a6). The strange idea of their war with cranes was perhaps derived from a lost Egyptian folk-tale, although Willcock *ad loc.* could be right that the birds' flying in formation may have something to do with envisaging them as an army. φόνον καὶ κῆρα φέροντες recurs at 2.352 (and φόνον καὶ κῆρα 2× *Il.* elsewhere); on the language see also the next comment.

7 ἠέριαι, 'through the air' here (cf. 1.497n. and Vergil, *Georgics* 1.375). For the second half of the verse compare 11.529 κακὴν ἔριδα προβαλόντες, *Od.* 6.92 θοῶς ἔριδα προφέρουσαι and (in the middle voice) *Od.* 8.210 ἔριδα προφέρηται ἀέθλων. The whole 3-verse addition about the cranes and Pygmies is heavily formular but has a naive tone (e.g. in the repetition of κλαγγῇ and φέρουσαι|, προφέρονται|) appropriate to its probable folk-tale origin.

8–9 For Achaean silence as opposed to Trojan and allied clamour see also 4.428–36, where the Achaean commanders give their essential orders but the rest advance in utter silence. Here, the silence indicates discipline and resolve (as well as unity of language in contrast with the Trojans), emphasized by μένεα πνείοντες and ἐν θυμῷ μεμαῶτες. The Trojans have had the hostile cranes to symbolize their martial spirit (and their foreignness, too); the Achaeans simply have this plain and factual statement of their calm determination.

ἀλεξέμεν ἀλλήλοισι, 'to come to each other's help'; the verb is common (most often meaning 'ward off'), the phrase not exactly paralleled in Homer. It does not imply so much as ἐν ταῖς φάλαγξι, as b writes.

10–14 Now comes a fresh simile that applies to both armies together; for the juxtaposition of similes, especially to illustrate general movement, cf. 2.144–6 and 147f., and exceptionally the sequence at 2.455ff. Formally this one illustrates the clouds of dust as they march, which restricts visibility to a stone's throw; but the shepherds high up in the mountains are one of

Homer's symbols of isolation and potential menace, and here everything is shrouded in mist and they are at the mercy.of sheep-rustlers.

10 Aristarchus (Did/A) accepted εὖτ' (ε) in the sense of ἠΰτε, 'as when', although the Chian and Massiliote texts had kept ἠΰτ' itself at the cost of following it with the post-Homeric contracted form ὄρευς. 19.386 is the only other similar use of εὖτε, which normally in Homer means simply 'when'.

11–12 The epigrammatic concision is typical of the simile-style, as is the inclusion of other minor comparisons (night, stone's-throw) and more broadly the sharp visual observation of details that are typical in a sense and yet moving and suggestive in themselves. That typical aspect is inconspicuously brought out by generalizing τε in 11 (as it also was in 4; both τ's in 12 are part of the τόσσον...ὅσσον construction).

13 ἀελλής is nothing to do with ἄελλη = storm, as Aristophanes (Did/bT) had thought; Aristarchus (Arn/A) corrected him on this and saw that ἀελλής is a different word, unique here in Homer, a form of (probably Aeolic) ἀολλής (ἀολλέες -ας 18x *Il.*), 'compact', cf. Ionic ἁλής and Chantraine, *Dict.* under that word (untypically, he misrepresents Aristarchus here).

14 = 2.785; see on 2–14.

15–120   Paris–Alexandros is shamed by Hektor into agreeing to fight a duel with Menelaos to resolve the issue. The two armies are overjoyed, and heralds are despatched to fetch king Priam, and also animals, for an oath-sacrifice

15 The first use of a formular verse that will appear 12x *Il.* in all.

16 προμάχιζεν: this means something more than merely to be πρόμαχος (38x *Il.*), a 'front fighter' in the usual sense of one of the front rank closest to the enemy. Like προμάχεσθαι the verb implies going out as a fighter by oneself – so Aias at 17.358f. tells the Achaeans that none of them should go out in front, προμάχεσθαι, above the others, ἔξοχον ἄλλων, but should remain in close formation; and at 20.376 Apollo tells Hektor not to challenge Akhilleus by going out ahead, μηκέτι πάμπαν 'Αχιλλῆϊ προμάχιζε. So Alexandros was behaving here like a challenger on behalf of the Trojans by constantly going out ahead of the rest as the armies approached each other. This was boastful and imprudent behaviour, typical of the man no doubt, and skilfully introduced as a credible piece of behaviour which diverts the expected clash of armies into an individual duel – and thus helps to fulfil the composer's evident purpose, partly exemplified in the catalogues of the preceding Book, of delaying the beginning of mass fighting for as long as possible.

Paris (as we tend to call him) is mentioned here for the first time in the

poem and is named not Paris but Alexandros. This is by far his commonest
appellation (45× *Il.*, including 21× in this Book, against 13× (including
Dusparis) and only 3× in this Book for Paris). There is no difference in the
nuance of the two names, and when Paris is used for the first time at 325
it is without any special comment or implication. The poet must, of course,
have found it useful to have two such metrical alternatives at his disposal.
Usually but not invariably he uses the longer form in the second part of
the verse, the shorter in the first part; 'Αλέξανδρος -ν θεοειδής -έα is his
regular description at the verse-end (12×), and it must have been sometimes
useful, as here, to mention his god-like beauty and consequent vanity. Yet
it would have been no insuperable hardship to make do without using the
name Paris at all. But it is clear that Priam's beautiful son had, and was
known by, both names; they are fixed in the tradition. Nilsson (*GgrR* 476
n.1) suggested not very plausibly (after P. Kretschmer, *Glotta* 13, (1924)
211) that he was a combination of two separate legendary or mythical
figures; it is probably more to the point that Paris is clearly a non-Greek
name – Illyrian according to von Kamptz, *Personennamen* 340f.; comparisons
with Thracian Πόρις = 'fighter' and Sanskrit *para* = 'best one' have also
been made – whereas Alexandros is Greek. Yet the status even of Alexandros
itself is disputed, since there was a Hittite name, Alakšanduš, of which it
might be a Greek form. This was F. Sommer's view, and is accepted by von
Kamptz, *op. cit.* 94f. Kretschmer on the other hand considered the name
to be unambiguously Greek (*Glotta* 24 (1935) 242ff.), and this is now
supported by the female name Alexandra on a Mycenae tablet (cf.
J. Chadwick, *The Mycenaean World* (Cambridge 1976) 61 and 66f.). Undoubted Greek compounds in -ανδρος, including names, are especially
frequent in the Asia Minor colonial foundations; cf. Chantraine, *Dict.* s.v.
ἀνήρ, and for further references *LfgrE* s.v. 'Αλέξανδρος.

17–20 Paris' costume and equipment are a surprise. He was admittedly
renowned as an archer (and shot Akhilleus with the fatal arrow according
to the post-Homeric tradition), and there was nothing to prevent him
equipping himself as such for the Trojan march-out; but in that case he
would not be prancing ahead of the rest, for archers operated from cover
(and certainly did not issue challenges implicit or otherwise). Nor did they
normally wear leopard-skins as here (17 παρδαλέην); Dolon wore a wolf-skin
for night work at 10.334, but that is different. Nor, above all, did they clutter
themselves with pairs of spears as at 18. Either the poet is making him out
to be quite eccentric, which is unlikely; or the poet is being a little
careless – carried away, perhaps, by the convenient and progressive cumulation of the harmless ξίφος into adding items which go with a sword but
not with the bow; or there has been subsequent elaboration. Both Zenodotus
and Aristarchus thought so; the former athetized 18–20 (Arn/A on 18), the

latter only 19–20 (Arn/A), which does not, of course, help the dilemma over equipment but is directed against the improbability of anyone so equipped issuing a challenge. Zenodotus' broader athetesis deals with the whole problem and should be taken seriously; 15–17 can be directly followed by 21 with no real loss, and with a certain gain not only over the mixed equipment but also over the interpretation of 16 προμάχιзεν which is implicit in προκαλίзετο in 19 – see on 19–20 below.

18 The two spears are especially strange equipment for one also carrying a bow, but they are also unusual for a spearman. The regular spear is a heavy thrusting spear, and only one of these is carried; that is what Paris will arm himself with when he comes to prepare for the duel at 338. On six other occasions in the *Iliad* a single warrior is specifically said to be armed with a pair of spears; these must have been light javelins, primarily for throwing rather than thrusting. Sometimes a description of combat becomes confused and conflates elements of both styles of armament, so that a thrusting spear is thrown like a javelin (which must have been difficult), or a warrior begins with a single spear and then is assumed to have a second one in reserve; such cases will be noted as they arise. The specific instances of εἵλετο δοῦρε etc. (i.e. a singular verb with the dual form of δόρυ, spear, as object) are interesting, since they show signs of a formular system concerning this dual-spear armament, which was therefore traditional – although not nearly so broadly established as the systems built round e.g. δουρί and ἔγχος, each used over 100x in the poem. The elements of the δοῦρε-system are illustrated by these three verses (including the present one):

   3.18 καὶ ξίφος· αὐτὰρ ὁ δοῦρε δύω κεκορυθμένα χαλκῷ
   11.43 εἵλετο δ' ἄλκιμα   δοῦρε δύω κεκορυθμένα χαλκῷ
   16.139 εἵλετο δ' ἄλκιμα   δοῦρε τά οἱ παλάμηφιν ἀρήρει.

Note that a dual noun can be qualified by a plural epithet, e.g. κεκορυθμένα.

19–20 He is actually wielding, πάλλων, these spears, presumably one in each hand. Moreover, either by this action or by words that are not reproduced, he is specifically challenging the Achaean champions to fight (προκαλίзετο, imperfect, 'was continuously challenging'). Whether that means in single combat or not is doubtful; Leaf has drawn attention to the implications of 20 ἐν αἰνῇ δηϊοτῆτι, which suggests a general encounter. That would accord with προμάχιзεν in 16, perhaps; it was noted there that Paris' behaviour was provocative, and could lead on to the concept of an individual duel; and yet it could also lead simply to engagement between the πρόμαχοι, that is, to fighting on the usual Homeric model. The uncertainty over the implications of προκαλίзετο is not incompatible with the idea that 18–20 may be an addition to the strict Homeric conception at this point.

21–37 There follows a carefully opposed pair of descriptions of Menelaos and Paris, introduced in each case by the formular phrase τὸν δ' ὡς οὖν ἐνόησεν and followed by an extended simile to illustrate the hero's particular emotions and reactions. The Menelaos passage consists of 9 verses, the balancing Paris one of 8, and they are followed by an exchange between Hektor and Paris, from 38 to 75, of equally symmetrical construction.

21–2 Menelaos can hardly fail to see Paris, as he 'comes with long strides in front of the throng'; μακρὰ βιβάς -άσθων is used six times elsewhere of powerful movement, and is echoed by ὕψι βιβάντα which implies an excess of confidence at 13.371.

23–7 His immediate reaction is of delight, as a lion is delighted when he comes on a dead stag or wild goat when he is hungry. He devours it avidly, μάλα γάρ τε κατεσθίει, even if the hunters with their hounds try to drive him off: this is the added detail that goes beyond the stated point of comparison (here, delight) and is typical of the developed Homeric simile. Sometimes, however, the addition creates a resonance with the main situation, and that may be so here; for Menelaos' delight is associated with determination to take his revenge, as will be implied in 28. The simile-action is set out with greater rhetoric than precision. Presumably the hunters have killed the dead animal, and the lion's determination is justified by his hunger, πεινάων; but one might have expected him to be able to make a kill, in this hunting country, by himself; also, as Aristarchus observed (cf. Ap. Soph. 148.23, quoted by Erbse 1, 360), σῶμα (etc.) in Homer seems to apply only to dead bodies (5× *Il.*, 3× *Od.*), and lions generally do not eat corpses – although they might eat an animal just killed. In any case the same problem arises in two other lion-similes, at 11.479ff. and 13.198ff. That may be an excess of criticism, and the fact is that lion-similes, in particular, tend to be somewhat vague. Lions were no doubt known, in northern Greece and parts of Asia Minor at least, but even so description of their habits would be prone to distortion by hearsay and imagination.

27–8 The poet's tableau of the two contrasting enemies is made even sharper by the juxtaposition of their names in 27; then the cumulative phrase which follows in 28, otiose in itself, renders the second half of the verse all the more striking: 'he believed he would (be able to) take vengeance on the transgressor', the man who had stolen his wife. φάτο in contexts like this, literally 'said' (i.e. to himself), often means little more than 'thought'.

30–1 In the preceding verse Menelaos has leapt down from his chariot (which in realistic terms should hardly be in the front line at this juncture – on chariots in front see on 4.297–300) and evidently means business; Paris sees him (in the same phrase as was used of Menelaos in the corresponding verse 21) and is shaken to the core, 31 κατεπλήγη φίλον ἦτορ, 'was smitten in his dear heart' – φίλον in the formula φίλον ἦτορ is always hard to translate, since it means more than 'own' and yet not exactly 'dear': it was *his* heart, and these were his own vital concerns to which he was strongly attached.

32 A formular verse (7× *Il.* + 2 variants) which does not usually imply any cowardice, but rather a sensible response to overwhelming odds. Menelaos is not one of the most powerful Achaean princes, but the mere sight of him puts an end to the Trojan's pretensions.

33–7 A concisely expressed and keenly observed simile: the subject is an anonymous person, a shepherd perhaps (33 τις, followed by the generalizing τε), 'who recoils when he sees a snake in the mountain glens, and trembling seizes his limbs beneath, and he moves backwards [35 ἄψ δ' ἀνεχώρησεν, less dramatic than 33 παλίνορσος ἀπέστη but emphatic by sheer repetition], and paleness takes his cheeks – so once again did he slip into the throng of proud Trojans, δείσας, in fear of Atreus' son'. The parataxis, once the comparison is established, is remarkable and effective; so are the 'gnomic' aorists. G. P. Shipp finds various 'late features' in this and other of these similes, including ὦχρος as a noun; 'The narrative', he adds (*Studies* 238), 'does not get clear of similes till 38'!

33 The rising threefold verse, with its emphasis on the culminating παλίνορσος ἀπέστη, suits the action. παλίνορσος occurs only here in Homer and has been diversely explained; Chantraine, *Dict.* s.v. ὄρρος goes so far as to connect it with that word, meaning 'rump' or 'bottom' ('a vulgarism', Shipp, *loc. cit.*); that is because the sigma is unexpected if the source is ὄρνυμι, but nevertheless I am sure J. Bollack is right in so deriving it in its Empedoclean occurrences (frags. 35.1 and 100.23 Diels–Kranz), where the meaning, as here, is something like 'moving rapidly in the reverse direction'.

38–75 Paris' hasty withdrawal brings an immediate and severe rebuke from his elder brother, leading to a reply from himself of roughly equal length in which he proposes a duel with Menelaos. The first speech is full of impassioned rhetoric, the second by contrast is calm and ingratiating. Supervening as they do on the formally opposed pair of similes of 21–37, these speeches maintain the impression of exceptionally careful composition as the whole episode develops.

38 ἴδον and ἔπος both originally began with digammas; the effect of the obsolete semi-vowel is more often observed than neglected in Homer, and there is little doubt that an earlier form of the text would have read νείκεσσε ἰδὼν αἰσχροῖσι ἔπεσσιν (rather than e.g. OCT's νείκεσσεν ἰδὼν αἰσχροῖς ἐπέεσσιν). νείκεσσε and ἰδών are in any event closely connected in sense ('rebuked him when he saw'), so the verse should be articulated as a rising threefolder, with some resemblance to 33.

Book Three

39-42 Hektor's first sentence consists of four verses whose colon-patterns are in strong contrast: 39 is broken by internal punctuation into four regular but exaggerated cola; 40 is a rising threefolder; 41 is a two/fourfolder with strong central caesura; 42 in conclusion is another rising threefolder, cumulated on to its predecessor in progressive enjambment.

39 Recurs at 13.769. Δύσπαρι is the same kind of ironical invention as 18.54 δυσαριστοτόκεια, and may provide support for the idea that the name Paris implied 'good' in some respect, see on 16 *fin.* The terms which follow represent three carefully selected and of course insulting characteristics of Paris as a person, in which as a matter of human nature the first tends to lead to the second and the second to the third; for he is (1) beautiful, (2) keen on women, and (3) a deceiver.

40 The last syllable of ὄφελες is artificially lengthened, as happens most easily at the regular colon-breaks; on the αἴθε construction see on 1.415-6. ἄγονος could be taken either in a passive sense ('unborn') or in an active one, not so much 'childless' (as the emperor Augustus evidently meant when he used the verse against his daughter) as 'unable to produce children' – and then not because sterile but because impotent. There is no particular meaning of ἄγονος which makes Hektor's wish absolutely logical and self-consistent – it is, after all, a highly rhetorical formulation; but what he wishes is that Paris had not been able to be γυναιμανής (as in 39) and so become involved in disastrous sexual unions (for that, rather than legal marriage, is the implication of ἄγαμος here). Nearly all editors understand 'unborn', nevertheless.

42 bT are probably right that ἄλλων goes only with ὑπόψιον: 'a cause of insult, and an object of contempt by others'; they also report that Aristophanes read ἐπόψιον, 'conspicuous (among others)', which is rather feeble.

43 καγχαλόωσι means 'laugh out loud', 'cackle' almost, and the choice of the formular description κάρη κομόωντες for the Achaeans (7× *Il.*, 4× *Od.*), with its repetition of k-sounds, is probably deliberately onomatopoeic. That is uncommon in Homeric style, where alliteration, although not infrequent, is usually unconnected with special semantic effects (as also in 46-51, on which see the comment below). κομόωντες is from κομάω (by epic diectasis, as indeed in καγχαλόωσι), itself from κόμη = hair: 'letting the hair grow', κάρη, on their heads. At 2.542 the Abantes were described as ὄπιθεν κομόωντες, which must mean with the hair long at the back, short on top (see comment there); the Achaeans generally, in contrast, must have had their hair long all over. Akhilleus at 23.141 cuts off the hair he had dedicated to the river Sperkheios on his departure ten years ago, but that was perhaps only a single lock. Long hair must have been inconvenient in some ways for warriors; presumably it was a distinguishing mark for the Achaeans in particular. Stephanie West, commenting on the expression's occurrence at

Od. 1.90, notes that long hair stayed in fashion among rich Athenians until the fifth century B.C. (cf. S. Marinatos, *Arch. Hom.* B 1ff.). She also observes that gods have long hair; but strictly it is only Zeus (whose locks fall forward in his great oath at 1.529) and Apollo (described as ἀκερσοκόμης at 20.39) who do so.

44–5 'Saying that a chieftain is ⟨chosen as⟩ their champion because of his beautiful appearance!'. πρόμος is a syncopated form of πρόμαχος: so Aristarchus (Arn/A). οὐδέ (οὔτε) τις ἀλκή is found 3x elsewhere in *Il.* (ἀλκή in all its cases being strongly disposed to the verse-end, 43/57x *Il.*), and ἀλκή -ήν is associated with φρεσίν on three other occasions.

46–51 Another complicated and closely-constructed sentence, twice the length of its two predecessors; it has the form of a rhetorical question ('was it as *such* a man that you did all that?'), in which alliteration is conspicuous, the p's in 46 and 47 being in subtle contrast with the r's, a's and e-sounds of ἑτάρους ἐρίηρας ἀγείρας. In 48f. 'mingling' and 'beautiful woman' are contemptuously associated in sound if not in grammar; then 'you carried her off to sea (ἀνῆγες) from distant land, kin of spearmen though she was' – νυός is strictly 'daughter-in-law', more generally member of the household. The sentence ends in the leisurely but strongly alliterative 50, 'a perfect pain to your sire, the city and all its citizens', followed by the antithetical and apophthegmatic 51.

46 Hiatus after the second-foot trochee, τοιόσδε ἐών, is usually avoided but is found at 2.8, 19.288, 23.263; cf. Chantraine, *GH* I, 91 (where 5.118 can be omitted from the list of parallels), also on 1.532–3. Emendation would in any event be easy, e.g. τοῖός περ ἐών (Bentley, van Leeuwen).

50 Compare 24.706, μέγα χάρμα πόλει τ' ἦν παντί τε δήμῳ: Hoekstra, *Modifications* 116, is surely right that the present verse gives the purer form of what was evidently a formula, μέγα πῆμα/χάρμα πόληί τε παντί τε δήμῳ (which justifies πόληι, πόληες against Shipp's suggestion, *Studies* 242, cf. 64, that their stem (with -η-) 'is likely to be late in Homer').

51 κατηφείην: so Aristarchus (Did/A), also Aristophanes, Sosigenes, the Argolic text and 'in nearly all the high-class ones', καὶ σχεδὸν ἐν ταῖς χαριεστάταις. Zenodotus and a small number of MSS nevertheless preferred the nominative, but the accusative is clearly right; it is probably, like the accusatives in the previous verse (for Helen as πῆμα cf. 160), in apposition to 48 γυναῖκ', although Leaf could be right that 'The acc. vaguely expresses the result of the preceding actions.'

52–3 The new question in 52 leads on to 53 (rather than following on from 51): 'Why don't you stand up to Menelaos? Then you would learn...'

54–5 The subjunctive with ἄν (οὐκ ἄν τοι χραίσμη) expresses a more confident view of a future result than the optative of the limiting clause, ὅτ' ἐν κονίῃσι μιγείης, which is partly determined by the temporal indefiniteness. The harsh climax of 'mingling in the dust' is carefully prepared by the soft erotic terminology of luscious wife, lyre, and Aphrodite's gifts of beauty.

Aristarchus(Arn/A) had to correct unnamed critics for substituting κίδαρις, a kind of hat, for κίθαρις, on the grounds that Paris is nowhere described as actually playing one; that is amusing in its way, but reminds us of how much Aristarchus had to defend Homer against.

56–7 The previous nine verses have been end-stopped or at most progressively enjambed; now the rhythmical pattern is varied (as often) in the concluding words, with a strong stop at the bucolic diaeresis in 56 followed by integral enjambment. The culmination of Hektor's address is also marked by abandoning its generally involuted syntax in favour of comparatively direct statement: 'The Trojans are very timid – otherwise you would long since have donned a stone tunic...', in which a final rhetorical flourish is provided by that unusual metaphor. Stoning to death is meant, despite 'being clothed in earth' implying burial in classical Greek.

59 Paris does not attempt to deny the charges outright, but will have excuses to offer.

60–3 His style will be less rhetorical than Hektor's but he begins, as a parenthesis, with a simile, not an especially elaborate one but developed beyond the main point of comparison nevertheless; and similes are rare in speeches and practically confined to narrative. The purpose of this simile is indeed rhetorical – in this case, to flatter, but also to delay a disingenuous and somewhat waspish conclusion – and not diversionary, or offering the contrast of a different scene, as so often in narrative. Hektor's heart (his nature, that is) resembles an unwearying axe which a man uses to shape a ship's timber, and which increases his power; he has his own skill, but the axe's potent indestructibility enables him to finish the task. The ship's timber, νήϊον, is a formular motif, 4x *Il.* elsewhere.

64–6 The parenthesis over, the sentence can be completed in a way that is not so mild after all: 'you are right to rebuke me, and relentless as ever, but do not throw a god's gifts in my face' – literally 'bring before me', 'confront me with', πρόφερε. The vocabulary of love was to be developed by later poets like Anacreon and Mimnermus, but some of it is found here already – the lovely gifts of golden Aphrodite which are not to be cast away.

65–6 'The glorious gifts of the gods are not to be rejected', he says, sliding cunningly from the particular to the general; 'one would not willingly choose them', he adds in a cumulated verse which makes his defence even more specious – for Paris *did* choose them, by awarding the prize to Aphrodite in exchange for μαχλοσύνη (24.30) and the most beautiful of women.

67–70 Now comes another surprise as he offers to fight Menelaos in a duel; in effect, to make good his previous behaviour as false πρόμαχος. The poet has no intention of making Paris out to be utterly contemptible – he has to be shamed into making this offer, but he has a sense of shame, of αἰδώς, nevertheless, and of the heroic concept of honour, τιμή, that goes with it. He will behave badly again, but then he can be truly heroic on occasions, also.

J. T. Hooker (*Iliad III*) observes that Hektor is addressed in the singular at 68, κάθισον, and in the plural at 70, συμβάλετ'; the latter recognizes that both sides are involved.

71–2 Both these verses sweep on to their different main caesuras without strong semantic pause: 71 to νικήσῃ (i.e. it is a two/threefolder), 72 to πάντα (i.e. it is a two/fourfolder). The observation has a practical use as well as drawing attention to a minor stylistic detail, since the superficially 'regular' colometry of 72 might at first suggest that εὖ should be taken with πάντα rather than ἑλών, whereas in fact it belongs with the whole phrase, 'taking all the property without omission'. These κτήματα (also in 70) must be the possessions, including some that were strictly perhaps Menelaos' rather than hers, which Helen and Paris took with them from Lakedaimon. When the oath is taken before the duel it includes the provision that if Paris succumbs then the Trojans are to *give back*, ἀποδοῦναι, all the possessions as well as Helen herself (285). There is also to be additional recompense, τιμή (286), which would hardly be envisaged here by a Trojan but which Agamemnon will naturally mention.

73–5 ὅρκια πιστὰ ταμόντες -ωμεν -ηαι is a traditional phrase (6× *Il.*, 1× *Od.*) for oath-taking, in the most solemn form of which a victim or victims are slaughtered. 'Cutting' applies to them, moreover they themselves embody the oath and can be called ὅρκια πιστά, as at 245 and 269. At the oath-ceremony which precedes the duel itself (not the oath referred to here) two separate acts of cutting are performed: first, hair is cut from the animals' heads and distributed to the participants (273f.); then, after the enunciation of the oath, their throats are cut (292). The almost metaphorical use of the 'cutting oaths' phraseology allows the addition of φιλότητα as object of ταμόντες by a form of hendiadys, 'swearing oaths of friendship'; the whole verse is repeated twice in this Book at 94 and 256, cf. also 323.

The various parties are loosely but effectively distinguished by Paris: the rest (that is, aside from Helen, Menelaos and Paris himself) are to take an oath of friendship; and (of them) you, the Trojans, may continue to dwell (ναίοιτε, concessive) in fertile Troy, and let the Achaeans return (τοὶ δὲ νεέσθων) to the Achaean land.

The final verse recurs at 258; καλλιγύναικα is applied twice to Hellas elsewhere (that is, to Akhilleus' homeland), and may have a special resonance here because of Helen's beauty.

Book Three

76–8 These three verses recur as 7.54–6, at the beginning of the second great duel-episode of the *Iliad*. They do not recur elsewhere, neither does the motif of a leader signalling by holding up his spear in this manner, nor does that of an army sitting down in response. Nothing closely similar is likely to happen in the ordinary circumstances of battle, so the unique idea and its expression are hardly surprising. The verses naturally contain certain basic formular elements, for example ὡς ἔφαθ', μῦθον ἀκούσας, ἐς μέσσον, φάλαγγας and ἅπαντες at the verse-end; but χάρη μέγα (the latter being adverbial) does not occur elsewhere, nor do ἀνέεργε and ἱδρύνθησαν exactly, both verbs being rarely used in the *Iliad*. In its present form this three-verse passage is specific to the two formal duel-scenes and was probably composed for one or both of them, or for a close archetype. Further similarities and differences will suggest that this duel cannot be taken simply as the model for that in book 7, or indeed vice versa; but in the present case 3 (or its archetype) may be prior in some sense, since Hektor's 'great joy' is more naturally engendered by Paris' offer to fight than by Helenos' cursory suggestion in 7. Moreover here the Achaeans will at first fail to respect Hektor's signal, whereas at 7.57 they respond immediately as though by then familiar with it. For full discussion of relations between the two duels see my 'The formal duels in Books 3 and 7 of the *Iliad*', in B. C. Fenik (ed.), *Homer, Tradition and Invention* (Leiden 1978) 19–40.

77 ᾽He was holding back, ἀνέ(ϝ)εργε, the ranks of Trojans': φάλαγγες (etc.), 35× *Il.*, implies nothing different from στίχες (etc.), 42×, 'rows' or 'ranks'; the choice between the two is determined by metrical requirements. Each has its own particular formulas, e.g. ∪∪–∪ φάλαγγες -ας|, as here, or στίχας ἀνδρῶν|, ἐπὶ (κατὰ) στίχας –∪∪–◡ |.

78 Like tragedy later, epic was not particularly sensitive to accidental repetitions as of μέσσου here after μέσσον in the previous verse.

79–80 Hooker (*Iliad III*) clearly brings out both the syntax and the different implications of the imperfect tenses here: 'And the long-haired Achaeans began to shoot at him; aiming with arrows and stones, they tried to hit him.'

82–3 Agamemnon calls in urgent tones for the bombardment of Hektor to cease, repeating and rephrasing both the word of command and the vocative for greater emphasis; then in contrast with these four strongly segmented cola comes the fluent and explanatory rising threefolder of 83. στεῦται is an old epic verb apparently meaning 'promise', 'threaten' or 'indicate' (rather than being connected with ἵστημι as used to be thought); ἔπος is lengthened before the felt digamma of (ϝ)ερέειν.

84 ἄνεῳ τ' ἐγένοντο|, compare ἄνεῳ ἐγένεσθε at 2.323; but Aristarchus (cited by Ap. Soph., Erbse I, 254) was probably right in seeing ἄνεῳ there as an adverb, 'in silence', without an iota (which was added by the majority

275

who took it to be a plural); see Chantraine, *Dict.* s.v. and *GH* 1, 249, who classes it as adverbial instrumental.

86–94 Hektor reports Paris' proposal in his words as far as possible, as is the rule in oral poetry, adapting only where necessary; thus 69 αὐτὰρ ἔμ' becomes αὐτὸν δ' in 90, συμβάλετ' in 70 becomes οἴους in 91. The concise κάθισον of 68 has to be expanded when it is reported; it is replaced by κέλεται and a fresh verse, 89, is added – a rather flowery verse, perhaps, showing some signs of inventive strain (τεύχεα are sometimes κᾱλά, but ἀποθέσθαι only appears once else in Homer, and then in a different sense, at 5.492, cf. 18.409). The last two verses of Paris' offer, 74f., are dropped entirely, perhaps because Hektor does not feel it necessary or diplomatic to elaborate on terms of departure at this stage.

86–7 |κέκλυτέ μευ is a formula meaning 'listen to me' (κλύω regularly taking the genitive of the person heard, the accusative of the thing heard): 9x *Il.*, 10x *Od.* Here that is altered in retrospect by the addition of 87 |μῦθον 'Αλεξάνδροιο, so that the sense becomes 'hear from me... the word of Alexandros'. In one way that is legitimate oral extension of a formula's normal use, especially perhaps in view of the Odyssean (not Iliadic) formulas κέκλυτέ μευ μύθων and κέκλυτε δὴ νῦν μευ, 'Ιθακήσιοι, ὄττι κεν εἴπω. But it is also relevant that 85f. recur (except for the first word of 85) as 7.66f., at the beginning of the second formal duel, where no similar difficulty arises; for the continuation there is 'that I may tell you what my heart bids me'. Even more remarkable is that 87 here (μῦθον 'Αλεξάνδροιο...) recurs only twice in the poem, and then precisely in book 7 and in reference to Paris' offer when the duel is over (at 374 = 388). It is clear that neither duel is simply based upon, let alone copied from, the other; there will be places where book 7 seems to be the borrower, but here it is clear that Homer has elements of the language he is to use in book 7 (and which will be more appropriate there) already in mind. The opposite was found to be probably the case with 76–8 – see the comment there.

95 A formular verse, 10x *Il.*, 5x *Od.* ἀκή is an old noun implying lack of agitation ('*douceur*') rather than strict silence; it perhaps comes from the same root as the Homeric ἦκα, 'gently', cf. Chantraine, *Dict.* s.v. ἀκή. In Homer it is used only in the accusative, adverbially. In the form ἀκέων (apparently a verbal derivative then also used adverbially), 5x *Il.*, 8x *Od.*, it certainly does imply silence, and even in ἀκὴν ἐγένοντο σιωπῇ the first word probably reinforces, rather than adding a new idea to, σιωπῇ. Compare ἄνεῳ τ' ἐγένοντο at 84, a separate formula, with a different metrical value, for the same idea.

97–110 Hektor's proposal was expressed in straightforward language (for example, it lacks virtually any internal punctuation); Menelaos' reply, by contrast, is more impassioned, as not only its content but also the short sentences and internal interruptions, down to 105 at least, reveal. His reaction, which is subtly imagined by the poet, is no longer the fierce delight of 23 ('he rejoiced like a lion...'), and for a good reason: there, he thought he was on the point of taking immediate revenge on his enemy; now the outcome is hedged around with conditions, and even if Paris dies the Achaeans will leave Troy intact. Moreover he and Paris are being treated as equals, which is no help to Menelaos' affronted sense of τιμή; that is why he feels not joy but grief, ἄλγος (97), and why he claims to be acceding to the proposal for the sake of his comrades rather than himself.

98–9 φρονέω...ἤδη is a difficult construction to determine; either 'I think they have already been separated' (i.e. are as good as separated) or 'I think they will soon be separated' is the usual choice of interpretation, with e.g. Hooker supporting the latter. But neither gives a satisfactory sense, and I prefer with Leaf to take φρονέω as meaning 'my thought is', i.e. 'I intend' (as at 5.564 and 17.286), followed by 'that they be separated now'. He has made up his mind to accept the challenge and put an end to hostilities.

99 πέπασθε is from πάσχω; the medieval MSS opted for πέποσθε (cf. πέπονθα in the singular), wrongly for the plural form as Aristarchus saw (Did/A).

100 ἐμῆς ἔριδος, '*my* quarrel' – not his fault, of course, but directly involving him and not the troops on either side. As last word of the verse the MSS read ἀρχῆς with Aristarchus against Zenodotus' ἄτης (Arn/A); but Zenodotus' version is not to be despised, since it is undoubtedly correct in two other passages with 'Αλεξάνδρου ἕνεκ' – –|, at 6.356 and 24.28. There, Alexandros' behaviour is seen (by Helen and the gods respectively) to involve a kind of delusion, but in the present passage Aristarchus argued that Menelaos would not use this term and so concede diminished responsibility to his enemy; ἀρχῆς would avoid that by meaning simply that Alexandros had initiated the crime and the quarrel. Such adaptations of an established phrase to special circumstances are not unknown, but other things being equal one would expect the wording of the other passages to be maintained. The point about ἄτη implying a kind of sympathy by Menelaos for Paris is a fine one, and I suspect that ἄτης is indeed the earlier reading; but with Aristarchus and the medieval tradition on the other side, one would not choose to alter the text.

103–4 Speed, τάχιστα, was the final thought of 102, so Menelaos proceeds urgently (and without connecting particle) to the practical details. He tells the Trojans directly here (οἴσετε, future imperative) to bring a white lamb and a black one, for Sun and Earth respectively (the order is reversed in the chiastic Greek construction), while the Achaeans will produce a third, of unspecified colour, for Zeus. bT ingeniously but erroneously explained that the sun symbolizes life, which the Trojans were fighting for, and the earth their land, whereas the Achaeans as foreigners sacrifice to Zeus Xenios. But Sun and Earth were regularly invoked to witness oaths, as was Zeus Horkios; perhaps Menelaos is being deliberately derogatory in suggesting that the two lesser and non-Olympian deities are more the concern of the Trojans, while the highest god is the responsibility of the civilized Achaeans (who in addition felt themselves to be under the protection of Zeus Xenios because of Paris' infringement of the laws of hospitality and marriage; to that extent bT were correct). See also on 276–8.

105 For ὅρκια τάμνῃ see on 73–5; in the event Agamemnon will perform the literal cutting, but Priam is there as chief Trojan representative and is 'cutting the oaths' in the metaphorical sense. For the idiom of Πριάμοιο βίην see on 2.658–60.

106 The insulting reference is inorganic, but is justified by Paris' proved untrustworthiness.

108–10 Aristarchus (Arn/A) athetized these three verses because they provide a kind of excuse for Priam's sons, who have been so strongly criticized in 106 – grounds analogous to those applied to ἄτης in 100. Proverbial material is quite often worked into Homeric speeches, not always with complete appropriateness, when a sententious effect seems justified, so that Aristarchus' objection is clearly overdone. At the same time the implied praise of Priam seems excessive in the circumstances, and is the sort of thing that would be more fittingly directed to Nestor elsewhere.

108 ἠερέθονται, 'float in the air', cf. 2.448, an epic development of ἀείρω = 'raise', used three times in the *Iliad* (cf. Chantraine, *GH* I, 327) and here applied to φρένες in a brilliant metaphor. Shipp, *Studies* 90 (cf. 238), shows convincingly that most such present forms in -θω (but not 231 ἠγερέθονται as it happens) are found in similes and digressions and are not what he considers 'old'. That can be accepted so long as 'old' is understood to mean 'relatively old in the development of the epic language', and so long as 'not old' is not classified (as it is by Shipp) as 'abnormal' and therefore by implication post-Homeric.

109 Shipp objects to οἷς, also, as abnormal (*Studies* 238), without good reason. ὁ γέρων is generic, and no more abnormal (or Attic, as Leaf claimed) than several other relatively developed Homeric uses of ὁ on its way to becoming the definite article. For ἅμα πρόσσω καὶ ὀπίσσω compare 1.343, 18.250, with comment on the former, in which some awkward cumulation suggested the possibility of rhapsodic expansion. Here the phrase with its following ὅππως-clause is used more naturally, and there is nothing in the language or style of these verses to make them definitely suspect; although the difficulty noted at the end of 108–10n. remains.

111–20 Both sides are delighted at the prospect of an early end of the fighting; they dispose themselves for the duel, and heralds are sent back for the oath-victims.

113 ἵππους refers not just to the horses but to the whole equipage or equipages, as often in Iliadic battle-scenes. Both sides drew up horses and chariots into ranks, and then dismounted; they are all envisaged as being chariot-borne at this point, although that can only have been so with the leaders and there must have been infantry, πεζοί, too.

114–5 They take off their armour and put it on the ground – a surprising detail, perhaps a token of their accepting the truce. It is a moot question whether 115 means that the sets of armour were close to each other, with little distance (ἄρουρα, literally 'plough-land') on each side, or that as the armies stacked their arms they themselves were close to each other with little space between them. T thought the latter, and I tend to agree; Leaf (for example) favoured the former, but on too literal an understanding of ἀμφίς.

116–20 Each act of despatch is closed off by a rising threefolder (117 and 120).

119 Most of the mss have ἄρν' ἐκέλευσεν, the remainder ἄρν' ἐκέλευεν. Patently ἄρν' represents ἄρνα, accusative singular, to accord with the single lamb mentioned as the Achaean contribution in 104, and it is a mystery why Monro–Allen printed the dual form ἄρνε in OCT. The correct reading is presumably ἄρνα κέλευεν (imperfect, to match 116 ἔπεμπε and 118 προίει).

121–60   Iris, disguised, tells Helen of the impending duel, and Helen hastens from home to the Scaean gate, where she finds Priam and his counsellors surveying the scene

121 There is no special reason why Iris should summon Helen – it is not in accordance with a decision of Zeus or any other god, as is regularly the case elsewhere (e.g. 2.786f.; only at 23.198f. does she act on her own initiative, and then in a completely different way). Presumably some or- dinary mortal, perhaps even Laodike herself, would in any event have told Helen what was happening. The scholia were aware of the difficulty but offered only superficial palliatives (δηλονότι παρὰ τοῦ Διός...ἐρωτική τε θεὸς ἡ Ἴρις, bT). One might feel that the meaning is no more than that Laodike was acting in accordance with the divine disposition of events in general, until one recalls that this duel is a purely human arrangement arising out of Paris' irresponsibility and Hektor's rebuke; the only specific divine plan in operation at present is Zeus's undertaking to Thetis, which is being delayed and even jeopardized by the duel. But presumably the poet wishes, nevertheless, to show the divine involvement even in these human proceedings; Helen in particular (who is in addition a daughter of Zeus) is almost a divine pawn after the Judgement of Paris, and her feelings about

Paris, Menelaos and her home (139f.) are a moving reminder of the confused moral and human issues of the war. In addition, the summoning by Iris prepares the way for that by Aphrodite which she tries to resist later in the Book.

122–4 Laodike is one of Priam's legitimate children (cf. 6.252), full sister of Hektor and Paris and sister-in-law, γαλόως, of Helen. She is married to one of Antenor's sons, Helikaon who does not recur elsewhere; five other of his sons are mentioned at 11.59f., 221 and 248f., the most prominent of them being Agenor; there is a seventh called Laodokos, indeed, and Athene will take his appearance at 4.86f. That repetition of disguise-motif and similar name can hardly be accidental, and Laodokos, and perhaps Helikaon too, look like *ad hoc* inventions by the poet. Laodike herself is shown by 6.252 to be more deeply rooted in the tradition, although the fairest of Priam's daughters according to 13.365f. is not she but Kassandra.

125–7 Compare 22.440f., where while Hektor is being pursued and slain his wife Andromakhe is weaving in ignorance at home, again a purple cloth and a double one ('large enough to be worn double', Leaf, cf. 10.134, and contrast 'single' cloaks, 24.230 = *Od.* 24.276). The pairs of verses are quite similar, especially 126 and 22.441:

> 3.126 δίπλακα πορφυρέην, πολέας δ' ἐνέπασσεν ἀέθλους
> 22.441 δίπλακα πορφυρέην, ἐν δὲ θρόνα ποικίλ' ἔπασσε.

ἐμπάσσω literally means 'sprinkle into', and there is no doubt that the patterns are woven into the cloth and not embroidered on afterwards; see A. J. B. Wace, *AJA* 52 (1948) 54ff. and H. L. Lorimer, *HM* 397f., who notes that figure-weaving was an Oriental import into Greece. Andromakhe's pattern of flowers (for that is what θρόνα probably means) in various colours is a purely formal one; it is tempting at first to wonder whether Helen's ἀέθλους might not be equally formal 'combats' of pairs of warriors disposed along the edges of the cloth, but the addition of 128 shows that something more elaborate was meant; also that ἀέθλους must mean not specific combats but trials or sufferings (at least 9x so in *Od.*, also 3x *Il.* in the formula ὑπ' Εὐρυσθῆος ἀέθλων). Helen's weaving of these sufferings while the duel is being prepared outside is a pathetic symbol of the omnipresence of war (and would be even more effective in the Andromakhe context).

128 The sufferings of Trojans and Achaeans are because of Helen herself, which makes her weaving of them even more poignant. ὑπ' Ἄρηος παλαμάων| is a unique and not completely successful phrase; the closest parallel is | Ἕκτορος ἐν παλαμῆσιν at 7.105 and 24.738, where victims fall 'in the palms of', i.e. at the hands of, Hektor; cf. also 21.469.

130–8 Why does the poet choose to develop this scene by reporting the preparations outside the city in the words of a third party? Partly, no doubt, because the speech gives a different and even more dramatic picture of the seated armies, and in addition because it helps to emphasize, in an almost visual way, Helen's direct involvement in the affair.

130 νύμφα is an Old Indo-European vocative preserved in a few feminine nouns in -ᾰ/η (Chantraine, *GH* 1, 200) and retained in Aeolic; νύμφη means 'young married woman', 'bride', and Leaf noted that it is still used to address a sister-in-law in modern Greek. θέσκελα ἔργα is also found 2x *Od.*; θέσκελος means 'marvellous', its first element being connected with θεός as in θέσπις, θεσπέσιος, θέσφατος.

131 This occurred only four verses earlier at 127 (as well as 2x elsewhere in *Il.*); it is the obvious way of including Trojans and Achaeans in the same verse, in the genitive, since |Τρώων (θ') ἱπποδάμων by itself occurs 8x *Il.*,'Αχαιῶν χαλκοχιτώνων| 22x *Il.* The mention of both sides together is independently required both here and at 127; moreover the repetition may be deliberate, to underline the correspondence between Helen's work and the world outside (125–7n.).

132–5 'They who previously made war...those very ones are sitting...'; onto each of these contrasting verses is cumulated a further description (133 and 135), making a balanced quartet. Both cumulations have striking features: the former, its emphatic rhyme ὀλοοῖο...πολέμοιο (cf. ὀλοοῖο...γόοιο, similarly disposed, 2x *Il.*); the latter, that they are leaning against their shields, a unique posture in Homer (partly echoed by Archilochus, frag. 2.2 West ἐν δορὶ κεκλιμένος) which goes beyond the description at 114 where they simply placed their armour on the ground.

136–8 After the dramatic and quite full description of the scene, its purpose is stated with a conciseness that seeks to be naive rather than brutal: 'they will fight *for you*, and for the winner you will be called his own dear wife'. Aristarchus (Arn/A) declared κε in 138 to be otiose, but it marks the indefiniteness of the future κεκλήσῃ (whose short final syllable, shortened by regular correption before the following initial vowel, is unpersuasively claimed as an 'abnormal feature' by Shipp, *Studies* 238, cf. 164).

139–40 The words of Iris–Laodike filled her heart with longing for her former husband and her home town and her parents (who must be Lede and Tundareos, although her actual father was Zeus as is explicitly stated at 199, Διὸς ἐκγεγαυῖα, and 426). No more than that is meant, and there is no intention of casting Iris in an Aphrodite-like role.

142 κατὰ δάκρυ χέουσα| (etc.), 4x *Il.*, 9x *Od.* (+variants); the formula can be made more pathetic by adding θαλερόν or, as here, τέρεν (cf. also θαλερὸν/τέρεν κατὰ δάκρυον εἴβεις| (etc.), 3x *Il.*, 2x *Od.* +variants). τέρην means 'tender' or 'soft', and Helen is shedding a charming tear for past as well as present as she veils herself and rushes out of her chamber.

143 This formular verse recurs 2x *Od.*, of Penelope (cf. also *Od.* 19.601);

οὐκ οἶος· ἅμα τῷ γε is found 3x *Il.* (including 2.745 and 822; see on 2.822–3), 2x *Od.* Stephanie West comments on *Od.* 1.331–5 that a woman would usually be accompanied by (two) maidservants when she went among men, and adds *Il.* 22.450 and *Od.* 18.182–4 as evidence.

144 In the Odyssean occurrences of 143 (at 1.331, 18.207) no names are attached to the maidservants in a following verse, as here, which adds some support to Aristarchus' (Arn/A) provisional athetesis of the present verse: if this Aithre is Theseus' mother, he maintained, then it should go, but if she is merely an accidental homonym, then it can stay. But the coincidence not only of Aithre but also of Pittheus (who was Theseus' grandfather and king of Troizen) is too much to swallow, and the verse is almost without doubt an Athenian interpolation. The story that Aithre was removed to be Helen's slave, when her brothers the Dioskouroi released her after her abduction by Theseus, was illustrated on the Chest of Cypselus according to Pausanias 5.19.3, which makes it no later than the sixth century B.C.; it was also mentioned in the *Iliou Persis* according to Pausanias 10.25.5, and that suggests that it was known somewhat earlier. Yet Theseus and his sons are foreign to the *Iliad* (see also on 2.552 *fin.*); it is strange that this interpolation made its way into the ancient vulgate, where so much else the Athenians might have been tempted to add did not.

βοῶπις is regularly restricted to Here, but its application to Klumene here cannot in itself be said to be a mark of post-Homeric composition, since it is applied to another mortal woman at 7.10. There is a Nereid called Klumene at 18.47, and it is suggestive that another Nereid in the same list, Halie at 18.40, is the other non-Olympian recipient of the epithet βοῶπις.

145 The Scaean gate (always plural in Greek, with πύλαι signifying double doors) is the main gate of Troy in the direction of the battlefield – its name presumably meant 'on the left' but reveals nothing further. It is mentioned 12x in the poem (3x in connexion with the 'oak tree', φηγός), whereas the Dardanian gate, πυλάων Δαρδανιάων|, is referred to 3x. If this is a separate gate, it might be expected to be on the eastern side of the walls, in the general direction of Dardanie (see on 2.819–20), with the Scaean gate to the north or north-west. There were probably other gates, too, since at 2.809 = 8.58 'all the gates' were opened for the army to march out – perhaps Troy was sometimes envisaged as having as many as seven, like Thebes (see on 2.809). Aristarchus, however (e.g. on 2.809 and 5.789 according to Arn/A and bT respectively), thought there was only one gate mentioned, the Scaean, for which Dardanian was another name. The latter scholium makes the good point that at 5.789 the Trojans are said not to have gone out in front of the Dardanian gate while Akhilleus was still in action, whereas at 9.353f. Hektor is said to have been unwilling to leave the protection of the *Scaean* gate in those conditions. Moreover of the three mentions of the Dardanian gate only one (5.789) indicates any particular locality, and that in the direction of the fighting; and in the other two cases, 22.194 and 413, πυλάων Δαρδανιάων| meets a metrical requirement, i.e. after ὁρμήσειε and μεμαῶτα, which the Scaean gate in the genitive case would not fill. The conclusion is that Aristarchus' opinion could very well be right.

146–8 'Those around Priam and Panthoos...as well as Oukalegon and Antenor', i.e. Priam and his companions Panthoos and so on; for the idea of including a person as among those who are 'around' him compare e.g. 2.445, 6.435–7. These are the Trojan elders and Priam's contemporaries, δημογέροντες in 149. Of them, Panthoos is father of Pouludamas, prominent warrior and Hektor's adviser; Thumoites does not recur; 147 names three of Priam's four brothers, sons of Laomedon, according to 20.237f. (in fact 147 = 20.238; Tithonos of course went off with Dawn). Antenor in 148 is the best-known of the group, husband of Theano and father of Agenor and several other and lesser warriors, see on 122–4 (including two Dardanian leaders at 2.822f.); he will describe Odysseus' and Menelaos' visit to Troy at 203–24 below. He is paired here, in a rising threefolder, with Οὐκαλέγων, 'Not-caring', who fails to find a mention elsewhere in Homer but is unforgettable (as by Vergil, *Aeneid* 2.311f.) because of his extraordinary name. Most Greek names, whether they belong to Achaeans or Trojans, are 'speaking names' in a sense, but their meaning is invariably heroic or at least tolerably complimentary, like all the others in the list. Oukalegon's name (he was son of Aisuetes and brother of Antenor, and therefore probably Dardanian, cf. 13.427f., according to T) is certainly not, but is hardly the sort of thing a poet would invent for a counsellor.

149 The 'community elders' were sitting on, or over, the Scaean gate, i.e. on a tower to one side of it as explained in 153, ἥντ' ἐπὶ πύργῳ.

150–3 They are beyond the age for fighting but valiant, ἐσθλοί, talkers; for the two complementary activities bT refer to 2.273. They are like grasshoppers who 'send forth a lily-like voice' as they sit in a tree.

152 λειριόεσσαν is formed from λείριον, 'lily' (or, sometimes, 'narcissus'): an opponent has 'lily skin', χρόα λειριόεντα, at 13.830; here the grasshoppers (cicadas) utter a 'lily voice', as do the Muses on Mt Olumpos according to Hesiod, *Theog.* 41; and a boy has 'lily eyes', λειρίων ὀμμάτων, at Bacchylides 17.95. Presumably therefore the comparison with a lily implies delicacy – a delicate voice, delicate skin and eyes; M. L. West on the Hesiod passage compares λεπταλέη φωνή at 18.571. That seems fairly straightforward, although the term has given rise to much argument and discussion from antiquity on. But can the chatter or clatter of cicadas really be 'delicate' or the like? Perhaps that is unfair, and 'chirruping' would be a better description of the noise, which the Greeks evidently enjoyed; in a probable development of this passage (or a common archetype) at

Hesiod, *Erga* 582–4, the cicada is said to pour out his voice in song as a harbinger of summer. There may, too, be an element of humour in the comparison; the cicadas certainly represent the ceaselessness of these old men's talk, for they are 'fine talkers' or 'noble orators' in 150f., and perhaps the 'lily voice' contains a similar touch of affectionate irony.

δενδρέῳ is the reading defended by Aristarchus (Arn/A) against Zenodotus' δένδρει. The difficulties of the former can be exaggerated; Wackernagel's view that it is an Atticism is not now often accepted, and δένδρεον ὑψιπέτηλον, evidently a formula, is found at 13.437 and *Od.* 4.458. Once the synizesis of δενδρέ(ϝ)ῳ across the lost digamma is accepted, there is surely no difficulty in the shortening (correption) of the resulting long syllable, although Leaf found it 'intolerable'. According to Chantraine, *GH* I, 37 this type of synizesis is rare in Homer, and he classes δενδρέῳ as 'linguistically late' (by which he does not mean necessarily post-Homeric), referring also to 153 ἧντο which is part of the same simile; but he also observes that without synizesis this form could not be used in hexameters. What all this amounts to is that this brilliant simile belongs to the most developed phase of the language of oral epic; that is, it is likely to be by Homer himself.

Synizesis and correption bind δενδρέῳ closely to ἐφεζόμενοι, so that the first part of the verse flows on almost without break, as indeed does the second part with its overrunning both of fourth-foot word-break and of the 'bucolic' one before the fifth foot. This creates a fluent contrast, and a sense of completion, after its two three/four-colon predecessors.

153 ἧντ': Chantraine, *GH* I, 476, disputes Wackernagel's view that this is an Atticism. The old form is εἵατο (ἥατο in 149), of which ἧντο is a relatively late artificial development; but he suggests εἵατο πύργῳ here (without ἐπί) as a possible emendation, or that ἧντ' replaced an old monosyllable ἕατ'.

155 Both Crates, the leader of the Pergamene school of critics (Nic/A), and Zenodotus according to Aristarchus (Arn/A) read ὦκα, 'swiftly', not ἦκα, 'softly', which is rightly defended by Aristarchus and accepted in the vulgate. As Helen approaches, the old men whisper their 'winged' comments to each other; for πτερόεντα see on 1.201.

156–60 This famous comment is constructed with extreme care. Its components are strongly formular, but are combined to form a sympathetic and quite subtle judgement ('no wonder they are fighting over her; for she is so beautiful; but, even so, let her return home and leave us in peace') which owes much to the type and arrangement of verses. Two contrasting pairs of enjambed verses are set around the simple and expressive whole-verse statement of 158; moreover there is an unmistakable modulation of the verse-pattern, from twofold 156 (in which the semantic division follows νέμεσις), to the technically fourfold but in effect threefold 157, to 158 which has an ambiguous three/twofold structure, to 159, almost paradoxical in content, which is an undeniable rising threefolder, to the cumulated concluding verse, 160, which re-establishes the regular fourfold pattern in accordance with its more logical statement of reasons and consequences:

156 οὐ νέμεσις Τρῶας καὶ ἐϋκνήμιδας Ἀχαιοὺς
157 τοιῆδ' ἀμφὶ γυναικὶ πολὺν χρόνον ἄλγεα πάσχειν·
158 αἰνῶς ἀθανάτῃσι θεῇς εἰς ὦπα ἔοικεν·
159 ἀλλὰ καὶ ὧς τοίη περ ἐοῦσ' ἐν νηυσὶ νεέσθω
160 μηδ' ἡμῖν τεκέεσσί τ' ὀπίσσω πῆμα λίποιτο.

156 νέμεσις in Homer implies righteous indignation by gods or men at an improper act. The noun is found 4x *Il.*, 4x *Od.*, without strong formular development (although οὐ νέμεσις itself is clearly traditional, possibly slightly colloquial); on the other hand the verbal forms νεμεσάω -άομαι -σητον -ίζομαι are common (33x *Il.*, 24x *Od.*). All derive from the root meaning of νέμω, namely 'assign something to its proper place, or in a regular way'.

157 Each of the three rhythmical elements of the verse is replete with significance: '(no one could think it wrong for Trojans and Achaeans) for such a woman, so long a time, to suffer griefs'.

158 The conventional comparison with a god or goddess (here, even more abstract, with goddesses) is as far as the poet chooses to go in describing Helen's famous beauty; his restraint, and his avoidance of perilous specifications of cheeks, lips and so on, have been much admired from antiquity on. There is something apophthegmatic about the verse, which gains much of its effect from the lingering introductory αἰνῶς, 'terribly' -- the English idiom is the same, but one should remain aware that the Greek usage belongs to the latest phase of the oral language (although Shipp failed to comment on it). αἰνῶς occurs 20x *Il.*, 13x *Od.*, but 17 of the Iliadic uses are with verbs of fearing (especially), being angry or ashamed, or being worn down; in other words 'terribly' or 'dreadfully' has its literal sense. Only 10.547 (again, something is 'terribly like' something else) and perhaps 24.198, as well as the present verse, have the metaphorical use. The proportions in the *Odyssey* are notably different: only 6 of the 13 occurrences are with verbs of fearing and so on, and of the remaining 7 no less than 4 give αἰνῶς a definitely pleasant meaning (including 1.208, another αἰνῶς...ἔοικας). That suggests that the idiom of this famous verse is Odyssean rather than Iliadic in character (especially since its other Iliadic uses are in the 'Odyssean' books 10 and 24).

159–60 |ἀλλὰ καὶ ὧς (9x *Il.*, 7x *Od.*) is a functional formula with an emotional ring, reinforced here by τοίη περ ἐοῦσ'. Moreover the alliteration of ἐν νηυσὶ νεέσθω in this rising threefold verse is clearly deliberate, a rhetorical touch heightened by the plural νηυσί and confirmed by ὀπίσσω πῆμα λίποιτο, with its mixture of plosive and liquid sounds (for πῆμα cf. 50).

161–244   Priam seats Helen beside him and asks her to identify for him some of the Achaean leaders in the plain below; she does so, but ends in distress because she cannot see her brothers among them

161–246 The Τειχοσκοπία or Viewing from the Walls (as it was known from the Alexandrian period on) is not so much a special kind of catalogue of Achaean leaders as a laudatory description and discussion of Agamemnon and Odysseus, followed by cursory references to Aias and Idomeneus and then brought to a close by Helen's growing concern about her brothers. Priam is depicted as not having set eyes on the enemy leaders before; after nearly ten years of siege (most of it close to the walls, as is shown by references elsewhere, e.g. 9.352–4) that is impossible in realistic terms; and it is generally considered that the episode, in an altered form, originally belonged to an early stage of the war and has been transposed to its present place for the purposes of the monumental *Iliad*. The way in which Priam's questions are introduced (especially 191 δεύτερον αὖτ' 'Οδυσσῆα ἰδών, 225 τὸ τρίτον αὖτ' Αἴαντα ἰδών) does indeed suggest that a systematic list of opponents lies behind the present attenuated survey; after the Catalogue of Ships it would, of course, be inappropriate to run through all the Achaean princes, even in somewhat greater detail. Our poet has evidently decided to use the traditional format of a Viewing in order to give an imposing description of Agamemnon and Odysseus, and from the enemy (or an objective) point of view – especially perhaps, in the first case, in order to counterbalance the king's ambivalent role so far. At the same time the identification-motif allows him to develop a sympathetic account of Priam and Helen and the relations between them. In a way it can be said that this peaceful scene (the two armies are, after all, seated and waiting for what they mistakenly believe to be the final act of the war) both introduces the second dimension of life within Troy and brings Helen, for whom the war and the duel are being fought, entirely to life as a creature both gentle and unhappy – something much more than the abstract and amoral pawn of ancient legend. The comments on Aias and Idomeneus, on the other hand, are meagre and uninteresting in themselves, and (as will be seen) are likely to be primarily a transition to Helen's search for her brothers, and so to a moving and disquieting end to the episode.

If the composer had been interested in making any kind of representative list, he would surely have included Diomedes and Nestor as well as Menelaos (who gets a brief mention in Antenor's speech about Odysseus, at 205ff.), and even perhaps the lesser Aias and the Asklepiadai; and Akhilleus would have been mentioned even in his absence. The presumed archetype might have been different, since Diomedes and Nestor, at least, could well have been made far more prominent in our *Iliad* than they had been in the earlier tradition about Troy – it is notable, for example, that the former is substantially confined to books 5, 6 and 10. The choice of Odysseus for description in detail is not surprising in view of his complex and contradictory character and his role both in the preparation for war and in the ultimate fall of the city.

Why did the monumental composer not take pains to remove the anachronism of Priam requiring this kind of information after so many years? It would, after all, have been a simple matter to have retained the outlines of the scene as a whole yet abandoned the device of his ignorance; he could, for example, have simply expressed surprise at Agamemnon's commanding presence, and so elicited Helen's comment at 172–80 much as it stands. Similarly he could have commented on Odysseus' relative lack of stature without suggesting that he had never seen him before, adding merely something like 'that *is* Odysseus, is it not?'; and Antenor's reminiscence could have followed virtually without change. A Homer who had been writing out his poem would probably have made such adjustments; but somehow the oral tradition of a Teikhoskopia must have persuaded the actual Homer, and his audiences, that this was not necessary, that the apparent anomaly could be overlooked or tolerated in the name of tradition.

The arrangement of the whole episode as it stands, and the relative length of the speeches of which it consists (except for 8 single verses of speaking, answering etc.), are significant both of careful construction and of the emphasis on the different persons under description. Of the 76 verses of speech, 9 are concerned with Helen (and Priam), 11 with Agamemnon, 6 with Priam's Phrygian reminiscences, 26 with Odysseus (and a further 4 with the Menelaos comparison), 3 with Aias, 4 with Idomeneus, 9 with the missing Dioskouroi; the rest are transitional verses. Thus Odysseus receives the greatest attention in quantitative terms, mainly indeed through Antenor's account of a particular occasion. The first three speeches, between Priam and Helen, are of exactly the same length, 9 verses each; Priam's second enquiry, about Odysseus, is slightly shorter (7 verses) and is followed by a very brief reply from Helen (3 verses) which leads to Antenor's long interjection (21 verses). Then a further brief 2-verse question from Priam about Aias stimulates Helen's final reply, of which a single verse deals with Aias, then 4 on Idomeneus lead to the 9 about her brothers. Thus the episode begins with a series of four quite leisurely exchanges of more or less equal length between Priam and Helen, then turns into quite abrupt questions and answers, except for Antenor's contribution and, at the end, Helen's disquiet addressed to herself rather than to Priam.

161 The other use of (ἐσ)ἐκαλέσσατο in the *Iliad* is at 24.193, ἐς δ' ἄλοχον Ἑκάβην ἐκάλεσσατο, φώνησέν τε, and is less obtrusively tautologous than ἐκαλέσσατο φωνῇ here – which is paralleled, however, by 171 μύθοισιν ἀμείβετο, in the very next verse of address, on which see 437n. The oral style was not antipathetic to the 'went with his feet' kind of locution, and there are many formulas of this kind, cf. e.g. on 169–70.

162–5 Priam's kindly address is in superficial contrast with what his companions were saying to each other just before; they did not assign blame, but they very naturally wished to be rid of Helen. Perhaps Priam did also, but he would hardly mention that to Helen herself, whom he clearly likes. He asks her to sit by him so that she can see her old friends and relatives by marriage, πηούς, and her former husband; does he understand her ambivalent feelings toward Menelaos – after all, she might be resentful and frightened? Questions like that are frustrated by the consideration that Priam is envisaged, here and there at least, as not yet realizing what is happening; for at 250ff. Idaios reports the situation to him as though he were ignorant of it, and at 259 Priam shudders, ῥίγησεν, at the news. And yet both armies are sitting down; he and the others *must* know that something unusual, probably a formal duel, is afoot, and that seems to be recognized at 195. Again the difficulty is presumably due to incomplete integration of the Viewing theme into its specific Iliadic context.

164 After the rising threefolder of 163, this verse with its repetition μοι αἰτίη ἐσσί...μοι αἴτιοί εἰσιν has an abrupt and almost dismissive quality; he clearly wishes to proceed to his questioning. Meanwhile he blames the gods in a truly heroic manner, when he might sooner (as bT hinted) have blamed his son Paris.

166 bT attempted to explain the apparent anachronism of Priam's enquiries by saying that on previous occasions the enemy would have been fighting, and in armour, which would have concealed their identity (they refer to Patroklos in Akhilleus' armour, cf. especially 11.798f.). This is a good try but far from convincing; for example 'this huge man' would have elicited a similar interest in the past even if he had been armed. His sheer size may be exaggerated here in view of 168, but Agamemnon was highly conspicuous according to the similes of 2.477–83.

167 An almost identical enquiry is made about Aias at 226. ἠΰς -ν τε μέγας -ν τε is used 8x *Il.* of 7 different warriors; ἠΰς is metrically lengthened from ἐΰς (Chantraine, *Dict.* s.v.), of which the adverbial form εὖ is better known; it is an old, assuredly Indo-European term meaning 'good' in a heroic sense, i.e. powerful, brave, noble.

168 κεφαλῇ here probably means 'in height', i.e. judged by the head (or as a dative of respect) and not, as Leaf and most commentators have thought, 'by a head', which seems excessive, especially after πελώριον in 166. At 193 Odysseus will be declared by Priam to be shorter κεφαλῆ than Agamemnon; if Odysseus were accordingly to be *two* head-heights shorter than several others (168), he would be practically a dwarf. At 227 Aias is outstanding κεφαλήν, with respect to his head (and broad shoulders); probably once again height is meant.

169–70 The extravagant praise is better paralleled in the *Odyssey* than the *Iliad*, mainly because the former has more meetings between strangers; see especially Odysseus to Nausikaa at 6.160 οὐ γάρ πω τοιοῦτον ἐγών ἴδον ὀφθαλμοῖσιν, and similarly of Odysseus himself at 4.269. ἴδον ὀφθαλμοῖσιν| is a common formula, 9x *Il.*, 14x *Od.*; for the redundant expression see on 161. With γεραρόν in 170 compare γεραρώτερος of Odysseus at 211 – this adjective, based on *γέραρ as equivalent to γέρας, privilege or honour (originally of age, cf. γέρων), does not recur in Homer. Odysseus will address his father Laertes with the same words, βασιλῆι γὰρ ἀνδρὶ ἔοικας, at *Od.* 24.253; ἔοικε (etc.) occurs frequently at the verse-end in both poems, but this particular locution (to say of someone unknown that he is like a certain kind of person) is commoner in the *Odyssey*. The phrase also exemplifies a common idiomatic use of ἀνήρ (or φώς) as appended to a noun expressing peoples, ranks or professions, e.g. Θρήϊκας ἄνδρας, ἡγήτορες ἄνδρες, τέκτονες ἄνδρες.

171 On μύθοισιν ἀμείβετο see 161n. and especially 437n.

172–80 The arrangement of Helen's reply corresponds with Priam's preceding comment and question: it is of the same length; it has a rising threefolder as its second verse; the first 5 verses (against Priam's first 4) concern her own position and emotions, the last 4 (against Priam's 5) the identity of Agamemnon. More generally, the first part of each speech includes the motifs of mutual respect, of Helen's friends and relatives, and of her feelings about having left home. The transition from sympathy and sorrow to the practical matter of identification is abrupt in each case; both speeches end in praise for the Achaean leader, although Helen's does so with a second rising threefolder and then reverts briefly to her own feelings of regret and self-blame. As a whole her words are more intense than Priam's, and the almost harsh enjambment of 173/4 contributes to that effect.

172 Hephaistos will refer to Thetis at 18.394 as δεινή τε καὶ αἰδοίη θεός; in both cases δεινός simply reinforces αἰδοῖος, 'revered', without implying anything more frightening. Helen's affection is suggested both by the intimate revelation of her feelings and by φίλε ἑκυρέ, 'dear father-in-law'. The aspiration of ἑκυρέ represents a lost (geminated) digamma, itself including the sigmatic element of *σϝεκυρός; cf. Chantraine, *GH* i, 146. It was because of those lost consonants that the final short syllable of φίλε could be treated as long.

173 'Would that evil death had pleased me', cf. ὡς ὤφελες in 428, and, more particularly, Helen's similar wish expressed to Hektor at 6.345–51. ἀνδάνειν implies definite pleasure, something more than 'be satisfied with', so there is an intended paradox, especially since death is κακός; indeed that is the main justification for an epithet which is otherwise weak here. The verse is evidently composed for its context; it is not especially formular, and δεῦρο occurs only here at the verse-end out of 22 Iliadic uses (and only 1/21× *Od.*).

174–5 θάλαμος is specifically the marital bedchamber at 423–5, and T is right to say that Helen is cryptically referring to Menelaos. She has left husband, relatives and friends of her own age (corresponding with those listed by Priam at 163); she now adds her only child (Hermione according to *Od.* 4.14), who is τηλυγέτη (6× *Il.*, 2× *Od.*, only here feminine), a word for which 'born late', and therefore especially cherished, would be a meaning that suits all its Homeric uses; the etymologies of Hesychius and of bT on 9.482, from τηλοῦ or τέλος and γίγνομαι, are nevertheless suspect.

176 τό is accusative, 'with respect to that', 'therefore'. κλαίουσα τέτηκα is a vivid phrase, 'melt away in weeping', only here in Homer.

179 |ἀμφότερον is formular, 6× *Il.* For the combination of qualities see on 2.201–2, and for the verse-end phrase cf. 4.87.

180 δαήρ is husband's brother; Helen addresses herself with equal savagery when talking to her other δαήρ, Hektor, at 6.344: δᾶερ ἐμεῖο κυνός... Kinship terms are frequent hereabouts, πόσις, πηός, ἑκυρός, δαήρ. 'Dog-faced' is a violent term, one flung at Agamemnon by Akhilleus at 1.159, but also used of his mother Here by Hephaistos at 18.396 – perhaps it was not quite so bad, for the Greeks, when applied to a woman as when applied to a man. See also on 1.225.

εἴ ποτ' ἔην γε is a formula, 2× *Il.*, 2× *Od.* (+ 1×, 1× similar). The Odyssean uses are fairly straightforward, since they all refer to Odysseus, who has disappeared and whose very existence, even in the past, seems remote; so *Od.* 19.315, οἷος Ὀδυσσεὺς ἔσκε μετ' ἀνδράσιν, εἴ ποτ' ἔην γε. The Iliadic applications are more oblique and consequently even more pathetic: at 11.762 Nestor says ὣς ἔον, εἴ ποτ' ἔην γε (so the vulgate – editors usually print ἔον γε), looking back to his youthful exploits; at 24.426 Priam says of the dead Hektor 'my son, εἴ ποτ' ἔην γε' (never forgot to sacrifice). Obviously the phrase expresses nostalgia and regret at how things have changed; it is 'a pathetic turn of phrase apparently peculiar to Homer' (C. W. Macleod on 24.426). Here it presumably refers to Agamemnon: 'he was my brother-in-law, if that relationship ever existed', i.e. if ever I lived in Lakedaimon and was married to Menelaos – it all seems so far off now. There is a bare possibility that ἔην here is first person and not third, and refers to Helen herself (she has just addressed herself as κυνώπιδος); at 11.762, as already noted, the vulgate reading is ὣς ἔον, εἴ ποτ' ἔην γε (but cf. 23.643, ὥς ποτ' ἔον, where ἔην would be metrically possible; there is no certain Homeric use of ἔην as 1st person singular imperfect of εἰμί). In any event it is unnecessary to suppose with Leaf, Hooker and others that εἰ in this phrase has a special and *unconditional* force.

182–3 μοιρηγενές, *hapax legomenon* in Homer, must mean 'born with (favourable) destiny' and comes to much the same as ὀλβιόδαιμον. Priam's almost excessive admiration of Agamemnon is based now purely on the number of troops he commands. That this is an important index of power and prestige is clearly shown by Agamemnon's catalogue-entry, especially 2.580: (he stands out above the other leaders) οὕνεκ' ἄριστος ἔην, πολὺ δὲ πλείστους ἄγε λαούς. In 183 ἦ ῥά νύ τοι πολλοί continues to express amazement: 'Many indeed (ἦ), then (ῥά νύ),...'

184–9 Priam's Phrygian reference is very much in the style of Nestor's reminiscences, although far briefer; the breathless admiration continues, and he reveals none of the perturbation that the sight of so large a force might be expected to arouse in one still under siege. That is probably a further result of adapted materials at this point, although he might also have been anxious to impress Helen.

185 The Phrygians are likewise αἰολοπώλους at *HAphr* 137, perhaps after this passage; otherwise the compound is unique in the epic, although cf. αἰολοθώρηξ (2x *Il.*), αἰολομίτρην (1x *Il.*) where αἰόλος presumably implies 'shimmering' rather than its basic sense 'rapid'. The latter is the probable meaning with horses (*contra* E. Delebecque, *Le Cheval dans l'Iliade* (Paris 1951) 167, who translates as 'aux coursiers frémissants (?)'); cf. 19.404, πόδας αἰόλος ἵππος. At 10.431 the Phrygians are ἱππόμαχοι (and the Maeonians ἱπποκορυσταί); but nothing is said of their horses in the brief entry in the Trojan catalogue at 2.862f.

186 Otreus and Mugdon are otherwise unknown; the latter's non-Greek name suggests that he may not be entirely fictitious.

187–9 The Phruges lived around the Sangarios river, which they are now defending, according to 16.717–19 where Hekabe's brother Asios is said to have 'dwelt in Phrugie by the streams of Sangarios'. They are a different people from those later called Phruges who swept down into Asia Minor from Thrace (cf. Herodotus 7.73) some time after the fall of Troy. Here the Trojans are their allies in keeping the Amazones at bay – Bellerophon had also fought against them down in Lycia according to 6.186. ἀντιάνειραι -ας in both passages shows the Amazons as already envisaged as women; in the Cyclic epic *Aithiopis*, ascribed to Arktinos and in some texts made to run on continuously from the end of the *Iliad*, they came to Troy to help Priam after Hektor's death, led by Penthesileia who was killed by Akhilleus. There is no detectable logic in all this: why should they be first the enemies of the Phrygians who were allied with Troy (naturally, since Priam's brother-in-law lived there), then come to help the Trojans? And what is this idea of a race of women based on? All the old matriarchal theories have collapsed. They were an ancient concept, affected no doubt by popular etymology ('breast-less'), integrated into the myths about Herakles for instance, and seem to have become a standard mythical symbol for exotic foreign raiders.

188 ἐλέχθην, 'I was counted with them', from λέγομαι.

189 Hooker comments on ὅτε τ', where τ' cannot be the generalizing particle, 'It seems that τε became so common with relative words in general expressions that it spread to other types of relative clause.'

192–202 Once again the poet lets Priam himself describe in some detail the physical appearance of the person he is asking about, and confines Helen's reply to a brief and traditional identification (almost epigrammatic in kind in the case of Odysseus, as AbT observe on 200–2); then comes further development, by Priam himself of Agamemnon and by Antenor (at 240ff.) of Odysseus.

193–4 On κεφαλῇ see 168n.; Aristarchus (Did/A) read κεφαλήν as at 227, and this could be right. Broad shoulders as a distinguishing characteristic, in addition to height, will recur at 210, where rather surprisingly Menelaos is said to surpass Odysseus in this respect, just as the latter here surpasses Agamemnon.

195–6 For the first time Priam refers to the unusual circumstance of the armies having taken off their armour; τεύχεα (literally 'things made') primarily describes defensive armour, and at 114 they ἐξεδύοντο, 'took it off', although swords and spears are doubtless included on the present occasion.

No strong contrast can be intended between the μέν and δέ clauses; or rather the particles provide a kind of pseudo-contrast to disguise the incongruity between the unarmed Odysseus and his parading around as though he were inspecting fully armed (and unseated!) troops. That incongruity arises from the inappropriate use of the formular half-verse ἐπιπωλεῖται στίχας ἀνδρῶν, suitable as it is to Agamemnon's inspection at 4.250.

197–8 The brief κτίλος comparison of 196 recurs in a more elaborate form at 13.492f. There is nothing surprising in the immediate repetition of a simile-motif; compare the Ares-comparisons at 13.295 and 298–305, with the comments of Moulton, *Similes* 21f. Here, however, there is special subtlety in the suggestion of how Priam thinks. It is as though he was pleased with the initial comparison and decided to develop it: 'he strides like a bell-wether – yes, I liken him to a thick-fleeced ram who moves through a great flock of gleaming sheep', in which the progressive element represented by 'yes' is to be found in the γε of ἔγωγε. For the use of ἐΐσκω cf. *Od.* 6.152, where Odysseus likens Nausikaa to Artemis; πηγεσι- must derive from

Book Three

πήγνυμι, 'with compact fleece'. Moulton, *Similes* 92f., stresses the parallel with Agamemnon as a bull among cattle at 2.480f., and at 93 n.14 develops an interesting argument about the ways in which one character may be used as a foil for another, as both Agamemnon and, later, Menelaos are for Odysseus.

199 M. W. Edwards, *Classical Philology* 64 (1969) 81–7, has observed that this formula of reply, together with those at 171 and 228, displays uneconomical variation (these being the only three verses of reply, as distinct from saying, connected with Helen):

171 τὸν δ' Ἑλένη μύθοισιν ἀμείβετο, δῖα γυναικῶν
199 τὸν δ' ἠμείβετ' ἔπειθ' Ἑλένη Διὸς ἐκγεγαυῖα
228 τὸν δ' Ἑλένη τανύπεπλος ἀμείβετο, δῖα γυναικῶν

Verses of address in general constitute a complex formular system, with some variation even for subjects (i.e. name–epithet groups) of the same metrical value; cf. e.g. M. Parry in Parry, *MHV* 10–16. That provides a certain justification for Edwards' conclusion that Homer may simply have preferred to have some variation of expression within a short scene; although variation for its own sake is rarely sought in the oral style. Yet there are other considerations. Thus the commonest of all reply-verses is τὸν/τὴν δ' ἀπαμειβόμενος/-η προσέφη ∪∪–∪∪–∘; but this will not fit with Helene, however positioned, mainly because of her initial vowel. Then no less than 28 different Homeric name–epithet groups follow the formular first half of e.g. 199, and Helen's is the only one beginning with a vowel – that is, the other 27 begin with a consonant and follow an unelided ἔπειτα. As a result, 199 becomes a slight but rather tiresome departure, not perhaps to be imitated or repeated, from an established formular rhythm. The poet is therefore pushed in the direction of simple ἀμείβετο, only 5x *Il.* but 14x *Od.*, of which ἀμείβετο μύθῳ| occurs 5x in all. It is presumably that formula which gave rise to μύθοισιν ἀμείβετο in 171 (although cf. also 6.343 τὸν δ' Ἑλένη μύθοισι προσηύδα μειλιχίοισι). Thus both 171 and 199 are exceptional adaptations, and as such not particularly satisfactory; perhaps that is why the singer chooses to replace μύθοισιν with τανύπεπλος (only here of Helen in *Il.*, but 2x *Od.*) when he comes to 228, since that does least violence to established formular systems.

200–2 Helen identifies Odysseus with an easy adaptation (using the epithet of πολύμητις 'Οδυσσεύς|) of the common address-formula διογενὲς Λαερτιάδη πολυμήχαν' 'Οδυσσεῦ (7x *Il.*, 13x *Od.*; it is of course a rising threefolder with its heavy patronymic bridging the central caesura). She then adds two further verses of compressed biography and characterization, nothing new but developing familiar information about him. The language of 201 is primarily par. alleled in the *Odyssey*, as one might expect (ἐν δήμῳ

'Ιθάκης 3x, κραναὴν 'Ιθάκην 4x); for the sentiment of κραναῆς περ ἐούσης compare *Od.* 9.27f., where Odysseus says that Ithake is rough, τρηχεῖ᾽, but a good nurturer of young men, than which he knows no sweeter sight. Verse 202 is an *ad hoc* amalgam of formular elements elaborating his traditional description as πολύμητις; Antenor will reuse μήδεα πυκνά| six verses later, and μήδεα εἰδώς| occurs 3x *Il.*, 2x (+2 similar) *Od.*

203 ἀντίον ηὔδα (17x *Il.*, 54x *Od.*) is a simple formula either of initial address, or of reply; Antenor enters the conversation with no special introduction – he is, of course, one of the elders among whom Priam and Helen are sitting (146ff.).

206–24 Antenor's description is introduced quite naturally as a personal confirmation of Helen's identification. It complements Priam's initial comments, at 193–8, on Odysseus' appearance (slightly confusing the issue at 209–11), then brings out his power as persuasive speaker – rather than the πολύμητις quality Helen had just stressed at 202.

203–8 Antenor's confirmation is useful (since Helen might not have known Odysseus well), but is further motivated by his obvious excitement as conveyed by ἦ μάλα τοῦτο... The theme of his entertaining Odysseus and Menelaos when they came to Troy before the war began was developed in the post-Homeric *Cypria*, but was certainly known to Homer since it is referred to again at 11.138–42, where the detail is added that Antimakhos had urged the Trojans to kill Menelaos there.

206 σεῦ ἕνεκ᾽ ἀγγελίης is a famous if overrated problem: does it mean 'for the sake of (bringing) a message concerning you' or 'as a messenger [ἀγγελίης, masc. nom.] on your behalf [σεῦ ἕνεκ᾽]'? Aristarchus (Arn/A) supported the latter against Zenodotus, who in spite of his unnecessary σῆς for σεῦ is probably right on this occasion. ὁ ἀγγελίης is in itself a doubtful form (despite νεηνίης, ταμίης etc., none of them from an abstract noun) according to M. L. West on Hesiod, *Theog.* 781 – an impossible one according to M. Leumann, who went on to argue, however (*HW* 168–72, also *LfgrE* s.v.), that this passage was misunderstood by other singers and then became the source of masculine ἀγγελίης at 11.140, 13.252, 15.640. Of these, 11.140 and 13.252 can be interpreted differently; only 15.640 favours Leumann's argument, and Zenodotus' ἀγγελίην would avoid the difficulty by making the construction similar to that of 11.140, where ἀγγελίην ἐλθόντα (of Menelaos coming to Troy) most probably means 'coming (for) a message-bearing', that is, coming on a mission, cf. 24.235 ἐξεσίην ἐλθόντι.

208 The reuse of μήδεα πυκνά after 202 is somewhat prosaic, especially since the earlier application to Odysseus was connected with his δόλοι and a development of his character as πολύμητις; Menelaos did not possess these traits.

209–11 ἀλλ᾽ ὅτε δή (38x *Il.*, 49x *Od.*) begins no less than 4 of the 21 verses of Antenor's speech; here and at 212 it lacks its usual adversative force. 'When they mingled with the assembling Trojans' in 209 probably means 'when they appeared in the Trojan assembly', as Leaf remarked, and does not therefore suggest that στάντων in 210 applies also to the Trojans. When the two of them were standing, Menelaos surpassed Odysseus 'in respect of broad shoulders'; Leaf is wrong on two scores in his comment that his 'shoulders stood out not only above his, but above all the Trojans', for if one wishes to say that a man is taller than another it is natural to mention the head (as at 168 and 193) and not the shoulders. Indeed the phrase (a formular one, 3× *Il.*, 1× *Od.* + 1 similar) looks like a misapplication of 193f., where Odysseus was said by Priam to be less tall than Agamemnon but broader in shoulders and chest, εὐρύτερος δ' ὤμοισιν ἰδὲ στέρνοισιν ἰδέσθαι. That makes sense: Odysseus is not especially tall but is powerfully built. His broad shoulders make him look especially impressive when he is seated (and his lack of commanding height does not show): that is the implication of 211, in which γεραρώτερος probably takes up γεραρόν in 170. These three verses are interesting but expressed with less than the usual Homeric clarity and ease; that does not apply to the change of construction between στάντων and ἑζομένω, which is nothing unusual, while for a nominative dual participle then distributed into ὁ...ὁ see especially 10.224.

212 ἀλλ' ὅτε δή is slightly more pointed than in 209: '(there was this physical difference between them), but when it came to words, then Menelaos was brief but fluent...'

μήδεα takes up the μήδεα πυκνά of 208, although in a rather sterile way (see on 208). The combination μύθους καὶ μήδεα has no exact parallel in Homer; there is nothing specific against it, but it is typical, nevertheless, of the strained diction of this part of Antenor's speech.

213–4 ἐπιτροχάδην, 'fluently', literally 'running on' in a good sense (as the context requires), as opposed to 'glibly' as Iros says of the disguised Odysseus at *Od.* 18.26. The term became part of the technical vocabulary of rhetoric, much later, and primarily implied 'cursorily' or 'passing rapidly from one point to another'. Our poet needs to say that Menelaos is a clear and fluent speaker, but a somewhat laconic one; even his fluency must be in a lower class than Odysseus' 'snowflake' delivery which he is about to describe. Therefore the two aspects – clearness and brevity – are listed alternately, twice over: he was fluent (ἐπιτροχάδην), with few words (παῦρα), but very clear ones (μάλα λιγέως), because he was not a man of many words (πολύμυθος).

215 οὐδ' ἀφαμαρτοεπής adds a third characteristic: his few, clearly-delivered words were to the point, did not miss their target. So far this cumulated verse is successful, even necessary; its second half is more difficult. Ancient doubts were concerned with whether ἦ, ἥ or εἰ should be read; Nicanor and Herodian (whose comments are reflected in A) were probably dependent on Aristarchus in rejecting the third, but this is probably right none the less; most of the мss thought so, mainly no doubt because it is intelligible while the others are not: Menelaos did not miss the target with his words, even if (εἰ καί) he was the younger (that is, presumably, than his brother Agamemnon). But even that does not make very good sense; Menelaos is not envisaged, after all, as a very young man, and it would only be in such a person that the power of sensible speaking would, according to the Greek view, be surprising enough to deserve comment. Incidentally γένος is not used exactly so elsewhere in Homer, to mean 'age' (Shipp, *Studies* 238); it is an understandable extension, but even so it adds a little more substance to the feeling that this central part of Antenor's speech was composed with some haste, or under some strain, or was perhaps so often cited in the post-Homeric period that it suffered minor rephrasing.

216–23 Now comes the most dramatic and effective part of Antenor's speech, to which the rest is preliminary in a sense: whenever Odysseus leapt to his feet he would just stand there with his eyes fixed on the ground (see the next comment), his staff held motionless as though he were a fool; but when he began to speak, he was beyond compare.

217 The language is a little imprecise, for ὑπαί means 'from underneath' as in ὑπόδρα ἰδών (see on 1.148–71), and, if he was looking up from under lowered brow, then his gaze can hardly have been 'fixed on the ground'. Taking ὄμματ' to mean 'face' not 'eyes', which is Leaf's solution, is out of the question – the term always refers to eyes elsewhere in Homer. Presumably we should understand that Odysseus first fixed his gaze on the ground, then looked up, or repeatedly looked up, without raising his head.

218–19 Holding one's staff quite still (it is the herald's staff, strictly, which is handed over as token of the right to speak, see on 2.109) is evidently the sign of a foolish or surly speaker. A good speaker, by contrast – except for Odysseus – moves it to and fro to emphasize the points he is making.

221–2 'But whenever he released his great voice from his chest...': the final ἀλλ' ὅτε δή (cf. 209–11 n. *init.*) introduces an expression of great power and simplicity, followed by the comparison of his words to snowflakes in winter. They come thick and fast, perhaps; or is Willcock correct in thinking rather of their 'slow inevitability and cumulative effect'? The answer is that one cannot be certain – it depends what kind of snowflakes they are. Are they driven by strong winds as in the snow-similes at 12.156–8 and 19.357f., or do they fall on a windless day as in a fourth snow-simile at 12.278–86?

C. Moulton, *Similes* 93, argues that there is a significant contrast between appearance and reality in this whole description of Odysseus, as earlier with

'Paris' exterior image and his true worth'; so that Odysseus here is a foil for Paris. That is probably going too far, but the contrast between a man's outward appearance and his true nature and capacities clearly fascinated Homer, most obviously in the *Odyssey* and with Odysseus in general, but also, for instance, with Akhilleus himself.

224 ἀγασσάμεθ': ἀγάασθαι, to rate something as substantial or excessive, can come to mean either 'admire' or 'be surprised or annoyed at'. Here it probably bears the latter sense, although Aristarchus (Arn/A) took the verse to mean 'we did not then admire his appearance as much' (as his power of speech). Bentley judged the verse un-Homeric because of its double ignoring of digamma in ἀγασσάμεθ' (ϝ)εῖδος (ϝ)ιδόντες, and Leaf characterized it as awkward and tautological. It is, however, a typically oral summation, not even really repetitive since Antenor has turned from a general judgement about Odysseus' incomparable oratory to a particular statement, and a telling reversion to the beginning of his speech, about how they felt in the Trojan assembly.

225 This closely follows the form of 191, which introduced Priam's previous question.

226-7 The question itself is much briefer than its predecessors, in fact the three questions become progressively shorter. It still includes the bare physical description that is required to supplement Priam's presumed act of pointing; again the criteria are height (cf. 168 of Agamemnon, 193 of Odysseus) and broadness of shoulders (cf. 194 of Odysseus). Verse 226 more or less repeats 167, applied there to Agamemnon; 227 makes Aias ἔξοχος, outstanding, in both respects, which means that he is one of those who outdo Agamemnon in the former (168) and that he surpasses even Odysseus in the latter (cf. 194). The tradition constantly remarked on Aias' great physique; Helen repeats πελώριος, 'huge', at 229 – that is an epithet otherwise applied only to Hektor, Agamemnon, Akhilleus and Ares (apart from, at 5.842 and 847, the exotic Periphas). Aias is often μέγας in the formula μέγας Τελαμώνιος Αἴας, and this corresponds with μέγας κορυθαίολος Ἕκτωρ, partly because of their metrically similar names no doubt (thus φαίδιμος is also shared between him (6x) and Hektor (29x)); but he alone is ἕρκος Ἀχαιῶν (at 229 and 2x elsewhere), and he alone wields the great tower-like shield, σάκος ἠΰτε πύργον, see on 2.558. Finally he is 'far the best' and 'much the strongest' after Akhilleus at 2.768-70 (see note there), and is the favoured choice as Achaean champion in the duel against Hektor in book 7.

228 For the reply-formula see on 199.

229-42 Helen's reply is astonishing, and brings the identification of Achaean heroes (which could have become monotonous if carried on for too long, especially after the great Achaean catalogue of book 2) to an unexpectedly early conclusion. She begins by naming Aias in a single verse, then passes on, unasked, to identify Idomeneus (who is next to him) and explains that she knows him well. This takes a further four verses, and allows her meanwhile to scan the whole army, as she says at 234, without being able to see her brothers Kastor and Poludeukes (the Dioskouroi). Her address ends with four verses in which she speculates, ironically and pathetically as it transpires, on why they are not present (239–42).

229 Aias is identified in almost the briefest possible way. That is remarkable in itself, especially after the relatively long descriptions of Agamemnon and Odysseus; but we should not conclude too hastily that interference with the text is the reason (see the next comment); on the contrary, the brevity is almost certainly intentional; and neither it nor the omission of Diomedes and Nestor, for example, are likely to be accidental in any sense.

230–3 That is virtually proved by the careful transition to Idomeneus, who is ἑτέρωθεν, to one side of, Odysseus (the term being metrically more convenient than the more exact ἑτέρωθι). Adam Parry correctly observed (in 'Have we Homer's Iliad?', *YCS* 20 (1966) 198) that 'the strongly formulary responses οὗτός γ' 'Ατρεΐδης (178), οὗτος δ' αὖ Λαερτιάδης (200), οὗτος δ' Αἴας ἐστί (229) here give way to the more abrupt 'Ιδομενεὺς δ' ἑτέρωθεν (230)'. The new emphasis on physical proximity – which, as Aristarchus (Arn/A) noted, accords with the position of Aias and Idomeneus at 4.251–74 – offers an adequate ostensible motive for Helen turning her attention to Idomeneus here rather than, say, to Diomedes. Equally important is the connexion he provides with her old life in Lakedaimon, where she often saw him; this begins to focus her interest in a more personal way, and also leads naturally enough through the thought of her old home to concern for her brothers. Idomeneus is, of course, quite an important person in his own right; with Meriones he is conspicuous at several points, especially in book 13, and there are signs in that Book of a special effort to emphasize the contribution of the Cretan contingent, on which see on 13.650–2; incidentally Cretans and Crete are mentioned no less than three times in the present four verses.

Shipp, *Studies* 239, remarks that 'the description of Idomeneus...is commonly considered to have been inserted, truncating the description of Ajax'; this is in relation to his classification of 231 ἠγερέθονται as an 'abnormal feature' (which is not justified by Chantraine, *GH* I, 327f.; forms in -έθω are secondary developments for metrical reasons, cf. ἠερέθονται, 3× *Il.*, and comment on 108). It is, indeed, tempting at first to think that the cursory nature of the description of Aias must be due to mechanical interference with the text, especially since the whole Viewing episode must have been developed from a different version set earlier in the war; but further reflection shows it to be brilliantly motivated in psychological terms and to form part of a description of Helen and her thoughts that is carefully worked out and extraordinarily subtle; see further Adam Parry, *YCS* 20 (1966) 197–200.

234–5 Helen continues in a style that in itself reveals little of her growing anxiety; indeed her whole speech is cast in a plain cumulative style (except for the integral enjambment of 230f. at its beginning) with uninterrupted verses and frequent progressive enjambment. Her manner, if we are to gauge it by her words, is melancholy rather than agitated, and 235, which is not strictly necessary, adds to the impression that she is making herself keep calm.

γνοίην is assimilated to the potential construction of (κεν) μυθησαίμην: she does not actually recognize them now, but she means that she could show that she recognized them, and name them, if necessary.

236–44 The description of her brothers as κοσμήτορε λαῶν, then as respectively ἱππόδαμον and πὺξ ἀγαθόν (237 = *Od.* 11.300), adds weight to her concern but may also suggest an almost dirge-like formality. Her closeness to them is brought out by the repeated emphasis in 238 that they are her full brothers, although this raises several questions about which version of the myth Homer primarily depends on. The development of the tale of the children of Lede and Tundareos is complex. The two brothers among them were known as the Diosko(u)roi only from the later fifth century B.C. on, or so it seems from surviving evidence. In Pindar, *Nem.* 10.49–90 Poludeukes and Helen are the children of Lede by Zeus, Kastor (together with Klutaimestre according to the common account) is her child by her mortal husband Tundareos. Zeus visiting Lede in the form of a swan is a commonplace of classical art, but Pindar stresses rather the different motif by which Zeus sleeps with a mortal woman on the same night as her husband does, and the consequence is twins, one of which is mortal, the other immortal or partly so – cf. Herakles and Iphiklos. Pindar also relates how when Kastor was killed by Idas, his brother Poludeukes surrendered half of his immortality to him, so that each spent alternate days on Olumpos and in the underworld. That is ignored here, but alluded to at *Od.* 11.301–4, where as sons of Lede (whom Odysseus sees in his visit to the underworld) they are 'possessed by the life-generating earth' in the same words as those of 243 here (on which see 243–4n. *fin.*), and 'now alive...now dead' (*Od.* 11.303f.). The Homeric tradition certainly knew that Helen herself had divine blood, since she is termed 'offspring of Zeus', Διὸς ἐκγεγαυῖα, three times (including at 199 and 418 in the present Book), and since at *Od.* 4.563–9 Menelaos is said to be destined for the Elysian plain because he is married to her. Is 238 perhaps carefully phrased to avoid this kind of issue by concentrating on Lede, who was certainly the mother of all three siblings, no matter who their father was? Whatever the possible relation of the Odyssean underworld passage, it is clear that 243 here implies that both brothers were dead in the normal sense – the verse would indeed lose much of its carefully prepared pathos if that were not so. Different versions of their birth, life and death certainly existed already in Homer's time (they had, of course, special characteristics as horsemen and as protectors of seamen), and he probably chose to draw here on a simple form which would not complicate the pathos and irony of Helen's reflection. In the *Odyssey* the main composer, or perhaps an elaborator, adds a gloss from a more sophisticated version, as also with Herakles at *Od.* 11.602–4.

239–42 Nicanor and Herodian in AbT disagreed about the accentuation of ἦ...ἦ in 239f., Herodian preferring ἤ for the latter, i.e. as interrogative; but Nicanor is probably correct: *either* they did not accompany (Menelaos) from Lakedaimon, *or* they did so, but now (αὖτ' being equivalent to δέ after μέν in 240) are unwilling to fight. The 'many shameful things and insults attaching to me, ἅ μοί ἐστιν', 242, would inevitably be directed also against her brothers, if they were there; but it is also true, as J. T. Hooker puts it, that 'Helen's self-disgust, already expressed at 180, comes to the fore again'.

Whether we should read δεύρω in 240 (not elsewhere in Homer), with Herodian in A and a few MSS, or the regular δεῦρο with metrical lengthening, remains doubtful – probably the latter.

243–4 It is unlikely, in view of the careful construction of Helen's whole speech and the pathetic tone of these two verses in themselves (especially in ἤδη, αὖθι and φίλη [ἑῇ Zenodotus (Arn/A)] ἐν πατρίδι γαίῃ), that 'life-generating earth', φυσίζοος αἶα, is to be taken just as a standard formular phrase, used at this juncture without special significance. Even if the idea of the fertile earth being also the repository of the dead has its own ironical or even hopeful paradoxicality, it still acquires additional meaning in relation to Helen's assumption that, whatever the reason for her brothers' absence, they are at any rate alive, when in fact they are dead. Milman Parry (*MHV* 125f.) argued that this like other standard epithets has no specific value; others have disagreed. In general it is true that formular epithets are not specially selected for their appropriateness to a particular occasion; but nevertheless the singer does from time to time choose language, including formular language, that takes on special significance or irony in an individual context. The matter is not seriously complicated by questions over the meaning of φυσίζοος; Chantraine, *Dict.* s.v. ʒειαί confirms the view of e.g. LSJ that the -ʒοος element is formed from ʒειά, 'barley', much as in the formula ʒείδωρος -ν ἄρουρα -ν (3× *Il.*, 3× *Od.*). Yet he accepts that popular etymology connected both ʒει- and -ʒοος with ʒωή, 'life', by the time of Empedocles and Aeschylus in the middle of the fifth century. In fact it is clear that the epic tradition already made this association, since the third Homeric instance of φυσίζοος (apart from the present passage and the possibly etymological development at *Od.* 11.301, on which see 236–44n.) similarly refers to γῆ φυσίζοος as the place which holds (back) the dead: *Il.* 21.63.

245–313   The heralds, accompanied by Priam and Antenor, arrive on the battlefield from Troy bringing sacrificial victims and wine. The oath-sacrifice, preliminary to the duel, is carried out by Agamemnon, after which the Trojan elders return to the city

245–8 After the distinctive conclusion of the Viewing episode that is implied by 243f., the poet reverts to the heralds who were despatched by Hektor back to Troy at 116f. in accordance with Menelaos' proposal at 103–5. In fact 245 could follow directly on from 120, immediately before the Viewing episode begins; that does not mean that the whole episode is any kind of later intrusion, but rather illustrates the simple way in which the monumental composer could amalgamate independent themes or songs, as well as the very direct transitions from one scene to another – in this case, from the battlefield to Troy and back.

The two Trojan heralds have by now (that is, we are to understand, during the conversation between Helen and Priam) got the two lambs specified by Menelaos at 103, as well as the wine which is an essential part of most sacrifices (cf. 269f., 295f.); Idaios in addition carries a mixing-bowl (247f.) and cups.

245 For the ὅρκια πιστά see on 73–5.

246 There is a developed formular system for wine, οἶνος, in which εὔφρονα here is a unique epithet, but as D. L. Page noted (*HHI* 268 n. 32), in this position in the verse it 'fulfils a need and has no duplicate'.

The primary application of καρπὸν ἀρούρης is clearly to cereal foods, as in ἀρούρης καρπὸν ἔδουσιν -οντες, 2× *Il.*; but the extension, through vines, to wine is occasionally paralleled in post-Homeric Greek.

250–8 Idaios now prepares for the second part of Menelaos' instructions at 105 by telling Priam about the proposed duel, and that he must take part in the preliminary oath-sacrifice. His words are at first formal (especially in the initial imperative, 250–2, with its rising threefolder at 250) and then practical, with mainly progressive enjambment.

255–8 His report of the terms on which the duel is to be fought and the oath taken uses preceding phraseology, as usual; especially in condensing Paris' initial proposition, 71f. = 92f., into 255, and in repeating 73–5 as 256–8 with minor adjustments.

259 ὁ γέρων comes very close to the developed use of the definite article, and interpretations like that of J. T. Hooker, 'he (ὁ) shuddered, old man as he was', seem strained.

At the end of the verse both Aristarchus and Zenodotus (Did/A) read ἑτάροις. The dative is perfectly possible after κελεύω, cf. e.g. 2.50, and may have a slight difference of nuance as compared with the accusative, 'give formal orders' (to perform a relatively complex task) rather than simply 'tell'; that could suit the situation here. Moreover the short dative plural in -οις is regular in this instance, as Shipp effectively demonstrated (*Studies* 50f.). Most modern editors, like Monro–Allen in OCT, print ἑτάρους with the great majority of mss.

261 Priam takes the reins with Antenor standing beside him; as bT point out, the former will have to drive his own chariot at 24.326. Antenor has not been specifically summoned, but a further Trojan presence at the oath is all to the good, he is Priam's chief counsellor and was with him on the walls, and he is known to Menelaos and Odysseus (cf. 207).

263 Σκαιῶν occurs only here without πυλάων (etc.); Aristarchus (Arn/A) noted the anomaly, also the unusual contraction as compared with 22.6 πυλάων τε Σκαιάων, where, as Shipp (*Studies* 239) commented, 'the monosyllable [i.e. τε] allows its use'; Shipp also added that 'One must allow for the difficulty of combining διά with Σκαιάων, with or without πυλάων.' Even so, Homer could surely have recast the verse – that would probably have meant adding a second verse – so as to include 'gates', had he wished to do so, and one can only conclude that 'the Scaean(s)' was an idiomatic abbreviation which happens not to be required elsewhere. See on 145 for the Scaean gate in general.

265 They descend from the chariot, not from the horses as ἐξ ἵππων might suggest; ἵπποι in epic language often refers to the actual chariot, and can even do so when associated with an epithet peculiar to horses (as Leaf observed), as at 17.504 καλλίτριχε βήμεναι ἵππω.

267–8 Agamemnon has played his kingly role in arranging for the oath demanded by Menelaos at 103ff., so as Priam approaches he rises to his feet; Odysseus, presumably to balance Antenor, follows suit.

269–70 The heralds assemble the ὅρκια, that is, the materials for the oath-sacrifice: the two lambs from the Trojans and the single one from the Achaeans (cf. 103f.), also the wine which they mix in the mixing-bowl carried at 247f. by Idaios. Aristarchus (Arn/A) correctly observed that this was not in order to mix wine with water (which is the regular function of the κρητήρ), but to mix the offerings of both sides: οὐχ ὕδατι ἔμισγον τὸν οἶνον, ἀλλὰ τὸν τῶν Τρώων καὶ ᾿Αχαιῶν. Admittedly there is no specific mention of the Achaeans providing wine, but neither is there of their producing the single lamb they had offered (the origin of the water in 270 is likewise not specified). The Trojan contributions, on the other hand, are detailed as part of the close description of movements within the city. The real support for Aristarchus' interpretation comes from 4.159 = 2.341

(which he cites), which mentions σπονδαί τ' ἄκρητοι, 'unmixed libations', as part of the oath. The wine will be drawn from the mixing-bowl, then poured on to the ground from cups after Agamemnon has completed his prayer and oath, at 295f. As they do so, the participants on each side pray that whoever transgress the oath shall have their brains, and those of their children, flow onto the ground like the wine (298–301).

There is no similar mention of wine in the corresponding oath-sacrifice at 19.250ff., which is less detailed. Here the wine probably has two distinct functions: (i) the first, which is not specifically described but is suggested by the prominence accorded to mixing the wine as part of the preliminaries, resembles that of wine at ordinary sacrifices, as for example at 1.462f. = *Od.* 3.459f. where the sacrificer roasts the divine portion on wooden spits and then pours a libation of wine, presumably on the fire. (ii) In its second function the wine enacts a curse against anyone who breaks the oath – it is an appendage to the oath-sacrifice itself, not part of it; similar symbolic acts are envisaged outside Homer, for example the shaking of priestly robes after the profanation of the mysteries in 415 B.C. (Parker, *Miasma* 191f.); see also on 300. The first function treats the wine as a regular libation; that is, as a shared offering to the gods which implicitly invokes their approval (in the case of burnt offerings it probably has additional implications which are irrelevant here). The second adapts the idea of libation to a specific symbolism; by pouring the wine, and praying that his own brain should be poured out similarly if he breaks the main oath, the participant is no longer involved in any kind of offering but is initiating a conditional form of sympathetic magic. Historians of religion and ritual have been inclined to call this 'pre-deistic': so Burkert, *Griechische Religion* 379; Nilsson, *GgrR* 129.

The water must have been brought by one side or the other in a special ewer; washing hands before sacrifice was a regular and obvious part of the preliminaries to ritual slaughter of any kind, as e.g. at 1.449 (χερνίψαντο), *Od.* 3.440f. and 445.

271–2 These verses recur as 19.252f., of the oath-sacrifice performed by Agamemnon as part of his reconciliation with Akhilleus. The μάχαιρα, which hangs down by the sword, is never mentioned as a weapon of war but was an all-purpose tool, for a ritual purpose as here or a surgical one at 11.844.

273–4 Agamemnon cuts off hairs from the animal victims' heads, and they are distributed by the heralds to the chieftains of both sides. In an ordinary sacrifice there would be a fire into which the hairs would be thrown as at *Od.* 3.446, 14.422; for oath-sacrifices no fire is needed and the hairs must have been simply discarded, thrown onto the ground, as casually no doubt as at 19.267f. the victim's body is thrown into the sea. The act of ἀπάρχεσθαι (the term does not appear in the present description, but see e.g. 19.254, ἀπὸ τρίχας ἀρξάμενος), or 'making a beginning or first offering', evidently consists in handing out the hairs rather than burning them – it is the action of receiving them that joins the participants with the victim, with each other and (in the present case) with the oath in which they are jointly partaking. If there *is* a fire, then burning the ritual hairs is an obvious means of disposing of them, and that might sometimes have been regarded as an additional symbolic offering to the gods. Much has been written (often in a highly speculative but at the same time rather dogmatic way) about the identification of sacrificer with victim in such rituals, for example among the Nuer by rubbing ashes on the animal before it is slaughtered; see E. E. Evans-Pritchard, *Nuer Religion* (Oxford 1956) 279ff., with my remarks in *Entretiens Hardt* xxvii (Vandoeuvres 1981) 48–53.

The short dative of ἀρίστοις| in 274 is no more objectionable than 259 ἑταίροις|, see comment there.

275 τοῖσιν, 'on their behalf'. Agamemnon holds up his arms and prays loudly, cf. 19.254f., where it is added that the rest of them listen in silence; in each case the words of the prayer follow immediately.

276–91 The prayer is implicitly an oath, since the gods are asked to be witnesses and guardians (280 μάρτυροι... φυλάσσετε) of the ὅρκια πιστά. It is symmetrically constructed and has the legalistic flavour proper to oaths, although it lacks any explicit statement that both sides swear to abide by such-and-such. Beginning with a five-verse invocation of the special gods and powers invoked (276–80), it proceeds to a balanced pair of three-verse 'clauses' with μέν and δέ: 'If on the one hand Alexandros kills Menelaos, then...; but if on the other hand Menelaos kills Alexandros, then...' (281–6). The second of these is elaborated by a fourth, cumulated verse (287), which serves the purpose, among others, of leading into a four-verse appendix (288–91) threatening what will happen if the Trojans fail to pay adequate recompense as specified in the second 'clause' at 286.

276–8 The deities addressed are those detailed by Menelaos at 104 (see on 103–4), except that earth, Ge or Gaia, is also elaborated by the rivers which are part of her, and by the avengers who dwell beneath her surface (278 ὑπένερθε). Zeus is involved in his local form, envisaged as overseeing events at Troy from his sanctuary on Mount Ida – not specifically as ὅρκιος (the epithet is not used by Homer, although cf. 107 Διὸς ὅρκια), but as supreme and highest god. The Sun (Ἥλιος is a vocative here, cf. 21.106 ἀλλά, φίλος, θάνε καὶ σύ) is concerned with oaths, like the Mesopotamian sun-god Shamash, because he sees and hears all and so cannot be deceived. Rivers are revered even more than springs (cf. Burkert, *Griechische Religion* 271f.); for example the Sperkheios, to which Akhilleus has promised offerings, is envisaged as having both sanctuary and altar in his waters at

23.148; coming from under the earth, they are also connected with the chthonic powers there – and perhaps too with the waters of Stux. Burkert also points out (at 377f.) the oriental and later Greek parallels for the conjunction in oath-invocations of sun, earth with its rivers, and underworld deities. At 15.36ff. Here herself swears by Gaia and Ouranos (which has a different value, however, from Helios) and the river Stux, as well as by Zeus's 'holy head' and their marriage-bed.

278–9 Those who 'take vengeance on men' for false oaths present certain problems. The ancient vulgate reading in 279 is τίνυσθον, a dual form which Aristarchus (Arn/A) referred to Plouton and Persephone, king and queen of the underworld who were also judges of the dead (and which Zenodotus, as usual, took to be equivalent to a simple plural). At 9.453–7 Phoinix describes how his father had called upon the Erinues, the Furies, to avenge an offence by his son, and how 'Zeus under the earth' (that is, Plouton or Hades) and Persephoneia had fulfilled his curses (9.456f.). That is in favour of Aristarchus; but in the roughly parallel oath-scene in book 19, it is the Erinues who are the subject of 19.260 (= 279 here): 'the Erinues, who under the earth | take vengeance on men, whoever swears a false oath' – the text there reads τίνυνται not τίνυσθον. On the whole the principle of formular economy makes it probable that the Erinues are envisaged here too, despite Aristarchus. What may have happened is that τίνυνται was adjusted to vocative τίνυσθε (for at 19.259 Earth and Sun etc. are in the nominative, after 258 ἴστω, and not directly addressed in the vocative as here), which was then mistakenly changed to τίνυσθον in order to avoid an (actually acceptable) hiatus before ὅτις. Incidentally one early papyrus (P. Hibeh 1, 19) read τίνυνται here also.

A further problem relates to the at first sight harmless-looking καμόντας, meaning 'when dead' (cf. εἴδωλα καμόντων at 23.72 and 2x *Od.*), and its counterpart ὑπὸ γαῖαν in the version of 19.259f. Punishment after death for sins committed in life, although illustrated by the great sinners Tituos, Tantalos and Sisuphos in the (probably elaborated) underworld-scene in the *Odyssey* (11.576–600), is not otherwise envisaged in the *Iliad*. In fact 19.259f. does not necessarily imply that; it depends on whether we apply ὑπὸ γαῖαν there to the Erinues or to their victims, and I agree with Nitzsch against Leaf and others that the former is more natural in terms of word-order and colon-break. That presents a different and more acceptable picture: the Erinues are chthonic deities; in a second mention in Phoinix' speech in book 9, at 571f., the Erinus hears Meleagros' mother's curse on her son ἐξ Ἐρέβεσφιν – that means, the Furies' dwelling-place is in the depths of the earth; but they punish mortals directly, on earth and when still alive, just as they do Orestes in Aeschylus' *Eumenides*. Indeed in the present episode transgressors against Agamemnon's oath will be envisaged at 299–301 as liable to punishment in life, not after death. The difficulty remains καμόντας in 278; a few mss read καμόντες, which sees the avengers as spirits of the dead – a slightly different conception, possible perhaps were it not for the virtual certainty that we are dealing here with the Erinues and not with chthonic daimons of the kind intended by e.g. Hesiod at *Erga* 141. Van Leeuwen considered μένοντες for καμόντας, but if emendation is envisaged it would be better to go the whole hog (especially since μένοντες gives a sense of μένειν not directly paralleled in Homer) and read ὑπένερθεν ἐόντες, which might then have been assimilated to the more developed Odyssean conception relatively early in the process of transmission.

281–6 The agreement to which the parties are swearing covers two main eventualities and one subsidiary one. If Paris kills Menelaos, then he is to keep Helen and her possessions (those she brought from Lakedaimon is what is meant), and the Achaeans are to go home. If Menelaos kills Paris, then they are to take Helen and her possessions, and appropriate recompense, τιμή, in addition. If the recompense is not appropriate (see on 287), then Agamemnon will stay and fight until the end: in a sense that is neither codicil nor subordinate condition, but a personal gloss on 286 ἥν τιν' ἔοικεν which he expects the Trojans to accept. What will happen if the duel is somehow aborted (as in the event it will be) is simply not considered – perhaps because the poet needs there to be some confusion over this at a later stage.

286 The idea of compensation is Agamemnon's; nothing has been said about it so far by Paris or Hektor (naturally enough), or even by Menelaos when he responds in general terms to their proposals, at 97–102 – not, as bT suggest, because he is only concerned to regain his wife, but rather because he wants to bring an end to the suffering on both sides.

287 This verse is a cumulated expansion on the concept of appropriateness as outlined in 286 ἔοικεν. It is no mere decorative elaboration, as might first appear, since Agamemnon here gives some indication of what 'appropriate recompense' might entail: it is to be one which will be remembered by future generations. This at the very least implies a substantial one, on a different scale from that of conventional penalties of, say, double the amount at issue.

289 The regular negative after εἰ ἄν/κε is μή; οὐκ here is to be explained as forming almost a single term with ἐθέλωσιν, much as in English 'unwilling'. Cf. 4.160 οὐκ-ἐτέλεσσεν.

290–1 The king is in one of his most imperious and impressive moods: *he* will stay and fight (although doubtless he will have to have the Achaeans with him, if the outcome is to be a τέλος of warfare, i.e. the fall of Troy).

292 ἦ, 'he spoke': 'with these words he cut the throats...' στόμαχος is the throat or gullet, part almost of the mouth, στόμα; later it was applied to other neck-like openings, into the bladder, womb or stomach – and hence to the 'stomach' itself. ἐπί...τάμε was the reading of most ancient texts before Aristarchus, but he opted for ἀπό...τάμε (Did/A); which is interesting not because of the actual change, which is minor, but because on this kind of point his text could prevail so completely over αἱ πλείους. 'Harsh bronze' (11× *Il.*, 8× *Od.*) can refer to any sharp bronze implement, usually spear-head but also sword, axe or, as here, the knife already used at 271f.

293–4 'He put them on the ground' is a slightly awkward way of saying that they collapsed, or he let them fall, to the ground; the verse (293) is perhaps based, too loosely, on a prototype like 6.473 of Hektor's helmet, καὶ τὴν μὲν κατέθηκεν ἐπὶ χθονὶ παμφανόωσαν.

The actual death of sacrificial victims is nowhere else in Homer so graphically described (although cf. *Od.* 3.449f., where the axe 'cut the neck-tendons and loosed the cow's strength', λῦσεν δὲ βοὸς μένος). Dying men are said to 'gasp', e.g. at 10.521, *Od.* 8.526, and the idea is elaborated here in the cumulated verse 294, where θυμοῦ δευομένους is an unusual phrase in which θυμοῦ means 'breath' if it is taken as an expansion of ἀσπαίροντας, or 'life-spirit' if the following γάρ-clause is understood strictly. Even this clause, which looks formular and is composed of common terms, has no direct parallel in Homer, and it begins to look as if the whole verse was constructed for this context, probably in order to increase the emphasis on the oath itself by unusual attention to the victims. At the same time the idea of animals gasping after their throats are cut is more dramatic to most modern readers than it would be to members of an ancient audience, to whom the event would be commonplace.

295–301 For the pouring of the wine and its application in the prayer see on 269–70, 2nd para.: this is not a regular libation, but the flowing wine becomes part of the oath, i.e. as a symbol of the fate of transgressors. No doubt there was a certain flexibility of practice, just as there were variations between these Homeric oath-rituals in general and those of later times; for example there is no sign in Homer of cutting up the animals and standing on parts of them while taking the oath (cf. e.g. Nilsson, *GgrR* 129, on τόμια), or of oaths taken by the σπλάγχνα of ordinary burnt offerings as at e.g. Herodotus 6.67–8, cf. Burkert, *Griechische Religion* 379.

296 ἔκχεον: bT noted that this purely descriptive term is used instead of a form of σπένδω (e.g. σπεῖσαν) because the poet 'knew in advance that their prayers would be ineffectual'. This looks Aristarchan in origin, but is probably wrong; for if there is any special significance in the choice of verb (which happens not to be used elsewhere in the poem in this form) and the avoidance of σπένδω, it is that this is not a typical libation – see preceding comment. It is true that what is 'poured' at a sacrifice is usually water, as at 270 here; when wine is poured it is for secular drinking (ἐν δ' οἶνον ἔχευεν, 3x *Od.*).

297–301 All present are evidently happy with the terms of Agamemnon's oath and confirm it by praying that whichever side breaks it will be drastically punished: their brains and those of their children are to flow like the wine which is being poured on the ground – their wives are to avoid this fate but are to be 'subdued by others' (301). This might seem to imply rape rather than capture and concubinage, but probably both are envisaged, since the poet seems to have in mind what actually happened when Troy was captured: most of the men and some of the children were murdered, some of the women were raped, others taken off to Hellas. The majority of mss (but not including A and B) actually read μιγεῖεν; nothing is recorded in the scholia, but the probability is that δαμεῖεν was in Aristarchus' text and is to be preferred.

This 4-verse prayer-curse is balanced by another 4-verse prayer at 320–3.

298 The gods invoked by Agamemnon at 276–9 are now compressed into a single verse, with Zeus still predominant and still κύδιστε μέγιστε. At 320, another invocation from unnamed people on both sides, the fuller form of 276, with Ἴδηθεν μεδέων, will be adopted, since this is not formally an oath and the 'other gods' do not need to be mentioned.

299 Whichever side transgresses is to be punished as a whole: nothing will happen immediately when Pandaros, spurred on by Athene, breaks the truce in the next Book, but the result, in a way, is the fall of Troy.

πημήνειαν is probably absolute (cf. 4.236 ὑπὲρ ὅρκια δηλήσαντο): 'do harm contrary to the oaths', in which ὑπέρ, 'beyond', implies 'against'. At 24.781 'doing harm' specifically means recommencing hostilities, and that is perhaps the meaning here (so Willcock), although a more general sense is also possible. The optative (rather than subjunctive with ἄν or κε(ν), as regularly with indefinite clauses in present time) is due to the influence of the optative ῥέοι, even though that expresses a prayer – not by mechanical attraction according to Chantraine, *GH* II, 248, but because the subordinate clause is 'drawn into the sphere of' the main clause; cf. also 6.59 and especially *Od.* 1.47, ὡς ἀπόλοιτο καὶ ἄλλος ὅτις τοιαῦτά γε ῥέζοι.

300 Leaf compared Livy 1.24, where Jupiter is asked to 'strike the Roman people as I shall strike this pig' (so too Nilsson, *GgrR* 128f.); but it is to be stressed that it is not implied here that the animals themselves serve any such symbolic function – that is reserved for the pouring out of the wine.

302 That the capture of the city is in the poet's mind is confirmed by οὐδ' ἄρα πώ, and this is a subtle comment. A pre-Aristarchan papyrus (P. Hibeh 19, third century B.C., containing parts of books 2 and 3) contrives to suppress this; it alters 302 and adds four verses as follows:

302 ὡς ἔφαν] εὐχόμενοι, μέγα δ᾽ ἔκτυπε μητίετα Ζεύς
302a ἐξ "Ἴδης βρον]τῶν, ἐπὶ δὲ στεροπὴν ἐφέηκεν·
302b θησέμεναι] γὰρ ἔμελλεν ἔτ᾽ ἄλγεά τε στοναχάς τε
302c Τρῶσί τε καὶ] Δαναοῖσιν ἀνὰ κρατερὰς ὑσμίνας.
302d αὐτὰρ ἐπεὶ ῥ᾽ ὄ]μοσέν τε τελεύτησέν τε τὸν ὅρκον...

Of these 302 = 15.377 with minor adjustment; 302b ~ 2.39; 302c ~ 2.40;
302d = 14.280. Only 302a cannot be exactly paralleled, but |ἐξ "Ἴδης occurs
3x elsewhere; βροντῶν happens not to recur, but βρόντησε (etc.) does.
More seriously, the combination στεροπὴν ἐφέηκε is not paralleled, and
ἐπὶ...ἐφ- is awkward. In any case the expansion is pointless; the thunder
and lightning pass without comment and seem out of place. Bolling (*External
Evidence* 81) justifiably remarks that 'The only value of this longer version...
is to show the sort of thing that was then being done in the way of
interpolation.' This is a typical 'wild text' of the sort that was put out of
business by the critical text and commentaries of Aristarchus.

304 Priam uses the same verse of address as Hektor at 86 (and also at
7.67). Again P. Hibeh 19 offers a different and expanded version:

304 κέκλυτέ μευ] Τρῶες καὶ Δάρδανοι ἠδ᾽ ἐπίκουροι
304a ὄφρ᾽ εἴπω] τά με θυμὸς ἐνὶ στήθεσσιν ἀνωγε[ν.

This makes Priam address just the Trojan side, not both sides as is
dramatically stronger; this version of 304 occurs at 456 and 3x elsewhere,
and was easily available to an interpolator. Bolling *loc. cit.* commented that
304a was often added to verses of address like 304 (as it is in a minority of
MSS after 86). It is a probable interpolation, or rhapsodic addition, here, but
was of course a genuine Homeric verse which could be cumulated or not
by an oral singer as desired.

305 This is the first occurrence of ἠνεμόεσσαν as a standard epithet of
Ilios at the verse-end (7x *Il.*). It was used of the obscure Enispe in Arcadia
at 2.606 and is probably to some extent conventional; but the site of Troy
at Hisarlik *is* very windy, as has often been observed.

306-7 bT commented on 305 that if Priam had stayed behind he would
have respected the oath and agreed to hand over Helen; that is ingenious
but certainly wrong, since the oath did not take account of what would
actually happen, namely that neither party would be killed. An adequate
motive for his departure is ascribed to him by the poet, that he 'cannot
endure' watching his son in the duel; this is noted, among other more fantastic suggestions, in the D-scholium. Thus the present passage foreshadows
the passionate sensitivity Priam will reveal both before and after Hektor's
death, in books 22 and 24; but the poet also has a practical motive for
removing him at this stage – to that extent bT were right – since his

presence at the scene of the duel would have been something of an embarrassment at its conclusion.

ἄψ in 306 is not so much a runover-word in a cumulated elaboration of meaning as a metrically convenient way of introducing a necessary ἐπεί-clause at the beginning of a verse. As for οὔ πω, Leaf and others urged that πω stands for πως, as οὔτω for οὔτως; there is no good evidence for this, and the meaning is probably 'not yet' as in 302 and elsewhere: 'I have not yet reached the point of enduring seeing my son...' (in which ὁρᾶσθαι is middle with active meaning as 4x *Il.* elsewhere).

308–9 'Zeus...and other immortal gods' were called on as witnesses of the oath at 298, but that oath has nothing to do with their role here, which is as associates of destiny over which of the two is to lose his life. Therefore the 'other immortal gods' here are no longer sun, rivers, earth and so on (see on 276–8 and 298), that is, the witnesses of oaths, but rather the other Olympians apart from Zeus, who support his maintenance of regular dealings among mortals. The phrase is very general, in any case, but is doubtless partly determined here, without special thought, by 298.

Priam speaks as though the question of guilt were an open one, as indeed the rest of those present will do at 321f.; but of course it is plain on the facts that Paris is the offender, see on 321.

310 ἦ ῥα, καί: compare e.g. ἦ, καί at 292; ῥα is added or not according to the metrical shape of what is immediately to follow.

The carcases of the sacrificed lambs (the two Trojan ones, presumably, with the Achaeans disposing of their own one somehow) are loaded on to the chariot to be taken back to Troy, and that is the last we hear of them. In the roughly parallel oath-sacrifice in book 19 the herald Talthubios flings the boar's carcase into the sea to be eaten by fishes (267f.). The conclusion from the two scenes taken together is that the victims of oath-sacrifices were not eaten by humans as in an ordinary meal-sacrifice; Burkert's assertion (*Griechische Religion* 379) that Priam takes them 'probably for profane use' is hard to accept. Pausanias 5.24.10 states that the ancient custom was not to eat the flesh of oath-sacrifices, but he seems to be relying on the book 19 passage, which he cites. It may also be concluded that the victims were disposed of by those who had contributed them – Priam does not simply leave the Trojan ones for the Achaeans to get rid of, by flinging them into the sea or whatever. The victims are themselves the ὅρκια, the oaths (see on 73–5), and are therefore sacred or even polluted in some way; throwing them into the sea is an ideal means of disposal, since the fish annihilate them and in any case the sea is a purifier, see on 1.313–4. Here the exegetical scholia are of some interest: oath-victims are correctly distinguished from τὰ...θεοῖς θυόμενα (AT); they were buried by locals, thrown into the sea by strangers (AbT). Obviously this is a mere inference from 19.267f. in particular – what would happen if the strangers were inland? (The inferences continue (AbT): perhaps Priam took them back to show them to those in the city, either to implicate them in the oath or simply to keep them informed.) Burying is indeed a probability, if the sea or a large river were not available; burning might be avoided as too similar to a divine offering. Variations in ritual uses of σφάγια (outside Homer) complicate the issue; for example the carcase could be cut into pieces which were then used for purification or protection (cf. e.g. Nilsson, *GgrR* 96f.).

311–12 The imperfects ἔβαιν' and τεῖνεν perhaps reflect a more detailed view of Priam's movements compared with those of Antenor in 312, who has the aorist βήσετο (a metrical variant, 4x *Il.*, for ἔβη); but the two tenses are sometimes used with little distinction, as is shown by the very similar 261: ἂν δ' ἄρ' ἔβη Πρίαμος, κατὰ δ' ἡνία τεῖνεν ὀπίσσω. It looks as though that verse has been adjusted here, because Priam has just been referred to (as ἰσόθεος φώς) and cannot be named again; hence the extended phrase, including imperfect ἔβαιν', in place of ἔβη.

The contrast of ἄν and κατά in both 261 and 311 is less artificial than it looks, since κατατείνειν means 'stretch *tight*' in post-Homeric Greek, and presumably here also. Moreover κατά...ὀπίσσω recurs in 19.394 with a different first half of the verse, and thus with no ἀνά in contrast.

313–82   After further preparations the duel takes place; Menelaos is victor, but Aphrodite snatches Paris away to the safety of his bedchamber

313–17 While Priam and Antenor return to Troy, Hektor and Odysseus prepare for the duel; the narrative continues in a straightforward style although with some longer sentences. Neither the measuring of the ground for the duel nor the drawing of lots for first throw will be exactly paralleled in the counterpart duel in book 7 (although lots are drawn there to choose the Achaean champion). Neither seems necessary, and their mention shows the poet as anxious to introduce some concrete detail at this point. The space for the duel was already limited in one direction by the lines of the two facing armies (see on 114–15), and in any case there was really no question of one contestant or the other trying to move away to gain some unfair advantage (let alone to get his bow, as bT suggest in some desperation). The measured space is not, however, immediately forgotten, for when the duel begins the two contestants stand in it close to each other at 344. As for first throw, in none of the hundreds of individual spear-fights in the rest of the poem is it suggested that this gave any advantage (if throwing rather than thrusting is in question, as here); but that is because the first throw always has to miss, for dramatic reasons; moreover further regulation is not unexpected in a formal duel.

318–23 As the lot-motif is repeated in the book 7 duel, but in different circumstances, so is this prayer-motif; 318 = 7.177, and the first halves of 319 and 7.178 also correspond – their second halves differ because both sides are involved here, but in book 7 only the Achaeans are (who pray for a favourable choice of champion).

This prayer by anonymous Achaeans and Trojans resembles that of 297–301; it is the second in a series of three 4-verse prayers (see also on 351–4), and starts out in similar terms to those of Agamemnon's longer prayer at 276ff.: 319 = 297, then 302 reverts to 276 (they ignore the 'other gods' here and pray to Zeus alone, who can therefore have his full local title; see on 276–8 and 298); ὁππότερος in 321 recalls ὁππότεροι in 299; then the prayers diverge. This latest prayer is that whoever of the two contestants started the whole affair should perish and go down to Hades, while the rest make oaths of friendship – 323 recalls the language of 73, 94 and 256 and stresses once again the theme of oath-taking that permeates this Book.

321 This renews the implication noticed in Priam's comment at 309 that the question of blame is an open one. There is no doubt that Paris was the sole offender; he had, after all, abducted Menelaos' wife, the most famous bride in Greece, and when he was a guest in his house, cf. 353f. The poet temporarily suppresses this to heighten the tension of the approaching duel by making it an equally-balanced affair. It is also conceivable that some prototype existed in which moral responsibility for events was less clear-cut.

μετ' ἀμφοτέροισιν: between both sides, Trojans and Achaeans.

324–5 The shaking of the lots has already been indicated at 316, but that must have been a loose way of saying that Odysseus and Hektor prepared them by placing them in the helmet. (Verse 316 recurs as 23.861, cf. *Od.* 10.206, in both cases of actually drawing lots; at least that tends to guarantee the form πάλλον, for which βάλλον might otherwise be a tempting conjecture.) The lots, κλῆροι, are probably pebbles in this case (the term ψῆφος is not found in Homer); they could be differentiated by size or colour, and would not need to be otherwise marked since there were only two of them. At 7.182ff., in the choice of Achaean champion, they were potsherds rather, since there were several participants each of whom had to scratch his mark. On similarities and differences between the lot-drawing in the two duel-scenes see G. S. Kirk, *op. cit.* on 76–8, pp. 30–2.

Hektor looks away – a neat detail – as he shakes the helmet to make one or other lot leap out. Why he rather than Odysseus performs the act is not explained, but perhaps the latter, as the more ingenious, had played the greater part in the associated preparation of measuring the ground.

On Πάριος see 16n.

326–7 For the στίχες of chariots and heaped armour see 113–15. κεῖτο applies only to the τεύχεα, and ἦσαν must be understood with ἵπποι (as Leaf remarked).

328–9 καλά is trochaic in Homer, because of the lingering effect of its original digamma, καλϝά. The final syllable of 'Αλέξανδρος, on the other hand, is metrically lengthened as often at the end of the first dicolon.

330–8 This is the first of four main arming-scenes in the poem; the others concern Agamemnon at 11.17–45, Patroklos at 16.131–44 and Akhilleus at 19.369–91 (for a selective description cf. Teukros' arming at 15.479–82). Basically the armour and weapons are the same in each case and are donned in the same order; the descriptions vary mainly in degree of elaboration, particularly of special pieces of armour like Agamemnon's corslet or Akhilleus' shield; see further Fenik, *Typical Battle Scenes* 78f., 191; J. Armstrong, 'The arming-motif in the Iliad', *AJP* 79 (1958) 337–54. This is shown by the following tabulation:

	Paris		Agamemnon		Patroklos		Akhilleus
bk 3		*bk 11*		*bk 16*		*bk 19*	
330–1	greaves	17–18	greaves	131–2	greaves	369–70	greaves
332–3	corslet	19–28	corslet	133–4	corslet	371	corslet
334–5	sword,	29–31	sword	135–6	sword,	372–3	sword
	shield	32–40	shield		shield	373–80	shield
	(σάκος)		(ἀσπίς)		(σάκος)		(σάκος)
336–7	helmet	41–2	helmet	137–8	helmet	380–3	helmet
	(κυνέη)		(κυνέη)		(κυνέη)		(τρυφάλεια)
338	spear	43–5	spears	139–44	spears	387–91	spear

Important points are as follows. (i) The greaves description and the basic corslet verse are the same for all four. (ii) Donning the sword is similar for all four (ἀμφὶ δ' ἄρ' ὤμοισιν βάλετο ξίφος), but then Par/Patr/Akh complete the verse with ἀργυρόηλον, Ag with ἐν δέ οἱ ἧλοι and two verses of development, to make his gold-studded and not silver-studded like the rest. Similarly Ag's shield is an ἀσπίς and its elaborate decoration is described; the rest share the same σάκος-verse. (iii) Par/Patr share the same helmet couplet; Ag varies the first verse, making his κυνέη grander, but shares the second one; Akh's helmet is a τρυφάλεια not a κυνέη like the others, and is developed by a simile over four verses. (iv) Par takes one spear, ἔγχος, in a single verse, εἵλετο δ' ἄλκιμον ἔγχος, ὅ οἱ παλάμηφιν ἀρήρει. Akh takes his special ἔγχος out of its spear-case in a unique verse, and it is then further described. Ag and Patr both take two spears, εἵλετο δ' ἄλκιμα δοῦρε, the verses being differently completed in each case (by a variant of the Par-formula, τά οἱ παλάμηφιν ἀρήρει, in that of Patr). It is then explained that Patr cannot wield Akh's special spear, which is described much as it is in the Akh passage. Thus there was a complex and interlocking formula-system for spears, single and double, and the singers combined elements of it as they wished; the same was so, although less markedly in these four passages, with shields and helmets – see further D. L. Page, *HHI* 270 n. 35.

In more general terms, the four arming-scenes all start out with the same three verses, and then share odd verses further on. They have much in common, and the motives for variations and elaborations can be clearly seen. The Patroklos arming-scene is identical with the Paris one (except for different single verses describing their corslet) until the last item, when Patroklos takes a pair of spears (unlike Paris' single one) because he cannot manage Akhilleus' great Pelian ash-spear. Agamemnon's corslet is a special gift from king Kinuras and is described at length; similarly his sword, shield and helmet are elaborated to make them superior objects. Akhilleus is likewise singled out for special treatment as he dons his divine armour, made for him by Hephaistos, and it is his shield (the subject of much of book 18), helmet and spear that are more elaborately described. Apart from these special items, the poet reverts to the plain descriptions of the Paris and Patroklos scenes for the rest.

With these conclusions in mind one can see one's way more clearly through ancient variants on the arming of Paris. Zenodotus athetized 334f. (Arn/A) and added a verse (ἀμφὶ δ' ἄρ' ὤμοισιν βάλετ' ἀσπίδα τερσανόεσσαν) after 337. The effect is to deprive Paris of a sword, which also necessitates recasting the shield verse (by using the first part of the discarded sword-verse followed by a noun-epithet formula, ἀσπίδα accompanied not by the common πάντοσ' ἐΐσην but by the exotic τερσανόεσσαν [or τερμιόεσσαν more probably]). Zenodotus has logic on his side in that Paris does not keep Menelaos at bay with a sword when Menelaos' own sword has shattered; but his changes result in the wrong order of arming (as Aristarchus objected), with the helmet put on before the shield with its strap, which would have fouled the plume. The agreement of all four major arming-scenes in their six items strongly suggests that the vulgate text is correct here. P. Hibeh 19 (see on 302) gave Paris two spears like Agamemnon and Patroklos, which is pointless. All these pre-Aristarchan variants, which were taken too seriously by Bolling, *External Evidence* 81–4, show that there was much detailed but confused discussion of the duel in antiquity; Aristarchus' text, which became the vulgate, is in all probability sound.

330–1 κνήμη is the 'point between knee and ankle', LSJ, and κνημῖδες are leg-guards or greaves, either of heavy cloth or leather (as with Laertes' rustic ones at *Od.* 24.228f.) or of metal. The Achaeans are 'bronze-greaved' at 7.41 (the common and slightly shorter term being ἐϋκνήμιδες, 'well-greaved'), Hephaistos makes them of tin at 18.613, and many examples of Late Bronze-Age metallic greaves have been found (early Iron-Age ones are a rarity; they become common again with the development of hoplite armour in the eighth century B.C.); cf. *Arch. Hom.* E 143–61 (H. W. Catling). Heroic greaves are surely envisaged as being of bronze; those in the arming-scenes have silver ἐπισφύρια, ankle-guards of some kind to which they were ἀραρυίας, attached, and therefore most probably to another metal object.

The bare description of a piece of armour in one verse, followed by a cumulated elaboration of it in a second, is an arrangement repeated with both corslet and helmet at 332f. and 336f., and slightly differently, with runover-word, with sword and shield at 334f.; on this cumulative technique see also pp. 34f.

333 Paris was light-armed, as an archer, at 17f., and so has no corslet; he borrows that of his brother Lukaon (a pathetic victim of Akhilleus at 21.34ff.), which fits him perhaps because kinsmen were assumed to have similar physique, as also in tragedy. On Homeric corslets and those of the Late Bronze and Early Iron Ages see *Arch. Hom.* E 74–118 (H. W. Catling), and comment on 4.135–6.

334 On silver-studded swords, a probable Mycenaean memory, see on 2.45.

335 The shield, σάκος, is 'great and heavy', although it is not to be confused with Aias' exceptional tower-like shield (7.219f.). When the description is elaborated in the Akhilleus arming-scene, it is the gleam of the shield that is emphasized; rarely, a σάκος is 'glittering', αἰόλον or παναίολον; an ἀσπίς is 'shining', φαεινή, more frequently; and there can be little doubt that the Homeric shield was regarded as being faced with bronze – this will be discussed at greater length later (cf. *Arch. Hom.* E 1–4, 48–52 (H. Borchhardt)). Like all matters of armament this one is confused by the conflation of elements and conventional poetical descriptions from different periods. In particular, σάκος and ἀσπίς were originally different, the latter being πάντοσ' ἐίσην and therefore circular and the former being rectangular or figure-of-eight and made of ox-hides (cf. ἑπταβόειον etc.); it is typical of the loose conventional vocabulary that Paris' σάκος has turned into an ἀσπίδα πάντοσ' ἐίσην by 356, cf. Menelaos' at 347.

336 The κυνέη, properly a dog-skin cap, became a common term for the helmet, including metal ones, in general. It can be made of other skins (10.257f., 335) or of bronze; the one used for the lots at 316 was 'bronze-fitted', χαλκήρεϊ, and three other helmets are so described in the poem. Three more have bronze cheek-pieces (χαλκοπαρήου), and bronze was clearly the standard material for most heroic helmets (Athene's divine one at 5.743f. is of gold); the gleam of helmets as well as shields is commonly noted. Cf. *Arch. Hom.* E 57–74 (J. Borchhardt).

338 The final verse of the list gives contrast by having no cumulated sequel, and reinforces its generally workmanlike quality. Again the tradition veers over weapons; the single Mycenaean thrusting-spear is confused with the pair of lighter throwing-spears which were adopted in the early Iron Age and were the commonest heroic armament. Paris at 18 had had a pair of spears; for the duel a single one is taken (Kirk, *Songs* 191, is confusing over this, but the discussion on pp. 190–2 can otherwise be consulted) – but it is used for throwing not thrusting (346, cf. 317, 356), much as Akhilleus' great Pelian ash-spear, a thrusting-spear if ever there was one, is thrown by him at 22.273.

339 Menelaos too has to arm, but there is no dramatic point in describing this in full; variations from Paris' armour would only show the contest as unbalanced. Some pre-Aristarchan texts did not agree: P. Hibeh 19 (see on 302 and 330–8 *fin.*) added at least three verses naming shield (ἀσπίς), helmet (πήληξ), greaves (in a compressed version of 330f.) and sword – probably all six standard items, in fact, but in an impossible order.

340 ἑκάτερθεν ὁμίλου is quite general in implication: 'on each side of the assembled armies'.

341 ἐστιχόωντο should strictly mean that they advanced together in a rank or file, and is correctly so used of Priam and Idaios in the earlier occurrence of this verse at 266; here they proceed independently from opposite sides. The reason for reusing 266 rather than the harmless standard verse ἐς μέσον ἀμφοτέρων συνίτην μεμαῶτε μάχεσθαι (= e.g. 23.814) seems to be the poet's desire to introduce once again the idea of both Trojans and Achaeans as grouped around, and so to sharpen the visual image of the duel taking place between the two seated armies: see further pp. 35–7 of the article cited at the end of 76–8n.

342 This verse is closely paralleled, not in book 7, but in the mock-duel in the funeral games for Patroklos at 23.815 (where also 813 = 340 here). Both passages seem derived from a similar oral prototype, although with individual adaptations; see further the article just cited, pp. 35f.

345 A unique verse, the hostility being inappropriate to the mock-duel of book 23 and being embodied in speeches between the contestants in book 7.

346–7 Paris exercises his right of first throw (cf. 317, 325); his spear, like Menelaos' at 355, is given the formular epithet δολιχόσκιον (δολιχόσκιον ἔγχος| 20x *Il.*, 4x *Od.*) which as well as being functional in a verse of this metrical shape conveys an imposing impression. Its sense has been debated, but there is no real objection to its most obvious meaning, 'with long shadow', to which no reasonable alternative has been proposed.

348–9 χαλκός not -όν is correct (here and at 7.259, 17.44, where 348 recurs); so Aristarchus (Did/AbT) and a minority of MSS: 'but the bronze [i.e. the bronze spear-head] did not break it, but its [οἱ] point was bent back | in the strong shield'. This is not only because χαλκῷ undoubtedly refers to spear not shield in the next verse, but also because χαλκός (etc.) frequently denotes a spear-head, and never elsewhere simply a shield (rather than a part of it, or its material, as at 7.267).

351–4 This is the third in a fourfold sequence of short addresses to Zeus, each composed of four verses (298ff., 320ff., 351ff., 365ff.), which are a dominant feature of this part of the duel-scene. Menelaos' prayer here, despite its reproachful sequel at 365ff., is a powerful reminder of his rectitude and in itself gives him the advantage over Paris, who can naturally attempt nothing similar. Zeus cannot, of course, respond immediately, because that would bring the war to an end (a historical impossibility) and go back on his oath to Thetis (a dramatic and theological one).

Aristarchus (Arn/A) athetized 352 on the wholly inadequate grounds that it is 'unnecessary' and the prayer should be concise, also that Menelaos would not call his enemy δῖον. In fact the four verses are carefully balanced, with marked breaks at alternate main caesuras, 352 and 354, and constitute a dignified statement of his moral position.

353–4 Even men of a later generation 'will shudder at doing ill to a host who (literally 'whoever', ὅ κεν with the subjunctive) shows him friendship': this well emphasizes the heinousness of Paris' crime.

355–60 The counter-throw itself is expressed in almost identical formular language (355f., cf. 347f., of which 355 occurs 7× *Il.*); but whereas Paris' throw failed to penetrate, Menelaos' goes right through shield and corslet. Even though it almost miraculously inflicts no wound, that penetration in itself is a symbol of Menelaos' ultimate superiority – for it is one of the rules of Homeric encounters that the warrior whose throw is too weak to pierce will lose (that is not so of a complete miss, however), cf. Fenik, *Typical Battle Scenes* 6f.

The whole of from 355 προΐει to 360 inclusive is exactly reproduced, of Aias, in the corresponding duel at 7.249–54. The spear-shot itself is conventionally expressed, but its further results are progressively less widely paralleled. Verse 357 = 7.251 (in which the metrical lengthening of initial διά in what ancient grammarians called a στίχος ἀκέφαλος, a 'headless verse', can be matched by other words whose first syllable is naturally short, Chantraine, *GH* I, 103; see also on 4.155), is also found as 11.435; and 358 = 7.252, with a weapon which 'pressed through decorated corslet', occurs twice in less formal encounters, for at 4.136ff. Pandaros' arrow then goes through the μίτρη and grazes the skin, and at 11.436f. the spear then grazes Odysseus' skin forthwith. Yet only in the two formal duels is there the remarkable sequel that 'straight onward beside the flank it sheered the tunic, | the spear did', and then that 'he swerved and avoided black doom' (359f. = 7.253f.).

These two verses have sometimes been suspected in modern times, and it is true that despite formular elements (|ἀντικρύ, χιτῶνα|, ἀλεύατο κῆρα μέλαιναν) there are signs of special and untraditional composition: thus διάμησε does not recur in Homer, although the simple verb, 'reap', does; ἔγχος occurs as runover-word in only one other out of over a hundred uses; and ἐκλίνθη recurs twice elsewhere but in a different part of the verse and of a less surprising action.

Fenik (*Typical Battle Scenes* 102–4) suspects that 358 has been displaced onto the formal duels from 11.436, and finds less difficulty in the spear piercing a tunic than a corslet; but we do not really know how closely the θώρηξ fitted, or how loosely the χιτών. In any case we should not take too literal a view of the sequence of events, a point on which these singers are often imprecise: perhaps Paris starts swerving when he sees the spear approaching, and does so just enough to make the spear-point miss his flesh by a fraction. There is no real problem here, just a singularly vivid and instantaneous, and admittedly daring, expansion by the monumental composer, for the sake of the two formal duels, of a special form of the passage-of-weapon motif which twice elsewhere results in superficial wounds; see further G. S. Kirk, *op. cit.* in 76–8n., pp. 32–4, and the comment on 4.135–6.

358 ἠρήρειστο: bT comment that 'the force of the blow is shown by the roughness of the word' – perhaps the relentless tearing, rather.

362–4 Atreus' son Menelaos, armed similarly to Paris according to the implication of 339, has a silver-studded sword like that of 334. Paris does not use his to defend himself – it simply is not mentioned – and this probably accounted for Zenodotus' adjustment of the text, see on 330–8 *fin.* and Aristarchus (Arn/A) on 361. The composer may well not have planned this minor apparent inconsequence, but could say (as we might) that Paris is obviously so discomposed by the near-miss and his strenuous efforts to avoid injury, as well as now by Menelaos' sword breaking into smithereens about his head, that he has no opportunity to draw his own sword before Menelaos grabs him by the helmet and half-throttles him with its strap at 369–72.

362 Menelaos strikes the φάλος, evidently the (or a) ridge or boss of the helmet (some had two or four, cf. ἀμφίφαλον, τετράφαλον, τετραφάληρον) – rather than a horn as some have thought; but the archaeological material casts little light, cf. *Arch. Hom.* ε 58f., 72–4 (J. Borchhardt). Some such protrusion would make a particularly solid part capable of smashing a thin bronze blade in a kind of accident which must have happened often enough in real life, too.

Aristarchus (Did/A) read αὐτῆ not αὐτῷ, referring to the helmet (κόρυς) rather than its ridge (φάλος), and this was the reading of the finer, χαριέστεραι, texts as well as the majority of texts according to T; despite which the medieval and modern vulgates have αὐτῷ. The difference of nuance is minimal; probably Aristarchus was right; but his lack of influence in some minor textual matters once again deserves note.

P. Hibeh 19 read ἐπαΐξας for ἀνασχόμενος, thus obliterating a vivid detail and spoiling the effect of ἐπαΐξας in 369; it also added a verse.

363 διατρυφέν from διαθρύπτω, 'shatter', only here in Homer. τριχθά τε καὶ τετραχθά is especially apposite to the noise of a tearing sail at *Od.* 9.71, and perhaps that was its favoured use, but it is effective enough here too.

364 Is closely similar to 21.272, which has Πηλείδης for 'Ατρείδης. There is a moderately developed formular system for ὤμωξεν (etc.), cf. e.g.|ὤμωξέν τ' ἄρ' ἔπειτα 3x *Il.*; groaning and moaning are perfectly heroic.

365–8 For the complaint compare 23.439, 'Αντίλοχ' οὔ τις σεῖο βροτῶν ὀλοώτερος ἄλλος; also Akhilleus to Apollo, θεῶν ὀλοώτατε πάντων, at 22.15 (on immortal insults to Zeus see on 1.552). Such an expression of annoyance did not call down thunderbolts, because despite the heavenward reproachful glance of 364 it was more like swearing than serious rebuke.

366 ἦ τ' ἐφάμην τείσασθαι, 'I thought I had had my revenge on'; although possibly τείσεσθαι, future, should be read as in 28, see on 27–8.

368 παλάμηφιν '*from* my hand', genitive-ablative (Chantraine, *GH* I, 234 and 237), probably dependent on ἐκ in 367 (which might, however, be in tmesis with ἤϊχθη). Ammonius according to Aristarchus (Did/A) read οὐδ' ἐδάμασσα in place of οὐδ' ἔβαλόν μιν, since Menelaos did in fact score a hit, although not a fatal one.

369–82 The rapid and simple narrative contains much progressive and only one integral enjambment, at 377/8.

369–70 Menelaos leapt forward and grasped the 'horse-bushy' helmet, perhaps indeed by the thick horse-hair plume itself, cf. Lorimer, *HM* 238f. and fig. 12 on p. 157. Then he began to drag him back, or was in process of doing so, toward the Achaeans, whirling him about, ἐπιστρέψας.

371–2 Meanwhile Paris was being strangled by the helmet-strap up against, ὑπό, his neck (which is 'tender' generically, not because Paris is like a woman as bT suggest). We do not hear of chin-straps elsewhere, which is perhaps why 372 is added as a slightly ponderous explanation. τρυφάλεια is another term for helmet, usually indistinguishable in sense from κόρυς or κυνέη; strictly it probably means 'with four φάλοι', (τε)τρυ-φαλος (cf. τρά-πεζα, 'four-foot' or table); see Chantraine, *Dict.* s.v., and on 362 for φάλοι; also Hoekstra, *Modifications* 96–9.

373–5 The motif and its dramatic form of expression are formular: X would have done Y...unless Z had sharply observed it (εἰ μὴ ἄρ' ὀξὺ νόησε,

Book Three

6x *Il.*, not *Od.*). Verse 374 = 5.312 (where *Aineias* would have perished unless Aphrodite had noticed it and saved him); the intervener can be either a god (Zeus, Poseidon as well as Aphrodite) or a man (Hektor, Diomedes).

Aphrodite thus continues to support her favourite Paris; it is she who makes the strap break – such accidents are regularly attributed to a god, but Aphrodite's involvement is part of the preparation for her ensuing confrontation with Helen.

The strap was 'much-embroidered' at 371, but is now (at 375) made of leather from an ox 'killed with a strong blow'; both epithets are conventional, but their slightly paradoxical succession adds to the bizarre flavour of the unusual scene as it develops.

376 The helmet came along empty, κεινή (Ionic; Attic κενή), without Paris' head inside it, together with (i.e. held by) his thick hand – this last being a formula (13x *Il.*, 5x *Od.*) proper to a heroic fist but also used of Athene's, twice in the Theomachy, and even of Penelope's in a well-known passage of the *Odyssey* (21.6).

378 ῥίψ' ἐπιδινήσας recurs at 19.268 when the herald throws the body of the sacrificed boar into the sea after Agamemnon's oath (see on 310).

379–80 Aristarchus (Arn/A) rightly noted a difficulty over this (second) spear; Paris had armed himself with a single one at 338, and Menelaos likewise according to the clear implication of 339. Menelaos therefore has no second spear with which to pursue his attack; indeed, now his sword is broken, he has no offensive weapon at all, while Paris, helmetless and probably confused, at least still has his sword. Aristarchus proposed that ἔγχεϊ χαλκείῳ is indirect object of ἐπόρουσε: he leapt upon the spear (the one that had pierced shield and corslet) to retrieve it. Word-order is against this, and more probably the poet is being slightly lax; 'with brazen spear' is a half-verse cumulation intended as an inconspicuous, almost automatic elaboration of κατακτάμεναι μενεαίνων, in order to lead into the fresh action of Aphrodite's intervention.

381–2 Verse 381 = 20.444, where Apollo snatches Hektor to safety with the same divine ease. ἀήρ, 'mist', confers invisibility; concealing with thick mist means here that Paris just disappears, although in the book 20 passage Akhilleus thrusts his spear into it four times before accepting that Hektor is no longer inside it (445–9). The present verses with their mellifluous ει/η and o sounds mark the passage from the rough-and-tumble of the fight to the fragrance of the bedchamber. κηώεντι -α (3x *Il.* of a θάλαμος) evidently means much the same as εὐώδεϊ, like κηώδεϊ of Andromakhe's bosom at 6.483; it is probably derived from *κῆϝος > καίω, 'incense' (Leaf) or 'fragrant wood for burning' (Chantraine, *Dict.*).

Book Three

383–461 Summoned home to the bedroom by Aphrodite, Helen attempts to resist but is frightened into compliance. She rebukes Paris but finally goes to bed with him; meanwhile on the battlefield Agamemnon claims victory for Menelaos

383–4 It was the more neutral Iris who fetched Helen to the Scaean gate at 129–45; now, in a repetition of the divine-summons motif, Aphrodite herself, as Paris' protector and embodiment of sexual love, impels her back home. After the Viewing and Priam's departure for the oath-ceremony she had evidently remained on the walls and watched the duel, among the Trojan womenfolk. That her movements around the city are on both occasions directed by a goddess emphasizes her dilemma and her helplessness.

385–7 Aphrodite disguises herself as an aged spinning woman who had accompanied Helen from Lakedaimon. That is consonant with the idea that Helen managed to bring many possessions with her (cf. e.g. 70, κτήμασι πᾶσι), but hardly with Paris' own description at 444f. of 'snatching' her away and making love to her on the island of Kranae. The oral tradition may have contained both versions; or the idea of a more elaborate removal may be the result of typical oral aggrandizement, comparable with the description of Akhilleus' hut in book 24 (or Eumaeus' homestead) in almost palatial terms.

385 νεκταρέου: 'smelling like nectar', 'fragrant', also of Akhilleus' tunic at 18.25; cf. ἀμβρόσιος, 2.19 and comment. The action (γραφικῶς, 'as in a picture', T) of twitching the robe to draw Helen's attention (rather than to draw her away from the other women as bT say) suggests an old servant's obsequiousness, and is in perhaps deliberate contrast with the elevated terms used for the robe itself.

388 Modern commentators have generally accepted T's assumption that the subject of φιλέεσκε is Helen.

389–94 One might expect to find some flavour in these words of the old servant whose appearance the goddess has assumed. That is not necessarily so in an oral style, but it is possible that the peremptory δεῦρ' ἴθι, the assumption that the husband's word is law and the φαίης locution reveal some such intention. The last of these is colloquial in the mouth of Antenor at 220, but it is also used thrice elsewhere by the poet himself, in narrative not speech; while the expansive description of the bed in 391 and the sophisticated oxymoron of 'gleaming with beauty and (clean) clothes' in 392 are more in the manner of a goddess.

391 κεῖνος ὁ γ' dramatically evokes the picture: 'there he is...'

δινωτοῖσι (cf. δῖνος = 'whirl'): either turned on a lathe or with thongs tensioned by twisting according to Aristarchus (Arn/A). The latter is improbable, the former possible if it refers to the legs; but at *Od.* 19.56 a

321

chair is δινωτήν with ivory and silver, and at 13.406f. a shield with bronze, which seems as if the term implies 'decorated with circles' or 'inlaid', rather. See Ventris and Chadwick, *Documents* 341, on *qe-qi-no-to* in no. 239.

392 οὐδέ κε φαίης...: a dramatic turn of speech; see also on 4.223–5.

393–4 Paris looks as though he were off to a dance: that has just the right hint of possible decadence, for although dancing was a regular part of life (for unmarried men at least, as bT comment), respectable enough when performed for a god, at 24.261 Priam will castigate his surviving sons as 'deceivers and dancers, distinguished at dance-steps'.

The distinction between being about to go to a dance and having just come from one is probably simply to emphasize the dancing idea in itself, by an almost polar construction; as well as to provide a suitably orotund close to this closely enjambed and ingratiating sentence. But perhaps the exertion of dancing might be held to increase a man's attractiveness, cf. στίλβων, 'gleaming', in 392.

395 Aristarchus (Arn/A) explained θυμὸν...ὄρινε as 'incited' rather than 'angered', and that is right; Leaf (followed by Willcock) is incorrect in his comment '*stirred her to anger*, as elsewhere'. The whole verse is a formular one and occurs (with varying pronouns) 4x elsewhere in the *Iliad*, always with the meaning 'stir on to action (by the words just spoken)'. Only at 14.459, where the phrase θυμὸν ὄρινε but not the whole verse recurs, is anger involved; the typical application is at e.g. 2.142, where Agamemnon's proposal of retreat stirs the troops to rush for the ships. Here, Helen is incited by Aphrodite's words – to obey her (we must understand) and return to her attractive consort. In her case the stirring of her θυμός is ultimately an erotic one.

396–8 But then she recognizes Aphrodite and does her best to resist her and the feelings she has inspired. These introductory verses to her speech of protest are full of ambiguity and possible contradiction, reflecting her own changing and conflicting feelings and the dubious role of the goddess.

Helen recognizes her by her beautiful neck, shining bosom and flashing eyes: has the goddess abandoned her disguise? Or do these features resist transformation? Or does Helen see through the outward disguise? And in any event, why does the goddess need to adopt a disguise at all – was it perhaps to escape the notice of the other women who surrounded Helen at 384? Surely they could simply have been ignored? Aristarchus (Arn/A) could not stomach either these problems or the impious tone of Helen's subsequent remarks, and athetized the whole of 396–418. Fortunately his stringent views had no effect on the vulgate, and one of the most profound, beautiful and emotive confrontations in the whole epic was allowed to survive unscathed.

One cannot help feeling that the unrealistic and incomplete nature of

Aphrodite's disguise is meant to reflect the poet's awareness that this goddess, in particular, is a projection of personal emotions. Not that the whole scene can be reduced to an allegory of Helen's instincts and revulsions; someone has to tell her that Paris (who had vanished into thin air) is back home, gleaming with beauty; but the role of the old woman, Helen's own feelings for Paris (over which Aphrodite had presided for so long), and her resistance to them, remain ambiguous.

398 θάμβησεν: compare 1.199, θάμβησεν δ' Ἀχιλεύς, when he recognizes Athene (again, the goddess's eyes are remarkable). θάμβος, 'wonder' or 'amazement', can be accompanied by fear as at 8.77, but both Akhilleus and Helen proceed at once to rebuke the goddess who has appeared to them. ἔπος τ' ἔφατ' ἔκ τ' ὀνόμαζε(ν) | is a common address-formula (17x *Il.*, 26x *Od.*), the person addressed being either named, in the vocative, or not, as here.

399–412 Helen's words to the divinity who has destroyed her life and happiness are passionate and bitter. They begin with an accusation of deceit put in the form of a terse question (399), then develop the ironical theme that Aphrodite is using her as a mere instrument: 'will you drive me even further afield to gratify some other favourite of yours?' (400–2). She follows this with a return to the present circumstances and another question hinging on Aphrodite's deceit: 'is it because Menelaos has won and wants to take me home that you have come here to deceive me (by inciting me to love Paris all over again)?' (403–5). Then comes a more startling and insulting development of the sexual theme: let Aphrodite abandon Olumpos and spend her whole time fussing over Paris – until he makes her his wife, or his concubine (406–9). Finally Helen reverts to her own position, and the controlled and elaborate rhetoric gives way to short and staccato, perhaps almost sobbing, assertions of refusal, shame and self-pity: she will not go to him; it would be wrong; the other women would blame her for it; she is so unhappy (410–12).

The whole speech seems to have been carefully planned by the main composer, and to owe relatively little to the tradition. After the initial single-verse question it consists of four sentences of either 3 or 4 verses. These alternate between the sarcastic idea that Aphrodite is using Helen as a surrogate and is in love with Paris herself, and speculation on what might happen to Helen in Troy. Alternatively the structure can be seen as three ironical sentences of roughly equal weight framed by the initial question and the downright refusal at the end. The style throughout is kept as simple as possible, given the necessary amount of enjambment (integral in three verses) and the ironic complexity of the thought.

399 On δαιμονίη see 2.200n.; here the term is directed to a goddess, and its implications are a little different – or rather they are made even more familiar and ironical, because the proper application is to a mortal. I doubt whether (as J. T. Hooker suggests) 'the use of this word...shows that the speaker is baffled by the motives of the person addressed'.

400–2 It is preferable to make this another question: 'Will you lead me on to some other well-populated city?', literally 'somewhere among... cities?'. They are envisaged as being in Phrygia or Maeonia because those regions seem even more foreign, and further afield, than Troy.

402 The spondaic monosyllables and the alliteration of εἴ τίς τοι καὶ κεῖθι increase the ironic effect; μερόπων ἀνθρώπων corresponds with 400 πολίων εὖ ναιομενάων, and creates the impression that almost anyone at all would do; moreover it isolates φίλος in a short third colon and throws special weight on it: 'dear', with more than a suggestion of 'sexually beloved', see on 453.

403–5 There is an obvious balance to the sentence created by οὕνεκα δὴ νῦν...τοὕνεκα δὴ νῦν; it is perhaps continued in the alliteration of the following word in each case, δῖον and δεῦρο; moreover στυγερὴν ἐμέ in the central verse of the three, deliberately pathetic as it certainly is, stands in a corresponding position to δῖον Ἀλέξανδρον just before, and possibly in intended contrast with it.

406 The medieval MSS all have ἀπόειπε κελεύθους, 'renounce the paths' of the gods, which was also evidently the ancient vulgate; it is both livelier and more elegant than Aristarchus' ἀπόεικε κελεύθου, 'keep away from the path' (Did/A), which is however accepted in e.g. OCT. Aristarchus' objections to the vulgate are not known.

408–9 Grieving over Paris and protecting him are restrained expressions in the circumstances, but are part of Helen's bitter sarcasm; that is what the goddess may profess to be doing, but it is tantamount to loving him. In the end he may make her his wife – or his concubine (Shipp, *Studies* 240 notes that δούλη, rare in Homer as against δμῳή, has that special sense and is not 'late').

410–12 Helen's emotional closing utterance appears artless but is carefully composed with its alternating themes: 'I will not go there [*sc.* to his bedroom] – it would be wrong – lying in that man's bed – the Trojan women will blame me for it.' Finally, and with no obvious logical connexion with what has preceded, comes her *cri de coeur*: 'I have infinite griefs in my heart.'

411 πορσανέουσα, literally 'to prepare' but commonly and metaphorically 'to inhabit' his bed, that is, make love to him. Helen has just said that such an act would incur νέμεσις, divine disapproval; now she adds a more immediate embarrassment, that the women who were evidently her friends would blame her for it. Presumably their reason would be indecent haste, rather than accepting her (second) husband again at some point after his apparent defeat in the duel; but in her mind and theirs there must be the thought already outlined in 404, that legally she may belong now to Menelaos instead.

413–17 It takes only a few words to break Helen's resistance; but the goddess is enraged (χολωσαμένη, cf. χωσαμένη in the next verse), and the threat she makes is a practical and powerful one: see on 416–17.

414 'Do not provoke me, wicked woman': σχετλίη is a strong term (see on 2.112), but here its use is unusual in that it has to be scanned either as σχἔτλῐη̄ or as σχῆτλῐη̄; elsewhere its first syllable is regularly long by position (it nearly always comes as first word in the verse). To ignore the effect of the consonant and liquid would, according to Leaf, be Attic, and Shipp tended to agree (*Studies* 240); but despite Chantraine's characterization (*GH* I, 109) of σχῆτλῐη̄, with a form of synizesis, as improbable, that may well be the preferable explanation. An organic Atticism here would be exceptionally surprising in a scene that carries all the marks of special composition by the monumental composer (Aristarchus' athetesis being nugatory, see on 396–8).

415 ἔκπαγλος means 'astounding', 'exceeding', as well as 'terrible' (< *ἔκ-πλαγ-λος cf. ἐκπλήσσω according to Chantraine, *Dict.*); see also on 1.145–6. The threat is to turn her exceptional affection into correspondingly (τὼς...ὡς) exceptional hostility. But the object of her affections is significantly changed in a clear reminiscence of the present passage at 5.423, where Athene maliciously suggests to Zeus that Aphrodite, now wounded in the hand by Diomedes, had been pricked as she fondled some Achaean woman to persuade her to follow the Trojans – τοὺς νῦν ἔκπαγλα φίλησε. It is *Paris* that Aphrodite really loves, as Helen knows.

416–17 The practical form Aphrodite's enmity would take is dangerous; the ἔχθεα λυγρά she could devise (μητίσομαι is aorist subjunctive after μή, like μεθείω in 414 and ἀπεχθήρω in 415) are not so much a mere revival of hostilities – that actually happens in any case, by the machinations of a more warlike goddess than Aphrodite – as hostility *directed against Helen* by both sides equally, and which would lead to an 'evil doom' for her (perhaps by stoning, as an adulteress?).

418–20 ἔδεισεν because of the original digamma, ἔδ(ϝ)εισεν. Helen, duly terrified into submission, must not be seen by her recent female companions; the poet remembers this detail and the complications their rebuke might cause. Wrapping herself in her cloak and moving silently are signs of her wish to remain inconspicuous, unlikely in themselves to ensure her invisibility – probably the goddess who is leading her does that. δαίμων is elsewhere applied to an unnamed god, not a particular one, but that probably has no significance here; it replaces θεός or θεά in order to pack the thought into the last colon.

421 It is Paris' house in a special sense, not only because he is there at present and is its lord and master, but also because he had personally taken part in building it (6.314f.).

422 The verse is constructed out of standard elements (for ἐπὶ ἔργα τράποντο cf. 23.53). The maidservants (as Professor R. M. Frazer reminds me) are the pair that accompanied Helen in 143, and not those awaiting her in the house; αἱ in 421 refers to Helen and them, rather than to Helen and Athene.

424 Zenodotus (Arn/A) substituted a single verse, 'and she sat facing lord Alexandros', for 423-6 on the ground that it was ἀπρεπές, unfitting, for the goddess to lift and place the chair for Helen. Aristarchus evidently refuted this by the observation that she is after all disguised as a servant; but in any case the objection is trivial. Athene carries a lamp at *Od.* 19.33f., as T noted; but it is probably more to the point that gods can do very corporeal things to mortals, when they need to: see e.g. 1.197 with comment.

Aphrodite is described here as φιλομμειδής, not as Διὸς θυγάτηρ which is metrically equivalent, as at e.g. 374: does that breach of strict oral economy mean that one or the other is chosen for its special aptness to a particular context? This does occasionally happen, but in other respects Aphrodite's verse-end system seems fairly normal:

> 'Αφροδίτη (etc.) (6× *Il.*, 1× *Od.*)
> δῖ' 'Αφροδίτη (4× *Il.*, 1× *Od.*)
> χρυσέην 'Αφροδίτην (etc.) (5× *Il.*, 5× *Od.*)
> φιλομμειδὴς 'Αφροδίτη (5× *Il.*, 1× *Od.*)
> Διὸς θυγάτηρ 'Αφροδίτη (8× *Il.*, 1× *Od.*)
> ἐϋστεφάνου τ' 'Αφροδίτης (1× *Od.*)

(note however that there is no formula in the nominative for the − − ∪ ∪ − ǒ | value, perhaps because of the hiatus that χρυσέη 'Αφροδίτη would create; it was however accepted in the dative).

The provision of metrical alternatives is paralleled in M. Parry's Table 1 (*MHV* 39) only by the variation between ἄναξ Διὸς υἱὸς 'Απόλλων (4× *Il.*, 1× *Od.*) and ἄναξ ἑκάεργος 'Απόλλων (2× *Il.*, 1× *Od.*). But again that turns on whether being a child of Zeus, or possessing some special personal characteristic, is to be mentioned; and in both cases it appears that the singer chooses between alternatives with that in mind. Aphrodite in particular is presented in two different lights in the epic: either as goddess of love and happiness (φιλομμειδής, in which the connexion with μειδιάω, 'smile', rather than μήδεα, 'genitals', as by Hesiod, *Theog.* 200, seems the earlier, cf. Chantraine, *Dict.* s.v. μειδιάω), or in a more serious aspect as daughter of Zeus. Thus at 374 = 5.312 she is the latter because she is shown as a powerful protectress; here, on the other hand, she is engaged in the game of love (and at 4.10 the title is even derogatory). The difference of epithet is well exemplified in book 14, where Aphrodite is Διὸς θυγάτηρ at 193 while Here is making her request to her but φιλομμειδής at 211 when she grants it and hands over her belt with its erotic properties. (Then at 224 she reverts to being Διὸς θυγάτηρ for a different reason, perhaps: because μείδησεν -ασα has occurred twice in the preceding two verses.)

426 Leaf noted that κούρη -η Διὸς αἰγιόχοιο is elsewhere applied only to Athene (3x *Il.*, 7x *Od.*); but it is a natural extension of Διὸς ἐκγεγαυῖα, used twice in the *Iliad* of Helen.

427 ὄσσε πάλιν κλίνασα is unique and well conceived; no one else in the poem has to deal with another person in quite this way. Helen evidently cannot bear to look directly at her lover -- it is surely something like that, rather than a contrived way of resisting Aphrodite's blandishments (or Paris' beauty?) as bT suggest. Some doubt about her precise motive, or mixture of motives, must remain, but the aversion of the eyes somehow suggests her own indirectness and probable confusion.

428–37 Her words to Paris are similar in several respects to those she addressed to the goddess – bitter and sarcastic, quite elaborate in expression, with much integral enjambment.

428–9 ἤλυθες or ἦλθες as first word in a speech is usually friendly, as at 24.104, *Od.* 16.23, 17.41; here it is the opposite. Telling your lover that you wish he had been killed is drastic enough, but then she rubs salt in the wound by declaring her former husband to be the better man. That is what the duel itself had suggested (although Paris will have an answer to that at 439f.); but Helen's jeering and almost triumphant tone must have been hard to endure.

430–6 She develops the idea at some length, with additional refinements: Paris had claimed to be better than Menelaos, so why does he not issue another challenge? That is of course unfair, since Paris might now feel that he was wrong, but it allows Helen to utter her histrionic prohibition: 'But *I* tell you to stop, not to fight him, lest you come to grief.' Some critics (including J. T. Hooker) take this as seriously meant – 'the old love suddenly resumes its sway' as Leaf put it (although he did not necessarily accept this view). That is hard to credit; nor can one easily agree with Willcock that 'The vehemence of her criticism shows that she still loves Paris.' The truth is that the whole address is of a piece, bitterly sarcastic and hostile; what she actually feels is hard to divine, although it seems to include resentment and even contempt; she will succumb quite soon to his logic and his charms, but perhaps even that makes undiluted contempt at this point more dramatically effective. There is a certain residual ambiguity about which it is unwise to be too dogmatic in this kind of literary *genre*.

Aristarchus (Arn/A) athetized 432–6 inclusive as prosaic (πεζότεροι), frigid and incongruous. That is surely unjustified.

434–5 Helen does, however, dwell somewhat on the idea of fighting, rather as in 431; πόλεμον πολεμίζειν is ungainly, made no less so by the (common formular) expansion of πολεμίζειν by ἠδὲ μάχεσθαι. The reason for this whole tortuous expression, which was used to good effect by Agamemnon at 2.121, is presumably the wish to get the most out of her rebuke and develop it as fully as possible.

436 This cumulated closing verse with its runover-word and change of rhythm succeeds in refining the irony by making the whole statement more hesitant and less dogmatic: it would be *unthinking* of him to fight again, and he *might* succumb if he did.

437 This is one of the least felicitous formulas of address; occasional redundant expressions are part of the oral style (see e.g. on 161), but μύθοισιν ἀμειβόμενος -η -ετο, especially when followed by προσέειπε which is itself repetitive, is unattractive. Its use is not infrequent (9× *Il.*, including with ἐπέεσσιν, : 2× *Od.*) compared with other extreme examples such as ποσὶ βήσετο (only 2× *Il.*); it is perhaps facilitated by phrases in which μύθοισι has an epithet, e.g. 6.343 μύθοισι προσηύδα μειλιχίοισι, which are perfectly acceptable. Even the primarily Odyssean ἀμείβετο μύθῳ (5× *Od.*, 2× *Il.* – and then in book 24 which has much Odyssean language) is preferable, since μύθῳ there can mean 'speech', therefore 'answered with (this) speech'.

438–46 Paris deals with Helen's rebuke in broadly the same way as he had with Hektor's at 64–70: by flattery (here delayed to the end), a simple prohibition ('don't criticize me'), based on the argument that men are in the hands of the god, followed by a rapid diversion to other matters (fighting the duel, making love). The tone is the same, of moderate reasonableness, and the style relaxed, with a mixture of whole-sentence verses and longer, moderately enjambed ones.

439–40 The point is elegantly made, and the assertion about gods has, as often, a proverbial ring (cf. 9.497, στρεπτοὶ δέ τε καὶ θεοὶ αὐτοί; 13.72, ἀρίγνωτοι δὲ θεοί περ; 21.264, θεοὶ δέ τε φέρτεροι ἀνδρῶν). Its weakness is that Athene is a far more powerful goddess, over fighting at least, than Aphrodite. Paris is evidently unperturbed by his experience and must be complacently aware that it was Aphrodite that spirited him away; perhaps he even recognizes her as she sets Helen before him.

441 ἀλλ᾽ ἄγε δή corresponds with the practical νῦν αὖτ᾽ in 67; τραπείομεν is from τέρπεσθαι, 'let us take our pleasure' (with metathesis of α/ε and ρ), rather than τρέπεσθαι as in 422. Paris softens his rather incisive conjugal suggestion by the assertion that his passion for her has never been greater. Zeus will say something akin to this to Here at 14.315f.

(after a similar invitation, in similar formular terms, at 314), although he regales her, with divine insouciance, with a list of mistresses who have not excited him so much.

Possible reasons for Paris' apparently ill-timed attack of ἔρως were discussed at length in antiquity; that is shown by bT but especially by Porphyry 1.65.22 (quoted by Erbse, I, 436). One theory was that he put on a show of exceptional attachment to assuage Helen's wounded feelings; Aristotle (frag. 150), on the other hand, had thought that his passion was sharpened by the consideration that he might not be allowed to gratify it. Such speculations reveal more about later psycho-sexual interests than about Homer, whose depiction of Paris is both consistent with the mythical tradition and (as also with Helen) intriguingly and perhaps deliberately incomplete. Paris seems both specious and imperturbable, secure in the gifts with which Aphrodite has rewarded him.

442 ἔρως 'enfolds' his heart (the φρένας here are the seat of the passions), conceals it all around, as also of Zeus at 14.294. ἀμφεκάλυψε(ν), ἀμφικαλύπτει (etc.) are formular at the verse-end (11× *Il.*, 10× *Od.*); their subjects vary from ἔρως here to death, sleep, a cloud, garment, shield, or funeral urn (also in the *Odyssey* the mountain, ὄρος like σορός, that threatened to cover the Phaeacians).

443–5 See on 385–7 for the contrast between this swift and romantic abduction and the idea that she took servants and possessions with her. According to Pausanias 3.22.1 Kranae was an island off Lakedaimon's port of Gutheion. Other possibilities were freely considered (Arn/A): that κρανέη is not a proper name but an epithet, 'rocky' (used of Ithake at 201 and 4× *Od.*); or that it was Kuthera, or the island called Helene (and therefore associated with her) off the south-east coast of Attica. They would hardly have 'sailed' for the Gutheion islet, which is now joined to the mainland by a short causeway; it might also have seemed uncomfortably accessible to irate husbands. On the whole we prefer the view that κρανάη is an epithet and that the rocky island is left mysteriously anonymous (compare the deserted island used for a very different purpose at *Od.* 3.270); the inhabitants of Gutheion would have claimed it in any case.

447–8 The poet does not attempt to explore Helen's motives; her acquiescence, conveyed in three formular words, is at first hearing shocking, but then seems almost inevitable.

There is no difference in implication between ἄκοιτις (only here of Helen, as T observed – except by implication at 138) and ἄλοχος, and they are sometimes equated (e.g. at 9.399). Both mean 'sharer of the bed' (κοίτη, λέχος) and can be applied either to a wedded wife or to a concubine; their choice in Homer is usually determined by metrical convenience, as here.

Book Three

τρητοῖσι (also of a (funerary) bed at 24.720) means 'bored with holes', either as mortises or for thongs to support the bedding; *Od.* 23.196–201 is not much help, *contra* Leaf.

449–50 As usual the poetical transition from place to place is made without effort, but with special contrast here between luxurious bed and the wild if unspecified beast. Menelaos resembled a hungry lion earlier, too, when he first saw Paris, but a joyful one as it came upon a hunter's prey (23); T adds that his searching for Paris when he is actually in bed with Helen has something comical about it, γελοίως 3ητεῖ τὸν ἀφροδισιάζοντα.

451–4 Paris is not to be found; no Trojan or ally could point him out – they were not trying to conceal him out of friendship, since they hated him like death: a violent indication of their feelings about war, Paris, and perhaps even (in view of Aphrodite's threat at 416f.) Helen.

453 φιλότης here has its commonest sense of affection, in contrast with sexual love at 445. It is Helen, not they, that is enfolding him in love (εἴ τις ἴδοιτο, 'if anyone were to have seen him'), which is ironical but perhaps not specifically intended.

456–60 Now Agamemnon, as Achaean leader and chief administrator of the oath, speaks out, in the same clear but unremarkable and mainly formular language as has predominated throughout the whole episode.

456 On the Dardanoi and this formular verse of address (4× *Il.*) see on 2.819–20.

457 φαίνετ'(αι): 'is plainly'; Paris was about to be killed and has strangely disappeared, but Agamemnon prudently avoids describing the position in detail since *his* conditions and Menelaos' for retrieving Helen were that Paris should actually be killed (κτείνῃ, 284, cf. τεθναίη, 102); whereas the Trojans themselves (Paris, Hektor and Idaios, at 71f., 92f., 255) had only talked in terms of victory (νικήσῃ κρείσσων τε γένηται, 92). This discrepancy, noted by AbT, is never referred to later, not even when the Trojans need an excuse for truce-breaking. It is, I think, quite deliberate on the part of the poet, at least, if only because Agamemnon would not have been able to claim success at all if killing had been the criterion. Yet the crucial factor, perhaps, is that neither side had envisaged an abortive result, one in which there would be no palpable loser whose corpse was there to prove it.

458–60 Agamemnon repeats the terms of the oath with slight necessary rephrasing (cf. 285–7); the verse about substantial additional recompense (see on 286 and 287) has an especially futile ring to it at this stage.

461 The Achaeans naturally applaud; the Trojans as naturally maintain (as we can infer) a pregnant silence, which brings the whole brilliant episode to a fittingly ironic conclusion.

BOOK FOUR

1–84   The gods are in assembly; Zeus maliciously suggests making peace after the duel, and Here and Athene are furious; he agrees that the latter should descend to earth to organize the breaking of the truce

1–4 The gods are on Mt Olumpos (as 74 will confirm), seated in the level space 'by Zeus'; that is, before his house.

1 ἠγορόωντο, by diectasis from ἀγοράομαι: 'were gathered in assembly'. ἀγορά is from the root of ἀγείρω, 'gather', but came to denote the place of speech-making (as well as of trade); hence ἀγορεύειν means 'make a speech in assembly', or simply 'speak' – ἀγορεύων in 6 could be either. ἀγοράομαι recurs only twice in the *Iliad*, at 2.337 and 8.230 where speech rather than assembly is indicated.

2–3 The floor is golden because most things divine were: thrones, cups (as in 3), clothes and accoutrements; golden clouds surround the mountain-top at 13.523 and 14.343f.

Hebe pours (literally 'wine-pours') their nectar; as Aristarchus noted (Arn/A), she is not here married to Herakles as in the probable rhapsodic addition at *Od.* 11.602–4. She recurs in the *Iliad* only at 5.722 and 905, where she performs other useful but lowly functions. It would have been too complicated to have the other divine wine-pourer, Ganumedes, in action here, because he had been a Trojan prince, snatched off by the gods to pour wine for Zeus because of his, beauty as 20.232–5 politely explains. The famous Archaic terracotta acroterion in the Olympia museum of Zeus abducting Ganymede more clearly indicates the real purport of this erotic myth.

ἐῳνοχόει: Zenodotus (Did/A) probably read ἐνῳνοχόει, which would only be plausible if the wine-cups had already been mentioned. ἐῳνοχόει results from pleonastic treatment of the temporal augment, the best parallel being ἑήνδανε at *Od.* 3.143; Herodian's discussion of the phenomenon is fully reported in A. Cf. on 1.598.

4 δηδέχατ' is the correct spelling of MS δειδέχατ'; the verb clearly signifies 'pledged' and probably derives from *δη-δε[κ]-σκ- (perhaps cf. Sanskrit *dāśnóti*, 'offer homage'), which gave rise to various Homeric forms, δήδεκτο, δεδισκόμενος, δηδισκόμενος and was assimilated to δείκνυμι ('point to') in the forms δεικνύμενος (9.196, *Od.* 4.59) and δεικανόωντο (15.86, 2x *Od.*): cf. Chantraine, *Dict.* s.v. δηδέχαται.

6 κερτομίοις, 'jeering', see on 1.539; παραβλήδην, 'deviously', because

Zeus really needs to get the fighting restarted to fulfil his promise to Thetis. There is no exact Homeric parallel for this meaning, which was disputed by some in antiquity, but 'with sidelong glance' was a common later usage and the middle παραβάλλεσθαι = 'deceive' occurs in Herodotus and Thucydides. Leaf, however, favoured 'provokingly', cf. παραιβόλα κερτομέουσιν, *HyHerm* 56.

8 The goddesses receive these epithets only here and in the single recurrence of this verse at 5.908, although 'Argive' must have been common for Here, the deity of the Heraion near Argos. 'Αλαλκομενηΐς is connected with Alalkomenai on the southern shore of Lake Kopais in Boeotia (p. 195), where there was a cult of the local hero Alalkomeneus. Athene's association with cult and hero is unknown, although she had a temple there in Pausanias' time (9.33.5).

9–10 The two of them are sitting apart and rejoicing (τέρπεσθον, dual) in what they see, i.e. Menelaos' success. τῷ in 10 refers to Paris; on φιλομμειδής see on 3.424 *fin.*

11 παρμέμβλωκε, perfect of παραβλώσκω, 'go beside', also at 24.73; she is always at his side and keeping death away from him, αὐτοῦ, a separative genitive.

13–16 Zeus refrains from raising the awkward question of the exact terms of the oath (see on 3.457), but still treats the matter as an open question. Verse 15 is a rising threefolder whose flow is brought to an abrupt halt by the runover-verb ὄρσομεν (subjunctive, like βάλωμεν), and seems to leave the terser alternative, ἤ φιλότητα..., as the more emphatic choice.

17 τόδε, the latter course, i.e. of making peace between them; the sarcastic tone (cf. κερτομίοις ἐπέεσσι, 6) comes out in the stress on πᾶσι and φίλον καὶ ἡδύ, since Zeus must know that general approval of the idea of peace is scarcely possible.

18–19 The optatives of οἰκέοιτο and ἄγοιτο, without ἄν or κε, are primarily potential, but 'not far removed from a wish. "The city of Priam may still be lived in "'' (Willcock, cf. Leaf): see Chantraine, *GH* II, 217.

20–5 These verses will recur as 8.457–62, after a more direct rebuke from Zeus. Another 6-verse passage shared with book 8 occurs at 446–51.

20 ἐπέμυξαν, only here and at 8.457 in Homer, 'muttered against him'.

21 Aristarchus (Arn/A?) probably assumed that πλησίαι here means 'near to Zeus' – on each side of him, in fact; but he was influenced by the parallel scene in book 8, where at 444f. the goddesses are seated Διὸς ἀμφίς. Without that addition it is more likely that they are envisaged as sitting close to each other, and muttering their complaints to each other.

The dual verbal terminations give a near-rhyme to the end of each half-verse, ἥσθην...μεδέσθην, emphasizing perhaps their mutuality but not particularly elegant in itself.

22   This (and the matching 8.459) and *Od.* 21.89 are the only cases where ἀκέων is definitely indeclinable; usually it declines as though it were a participle, which it probably originally was (cf. Chantraine, *Dict.* s.v. ἀκή). See also on 3.95.

23   Athene is seized by wild anger, but in a daughterly fashion confines herself to scowling in silence; Here cannot contain her χόλος within her breast (it 'swells in the breast even of sensible people' according to 9.553f.), and it bursts out of her in words.

25   This formular verse occurs 5 times elsewhere in the *Iliad*.

26–8   Herē chooses to base her complaint on the sweat she and her horses had expended on assembling the Achaean army (although according to 2.446–52 the practical work had been left to Athene). She will repeat the argument more calmly at 57–61, backing it up by stressing that she is a senior goddess and also Zeus's wife.

29   This verse occurs 3× *Il.*, not *Od.*; at 16.443 it follows shortly after the αἰνότατε Κρονίδη verse, cf. 25. Herē rebuking Zeus is an established Iliadic theme, a 'formula' at a different level, which sometimes calls up the same language. The theme can of course be varied; sometimes it follows an initial rebuke by Zeus, and it does not always end in the same way; for example in the parallel scene in book 8 Zeus has already threatened action, and there is nothing more he can be told to 'do', ἔρδ'; so Here ends differently by saying they will still offer advice.

30   Another formular verse, 3× *Il.* including 1.517 (to Thetis); but its first part, τὴν/τὸν δὲ μέγ' ὀχθήσας, is far commoner (10× *Il.*, 3× *Od.*) and is joined with a variety of name–epithet formulas.

31–49   Zeus's reply disguises his own need to continue the war and so fulfil his promise to Thetis. He begins by almost humorously reproaching Here for her consuming hatred of Priam and his sons, but then turns quite surprisingly to what he will expect in return for giving in to her. He ends, in an obvious form of ring-composition, by describing his own particular affection for Troy and Priam. This may cause the listener to wonder why, nevertheless, he allows the city to fall, even after he has discharged his promise to Thetis. The answer is that this has been made inevitable by Paris' offence against hospitality, which is protected by Zeus ξένιος himself, and by the Trojans' condoning of it by receiving him and Helen.

31–3   δαιμονίη is hardly affectionate here, as it was to some extent when Zeus addressed Here so at 1.561 (see the comment there); but it accords with the irony of the question that is to follow: What are the many evils they do you, that (ὅ τ') you vehemently desire to ravage Ilios? In fact it was only Paris that had offended her, and then by favouring Aphrodite at her expense in the Judgement; for Aristarchus (Arn/A on 32) was almost certainly wrong in saying that Homer did not know of this, even though he ignored it at 14.188ff. (bT on 51) and made explicit reference to it only at 24.25–30 (athetized by Aristarchus, cf. C. W. Macleod *ad loc.*).

34–6 A brilliant *tour de force*: feminine threats of blood and vengeance (compare Hekabe at 24.212f., who says she would like to eat Akhilleus' liver out of his body) are made less rhetorical and more realistic by the idea of the goddess passing through the gates and walls of the city to carry them out. 'Priam and Priam's children' is repeated in a more sinister way from 31, and the other Trojans are thrown in for good measure; only through having devoured them (βεβρώθοις, perfect optative) would she *cure* her rage – which is thus implied to be a kind of disease. A desire to eat human flesh, whatever the circumstances, would indeed be a psychotic deviation in a god, whose proper food is ambrosia. That shows the savagery of Zeus's sarcasm – if it is not the result, rather, of loose oral deployment of a motif primarily applied to mortals.

37 ἔρξον: so too when Zeus makes a concession to Athene at 22.185; the whole formula ἔρξον ὅπως ἐθέλεις is otherwise Odyssean (3×).

μὴ τοῦτό γε νεῖκος: 'let not so small [that is the force of γε] a disagreement as this...'

39 On this whole-verse formula see 1.297n. Its purpose here is not so much to introduce a completely new point as to reassert Zeus's authority despite the concession he is making.

40–1 μεμαώς (-ῶτες etc.) occurs in a variety of formular uses. Listening to 40, one would expect πόλιν ἐξαλαπάξαι to depend on it, cf. e.g. 13.182 μεμαώς ἀπὸ τεύχεα δῦσαι; but the completion of the sense in 41 might suggest that the infinitive depends on ἐθέλω, rather, in which case μεμαώς would be used absolutely as at e.g. 11.258, ἕλκε πόδας μεμαώς. It is nevertheless preferable to accept the construction initially indicated by 40 and understand ἐξαλαπάξαι again after ἐθέλω: 'whenever I, too, eager to sack a city, wish to sack one where men live whom *you* favour...'; the slightly awkward sequence being the result of extending a common formular expression, i.e. μεμαώς + infin.

43 ἑκὼν ἀέκοντί γε θυμῷ: 'of my own choice although not willingly', a pregnant and paradoxical use of a contrast normally applied to different people, cf. 7.197 ἑκὼν ἀέκοντα. Zeus knows that one can do something even though one does not really want to, and he states the idea neatly so as to strengthen his position against Here. It is a subtle piece of psychology on Homer's part.

44 'All X's under the sun and starry sky' looks like a useful formular expression, but does not exactly recur. It contains one important formular component: οὐρανοῦ -ν ἀστερόεντος -α occurs 6× *Il.*, 4× *Od.*, although found only here in the dative. 5.267 ἵππων ὅσσοι ἔασιν ὑπ' ἠῶ τ' ἠέλιόν τε looks like a close parallel, but is a clumsy (because the idea of 'east'

implicit in dawn is irrelevant) and relatively late adaptation of πρὸς ἠῶ
τ' ἠέλιόν τε (12.239 and *Od.* 13.240).

45 ναιετάουσι, 'are inhabited', as at *Od.* 9.23. ναιετάω is an artificial
form based, no doubt for metrical convenience, on ναίω, 'inhabit' (cf.
λαμπετάω, εὐχετάομαι), which is especially common in the formula εὖ
ναιόμενον πτολίεθρον etc. but is also used intransitively at 2.626. For
intransitive ναιετάω, as here, compare especially 6.370 = 6.497 δόμους εὖ
ναιετάοντας and 2.648 πόλεις εὖ ναιεταούσας, which appear to be developed
after the model of εὖ ναιόμενον πτολίεθρον etc. See Chantraine, *Dict.* s.v.
ναίω; there is little to justify Shipp's feeling (*Studies* 242) that the finite verb
ναιετάουσι, as opposed to the participial form, is an 'innovation' (with the
implication that it is also an 'aberration'), although it may well represent
the final stage of a process of formular development from εὖ ναιόμενον
πτολίεθρον. On the form πόληες see 3.50n.

46 περὶ κῆρι: in the decision whether περί is adverb ('exceedingly') or
preposition, the repetition at 53 must be taken into account: ἀπέχθωνται
περὶ κῆρι (cf. also *Od.* 6.158), in which the placing of the phrase after the
verb might seem to favour taking περί as a preposition, 'around the heart',
i.e. deep in the heart. Most scholars, however, prefer the adverbial
interpretation; Chantraine, *GH* II, 126, is confident that in the Homeric
instances 'περί is adverbial and κῆρι is locative', but goes on to say that
prepositional phrases like περὶ φρένας may have affected the matter.

Aristarchus (Arn/A) noted that Ἴλιος is regularly feminine (hence Ἴλιος
ἱρή (etc.), 20x *Il.*); only at 15.71 does it have a neuter epithet.

47 bT cited 20.306 as contradicting this verse; that belongs to an
unusual passage in which Zeus is claimed to be hostile to Priam and his
family and to favour the descendants of Dardanos (see on 2.819–20), but
here Priam and his people simply represent Troy's inhabitants in general.

48–9 = 24.69f., where it is specifically Hektor who keeps the altar
loaded with offerings (for his piety in this respect see also 22.170–2). The
language of these two verses is carefully chosen: Zeus's *altar* 'never lacked
equal [i.e. fairly divided, generous] feast' – although he himself as a god does
not exactly 'feast on' the offerings there, hence the feast is qualified as λοιβῆς
τε κνίσης τε, that is, libations and the savour of burning fat-encased
thigh-bones: cf. 1.460–3. Finally Zeus stresses that such offerings are the
gods' rightful privilege; it is the principle of the thing rather than the savour
of fat itself that matters to him (see my remarks on the epic tradition's
'progressive de-incarnation of the Olympian gods' in *Entretiens Hardt* XXVII
(Vandoeuvres 1981) 77–80; but also on 34–6 above). There is also some
truth in bT's comment that the addition to τὸ γὰρ λάχομεν... is made 'so
that he should not seem to be exulting over little things'.

51–67 Herē's reply to Zeus has the appearance of being straightforward and spontaneous, beginning with whole-verse statements and moving on to slightly more complex ones. Yet it constitutes a carefully thought-out and quite subtle response to Zeus's offer; its main purpose is to engage him in immediate action, which it does by making four points: (i) you can destroy three cities dear to me, in the future, if they offend you; (ii) in any case I could not prevent you, since you are supreme; (iii) but I too have my rights, so let us two agree and the other gods will follow; (iv) so despatch Athene forthwith to get the fighting restarted.

Some of the cumulative techniques of composition employed in this speech are analysed in chapter 2, pp. 35f., where it is shown that 51–61 'contains almost nothing in the way of decorative progression and runover cumulation; rather the flow of ideas is transmitted in a series of apparent afterthoughts...each of which...arises as a kind of gloss on its predecessor'; and of 62–7 that 'This long sentence is formed by alternating progressive and integral enjambments.'

51–3 Zeus has demanded the right to destroy one city favoured by Here; she offers him three. This has caused confusion among commentators, but can be understood in terms of simple psychology; for example the goddess may be only concerned with the present, and in any case there is no reason for her to suspect that the three cities will ever incur Zeus's rage and enmity – and if they do, as she will say at 55f., then they are doomed anyway. Therefore she might just as well offer all three to keep Zeus in a good humour. That is one possible reading; Willcock (on 50) on the other hand insists that her response shows her 'utter ruthlessness and selfishness', which is less likely as well as too dogmatic, although gods can be indifferent to human suffering. Quite apart from the Judgement of Paris (on which see 31–3n.) as cause of Here's hatred of Troy, her cult was deeply rooted in the Peloponnese, especially at the Argive Heraion midway between Mukenai and Argos, but also at Sparta; Aristarchus (Arn/A on 52) is no doubt right that this by itself would explain her support of the Achaeans, as it also justifies her mention of the three cities as especially dear to her.

Shipp (*Studies* 242) seems to be repeating Leaf's misapprehension that Argos was a Dorian foundation which never co-existed with Mukenai when he calls the mention of Sparta and Argos 'a well-known anachronism' – actually it was continuously inhabited from the Bronze Age on, and even seems to have escaped major damage at the end of LHIIIB (see on 2.559–62). This may tell against the otherwise attractive idea in Leaf and others that Here's concession over the three cities was a hint at the collapse of the Mycenaean empire after the Trojan War.

53 On περὶ κῆρι see 46n.

54 οὐδὲ/οὔ τι μεγαίρω| 2x *Il.*, 2x *Od.*; compare too the general shape of 5.809, παρά θ᾽ ἵσταμαι ἠδὲ φυλάσσω.

Book Four

55–6 Aristarchus (Arn/A) athetized, on the feeble ground that they weaken the favour which Here is anxious to appear to be doing Zeus. Actually she is attempting to ingratiate herself in several different ways, not all consistent with each other.

57 'My labour, too, should not be rendered quite without result', which adapts the wording of her original protest at 26, πῶς ἐθέλεις ἅλιον θεῖναι πόνον ἠδ' ἀτέλεστον;

58–61 She now tries to establish her claim on quasi-legal grounds: (i) she is, after all, a god; (ii) and one of the ruling family of gods (being Zeus's sister); (iii) senior of all goddesses, at that; (iv) both because she is Kronos' eldest daughter and because she is married to Zeus who rules over all of them. She must know that all this amounts to very little; Zeus has ignored her wishes before (e.g. at 1.561–8) and will do so again, beating her up if necessary (1.586–9), just as he can take on all the other gods combined (8.5–27).

60 ἀμφότερον as at 3.179 and 4× *Il.*, 2× *Od.* in addition, including 18.365f. which repeats 6of. here.

62–7 Her tone becomes confidential and ingratiating, then (at ἐπὶ δ' ἕψονται...) positively brisk, with internal punctuation and heavy enjambment; see also the analysis on p. 36.

66 πειρᾶν δ' ὥς κε, 'to try how', i.e. 'try to arrange it that', probably does not entail any real doubt of Athene's ability to succeed, but implies rather that the matter is not entirely straightforward and she will have to make an effort to devise appropriate means.

ὑπερκύδαντας is found only here and in the repetition of this verse at 71; also ὑπερκύδαντα Μενοίτιον at Hesiod, *Theog.* 510. For the form M. L. West on the Hesiod passage compares ἀκάμας, ἀδάμας etc., after Leaf; more to the point may be the Attic deme-name Κυδαντίδαι cited originally by Wackernagel (see Chantraine, *Dict.* s.v. κῦδος). The form was evidently discussed at length by Herodian, cf. Choeroboscus in A (Erbse I, 457f.); it has the appearance of an artificial creation, nevertheless, and is unusual in that it replaces the standard and extremely frequent epithet for the Achaeans in the nominative and accusative, beginning with a vowel, namely ἐϋκνήμιδες -ας. Such departures from oral economy are of course extremely rare; is there perhaps a special need for a word meaning 'arrogant' here? bT claim that the Achaeans were arrogant in hailing Menelaos' victory in the duel, but that is untrue; their response was the normal heroic one. Admittedly their description as 'well-greaved' at this point would be somewhat irrelevant, but formular epithets often are. Perhaps the use of the term can be justified as part of Here's continuing and subtle persuasion of Zeus – she is deliberately disguising her favouring of the Achaeans, and suggesting that breaking the truce would be no more than they deserve.

Rhapsodic 'improvement' remains a possibility, even perhaps after the model of Hesiod's more certainly relevant application of the epithet to Menoitios.

67 The formular language for truce-breaking recalls Agamemnon's alliterative words at 3.299, ὁππότεροι πρότεροι ὑπὲρ ὅρκια πημήνειαν.

68–72 Zeus agrees and at 70–2 gives concise instructions to Athene, using Here's exact words where possible, i.e. by adjusting 65 and repeating 66f.

73 πάρος μεμαυῖαν 'Αθήνην: so too at 19.349, 22.186 and *Od.* 24.487, all when Zeus sends the goddess to do something she (or Here) has urged on him. This is a specially-devised noun-epithet group, but does not (like ὑπερκύδαντας, see on 65) replace any regular one for Athene in the accusative at least, since she only appears as direct object in one other Iliadic passage apart from these three similar ones (but 8x *Od.*, where she is μεγάθυμον 2x, γλαυκῶπιν 1x).

74 Occurs 5× *Il.*, 2× *Od.*; first at 2.167, cf. 1.44 and see 7.19n.

75–8 She descends like a bright 'star' trailing sparks, the kind that is thought to be sent by Zeus as a portent, whether to sailors at sea or to an army on land (the former see such phenomena on night watch, the latter are alert to portents of any kind). Is this a comet (in space) or a meteor (in the atmosphere)? Probably the poet combines elements of both. Comets are scarce but spectacular (Halley's comet, for example, made a deep impression before the Battle of Hastings and is portrayed on the Bayeux Tapestry); large meteors or 'fireballs' can also appear to have a tail, but are rarely observed to strike the ground; most meteors burn up in a fraction of a second once they have entered the atmosphere. For the actual point of comparison between goddess and 'star' see the next note.

This is one of ten Iliadic similes concerning stars and the like, the brightness of which is also noted at 5.6 (λαμπρόν) and 22.27 (ἀρίζηλοι...αὐγαί); but here the sparks discharged are a unique detail deserving special description.

78–84 'Resembling that did Pallas Athene rush toward the earth and leap into the midst (of them)': that does not of itself mean that she still had the appearance of the 'star' as she did so. The description of the amazement provoked among the onlookers (79) admittedly follows immediately on her 'leaping into the midst', but ἔχεν is imperfect and does not necessarily suggest anything very sudden. AbT thought the amazement to be at the goddess's energy and force, and b (on 75–9) had already commented that she descended to earth while they were pondering the portent. That is probably correct, and avoids the improbability of a meteor still trailing a tail as it strikes the earth. By 86 Athene has adopted the appearance of the Trojan Laodokos as she moves across to the Trojan side. The whole passage conflates several different ideas and impressions: the rapidity of Athene's descent through the air, its unusual nature, the appearance of a comet or large meteor apparently trailing fire, its naturally being taken as a portent, the sense of these Achaeans and Trojans that something portentous has occurred. Divine epiphanies, Athene's in particular, often give rise to similar doubts about whether she was actually seen as that to which she has been compared in a simile – a bird, for instance – or not; see S. West on *Od.* 1.320, with references, and in particular *Il.* 17.547–52, where Athene takes on much of the appearance of a rainbow (similarly a portent) as she moves among the Achaeans.

In any event the onlookers are conscious of a portent not dissimilar from that described at 76 itself, although they cannot tell whether war or peace (that is, the φιλότης envisaged in the terms of the truce, e.g. at 3.323) is indicated.

84 = 19.224, which shows that the verse does not simply refer to Zeus as ὅρκιος and thus guarantor of the issue of peace or war in this particular case.

85–219 Persuaded by Athene, Pandaros shoots at Menelaos and wounds him superficially. Agamemnon is enraged at the breaking of the truce and fearful for his brother, but Menelaos reassures him and Makhaon is summoned to dress the wound

85 A resumptive adaptation of 81; for the comment by undefined bystanders see on 2.271.

87 This Laodokos, a son of Antenor, is not mentioned elsewhere. The rising threefolder, a rarity in this Book so far, is forced by the heavy patronymic. See also on 3.122–4.

88 εἴ που: see on 1.207, 2.72, also 66n. *init.* Zenodotus (Arn/A) rewrote the verse to get rid of the construction, which he thought inappropriate for a god; and Aristarchus defended it on the wrong grounds, i.e. that Athene is disguised as a mortal and therefore subject to human contingency.

89 The marked asyndeton is not unusual with εὗρε (etc.), cf. 2.169, 4.327 and 4× elsewhere in the *Iliad*; see further on 5.168–9. The verse is rhythmically inelegant, perhaps deliberately so, with its bouncing first half (caused by trochaic breaks in conjunction with the break after the second foot) made more prominent by the continuously flowing second half.

90–1 The runover-word in each case adds little in meaning or decoration, but serves to generate further information in the rest of the verse. On the river Aisepos see on 2.824 and 825; in short, Pandaros (cf. 2.826–7n.) comes from Zeleia in the Aisepos valley some 70 miles ENE of Troy. At 5.105 and 173 he is said to come from Lukie; that can hardly be the same as the land around the river Xanthos in south-west Asia Minor, home of Sarpedon and Glaukos, and must be a local name. The Trojan catalogue, at least, is clear on this, since his troops are described at 2.826 as Τρῶες; but see also on 101.

His men are ἀσπιστάων, 'shield-bearers', which might at first sight seem incompatible with his own role as an archer. But the Achaean archer Teukros often needs the protection of Aias' shield (σάκος not ἀσπίς); Pandaros too is an isolated figure as bowman, and at 5.192–205 will regret having left his chariot at home. His contingent is not light-armed like the Locrians.

93–103 Athene's speech is full of optatives, giving it a persuasive and ingratiating tone – perhaps as befits Laodokos, a less conspicuous warrior than Pandaros. She says nothing about breaking the truce, and Pandaros will ignore that aspect of the matter.

93 μοί...πίθοιο, 'may you obey me', cf. *Od.* 4.193.

94–5 τλαίης κεν and κε...ἄροιο are apodoses after the virtual protasis in 93: 'may you obey me; ⟨if you were to,⟩ then you would endure to...'

99 Most of the Iliadic references to pyres are specific ones, especially to Patroklos' in book 23. The only other general use, where 'going on the pyre' or 'sending on to the pyre' is a circumlocution for being killed or killing, is in the Meleagros tale at 9.546, πυρῆς ἐπέβησ᾽ ἀλεγεινῆς, which suggests the existence of a formular system that happens to be lightly represented in the *Iliad*.

101 Apollo is Λυκηγενής only here and in the near-repetition of this verse at 119. The epithet may be related to his common title Λύκειος, the meaning of which is much debated and still quite uncertain (connexion with 'light' is now generally rejected, but 'wolf', λύκος, and Λυκίη in some geographical sense are still mooted). Or it may refer to the particular Λυκίη near the Troad with which Pandaros is associated in book 5, see on 90–1 above; Pandaros' father's name Λυκάων (shared by Priam's son killed by Akhilleus at 21.34ff.) might have the same connexion, although the people called Λυκάονες came from south-west Asia Minor: see von Kamptz, *Personennamen* 327 for further references. The mythical king Lukaon and Mt Lukaion in Arcadia had wolf-elements, but Apollo, whose origins are West Asiatic (more probably than northern, cf. the Hyperboreans) has little claim to anything similar. M. P. Nilsson, *GgrR* 505f., dismissed his hostility to wolves in his role as herdsman-god as literary and relatively late, and on p. 530 summarized the objections to Wilamowitz' view that he was specifically connected with Sarpedon's Lycia.

102–3 Verse 102 recurs (as well as in its repetition at 120) twice in the archery contest in the funeral games for Patroklos, at 23.864 and 873; that improbable episode is highly likely to be a rhapsodic expansion, but this does not impugn the present context. Hecatombs are 'famous' 7x *Il.* in all;

sometimes they are 'holy', but this epithet is reserved here for Zeleia, cf. Thebe as ἱερὴν πόλιν 'Ηετίωνος at 1.366, also 378n. For ἄστυ with the town-name cf. ἄστυ μέγα Πριάμοιο (8x *Il.*), as well as 14.281.

104 He is ἄφρονι, presumably, because he does not think about the truce and the consequences of breaking it. The alliteration of φ's (and the π of πεῖθεν) should be remarked.

105 'Without delay he stripped the polished bow made from a full-grown goat': συλάω most often means to strip armour from a dead enemy, but here and at 116 (of the lid of a quiver) it evidently means stripping off a protective cover or casing to make a weapon accessible; H. L. Lorimer, *HM* 292, thought that 'he "detached the bow"', which was carried strapped to the quiver', but that is uncertain. As for ἰξάλου, here translated 'full-grown' *exempli gratia*, it is an unknown word for which bT suggested various meanings, of which T's ὄνομα ἡλικίας is the only plausible one, cf. D's ἤτοι τελείου ἢ πηδητικοῦ, 'full-grown or bounding'; this last is also possible, but in Hellenistic epigrams, where the term is occasionally imitated, Gow and Page (*The Greek Anthology* 1, vol. 11 (Cambridge 1965) 342) find the former to be the more generally appropriate sense for what that is worth. At least the word contributes to the continuing alliteration, here of ξ-sounds followed by the γ's of αἰγός and 106 ἀγρίου.

106–7 It is a wild goat shot in the chest by Pandaros himself as it emerged from rock or cliff; ἐν προδοκῆσι, in a place of ambush, is connected with δέχομαι and therefore repeats the idea of δεδεγμένος.

108 Aristarchus (Arn/A) observed that it must have been driven on to its back by the force of the blow (perhaps also because it leaps into the air from the shock). It fell back into the rock, perhaps a rock cleft; ἔμπεσε balances ἐκβαίνοντα in 107, but the picture is not entirely clear.

109 δῶρον can mean a unit of measurement, the palm or width of four fingers; Hesiod, *Erga* 426, mentions a ten-palm cart. The goat's horns measured about four feet; that must mean the total span, which is just possible.

110 'Homer's account of (Pandaros') bow...has a specious appearance of detailed precision which does not survive examination' (Lorimer, *HM* 290). The description suggests at first hearing that the 'horn-polishing craftsman' simply joined, ἤραρε, the entire horns together, presumably with a wooden handle or bridge; but that would provide almost no flexibility and is entirely out of the question. Commentators have therefore rightly accepted Reichel's view that Pandaros' bow must have been of 'composite' type: that is, made out of wooden staves reinforced by inset strips of horn (keratin) on the inner side and sinew on the outer side, all bound together; see Lorimer, *HM* 290f. and F. H. Stubbings in Wace and Stubbings, *Companion* 519. Such a bow is strung by bending it backwards, i.e. into a reflex shape. These composite bows are Asiatic in type and origin (as opposed to the longer but less powerful single-stave European type); the *Scythian* bow is a double-curve or Cupid's bow version of this Asiatic type and could only be strung in a crouching position, by placing one end of the bow under one thigh, and the other over the other knee. It is important to note (see on 112–13) that Pandaros' bow is not of this special Scythian kind; nor, incidentally, is Odysseus' famous bow in *Odyssey* book 21, since at 128 Telemakhos could have strung it while standing.

111 The 'smoothing' of the horns, λειήνας, now takes on extra significance; it is not the whole horns but the long strips of their outer casing (the longer the better, hence perhaps the emphasis on the length of the horns themselves) that have to be carefully cut and polished before insertion into the groove in the wooden stave. The κορώνη is the curved hook round which the loop of the bow-string had to be fitted at one end of the bow; often, no doubt, there would be a hook at the other end too, but the string could be attached there (when there was no tension on it) in various other ways. That the hook should be gold-plated is not impossible, but is probably poetic exaggeration.

112–13 εὖ κατέθηκε...ποτὶ γαίῃ: literally 'placed it down well... against the ground'; he does so in order to string it, stretching it (τανυσσά-μενος) and bending it into a reflex shape (ἀγκλίνας). Meanwhile his companions shelter him with their shields, much as Aias did with Teukros (e.g. at 8.267).

117 The arrow is 'winged', probably swift rather than literally 'feathered', and never used before. ἕρμ' is puzzling, and, together with an unfounded objection to ἀβλῆτα, caused Aristarchus (Arn/A) to athetize the verse; elsewhere in Homer it means (apart from 'ear-pendant', from εἴρω, 2x) 'prop', either literally of ship-supports or metaphorically as a support or bulwark, as for instance Hektor is of Troy. None of these clearly suits the present passage; attempts to explain it either as connected with ὁρμή, i.e. as 'origin', or with later ἕρμα = ballast are unconvincing. Perhaps after all, and as bT suggest, the metaphorical 'support' idea is least objectionable. The phrase is a special application in any case; μελαινάων ὀδυνάων| occurs 2x *Il.* and was probably the model; μελαινάων is in fact the vulgate reading, but as Aristarchus noted (Did/A), μελαινέων is necessary for the metre, the -έων form with synizesis being a common Ionian form in Homer, cf. Chantraine, *GH* I, 69 and 201.

118 κατεκόσμει, he 'arranged' it onto the string; the unusual verb continues to emphasise the care Pandaros is giving to the crucial shot.

119–21 = 101–3, with the necessary adjustment of εὔχεο to εὔχετο.

122 The γλυφίδας are probably notches or nocks in the butt of the arrow-shaft, into one of which the string is fitted; there are presumably two of them in an X pattern to make fitting easier (they would not necessarily cause splitting as has been objected). This interpretation is preferable to taking them as transverse notches further down the shaft, as finger-grips, as urged e.g. by Lorimer, *HM* 293f.

123–4 He draws string and arrow-butt back to his chest; this is the Cretan draw as opposed to the Scythian one to the shoulder, as bT observe (but to the left breast, T!). That would not suffice to bend the bow into a half-circle or anything like it, but then κυκλοτερές need only imply 'in a curve'.

That the arrow-head is of iron not bronze has caused much discussion; it is surely nothing to do with this bow as an Asian weapon, or Pandaros as particularly Asian, as Lorimer 294 thought. Homeric arrows were otherwise tipped with bronze on the rare occasions when the metal was specified (especially χαλκήρε' ὀϊστόν, 2x *Il.*, also χαλκοβαρής); but occasionally iron replaces bronze as the standard metal for these singers, as of the axes in the trial of the bow in the *Odyssey* and of the knife with which Akhilleus might damage himself at 18.34, μὴ λαιμὸν ἀπαμήσειε σιδήρῳ. Iron cutting-implements are admittedly commoner than iron arrow- and spear-heads in the early centuries of the Iron Age, but even the latter are occasionally found. As often, metrical reasons may play some part.

125 λίγξε, only here in surviving Greek, 'made a shrill sound'; an onomatopoeic word probably connected with λιγύς, 'clear' or 'shrill'. The verse is an expressive one, with the idea of the twanging noise further developed in the string's 'loud cry', μέγ' ἴαχεν.

126 The singers of the heroic oral ·tradition liked giving inanimate objects, especially missiles, human desires and aims; compare λιλαιόμενα -η χροὸς ἆσαι, of spears, 3x *Il.*, also the 'shameless stone' of 521 (see comment there).

127 The apostrophe, or direct address by the singer to one of his characters, is an emphatic and pathetic device applied to Menelaos five times elsewhere (at 146, 7.104, 13.603, 17.679, 23.600), but most powerfully in addressing Patroklos before his death in book 16 (no less than eight times, at 20, 584, 693, 744, 754, 787, 812, 843). There, something of a formular system was developed: |Πατρόκλεις, |‒ ∪ ∪ ‒ Πάτροκλε, Πατρόκλεες ἱππο-κέλευθε|, Πατρόκλεες ἱππεῦ|. Menelaos is always addressed in apostrophe in the first half of the verse as here, |‒ ∪ ∪ ‒ Μενέλαε; some names were evidently felt to be more suitable for this kind of treatment than others, since Hektor is not so addressed before his death in book 22, although the pathetic tone is generally no less strong there than in book 16.

128 πρώτη: *ad sensum*, 'first not to forget you was Zeus's daughter'. ἀγελείη is an epithet of Athene (only) 6x *Il.*, 3x *Od.*, the latter including the same formula as here, Διὸς θυγάτηρ ἀγελείη (2x). It is either from ἄγω and ληΐη, 'bringing booty', in her role of war-goddess (for which see e.g. 2.446–52), which derives support from 10.460 Ἀθηναίη ληΐτιδι and is followed by Chantraine, *Dict.* s.v. λεία; or from ἄγω and λαός, 'leader of the host', cf. the name Agelaos and her epithet ἀγέστρατον at Hesiod, *Theog.* 925. M. L. West on *Theog.* 318 argues for the latter, 'from *ἀγελήης by dissimilation', and cites F. Bechtel's point (*Lexilogus zu Homer* (Halle 1914) 6) that for the λεία meaning one would expect *ἀγελήίη (which is metrically different).

129 βέλος ἐχεπευκές: see on 1.51.

130–1 The goddess brushes the arrow to one side as a mother does a fly from her sleeping child. There are three other fly-similes in the poem, two of flies around milk-pails but one not dissimilar to the present one, when at 17.571 a fly persists even though brushed aside, καὶ ἐργομένη. There it is courage, here it is the ease of the goddess's movement that is primarily in question, but the pathos of 125, also, is reflected in the child and its sweet, ἡδέϊ, sleep; for tender mother-and-child images see also 8.271, 16.7–10. Leaf was correct in saying that τόσον means 'just so much' (cf. 22.322 and 23.454), and therefore that ὡς ὅτε does not depart from an expected correlation with ὅσον.

132–40 The course of the arrow: Athene's action directs it onto the clasps of the ζωστήρ, where the corslet is double. It penetrated these, then too the μίτρη, which resisted it most of all – but nevertheless reached the skin and just grazed it. The passage is lightly enjambed, mainly consisting of whole-verse sentences; its drama comes from the detail of the arrow's course through one defence after another, with a kind of inevitability which in the end is partly frustrated.

132–3 Neither the ζωστήρ (belt or girdle) nor the μίτρη in 137 (see comment on 137–8) are well understood, but probably the former protects the upper abdomen, the latter the lower; cf. H. Brandenburg, *Arch. Hom.* E 119–22. Verses 132 (from ὅθι) and 133 recur at 20.414f., where Akhilleus' spear strikes Poludoros in the back – presumably a misunderstanding by the poet there, since the clasps of the ζωστήρ must in any case be in front. Why the corslet is double here is again uncertain; if it is a leather one, for example (see the following comment), it might overlap like a jacket.

135–6 The girdle itself, not simply the pair of golden clasps of 132f., is implied to be metallic by δαιδαλέοιο, see also on 186–7. So too is the corslet, unless πολυδαιδάλου could refer to applied metal disks or the like such as are suggested by one, but only one, of the corslets on the Late Mycenaean (LHIIIC) Warrior Vase (illustrated in e.g. Lorimer, *HM* pl. iii, 1b; Wace and Stubbings, *Companion*, Pl. 29 (a)). θώρηκες still present problems; the archaeological record (on which see H. W. Catling in *Arch. Hom.* E 74–118) suggests that metal ones of different kinds, mainly plate-corslets, were used in the Late Bronze Age, but that in the Early Iron age, and until the development of hoplite armour from the late eighth century B.C. on, they were non-metallic and of leather or the like – resembling, indeed, most of those on the Warrior Vase. If Homeric ones were usually so envisaged, that would help to explain why they were standard items in the arming-scenes (on which see 3.330–8n.) but could be ignored when wounds and the exact paths of spears were described.

On the lengthening of |διά see 155n. Specific objection has been taken to 136, a verse which recurs at 3.358, 7.252 and 11.436. To the first two of these it is objected that there could be no swerve after the spear had pierced the corslet (on which see the last paragraph of 3.355–60n.), and to the present use that the corslet is ignored when the wound is exposed by Makhaon at 215f. (so for example Fenik, *Typical Battle Scenes* 102). Only 11.436, in the wounding of Odysseus, is free from all these criticisms, and Fenik surmises that it is a basic item which is compounded almost unconsciously with other and sometimes inconsistent details of armour or a wound.

137–8 Apart from this Book, the μίτρη is mentioned at 5.857 where Ares is wounded νείατον ἐς κενεῶνα, ὅθι ζωννύσκετο μίτρῃ, which reinforces the connexion with ζωστήρ at 134f., and in the epithets αἰολομίτρην (5.707) and ἀμιτροχίτωνας (16.419). At 187 both it and the ζῶμα (separate from the ζωστήρ of 186) are made by bronze-smiths, which confirms the implication of αἰολομίτρης. The μίτρη may therefore resemble the roughly semi-circular bronze aprons of the early seventh century B.C. found in Crete and at Olympia (H. Brandenburg in *Arch. Hom.* E 135–42), designed to hang down from a belt and protect the lower belly. Such an item of defensive equipment would be under development in Homer's time, as bronze defensive armour became more elaborate; its lack of formular status and its absence from the arming-scenes confirm that it was a relatively late addition to the language of the oral heroic tradition.

140 Aristarchus (Arn/A) athetized this and 149 on the ground that ὠτειλή, etymology unknown, means a wound made by a thrust and not by a missile. His grounds for this dogma are uncertain, beyond a slight resemblance to οὐτάσαι; probably the term in post-Homeric Greek applied particularly to large open wounds, and that might have something to do with it, although such a specialized sense in the early poetical tradition seems unlikely. This verse and 149 are admittedly inorganic, but it is clear that most critics did not share Aristarchus' objections.

141–7 Menelaos' thighs and legs become stained with blood as an ivory cheek-piece for a horse is stained with purple by an Asiatic craftswoman: one of the most striking and unusual of Iliadic similes. The bare facts of the comparison are briefly stated in the first two verses, then the next three expand on the desirability of the finished royal possession. This is partly development of the simile-situation for its own sake, but partly, too, it reflects on the subject of the comparison, here by implying the unique value of Menelaos to the Achaeans – for C. Moulton, *Similes* 93 n. 14, is surely wrong in claiming that 'association with women and children...begins to complicate our conception of Menelaus'. For the cumulative composition of the simile see p. 35.

141–2 141 can be heard either as four-colon or as a rising threefolder, more intelligibly and forcefully as the latter.

μιαίνω meaning 'stain' in a purely technical sense is a virtually unparalleled use of a word of which the basic meaning is 'the impairment of a thing's form or integrity' (Parker, *Miasma* 3); it must surely be determined by 'stained with blood' in the resumption at 146.

Ivory is mentioned only twice in the *Iliad* (here and at 5.583), both times of horse-trappings, but eight times, and with a greater range of applications, in the *Odyssey*. Many elaborately carved ivory objects, especially decorative appliqué pieces, have been found in Mycenaean graves and occasionally in Early Iron Age ones; many were West Asiatic in inspiration or workmanship, being imported from Syria and Phoenicia in particular; Lorimer, *HM* 508, draws attention to ivory horse-trappings from Nimrod, also. Nothing is specifically known of Carian or Maeonian work, although these regions (on which see also on 2.864–6 and 867–9) bordered on one with which Homer was probably familiar, roughly from Smurne to Miletos. The singling out of the craftswoman and the dyeing operation may suggest personal observation. Moulton, *Similes* 91 n. 8, notes other Homeric technical similes; 18.600f. (potter) and *Od.* 6.232ff. = 23.159ff. (inlayer of gold and silver) are closest in this respect.

The plural ἵππων has caused surprise, since the ornament is naturally only for one horse (ἵππῳ in 145); but the plural is generic, 'equine cheek-piece'.

143–5 An elaborate and carefully enjambed sentence, predominantly paratactic for aesthetic and pathetic effect rather than through syntactical *naïveté*: the cheek-piece lies in a store-room (cf. 6.288), many horsemen have coveted it but it lies there to delight a king, to adorn his horse and bring glory to its owner.

144 ἄγαλμα: only here *Il.*, 7× *Od.*; from ἀγάλλομαι, 'delight in', it probably has its literal sense here.

145 Another rising threefolder. Leaf noted that ἐλατήρ in Homer is elsewhere applied only to the driver in a chariot-race, as appropriate to 'an ornament which would be used for purposes of display rather than of warfare'. Armour for horses is of course unknown in Homer.

146 Another apostrophe, cf. 127n.; on μιάνθην see on 141–2 *init.*; the resumptive word τοῖοι departs from the introductory ὡς ὅτε formula of 141, as not infrequently.

147 His well-formed thighs and beautiful ankles reinforce the high valuation of Menelaos and the outrage of defiling him.

148–54 The reactions of Agamemnon, then Menelaos, then Agamemnon again are concisely given in alternating and balanced verses: ῥίγησεν δ'...ὡς εἶδεν...ῥίγησεν δὲ...ὡς δὲ ἴδεν. The wound's superficial nature is quickly discerned by Menelaos, but Agamemnon does not yet know this.

149 See on 140; the matching of ὡς εἶδεν here with ὡς δὲ ἴδεν in 151 is further support, if any is needed, for accepting the verse as genuine, against Aristarchus (Arn/A).

151 The νεῦρον is not of course the bow-string (usually νευρή, feminine, but plural νεῦρα at 122 and 16.316), but must be a binding to help fix the arrow-head to the shaft. It and the barbs remain 'outside', i.e. visibly embedded in the μίτρη etc.

152–4 His θυμός had temporarily left his chest, it seems, and he was breathless with shock; compare 22.475, ἣ δ' ἐπεὶ οὖν ἔμπνυτο καὶ ἐς φρένα θυμὸς ἀγέρθη, where Andromakhe recovers from an actual faint. Now the breath-soul is 'gathered back again in his chest'.

155–82 Agamemnon's address to his brother is divided into two contrasting portions. In the first, down to 170, he heaps reproaches on himself for having permitted Menelaos to be (possibly) killed, and affirms his conviction that Zeus will avenge it; in the second, from 171, he deplores the disgrace this death would bring on himself through the failure of the expedition and the boasting of the Trojans. The most stirring and dignified part is his passionate statement of belief in the inevitable vindication of the oath; his subsequent descent into self-pity is vivid and imaginative in its way, typical of Agamemnon but also of the heroic character in adversity.

155 θάνατόν νύ τοι ὅρκια τάμνον, a powerful adaptation of the language of oaths (on which see on 3.73–5): 'the oaths I "cut" were death to you'. The metrical lengthening of φίλε recurs twice in the poem in the same address-formula |φίλε κασίγνητε (in which the lengthened second -ε before masculine caesura can also be paralleled); that treatment of a short opening syllable in a so-called στίχος ἀκέφαλος is a special licence (on which see also 3.355–60n.), perhaps reflecting an emphatic musical accompaniment and giving additional emphasis in itself, cf. e.g. |δία at 135 (+ 3× *Il.*).

156 If bT are right that προστήσας is metaphorical and implies 'put you forward *as a sacrifice*', μεταφορικῶς ἀπὸ τῶν θυμάτων ἅπερ προΐστῶσι τῶν βωμῶν, that greatly strengthens Agamemnon's point; but no good parallel is known for such a use.

158–9 The oath itself, the blood of the sacrificial lambs and the libations were not in vain: these are the main ritual acts which sealed the compact. The libations were described at 3.295f.; on their being 'unmixed' see on 3.269–70 *init.* As for δεξιαί, they are usually taken as 'trustworthy right hands', metaphorical perhaps since no handshakes were mentioned in book

3 (or indeed at Aulis – for 159 = 2.341). bT took δεξιαί as an epithet of the libations, but 'unmixed and favourable' would be an odd connexion, and there are other difficulties too.

160–2 A solemn and moving profession of faith, proverbial in tone and language (with the gnomic or generalizing τε in protasis and apodosis (εἴ περ γάρ τε...ἔκ τε) as well as the gnomic aorist ἀπέτεισαν, which by themselves disqualify Zenodotus' attempt, Arn/A, to make the text apply to the Trojans specifically). The solemnity is increased by the accurate accretion of particles and conjunctions: εἴ περ γάρ τε καὶ αὐτίκ'... ('for even if, indeed, he has not immediately...') and ἔκ τε καὶ ὀψὲ τελεῖ ('he will fulfil them completely, even if late...'). τελεῖ is future rather than present, a relatively recent (i.e. Homeric or shortly before) contraction in either case.

They will pay, when they do, σὺν...μεγάλῳ, 'together with a great (price)' – or great evil according to bT: their own heads (i.e. lives) and their wives and children. What this might entail was described in the curse on breakers of the oath at 3.300f., 'may their brains flow on the ground like this wine, theirs and their children's, and may their wives be subjected to other men', on which see on 3.297–301. This is the first general statement in Greek literature of the powerful dogma that Zeus always exacts vengeance in the end, and that it may spread into the transgressor's family. Agamemnon stops just short of saying that a man might die unpunished himself, but that then his descendants will suffer, a refinement developed in Solon and Aeschylus – see also Hesiod, *Erga* 282–5, Parker, *Miasma* 201 and H. Lloyd-Jones, *The Justice of Zeus*[2] (Berkeley 1983) 7f., 37, 44.

163–5 Agamemnon follows his theological pronouncement with an equally serious but more specific prophecy about the fate of Troy.

163 οἶδα as opening tends in any event to introduce a very personal declaration; εὖ...οἶδα is still more emphatic, cf. 19.421 as well as the recurrence of this verse and its two successors at 6.447–9, movingly spoken by Hektor to Andromakhe. The addition of the formula κατὰ φρένα καὶ κατὰ θυμόν (on which see 1.193–4n.) increases the sense of passionate conviction.

164 ἔσσεται ἦμαρ: the passionate and prophetic tone continues. ἦμαρ tends to be sinister in its Homeric uses, and to be qualified as νηλεές, αἴσιμον, μόρσιμον, δούλιον, ὀλέθριον or simply κακόν; for the idiom with ἔσσεται compare Akhilleus' melancholy foreknowledge of his own death at 21.111, ἔσσεται ἢ ἠὼς ἢ δείλη ἢ μέσον ἦμαρ, again with ἦμαρ.

'Holy' Ilios seems pathetic here, although it is standard with Ilios at the verse-end, cf. 46n. *fin.*

166–8 The poet, through Agamemnon, broadens the vision of Troy's destiny by imagining Zeus shaking his aegis over all its inhabitants in anger at the deceit. The god is described in the grandest terms; compare

Agamemnon's prayer to him at 2.412 (and see on 2.427–8). For the αἰγίς see on 2.446–51; only here is it ἐρεμνήν, dark, no doubt to mark it as especially sinister and portentous. Agamemnon ends this section of his speech by reverting to the idea of fulfilment, as well as to ἔσσεται (which through 164 has temporarily acquired serious overtones), in almost punning language: τὰ μὲν ἔσσεται οὐκ ἀτέλεστα (cf. Here's different application of ἀτέλεστον| at 26 and 57).

169 Now he turns directly to the possibility of Menelaos' death, which would cause him terrible grief, αἰνὸν ἄχος (8x *Il.*, 1x *Od.* in this position in the verse).

170 πότμον ἀναπλήσαντες is straightforward enough at 11.263, as is κακὸν οἶτον ἀναπλήσαντες 3x in book 8; the addition here of βιότοιο ('the fate of life') is undoubtedly awkward, which is perhaps why the ancient vulgate had μοῖραν, 'portion', in place of πότμον. The latter was read, however, by Aristarchus (Did/A) and is generally accepted in modern texts; it may well be correct in view of 11.263, but still represents a curiously loose expansion in such a carefully composed passage as this.

171–5 Agamemnon's grief often turns quickly to self-pity, as here. It was natural for a Homeric hero to consider any new development in the light of its effect on his own honour, but Akhilleus at 18.79ff., for example, although concerned at the loss of his armour, is genuinely and deeply affected by Patroklos' death.

These are the considerations that occur to Agamemnon in paratactic sequence: 'I shall be an object of reproach at home – for the Achaeans will quickly want to return there – and we should be leaving Helen behind for the Trojans to boast over – and *your* bones will rot in the soil of Troy, and the whole undertaking be brought to nothing.'

171 As Aristarchus evidently thought (Arn/A), Argos here does not mean the city (which belonged to Diomedes) but the Peloponnese, rather. It might refer to the country in general, but something more local to Agamemnon is more pointed; also 'thirsty' Argos (the epithet occurs only here) suits the Peloponnese in particular, since there were various myths, like that of Herakles and the Lernaean Hudra, to explain how it became better irrigated.

173 This verse first occurred (together with Ἀργείην Ἑλένην in 174) at 2.160f.

174 'The land will rot your bones' implies simple inhumation, without the special treatment that would normally be accorded a great hero who had to be left behind, as Patroklos was to be. Funerary terminology in the epic tradition tends to be loosely used; here the most undignified possible description is chosen, but see 177 and comment.

176 The normal epithet for Τρώων at the verse-end is ἀγερώχων (5x

Il.); the singers evidently did not often need to fill the whole of the second half of the verse with a name–epithet group for Trojans in the genitive, so that ὑπερηνορεόντων here may be specially chosen for the arrogance they would show at Menelaos' death. κυδαλίμοιο of Menelaos in the next verse, on the other hand, is regular (7x *Il.*).

177 Leaping on an enemy's tomb must have been intensely satisfying in itself, as well as annoying to the other side. Elaborate tombs invited such treatment, and one wonders that the Achaeans consented to leave any part of Patroklos, for example, behind – presumably it was out of confidence that they would win in the end. Here the picture in 174f. of Menelaos' bones rotting is implicitly amended; presumably they would be treated like those of Patroklos or Hektor, that is, collected after the corpse was cremated, then carefully encased in fat and placed in a golden jar in the case of the former (23.243f.), or wrapped in purple cloths and placed in a golden coffin in the case of the latter (24.795f.). In each case the purpose was no doubt to preserve the bones more or less indefinitely, *contra* 174.

178–81 The Trojan speech of triumph that Agamemnon imagines is quite restrained in the circumstances, and (naturally enough since it is devised by Agamemnon himself) contains no real personal abuse or detailed criticism of his leadership. It focuses entirely on the ineffectiveness of his anger and the failure of the expedition to achieve its ends; that insult to his royal τιμή is what he really fears, and would make him wish to sink into the earth (182).

181 The ships are empty, κεινῇσιν, not only of booty but also (cf. 173f.) of Helen.

182 Diomedes likewise says τότε μοι χάνοι εὐρεῖα χθών at 8.150 (and the last two words are a formula occurring 4x *Il.* in all).

184–7 Menelaos reassures him with a reply which, after a concise and comforting initial imperative, consists of a rhythmically varied and strongly enjambed 3-verse sentence. Verse 185 is unusual in its colon-structure: the main caesura, separating ὀξύ from ...βέλος, can hardly be strongly felt, but the sentence-break at the bucolic caesura forbids taking the verse as a rising threefolder. The 4-colon 186 and essentially 2-colon 187 restore the rhythmical balance.

185 πάροιθεν could be either local ('in front of the skin') or temporal ('before it reached there').

186–7 Menelaos' description does not completely accord with the arrow's course at 135–8; it omits the corslet and adds the mysterious ζῶμα (on which see H. Brandenburg, *Arch. Hom.* ε 121–3). It is implied that ζωστήρ and μίτρη are both of bronze, which suggests if anything that the ζῶμα was non-metallic. Aristarchus (Arn/A) speculated that it was joined to the corslet, but it may have been a thick belt to which the μίτρη was attached. Both verses recur (with minor adjustment) at 215f.

Book Four

189–91 Agamemnon's reply is equally practical, his expression of relief being confined to a simple 'may it be so' before he turns to the matter of medical aid, which is to be the subject of the next 30 verses. This is perhaps surprising, considering that Menelaos' wound is superficial and he has not even complained of the 'black pains' surmised in 191. The poet must have felt that the diversion increased the dramatic force of Menelaos' wounding; medical attention was a topic not without its own interest, although once Makhaon himself is wounded in book 11 it is virtually ignored.

189 φίλος as a vocative is found also at 9.601, 21.106 and 3x in book 23, but only here with a proper name in the normal vocative form.

190 The doctors will 'lay hands on' the wound (from ἐπιμαίομαι, which can also have a metaphorical sense, 'strive for') as well as applying soothing ointments (for φάρμακα are medicaments in general).

192 A herald is not described as θεῖος elsewhere (but it is a common epithet in the genitive for e.g. Odysseus or Akhilleus, and heralds are 'messengers of Zeus', Διὸς ἄγγελοι, at 1.334 and 7.274, as well as being 'dear to Zeus' at 8.517). On Talthubios see on 1.320; he has already been used as a messenger by Agamemnon at 3.118.

193–4 Makhaon and his brother Podaleirios were the leaders of the contingent from around Trikke in Thessaly at 2.729–32 (see 2.731–2n.), where they are described as the two sons of Asklepios and as good doctors, ἰητῆρ' ἀγαθώ, much as their father is ἀμύμονος ἰητῆρος here. Makhaon is much the more important for Homer, in fact Podaleirios is only mentioned once again, in the fighting at 11.833. Both names are usually taken as Greek, Makhaon from μάχη and his brother as 'lily-footed', which seems improbable to say the least; their father's name is unintelligible (see von Kamptz, *Personennamen* 216, 242, 369f.). Both the sons are associated with Asklepios in cult, and Homer's neglect of Podaleirios (which is not, after all, due to any metrical intractability) is surprising; conceivably bT on 193 were on the right track, that Makhaon was the surgeon, Podaleirios the physician.

195–7 Aristarchus (Arn/A) athetized these verses here, wrongly, on the grounds that they reappear at 205–7 (and that 195 is unnecessary here since Talthubios can see why Makhaon is needed).

195 An interesting use of ἰδεῖν; when he 'sees' Menelaos (and his wound, cf. 217), he will sum up the situation and treat him accordingly. The English idiom whereby a doctor sees his patient is similar.

197 The Lycians are likewise associated with the Trojans as major allies at 6.78, also 6x in the address-formula Τρῶες καὶ Λύκιοι καὶ Δάρδανοι ἀγχιμαχηταί. No reference need be intended to Pandaros as from a 'Lukie' around Zeleia, see on 90–1 (although the Λύκιοι of the address-formula are admittedly sandwiched between those from the Troad).

Agamemnon chooses to think that the successful archer will win glory for his deed, even though it breaches the truce; the antithesis of abstracts in κλέος and πένθος makes a neat and rhetorical ending.

198–207 A straightforward, very formular narrative, ending in the 3-verse repetition of Agamemnon's words of instruction. παπταίνων in 200, although itself formular, adds an anxious human touch.

201–2 ἑσταότ' -ας, 13x *Il.*, occurs 6x as runover-word, a weak one here in terms of additional meaning conveyed (but see on 303–5); λαῶν in 202 is little stronger, but both serve to lead on to further information, not absolutely essential but helping to fill out the scene. Verse 201 is identical with 90, where Athene comes upon Pandaros, and 202 is closely similar to 91.

The abbreviation of Τρίκκη (2.729) to Τρίκη, purely for metrical purposes, is startling of its kind, although cf. e.g. 'Οδυσσεύς/'Οδυσεύς.

208 A formular verse (5x *Il.* + 2 variants, 1x *Od.* + 2 variants).

211–13 The wounded Menelaos is surrounded by other chieftains and Makhaon enters the circle to stand at his side, παρίστατο; the δ' is 'apodotic', see on 1.194. ἰσόθεος φώς| occurs 12x *Il.*, 2x *Od.* of a variety of heroes.

213 The girdle, ζωστήρ, is ἀρηρότος, presumably 'close-fitting', as it was ἀρηρότι at 134 (and παναίολον, i.e. metallic or faced with metal, at 215 as it was δαιδαλέοιο at 135). It is a slightly odd description when used absolutely, or when 'the body' has to be understood, and is perhaps loosely derived from descriptions like that of the corslet at 15.529f. which is γυάλοισιν ἀρηρότα, fitted with curved pieces of some kind.

214 The barbs are 'broken back', πάλιν ἄγεν, (from (ϝ)ἄγνυμι which explains the lengthening of πάλῑν), as the arrow is drawn out. They were 'outside' at 151, but that meant simply that they were not embedded in flesh, and they could easily be imagined here as catching on the broken metal of the ζωστήρ etc. as the arrow was withdrawn.

215–16 He now undoes the various bits of armour (these verses repeat 186f. except for λῦσε δέ οἱ in place of εἰρύσατο, and the consequent change of cases) in order to see the wound.

218–19 Makhaon 'sucks out' the blood and expertly, εἰδώς, spreads on healing unguents (in an explosion of p-sounds which has no relation to meaning) which the kindly Centaur Kheiron had given his father Asklepios. At 11.829–32 the wounded Eurupulos asks Patroklos to wash (not suck) the blood from his arrow-wound and apply healing drugs (in similar language to that used here) which he had learned from Akhilleus, himself taught by Kheiron. Leaf notes that Homer restricts his references to Kheiron to the theme of him as teacher of Asklepios, Akhilleus and other heroes, of medicine among other accomplishments, and as donor to Peleus of the 'Pelian ash-spear'. Other myths of the 'most just of the Centaurs' must, of course, have been known to the epic tradition.

*220–421   Meanwhile the Trojan ranks approach and the Achaeans rearm. Aga-
memnon moves through the contingents inspecting their readiness and distributing
praise and blame among the leaders*

221 = 11.412; for 'ranks of shield-bearers' see also 201 = 90. bT not
unreasonably raised the question why the Trojans, if they really wanted to
end the war, did not seek out the truce-breaker rather than moving instantly
to attack, and suggested various answers: because they assumed their
leaders had ordered the shot, or because they expected the enemy to be
either despondent or unprepared, or because they considered the situation
irretrievable. If the composer had any particular reason in mind, it was
probably the last of these.

222 Difficulties have been raised over χάρμης (22× *Il.*!), clearly derived
from χαίρειν, on the grounds that warfare in this epic tradition is usually
described as grievous or hateful; but 2.453 and 11.13, where war becomes
'sweet', are enough to dispel scepticism, moreover the 'joy of battle' is a
commonplace idea in militaristic societies.

223–421 The Epipolesis or Tour of Inspection, as the ancient critics
termed it after ἐπεπωλεῖτο in 231 and 250, is a self-contained episode of
almost two hundred verses which can be compared with the Teikhoskopia
in book 3 or the catalogues in book 2. Once again battle is imminent – the
Trojans are almost upon the Achaeans, who themselves are ready for the
fight; once again it is delayed, although for the last time. When the
Inspection is over, the two armies really will, at last, engage. The episode
is successful and intensely dramatic in itself; it serves, moreover, to extend
the audience's knowledge of the Achaean leaders, already deepened in
certain cases by the Viewing from the Walls. Yet the Inspection could in
theory have been a special and separate composition inserted when the
full-scale poem came to be constructed by the monumental composer, or
even after that. It is, indeed, strictly 'inorganic' in that 222 could be directly
succeeded by 422. We should raise no objection to that sequence, supposing
the Inspection had never existed. Yet the repeated themes of armies on the
move, of elaborate similes and major diversions, suggest strongly that the
Epipolesis belongs to a general scheme of delay followed by the main
composer throughout books 2, 3 and 4:

2.442–54	Achaeans assemble for war; Athene shakes the aegis
2.455–83	similes (glare, noise, number etc.)
2.484–877	diversion: catalogues
3.1–14	similes (noise, [silence], dust)
3.15ff.	diversion: Paris, truce, Viewing, duel
4.220–3	armies ready to engage
4.224–421	diversion: Epipolesis

4.423-38   similes (noise and rush, [silence], noise)
4.439-45   Athene, Ares etc.
4.446ff.   armies finally engage.

The episode itself is a complex one:

(i)   223-31   Agamemnon is keen for war, prepares to inspect his army
(ii)   232-9   encourages the eager ones
(iii)   240-50   criticizes the slack ones
(iv)   251-72   praises the Cretans, Idomeneus replies
(v)   273-92   praises the Aiantes
(vi)   293-326 finds Nestor instructing Pylians, praises him, Nestor replies
(vii)   327-64   criticizes Menestheus and Odysseus, Odysseus replies, Agamemnon conciliates
(viii) 365-421 criticizes Diomedes, Sthenelos replies, Diomedes rebukes him.

After a brief introduction, therefore, there are short representative speeches of encouragement and blame, then three longer speeches of praise directed to specific leaders, followed by two of blame. Each of these last five is slightly varied in arrangement: (iv) praise / reply; (v) praise / no reply; (vi) Nestor addresses his men / praise / reply; (vii) blame / reply / conciliation; (viii) blame / reply by Sthenelos / rebuke by Diomedes. The whole episode appears to be carefully composed, but as with all catalogue-type sequences there was opportunity for elaboration here and there.

223-31 Introductory: Agamemnon is eager for action, sets off on foot to tour the ranks with his chariot following behind.

223-5 A deliberately rhetorical statement with its four parallel participles in -οντα: 'not dozing (βρίζοντα, unique in Homer), not cringing back, not unwilling to fight, but being eager for battle...' For the potential construction in the 2nd person singular, οὐκ ἄν...ἴδοις, compare οὐδέ κε φαίης, 3x *Il.* including 429; see also on 3.392.

226 ἔασε can mean 'left behind', as in |τοὺς μὲν ἔασε, ὁ δ'... (3x *Il.*), but here seems to imply no more than that he descended from the chariot. He does not leave it behind, exactly, since the charioteer is told to keep horses and chariot close at hand.

227 The θεράπων, attendant or charioteer, was keeping them ἀπάνευθ', 'apart'; is that why in 229f. Agamemnon kept on telling him (very frequently, μάλα πόλλ' ἐπέτελλε) to have them close by, παρισχέμεν? And are the horses snorting, φυσιόωντας, to show that they are difficult to control? One might be forgiven for thinking so; the commentators in any event have ignored the matter, which is explained in the comment on 229-30.

Book Four

228 Eurumedon is not mentioned elsewhere as Agamemnon's chariot-eer, although Nestor has one of that name at 8.114 and 11.620. One might compare Eurubates as generic name for a herald, 1.320 and comment; although with charioteers, at least, it is probably the singers' relative indif-ference rather than possible guild connexions that is responsible for the duplication.

229–30 The emphasis on the king's possible need for his chariot, for whenever he might become exhausted through his long tour of inspection, is a little bizarre. This motif, of the charioteer keeping horse and chariot close behind a warrior, properly belongs to descriptions of fighting in which the warrior might need to beat a hasty retreat. That is exemplified at 13.385f., where Asios is πεзὸς πρόσθ' ἵππων, fighting on foot in front of his horses, which his charioteer keeps so close that they breathe on his shoulders. That, too, is what Agastrophos failed to ensure at 11.338–42; Diomedes wounds him, 'but his horses [or, chariot] were not near for him to escape, a great oversight on his part; for his attendant was keeping them apart, while he on foot was raging through the front fighters, until he lost his life'. In fact 11.341, τοὺς μὲν γὰρ θεράπων ἀπάνευθ' ἔχεν, αὐτὰρ ὁ πεзός, is clearly the kind of source from which 227 was drawn (cf. 231 | αὐτὰρ ὁ πεзὸς ἐών, which is exactly paralleled earlier in book 11 at 11.230); one might add 16.506, where the Murmidones hold the dead Sarpedon's captured horses, σχέθον ἵππους φυσιόωντας. Our poet, therefore, seems to have compounded 227 out of other verses known to the tradition and appropriate to different circumstances; the same is so, less strikingly, of 229f. (where for τῷ μάλα πόλλ' ἐπέτελλε, for instance, cf. τοῖσι δὲ πόλλ' ἐπέτελλε of Nestor at 9.179). This goes further than ordinary oral flexibility in the deploying and extending of formulas and basic motifs, since the poet has thereby created a specific situation which is ultimately improbable, and for no clearly discernible purpose. Was it really to show that Agamemnon did not shirk the physical labour of walking, as bT maintained? Hardly; on the other hand there might be just a hint of the physical effort involved in deploying a whole army in Here's complaint to Zeus at 26–8, q.v. with comment.

230 On κοιρανέοντα see 2.207n., which draws attention to the parallel between Agamemnon's short speeches of encouragement and rebuke which follow, and those of Odysseus in book 2 as he restores morale after Agamemnon's disastrous Testing. The conclusion is drawn there that both episodes are due to the same main poet developing a standard theme in ways that are distinct in detail.

231 On πεзὸς ἐών cf. 11.230 and 229–30n. ἐπεπωλεῖτο στίχας ἀνδρῶν is repeated, preceded by κοιρανέων (cf. 230 κοιρανέοντα) at 250; it is used again of Agamemnon at 11.264 and of Hektor at 11.540. The linguistic parallels with book 11 are quite striking so far.

232–3 Compare 2.188f. (especially for the frequentative verb with ἐπέεσσιν and παραστάς, cf. θαρσύνεσκε παριστάμενος ἐπέεσσιν here) and see on 229–30.

235 ἐπὶ ψευδέσσι: Zeus will not help the Trojans 'on the basis of falsehoods', i.e. for breaking the oath (cf. LSJ s.v. ἐπί, III.1); unless ψευδέσσι is from ψευδής, 'liar', ('be a helper for liars'), not otherwise in Homer (who uses ψεύστης in book 24) but supported by Aristarchus against Hermappias (Hdn/A).

This verse gives the theme of Agamemnon's whole brief address: it is the Trojans' crime he dwells on, as providing encouragement for an eventual Achaean victory, rather than on any specific praise for these eager contingents.

236 The phraseology is familiar, cf. 67, 72 and 271, and that of the actual oath at 3.299.

237 A striking combination of two formulas, τέρενα χρόα (3x *Il.*, and in this position) and γῦπες ἔδονται| (4x *Il.*).

238–9 The language here is mainly but not entirely formular: νήπια τέκνα 11x *Il.*, 3x *Od.*, including Τρώων ἀλόχους καὶ νήπια τέκνα 4x *Il.*, but πτολίεθρον ἕλωμεν elsewhere only at 2.228 (usually πτολίεθρον is last word in the verse). The threats of 162 against Trojan women and children are now seen to imply captivity only (possibly preceded, one supposes, by other unpleasantness in the case of the former), although the curse on transgressors of the oath at 3.300f. had entailed death for the children. See also on 160–2.

240–1 Verse 240 follows the pattern of Odysseus' balanced speeches introduced by 2.188f. and 199f.: there, ὅν τινα μέν... and ὃν δ' αὖ..., here, οὕς τινας αὖ. 241 corresponds closely with 233: τοὺς μάλα θαρσύνεσκε/ νεικείεσκε. If Agamemnon's previous encouragement was rather muted, his blame is now unstinted.

242 ἰόμωροι here and at 14.479 is clearly abusive, but its exact sense is debatable. It might seem parallel to ἐγχεσίμωροι (3x *Il.*, 1x *Od.*) if ἰο- is from ἰός, 'arrow'; but ἐγχεσίμωροι is plainly laudatory, and ἰο- here has a short iota whereas ἰός has a long one (although not in Pindar, *Py.* 2.9, as e.g. Leaf observed). Moreover this would not make a particularly effective term of abuse even if archers were held in disrepute, cf. 11.385–7. That apparently leaves ἰά or ἰή meaning 'voice' or 'cry', Homeric ἰωή; 'all voice', or the like would suit the second part of 14.479, 'Αργεῖοι ἰόμωροι, ἀπειλάων ἀκόρητοι. As for the -μωροι element, that is equally speculative. Dogs are ὑλακόμωροι at *Od.* 14.29; if -μωροι meant 'glorying in' *vel sim.*, that would cover all three compounds; here, 'glorying in voice', i.e. mere boasters. See also Chantraine, *Dict.* s.v.

ἐλεγχέες is found here and at 24.239, cf. κακ' ἐλέγχεα 3x elsewhere (and 3 other Homeric uses of ἐλέγχεα): the -έες termination obviously represents an adjustment, probably unnecessary and perhaps post-Homeric, of -εα to avoid hiatus at the bucolic diaeresis. σέβεσθε, not elsewhere in Homer, 'are you not ashamed?'.

243–6 They are τεθηπότες (from τάφω), 'amazed', like fawns; the same phrase comes at 21.29 and a similar one, with πεφυζότες for τεθηπότες, at 22.1. At 13.102–4, similarly, deer are spiritless (ἀνάλκιδες, cf. 245 ἀλκή) and prone to flight (φυζακινῆς, cf. 244 θέουσαι); they are natural victims of carnivores in the poem's five remaining deer-similes. Here the fawns are particularly well observed: they cover much ground in flight, stand still when tired, have no inclination to resist, but look puzzled (mainly because they are listening, in fact?). That apparently vacant inactivity is what annoys Agamemnon about some of his troops.

247–9 This is a relatively common motif of exhortation and rebuke later in the poem as the fighting draws near to the ships; compare for instance a similarly sarcastic enquiry from Aias at 15.504f., 'do you think if Hektor fires the ships that you will walk home?'.

250 The pair of contrasting general speeches is rounded off by ἐπεπωλεῖτο στίχας ἀνδρῶν, balancing 231 (with κοιρανέων taking up κοιρανέοντα in 230); here the phrase is continuative as well as resumptive.

251 First, of the contingents specially identified, he comes to the Cretans: no particular reason, perhaps, although they are often singled out for praise, as indeed is suggested at 257ff. Perhaps the composer had special Cretan audiences to please, or did he draw on a special Cretan tradition of heroic poetry? These questions will be discussed more fully under book 13. Idomeneus, at least, is always a tireless and reliable fighter, and can safely be placed among those to be congratulated.

κιὼν ἀνὰ οὐλαμὸν ἀνδρῶν is repeated when Agamemnon moves on to the next contingent at 273; οὐλαμός is otherwise found only 2x *Il.* It is evidently formed from the root of εἰλέω, 'press', with the same suffix as in ποταμός, πλόκαμος: Chantraine, *Dict.* s.v.

252–4 The Cretans were putting on their armour, θωρήσσοντο (on which see 274n.), with Idomeneus among the front fighters like a wild boar in his ἀλκή, his courage and martial spirit (in contrast with those who lacked ἀλκή, like fawns, at 245), while the ranks behind were being urged on by his second-in-command Meriones.

φάλαγγες (etc.), 35x *Il.*, means much the same as στίχες, lines of troops usually abreast.

253 A main verb has to be understood, either ἦν, or, less probably, ὤτρυνε (φάλαγγας) from 254.

256 μειλιχίοισι(ν) is usually an epithet of μύθοις or ἔπεσσιν, but here and at 6.214, 17.431 and *Od.* 20.165 it is used by itself and 'words' has to be understood: an unusual idiom, but compare κερτομίοις at 6, and comment on 1.539.

257–64 Agamemnon's address to Idomeneus consists of two longish sentences indicating general esteem followed by a closing single-verse injunction.

257 He begins with a rising threefolder, rare in this Book and particularly emphatic for that reason.

259 The cumulated phrase ἠδ' ἐν δαίθ' is slightly illogical in itself (since Agamemnon honours him for his performance in war and other things, but not at feasts – this is where the honour is shown), but serves to introduce an idea which is developed at some length.

αἴθοπα -ι οἶνον -ῳ (12× *Il.*, 12× *Od.*) is γερούσιον only here and at *Od.* 13.8; the word is from *γερόντιος, i.e. belonging to the γέροντες or elders, in this case Agamemnon's close colleagues, the other kings, the ἄριστοι of 260.

260 The medieval vulgate has κρητῆρσι in the plural, but only one mixing-bowl would be needed for these relatively small parties and Aristarchus (Did/A) was right to support the singular.

261–3 There is no direct mention of the δαιτρόν elsewhere; it is a 'share' or 'portion', from δαίω; each of the ordinary guests thus has so many cups each, but the host and anyone specially honoured have as much wine as they wish. But Sarpedon and Glaukos according to 12.311 had the privilege of πλείοις δεπάεσσιν, full cups, in Lukie, and Hektor at 8.161 assumes that Diomedes is also so honoured among the Achaeans; the latter instance may suggest the kind of arrangement Agamemnon refers to here. But why is Idomeneus specially singled out? Partly perhaps because he is older than the others (μεσαιπόλιος, 'half-grey', at 13.361), except of course Nestor who must have had the same privilege. Probably nothing too formal is intended – a definite system would be too likely to provoke heroic resentment – and Agamemnon means that he takes special care that Idomeneus' cup does not remain empty.

264 The king is scarcely tactful; even Idomeneus, who is preparing vigorously for war, has to be told to ensure that he lives up to his previous claims.

266–71 Idomeneus accepts the encouragement in good part, however, and makes an egregious reply in which he promises to be a trusty comrade (a good scout, almost), as indeed he had undertaken to be. He then suggests that Agamemnon should urge on others, and echoes the king's own words about the Trojans' oath-breaking and its consequences.

267 His previous undertaking is described, especially through κατένευσα, in quite formal terms; presumably it refers to the general oath taken by Helen's suitors (of which he was one according to Hesiod, *Ehoiai*, frag. 204.56 M–W, ἐκ Κρήτης δ' ἐμνᾶτο μέγα σθένος Ἰδομ[ενῆος]); or was there some special Cretan commitment?

269–71 Although the content of the developing sentence is rather stale, it is conveyed quite dramatically, with the bouncing first half of 269 and its unusual three trochaic breaks followed by a long and uninterrupted second colon, leading to runover Τρῶες and a further runover-word in 271.

272–3 Verse 272 will recur at 326, and κιὼν ἀνὰ οὐλαμὸν ἀνδρῶν has already been used in 251. For the Aiantes see on 2.406 and 527; there can be little doubt that here they are the greater Aias *and Teukros*, since the Locrian Aias' light-armed contingent (on which see 13.712–22) would hardly be described as 'bristling with shields and spears' as at 282 here.

274 κορύσσομαι is from κόρυς, 'helmet', and strictly means 'put on the helmet'; but it usually has the sense of arming in general, as here, exactly as with θωρήσσομαι (e.g. at 252) from θώρηξ. For other applications see on 424–6.

νέφος εἵπετο πεζῶν recurs at 23.133, the cloud-metaphor being based presumably on the troops' denseness and darkness (cf. 16.66, κυάνεον Τρώων νέφος; the ranks are κυάνεαι at 282); but further implications are added by the simile which follows. AbT are on target here: 'He included the column's dense and striking character in a single word, by likening it to a black and lowering cloud; and made a simile out of the metaphor'; see also on 452 *fin*.

275–9 The simile is brilliant in observation, language and deployment, with the goatherd in that high place, the black cloud driven over the sea by a westerly gale, his shiver as he leads his flock to shelter. Many of Homer's favourite images are here: mountains, sea, storm, lonely observer. The elements of the simile are set out paratactically for the most part, with careful alternation and repetition: the herdsman sees the cloud coming over the sea – he is high up and far off – it looks blacker than pitch as it moves over the sea bringing strong wind – he shivers and drives his goats into shelter. The movement of the cloud is stressed by literal repetition: 276 ἐρχόμενον κατὰ πόντον, 278 ἰὸν κατὰ πόντον. Yet the position and response of the herdsman himself are no less important, for he helps us to see and feel the scene almost as he does. It gains solidity through him, yet also contrives to hint at man as under the power of nature, but as somehow dignified thereby.

The herdsman in the mountains (for that is the implication of σκοπιῆς, 'look-out place') recalls the shepherds of 3.10ff. (see on 10–14 there), and is echoed too at 8.559; but especially he recalls the shepherd who hears from afar (455 τηλόσε, cf. 277 ἄνευθεν ἐόντι) the roar of mountain torrents later in this same Book at 452–6. C. Moulton, *Similes* 42–5 and 52–5, is especially good on these developed similes of the Epipolesis and its sequel and on their relation to each other. There is no further instance in the Epipolesis itself, but it is followed at 422–8 by the movement of the ranks like a wave breaking on the shore, echoing the threatened violence of the storm-cloud over the sea here. The Trojans are like bleating sheep at 433-8, which is a little different; but then at 452-6, in the general clash of arms, comes the image of the mountain torrents whose roar, as well as the lonely shepherd who hears it, recalls the breaking wave of 422ff. and the impending λαῖλαψ of 278.

280-2 τοῖαι, just like the cloud in the simile; there are several detailed points of resemblance, for the ranks are πυκιναί, dense, like the cloud; they κίνυντο, move swiftly as it does, and are κυάνεαι, dark like it; even their bristling, πεφρικυῖαι, with weapons might be thought to recall a wind-driven storm-cloud's ragged edges.

283 A rare example of formular variation with no further discernible purpose, for at 255 we find τοὺς δὲ ἰδὼν γήθησεν ἄναξ ἀνδρῶν ᾿Αγαμέμνων; cf. 311. But perhaps 279 ῥίγησέν τε ἰδών provides a motive.

285-7 A contrast with 264, since Agamemnon now sees that further urging is unnecessary and unfitting.

288-91 This four-verse compliment in the form of a prayer only differs in one verse (289) from that addressed by the king to Nestor at 2.371ff. If everyone had the spirit of the Aiantes (or ten counsellors like Nestor), Priam's city would quickly fall; 291 = 2.374 also occurs at 13.816, and |χερσὶν ὑφ' (etc.) 6x in addition elsewhere.

292 The description of Agamemnon moving on to another contingent will be used again at 364; it is compounded from formular elements.

293 On Nestor as 'clear-voiced orator of the Pylians' see 1.247-52n.

295-6 In the Achaean catalogue only Nestor was mentioned as Pylian leader, at 2.601. The present list of five names is clearly invented and not traditional, since most of the names are part of the common stock drawn on for minor figures elsewhere in the epic. Thus this Pelagon does not recur, but there is a Lycian one at 5.695; Alastor and Khromios are also Lycians, victims of Odysseus at 5.677; another Alastor seems to be a companion of Antilokhos, and therefore Pylian, at 13.422, but that verse also occurs at 8.333 where he is a companion of Aias and therefore Salaminian. There is a Priamid Khromios at 5.160, a second Trojan victim of that name at 8.275, and a third and more successful Khromios at 17.218, 494, 534 (he is the same as the Mysian Khromis of 2.858); Aristarchus (Arn/A) noted that the present, Pylian Khromios makes a third, but actually it is a fourth. Haimon does not recur (except as a patronymic, Haimonides, a Theban of two generations back mentioned at 394); at 13.691 Bias is an Athenian (also father of two Trojan brothers at 20.460). It is noticeable that books 5 and 8 are conspicuous *loci* for these names, and they too show signs of *ad hoc* invention here and there. Finally, to return to a real Pylian and an important one, why was not Antilokhos, Nestor's son, named as one of these commanders?

297-300 A remarkable example of Nestor's tactical ideas (on which see the comment on 2.360–8): he appears to be marshalling (294 στέλλοντα) the chariot-force in front, the infantry behind, and the cowards in the middle. The last is distinctly odd (even despite Caesar, *B.G.* 3.24, *duplici acie instituta, auxiliis in mediam aciem collectis*, to which Dr J. A. Fairweather has drawn my attention); it is what the Greek clearly says, but by stretching things a bit we might understand the meaning to be that the cowards, or bad fighters (and κακούς properly means the former in a martial context), were placed in the middle of, i.e. among, the infantry. Having the chariots out in front is almost as strange. Normal Homeric tactics are for chariots to convey the great warriors up to the front line of fighting, where they dismount. (If they attempt to fight from the chariot, as Trojans occasionally did, they are always killed.) The chariot is then kept close by, in case a quick retreat becomes necessary. It is true that at 11.47–52 chariots and infantry (there, πρυλέες) are marshalled as two groups; the former are to restrain their horses and keep together, as here – but there is an important difference, since they are behind and the infantry in front. A hundred verses later the infantry forces on each side are engaged, and so are the charioteers (11.150f.); this confirms the idea of the latter as an autonomous group, at least. Nestor's own reminiscence of chariot-fighting against the Epeans at 11.743–9 is not detailed enough to be relevant. None of this serves to justify, or rather to reveal as less than eccentric (or sheerly anachronistic), the present disposition, which envisages something like a massed clash of chariots before the infantry gets to grips. H. L. Lorimer, *HM* 324f., considered such tactics to be more probably a confused reminiscence of Hittite chariots in the Late Bronze Age (since their fighters used thrusting-spears, as here) than of Assyrian or Egyptian forces of closer to Homer's own period, since their chariots carried archers. In any case massed chariot tactics required the horses to be armoured (as Mesopotamian ones, for instance, were; see Elena Cassin in Vernant (ed.), *Problèmes de la guerre* 304). That is something of which the *Iliad* offers no hint, beyond the ceremonial ivory cheek-piece of the simile at 141ff.

The ancient critical tradition from Aristotle on (he is cited by Porphyrius 1.73.10, quoted by Erbse, 1, 501) identified the difficulties but tried to reduce them by suggestions that were sometimes far-fetched: that πρῶτα and ἐξόπιθε in 297f. refer to the right and the left wing, with the cowards in the middle; or that these are sandwiched, man for man, between sound troops. A more erudite suggestion was that gaps or pathways would be left so that the chariot-force could retreat through the infantry, if it were repulsed. None of this, unfortunately, is of much help.

299   It is tempting to look to ἕρκος ἔμεν πολέμοιο for some kind of sense; for if the foot-troops are regarded as a solid and impenetrable bastion, which is what ἕρκος might suggest, then the chariot-force, by contrast, are more fluid. Yet they cannot be understood as being sent ahead as patrols, for example, since Nestor's detailed instructions at 303ff. make it clear that they, too, are to stay in close formation. Moreover the use of ἕρκος... πολέμοιο at 1.284 suggests that the phrase is a general one, and that no such specific implication should be read into it.

301–9 Nestor's instructions to the charioteers involve a curious slide into direct speech, without the normal verse or half-verse of address. That has to be read into 301 ἀνώγει, as also in the only Homeric parallel, the dubious archery-contest at 23.854ff. At all events Nestor insists (i) that they should keep together, and neither advance out of bravado nor retreat individually; (ii) that they should thrust with the spear only when another chariot came within reach (which must mean, practically touching) – that is, they are not to throw their spears. Nestor concludes by saying 'this is how the men of old used to sack towns and fortifications', from which it is probably wrong to conclude (like Leaf) that the instructions refer specifically to ancient siege tactics; admittedly τείχεα are emphasized, but, even so, the meaning may simply be 'this is how they won wars such as we are fighting against Troy'.

The tactics as described are hard to imagine as being successful, and have only a slight relation to anything else in Homer – or in later Greek warfare, for that matter, although many commentators have been tempted to make 'Attic interpolation' a key to the difficulties. The development of the hoplite phalanx precluded any further development of chariot tactics after the time of Homer – and even before that, in the Geometric age itself, chariots seem to have been reduced to mere ceremonial uses, or, in battle, to something like the auxiliary role depicted with some confusion in Homer. Therefore the notion of Nestor's tactics being an Attic interpolation of the sixth century B.C. (most probably) is even harder to credit than the idea that they are a confused reminiscence which had descended in the oral tradition and perhaps from Mycenaean times. For the Linear B tablets from Knossos reveal that large chariot forces were kept there; see, for example, M. Detienne in Vernant, *Problèmes de la guerre* 313ff. Even so, it is hardly credible that Mycenaean chariots were deployed in the way outlined by Nestor here, although they might have adopted the pursuit-tactics suggested in his Epean reminiscence in book 11 – the lack of armour for the horses is again a crucial point. In that case, we come back to the possibility that Nestor's advice reflects a distorted memory of Mycenaean knowledge of Near Eastern uses of chariots in the second millennium B.C.

301 μέν may suggest that Nestor intended to give corresponding advice, with a δέ, to the infantry; but 302f. continues to stress his role as counsellor of the chariot-force alone.

305–7 These three central verses of his speech are themselves symmetrically arranged, since the first and third consist of an instruction in the first part followed by a vague general justification in the second; whereas the second verse of the three is a rising threefolder with a quite different ring to it.

308–9　See also on 301–9, end of the first paragraph. In 308 οἱ πρότεροι is a developed use of the definite article, more so than e.g. Ἀργείων οἱ ἄριστοι at 260; see on 1.10–11. On ἐπόρθουν see on 2.690–1; πέρθω is the common Homeric verb, but the name of Oineus' father Portheus (14.115) shows that we are not necessarily dealing here with a later Ionic or Attic form. ἐπόρθουν is described by Shipp, *Studies* 242f., as 'really remarkable... with Attic contraction', but in any case ἐπόρθεον (i.e. with synizesis of -εον) occurs in a minority of mss including A, Ge and T, and is printed in OCT. The verse, and probably the whole tactical description, were certainly formed late in the oral tradition, but we need go no further than that.

313–16　Once again, as with the Aiantes, Agamemnon's approval takes the form of a rhetorically-expressed wish, here that Nestor's physical strength equalled his spirit. It echoes Nestor's own wish, three times later in the poem, εἴθ' ὡς ἡβώοιμι, βίη δέ μοι ἔμπεδος εἴη (at 7.157, 11.670 and 23.629); in all these cases the epic spelling αἴθε has been adjusted to later practice.

315　This use, together with those at 444 and *Od.* 3.236, of ὁμοίϊον = 'making equal' is almost certainly derived from the obviously old formula ὁμοιΐοο πτολέμοιο (6x *Il.*, 2x *Od.*).

318–25　Nestor's reply develops Agamemnon's previous comment about irreversible old age. He stops short of expanding the reminiscence about Ereuthalion – that will follow at 7.136ff. – and returns to his role as adviser to the chariot-force: that is his speciality, as is shown elsewhere by 2.555, by his epithet ἱππότα, by his feat against the Epeans in book 11, and by his technical advice to Antilokhos before the chariot-race in book 23.

320–1　Verse 320 was athetized by Aristarchus (Arn/A) as being better in place at 13.729 (where, however, the mss have a different ending to the verse) and logically defective here, since one would not choose both youth and old age. But the meaning is that the gods have not given everything to all men; ἅμα fits the other context better, but is acceptable here. The reflection is aptly put, and is finely complemented by 321 (characterized by Leaf as 'flat and empty'), which has a 'late' form, ἔα = 'I was', once elsewhere in *Il.*, 2x *Od.*

324–5　Aristarchus (Arn/A) distinguished between νεώτεροι as implying absolute youth and ὁπλότεροι as those younger than Nestor himself.

αἰχμάσσουσι in 324 is *hapax legomenon* in Homer but found in tragedy, therefore a probable Atticism according to Shipp, *Studies* 243; but αἰχμή is an extremely common Homeric word, -άζω terminations are also frequent

(Chantraine, *GH* I, 336–8), and verbs with internal accusatives formed from the same root are represented by e.g. δαίνυ/δαίνυντ'...δαῖτα (as at 9.70).

326 This verse has occurred already at 272, as Agamemnon left the Cretan contingent.

327–35 Now he arrives at the oddly-matched contingents of the Athenians and the Kephallenes. The passage contains a battery of rising threefolders at 328, 329 and 332, only the last of which is due to the need to accommodate an unusually heavy word (συνορινόμεναι). The effect is clearly not planned, and is not entirely felicitous.

327–9 For the lack of connective with εὗρε cf. 89 and comment. Menestheus (on whom see also 2.552n.) is 'horse-whipping'; he was a good organizer of chariots and shield-bearing warriors, second only to Nestor, at 2.553–5, and perhaps that is what makes the poet think of him directly after Nestor here. His association with Odysseus is surprising in any case, see on 338–40. On Πετεῶο cf. Shipp, *Studies* 56; the form of the genitive might be Attic for this Attic hero, but as old as Homer or his close predecessors nevertheless.

328 μήστωρες -ας ἀϋτῆς, 'devisers of the war-cry' (4× *Il.*, not elsewhere of the Athenians); note that the war-cry is replaced by 'rout' in the dual and singular: μήστωρε -α φόβοιο, 'deviser of rout' (6× *Il.*), the two versions being part of a formular system. The singer does not hesitate to give the Athenians a martial epithet despite circumstances, as with Odysseus' ranks of Kephallenes at 330 which are οὐκ ἀλαπαδναί.

331 The repetition of ἀϋτῆς| after 328 is presumably fortuitous; at any rate the Athenians have not heard the war-cry now. Middle ἀκούετο, especially with σφιν, is unusual, but may contain the nuance that they were not yet consciously listening for it.

332 κίνυντο φάλαγγες| occurs also at 281 and 427; obviously much of the language of the Epipolesis is repetitious, sometimes designedly so to mark Agamemnon's systematic progress and the army's deliberate preparations.

333–5 οἱ δὲ μένοντες | ἕστασαν completes the sequence of 328 ἑσταότ', 329 ἑστήκει, 331 ἕστασαν; if we doubt that 'standing' means 'standing around', Agamemnon's words at 340 will make the matter plain: καταπτ-ώσσοντες ἀφέστατε. They are waiting 'until another battalion of Achaeans should approach and set off against the Trojans and start the fighting'; an ancient variant in the 'polystich' text (according to Didymus in A) suggested that they were waiting for Trojans to attack, but there is no real point in this.

Too much can be made of πύργος, of troops, in 334; it occurs so only here and at 347, but πυργηδόν, 'like a tower', is well established in three Iliadic uses (of which only one, *contra* Shipp, *Studies* 243 n. 4, is in a simile).

336–7 Nearly the same couplet recurs at 368f., where 368, however, becomes a rising threefolder. Verse 337 might appear superfluous, but the fact is that νεικέω is not regarded as in itself a verb of speaking, at least prospectively, and needs bolstering by μύθῳ, ἐπέεσσιν or the like (as at e.g. 2.224, 3.38), or at least by the addition of a verb like ὀτρύνω (at 10.158). Here it receives an entire verse of address to supplement it.

338–40 Menestheus and Odysseus make a strange pairing in this encounter, but they continue to be both mentioned, at least until the latter's riposte to Agamemnon at 350ff.

339 κερδαλεόφρον is deeply insulting, and was applied by Akhilleus to Agamemnon at 1.149 at the height of their quarrel. One can see why Zenodotus (Arn/A) tried to replace it with φαίδιμ' 'Οδυσσεῦ; but 'skilled in wicked deceits', which immediately precedes, is an equally malicious interpretation of Odysseus' reputation as πολύμητις – at worst, of 'knowing all kinds of deceits' as Helen put it at 3.202. 'Cringing' in the next verse confirms the unfairness of Agamemnon's criticisms, which are quite unjustified by the circumstances but reflect a tendency to rhetorical exaggeration in this general theme of praise and rebuke on the battlefield; compare his general criticism at 242ff., and what he will say to Diomedes at 370ff.

341–2 After the sequence of ἑσταότ' etc., on which see on 333–5, the positive use of ἑστάμεν at 342 is slightly ironical; it is explained by μετὰ πρώτοισιν ἐόντας in 341 (where the accusative ἐόντας, despite the dative of σφῶϊν, is 'because the participle's main syntactical relationship is as subject of the infinitive ἑστάμεν' (Willcock); cf. 1.541).

343 Leaf's complaint of 'hopeless syntax' was approved by Shipp, *Studies* 243; the syntax is admittedly strained, but Aristarchus' paraphrase (Did/A) as πρῶτοί μου ἀκούετε περὶ δαιτός explains what was intended. He also observed (Arn/A) that Menestheus was not, in fact, one of Agamemnon's privileged companions, and not among the seven guests at 2.404–9 (see the comment there). He was not, after all, in the top class of Achaean commanders.

345–6 The motif of food and wine offered to the senior kings is repeated, in a reverse sense, from what was said to Idomeneus at 259ff.; but drinking wine 'as long as you wish' ignores the idea there of the δαιτρόν, on which see 261–3n.

347 φίλως takes up φίλ' in a corresponding position in the verse at 345. For πύργῳ see on 333–5.

349 A common form of address (13× *Il.*, 7× *Od.*), applied to various displeased heroes (as well as to Zeus). On ὑπόδρα see 1.148–71n.

350–5 Odysseus is very restrained in the circumstances (as Diomedes will be at 411ff.). He does not, however, specifically deny that they *have* failed to notice that the army is preparing for battle.

350 'What a word is this that has escaped the barrier of your teeth!' is a vivid formular expression (exclamatory rather than interrogative) that occurs only 2x *Il.* but 6x *Od.* (with one variant in each case). Its other Iliadic use is at 14.83 and it is again directed by Odysseus at Agamemnon, who has proposed a premature retreat. The teeth look like a fence, and should act like one against certain utterances.

351–2 Aristarchus (Nic/A) seems to have preferred ending the question at μεθίεμεν and envisaging a comma after Ἄρηα in 352; but Leaf was right to object that it would be unusual for a long sentence to begin at the bucolic caesura; that ἐγείρομεν (subjunctive) should properly have κε if it referred, as it then would, to the future; and that asyndeton before ὁππότ' would be difficult. That being so, we must understand the sentence as meaning 'How can you say that we are lax in fighting, whenever we Achaeans stir up war against the horse-subduing Trojans?', in which the ὁππότ' clause directs the idea of fighting (351 πολέμοιο) to actual engagement rather than the preparations on which Agamemnon is unfairly concentrating.

353 The verse recurs at 9.359 (cf. also 8.471), where Akhilleus tells Agamemnon that he (Agamemnon) can watch him departing on the next morning if he cares to do so. Here it is even more sarcastic, with its possible sneer that the king may not be interested in watching fighting at close quarters.

354 Odysseus has already referred to himself at 2.260 as father of Telemakhos. There it is a truism, part of a rhetorical form of assertion: 'let Odysseus' head not be on his shoulders, and let me not be called Telemakhos' father, if I do not lay hands on you...' Here the intention is also rhetorical, no doubt, but some feeling of pride is also conveyed, as φίλον suggests. Aristarchus (Arn/A) remarked that the composer is evidently aware of the Odysseus of the *Odyssey*.

355 ἀνεμώλια, 'like the wind', i.e. insubstantial or unstable, a vivid metaphor, of words only here and twice in the *Odyssey*.

356–7 The first part of 356 occurs 3x *Il.*, 1x *Od.*, with different nuances: at 8.38 Zeus smiles benevolently at Athene as he grants her request; at 10.400 Odysseus smiles ironically and deceitfully at the captured Dolon; at *Od.* 22.371 he smiles in an amused way as Medon emerges from hiding. Here Agamemnon's smile is an ingratiating one; he sees how angry Odysseus is and tries to smooth over what he himself has said. The different possible applications of a fixed formular expression are well exemplified here.

γιγνώσκω (etc.) with the genitive recurs at *Od.* 21.36, 23.109, but not elsewhere in the *Iliad* (and that includes 23.452f.); here it governs a participle as occasionally with other verbs of knowing (as e.g. at 1.124), cf. Shipp, *Studies* 144.

358 The use of this standard form of address to Odysseus (already at

2.173), with its flattering but ambivalent πολυμήχαν', 'of many devices', is an ingenious way, if it is not accidental, of softening Agamemnon's insults at 339.

359 περιώσιον, 'in a superfluous way', developed (like περισσός) from περί. Agamemnon can hardly mean that he is not chiding Odysseus superfluously, i.e. that he is justified in doing so; rather that he is not, in fact, chiding him, since that would be unjustified and superfluous. This is indirect and unclear, and as usual Agamemnon seems intent on evading any admission of responsibility for past actions.

360–1 He goes on to say in singularly cloying language that Odysseus 'has kindly thoughts', i.e. towards Agamemnon, because he is 'of the same mind'. This last phrase, τὰ γὰρ φρονέεις ἅ τ' ἐγώ περ, may conceal some recognition of Odysseus' recent role in preventing precipitate withdrawal after the king's misconceived 'testing' in book 2. Its predecessor, ἤπια δήνεα οἶδε, quite apart from the recurrence of οἶδε so soon after οἶδα in the previous verse, may be judged inelegant and forced – appropriately so, perhaps – both rhythmically and assonantally; it has no close Homeric parallel. δήνεα, related to δαῆναι, διδάσκω, is rare, only 2x *Od.* elsewhere in Homer.

362 |ἀλλ' ἴθι is a common formula of mild exhortation, 11x *Il.*, 4x *Od.* The central part of the verse recurs in Hektor's words to Paris as they go out to battle at 6.526, ἀλλ' ἴομεν, τὰ δ' ὄπισθεν ἀρεσσόμεθ', αἴ κέ ποθι Ζεύς (and in general the two verses are constructed very similarly). ἀρέσκω means 'conciliate' or 'make amends': here, 'we shall make amends to each other for these things'.

363 Agamemnon's words end, like those of Odysseus at 355, with a word based on 'wind', but in a different sense and again with a subtle glossing over of the past; there Agamemnon's words were described by Odysseus as ἀνεμώλια, 'wind-like' in the sense of unstable or foolish; here the gods are asked by Agamemnon to make everything be 'carried away with the winds', μεταμώνια from *μετανεμώνια, i.e. μετ' ἀνέμων (so Chantraine, *Dict.*).

364–9 Now it is the turn of Diomedes and Sthenelos; Agamemnon's progress to the next rebuke is described in by now familiar terms, with 364 = 292 and 368f. closely similar to 336f.

365 The asyndeton with εὗρε of 327 is not repeated, as it doubtless would be if metre made it convenient. ὑπέρθυμον, 'with an excess of spirit', is a fairly common martial epithet, 5x of |Τρῶες ὑπέρθυμοι but also of various Achaean heroes.

366 ἑσταότ', 'standing' (or 'stationary', even), is again used (see on 333–5) to convey the fault which evokes criticism, as also with Sthenelos who ἑστήκει in 367. The singer chooses to use a formular verse not clearly suited to this particular situation; it recurs at 11.198 and, with variations, at 23.286. In the former, standing is no reproach; Hektor is simply standing in his chariot, and descends from it immediately at 11.211. That shows, at least, that ἵπποισι καὶ ἅρμασι there is taken as a kind of hendiadys; ἵπποι often refers to chariot rather than horses, and it is sometimes difficult to tell which. At 419 Diomedes, too, will descend from his chariot; but is he really envisaged as standing in it throughout Agamemnon's long rebuke? One might feel that his being there in the first place is hardly a sign that he is not preparing for war. At 23.286 ἵπποισίν τε...καὶ ἅρμασι κολλητοῖσιν almost certainly refers to horses *and* chariots, and one suspects therefore that Diomedes here, despite 367, Hektor at 11.198 and his own 'leaping to earth' at 419, is 'stationary among the horses and riveted chariots'.

370–400 Agamemnon puts his rebuke to Diomedes in the form of an unfavourable comparison with his father Tudeus, one of the Seven against Thebes. That allows him to recount, in an abbreviated form, one of Tudeus' feats, derived no doubt from a longer oral poem on the Theban theme; Athene herself gives a slightly different version at 5.800ff. Why Diomedes is chosen for rebuke is not clear, any more than it was with Odysseus, but probably the opportunity for just such a digression was itself attractive from a narrative and dramatic point of view. For the series of three laudatory encounters and two rebukes is carefully varied, not only in the responses of the recipients but also in the dominant motifs: privilege at the feast with Idomeneus, developed simile with the Aiantes, tactical advice with Nestor, reversal of the feast-motif with Odysseus, and now the reminiscence-motif with Diomedes.

The speech advances in whole-verse sentences and clauses for the most part, with much progressive enjambment, as might be expected in a simple narrative of events. Only 374f. are interrupted by internal punctuation; there are three integral enjambments (374, 387, 399) and four rising threefolders (371, 373, 376, 387), most of the rest being four-colon verses. Most of those seven instances are associated with special emphasis and emotion, as can be seen in 370–6 and 387f.

370 It is an obvious device to address Diomedes by the patronymic phrase, to introduce Tudeus without delay.

371 This rising threefolder makes a dramatic exordium with its repeated and vivid verbs of enquiry – πτώσσεις again (reinforced by 372 πτωσκαζ-έμεν, cf. 340 καταπτώσσοντες) and ὀπιπεύεις, i.e. just gazing at something without taking action – followed by the wonderful old formula π(τ)ολέμοιο γεφύρας (5× *Il.*): 'why are you just eyeing the bridges of war?'. This intriguing phrase, probably ἀνὰ πτολέμοιο γεφύρας in its regular use as in three of the Iliadic occurrences, evidently referred to the open pathways of the battlefield, clear space between the ranks or groups of combatants (cf.

Book Four

τὰς διόδους τῶν φαλάγγων, T). γέφυραι are embankments at 5.88 and it is implied that they are causeways at 15.357 (γεφύρωσεν), rather than actual bridges. See also on 5.87–8.

374–5 The stress on Agamemnon's reliance on hearsay seems unnecessary, but 376 follows better on 375 than on 373.

376–9 A rising threefolder (since ἄτερ cannot be separated from πολέμου) introduces the tale of this particular feat of bravery on the part of Tudeus. 'Without war' draws the listener's attention away from the idea of fighting, as in 373–5, to that of a peaceful preliminary mission. Tudeus accompanied Poluneikes (who had been deprived of the rulership of Thebes by his brother Eteokles) to Mukenai for reinforcements – which they would have got, according to Agamemnon, had it not been for unfavourable omens from Zeus.

378 The walls of Thebes are 'holy', according to T because they had been built through the power of Amphion's lyre; but more probably because ἱερός is a conventional epithet applied fairly indiscriminately to different places (primarily to Troy, cf. Ἴλιος ἱρή (etc.), 20× *Il.*, but also e.g. to Euboea at 2.535).

381 These 'signs' are very unspecific, either because they disguise a more political motive or more probably as an oral expedient for condensing a longer account; compare the equally vague 'obeying the portents of the gods' at 398. On παραίσια see the next comment.

382 πρὸ ὁδοῦ: 'forward on their road' – not elsewhere in Homer, but not therefore Attic as Shipp argued, *Studies* 243. He also noted a few other 'late' linguistic features in this Tudeus digression, more perhaps than in the Epipolesis as a whole; as well as others which are unusual but acceptable in themselves, like 381 παραίσια or the expanded form Καδμείωνας in 385. The language hereabouts is not so rich in 'late' features as other condensations of non-Trojan material, notably Nestor's reminiscences in books 7 and 11 and Phoinix's Meleagros-*exemplum* in book 9.

383 The Asopos river, south of Thebes, is 'deep in rushes' and with grassy banks (if that is what λεχεποίην, literally 'bed-grassy', implies here; the epithet is used of a town, Pteleon, at 2.697).

384 ἀγγελίην, 'on a message-bearing mission', cf. 11.140 and on 3.206. The mission was presumably to demand that Eteokles step down in favour of his brother.

385–98 From now on the tale proliferates folk-tale motifs, some exemplified on a larger scale in the *Odyssey*: the solitary visitor appearing before the king and nobles at dinner; his getting involved in contests and winning against all odds; the ambush and the sole survivor. There are close parallels with the opening of *Odyssey* book 8, where Odysseus is challenged by the

369

Phaeacians to various athletic contests; he reluctantly takes part in one, which he easily wins with the help of Athene, as Tudeus does here.

386 βίης 'Ετεοκληείης, compare βίη 'Ηρακληείη (etc.) (6x *Il.*) and 2.658–6on.

387 ξεῖνός περ ἐών: the Homeric guest is protected by Zeus and is usually received with kindness, but even so Tudeus' position must have been daunting since he is among enemies. οὐδέ and ...περ do not fit altogether smoothly, but there is probably no need to impute a later use of the term ξεῖνος, i.e. as 'alien', like Shipp, *Studies* 243f. after Leaf.

389–90 Tudeus' boldness at Thebes will be evoked again at 5.800–13, by Athene herself as like Agamemnon she spurs Diomedes (wounded now) into action. That account, shorter than the present one, omits the preliminaries and takes up the tale with Tudeus' arrival πολέας μετὰ Καδμείωνας (804, cf. 385); he is bidden to join them at the feast, 805, which goes beyond 385f. here, and challenges them (ἀεθλεύειν being understood), προκαλίζετο as here and twice elsewhere. Verses 807f. then continue much as 389f. but with τοίη οἱ ἐγὼν ἐπιτάρροθος ἦα instead of τοίη οἱ ἐπίρροθος ἦεν 'Αθήνη. Which of these was the primary version is hard to say (although Aristarchus, Arn/A, athetized 5.808 on the ground of repetition and lesser suitability), especially since both ἐπιτάρροθος and ἐπίρροθος have their difficulties. The former is well established in the Homeric vocabulary (7x *Il.*, 1x *Od.*), the latter recurs only at 23.770. The latter seems to be formed from ῥόθος, the resonant noise e.g. of waves, but Leaf's 'coming with shouts (to the rescue)' is not compelling. ἐπιτάρροθος on the other hand is shown by its Homeric uses to mean something like 'bringing help', and has no obvious etymology apart from its superficial resemblance to ἐπίρροθος. This detail, then, reveals little about the relationship of the longer and shorter versions of Tudeus at Thebes, the slight differences of which (the latter adds that Tudeus was a small man) suggest that they were separately derived from a common source, probably a fully developed hexameter narrative.

391 We are left to judge whether the Cadmeans' anger was primarily caused by their defeat in the athletic contests, or by the nature of Tudeus' message, or by a combination of the two.

392 Most MSS have ἄψ ἀνερχομένῳ, which is metrically defective; some supply the deficiency by reading ἀναερχομένῳ, where the internal hiatus might be paralleled by e.g. 13.262 ἀποαίνυμαι, or less satisfactorily ἐπανερχομένῳ where the ἐπ- component is pointless. Bentley's ⟨ἄρ'⟩ ἀνερχομένῳ is certainly correct, since it recurs at 6.187 in the narrative of a similar ambush (of Bellerophon). ἄρ' in the book 6 version is fully justified, which is not the case here – but that is typical of slight oral imprecision in the adaptation and relocation of traditional phraseology. The two verses also resemble each other in formular construction and the echoing of δόλον and λόχον:

6.187 τῷ δ' ἄρ' ἀνερχομένῳ πυκινὸν δόλον ἄλλον ὕφαινε
4.392 ἂψ ⟨ἄρ'⟩ ἀνερχομένῳ πυκινὸν λόχον εἷσαν ἄγοντες

The phrase εἷσαν ἄγοντες| recurs at 23.698, where the idea of 'leading' is more appropriate than here; it seems to be part of a formular system, cf. 1.311 |εἷσεν ἄγων of Agamemnon putting Khruseis on board ship to return to her father. εἷσαν is from ἵζω, literally 'seat' but often simply 'set' or 'put in place'.

393 Fifty is a conventional number applied to different groups in various myths (or rather folk-tales); so with the fifty Danaids and their fifty cousins, also the fifty Argonauts. The sole-survivor motif in 397 is equally conventional, cf. e.g. Lunkeus alone spared of the fifty Egyptian cousins, or Thoas of the Lemnian men slain by their womenfolk. The pair of leaders is not in the same class, although five contingents in the Achaean catalogue have two commanders.

394-5 Maion, only here (and at 398) in Homer, probably means 'he who reaches for, or pursues', cf. μαίομαι; so Frisk, although Chantraine, *Dict.* s.v. μαίομαι is not so sure. Whether this is intended as a 'speaking' or significant name here, as von Kamptz, *Personennamen* 238 assumes, is uncertain, despite the names in 395; he is, after all, spared (398), which distinguishes him from the bloodthirsty remainder. According to Statius 4.598 he was a priest of Apollo, which as Leaf thought might explain θεῶν τεράεσσι πιθήσας in 398 – if it is not a deduction therefrom; and there was a Theban tradition that he buried Tudeus in Thebes (cf. 14.114) according to Pausanias 9.18.2.

His father is Haimon, a name given also to one of the Pylian commanders at 296; see on 295–6, where this and other names in the list are seen to be part of a common stock that could be drawn on for minor characters *ad hoc*; a third Haimon was grandfather of the Myrmidon Alkimedon at 17.467. Various explanations have been offered for the Pylian and Myrmidon applications, cf. von Kamptz, *Personennamen* 237 and 319f., but here Αἵμων is usually taken as a significant name, that is, as 'he who hunts, or seizes', cf. 5.49 αἵμονα θήρης, with a savage ring like that of Autophon and Poluphontes in 395. That remains doubtful in view of its uncertain etymology and of what was just observed about his son Maion.

There can be no doubt, however, about Autophon and Poluphontes themselves; the φόνος element in their names is too conspicuous for them to be named here accidentally – they are 'slaughterous' because they have been despatched to kill Tudeus. For Poluphontes compare the name of

Bellerophontes, whose ambush at 6.187–90 is so similar (although he of course is ambushed rather than ambusher); Aristarchus (Did/A) noted Lukophontes as a variant, and that was the vulgate reading (in all MSS except A itself) – it has the advantage of being applied to a minor Trojan, also, one of Teukros' victims at 8.275, another being son of Poluaimon in the following verse. As for significant names, they are commoner in the *Odyssey* (see W. B. Stanford, *The Odyssey of Homer, Books I–XII*[2] (London 1961) xxif.), as with e.g. Phemios Terpiades, but the *Iliad* has the outrageous Oukalegon (3.148, see 3.146–8n.) as well as the craftsman Tekton Harmonides and the seer Poluidos among others. Many warriors have martial names of one sort or another; only occasionally can we be sure that they have been specially selected or even invented by the poet, or a predecessor, for some particular martial context.

396 ἀεικέα πότμον ἐφῆκε (etc.) occurs only here in the *Iliad* but 6x in the *Odyssey* (which also has ἀεικέα πότμον ἔπεσπον (etc.) an additional 3x). This does not suggest an especially Odyssean origin for the Tudeus episode or the ambush motif, or anything like that, since the whole phrase is built up out of components well established in the *Iliad* itself: κήδε᾽ ἐφῆκεν 2x *Il.*, not *Od.*; ἀεικέα λοιγὸν ἀμῦναι (etc.), 5x *Il.*, not *Od.* (ἀεικέα in this position in the verse 12/12x *Il.*, 15/19x *Od.*); πότμον ἐπίσπῃ (etc.) 6x *Il.*, 14x *Od.*

καί in καὶ τοῖσιν does not imply that he had also killed the defeated athletes (as bT thought), but is perhaps motivated by ἀεικέα: losing at the contests had also been disgraceful, although less fatally so.

397 The parallel Bellerophon tale lacks the single-survivor motif (6.189f.), on which see 393n.

398 θεῶν τεράεσσι πιθήσας: so too at 6.183 of Bellerophon killing the Chimaera, just four verses before the ambush-passage; cf. 408 and comment, also on 2.73–5 *fin.* The formula, which reinforces the impression of a similar history for the two ambush narratives, is a convenient one for summarizing a longer version, compare the παραίσια σήματα of 381 and the comment there.

399 On Tudeus as Aetolian, which is emphasized here, compare the description of his son Diomedes at 23.471, Αἰτωλὸς γενέην, μετὰ δ᾽ Ἀργείοισιν ἀνάσσει. Tudeus' father Oineus was expelled from Kaludon by his brothers and restored by Tudeus according to Hesiod, *Ehoiai*, frag. 14 M–W; but the reason for his move to Argos is left vague by Homer at 14.119f., according to which Oineus stayed in Kaludon but Tudeus lived in Argos 'after wandering – for such must have been the will of Zeus and the other gods', a vague formula not unlike θεῶν τεράεσσι πιθήσας in 398.

400 See pp. 22f. for the remarkable rhyming of ει/η sounds, each in the first syllable of the metrical foot; clearly this is intended to make a strongly rhetorical ending to Agamemnon's speech. The shortened form of χερείων recurs at 1.80 (q.v. with comment) and 14.382, both of them, like this verse, strongly apophthegmatic in style and concision.

The addition 'but better in assembly' (i.e. at speaking, see on 4.1) is irrelevant to Agamemnon's general point; it may be meant to soften the rebuke, but is more probably malicious; it also reflects a desire for strong closing antithesis.

401–2 κρατερός is Diomedes' standard epithet at the verse-end (18x *Il.*, including at 411), and does not imply (as bT thought) special emphasis on his courage after Agamemnon's rebuke. That so great a warrior should accept it in silence is unexpected; even more so that he 'respected', αἰδεσθείς, the royal reproach, especially because at 9.34–6 he will remind the king of his insult. But at 413–17 he will explain to Sthenelos that he does not blame Agamemnon because it is in the king's interest to encourage the Achaeans to fight; this solves the difficulty of αἰδεσθείς, at least, since it shows that Diomedes respects the kingly office, merely, and understands the kind of behaviour it tends to elicit.

αἰδώς, αἰδέομαι, αἰδοῖος cover a wide range of feelings from fear to shame to respect: respect for an elder, or for the interests of one's comrades, or for a status, function or office (e.g. of a suppliant, a god, or a king as here). An adequate parallel is provided by 1.23 = 377, where Agamemnon is urged (in vain) to 'respect the priest', which means Khruses *qua* priest. αἰδοίοιο here supports this interpretation; not a standard epithet with βασιλεύς, it is evidently selected to emphasize the point Diomedes is making. That is perhaps confirmed by the rather inelegant repetition of αἰδ- in first and last word of the verse.

403 The 'son of glorious Kapaneus' is Sthenelos, cf. 2.564 and 5.319; he is also Καπανήιος υἱός 3x (including 367). κυδαλίμοιο usually occurs in the formula Μενελάου κυδαλίμοιο| (7x *Il.*, 7x *Od.*), but is occasionally applied to other heroes too (Aias, Nestor, Akhilleus as well as Kapaneus here). Sthenelos no doubt deserves an honorific description, but it is not a special one, being but one functional item in a developed name–epithet system for the nominative and accusative cases:

2.564	– Σθένελος Καπανῆος	ἀγακλειτοῦ φίλος υἱός
4.403	– υἱὸς Καπανῆος	∪ – ∪ ∪ κυδαλίμοιο
5.108	– – – Σθένελον	∪ ∪ – Καπανήιον υἱόν
4.367	– ∪ ∪ – – –	Σθένελος Καπανήιος υἱός
5.111 etc.	– ∪ ∪ – Σθένελος(ν) ∪	∪ – ∪ ∪ – ∪ ∪ – ⏑
23.511	ἴφθιμος Σθένελος	– – ∪ ∪ – ∪ ∪ – ∪

404–10 Sthenelos, unlike Diomedes, refuses to keep silent and refutes Agamemnon's unfavourable comparison with Tudeus by the simple argument 'they failed, we succeeded, therefore we are better than they (and not the reverse)'. His words are simple and direct, with no runover cumulation or integral enjambment and in mostly whole verse sentences; the one longer sentence, progressively enjambed, culminates quite effectively in 408, a rising threefolder; see also on 412–18.

404 ψεύδε' for ψεύδεο: 'do not lie, when you know how to speak clearly'. σάφα as an adverb occurs 9x *Il.*, 12x *Od.*, only here in the *Iliad* with a verb of speaking, otherwise with verbs of knowing; but in the *Odyssey* the distribution is equal (i.e. 6x with a verb of speaking as here). 'Clearly' means 'truly' – it is false to describe this as a particularly Attic usage, as Leaf and others do.

405 Sons are often held to be inferior to their fathers; this stirring claim to the contrary is based on the specific and unusual case of the successive attacks on Thebes. The repeated ἡμεῖς, first word both of this verse and the next and followed by a monosyllable in each case, reinforces the proud claim; so does εὐχόμεθ', a favourite heroic verb in different senses which all depend on the basic idea of 'an insistent and solemn declaration' (Chantraine, *Dict.*, s.v.): so 'affirm', 'claim', 'vow', 'pray aloud'.

406 καί goes closely with εἵλομεν: 'we actually captured it' (unlike their fathers). ἕδος has exalted associations, being normally used of Olumpos, the seat of the gods.

407–9 These three verses were wrongly athetized by Aristarchus (Arn/A), partly on the trivial ground that the dual ἀγαγόνθ' (for ἀγαγόντε) in 407 ignores the other five Epigonoi, but partly because they only win with the help of the gods and are not therefore superior. Yet throughout the *Iliad* divine help and consequent success are in themselves a mark of superiority.

407 A strongly rhetorical verse with its chiastic arrangement (epithet–noun–participle–noun–epithet) and antithesis of the two enclosing epithets. We are not told elsewhere either that the Epigonoi were weaker in total numbers than the Seven, although that is plausible enough; or that the walls of Thebes were stronger than before (for that is what ἄρειον means, cf. τεῖχος ἄρειον also at 15.736 – nothing to do with Ares as LSJ, Shipp and others have thought, or with being stronger than the walls of Troy which is what A believed), although that too seems a reasonable assumption.

408 See on 398 for the 'portents of the gods', and compare 381 for Zeus's involvement. The portents are again unspecified; the composer clearly finds the formula generally useful, and reverses its words (τεράεσσι θεῶν not θεῶν τεράεσσι as at 398 and 6.183) to make it follow πειθόμενοι and constitute a rising threefolder.

ἀρωγῆ (etc.) occurs 8x *Il.*, always at the verse-end.

409 The Seven lost through their own reckless folly, ἀτασθαλίῃσιν, which is what Hektor accuses himself of at 22.104. Most of the verse recurs at *Od.* 1.7, and there are two other references in similar terms to the Suitors'

Book Four

folly. That does not make the present verse an 'Odyssean' one exactly, as has been suggested. Yet a number of Odyssean parallels have already been noted in the language of this encounter with Diomedes and Sthenelos, in particular. That may merely suggest a heavy contribution from the monumental composer's own vocabulary (particularly if he was indeed, although at a later stage of his career, the composer of the monumental *Odyssey*).

410 μή with the aorist imperative is rare, although cf. 18.134.

411 See on 349, where Agamemnon earns a similarly scowling reply from Odysseus.

412–18 Diomedes' 7-verse speech of rebuke to Sthenelos formally corresponds with that of Sthenelos to Agamemnon in both length and arrangement: a more complex 3-verse sentence (here with integral enjambment at 415/16) enclosed by shorter, whole-verse ones. The correspondence is not quite exact, since here the opening two verses are extended by progressive enjambment into a third, and there is just a single statement, 418, at the end; whereas Sthenelos had begun and ended with an exactly balanced pair of short statements.

412 On τέττα, only here in surviving Greek, see Chantraine, *Dict.* s.v. τᾶτᾶ; it is clearly a hypocoristic, familiar form of address, compare ἄττα (2x *Il.* in the formula ἄττα γεραιέ; 6x *Od.*) – surely a friendly one as Aristarchus thought (Arn/A), although AbT considered it disparaging.

σιωπῇ ἦσο, 'remain silent', simply (for obviously Sthenelos was not seated, and would not be so); see on 2.252–6.

413 Once again (see on 401) a regular formular usage may give a misleading first impression of special subtlety on the part of poet or speaker: Diomedes is not being sycophantic when he calls Agamemnon ποιμένι λαῶν here, or anticipating his own point about the king's natural concerns; rather 'shepherd of the peoples' is a regular verse-end formula applied to several different heroic characters in the dative, including Diomedes himself at 11.370. The poet may nevertheless have been quite pleased with its suitability here.

415–17 The first and third verses of this 3-verse sentence begin with τούτῳ μέν... τούτῳ δ'... respectively; πένθος in the third balances κῦδος in the first; and the Achaeans are neatly varied between conditional clause (εἴ κεν Ἀχαιοί...) and genitive absolute (Ἀχαιῶν δῃωθέντων).

415 Agamemnon's 'great grief' would be at his own failure rather than for his defeated troops as such.

418 The last verse of the speech (= 5.718, cf. 24.618) is concise and practical, much like 410. It may concede, incidentally, that they have not until now been too concerned with martial preparations.

419 Diomedes is now envisaged as having been standing fully armed

375

in his chariot during Agamemnon's rebuke, although see on 366. This is a common formular verse (8x *Il.*, with variations at its beginning), already applied to Menelaos at 3.29. 'Together with arms-and-armour' (for τεύχεα often implies both) is part of the formula, a little casual perhaps but given special point here by the addition of 420f., describing how the armour resounded and how frightening it was.

420–1 The first half of 420 does not recur elsewhere in so many words; however δεινός -v is formular as first word, and for ἔβραχε cf. 16.566. Similarly the second half is not reproduced exactly elsewhere, but cf. 13.497f., 21.254f.; ἐνὶ (rather then ἐπὶ) στήθεσσι -v is frequent in this position. |ὀρνυμένου in 421 is again a little unusual, and ταλασίφρονα is not formular outside name–epithet groups; although δέος εἷλεν/ἑρεῖν (etc.) occurs 5x *Il.*, 6x *Od.* It looks as though these two verses have been specially composed, although as usual with some help from traditional phraseology, in order to re-establish Diomedes as formidable.

422–544   The two armies advance against each other and at last join battle. After a short description of general combat the first individual encounters are described

422–56 Once again the armies are on the move, this time with no impending diversion to delay a full-scale engagement. Motifs from earlier descriptions, especially from book 2, are successfully repeated: the gleam of weapons, the leaders, the contrast between Achaean silence and the volubility of Trojans and their allies – this last illustrated by a simile, as are the massed Achaean ranks. The armies meet (446–56), and this is described at first in general terms: the clash of weapons, the boasts and groans, the blood flowing, the whole din of battle resembling the roar of mountain torrents. The correspondence with the first elaborate march-out which culminated in the catalogues in book 2 is especially striking. That began with Athene inciting the Achaean troops (2.446ff.); here Athene, Ares and others are similarly involved on both sides, 439ff. It continued with the series of five similes (2.459ff.) illustrating the gleam of arms, the numbers involved and the skill of the Achaean commanders. Those similes were different in subject from the ones here (fire, birds, flies, goatherds, bull, against waves and ewes here); the motifs of gleaming weapons and conspicuous leaders are noted here also (431ff., 428–31), but not by similes. The Trojans and their allies receive more attention here, although the account still favours the Achaeans. The motif of silent Achaeans and noisy Trojans (or allies) at 428–38 was not used in that earlier Achaean march-out, but the polyglot character of the allies was remarked in the corresponding passage introducing the Trojan catalogue at 2.802–6, itself a counterpart to Nestor's advice to Agamemnon at 2.362f. The motif is deployed in the opening verses of book 3, including the crane-simile to illustrate Trojan clamour, and more fully developed here both by the ewes-simile and by the incorporation, apparently after 2.803f., of the explanation about different tongues.

422–8 The Danaans (Achaeans) move forward relentlessly, rank upon rank, like wave upon wave breaking on the shore. The developed simile, as often, marks the transition to a new episode, and that is helped by the very frequent ὡς δ᾽ ὅτ᾽ type of introduction and consequent postponement of the Danaans' name until the end – which makes the simile itself apparently neutral at first and avoids a direct association with Diomedes in 419–21. The simile echoes two earlier ones about waves, at 2.209f. and 2.394–7; they too were evoked by massed movements of the Achaean troops, from ships to assembly and assembly to ships. The first of them briefly compared the thunder of waves breaking on a great beach (αἰγιαλῷ, as here); the second, the noise of waves driven by a south wind against a high cliff. In the present passage, too, the wind is specified, although as west rather than south; and the unending procession of waves is another common element (2.396f. and 4.423). This is indeed the explicit point of comparison here, although the noise, also, is heavily stressed by 422 πολυηχέϊ and 425 μεγάλα βρέμει (cf. πολυφλοίσβοιο and βρέμεται in 2.209f.); in the earlier pair the point of comparison was noise, rather (of shouts rather than thunderous motion at 2.394). A third simile related to the present one, in which Aias' troops are likened to a dark cloud driven by the west wind across the sea, came early in the Epipolesis at 4.275–82, and there will be further connexions in the torrent-simile at 452–5. See the individual comments on all these related similes, as well as Moulton, *Similes* 42–4.

The effect of these repeated images of the noise and surge of waves and torrents is to give an unforgettable impression of the size and power and serried ranks of the Achaeans in particular, almost like a force of nature itself; and incidentally to suggest how earlier scenes of near-pandemonium in the Achaean camp, and the grand but ultimately frustrated march-out of both sides later in book 2, lead in the end to the vast clash of arms which is now to follow.

422–3 κῦμα...ἐπασσύτερον, 'one wave after another'; the general sense of ἐπασσύτεροι (etc.) in its seven Homeric appearances (6x *Il.*, 1x *Od.*) is clear enough, although its etymology is disputed (either from *ἐπ-αν-(σ)σύ, cf. σεύομαι; or from ἆσσον, comparative of ἄγχι and frequent in Homer, with ἀσσοτέρω 2x *Od.* and ἐπ- implying repetition; cf. Chantraine, *Dict.* s.v. ἐπασσύτεροι).

Wave upon wave rushes (ὄρνυτ᾽) against the beach with a roar of surf (πολυηχέϊ, 'resounding'), as a westerly gale drives them on. This has been taken by modern critics as a specifically Ionian detail, since Ionia has a west-facing coast; but so do the Peloponnese and many islands, for example.

Moreover in a heavily indented coastline beaches can be found facing in almost any direction. Little that is useful can be determined from the prevalence of different winds in different parts of Greece, and in any case Homer's wind-terminology is far from precise. The Etesians blow more from the north-west than from the north-east in the eastern part of the Aegean (Boreas and Zephuros together 'blow from Thrace' at 9.5); the scirocco in western Greece often comes from the south-west; true westerly gales over open sea are rare, but the words of the *Admiralty Pilot* vol. III (strictly on western Greece) apply all over: in the open sea 'strong winds and gales can blow from any direction', and 'since a large part of the coastline...is very indented, and is backed by rugged mountainous country, local variations of coastal wind are very numerous'.

424–6 πόντῳ, locative, 'in the sea', i.e. offshore. κορύσσεται, 'raises its head', is an extension of the basic connexion with κόρυς, 'helmet'; further development of the metaphor is to be found at 442, closely related to the present verse (see comment there), in the allegorical description of Eris, also at 2.273 and 21.306; see also 2.272–7n. and Leumann, *HW* 210. Each wave 'first lifts its head out at sea, then breaks on the land with a great roar, and around the headlands, arched as it goes, comes to a peak and spits out sea-spray'. The parataxis is far from straightforward, combined as it is with the integral enjambments of 424 and 425; 'coming to a peak' presumably describes the wave on the point of breaking and *before* it hits the shore – in an impressionistic account such matters of literal sequence hardly count. ἀμφὶ δέ τ' ἄκρας is more puzzling. Headlands are not needed when the waves are breaking along the shore, as here; but in another wave-simile at 17.263–6 the waves are breaking at the mouth of a river, and headlands, its projecting banks, are in order – the phrase is the same, ἀμφὶ δέ τ' ἄκρας (unless the accepted vulgate reading there, ἄκραι, which presents great difficulties, is correct), and seems to have been applied loosely here to a slightly different situation.

ἰόν in 426 is Aristarchus' reading (Did/A); the vulgate has the less vivid ἑόν, printed in OCT. κορυφοῦται, 'rises to a peak', occurs only here in Homer; there is little difference in meaning (metre is another matter) between it and κορύσσεται. The curved or arching (κυρτόν) and fast-moving (ἰόν) wave, then its crest and the spray it spits out, are keenly observed and expressed, with sharp alliteration and assonance of k- and a-sounds especially from ἄκρας on.

427–8 ὡς τότ' ἐπασσύτεραι very precisely picks up the ὡς δ' ὅτ'... ἐπασσύτερον of 422f.; despite this, the formal point of comparison (the succession of ranks and waves) is a relatively minor aspect of the whole simile, which is concerned with the powerful breaking of the waves more than anything else. The power (but not of course the noise) may colour, as much as the formal comparison of line upon line, the impression a listener might form of the advancing Achaeans.

φάλαγγες -ας is regular (30/32× *Il.*) at the verse-end, but κίνυντο φάλαγγες| is confined to this Book, cf. 281 and 332. |νωλεμέως (4× *Il.*, 5× *Od.*, cf. νωλεμὲς αἰεί|, 4× *Il.*, 2× *Od.*), 'ceaselessly', is of uncertain derivation.

428–9 The half-verse cumulation of νωλεμέως πόλεμόνδε, almost an afterthought, leads on to a new observation of the leaders giving their orders, with runover-word cumulation and a sense of urgency conveyed by the internal stops. For the leaders see on 422–56 above, and compare 2.805, τοῖσιν ἕκαστος ἀνὴρ σημαινέτω, of the Trojans.

429–31 The leader-motif is now connected with that of Achaean discipline and silence: only the leaders utter their commands, the troops silently obey. Then the dramatic οὐδέ κε φαίης (see on 3.392) leads to a conclusion in 430 which conflates two slightly different ideas marked off by the main caesura: (a) you would not think so large an army was involved, so silent were they, and (b) you would not think so large an army had a voice to utter, so silent were they. The sentence is rounded off in 431, by a kind of ring-composition, with a cumulated reversion to the leaders, now called σημάντορας, whom they 'fear' in silence.

431–2 The second part of 431 moves on to the gleam of their armour, a standard detail in descriptions of an army advancing, see 2.455–8 and the comment on 422–56 above. The detail is briefly dealt with, the last half of 432 being little more than padding, although the flowing dactylic verse makes a suitably rhythmic conclusion.

Looking back at the whole description from 427 one can see how intricate and yet harmonious its expression has been:

427 whole-verse sentence,
428 half-verse cumulation; then new sentence,
429 runover-word cumulation; new sentence; comment begins with 4th colon
430 (integral enjambment) and is completed in a flowing verse,
431 cumulation, 'ring' completed; new sentence begins with 4th colon
432 (integral enjambment) and is completed in a flowing but plethoric verse.

433–5 The Trojans, on the other hand, are raising a great clamour, as they did at 3.2–8 where they were compared to cranes. Here they resemble countless ewes in a rich man's yard waiting to be milked. ἀμέλγω (4× *Od.*) is also implied in the naive and presumably old formula νυκτὸς ἀμολγῷ, 'in the milking-time of night', 4× *Il.*, 1× *Od.*; they bleat incessantly (ἀzηχές, probably from *ἀ-δι(α)-εχές, cf. συνεχής) in response to their lambs.

Book Four

436 ἀλαλητός (7× *Il.*, 1× *Od.*) is an onomatopoeic word either for the war-cry, its commonest use, or more generally for confused shouting, as also at 2.149.

437–8 Compare the words of Iris–Polites to Hektor at 2.803f.

πολλοὶ γὰρ κατὰ ἄστυ μέγα Πριάμου ἐπίκουροι,
ἄλλη δ᾿ ἄλλων γλῶσσα πολυσπερέων ἀνθρώπων

and the conclusion that each group should be given orders (805 σημαινέτω) by its own leaders, on which see 2.802–6n. Here the idea is similar but the expression completely different. The ἐπίκουροι are now πολύκλητοι... ἄνδρες, 'men summoned from many places', cf. 10.420 πολύκλητοι ἐπί-κουροι – the phrase echoes τηλεκλειτοὶ ἐπίκουροι (etc.), 5× *Il.* Then the proverb-like 2.804 is replaced by a more specific statement which, judging by its unformular quality and use of terms not otherwise found in Homer (but not particularly 'late' in form), was composed for this particular place. Thus θρόος is paralleled only by ἀλλόθροος once in the *Odyssey*; it is a poetical word denoting cries or shouts from many people at once (probably from the same root as θόρυβος and θρῆνος, cf. Chantraine, *Dict.* s.v. θρέομαι). Neither γῆρυς nor γηρύω are otherwise found in Homer, although that is surely accidental; it is a 'terme noble et religieuse' according to Chantraine s.v., found in poetry and late prose. Finally both ὁμός (predecessor of ὁμοῖος), 'common', and Aeolic ἴα for Ionic μία are infrequent in Homer, although they are old forms. The use of three separate terms for speech or voice, namely θρόος, γῆρυς and γλῶσσα, might suggest that some attempt is being made to distinguish differences of dialect from those of separate languages; more probably, however, it is simply to emphasize the point being made, which is aetiological, almost learned, in character.

439–45 Divine incitement is probably a standard part of the theme of armies marching out to battle; at 2.446–52 it was Athene who urged on the Achaeans with her aegis; here there is no aegis but Ares is added as divine supporter of the Trojans, together with the abstract trio Terror, Rout and Strife, the last of which receives further elaboration. The passage has much progressive enjambment, a symptom of cumulative composition; it is as though the composer has gradually expanded it, adding detail after detail in succession. The possibility of post-Homeric elaboration exists, but see on 444–5.

439 As usually but not invariably in Homer, the μέν-clause refers to the last to be named of a preceding pair (here, the Trojans) and the δέ-clause to the first, in a chiastic arrangement. Ares is Athene's pro-Trojan counterpart as war-deity.

440–1 Despite the close relationship of Eris, Strife, to pro-Trojan Ares, these three are to be understood as spreading the spirit of war among both

380

Book Four

sides equally. They are not fully personified, and have few characteristics beyond what is implied by their names. At her most concrete Eris is depicted on the Shield of Akhilleus as associated with Ker, Doom, in dragging wounded men and corpses about the battlefield (18.535–7), or imagined as rejoicing among the fighting at 11.73; Ares himself will be discovered stripping a dead warrior at 5.842–4. These other beings are usually his pale shadows, introduced to support or emphasize his actions: Eris joins him in stirring up strife at 5.518, Phobos follows him into battle at 13.299f., Ares tells Deimos and Phobos to yoke his horses at 15.119, Eris, Ares and Athene stir up war among the gods at 20.48ff. At 13.299 Phobos is his son, here Eris is his sister – she has to be feminine because of the gender of the common noun she represents, and is promoted to Ares' own generation to compensate for that, in a purely *ad hoc* description like Hesiod's of her as a child of Night at *Theog.* 225. Such figures find their counterparts in the winged or multipartite demon-like figures of contemporary orientalizing art, primarily of the late eighth and early seventh century B.C. The poetical tradition probably reflects such images in the description of Agamemnon's decorated corslet at 11.24ff., where Deimos and Phobos are grouped around the central gorgon-head at 11.37; or of Athene's aegis at 5.738–42, which contains not only a gorgoneion but also Phobos, Eris, Alke and Ioke.

The lengthening of Ἔρῑς before ἄμοτον is strained and irregular, and clearly arises out of the omission of τ' (a necessary omission here because of the preceding connectives) from the phrase Ἔρις τ' ἄμοτον μεμαυῖα as at 5.518. Ἄρεος for Ἄρηος is also unusual (unlike the metrical lengthening of Ἀ- at the beginning of the verse, which is well established), being paralleled by 19.47 Ἄρεος θεράποντε| (itself due to the adaptation of the formula θεράποντες Ἄρηος|) and *Od.* 8.267 ἀμφ' Ἄρεος φιλότητος, in the preamble to the sophisticated song about Ares and Aphrodite; cf. also 491 Ὀδυσσέος, with comment. κασιγνήτη ἑτάρη τε is paralleled by κασίγνητοί θ' ἕταροί τε at 24.793, cf. Here as Zeus's κασιγνήτην ἄλοχόν τε (2× *Il.*).

Either 441 or both it and 440 could be omitted, the latter carrying with it either 442f. or 442–5; but see on 444–5 below.

442 This and the next verse give a graphic allegory of the power of Eris: first she is small, then immense. Verse 442 is closely related to 424, from the wave-simile:

424 πόντῳ μέν τε πρῶτα κορύσσεται, αὐτὰρ ἔπειτα
442 ἥ τ' ὀλίγη μὲν πρῶτα κορύσσεται, αὐτὰρ ἔπειτα.

Here πρῶτα κορύσσεται is common to both, but unlike αὐτὰρ ἔπειτα is not a well-established formula; for the sense of κορύσσεται see on 424–6. These are the only two metaphorical uses of the verb in the middle voice, and there is a strong probability in this case – which cannot often be

381

said – that one is the model for the other. Which, then, is the model? Almost certainly 424, not because it comes first in our text but because the wave 'lifting its head' is appropriate to context and the envisaged sequence of events, whereas that Strife 'first lifts her head ὀλίγη, being very small', is difficult in the latter respect especially; what is really needed is something like 'being at first very small, she then lifts her head until it touches the sky'. Vergil in his adaptation at *Aen.* 4.176 says something very like that.

443 On ἐστήριξε compare 11.28 στήριξε, in a short simile – more to the point, in that same description of Agamemnon's corslet in which Deimos and Phobos occurred (see the end of the first para. of 440–1n.). Eris 'fixes her head against the sky', i.e. touches the sky with her head while her feet continue on the ground.

The occasionally strained language, the taste for allegory, the slight formular content – all this marks the couplet, and perhaps 440 also, as relatively late in composition. Whether in this case that implies 'by Homer himself' or 'post-Homeric' will be further discussed in the next comment.

444–5 An important factor is 444 καὶ τότε, 'then also', which, inconspicuous as it is, presupposes some kind of immediately preceding general statement about Eris – and therefore, probably, the previous couplet. The verse as a whole, although still not formular, presents no special difficulty; 445 is closer to the style of ordinary Homeric narrative ($|-\overline{\smile\smile}-$ καθ'/ἀν' ὅμιλον is a common formula (17x *Il.*), and στόνος ἀνδρῶν occurs at 19.214), and the whole of its first half, ἐρχομένη καθ' ὅμιλον, will recur precisely at 516 with Athene as subject, and nowhere else. That suggests a connexion between the two verses; the phraseology is too general to argue for a model–copy relationship exactly, but 515f. is almost certainly organic to the whole account of individual fighting which fills the last 90 verses of this Book, and that gives some support to the idea of 445 as genuinely Homeric. Alternatively, a later elaborator created 445 on the basis of his knowledge of 516 – but that is not the usual way of late-aoidic or rhapsodic expansion. But if 445 presupposes 444, and 444 evidently 442f., and they 440 at least, then the whole elaboration, despite one or two signs of strain, is likely to be due to the main composer, probably at one of the latest stages of his creation of the monumental poem.

446–56 The two armies meet and become locked in close combat; blood flows. Down to 451, this general description recurs at 8.60–5 (see also on 20–5); here, however, it is reinforced by a simile of mountain torrents meeting, and thus brings to a strong conclusion the episode of the armies marching out to battle. Similes throughout this episode mark changes of emphasis, first on the Achaeans, then on the Trojans, then on both sides interlocked: 422 wave-simile (Achaeans); 429 silence/noise motif (both sides); 433 ewes-simile (Trojans and allies); 439 gods spur them on, Eris-allegory; 446 the armies clash, simile of the torrents.

446–51 These verses are organic at 8.60–5 – that is, some description of general engagement is required there. Admittedly book 8 has several untypical and distinctly 'late' features, so that does not of itself assure authenticity here. On the enjambments in 446–9 (which are regular enough) see p. 33.

446 The 'single space' into which the armies come together does not recur exactly (apart from at 8.60), but is simple and evocative.

447 ῥινούς, literally 'hides', i.e. leather-covered shields; not elsewhere (except at 8.61) as a metonym, but compare Idomeneus' shield at 13.406, which is a round ἀσπίς worked with 'cattle skins, ῥινοῖσι βοῶν, and shining bronze'; also 7.238 and 16.636, where βούς/(βῶν) itself connotes a shield. The repetition of σύν and the conjunction of 'hides, spears and men's might' are highly rhetorical, as suits an impressionistic description like this one.

448–9 The couplet has often been considered a post-Homeric elaboration; that is possible but no more. The runover-word χαλκεοθωρήκων is found only here (and at 8.62); it is clearly (as Shipp suggested, *Studies* 244) an equivalent at the beginning of the verse of the common verse-end formula χαλκοχιτώνων (etc.). The -εο- formation is 'linguistically noticeable' (Shipp), since the regular form of such compounds is as in e.g. χαλκοβατής; but Stentor is χαλκεοφώνῳ at 5.785, and metrical exigency probably justifies the licence in the later stages of the oral tradition.

ἀσπίδες ὀμφαλόεσσαι (etc.) is a formula, 10x *Il.*, 1x *Od.*, as is πολύς δ' ὀρυμαγδὸς ὀρώρει (4x *Il.*, 1x *Od.*) in 449. The idea of leather shields being round or bossed is a typical Homeric imprecision, but cf. Idomeneus' shield cited in 447n.; their being 'close to each other' (ἔπληντ' from πελάζω, 'approach', cf. πέλας, also at 14.468 πλῆντ' and *Od.* 12.108 πεπλημένος) has suggested hoplite tactics to some (e.g. T. B. L. Webster, *From Mycenae to Homer* (London 1958) 219). That is just possible, although the present description is far less indicative of organized, closely-packed, side-by-side fighting than e.g. 13.130–3; see p. 9, where it is suggested that early experiments in something like hoplite deployment could go back at least to 725 B.C. Thus, even if the present couplet did suggest something of the kind, that would not make it necessarily post-Homeric. Moreover generic descriptions of massed fighting clearly invited a certain exaggeration, to the point at least of saying that shields were in contact with the shields of enemies, without any necessary implication of hoplite warfare. For that to be implied, the shields and helmets of warriors *on the same side* must be in virtually continuous (sideways) contact, as at 13.131–3 = 16.215–17.

450–1 This makes a powerful continuation of the generic description, rhetorical in its chiastic arrangement (the groans and boasts of victors and victims, in that order as Aristarchus noted, Arn/A) and the rhythmical contrast of 451, a rising threefolder – or perhaps rather a two-colon verse with 4th-foot work-break, throwing extra emphasis on the ground running with blood at the end.

452–5 This is the first of four torrent-similes in the poem (compare especially 11.492–5, where a river in flood descends χειμάρρους κατ' ὄρεσφιν and carries debris down into the sea). It is as brilliant in its power and precise observation as the two sea-similes with which, together with that of the ewes, it is closely related: those of the waves breaking at 422ff. and of the dark cloud over the sea at 275ff., see Moulton, *Similes* 44f. The second of these belongs to the Epipolesis not to the march-out, but the idea of massed troops is the same, as also is the solitary herdsman (on whom, however, see 455n.).

452 'Winter-flowing rivers', literally, are torrents which rush down and fill the dry river-beds of summer. ὄρεσφι is genitive not locative (for tmesis of κατ' is not possible with κατ' ὄρεσφιν at 11.493); see Chantraine, *GH* I, 237, who emphasizes the great flexibility with which the -φι termination is used in the Homeric poems, obviously for metrical convenience. ῥέοντες, 'flowing', seems directly to echo the flowing blood of the previous verse, and may be prompted by it in a style of composition which, especially where developed similes are concerned, is linear and associative (cf. Moulton, *Similes* 45 n. 50; the connexion between 453 μισγάγκειαν and 456 μισγομένων is, however, directly resumptive). The repetition of νέφος in 274 and 275 is somewhat similar, see 274n. *fin.*

453 The two rivers in spate (cf. the dual συμβάλλετον) hurl together their heavy weight of water (ὄβριμον ὕδωρ after ὄβριμον ἔγχος, 13× *Il.*) into a μισγάγκειαν, a rounded combe or basin (ἄγκος) in which waters mingle.

454 The 'great springs' feed the torrents high up in the mountains; 'within a hollow gorge', if the singular is taken literally, must refer to the single ravine into which the combined waters flow down from the combe; otherwise, and perhaps more probably, it applies to each of the two separate torrents higher up.

455 The shepherd hears the roar of water τηλόσε, literally 'to afar'; bT preferred τηλόθι, 'far off', simply, but Leaf observed that the idea of hearing being projected to the source of sound can be paralleled in Homer, cf. 11.21 and especially 16.515, where Glaukos tells Apollo δύνασαι δὲ σὺ πάντοσ' ἀκούειν (but a god is slightly different).

It is debatable whether the shepherd is meant to remind the audience specifically of the goatherd of 275ff. Rather it seems that each is an essential part of the poet's vision of the power of nature in remote places – not so remote that they seem unreal or artificial, since the herdsman witnesses that

Book Four

power and is stirred by it; similarly H. Fränkel, *Die homerischen Gleichnisse* (Göttingen 1921) 30.

456 The ancient vulgate reading was φόβος, but Aristarchus (Did/A) and a minority of MSS read πόνος. This is a conjecture based on no textual authority, on the grounds (as given by Didymus) that οὐ γὰρ γέγονέ πω φυγή – for φόβος in Homer means 'rout' or 'retreat'. That is correct, but the fact is that γένετο ἰαχή τε φόβος τε is a formula which appears three times elsewhere in the *Iliad*. Even that does not quite settle the matter, since formulas were sometimes adapted, and πόνος, 'toil' (as e.g. at 12.348, πόνος καὶ νεῖκος ὄρωρεν, cf. 14.480) is indeed more suitable in this context.

457–544 After the preliminary description of general warfare, the Book ends with the first series of detailed encounters in the poem. The clash of individual warriors, ending in the death of one or the other of them, is the typical mode of warfare in the *Iliad*, to be developed in enormous variety and detail in the central Books of the poem. Here, for less than a hundred verses, is the initial – almost, one might say, the initiatory – exercise in this kind of battle-poetry, arranged with exceptional precision and exemplifying several of the standard motifs and motif-sequences of the genre. It will lead on, in the following Book, to a continuation centred around the special exploits of Diomedes; but the alternation here of Achaean and Trojan successes and the intervening short impressions of general fighting confirm that this final section of book 4 is intended as an artistic unity. The division between books 4 and 5 is not a particularly strong one, marked by a move from earth to Olumpos or by nightfall, for example; even so, it is more than an arbitrary break.

A summary of events to the end of the Book shows something of the variety and careful symmetry of the action:

457–62 Antilokhos (Achaean, son of Nestor) kills Trojan Ekhepolos with a spear-thrust to the head; short simile of his falling

463–6 Elephenor (Achaean) grabs Ekhepolos' body, intending to strip it

467–70 Agenor (Trojan) kills Elephenor with a spear-thrust to his unprotected ribs

470–2 General fighting round Elephenor's body (short wolf-simile)

473–89 Aias kills Simoeisios
  (474–9: brief account of his birth
  480–2: detail of wound
  482–7: developed simile of his falling like a poplar tree)

489–93 Antiphos (Trojan) throws his spear at Aias, misses but kills

385

Leukos, companion of Odysseus; detail of wound; he falls on top of Simoeisios' corpse which he was trying to drag away

494-504 Odysseus is enraged, Trojans retreat, he throws his spear and kills Demokoon from Abudos; detail of wound and his falling

505-7 Brief general description of Trojans being pushed back

507-13 Apollo from high up in Troy rallies the Trojans, points out that Akhilleus is absent from the fighting

514-16 Athene spurs on the Achaeans, moving among them

517-26 Diores (an Epean) is killed by a rock thrown by Thracian Peiros; it smashes his leg, Peiros finishes him off with a spear-thrust in the belly; detail of wound

527-31 Thoas (Aetolian leader) kills Peiros as he retreats, hitting him first with the spear, then with a sword-thrust in the belly

532-5 Thracians prevent Thoas from stripping Peiros' body; he retreats

536-8 The corpses of Diores and Peiros lie side by side; many others are slain around them

539-44 Rhetorical description of general fighting, as both Trojan and Achaean dead lie stretched out side by side.

The description thus falls into five sections: (i) killing of Ekhepolos and Elephenor, general fighting round Elephenor's corpse; (ii) killing of Simoeisios, then Leukos and Demokoon; (iii) general description of Trojans being pushed back; Apollo rallies them, Athene spurs on the Achaeans; (iv) killing of Peiros and Diores, whose corpses lie side by side; (v) rhetorical summary of general fighting, with many Trojan and Achaean dead.

457 Antilokhos is Nestor's son and the first man in the *Iliad* to slay an enemy, although this earns no special comment in the poem (Aristarchus' explanation, Arn/A, that it was because of his speed of foot, cf. 18.2, is wholly unpersuasive). He has not been mentioned so far, which is surprising, and finds no place in the admittedly eccentric list of five Pylian commanders at 295-6 (see comment there). He will recur quite often in subsequent fighting, and is prominent in the chariot-race of book 23.

ἕλεν is a standard expression for 'slew' in these encounters; ἄνδρα κορυστήν (3× *Il.*) implies a fully-armed warrior, cf. 274n.

458 ἐν(ὶ) προμάχοις(ι) occurs 9× *Il.*, 7× in this position. This Ekhepolos only appears here, at his death; his patronymic is unusual and intriguing, being based on θαλύσια, 'harvest offerings' as at 9.534.

Book Four

459–62 As so often in Homeric duels (i.e. man-to-man encounters in battle, not formal duels like that of Paris and Menelaos in book 3), there is no elaborate exchange of blows, and the first man to thrust (presumably) with his spear inflicts an immediately fatal wound. Fuller detail is given (a) on the path of the weapon and exact nature of the wound – here, through the ridge or boss (φάλος, see on 3.362) of the helmet and into his forehead; and (b) on the victim's death and collapse to the ground – in the present passage (in which 461 is repeated at 503, and the whole of 459–61 recurs as 6.9–11) darkness covers his eyes (σκότος ὄσσε κάλυψεν, 12x *Il.*) and he falls like a tower. Finally ἐνὶ/κατὰ κρατερῇ/ἢν ὑσμίνῃ/ην is another common martial formula (18x *Il.*); most of these encounters are rich in standard phraseology in many different combinations. The normative effect of the fighting so far is reinforced by regular colometry and, with the exception of (integral) half-verse cumulation at 461, progressive enjambment.

463–70 Bronze armour was valuable, and stripping it from a dead enemy an important priority. It could also be dangerous, and the death of a warrior so engaged is a standard motif of battle-poetry. Its use facilitates the transition from one duel or victim to another: A kills B; A or X (someone else, as here), tries to strip the armour; C kills A or X. There are possible variations: for example X can either be on the same side as A, as here, or a companion of B who is anxious to rescue his body, rather.

463–4 Verse 463 is a rising threefolder (since stressing the main caesura destroys the sense). Elephenor is sole leader of the Euboean Abantes at 2.540f. (see 2.542n.), indeed 464 = 2.541. It seems surprising that such a relatively prominent contingent in the catalogue, with seven towns listed, should lose its commander so early in the poem and without further comment.

465 For ὄφρα after λελιημένος, meaning simply 'eager to...', compare 5.690, and, after other verbs, 6.361 and 16.653.

466 The pathetic or ironical comment, 'but his effort was only for a short while', is again typical of these descriptions of battle, cf. 477–9 of Simoeisios. For μίνυνθα in pathetic comments cf. 1.416, 13.573, 17.277f.

467–9 Agenor is son of the Trojan counsellor Antenor and will be heard of later in the poem; he sees Elephenor's side (literally πλευρά, ribs) protruding outside his shield, παρ' ἀσπίδος, as he bends and drags Ekhepolos' body; 469 = 11.260, also of a man dragging a body. λῦσε δὲ γυῖα etc. is often used of these martial deaths (8x *Il.* + variants); it is a vivid and slightly naive formula probably long established in the heroic tradition. ξυστόν, on the other hand, is an unusual word for the regular battle-spear. Properly an adjective, it is derived from the root of ξύω (smooth, scrape, sharpen, polish); why it should be specially applied to a spear is not clear, unless the great ship-spear, ξυστὸν μέγα ναύμαχον, of 15.677 (cf. 15.388) was the original form and had a sharpened point (cf. *Od.* 9.326) instead of a bronze spear-head.

470–2 This sequence of deaths is separated from the next by a short description of general fighting, arising out of the resumptive half-verse cumulation in 470. The 'harsh work' of battle (cf. the ἔργον of 539 and the φυλόπιδος μέγα ἔργον of 16.208) took place ἐπ' αὐτῷ, 'over him'; there is no need to see a special contrast between αὐτῷ and his θυμός just before, despite ψυχὰς...αὐτούς at 1.3f. Trojans and Achaeans attack like wolves (another brief comparison, cf. 462 ὡς ὅτε πύργος) and 'man was grappling with man' *vel sim.*; δυοπαλίζω is a rare and striking term, only here in the *Iliad*, perhaps an expansion of πάλλω, 'I shake'. It is used of throwing on a beggar's rags at *Od.* 14.512, which does not greatly help. At least this seems to be a verse-end variant of |ἔνθα δ' ἀνὴρ ἕλεν ἄνδρα as at 15.328, 16.306.

473–89 The description of individual clashes resumes with one of the most carefully formed and moving encounters in the whole *Iliad*. Simoeisios is a young Trojan whose birth and parentage are briefly described, and whose short life is stressed as he succumbs at once to Aias; he falls and lies like a tree, which he resembles in several different respects. Homer is here assembling motifs used in different combinations elsewhere: the victim who had been born by a river, like Satnios at 14.442ff. – to a nymph there, but not here, recalling Iphition at 20.382–5, born of a nymph but 'under Mount Tmolos'; or the twin brothers Aisepos and Pedasos at 6.21ff., born of a nymph to Boukolion, who made love to her when he was pasturing his sheep. It is the addition of the simile that makes the Simoeisios passage 'outstanding as the poet's portrait of a doomed young warrior, come to the war from his parents, and soon to perish' (Moulton, *Similes* 57). That, too, has its close parallel when the Trojan Imbrios falls at the hands of Teukros at 13.170ff., like an ash-tree conspicuous on a mountain-top, which is cut with a bronze axe and its tender foliage brought to the ground; on the detailed thematic similarities see also Fenik, *Typical Battle Scenes* 125–7.

bT on 473–9 comment that the poet gives not merely the victim's name, but all the other details as well, 'so as to make the narrative easily believable, as though the author had seen the event in person', πολλὴν πίστιν ἐπιφέρων τῷ λόγῳ ὡς αὐτόπτης ὤν. But pathos, rather than vividness or credibility, is the chief aim.

473 Anthemion's name is presumably related to ἄνθος, perhaps by way of the Homeric epithet ἀνθεμόεις, and is perhaps the result of association with the river, cf. the 'flowering Scamandrian meadow' of 2.467.

474 ἠΐθεον, an unmarried young man, the male equivalent of παρθένος; his youth is pathetic, and this is reinforced by θαλερόν, for he is 'in bloom', in the prime of life. His name, like that of the other young Trojans Satnios (see previous note) and Skamandrios at 5.49 (cf. 6.402), is based on one of the rivers of the Troad; see von Kamptz, *Personennamen* 302. Willcock may be right that it is invented for the occasion; at least it allows the poet to move straight to the place and circumstances of his birth.

475–6 His mother, not named, had gone with her parents into the foothills of Ida to pasture the family flocks (to 'see' them, ἰδέσθαι, literally, cf. on 195), in a poignant little evocation of peacetime; it was on her way down that she gave birth to her son by the banks of the river after which he was named.

477–9 His being unable to pay back to his parents (repeated now from 476 with the added pathos of φίλοις) the θρέπτρα or cost of his upbringing maintains the emotional tone, as does the shortness of his lifetime, αἰών, through Aias' spear; on μινυνθάδιος cf. 466 and note. The alliteration of 479 δουρὶ δαμέντι| introduces a certain brusqueness at the end of these fluent and closely enjambed verses from 474 on, in which the expression, dense and heavily punctuated at times, is relieved by the more restful 475 and the earlier part of 479; and so leads on to the harsh reality of the fatal blow.

θρέπτρα from θρεπτήρια (cf. τρέφω), as λύτρα from λυτήρια: so Aristarchus (Arn/A) on 478.

480 πρῶτον: 'among the front fighters', bT. Simoeisios does not have the chance to attack Aias, indeed it is uncertain whether he had even seen him. The swift and unexpected death is appropriate to the pathetic young victim.

481–2 The runover-words in each verse, followed by strong stops, provide a violent transition first to the spear's fatal course, then to the victim's collapse.

482–7 Falling 'in the dust', in various formular expressions based on κονίη, is extremely common; cf. e.g. Diores at 522, also 536–8n. The simile which follows (of which bT comment on 482, not very imaginatively, that the poet adds details διώκων ἡδονήν, so as to make it more attractive) has a close and complex reference to the narrative at different levels. Simoeisios *fell* like a poplar tree (a more elaborate version of Ekhepolos falling like a tower at 462), but its implied verdure is also suggestive, as is its lying there by the river – which recalls not only Simoeisios' present fate but also his birth by the river, before the war.

483 'And it was growing in the hollow of a great water-meadow': εἰαμενή, according to later uses, is some kind of hollow; formed from a participle, like δεξαμενή (so T), the word is of uncertain derivation. Chantraine, *Dict.* does not mention its traditional connexion with ἧμαι as that which 'sits', which surely cannot be discounted.

484 It is smooth, with branches growing out at the top; in other words,

389

it has had its lower branches lopped as one still sees in Mediterranean lands: so Leaf after Mure, but the intention of mentioning this detail is surely *not* to suggest a comparison with Simoeisios' helmet-plume. This was evidently the regular way of arboriculture.

485–6 The chariot-maker (or '-joiner', -πηγός from πήγνυμι) cuts down the tree – either cuts it 'out', literally, from a grove, or shapes it, cf. 3.62 – with his axe of shining iron. Moulton, *Similes* 58, supposes an implicit comparison with the man being felled, but χαλκῷ rather than σιδήρῳ would have made this point better; compare the parallel simile at 13.178–81, where the ash-tree is cut with bronze. bT on 484 suggested that 'branchless trees are ready for bending', but that is too facile; if anything, systematic lopping of the lower branches would make for less rather than more flexibility. The choice of poplar wood, which is soft, for the felloe of a wheel is a little surprising, even if the light-weight Rosellini chariot from Egyptian Thebes had wheels of bent ash-wood without tyres (Lorimer, *HM* 317 and 328). One might expect the two-man Mycenaean, Geometric or Homeric war-chariot with its normally four-spoked wheels to have had felloes of a hard wood like ash, probably made up in sections like a modern cartwheel, in which toughness rather than extreme flexibility was the prime consideration. Yet the chariot-wheel tablets from Knossos and Pulos present a different picture. Most of the Knossos wheels are elm or willow, *pe-te-re-wa* (cf. πτελέη) or *e-ri-ka* (cf. Arcadian ἑλίκη), and the only wood mentioned in the Pulos chariot-wheel series is cypress (*ku-pa-ri-se-ja*, cf. Homeric κυπαρίσσινος): see Ventris and Chadwick, *Documents*, nos. 278–82 and pp. 369–75, with a brief discussion of Egyptian wheels on pp. 369f.; also R. Meiggs, *Trees and Timber in the Ancient Mediterranean World* (Oxford 1982) 105–15, whose comment on p. 114 that 'Poplar, a wood that is easily bent, might be chosen for the felloe of a wheel at either date' (*sc.* Mycenaean or eighth/ninth century B.C.) fails to take account of the softness issue. Poplar is a softer wood than ash, elm, cypress or even willow.

487 ἀζομένη, 'drying': the trunk is left to season for a while – a valid observation, perhaps, of one of the sights of the countryside, but also with a suggestion of Simoeisios' extended corpse, just as the river banks hint at his birth.

Aristarchus (Arn/A) has a different idea, that the timber was left beside the river to be carried down when it flooded; but that neglects ἀζομένη, or rather connects it erroneously with another simile at 11.492–4, in which a torrent rushing down from the mountains carries with it into the plains many dry oaks and pines. Probably these are dead trees from the banks of the ravine.

488 The return to the narrative situation includes Simoeisios' patronymic (in an abbreviated form, Anthemides from Anthemion like Deukalides

from Deukalion); this formal detail, which reverts to his first mention at
473, completes the ring-composition but also helps to stress, perhaps, that
he was a real person, not simply a symbol of youth and the pathos of war.

489–90 The half-verse cumulation leads into the next in the chain of
killings: now Priam's son Antiphos (there are two other Antiphos's in the
poem; this one will be killed by Agamemnon in book 11) hurls his spear
at the victorious Aias. The verb is specific, ἀκόντισεν; it is a throw not a
thrust, and throws (which unlike thrusts often go astray) are necessary when
a fatal wounding is required by the poet, although not of the intended victim
but of someone else.

491 |τοῦ μὲν ἅμαρθ᾽ recurs at 15.430. Leukos is not heard of elsewhere
in Homer; more remarkably, the reduction of η to ε in ᾽Οδυσσέος is unique
(against ᾽Οδυσσῆος 7× *Il.*, 71× *Od.*, ᾽Οδυσῆος 5× *Il.*, 61× *Od.*), paralleled only
by ῎Αρεος for ῎Αρηος in 441 and at 19.47 and *Od.* 8.267; see the comment
on 441. Ares is in any case prone to metrical variation, whereas Odysseus
has a variety of forms (especially with -σ- or -σσ-) which make such
measures wholly unnecessary. Emendation is not easy: ᾽Οδυσσεύς is unattractive, cf. ᾽Οδυσεύς at *Od.* 24.398, itself usually emended; ᾽Οδυσσῆος
θεράποντα would be possible, unless the tradition knew that Leukos was
not a θεράπων but his equal. The verse can hardly, in any event, be dis-
pensed with.

492 The alliteration of β's is perhaps expressive of the harsh wound in
the groin (βουβῶνα is *hapax legomenon* in Homer). The pluperfect βεβλήκει
is common in a 'resultative' sense (Chantraine, *GH* 1, 437): 'had succeeded
in hitting'.

493 The victim who falls on another corpse as he is trying to drag it
away is a common motif.

494 The poet may feel that Odysseus needs to be shown in heroic action
as soon as possible after his rough handling by Agamemnon at 336ff., which
is perhaps why he takes over from Aias here.

495–8 Many elements of this and other encounters are formulas, not
only whole and half-verses but also motifs like the victor's anger at a friend's
death, or the victim who had been dragging away a corpse, or the bastard
son, even. Here, 495 is a formular verse, 7× *Il.*; 496 recurs at 5.611 and
17.347, with its first half recurring once else in addition and its second half
being a common formula, 14× *Il.*; whereas 497f. recur *in toto* as 15.574f.

496 Like Antiphos in 490, Odysseus throws and does not thrust, and
in a metrically similar phrase; he too hits someone other than his intended
victim (who was presumably Antiphos himself – it is to him that μάλ᾽ ἐγγὺς
ἰών must refer).

497 He looks around him not so much to avoid hostile action, as bT
suggest, as to pick out his target, or just in a threatening way.

499–500   Demokoon is mentioned only here (and does not occur in the catalogue-entry on Abudos etc. at 2.835ff.); for the form of his name, which means 'paying attention to the community', cf. von Kamptz, *Personennamen* 84. Abudos is near Troy, on the Hellespont, and was evidently in close touch with it; Hektor had a special friend there, Phainops, according to 17.582–4. Modern editors and translators have followed Aristarchus (Arn/A) in interpreting παρ' ἵππων ὠκειάων as a further specification of 'Αβυδόθεν, namely as 'from the swift mares' (which he kept there) in a kind of stud-farm for Priam; at 2.838f. the horses of Asios from neighbouring Arisbe are specifically mentioned. But bT add οἱ δὲ ἀντὶ τοῦ ἐφ' ἵππων, showing that some people in antiquity took the phrase with βάλε in 499, i.e. he hit him (as he stood) in his chariot. That cannot be entirely dismissed; 'swift mares' refers to a chariot in battle at 7.15 and 240, and, surprisingly, never elsewhere to horses by themselves. But παρ' would have to mean 'beside', as at 468; it is not true, as Leaf objects, that word-order is strongly against this. Another possibility, for those who feel that the 'swift mares' are too vaguely expressed for the stud-farm interpretation, might be to read ἦλθεν, ἀφ' ἵππων, cf. ἐκ δ' ἔβαλ' ἵππων (of Antiphos, indeed) at 11.109, also ἀφ' ἵππων ὦσε χαμᾶζε, 4× *Il.*

501–4   As often after a special description of the victim, there is ring-composition by means of a resumptive verse or two; here Odysseus' anger is referred to again before the weapon's course is described.

κόρση is usually interpreted as 'temple', i.e the same as κρόταφος, in which case Demokoon must have been sideways on to the spear's flight, since it passes through both temples. Aristarchus (Arn/A), however, evidently took it to mean 'head' in some more general sense, and that would be confirmed if Chantraine, *Dict.* s.v., is right in claiming the noun to be related to κείρειν, 'cut' (of the hair).

The description of Demokoon's death is strongly formular: σκότος ὄσσε κάλυψε occurs 12× *Il.* (see on 459–62), and the whole 'clattering as he fell' verse (504) 7× *Il.*, with its first half by itself another 12× and its second another 3×. δοῦπος is the din of battle, but also of the roar of water at 455; ἀράβησε is another onomatopoeic word, the corresponding noun being used of the chattering of Dolon's teeth at 10.375. There is a subtle if artificial distinction between the two noises: 'he fell with a thud, and his armour clattered about him'.

505–6   There has been little rhythmical variation in the battle-poetry so far, so that 505, which is most likely to have been sung as a rising threefolder, stands out as the Trojan front-fighters give way to Odysseus' wrath, allowing the Achaeans to retrieve not only Leukos' body but also that of the enemy Demokoon.

506–7   These two verses are an almost perfect rhythmical match, confirming the idea of a fresh impulse on the singer's part.

507 νεμεσάω (at least 12x *Il.* in various forms) implies annoyance or indignation – often, although not here particularly, righteous indignation. Based ultimately on νέμω with its great variety of applications, it is closely associated with νέμεσις, strictly the assignment of blame by a legal authority for some kind of disorder; see also on 3.156.

The verse is hardly a rising threefolder, because of its strong stop at the 4th-foot caesura and its irregularly long first colon ἴθυσαν δέ (which technically breaches Meyer's Law by emphasizing a break after the second trochee).

508 Pergamos (feminine) is the acropolis or highest part of Ilios, the city of Troy. Paris descends κατὰ Περγάμου ἄκρης at 6.512, presumably because that is where his house as well as Priam's is; Kassandra is on Pergamos at 24.700 when she sees Priam returning across the plain. It is also where Apollo has his temple, 5.446, cf. 460, and that is no doubt where he watches the battle from (cf. 4.514, where he exhorts the Trojans ἀπὸ πτόλιος); the same phrase Περγάμου ἐκκατιδών is also applied to him at 7.21. These are the only six Homeric uses of the name, which is related to πύργος, 'tower' (cf. Chantraine, *Dict.* under that word), and in neuter forms (cf. Ἴλιος becoming Ἴλιον) became common later for a high citadel, cf. especially Pergamon in Mysia.

509–13 Apollo's exhortation is quite complicated in expression, with its varying degrees of enjambment and runover, but logical in argument: (i) you should not retreat before the Argives; (ii) because they are not invulnerable; (iii) especially since Akhilleus is not among them.

509 The opening verse of Apollo's speech is a rising threefolder, as the natural punctuation suggests – not a very marked one since the first and second words can be envisaged as separate cola despite the close connexion of the latter with Τρῶες.

ὄρνυσθ'(ε) as first word occurs 6x *Il.* ἱππόδαμοι is a regular epithet for the Trojans, based no doubt on their real interest in raising horses (many horse-bones were found by the excavators, see C. W. Blegen, *Troy* iii.1 (Princeton 1953) 10f.; Page, *HHI* 57 and 252 with notes). It is designed primarily for the genitive and dative cases (18x *Il.* together, against 2x in the vocative as here and 3x in the accusative).

510–11 Their skin is not made of stone or iron, for withstanding bronze when they are struck: the last two words of 511 complicate the sense, but make a striking verse out of four words of increasing weight; the rhetoric is deliberately indirect and ironical. The motif is reused in slightly different words (τρωτὸς χρὼς ὀξέι χαλκῷ) but with enormous pathetic effect by Hektor as he faces Akhilleus at 21.568–70.

512–13 οὐ μὰν οὐδέ: cf. also 2.703 = 726, οὐδὲ μὲν οὐδ' οἱ ἄναρχοι ἔσαν for this locution, common in later Greek, which normally follows a negative clause as here. μάν/μήν/μέν is an affirmative particle (Chantraine, *GH* i,

16) often with a strong progressive sense; it 'adds a fresh point' (Denniston, *Greek Particles²*, 336, cf. 338), as here.

The dramatic expression χόλον θυμαλγέα πέσσει/ων recurs, of Meleagros, at 9.565. πέσσω means 'ripen' or 'cook', hence 'digest' – but the point about Akhilleus is that his anger remains and he fails to digest it; it stays as a 'grief to his spirit', θυμαλγέα, inside him. In these cases, therefore (and in similar uses with κήδεα, cf. also 8.513) it implies absorption into the body rather than actual digestion (or being contained for a long period as bT assert).

513–16 Athene matches Apollo's exhortation by urging on the Achaeans; she has no special base, like Pergamos for Apollo, from which to do so, and moves directly among the troops (516) to identify (ἴδοιτο, another application of this useful verb, cf. 205 with comment and 476) the slacker, μεθιέντα – both the word and the idea remind one of Agamemnon's rebukes, e.g. at 240.

Τριτογένεια is the first occurrence in the poem of this title for Athene (which occurs 3x *Il.*, 1x *Od.*). The etymology is unknown, see Chantraine, *Dict.* s.v., and M. L. West on Hesiod, *Theog.* 895 for references to modern discussions. Various explanations were naturally offered in antiquity, none persuasive; some are summarized by bT on 8.39, others in the D-scholium on the present passage. A common version is that after the goddess was born from his head, Zeus gave her to the river Triton in Boeotia or Thessaly, or to Lake Tritonis in Libya, to rear; connexion with the sea-deities Triton and Amphitrite is likely in these names, but Athene herself has no special associations with water. Chantraine considers the most plausible etymology to be from τρίτος, 'third', with metrical lengthening of the iota; he compares the Athenian Tritopatores, i.e. genuine ancestors, in which case Athene would be the 'genuine daughter' of Zeus.

517–26 The description of fighting resumes with another carefully elaborated death, this time of an Achaean, the Epean leader Diores. First comes a short general statement that destiny detained him (517); then he is struck by a stone thrown by the Thracian Peiros (518–20); then come further details of the damage inflicted (521–2). He falls on his back, stretching out his arms to his comrades as he lies dying (522–4); Peiros runs up and spears him in the belly, and he expires (524–6). The rhythmical pattern is straightforward throughout, but the cumulations, enjambments and internal stops are exceptionally varied.

517 The sense of μοῖρα πέδησε is more fully brought out at 22.5, where destiny binds Hektor to stand firm outside the walls of Troy although the others are rushing inside for safety. In the present context the phrase is less exact, in the sense that the Achaeans are already on the attack, and Diores with them; but it has a satisfactory general sense, in that destiny (literally his portion) shackles or holds him there to be a victim.

Book Four

Diores is commander of one of the four Epean squadrons at 2.622 (a homonym is father of the Myrmidon Automedon at 17.429), and Nestor took part in funeral games for his father Amarunkeus according to 23.630. This last name is pre-Greek, probably West Asiatic, with 'Αμαρυ- as in the place-name 'Αμάρυνθος in Euboea, and -νκ- equivalent to -νθ- there (von Kamptz, *Personennamen* 347). Diores himself is Διϝο-ήρης, 'pleasing to Zeus', cf. e.g. ήρα in the formula ἐπὶ ήρα φέρειν (von Kamptz, *op. cit.* 88).

518 χερμάδιον is something you can take in your hand, χείρ, hence a large stone rather than a boulder. Such stones are regular missiles, 14× *Il.* (including ὁ δὲ χερμάδιον λάβε χειρί 3× and μεγάλοισί τε χερμαδίοισιν 2×), and are evidently not regarded as unheroic. χερμαδίῳ itself as first word in the verse is formular (5× so out of 6 occurrences). Being hit by such a stone is often fatal; here the shattering of the lower leg is held to be so, and is made to sound especially fearful by the description of the stone as jagged, ὀκριόεντι (518), and shameless, ἀναιδής (521).

519–20 Πείρως is abbreviated from Πείρεως; at 2.844 he is Πείροος, leader of the Thracians together with Akamas. There is a slight discrepancy between this brief catalogue-entry and the present passage; there, at 2.845, the Thracians are from around the Hellespont, here he comes from Ainos a little further away.

521 The 'shameless' stone is a famous example of treating something inanimate as subject to human emotions, compare 126 on Pandaros' arrow, with comment, and the spears which 'desire to satiate themselves with flesh' (11.574 and 2× *Il.* elsewhere). It is, of course, no more than a metaphor, but the idea of missiles which enjoy finding their target is peculiarly unnerving.

The stone shatters both tendons, τένοντε – Aristarchus (Arn/A) on 20.478 says that Homer applied the term to all sinews. Homer also regarded them as coming in pairs, since the singular is never found, and five out of eight occurrences of the term are in the dual number.

522 ἀπηλοίησεν, only here in Homer, is aorist of ἀπ-αλοιάω, the verb being evidently an epic form of later ἀλοάω, 'crush', perhaps to be connected with ἀλέω, 'thresh'.

ἄχρις clearly means 'utterly' or something similar, but no one knows why, since ἄχρι as preposition means 'up to', 'until', much like μέχρι. Chantraine, *Dict.* s.v. ἄχρι is uninformative; Leumann does not mention it in *HW*, although the probable explanation is of the kind with which he is there concerned – for 17.599f., γράψεν δέ οἱ ὀστέον ἄχρις | αἰχμή, suggests 'up to', more or less precisely, as the sense, as the spear-point merely 'scratches' the bone. But then at 16.324, as in the present passage, the bone is not just touched but totally smashed, ἀπὸ δ' ὀστέον ἄχρις ἄραξε. These are the only three Iliadic instances of the term (which occurs once in the *Odyssey* meaning 'until'), and it seems likely that the 'utterly' applications are due to a misunderstanding, within the oral tradition itself, of 17.599f. or other similar uses not represented in surviving poetry.

523 This verse recurs, also with ὁ δ' ὕπτιος ἐν κονίῃσι preceding, at 13.549. ὁ δ' ἕζετο χεῖρε πετάσσας, in addition, is found 2x *Il.*, at 14.495 of a mortally wounded man spreading his arms out behind to support himself and at 21.115 of a gesture of supplication or resignation. Perhaps those cases are easier to envisage than the wounded man who is flat on his back, ὕπτιος, yet stretches out his arms; in any case the gesture is a hopeless and pathetic one, implying an appeal to retrieve his body, or even perhaps a kind of farewell, rather than any conscious expectation of rescue. χεῖρε πετάσσας is a formula of multiple applications; in the *Odyssey* it is used of an embrace, also of Odysseus swimming.

524 'Breathing out the θυμός' exemplifies the basic meaning of θυμός as breath-soul.

525–6 Peiros now runs up and delivers the *coup de grace*, which causes the innards to spill out on to the ground, a vivid and gruesome phrase with its three initial χ's, χύντο χαμαὶ χολάδες. Darkness covers the eyes in the same formula as in 503.

527–38 The final act in the drama of the death of Diores and its consequences takes place when Thoas avenges him by killing Peiros. The other Thracians prevent him from despoiling the body, and the two victims lie stretched out side by side in the dust: a powerful and pathetic climax to this first major scene of battle in the *Iliad*, apparently rounded off by a short evocation of the general fighting which continues; but see on 539–44.

527–8 Thoas is sole leader of the Aitoloi and a prominent figure; he strikes Peiros in the chest and penetrates to the lung as Peiros rushes away. Aristarchus (Did/A) evidently hesitated between ἀπεσσύμενον and ἐπεσσύμενος (of Thoas), favouring one in one edition and the other in the other. The vulgate reading was in fact ἐπεσσύμενον, i.e. of Peiros, probably because he is wounded in the chest and not the back. The objection to it is that Peiros' 'running up', 524 ἐπέδραμεν, must have been completed when he eviscerated Diores, and that he himself cannot have been hit before then; but the epic poets were sometimes imprecise over that kind of fine chronological distinction.

529–31 The wound in the lung was clearly fatal, but Thoas now comes close (implying that his spear had been thrown not thrust), pulls out the spear and, instead of using it again for a final thrust – that is never done – draws his sword and cuts open the belly, in an action roughly parallel, and presumably intentionally so, with that perpetrated by Peiros himself just before.

532–3 Thoas is too important to be killed, and the chain of killings has to be terminated somehow. Therefore the dead man's troops, the 'top-knotted Thracians' (the phrase is repeated in Hipponax, frag. 115.6 West, if that poem is not to be attributed rather to Archilochus), keep him at bay with their long spears – see on 2.542f., where the Abantes also have an unusual hair-style and are famous for their spears.

534–5 These verses recur at 5.625f., in a broadly similar context, where Aias has just killed Amphios with a wound in the stomach and is prevented by the Trojans with their spears from stripping his armour.

535 πελεμίζειν means 'to shake' (its exact semantic relation to πόλεμος is debated); Thoas was shaken, rebuffed, by being 'thrust away from them' and so retreated, χασσάμενος.

536–8 Diores had fallen in the dust at 522, just as Simoeisios had done at 482; now the poet repeats the detail and the phrase as Peiros, slayer of Diores, joins him ἐν κονίῃσι. They were 'both stretched out beside each other'; the tableau is strongly pictorial, the motif of the two corpses being not exactly paralleled elsewhere in the poem, and their symbolic opposition and union in death are stressed by the formal antithesis of 537. The runover-word enjambment of 537/8, following on from the whole-verse 536 and the twofold 537, and leading into a brief general statement about all the others who were being slain around them, constitutes a marked and apt conclusion to what may well have been intended as the final verses of this opening scene of battle – see the comment which follows.

539–44 There is, unfortunately, a serious doubt over whether these verses are completely authentic, or whether (as Bentley and Heyne among others have thought) they might have been added as an additional conclusion by a performer, whether post-Homeric singer or rhapsode, who wished to make a major break and not to continue with the exploits of Diomedes in book 5. It was noted above that 536–8 make a suitable ending to the previous sequence of events; the present passage, despite an obvious effort to create a powerful generalization of a rhetorical kind, might be heard as something of an anticlimax. Moreover it contains some rough edges which could be due to post-Homeric elaboration of the more skilled kind.

539 Similar expressions, although with a god not a (typical) man as subject, are found twice elsewhere:

13.127 (phalanxes) ἃς οὔτ' ἂν κεν Ἄρης ὀνόσαιτο μετελθών
17.399 (nor would Ares or Athene) τόν γε ἰδοῦσ' ὀνόσαιτ'

These passages are themselves closely related, since Athene is joined with Ares in the first (at 13.128) as well as the second, and the epithet λαοσσόος is applied first to the one deity and then to the other. The reference of τόν in 17.399 is to μῶλος two lines before, which may be compared with ἔργον (cf. 470) in the present passage – which therefore seems to develop the motif slightly, although in a perfectly acceptable way so far: a man would not make light of entering this battle (i.e. so fierce was it).

540 Now comes a slight weakness of sense rather than expression, which might well pass unnoticed in ordinary performance; for, in order to make this hypothetical warrior a powerful symbol and to show how bitter the fighting was, the composer needs to show him as exceptionally able to cope with the dangers of battle. This he now begins to do by describing him as *unwounded* so far, either by throw or by thrust (that is the distinction between ἄβλητος and ἀνούτατος, neither of them a standard term). But a wounded man would not enter the fighting in any case, as is shown by the Achaean leaders wounded in book 11 – as Nestor says at 14.63, 'it is in no way possible for a wounded man to fight'. What is required, rather, is that this imaginary man should be fresh, untired, as at 11.802 = 16.44, where 'easily would you, being untired, ἀκμῆτες, (push back) men tired by the battle-throng'.

541–2 δινεύειν is not exactly so used elsewhere, but is a striking expression none the less; κατὰ μέσσον is lightly formular (3× *Il.*). Now the poet introduces the Athene part of the motif: (he would not make light of it) even if Athene led him by the hand and kept away missiles. Verse 542, as Shipp, *Studies* 245 noted, is compounded of a phrase used at 17.562, where Menelaos prays that Athene should βελέων δ' ἀπερύκοι ἐρωήν (the 'rush' of missiles, cf. ῥώομαι), and a version of the |χειρὸς ἑλόντ' etc. formular pattern – the feminine |χειρὸς ἑλοῦσ' occurs only at 5.30, in fact, where it is Athene that grasps Ares' hand. But the connexion of the two phrases is made by a wholly untypical placing of αὐτάρ, which elsewhere begins with the metrical foot, i.e. 'always has its first syllable in arsis' (Leaf); in a formular tradition, and with such a common connective, that would be a bold variation even if it does not sound wholly wrong to the modern ear. The MSS veer between the impossible ἑλοῦσ', ἀτάρ (the majority reading), ἑλοῦσ', αὐτάρ, and, from a small minority and Eustathius, ἑλοῦσα, ἀτάρ, which may have been the ancient vulgate reading; unfortunately the Aristarchan tradition left no comment. The hiatus in this last case would be difficult, although not impossible as Leaf claimed. In any event the junction of phrases is not managed quite smoothly; of course this affects 542 only, and the verse could be omitted.

543–4 The final sentence is skilfully deployed in a regularly formular style, and developing 538; but objection has been made, e.g. by Leaf, against ἤματι κείνῳ (5× *Il.*) and the pluperfect τέταντο, on the ground that both imply this to be the end of the day's fighting, which in any case it is not. The objection is probably overdone, since a degree of perhaps excessive finality is to be expected in a conscious conclusion of this kind; but no other ending of a Book, at least (not even of book 17), is closely similar. At the same time, and remembering that 536–8 have already provided an acceptable and even a strong conclusion, one might reasonably prefer to regard these last six verses as a special extension, aoidic rather than rhapsodic in kind, of the version Homer himself usually sang.

INDEX

A few minor Homeric names are omitted but their line-reference can be found through the index in OCT.

Readers familiar with e.g. R. Lattimore's translation are reminded that upsilon is here transliterated as 'u' (not 'y'), and chi as 'kh' (not 'ch').

Index

Index

Index

Lightning Source UK Ltd.
Milton Keynes UK
UKHW010003190721
387346UK00007B/142